D1552612

ARISE, AFRICA! ROAR, CHINA!

THE JOHN HOPE FRANKLIN SERIES IN AFRICAN AMERICAN HISTORY AND CULTURE

Waldo E. Martin Jr. and Patricia Sullivan, editors

ARISE, AFRICA! ROAR, CHINA!

Black and Chinese Citizens
of the World in the Twentieth Century

GAO YUNXIANG

高云翔

THE UNIVERSITY OF NORTH CAROLINA PRESS

Chapel Hill

Publication of this book was supported in part
by a generous gift from Kim and Phil Phillips.

Designed by Jamison Cockerham
Set in Arno, Scala Sans, and Aller
by Tseng Information Systems, Inc.

Cover illustrations: *From top, clockwise*: Liu Liangmo (from *Green Bay [WI]
Press-Gazette*), Langston Hughes (courtesy New York World-Telegram & Sun
Newspaper Photograph Collection, Prints and Photographs Division, Library of
Congress), Si-lan Chen (courtesy New York Public Library), W. E. B. Du Bois
with Mao Zedong (courtesy of W. E. B. Du Bois Papers, Special Collections
and University Archives, University of Massachusetts Amherst Libraries),
and Paul Robeson (author's collection); background courtesy iStock.

Manufactured in the United States of America

The University of North Carolina Press has been a member
of the Green Press Initiative since 2003.

LIBRARY OF CONGRESS CATALOGING-IN-PUBLICATION DATA
Names: Gao, Yunxiang, author.
Title: Arise, Africa! Roar, China! : Black and Chinese citizens
of the world in the twentieth century / Gao Yunxiang.
Other titles: Black and Chinese citizens of the world in the twentieth century |
John Hope Franklin series in African American history and culture.
Description: Chapel Hill : The University of North Carolina Press, 2021. |
Series: The John Hope Franklin series in African American history
and culture | Includes bibliographical references and index.
Identifiers: LCCN 2021027388 | ISBN 9781469664606
(cloth ; alk. paper) | ISBN 9781469664613 (ebook)
Subjects: LCSH: Du Bois, W. E. B. (William Edward Burghardt), 1868–1963. |
Robeson, Paul, 1898–1976. | Hughes, Langston, 1902–1967. | Leyda, Si-lan
Chen. | Liu, Liangmo, 1909–1988. | African Americans—Relations with Chinese. |
African Americans—Political activity—20th century. | China—Politics
and government—20th century. | BISAC: HISTORY / World | SOCIAL
SCIENCE / Ethnic Studies / American / Asian American Studies
Classification: LCC E185.61 .G218 2021 | DDC 327.1/708996073—dc23
LC record available at https://lccn.loc.gov/2021027388

To my transpacific family,

spreading from Xinjiang and Inner Mongolia to Toronto and New York,

and to the memory of my father, Gao Zhen (高珍 [1941–2011])

Contents

Acknowledgments

I have received generous support from numerous friends and colleagues across the globe in writing this book. Zhang Juguo of Nankai University and Pan Huaqiong of Beijing University facilitated my navigation of the enormous number of Chinese sources available at their universities. Hang Yao of the Soong Qingling (Madam Sun Yat-sen) Foundation provided me with valuable materials from the organization's collections. Alan Smith of Toronto enthusiastically shared private photographs of Paul Robeson and hundreds of newspaper articles in English.

Chen Yuan-tsung, Sylvia Si-lan Chen's surviving sister-in-law, and Ji Xiao-bin, Ji Chaoding's nephew, offered insights on the Chen and Ji families, respectively. Lynn Garafola of Columbia University, who had interviewed Chen on her collaboration with the legendary Soviet dancer-choreographer Kasyan Goleizovsky, patiently answered my questions and offered valuable criticism of the chapter on Chen. I enjoyed discussing the history of dance in China with Eva S. Chou of Baruch College, City University of New York. Stella Dong, a writer and family friend, enchanted me with the stories of her interviews with Sylvia Si-lan Chen's brother Jack in the 1980s. I have been inspired by my conversations with Louise Edwards at the University of New South Wales (Sydney), Keisha N. Blain at the University of Pittsburgh, and Phillip Luke Sinitiere at the College of Biblical Studies (Houston), and by their distinguished work. The knowledge I gained from Marc Gallicchio at Villanova University, Emily Wilcox at the University of Michigan, Bill V. Mullen at Purdue University, and other scholars has been of great help. I would like to acknowledge in particular Wilcox's collegiality in providing a rare image of Sylvia Si-lan Chen from the Pioneers of Chinese Dance Digital Collection at the Asia Library of the University of Michigan.

Gail Hershatter at the University of California, Santa Cruz, offered important support, collegiality, and insights into the meaning of this book, as befits her position as a preeminent scholar of China. Andrew Morris at California Polytechnic State University provided generous and insightful evaluation of the manuscript; his warm friendship and collegiality are inspirational. My teacher and valued friend Charles Hayford, an active independent scholar, read and edited much of the manuscript and offered extraordinary advice for navigating the publishing process. His late father, Harrison Hayford, a professor of English at Northwestern University, happened to be a fellow Herman Melville scholar and a close friend of Jay Leyda, Sylvia Si-lan Chen's husband. This book has benefited from the valuable comments of Marc Gallicchio of Villanova University and two other anonymous readers. I feel blessed to now consider Professors Hershatter, Morris, Hayford, and Gallicchio as friends and colleagues.

I was inspired by exchanges with colleagues at the University of Michigan's Lieberthal-Rogel Center for Chinese Studies during my invited lecture there in 2019. I benefited from wisdom of colleagues at the following conferences: the Annual Meetings of the American Historical Association in New York in 2015 and 2020; the Ninth Annual Harriet Tubman Summer Institute—"New Geographies: Africa and African Diasporas" at New York University, the Third Annual Conference of the African American Intellectual History Society at Brandeis University, and the White Privilege Conference Global in Toronto, all in 2018; the Annual Conferences of the Association of Asian Studies in San Diego in 2013 and in Toronto in 2017; the Annual Meeting of the Organization of American Historians, the Southeast Annual Conference of the Association for Asian Studies, and the Annual Conference of ASIANetwork, all in 2021. A portion of chapter 1 appeared in my article "W. E. B. and Shirley Graham Du Bois in Maoist China," published in the *Du Bois Review: Social Science Research on Race* 10, no. 1 (2013): 59–85. Lawrence Bobo, the W. E. B. Du Bois Professor of the Social Sciences at Harvard University, carefully edited the piece.

I wish to thank the staffs at the following libraries and archival institutions: the Shanghai Municipal Library, China National Library (Beijing), the Nankai University Library, the Beijing University Library, the Archives of the Pearl S. Buck House (520 Dublin Road, Perkasie, Pennsylvania), the Special Collections and Archives of the University of Massachusetts Amherst Libraries, the Arthur and Elizabeth Schlesinger Library of the Radcliffe Institute for Advanced Study at Harvard University, the Tamiment Library and

Robert F. Wagner Labor Archives of the Elmer Holmes Bobst Library at New York University, the Beinecke Rare Book and Manuscript Library at Yale University, the Manuscript Department of the Huntington Library (San Marino, California), the Seeley G. Mudd Manuscript Library at Princeton University, the Butler Library at Columbia University, the Manuscript and Prints and Photographs Divisions at the Library of Congress, the Moorland-Spingarn Research Center at Howard University, the Special Collections Research Center of Bird Library at Syracuse University, the New York Public Library for the Performing Arts and General Research Division, the National Archives at San Francisco and San Bruno, and Colgate University Library. The Faculty of Arts at Ryerson University provided grants for final preparation of the book.

I am indebted to Brandon Prioa, my editor at the University of North Carolina Press, for his superb editing and ongoing enthusiasm for this book. I wish to thank other staff members at the press for their constant professionalism. I am also grateful to Waldo E. Martin Jr. and Patricia Sullivan for including this book in the distinguished John Hope Franklin Series.

Without the devotion and unyielding support of my beloved mother, Du Xiuhua (杜秀花), to our family, creating this book would have been impossible. My husband, Graham Russell Gao Hodges (郝吉思), shared his knowledge of African American history, enthusiastically acquired valuable scholarly materials on my behalf, read every draft, and offered valued commentary. Our twin sons, Graham Zhen (高然墨) and Russell Du Gao-Hodges (高然诗), remain my permanent inspiration.

My family associations to figures in this book illustrate the intertwining of personal and global histories. Going through his mother Elise Russell Hodges's 1938 yearbook at Mt. Holyoke College, my husband noted a Barbara Yen, who turned out to be a daughter of the noted Chinese diplomat Weiching Williams Yen (Yan Huiqing) and a cousin of aviatrix Hilda Yank Sing Yen. The Yens' friendship with Sylvia Si-lan Chen's family remained constant from Guangzhou and Wuhan to Moscow and the United States. My husband's father, Reverend Graham Rushing Hodges, was a roommate of Tracy B. Strong, a nephew of journalist Anna Louise Strong, at the Divinity School of Yale University. During Tracy's last visit with Hodges, who was in hospice care at age eighty-eight, in 2004, the old friends recalled their meeting the noted journalist who had just sailed from China to New York Harbor in 1939. They were still impressed that she had greeted them, asking about the current fashion of women's hats in the United States.

Lastly, I wish to acknowledge the loss of my dear graduate school mentor at the University of Iowa, R. David Arkush (1940–2018).

ARISE, AFRICA! ROAR, CHINA!

Introduction

In 1941, the most famous African American singer and actor of the era, Paul Robeson (1898–76), recorded an album of Chinese resistance and folk songs, featuring "Chee Lai!" which later, under the title "March of the Volunteers," became the national anthem of the People's Republic of China (PRC). Collaborating with Robeson on the album's overall production was Liu Liangmo (ca. 1909–88), a Christian activist and journalist who had recently arrived in the United States after launching the mass singing movement in China. The selection of "Chee Lai!" was no accident — Robeson was attuned to the power of anthems. He also recorded the Soviet national anthem in 1944 and had often sung "Lift Every Voice and Sing," commonly known as the Black national anthem, at Mother Zion African Methodist Episcopal Church, one of Harlem's most famous houses of worship. Such songs create emotions Benedict Anderson has termed "unisonance," or, "a way of feeling that resonates through one's body and sustains a collective membership in a national community."[1]

That collective feeling permeated the lives and political activism of the five citizens of the world whose global interactions are the subject of this book. *Arise, Africa! Roar, China!* unpacks the close relationships between a trio of famous twentieth-century African Americans and two little-known Chinese during World War II and the Cold War. W. E. B. Du Bois, Paul Robeson, and Langston Hughes need no introduction, but their Chinese allies, journalist and musician Liu Liangmo and Sino-Afro-Caribbean dancer-choreographer Sylvia Si-lan Chen (ca. 1905–96), have, until now, been consigned to the dustbin of history. The chapters on the three African American intellectuals examine their interactions with China and its people, tracing evolutions of their mutual perceptions within shifting global politics. Biographical narratives of Liu and Chen are comprehensive, highlighting their sojourns in the United States.

These activists were not alone. Their spouses impacted their careers and ideologies. Shirley Graham Du Bois (1896–77) and Eslanda Robeson (1895–65) pushed their husbands into an embrace of Chinese Communism. Liu's wife, Chen Weijiang (Wei-Giang, ca. 1911–95), was even more radical than he. Occasionally collaborating with Liu in writing and speaking, she steered his attention to gender issues. Chen took care of their extended family while Liu traveled throughout China and the United States during the war. Sylvia Si-lan Chen's husband, Jay Leyda (1910–88), the noted film historian and writer, was her principal supporter in a marriage that survived decades of political and immigration turbulence. Their union came as a blow to Hughes. In Moscow, Chen and Hughes had embarked on a love affair, leaving an emotional stamp evident in their numerous letters written from around the globe. She was the major heterosexual love of his life. The romance may have been unsustainable, but it resonated in other ways for Hughes, enabling him to meet several of Chen's family members and friends and further inspiring his historic trip to China.

These five figures' passages over murky and often treacherous political and ideological landscapes were facilitated by powerful white and Chinese liberal figures and institutions that controlled the transpacific flow of resources, and many lesser-known friends. Prominent in their networks of support were First Lady Eleanor Roosevelt; Pearl S. Buck, Nobel laureate and the gatekeeper of China matters in the United States; Agnes Smedley, the American journalist and agent for the Comintern and Soviet military intelligence based in Shanghai in the 1930s; Madam Sun Yat-sen, the leftist sister of Madam Chiang Kai-shek; Lin Yutang, the famous Chinese philosopher and writer whose book *My Country and My People* powerfully influenced American perceptions of China;[2] "The King of Beijing Opera" Mei Lanfang, whose company successfully toured the United States during the Great Depression; Lu Xun, the revered father of China's modern literature; United China Relief Inc., the largest-single contributor of aid to wartime China; and the semiofficial China Institute in New York City. These five individuals' trajectories illuminate the networks of Chinese and Americans close to them and shed light on the Sino-American cultural and political contacts that shaped the course of the twentieth century.

While most scholarship on Sino-American relations treats the United States as default white, this book breaks new pathways by foregrounding

African Americans, combining the study of Black internationalism and the experiences of Chinese Americans with a transpacific narrative, and understanding the global remaking of China's modern popular culture and politics. Du Bois, Robeson, and Hughes were central players in the push to broker connections between African Americans and the wider world. Black internationalism most notably set its sights on Africa, the Anglophone West Indies, Europe, and the Soviet Union, yet China was also an important target.[3] Excellent studies have examined African American interactions with China, but these are often limited to Black appropriation of Chinese culture and thought, or only go so far as to indicate that such contacts existed.[4] Recently scholars of Pacific diaspora arts have emphasized how Americans and Chinese interacted through soft power. Valuable as cultural history, these works still rarely place their subjects within a full historical context.[5] Julia Lovell powerfully illustrates how international events transformed Chinese politics and how Mao Zedong's ideology was enduringly refashioned by different countries and peoples, including African Americans and Africans.[6] This book reveals much earlier and widespread interaction between Chinese leftist figures and Black ones than Lovell's book accounts for. It traces China's transnational entanglements even during periods when the nation has commonly been regarded as insular and unconnected to the wider world.

Arise, Africa! Roar, China! expands the scholarship on Sino–African American exchanges by illustrating how three African American cultural giants were perceived, studied, and critiqued among the Chinese, and by introducing Liu and Chen as significant new subjects in this discourse. This book examines the intertwined lives of people usually perceived as inhabiting nonoverlapping domains. It is about individuals who strove in their own ways to create a politicized transpacific discourse and enable global communication between African Americans and Chinese. While situating each of the five figures in a complex and shifting political context, this book formulates an account of the personal, artistic, cultural, and political networks they established. It illustrates their formative effects both on Chinese views of the Black diaspora and African American views of China's place in an emergent imaginary of anticolonial and racial liberation. Directly comparative works about the three famed African Americans are somewhat rare among current studies; discussions of individual Afro-Chinese relationships are hard to find, and narratives of interactions between Chinese and African American women are even scarcer. Keisha N. Blain has recently broken new ground by demonstrating the efforts of ordinary African American women to create a Black internationalism.[7]

Travel and physical mobility beyond national boundaries powerfully affected the politics of those five citizens of the world. Largely by train and boat before the advent of mass air transportation, travel was a global, deeply personal, yet nonetheless social experience. W. E. B. Du Bois visited China three times between 1936 and 1962, in addition to his many trips to Europe, Russia, and Africa. Shirley Graham Du Bois accompanied her husband on the last two occasions and made China her principal home after his death. Robeson traveled widely in Europe, the Soviet Union, Africa, Canada, and Latin America to advance his career and seek a spiritual home and cultural roots. Hughes chronicled his trips to Haiti, Cuba, Mexico, Africa, Europe, the Soviet Union, and China in his autobiographies *The Big Sea* and *I Wonder as I Wander*.[8] Chen was truly cosmopolitan: born in Trinidad of French Creole and Chinese parents, she crisscrossed the globe, juggling several nationalities and passports, and lived in Trinidad, London, Guangzhou, Wuhan, Moscow, Shanghai, Hollywood, Beijing, East Berlin, Toronto, and New York City. For Liu, the Pacific was a vast, watery border to be traversed numerous times. He zigzagged around China and the United States for nearly two decades to mobilize Chinese morale for the resistance and bolster support among the American public for a besieged China through singing and giving speeches. He visited East Berlin and Australia for the world peace movement in the 1950s.

Travel and its lived experience transformed the ideologies of these subjects. While African Americans and Chinese roamed the world to find sustenance and meaning, the historical memory of the diaspora holds substantial emotional value. For Blacks, the diaspora was linked to the slave trades (Atlantic and internal) and later to the flight north through the Underground Railroad and the Great Migration of the late nineteenth and early twentieth centuries. For more recent African Americans, especially the three discussed in this book, travel meant at least temporary respite from the burdens of homeland segregation. Du Bois relished his freedom of movement and the treatment he received in the Japanese Empire in 1936 and the Soviet Union and the PRC in 1959. Similarly, Robeson took advantage of England's relative tolerance to advance his career; receptions in the Soviet Union thrilled him, including a memorable occasion when Du Bois and he crossed a crowded room to embrace each other. The wandering Hughes found comfort and celebration in the Soviet Union and China. He shared with Du Bois and Robeson a renewed leftist political commitment along with material for his writing.

The three African American intellectuals' presence in China and their alliances with Chinese sojourners facilitated the shifting dynamics of Pan-Africanism and Pan-Asianism and ultimately the color line of Mao Zedong's Third World theory. The transformation started with the gradual changes of Blacks' image in the Republic of China. Stung by the humiliating image of the "sick man of Asia," alarmed by Nazi racism and Japan's imperialist ambitions, China was acutely frustrated by the continuous defeats of Chinese athletes at the 1932 and 1936 Olympics. Thus Chinese media celebrated the "natural" physical prowess of the boxer Joe Louis (the "Brown Bomber") and track and field athlete Jesse Owens on behalf of the world's people of color. The front cover of China's leading cartoon magazine, *Modern Sketch*, devoted to the 1936 Olympics, found inspiration in Owens's triumph. Its back cover featured the drawing of a muscular Black woman resembling the American chanteuse Josephine Baker, clad in a banana skirt, with the caption "Victory of Colored People at the Olympics." Those images exemplified Chinese portraiture of African Americans. Du Bois, who was visiting China around that time, announced that the race "must be represented, not only in sports, but in science, in literature, and in art."[9] Indeed, jazz musicians in nightclubs, who were dismissed as "foreign musical instrumental devils [*yangqin gui*]," or caricatured in advertisements for toothpaste and white towels, dominated Blacks' representation in the Republic of China's media. The presence of these three figures started to alter such stereotypes there.

Chinese people migrated to the United States and elsewhere in the late nineteenth century for economic reasons or to escape wars and revolutions. Arriving in the United States, many would face racial terror and segregation, forces to which Liu and Chen were not immune. However, their brave journeys brought Sino–African American cultural alliances into new historical settings. The Chinese intelligentsia had long connected through literature and drama the shared "enslavement" of the Chinese nation as a semicolony and of African Americans. In the introduction to their 1901 translation of Harriet Beecher Stowe's *Uncle Tom's Cabin* (1852), Lin Shu and Wei Yi argued that the tortures "yellow" people faced were even worse than those endured by Black Americans. Chinese people needed the book because "slavery is looming for our race. We had to yell and scream to wake up the public." Diaspora Chinese in Tokyo pioneered modern Chinese drama in 1907, staging a play based on Stowe's classic.[10] Liu and Chen brought modern Chinese popular cultural forms such as music, dance, and print journalism brewed in the pressure cooker of war into the politicized Sino–African American cultural connection based on racial sympathy. In the rigidly segregated United States, while leaders and audiences might occasionally cross over the color line, separation by race was the norm. That fact affected the approaches of Chinese sojourners such as Liu and Chen, who strove to redefine the image and narrative of China for their readers and audiences.

Diasporas are extraordinarily diverse and personal, bound together primarily by shared politics. Indeed, because of their ideological bents and celebrity, the experiences of this book's five subjects take on global significance. Their political activism was riddled with ambiguities. Keisha Blain has noted the often-contradictory behavior of the women she studies — they did not always follow progressive paths, and even collaborated with white supremacists at times. While none of the characters in this book veered right, their lives did take twists and turns that made political contradictions inescapable. Vaughn Rasberry has recently pointed out the predilection of Black internationalist intellectuals to admire totalitarianism.[11] As committed leftists resorting to communism to defend their race and color, the figures in this book necessarily accepted mass rule. Du Bois flirted with support for Japanese military aggression against China, arguing that an Asian dictatorial power was better than Western colonial governance. Influenced strongly by his wife, he enthusiastically endorsed the PRC during the 1950s and early 1960s, when the regime launched several radical mass campaigns with catastrophic consequences. Robeson voiced unstinting support first for the Soviet Union and later for the PRC. Hughes was initially enthusiastic about the Soviet Revolution then drifted to the middle during the McCarthy era, though his ongoing admiration for the Chinese Communist Party (CCP) persisted in his writings. Liu, a dedicated Christian, delicately balanced his loyalty between the Nationalist and Communist forces in the Republic of China, fended off allegations of communist affiliation in the United States, but enthusiastically helped inculcate the new socialist order among his fellow believers upon returning to the PRC. Chen was less directly involved in political movements but believed firmly in the Soviet system and worked closely with alleged communist front organizations in the United States between the late 1940s and early 1950s. The Federal Bureau of Investigation (FBI) regarded her husband, Jay Leyda, as a communist, and the Chen family wandered the globe as unyielding leftists. By examining each individual's radicalism, this book displays the variety of Sino–African American cultural politics, allowing a greater appreciation of left influences on African Americans, Chinese Americans, and American attitudes in general.

While physical mobility and transnational influence transformed these subjects into citizens of the world, none of them traveled freely. They faced constant obstacles juggling the treacherously slippery transpacific politics entailed by their races and leftist activism. Close surveillance and persecution by a global network of intelligence and immigration agents, incessant uncertainty about their legal residence status, denial of passports over allegations of Communist Party membership, forced shifting of nationalities, and the changing doctrinal demands of the CCP highlighted the ambiguities of their citizenship. The FBI cast a dark shadow over the lives of all five figures. The U.S. government famously canceled the passports of Du Bois and Robeson. The Japanese authorities expelled Hughes. The 1882 U.S. Chinese Exclusion Act deemed a person of Chinese ancestry "an alien ineligible for citizenship." Such an "alien" could only be admitted into the United States as a "nonquota immigrant"—a returning legal immigrant; a minister of a religious denomination, or a professor of a college, academy, seminary, or university and "his wife, and his unmarried children under eighteen years of age"; or a student "at least fifteen years of age."[12] Liu thus entered the United States as a student, a status difficult to maintain for long. He and his family left under threat of deportation in 1949. Chen, though married to a U.S. citizen, suffered years of exclusion because of her partial Chinese ancestry. She was admitted as a visitor under strict limitations and faced the constant nerve-wracking threat of deportation for four decades. All of these administrative actions were linked to their politics. Meanwhile, such exclusions and denials exacerbated feelings of otherness and racial discrimination. Du Bois and Chen were at points nearly stateless. Liu was later marginalized by the totalitarian PRC regime to which he had been devoted (he was rehabilitated later), while the three African Americans' fame and popularity reached a peak there. The PRC granted Chen, who fell in between the categories of Chinese and foreigner, a reserved welcome during her uncomfortable five-year exile there.

A broad vision of issues of race and nationality, as well as world travel, created a cosmopolitan outlook for the five figures in this book. Scholarship on race and cosmopolitanism has expanded our understanding of activism beyond national borders. However, little attention has been paid to Sino–African American activism, especially in the period of Jim Crow and the Chinese Exclusion Act. Paul Gilroy and Kwame Anthony Appiah, two of the foremost scholars of cosmopolitanism, rarely have set their gazes across the Pacific, though Gilroy has called for attention to communication networks far beyond the United States. African American and Chinese freedom struggles within a global context greatly enhance understanding of their meaning.[13]

My sources reflect that deep meditation. Such transnational/transcultural history requires a fluent multilingual approach to comprehensively and thoroughly survey the massive, yet rarely used, sources. The multiple archival streams of scattered materials illustrate the diverse and even conflicting perceptions of these five citizens of the world. I checked each figure's archives, published and private, FBI files, Immigration and Naturalization Service (INS) records in numerous locations, and the manuscript holdings of such major social institutions as United China Relief and such prominent individuals as Pearl S. Buck. I have spent much time combing through English-language newspapers and other media published in the United States, Great Britain, and Shanghai, and Chinese-language periodicals published in China and New York City's Chinatown from the 1930s to the present. I have found numerous monographs and pamphlets on and by my subjects, written in or translated into Chinese. Doing so has given me new insights into how first the Nationalist government and then the PRC regarded and used the artistry and writings of the five figures.[14] This method breaks new ground for the well-known stories of Du Bois, Robeson, and Hughes, even beyond their official biographies, and brings back to life the sagas of Liu and Chen.

I have divided the book into five chapters, using a chronological method in each one. Chapter 1, "Africa, Arise! Face the Rising Sun! W. E. B. and Shirley Graham Du Bois," illustrates the Du Boises' complex and shifting connections, during times of political turmoil, to Pan-Africanism and Pan-Asianism by scrutinizing their writings and multiple visits to China from 1936 to 1977. Chapter 2, "Arise, Ye Who Refuse to Be Bond Slaves! Paul Robeson, 'the Black King of Songs,'" rediscovers Robeson's profound affection for China, his enthusiasm for its resistance against Japan, his long-term friendship with leftist Chinese sojourner artists, and the reciprocal embrace of Robeson and the PRC. Chapter 3, "Transpacific Mass Singing, Journalism, and Christian Activism: Liu Liangmo," explores Liu's launch of the mass singing movement for China's war mobilization and his popularization of China's fighting and folk songs globally through cooperation with Robeson. It discusses his simultaneous interactions with African, Chinese, and white Americans through music, speeches, and journalism. The chapter follows how Liu actively participated in the "Three-Self Reform Movement" in the PRC to bind Christian churches to the new regime and how, as a high-level cultural official, he promoted the receptions of the Du Boises and Robeson. Chapter 4, "Choreographing Ethnicity, War, and Revolution around the Globe: Sylvia Si-lan Chen Leyda," unpacks Chen's journey through the Caribbean, Europe, China, the Soviet Union, and the United States as the first "modern Chinese/Soviet dancer." She choreographed political and folk material from China, Soviet Asia, African America, and the Caribbean, borrowing techniques from China's wartime cartoons and caricatures. As a daughter of Eugene Chen, the left-leaning minister of foreign affairs of the Republic of China, her mixed background forced her to navigate complex racial and political hurdles. Yet Robeson and Hughes saw and depicted her as personifying the "perfect" union of Black and Chinese. Chapter 5, "Roar, China! Langston Hughes, Poet Laureate of the Negro Race," explores the unique role Hughes played, as the first Black intellectual celebrity in China, in connecting the liberation campaigns of Chinese and African Americans. There, his image foregrounded his intellectual capacity as opposed to stereo-typical "primitive" athletic and musical personas and the commercialized exoticism of Blacks. The chapter addresses his epic visit to China in 1933, his romance with Chen, his extensive writings about China, and the reception of his work there within shifting ideological contexts. An epilogue briefly discusses contemporary understanding of these five citizens of the world.

FIGURE 1.1. W. E. B. Du Bois lectures at Beijing University
in a celebration of his ninety-first birthday, February 23, 1959.
*Courtesy of W. E. B. Du Bois Papers, mums312-io685, Special Collections
and University Archives, University of Massachusetts Amherst Libraries.*

1

Africa, Arise! Face the Rising Sun!

W. E. B. and Shirley Graham Du Bois

On February 23, 1959, W. E. B. Du Bois (1868–63), accompanied by his wife, Shirley Graham Du Bois, celebrated his ninety-first birthday by speaking to more than 1,000 faculty members and students at Beijing University, China's most prestigious institution of higher learning, and to the world by radio (fig. 1.1). In his epic speech, Du Bois proclaimed Chinese and African dignity and unity in the face of Western racism, colonialism, and capitalism. He opened his speech grandly, "By courtesy of the government of the six hundred and eighty million people of the Chinese Republic, I am permitted . . . to speak to the people of China and Africa and through them to the world. Hail, then, and farewell, dwelling places of the yellow and Black races. Hail human kind!" Du Bois declared that the "ownership" of "my own soul" led him to dare "advise" Africa to follow China's leadership and recognize its understanding of the color line. "China after long centuries has arisen to her feet and leapt forward. Africa, Arise, and stand straight, speak and think! Turn from the West and your slavery and humiliation for the last 500 years and face the rising sun. Behold a people, the most populous nation on this ancient earth which . . . aims to 'make men holy; to make men free.' . . . China is flesh of your flesh and blood of your blood." He urged China in turn to recognize that it is "colored and knows [to] what a colored skin in this modern world subjects its owner." Du Bois answered his own concern by noting that "China knows more, much more than this; she knows what to do about it." He concluded the speech pleading that Africa and China "stand together in this new world and let the old world perish in its greed or be born again in new hope and promise. Listen to the Hebrew prophet of Communism: Ho! Every one that thirsteth; come ye to the waters; come, buy and eat, without money and without price!"

Afterward, the speech was reprinted and distributed widely. Du Bois proudly recalled how his birthday was accorded a "national celebration ... as never before." The *People's Daily*, the mouthpiece of the Chinese Communist Party, praised his speech and headlined its full coverage with the title "Du Bois Issues a Call to the African People: Africa, Arise! Face the Rising Sun! The Black Continent Could Gain the Most Friendship and Sympathy from China." The speech was soon published in *Peking Review*, a popular global mouthpiece of Communist China. To accompany Du Bois's speech, Jack Chen, an editor of the magazine and Sylvia Si-lan Chen's brother, contributed a cartoon illustrating Uncle Sam offering a new gilded chain of dollar signs to a muscular Black man breaking his old one. Footage of the speech would be prominently featured in a documentary on the Du Boises' visit made by the Central News and Documentary Film Studio on behalf of the Chinese People's Association for Cultural Relations with Foreign Countries (*Zhongguo renmin duiwai wenhua xiehui*, CPACRFC).[1] Outside of China, the *New York Times*, a less sympathetic newspaper, reported, "Dr. Du Bois summed up his bitterness at the United States by saying in his speech that 'in my own country for nearly a century I have been nothing but a nigger.'"[2]

W. E. B. and Shirley Graham Du Bois's visit was part of their triumphal world tour from August 8, 1958, to July 1, 1959, which Du Bois called "the most significant journey" of his life. It became possible after the Supreme Court of the United States ruled that the U.S. State Department lacked the authority to deny passports to citizens who refused to sign the affidavit that they were not communists. The Du Boises responded by immediately applying for and securing their passports.[3] The Soviet Union and the People's Republic of China (PRC) both extended welcoming hands to the long-isolated couple, who eagerly added China to their itinerary.

Du Bois's milestone trip and speech afforded the PRC a measure of political dignity and status that it badly needed in 1959. During the Great Leap Forward, the CCP's first major crisis, and increasing Sino-Soviet tensions, Mao Zedong wished to cultivate alliances with emerging African nations and regarded Du Bois, with his immense international reputation, as key to that effort.[4] Du Bois felt honored and enlightened in turn by what he saw in China. He regarded China and Africa as joined in their present and future battles against Western imperialism and capitalism. If the Chinese wanted to teach Du Bois about the need for international revolution, he was ready to applaud and support their efforts. With Communist China now replacing Japan as the beacon of hope in Asia, Du Bois's advocacy of a joint Pan-Africanism and Pan-Asianism reached a new height.

W. E. B. and Shirley Graham Du Bois

Historically, Du Bois's views of China and Asia had evolved within shifting political and ideological contexts. The message of his 1959 visit to China stood in sharp contrast to the statements he delivered after his little-noticed first trip to Asia in 1936. In the midst of China's national crisis stemming from Japanese military aggression, Du Bois had proclaimed, "I believe in Japan. It is not that I sympathize with China less, but that I hate white European and American propaganda, theft, and insult more. I believe in Asia for the Asiatics and despite the hell of war and fascism of capital, I see in Japan the best agent for this end." Finding a lack of racial strength in the Nationalist government, Du Bois then anointed imperial Japan as the pillar of Asia, a position that sparked outrage in the United States and China—and that he did remark upon twenty-three years later.[5]

The Du Boises' visits to China are well known, but scholars have not accorded them much importance. Their high-profile 1959 trip has received the most notice, yet David Levering Lewis, Du Bois's most significant biographer, dismisses it as naive, a common perception.[6] Most scholarly attention has focused on the consequences of this trip in the United States. Robin D. G. Kelley, Bill V. Mullen, and other scholars have detailed its importance for understanding Du Bois's philosophy of the unity of people of color and the trip's impact on Black radicals of the 1960s. Mullen, the leading commentator on Du Bois's writings on Asia, contends that this visit stoked Du Bois's anticolonialism, a major theme in the later decades of his active life.[7] Looking through the lens of China's official coverage of the event, it becomes clear that the time that the Du Boises spent in China was mutually beneficial for the guests and their hosts. Du Bois learned much from China and from his wife's experiences there. In turn, the Chinese benefited from their influence among Black and national communities.

Shirley Graham Du Bois played an important role in their visits to China and their aftermath. Her biographer Gerald Horne has done much to enhance Graham Du Bois's reputation after several decades of neglect and disdain.[8] Yet even Horne's work has not fully analyzed the couple's visits to China in 1959 and in 1962 or credited Graham Du Bois's contributions. This chapter reveals how Graham Du Bois became a key interpreter of her husband's vision of China. Her devotion to the cause of women there during and after the visits helped Du Bois change his views of China as weak to the new understanding of a developing nation inhabited by robust men and women. After Du Bois's death, Graham Du Bois's personal involvement with significant actors in the Cultural Revolution (1966–76) added new dimensions of the ties between Red China and Black America.[9]

W. E. B. Du Bois's famous dictum that the question of the twentieth century is that of the color line takes on even broader meaning in the light of these visits. The Du Boises' trips to China and comments on China and Asia within the context of race, colonialism, capitalism, and socialism or communism enlarged the story of their lives and thought. It becomes clear that Du Bois's story of the color line in the twentieth century is incomplete without the Chinese perspective.

DU BOIS'S EARLY VIEWS: "ASIA FOR THE ASIATICS"

In his semiautobiographical *Dusk of Dawn*, published in 1940, W. E. B. Du Bois wrote that, beyond the "badge of color," the "social heritage of slavery" and "the discrimination and insult . . . binds together not simply the children of Africa, but extends through yellow Asia and into the South Seas. It is this unity that draws me to Africa." He further articulated this sentiment in his 1958 letter to Madam Sun Yat-sen: "From my boyhood I feel near them [the Chinese]; they were my physical cousins."[10]

China had played a part in Du Bois's hopes for the unity of people of color since the publication of *The Souls of Black Folk* in 1903. The "martyr-dom [in Africa in 1885] of the drunken Bible-reader and freebooter, Chinese Gordon," who had helped to suppress the Taiping Rebellion, had first signaled for him white dominance in both Africa and China. Du Bois noted that white colonialism in Asia ushered in "a particular use of the word 'white'" in the colonial vocabulary of race. White imperial powers' attempt to divide China in the late nineteenth century marked the climax of colonialism, Du Bois announced at the 1909 National Negro Conference.[11]

China and Asia helped Du Bois debunk a white supremacism that sustained colonialism through pseudoscience and religion. In his 1897 essay disputing the classification of human races through comparative anatomy, Du Bois prominently noted the allegedly "yellow" skin, the "obstinately" straight hair, and the monosyllabic language of the Chinese. Citing the cultural giants of China and other Asian countries, Du Bois asserted that white "brains and physique" were not superior to those of the "Indian, Chinese or Negro." "Run the gamut," he demanded in 1920, "and let us have the Europeans who in sober truth overmatch Nefertiti, Mohammed, Rameses, and Askea, Confucius, Buddha." Du Bois went on to affirm the advancement of Chinese civilization in 1931: "China is eternal. She was civilized when Englishmen wore tails. . . . Before Civilization was, China is." He proposed inserting photographs of Paul Robeson, Sun Yat-sen, and President Calvin

W. E. B. and Shirley Graham Du Bois

Coolidge in American geography textbooks as visual representatives of the "three great branches of humanity."[12] Du Bois predicted that the discovery that color and racial prejudices were "largely lies and assumptions" rather than science would empower the oppressed races. He asked rhetorically in 1920, "What is this new self-consciousness leading to? Inevitably and directly to distrust and hatred of whites; to demands for self-government, separation, driving out of foreigners — 'Asia for the Asiatics,' 'Africa for the Africans,' and 'Negro officers for Negro troops!'"[13]

By embracing China's 1911 Revolution and World War I as vehicles for the social and economic uplift of nonwhites, Du Bois directly linked the struggles of African Americans and those of nationalist forces in China. His editorial in the *Crisis*, the magazine of the National Association for the Advancement of Colored People (NAACP), predicted that the establishment of the Republic of China would usher in "a world where Black, brown and white are free and equal." Du Bois was confident that the Great War would lead to "an independent China, a self-governing India, an Egypt with representative institutions, and an Africa for Africans' sake and not merely for business exploitation," in addition to "an American Negro, with the right to vote and the right to work and the right to live without insult."[14] During the First Pan-African Congress in Paris, Du Bois presented a memorandum to U.S. president Woodrow Wilson at the Versailles Peace Conference, urging that the principle of self-determination be universally applied to "inaugurate on the dark continent a last great crusade for humanity. With Africa redeemed, Asia would be safe and Europe indeed triumphant." The *Chicago Tribune* dismissed his "scheme" as "quite Utopian, and it has less than a Chinaman's chance of getting anywhere in the Peace Conference, but it is nevertheless interesting."[15] Even so, Vladimir Lenin and, later, the CCP echoed Du Bois's views.

Du Bois closely monitored events unfolding in China following the 1911 Revolution. In the *Crisis*, he discussed how the Northern Expedition jointly launched by the Nationalist Party and the CCP between 1926 and 1927 overcame setbacks under warlords. For Du Bois, it signaled the painful birth of a free modern China, one "slowly and relentlessly kicking Europe into the sea." He initially refused to believe that the Northern Expedition was falling apart and condemned threats of foreign intervention, particularly by the United States. After Chiang Kai-shek's bloody purge of the CCP, Du Bois repeatedly denounced him as a "traitor." When Chiang, influenced by his new wife, May-ling Soong, converted to Methodism, Du Bois poured scorn on the general. "China has had enough troubles, but now that it is reported that

Chiang Kai-shek has embraced Christianity. 'We can confidently expect anything.'" Nonetheless, Du Bois remained optimistic that revolutionary forces in China would rid the land of "home grown exploiters and foreign leeches." Soon he led the Fourth Pan-African Congress in New York City to pass a resolution demanding "real" national independence of China, India, Egypt, and Ethiopia and the rights of Africans and African-derived peoples.[16]

Insisting "Asia for the Asiatics" in opposition to white colonialism, Du Bois could not avoid the complex position of Japan in imperial struggles over the color line. While Japan rose as the only colonial power in Asia at the expense of China and Korea following the first Sino-Japanese War (1894–95), Du Bois welcomed "the sudden self-assertion of Japan" for breaking down "a whole vocabulary" of white colonialism on racial supremacy. He further applauded the maneuvers of "yellow" Japan during World War I, which defied "the cordon of this color bar" and threatened "white hegemony."[17] However, as early as 1885, the influential Japanese philosopher Yukichi Fukuzawa had explicitly advocated that Japan "leave the ranks of Asian nations and cast our lot with the civilized nations of the West." U.S. president Theodore Roosevelt granted Japan the status of honorary Aryan to carry on the "white man's burden" at the end of the 1905 Russo-Japanese War. Du Bois expressed concern about such an alliance: "If, of course, Japan would join heart and soul with the whites against the rest of the yellows, browns, and Blacks, well and good. There are even good-natured attempts to prove the Japanese 'Aryan,' provided they act 'white.'" Even so, he opted to ignore the aggressive Twenty-One Demands Japan had slapped on China in 1915, and reasoned that "blood is thick, and there are signs that Japan does not dream of a world governed mainly by white men." Furthermore, he warned that fear of the "yellow peril" might entail "a world crusade against this presumptuous nation which demands 'white' treatment." Considering China and Japan to be fellow challengers of white supremacy, he concluded that post–World War I hope lay "in the Orient, [with] the awakened Japanese and the awakening leaders of New China."[18]

Supported by Du Bois, the First Pan-African Congress petitioned the Versailles Peace Conference to turn over German colonies to an international organization instead of various colonial powers. However, despite strong protest from China, which had just made war contribution to the Allies, the conference transferred German colonial interests in China to Japan. In the 1917 Lansing-Ishii Agreement, the United States recognized Japan's "special interests" in China. Celebrating the agreement as U.S. acknowledgment that "Asia is primarily for the Asiatics," Du Bois advised

W. E. B. and Shirley Graham Du Bois

China to unite with Japan in order to "present an unbroken front to the aggressions of the whites."[19]

Du Bois's first trip to the Soviet Union in 1926, amid China's Northern Expedition sponsored by the U.S.S.R., allowed him to count on the communist country to help uplift the darker races. He acknowledged, probably only this one time, that "Japan is the logical leader of Asia and yet has been among the severest oppressors of China." Du Bois hoped Japan's severe financial trouble, partially caused by its "seeking to play both ends against the middle, in the fight between Europe and Asia," would eventually "align Japan with the colored race where she belongs." He applauded the Soviet Union for never drawing a color line but rather courting the "yellow races" and "alone" assisting "China's true interests." Encouraged by Du Bois, the resolution of the Fourth Pan-African Congress "thanked" the Soviet Union for such "liberal" endeavors and its decision not to confront China following the collapse of the Northern Expedition. He declared, "China and Russia are becoming the beacons of all oppressed peoples." Du Bois was alarmed that the British proposed a naval base in Singapore in 1930 to facilitate whites' penetration into China. He avowed that would never happen, because "yellow Asia and Red Russia forbid it, which is another lesson in race superiority."[20]

Immediately after Japan launched the full-scale war on China in 1937, Du Bois would cast a nostalgic look at the Northern Expedition, which he now interpreted as a "magnificent providence of God" carried out by China and the Soviet Union to emancipate the working class across the world. Armed with a newly acquired class perspective, Du Bois blamed capitalist and imperialist domination following the death of Sun Yat-sen for disrupting a chance to reshape the geopolitical landscape in Asia. When Cold War tensions intensified near the end of World War II, Du Bois would quickly remind the world that Western racial contempt toward the darker races had been similarly poured upon the Balkans and Russia as "quasi-Asiatic," leading to the staging of "almost a race war to uphold tottering capitalism" following the 1917 Bolshevik Revolution.[21] Such perceptions long anticipated his late-life conversion to communism.

DU BOIS DEFENDS JAPAN'S MAKING "MANCHURIA ASIATIC"

After Japan boldly challenged the post–World War I territorial arrangement by seizing Manchuria following the Mukden Incident on September 18, 1931, the League of Nations ordered a commission headed by the British statesman Lord Victor Bulwer-Lytton to investigate the invasion. While Japan maneuvered for international recognition of its puppet Manchukuo, Chinese and Japanese diplomats vigorously argued for their own cases with the League. Paul Chih Meng (Meng Zhi), associate director of the China Institute then located at 119 West 57th Street in New York City, compiled a monograph titled *China Speaks: On the Conflict between China and Japan*. Weiching William Yen (Yan Huiqing), China's chief delegate to the League of Nations and its minister to the United States, and W. W. Willoughby, professor of political science at Johns Hopkins University and a frequent adviser to the Chinese government on international affairs, contributed introductions. The book was in dialogue with *Japan Speaks on the Sino-Japanese Crisis* by K. K. Kawakami, a veteran news correspondent in Washington, D.C., with an introduction by the Japanese prime minister, Ki Tsuyoshi Inukai. *China Speaks* apparently drew enough attention from the Japanese side that the South Manchuria Railway Company office in Manhattan's Lincoln Building acquired a copy.[22]

As an outspoken exemplar of the pro-Japanese mindset among African Americans, W. E. B. Du Bois unambiguously defended Japan's new round of aggression. He asked rhetorically, "Could China have been saved from exploitation if Japan had not made Manchuria Asiatic by force?" After the investigation commission was announced in November, he immediately asserted that the League could not stop Japan because of its members' "bloody hands." He then repeatedly denounced their "Hypocrisy of Hypocrisies," comparing Great Britain and France defending China against Japan to "two fat tabbies taking charge of the interests of mice."[23] Meanwhile, Du Bois warned China loudly not to trust the League, as "a word from twelve little Black millions who live in the midst of Western culture and know it." He insisted that the League's intervention "bodes ill" for China and "all colored folk," because the white imperialists behind the League were there only for the chance to "crush and exploit" both China and Japan among "blood and smoke of Shanghai and Manchuria."[24]

After the League of Nations recommended that Japan return Manchuria to the status quo prior to the Mukden Incident, Japan withdrew from the League and accelerated its aggressions in China. Du Bois observed the League's inaction with contempt: "We seem dimly to remember that the League of Nations, armed with several notes from Mr. [Secretary of State Henry L.] Stimson, started to make Japan do something sometime.... Here is Mr. [Kikujirō] Ishii telling America to keep out of China, and yet we have not mobilized the fleet." Du Bois warned of a potential alliance between

W. E. B. and Shirley Graham Du Bois

the 12 million African Americans and Japan, when the United States fights a "colored nation." He pressed, "Don't let that slip your mind for one little minute."[25]

Du Bois forcefully defended "Japanese imperialism" as a lesser evil than the European variety. He insisted that "Japan's assault upon China [was] not simply naked aggression" but sought to protect China and Asia from the "rapacity of the white imperialist nations," which had "forced her [Japan] to choose between militarism or suicide." He recast Japan's actions from the first Sino-Japanese War to the Russo-Japanese War as acts of resistance against European domination over Asia. Ultimately, Du Bois urged that "us as colored people" must recognize that "Japanese imperialism" would offer "infinitely" greater economic benefits than the most advanced white countries, "except . . . Russia." During his student years in Germany, Du Bois had learned his earlier lessons on color-blind racial brutality exercised by Germans against Poles and Jews. Nonetheless, he insisted otherwise when Japan and China were concerned.[26] His argument dovetailed with Japanese claims of a Pan-Asianism, which justified Japan's colonial aggression in Asia as protecting the continent from white colonial powers.

Du Bois thus appealed to China and Japan to cease fighting and unite with India in order to drive their real enemy, the white exploiters, out of Asia entirely. He pleaded his case earnestly in the *Crisis* editorial of January 1933:

> Colossi of Asia and leaders of all colored mankind: for God's sake
> stop fighting and get together. Compose your quarrels on any
> reasonable basis. Unite in self-defense and assume that leadership
> of distracted mankind to which your four hundred million of people
> entitle you. . . . Unmask them [the White imperialists], Asia; tear apart
> their double faces and double tongues and unite in peace. Remember,
> Japan, that white America despises and fears you. Remember, China,
> that England covets your land and labor. Unite! Beckon to the three
> hundred million Indians; drive Europe out of Asia and let her get her
> own raped and distracted house in order. Let the yellow and brown
> race, nine hundred million strong, take their rightful leadership
> of mankind. Let the young Chinese and Japanese students and
> merchants of America and Europe cease debate and recrimination
> while gleeful whites egg them on. Get together, China and Japan,
> cease quarreling and fighting! Arise and lead. The world needs Asia.

In vain, Du Bois warned, "Careful, careful, Nordics; Japan and China are nearing understanding."[27] Such an alliance was not to be.

Du Bois vaguely imagined a joint Pan-Asianism and Pan-Africanism with Japan as the leader. He forecast that "unification and reasonable oneness of purpose . . . between yellow Asia and Black Africa" would usher in a new era free of white dominance. Du Bois believed an unconfirmed report of a treaty between Japan and Ethiopia, by which Ethiopia was to provide 16 million acres for Japanese colonization in exchange for "Japanese ingenuity, trade and friendship," exemplified affinity between the two continents. He had no illusions that Japanese motive in Ethiopia was other than profit but insisted that the Western powers' "selfish and outrageous" conduct there was worse.[28]

1936 TRIP: A RACIAL PARADISE IN MANCHUKUO VERSUS "ASIAN UNCLE TOMS" IN SHANGHAI

Propelled by his dream of a unified Asia and Africa, Du Bois prepared to visit the East. An opportunity finally arose in 1936 when he received a $1,600 travel fellowship from the Oberlaender Trust in Philadelphia to study education developments in Germany. During a seven-month trip, he visited the Third Reich, England, and Austria before entering China and Japan from the Soviet Union. On this second trip to the Soviet Union, Du Bois observed a nation "sure of itself." New construction, general prosperity, law and order, and military might were in widespread evidence.[29] Du Bois chose to ignore Joseph Stalin's steady repression, an indifference to tyranny that would become apparent in his subsequent visits to Manchukuo and Maoist China.

Despite Du Bois's friendship with the Soviet Union, the Japanese authorities, who had noted his unambiguous pro-Japanese position in the aftermath of the Mukden Incident, sagely realized the potential value of Du Bois's backing. They sought to use Du Bois to stimulate antiwar sentiment among African Americans, whom they rightly perceived as a potentially significant fighting force for the U.S. military. With this goal, the Asian leg of Du Bois's trip was facilitated by Yasuichi Hikida, "one of Imperial Japan's most effective agents in the United States," as observed by David Levering Lewis. Hikida was particularly adept at cultivating Japanese–African American alliances. He was well acquainted with Du Bois and his wife Nina before Du Bois requested contacts in Japan to deliver lectures in exchange for travel expenses and advice on places to stay in the segregated parts of China. They communicated frequently on these matters between the summer of 1935 and October 1936. Hikida mentioned that, like Black athletes in the forthcoming 1940 Tokyo Olympics, Du Bois's trip to the East would be of "tremendous

W. E. B. and Shirley Graham Du Bois

interest and importance" to the "mutual propaganda of the darker races, particularly that of [sic] between Japanese and American Negro." He suggested that in connection with Du Bois's scheduled visit *Darkwater* or *The Souls of Black Folk* should be translated into Japanese. Hikida made arrangements for accommodations from Manchukuo, China, to Japan to ensure Du Bois's trip to the East was both "comfortable and profitable." At the Inner Mongolia border, a Japanese official from the Manchukuo State Railways, "the billion-yen quasi-state corporation [dominated by the South Manchuria Railway Company] that had become Japan's largest business enterprise," awarded Du Bois two first-class "complementary" tickets across Manchukuo, a tactic guaranteed to please the traveler. Du Bois compared this gift with Jim Crow practices in the United States, in which nonwhite travelers were forced to buy undesirable train seats at premium prices.

In his *Pittsburgh Courier* articles in early 1937 chronicling his trip, Du Bois exhaustively covered the range of interactions during his weeklong stay in Manchukuo to ensure that his observations sounded thorough and credible: "I have seen its borders north, west and south; its capital and their chief cities and many towns; I have walked the streets night and day; I have talked with officials, visited industries and read reports." As he traveled east through Harbin and on to Changchun (the Japanese renamed the city Xinjing) on November 13, he marveled at the perfect service and comfortable trains and roadbed. Long convinced of the immense value of Japan's triumph in Manchuria, Du Bois visited Yosuke Matsuoka, the president of the railways and the most important Japanese official in China, in Shenyang (Mukden). As Japan's last delegate to the League of Nations, Matsuoka previously "had led the dramatic exit of the Japanese delegation" from the organization. After stopping by Dalian, Du Bois capped his schedule with a ride, arranged by Hikida's contacts, to Port Arthur, where he, accompanied by graduates of several American universities, was entertained at lunch and dinner. Dinner was followed by a lecture and discussion on race segregation through an interpreter, and an evening call from the U.S. consul.[30]

Du Bois's visit to Manchukuo was, he proudly noted, "marked by courtesy, sympathy and hospitality." His experiences further convinced him that "colonial enterprise by a colored nation need not imply the caste, exploitation, and subjection," as it did with "white Europe."[31] He declared, "I brush aside as immaterial the question as to whether Manchukuo is an independent state or a colony of Japan. The main question for me is: What is Japan doing for the people of Manchuria and how is she doing it? Is she building up a caste of superior and inferior? Is she reducing the mass of the people to slavery and poverty? Is she stealing the land and monopolizing the natural resources? Are the people of Manchuria happier or more miserable for the presence of the foreign power on their soil?" Du Bois then enthusiastically embraced this exceptionally benign form of colonialism, depicting Manchukuo as a racially harmonious paradise: "I have come to the firm conclusion that in no colony that I have seen or read is there such clear evidence of . . . absence of racial or color caste [and] . . . no apparent discrimination between motherland and colony. . . . Nowhere else in the world, to my knowledge, is this true. And why? Because Japanese and Manchukuoans are so nearly related in race that there [neither] is nor can be . . . race prejudice." Du Bois lauded the "marvelous" achievements in Manchukuo that had come about within four years of the invasion. He witnessed fully employed "happy" people under impartial "public peace and order," excused "separate schools for Manchukuoans and Japanese" as for pure linguistic reasons, and declared "a lynching in Manchukuo would be unthinkable." He naively insisted that "the Japanese hold no absolute monopoly of the offices of the state," since "the natives" were fully incorporated. Du Bois was most enthusiastic about the state ownership and "public services" in electricity, water, gas, telegraph, telephone, and even crop management, boasting that "the largest open cut coal mine in the world is in Manchuria," employing 30,000 miners and owning its own infrastructure. He acknowledged that, unlike in the Soviet Union, the government control over capital in Manchukuo was not "for the benefit of the workers. But neither, so far as that is concerned, is Japan's."[32]

Nationalist China under the despised Chiang Kai-shek offered a sharp contrast. Du Bois was horrified by open displays of racial arrogance and imperialist oppression in Shanghai. In his third, posthumously published autobiography, he recalled his distress at observing that "the greatest city of the most populous nation on earth" was owned, governed, and policed by foreigners, with their warships floating calmly nearby. He provided the shocking statistics: in "this city of nations," 3 million Chinese were ruled by 19,000 Japanese, 11,000 Britons supported by "black-bearded Sikhs," 10,000 Russians, 4,000 Americans, and 10,000 foreigners of other nationalities. During his one-week stay in the treaty port, Du Bois witnessed a shocking racial incident. "A little English boy of perhaps four years of age ordered three Chinese children out of his imperial way on the sidewalk on the Bund; and they meekly obeyed and walked in the gutter." It reminded him of Mississippi. Adding to the irony, "And, too, I met a 'missionary' from Mississippi," teaching in the Baptist University of Shanghai, from which Liu Liangmo had just graduated. Du Bois caricatured that at least matters had improved, since rich

Chinese could visit the racetrack, from which they and dogs had long been excluded, and the notorious abuse of coolies and rickshaw pullers had become less common.[33]

Du Bois made controversial statements that further endeared him to the Japanese but alienated Chinese nationalists and Americans alike. Concern over Japanese aggression was widespread from Geneva, Manchukuo, and Shanghai to New York City. While arranging his trip with Hikida, Du Bois reached out to the Chinese embassy, which referred him to the China Institute. Du Bois was well acquainted with the institute's director. In the early 1920s, he had arranged for Chih Meng, then a Columbia graduate student, to visit southern Black colleges to correct Meng's "too rosy" impressions of the United States. Surprised by Meng's report that most Blacks' "prejudices and misinformation on China are just as bad" as whites' toward Blacks, Du Bois and Meng introduced Chinese faculty members and students to Fisk, Tuskegee, Howard University, and the Hampton Institute to promote "mutual understanding." Now, at the behest of Meng, Du Bois "went by invitation" to the University of Shanghai, Liu Liangmo's alma mater. Its first Chinese president, Herman Liu Zhan'en, was Meng's schoolmate at Nankai and Columbia Universities and was on the China Institute's board of advisers. Liu Zhan'en was familiar with Du Bois's scholarly stature, and they had corresponded in 1930 about the University of Shanghai library subscribing to the *Crisis*. However, Meng and Liu's earnest gesture did not ultimately win the leading Black scholar's favorable opinion. In contrast to what Hikida's network offered to Du Bois, they stressed that he had to give lectures "gratis," despite the traveler's explicit statement that payment for his travel expenses depended on paid lecture engagements. Meng cited "recent political and economic conditions" in China and the steep currency exchange rate, which could hardly impress the proud scholar. Beyond trivial material gains, physical comfort, or vanity, Du Bois obviously perceived his reception as the measurement of attitudes toward his race.

At the university, Du Bois "occupied a seat on the dais," listened as a Rockefeller Foundation representative spoke about scholarships to the United States, but "declined to say even a few words," when requested by Liu Zhan'en. Instead, "I said to the president that I should like to talk to a group of Chinese and discuss frankly racial and social matters," Du Bois reported. Liu complied and arranged a luncheon at the Chinese Bankers' Club at 59 Hong Kong Road on November 30. Among the attendees were T. N. Dzau, one of the editors of the China Press; T. C. Tai, the secretary-general of the Bank of China; Hollington K. Tong, the general manager of the China Publishing Company; H. C. Chen, director of the Educational Bureau for Chinese, Shanghai Municipal Council; and Poeliu Dai, the executive secretary of the China Institute of International Relations. Du Bois's vivid description of the gathering, into which he "plunged . . . recklessly," first appeared in one of his *Pittsburgh Courier* articles and was reprinted in his 1954 essay "Normal US-China Relations" and in his *Autobiography*. After introducing his slave ancestors, his education and travels, and the "Negro problem," Du Bois bombarded his hosts with a series of questions on various issues, ranging from escape from the dominance of European capital, a future world with Asia and the colored races as its spiritual center, to the progress of China's working classes. Most important, he would like to know, "Why is it that you hate Japan more than Europe when you have suffered more from England, France, and Germany than from Japan?" If Japan and China worked together, he continued, perhaps Europe could be eliminated permanently from Asia. Du Bois calmly reported, "There ensured a considerable silence, in which I joined."[34]

His hosts politely acknowledged that they knew little of India or Africa, or "Africa in America," and "Asia is still under the spell of Europe," but they specified their plan to seek control of capital and boasted of China's achievements, such as a stabilized currency, increased wages, budding labor legislation, and a campaign against illiteracy. Unimpressed, Du Bois reported his shock over "cheap women; cheap child-labor; cheap men" and the "vast poverty" amid a "glittering modern life of skyscrapers, majestic hotels, theaters and night clubs." Workers were paid "less than an average of 25 cents a day" under the heels of omnipresent European capital. He trusted that the Chinese seconded his argument that the core of China's "emancipation" was "European capitalist control," rather than imminent Japanese military brutality.[35]

Du Bois's dismayed hosts responded that whatever problems China suffered, Japan's militarism hindered any progress. Unconvinced, Du Bois commented in the *Pittsburgh Courier* that "the most disconcerting thing about Asia is the burning hatred of China and Japan [for each other]." Until 1954, Du Bois insisted how wrong his hosts were: China "bitterly resented the intrusion of Japan, coming in as though she were a Western power destined to dominate Orientals." In his *Autobiography*, Du Bois lamented his fruitless argument in 1936 with the "several leading Chinese" and realized that even after three hours of debate, nothing had been said about the Soviet Union, or about the CCP's Long March; America was mentioned "only for its benefactions and scarcely for its exploitation"; little was said about the Nationalist

Party or Chiang Kai-shek; only hatred of Japan was in the air.[36] Du Bois attempted to reach Madam Sun, who had been known for hosting high-profile leftist foreign guests, including Langston Hughes and Sylvia Si-lan Chen, "but failed," as he would reveal in his 1958 letter to Madam Sun expressing his desire to revisit China.[37]

While Du Bois's contemporary notes focused on the sharply contrasting racial landscapes in Manchukuo and Shanghai, his writings decades later mentioned his visit to the two ancient capitals Nanjing and Beiping (now Beijing) but omitted his trip to another treaty port, Tianjin, sponsored by the Hikida network. He dismissed the historic Nanjing, now capital of the Nationalist government, as "a thing half-begun and half-done" and an abandoned "ghost capital," evidently due to lack of funds. Writing in the *Pittsburgh Courier*, Du Bois briefly acknowledged China's history, landscapes, and its striking "myriads of people." China "is inconceivable. . . . Never before has a land so affected me"—not even Africa. Its vastness, its teeming millions, and its ancient quality overwhelmed him. In romantic terms, Du Bois shifted his gaze in the 1950s from Japan to the PRC as the pillar for the "darker world." For example, he retrospectively elaborated his marvel at standing on top of the Great Wall, the acclaimed "only work of man visible from Mars," to which he rode on the shoulders of four men up and down, paying only seventy cents. "I write this now as things were in 1936," Du Bois insisted.[38]

As he sailed from Shanghai aboard the S.S. *Shanghai Mari* to Nagasaki on December 1, 1936, Du Bois hurled a final insult, claiming that the Chinese Nationalists were "Asian Uncle Toms" and likening them to willing Black menials of white racism in the United States. Japanese newspapers had widely advertised the forthcoming lectures by the "father of black folk" on "overthrowing White men," which was associated with Black athletes' triumph at the 1936 Olympics. Upon his arrival in Japan, Du Bois was again treated like a celebrity, captured in numerous photographs preserved in his papers. Though he noted poverty and a lack of democratic freedom in Japan in his private diary, Du Bois publicly exulted in his reception, arranged by Hikida's associates, in elite circles, and marveled at its prosperous cities, shrines, and theaters (fig. 1.2). He announced that the hospitality heaped on him was a gesture from one colored people to another and "for this reason, my visit is not to be forgotten." For decades, a framed Japanese-language poster advertising Du Bois's lecture titled "The Future of the Black Race" hung above the bound first editions of his books, neatly arranged on a desk in the living room of his Brooklyn Heights home.[39]

FIGURE 1.2. W. E. B. Du Bois (*center*) at a dinner party
given by faculty members of the University of Tokyo in 1936.
*Courtesy of W. E. B. Du Bois Papers, mums312-i0460, Special Collections
and University Archives, University of Massachusetts Amherst Libraries.*

After Du Bois returned to the United States in early 1937, his interviews
from his recent trip abroad were published in the then liberal *New York Post*
and the German-language *Staats-Zeitung und Herold*. His essay on the same
subject appeared in the *Amsterdam News* in 1939. There he repeated his belief in the virtues of Japanese rule and firmly urged a Sino-Japanese alliance,
which would "save the world for the darker races." He steadfastly maintained
such views after Japanese forces occupied Beiping and Shanghai, and even
after the world learned of Japan's genocidal occupation of China's Nanjing
in the winter of 1937–38. To the news of the Nanjing Massacre, one of the
worst slaughters of the twentieth century, Du Bois responded that few of the
white American protestors had said much about depredations in Ethiopia.
In contrast, he maintained, the Japanese classed themselves with the Chinese, Indians, and Negroes as "folk standing over against the white world."
In 1938, the U.S. *China Weekly Review* returned the taunt when it alleged that
Du Bois was a paid propagandist for the Japanese. To a letter asking him to
affirm that he was not a paid agent for Japan, Du Bois replied that, while he
had never received a cent from the Japanese government or from any Japanese person, he had faith in Japan. He tossed aside appeals for nonviolence
and contended that it was Japan's duty to "persuade, cajole and convince

W. E. B. and Shirley Graham Du Bois

China. . . . But China sneered and taught her folk that the Japanese were devils."[40]

Soon Du Bois asked for Chih Meng to recommend a "small textbook" of Chinese history and culture for his "Asiatic Culture" course at Atlanta University. In his 1958 letter, Du Bois would acknowledge to Madam Sun that China remained far from his "touch and knowledge," despite his brief work on the board of directors of China Welfare Appeal Inc. in New York City following his 1936 trip. Headed by YMCA employee Talitha Gerlach, the organization worked closely with Madam Sun. Du Bois died unrepentant about his 1936 scolding of the Chinese Nationalists.[41] Du Bois's arrival in the Republic of China had attracted little notice. His attacks on the elites further alienated the official and semiofficial media, which had little interest in Black intellectuals. His lauding of the Japanese invasion repelled the leftist cultural circles, who had just warmly received Langston Hughes, despite their harsh criticism and rigid judgment of Hughes's work.[42]

PERCEIVING WORLD WAR II THROUGH A RACIAL LENS

W. E. B. Du Bois continued to look with suspicion on the motivations behind European and U.S. actions into the 1940s. At the outset of World War II, Du Bois insisted on the war's racist nature. He regarded it as a means of enabling "white folk's" more successful "mastery of Asia and Africa," citing remarks by Wendell Willkie in the *New York Times*, Pearl S. Buck, Eleanor Roosevelt, and Dorothy Thompson. He quoted Buck at particular length, praising her great "courage" in disputing that the war was being fought for democracy and freedom.

Along similar lines, Du Bois continued to justify Japan's expansion in the Asia-Pacific region. He sympathized with the country's having to defend "her very existence" against Europe, which had sought to "conquer China and thus inhibit Japan." He announced Japan's seizure of Saigon and British fortification of Singapore as reciprocal threats. In 1944 he asserted that the "long trail of blood and tears" China had suffered at the hands of Western colonial powers since the Opium War allowed few illusions as to their imperial intention there. Ignoring Japan's ongoing atrocities against China, Du Bois continued to insist that the two nations shared the goal of driving Europe out of Asia and "substitut[ing] the domination of a weak Asia by a strong Japan." While China's method was "cooperation and gradual understanding," he argued, "Japan['s] was to invoke war and force." Du Bois identified "several hundred million Chinese, Filipino, Malays, and East Indians" as Japan's supportive fellow "yellow bastards."[43]

Du Bois vehemently opposed U.S. involvement in the war, finding support for war among the nation's liberal press "disquieting." In early 1940, Henry L. Stimson, now secretary of war, sent a letter to Du Bois soliciting his aid in deterring Japan. Du Bois declared bluntly and publicly, "He will not get my help," noting that he had received no such letters about Italy and Ethiopia. Among the perceived obstacles for Franklin D. Roosevelt's presidential campaign, Du Bois listed the fact that "his Secretary of State [Cordell Hull] hates Japan." Hull would deliver an ultimatum "for the peace of the Pacific," commonly referred to as the "Open Door Note," to Japan on November 26, 1941. The document requested withdrawal of all Japanese military forces from China and thus affirmed long-established U.S. support of Chinese territorial integrity and equality of commercial opportunity in China. On the same day, Japan sent its naval fleet toward Hawaii.

Du Bois refused to adjust his position even after Japan attacked Pearl Harbor. Echoing his attitude toward the League of Nations following the Mukden Incident, Du Bois ridiculed the chance of U.S. victory: "If General MacArthur is fighting as hard in the Philippines as he is in the American newspapers, the Japanese are doomed." If Japan refused to surrender quickly, he snorted, "why not send Dorothy Thompson over there to talk them to death?"[44]

Du Bois tackled the problems of domestic racial relations to back up his opposition to U.S. war policy. He repeatedly denounced the forced resettlement of 10,000 Japanese Americans as the "most foul example of racism and greed" with the war against Japan as its backdrop. Du Bois called out the harsh treatment of Chinese and Filipino residents, and the racist practice of the Census Bureau in lumping together Blacks, Chinese, Indians, Japanese, and others as "non-whites."[45] To African Americans, he strove to drive home the message that Japan was fighting for "Asiatic freedom," while U.S. racist hostility toward Japan was motivated by his nation's own desire to exploit China. He warned his alma mater, Fisk University, not to fall victim to the "mounting hysteria" for U.S. entry into the war. Du Bois was not alone in his blindness to the horrors of Japanese militarism. Other African Americans contended that the Sino-Japanese conflict was none of their business. To the dismay of such disparate forces as the Communist Party USA and such pro–New Deal Black newspapers as the (New York) *Amsterdam News*, some Black journalists expressed pride in Japanese authorities lording over British, French, and U.S. citizens in occupied Shanghai.[46]

Du Bois's views softened only slightly after the war. Immediately following Japan's surrender, he wondered, "What have we lost and what have we gained from the war?" He concluded, "Japan's defeat and humiliation is a setback for colored peoples," which "most of us have been unhappy about." Yet, drawing upon a class perspective, he conceded, "Insofar as a Japanese exploitative ruling clique was trying to capture all of Asia, we welcome its defeat." He blamed Japanese adoption of Western imperialism for its downfall and terrible abuse of China.[47] Even so, Du Bois remained suspicious of British and U.S. motivations in Asia, contending that their lingering colonial power there constituted "the greatest and most dangerous race problem today." He was concerned that the West's ongoing fears of "yellow peril" and its long-held bogus belief that "the Black and brown and yellow people" were biological inferior and unfit for self-government threatened to dictate the postwar arrangement. Du Bois strongly opposed U.S. occupation of Japan "or any effort to repress the people there." He challenged, "But why? If Asia is going to develop as a self-governing, autonomous part of the world, equal to other parts, why is policing by foreigners necessary? Why cannot Asia police itself?"[48]

Reviving his old hope that world war would lift up the darker races, Du Bois forecast major roles for a freed Asia and Africa in the postwar world. He wrote in early 1943 that the Holocaust screamed "a fierce condemnation" of the entire Western civilization, beyond Hitler or Germany. Du Bois asked rhetorically, "Must we turn to Asia and Africa for the saving of civilization?" The war pushed China and all of Asia to "the center of history again," made the impending "upheaval in Pan-Africa" relevant, and allowed "very significant advances on many fronts by Afro-Americans," as Du Bois saw it. He was confident that "the colored and colonial world" would not allow a Western monopoly of the atomic bomb, the ultimate symbol of power. Du Bois predicted that the nations of the East such as China, India, and Japan, from which now "the sunlight is streaming," would lead the breakthrough.[49]

Du Bois hoped that the future of China would involve allying with both the Soviet Union and the United States, who allegedly "do not depend on the exploitation of colonies," but he was soon disappointed. At the 1944 Dumbarton Oaks Conference, with Great Britain, the two superpowers negotiated alliances and included China only after major decisions were sealed, to Du Bois's dismay. He favorably compared China's antiracist and anticolonial proposal to the one presented by Japan at the League of Nations, but he quickly noted its omission in the published proposals of the conference. In his radio address "The Negro and Imperialism," delivered over WEVD in

New York City on November 15, Du Bois criticized the conference's plan for the United Nations, particularly the UN Security Council. He was concerned that the organization would be dominated by white nations, while "the three hundred and fifty million yellow people represented by China" would not be recognized as racial equals. In his book *Color and Democracy*, produced as the conference unfolded, Du Bois proclaimed famously that "the colonies are the slums of the world."[50] Du Bois's attitude signaled his belief in China's leadership in a postcolonial world.

DU BOIS, INTERNATIONALISM, AND CHINA

In the 1940s Du Bois moved toward a more internationalist approach. His battles with the NAACP leader Walter White left him more marginalized in the U.S. civil rights movement, a pattern exacerbated by his increasingly leftward tilt just as anticommunism was increasing its influence on postwar U.S. domestic policies.

Du Bois grew increasingly enthusiastic about the Soviet Union. He later even claimed, in his *Autobiography*, that none of the NAACP's triumphs, including the fabled *Brown v. Board of Education* decision of 1954, would have been possible without the "world pressure of Communism led by the Soviet Union." In his refusal to accede to the anticommunist party line, Du Bois was exhibiting what Vaughn Rasberry has called his "refusal to be white."[51] The efforts of Paul Robeson, with whom Du Bois drew closer during this time, and Liu Liangmo doubtless influenced Du Bois. Graham Du Bois knew Robeson well, having published a biography of him in 1946. Both Du Boises knew Liu, as they shared social circles in New York City.[52]

Du Bois was concerned that capitalist Japan's alliance with fascism "sets her down as an enemy of Russia," despite his persistent defense of Japanese aggression in Asia. After the 1939 Soviet-Germany agreement, he blamed "the tactics of Britain and France" for driving both the Soviet Union and Japan close to the Nazis. He applauded how the war highlighted the "great prestige and endurance" of the Soviet Union. Du Bois was confident that the communist nation, which had uplifted its "debased masses," cutting across racial lines, in a single generation, would protect Asia and Africa from Western attempts to restore colonialism. He lauded consistent Soviet support for the Chinese Revolution, showing "the greatest sympathy with coolie labor and no love for Chiang Kai-shek." He was pleased that T. F. Tsiang (Jiang Tingfu), a Chinese diplomat and historian, indicated that China's future industrialization would follow the Soviet rather than the U.S. model.[53]

W. E. B. and Shirley Graham Du Bois

Intellectually primed by his support for the Soviet Union, Du Bois encouraged Indian nationalism until he perceived Jawaharlal Nehru's rightward politics after independence, and he found much to admire in Mao Zedong's efforts in China. In contrast, he found little racial solidarity with Chiang Kai-shek and his associates, whom he regarded as soft on white colonialism. In his *Amsterdam News* column, Du Bois summarized Leland Stowe's book *They Shall Not Sleep*, highlighting the corrupt nature of the Chiang regime.[54] Nor was he impressed with the highly popular speeches Madam Chiang made while visiting the United States, criticizing their "generalities" and failure to address China's suffering and exploitation by imperialists. Surprisingly, he did not comment on her omission of African Americans as she praised the contributions of white immigrants to the war effort in her famous addresses to Congress on February 18, 1943.[55] After the "Soong sister had swept in on us with her retinue, jade, and jewels," Du Bois scoffed that British "courtesies" and meager U.S. "justice" could hardly "reassure China." Chiang's brother-in-law T. V. Soong, along with Lord Halifax and Anthony Eden of Britain and Jan Smuts of South Africa, was awarded an honorary degree at the University of California, Berkeley, in 1945. Du Bois ridiculed their qualifications: Soong "for saying nothing," Halifax and Eden for maintaining colonialism, and Smuts for "keeping the Negro in his place."[56]

After the civil war broke out in China in 1946, Du Bois lent his unambiguous support to the CCP. He contended that opposition to President Harry S. Truman's policy to support Chiang's "puppet government" was far from "treason." He applauded the 1948 Conference on the American Policy in China and the Far East in New York City for its objection to identifying "the corrupt and reactionary Chiang Kai-shek" with China. Du Bois congratulated the Communist takeover of Hainan Island in 1950, asking optimistically, "Where will Chiang go when Taiwan is so liberated?" The *People's Daily* noted that he wrote to newspaper editors across the United States condemning a potential U.S. invasion of Taiwan in 1955. As in many political arenas, Du Bois's increasing support for Mao's brand of communism put him further at odds with Walter White, who endorsed Chiang's Nationalist government and was openly anticommunist.[57]

Du Bois repeatedly demanded that the United States recognize the PRC, support its seating at the United Nations, and form mutually advantageous relations with the "great Chinese people." He condemned U.S. refusal to take these steps as "reprehensible" and against diplomatic "common sense[,] ... ethics and philanthropy." Du Bois tirelessly campaigned against U.S. involvement in the Korean War, which he called "the deepest tragedy," and he dismissed the media's claim that the Soviet Union was manipulating the PRC and North Korea.[58] He called Douglas MacArthur "the Wild Man of Tokyo" who was turning Korea into a "stinking desert" and accused MacArthur of seeking to conquer China and Southeast Asia and "drop atom bombs on Moscow." Du Bois attributed U.S. hostility toward the PRC to imperialism, which had been sustained by Black slaves, "yellow coolie[s]," and "all 'lesser breeds without the law.'" These groups "could furnish a 'white man's burden' and let him strut over the world, and lord it in Asia and Africa, and rule and rule without end, forever and forever," Du Bois wrote indignantly. At the 1952 Progressive Party convention in Chicago and meetings of the American Peace Crusade organization, he reiterated his call to end the Korean War, offer friendship to the Soviet Union and China, and reduce the threat of another world war.[59]

The CCP victory in 1949 had placed China and Asia at the center of colored peoples' revolutionary struggle. Communist China was anticolonial and had a policy of constructive engagement with African nations. Mao's mass or peasant-based theory of revolution, in Bill Mullen's words, "displaced the [white] industrial proletariat at the center of Marxist revolution." It thus provided a counterthrust, in Du Bois's mind, to Euro-American imperialist hegemony. Chinese rural proletarians could serve as a model for an African socialism, likewise "based on old African communal life."[60]

In 1954, Du Bois passionately portrayed the PRC as the new pillar of Asia and the colored world, after reviewing how "since 1936, the world has moved, and fast." World War II proposed Japan as "master of Asia," and when Japan was overthrown, Du Bois observed, the United States emerged as "imperial owner of China" by buying Chiang and his "wealthy gang." However, the long-forgotten "peasantry of China" turned things upside down by launching "the most extraordinary revolution of our day" and adopting socialism. Du Bois quickly focused on how the commercial capacity of the new China could overcome the "fatal limitation of colonialism," "too poor and sick to buy much." Invoking China as the legendary world trade center during "the days of Marco Polo," he argued that China's market of 500 million potential consumers could provide economic salvation for the West and Japan. He chided the West, long used to "sneering at" and "stealing from" Asia, for remaining blind to this possibility. Du Bois urged the United States to admit that its own forces were the "scoundrels" in this situation, to quit questioning "who lost China," to give in to trade with "the East," and to respect the freedom of colored peoples worldwide.[61]

Du Bois's enthusiasm for the Soviet Union and the PRC translated into a renewed vision of socialism, to which he had been attracted since 1904, for the world's oppressed, including Black Americans. Consistent with his long-standing views on white supremacy, he highlighted in 1944 that the "so-called race problem" was rooted in socioeconomic issues irrelevant to biology. In his final speech before the NAACP at its thirty-eighth annual convention in Washington, D.C., in 1947, Du Bois argued that "socialism is an attack on poverty," which plagued former colonies across the world to the "harshest and crudest" degree. Tying his analysis of race and colonialism to class, wage, and labor, Du Bois was concerned that "fear of being called Communist" made people avoid "the truth about work and income." He articulated how colonial powers bribed white laborers for support with a living wage and job security at the expense of "the East Indian, the Chinese coolie," and Blacks in South Africa and the U.S. South. He compiled statistics to illustrate that hundreds of millions of families in these demographic groups lived on an annual income averaging roughly from $25 to $50. Lamenting that racial prejudices kept white and colored workers across the world "separated and unacquainted," Du Bois called on white workers to recognize that their advancement would remain incomplete "so long as colored labor is exploited and enslaved and deprived of all political power."[62]

Du Bois predicted that the "darker world" would adopt socialism as "the only answer to the color line," and that the status of African Americans would thereby be elevated. Throughout the 1950s, he published several essays, including two in *United Asia*, a magazine based in Bombay (today's Mumbai), discussing Pan-Africanism and African Americans' relations with socialism. Du Bois questioned rhetorically, "What will be American Negroes' answer to the challenge of socialism?" He was confident that they would be inspired by the Soviet Union, which could not "conceive such barbarism" as the color line, and that they would inevitably accept the "tremendous" impact of Communist China. He observed optimistically in 1958 that the majority of mankind was living under either complete socialism in the Soviet Union and China, or partial socialism in India and Scandinavia.[63] While Du Bois's predictions might not come to pass, he soon found an enthusiastic audience in China.

THE CHINESE COMMUNIST PARTY'S
EMBRACE OF DU BOIS

As Vaughn Rasberry points out, W. E. B. Du Bois had celebrity status and was widely revered in the Soviet Union, then still the CCP's closest ally. Choosing to ignore Du Bois's earlier endorsement of Japanese aggression in China and echoing his comments about the Nationalist government, the CCP began reporting favorably about him as early as February 1949. The *People's Daily* quoted Du Bois when he declared that African Americans must move beyond antilynching and anti–poll tax reforms to join "the worldwide struggle between reaction and democracy," something he viewed as impossible within the U.S. political system.[64] His comment fit well with Liu Liangmo's 1940s arguments in his *Pittsburgh Courier* columns and communist belief in the predominant importance of world revolution over local concerns. The CCP established an Office for Foreign Affairs (Shewai shiwu bangongshi, abbreviated as Waishiban) to oversee foreigners in China and foreign commentary about China. Controlled by Premier Zhou Enlai, the office regularly scoured foreign newspapers and was well apprised of Du Bois's statements.[65]

Treating the organized regional and world peace movement as a powerful popular rebuke of U.S. involvement in China's civil war and the Korean War, China's state media reported intensively on the involvement of Du Bois and Paul Robeson in the campaign. Du Bois and Shirley Graham, along with Robeson, the African American baritone Aubrey Pankey, and the popular young actor Marlon Brando, attended the Cultural and Scientific Conference for World Peace arranged by the National Council of the Arts, Sciences, and Professionals at the Waldorf-Astoria Hotel in New York City in March 1949. Pablo Picasso was refused a visa to attend. Du Bois made a speech, lauding the conference for bringing "cultural leaders of the Soviet Union" and highlighting that "the sessions were picketed" and media coverage was distorted. The recently formed infamous House Un-American Activities Committee immediately compiled a sixty-four-page review of the conference, calling it a "forerunner" of the forthcoming Paris peace congress amid the "Communist world-wide 'peace' offensive."[66]

The *People's Daily* lauded the opening of the International Congress for Peace in Paris, chaired by the Nobel Laureate and French communist atomic scientist Frédéric Joliot-Curie, the following month. The newspaper praised Du Bois and Robeson for their presence, announcing that Du Bois led the U.S. delegation and was elected president of the conference. The CCP would repeatedly refer to this event in later evaluations of his career. It protested France's refusal to grant visas to 1,784 representatives of sixty-nine nations, who held a separate peace congress in Prague. Among them were CCP delegates, including Xu Guangping, widow of the noted writer Lu Xun, and Dai Ailian (Tai Ai-lien, Eileen Tai, 1916–2006), Si-lan Chen's cousin and a student of dance.[67]

W. E. B. and Shirley Graham Du Bois

The state media in China cited and applauded Du Bois's arguments about nuclear warfare. The *People's Daily* noted that the Peace Information Center under Du Bois's leadership obtained 2.5 million signatures for the 1950 Stockholm Peace Declaration initiated by Joliot-Curie demanding a ban on nuclear weapons.[68] On July 13, 1950, U.S. secretary of state Dean Acheson published an article in the *New York Times* attacking the Peace Information Center for promoting the "bitter hypocrisy of the Communist 'peace appeal.'" Du Bois responded immediately, insisting on the necessity of cooperating with the Soviet Union and China against "utter atomic disaster" as the Allies had against "the menace of Hitler."

The Chinese protested when the U.S. government arrested Du Bois under the Smith Act in 1951 for "spying for foreign countries" through the center. During his lecture tour to counter a press blackout and prepare for his trial, Du Bois announced that his persecution was meant to silence U.S. citizens from objecting to U.S. corporations' efforts to renew their control over former colonies, dominate Asia, and "above all to crush socialism in the Soviet Union and China." Since "American exploiters and overlords drove the Chinese peasants straight into the arms of Communism," he warned, "the same thing" could happen in all former colonies. After Du Bois and his codefendants appealed to the World Defenders of Peace, letters of support began to pour in from China. Du Bois noted that the Shanghai *China News* joined media worldwide in publishing supportive articles and that four Chinese served on the International Committee in Defense of Dr. W. E. B. Du Bois and His Colleagues. The *People's Daily* proclaimed that people around the globe, including citizens of the Soviet Union and China, protested "this baseless behavior of the U.S. government."[69]

Under pressure, the poorly prepared charges collapsed, and the U.S. government was forced to concede Du Bois's innocence. "Blessed are the Peacemakers, for they shall be Communists," the unyielding Du Bois announced in 1952. In 1953, to show its appreciation of Du Bois, World Affairs Press, affiliated with China's Ministry of Foreign Affairs, published a translation of *In Battle for Peace*, an account of his arrest, subsequent trial, and ultimate acquittal as an "unregistered foreign agent." In the book, Du Bois discarded his earlier belief in the Talented Tenth as narrow and replaced it with devotion to the international community of the downtrodden. This was the first full translation of Du Bois's work into Chinese. He was "thrilled to hear" that Talitha Gerlach, who had moved to Shanghai, came across it in a bookstore and eagerly requested a copy. Since the Du Boises felt they were being censored by U.S. publishers, the news inspired Du Bois's plan to "appeal to

China" to publish his long novel in progress "reflecting African history from 1876 to 1954." The People's Daily quoted Du Bois's 1952 letter to twelve South American leaders about the peace conference of American nations, urging them to fight for peace, industrial reform, and a fair distribution of wealth. During their 1959 visit, over 1,200 people would gather in Beijing to celebrate the tenth anniversary of the world peace movement and the leadership of Du Bois and his wife.[70]

The People's Daily would publish a summary article that indicated how closely the Chinese government followed and appreciated his actions throughout the 1950s. It reviewed and judged Du Bois's friendship with the Chinese people and were highly positive about his position on Taiwan and peace. The paper's next comments set the correct line for genuine ideological engagement between Du Bois, Graham Du Bois, and their Chinese hosts. The People's Daily acknowledged that Du Bois worked to unite the struggles for liberation of Blacks and other laboring people in the United States but emphasized that he needed to understand that the Black struggle for freedom and rights and the American people's struggle for world peace could only be ultimately victorious through close cooperation with international proletariats, under the leadership of communist parties.[71] While this ideological line the Chinese pushed throughout the Du Bois's visit may be regarded as standard communist rhetoric, it opened the possibility that the Chinese and Du Bois might learn from each other.

SHIRLEY GRAHAM DU BOIS, CHINA, AND COMMUNISM

In his embrace of China and Chinese communism, W. E. B. Du Bois had his wife's strong support. Shirley Graham Du Bois had become an important figure in Du Bois's life in the 1940s, and they married on February 27, 1951, shortly after the death of his first wife. The PRC emphasized his favorable positions since Graham Du Bois had entered his life. Although Graham Du Bois was already a communist, Gerald Horne argues convincingly that she was not the principal reason that her husband joined the party, an event that occurred more than a decade after their marriage. What she did do, however, in addition to invigorating his life and helping him survive some tough times, was to expose him to groups and contacts that would eventually lead to a better reception in China. She expanded his cooperation with people of other races and brought him closer to the party, if not yet to membership.[72]

In China, Graham Du Bois, like her husband, received much praise. Facilitated by Liu Liangmo, state publishing houses published translations of her biographies of the African American scientist George Washington Carver and Robeson between 1949 and 1950. In addition to celebrating Robeson, the second book created an association in Chinese minds between Graham and the revered singer. The translator stressed that Graham was a Black woman and an active participant in the international peace movement.[73] The *People's Daily* recognized her as a member of the World Peace Council and of the National Council of American-Soviet Friendship. It applauded her, along with Eslanda Goode Robeson, wife of Paul Robeson, who had visited the PRC as early as 1949, for tearing down Taiwan's flag from the assembly hall at the All-Africa Congress in Ghana in December 1958 to break the U.S. government's "two China" conspiracy. Du Bois noted that their action was assisted by Tom Mboya, chair of the All-Africa Congress.[74]

In a sign of appreciation, Du Bois ensured that his wife's name also appeared on the cover of *In Battle for Peace* ("With Comment by Shirley Graham"). As Kate Baldwin observes, nowhere in the book does Du Bois indicate any awareness of his wife's intellectual presence or equality. Rather, she demonstrates Graham Du Bois's remarkable "capacity for self-forfeiture." Baldwin's comments align with Hazel Carby's argument about Du Bois's wholly masculine intellect. Baldwin does show, however, that Graham Du Bois exhibited agency, as her husband's bedrock companion, in her fundraising and, increasingly, by substituting for him at international conferences so he could avoid arduous travel.[75] As we will see, Graham Du Bois was developing an international presence in her own right, with China playing a major role.

ON TOUR OF THE SOVIET UNION AND CHINA IN 1959

In 1959, the Chinese government had immediate reasons to welcome the Du Boises' public support. Despite early optimism and reports of a fine harvest in 1958, the Great Leap Forward had stumbled badly, leading to famine for more than 10 million people. Collectivization of agriculture had faltered, and the backyard steel furnace movement was a disaster.[76] These problems called into question the CCP's leadership and policies for the first time since 1949. Mao and his fellow officials needed a new domestic perspective to reinvigorate the revolution and socialize the nation.

In addition, the PRC required new diplomatic defenders and tactics as it contested Soviet dominance of world communism and aspired to leadership of the Third World. The CCP needed Du Bois's prestige and acumen as it attempted to lessen its dependence on the Soviet Union by seeking stronger alliances with Asian and African nations. At the Bandung Conference in Malaysia in 1955, Premier Zhou diplomatically fenced with other national delegates over inclusion of the Universal Declaration of Human Rights as a core principle of the meeting. Yet P. C. Chang (Zhang Pengchun), a representative of the Republic of China at the United Nations and a brother of the noted educator Zhang Boling, had co-authored the document. Zhou, Chang's former student and protégé, eventually accepted the declaration to avoid alienating nations China regarded as potential allies. African Americans, in turn, watched the proceedings with fascination. Richard Wright, the exiled novelist, attended the conference and praised its accomplishments while other African American leaders hesitated to do so. Du Bois wanted badly to attend, but the U.S. government's seizure of his passport made his presence impossible, leaving him frustrated and bitter. He praised the "pan-colored" conference as one that would have lasting and decisive influence.[77]

The Bandung Conference was the first step toward establishing China's independence from Moscow and escaping the isolation of the previous decade. To further these aims, Mao devised a new worldview that moved from two blocs (imperialist capitalist vs. communist) based on ideology into three camps based on history: the superpowers (the United States and the Soviet Union), the industrial nations (Europe plus Canada), and a Third World that encompassed China and former agricultural colonies in Asia, Africa, and Latin America. The Du Boises arrived in China at a turning point in CCP history, when Mao was deeply bothered by the Soviet refusal to back him in a tinderbox dispute with the United States over the offshore islands of Quemoy and Matsu. Disappointed by the Soviets, the CCP was already reaching out to Africa for friendship, but newly independent African states met Chinese overtures with caution and reserve.[78] Du Bois's immense intellectual stature in Africa could open doors for alliances with postcolonial nations there. Lacking trade and diplomatic ties, China sought inroads through cultural affinities, in which Graham Du Bois was eager to help. Du Bois's willingness to endorse Mao's plans enabled the Chinese to overlook the Black intellectual's 1936 comments. At the same time, the Du Boises saw the visit as a means to advance Pan-Africanism in China and Asia.

The couple sailed from New York to England in August 1958. Du Bois lectured, broadcast, and recovered from ailments in London, Holland, and Paris. They spent four weeks relaxing in Paul Robeson's London apartment while the singer was visiting the Soviet Union, and Du Bois attended the memorial for Joliot-Curie in Paris. An abrupt cablegram prompted them to fly to Tashkent in Soviet Asia for a meeting of African and Asian writers, an

W. E. B. and Shirley Graham Du Bois

FIGURE 1.3. W. E. B. and Shirley Graham Du Bois, Senegalese
writer and activist Majhemout Diop, Zhou Yang, and leader of the
Chinese delegation Mao Dun (*first on right*) at the Afro-Asian Writers'
Conference in Tashkent, Uzbekistan (USSR), October 1958.
*Courtesy of W. E. B. Du Bois Papers, mums312-io649, Special Collections
and University Archives, University of Massachusetts Amherst Libraries.*

event that somewhat made up for his absence at the Bandung Conference.
In Tashkent, the Du Boises connected with China's leading intellectuals and
cultural officials: Guo Moruo, vice premier, head of the Chinese Academy
of Sciences, the China Federation of Literary and Artistic Circles, and the
China Peace Council; Mao Dun, minister of culture, vice chair of the Afro-
Asian Solidarity Committee, and one of China's most important twentieth-
century writers; and Zhou Yang, nicknamed the "Cultural Tsar" and director of the powerful Propaganda Department of the CCP Central Committee
(fig. 1.3). The couple were "entertained by Indians, Chinese, Africans, and
Russians and then whisked back to Moscow," Prague, and East Berlin as
honored guests, with Du Bois receiving a couple of honorary degrees in the
process.

They flew back to Moscow in time to attend the forty-first anniversary
celebration of the 1917 Bolshevik Revolution on Red Square "with half a million spectators." Du Bois wrote to his daughter Yolanda, "A gaily uniformed
major escorted me, Shirley and our official interpretor [*sic*], from the Square
to the hotel and on the way he stopped and saluted Kruitchef [*sic*], and

Kruitchef [sic] raised his hat to me. That night we attended a reception at the Kremlin, met the Government, and I talked alone with Kruitchef [sic]." Nikita Khrushchev feted them again at the Kremlin at a New Year's Eve dinner and announced that Du Bois had won the 1959 Lenin Peace Prize. Robeson arrived after the Du Boises. When the two men spotted each other, they weaved among tables and embraced in the middle of the banquet hall. The crowd applauded as Du Bois and Robeson burst into joyous laughter. Du Bois met the Soviet leader privately in January to discuss "vital questions concerning the struggle for peace."[79] Despite tensions, the Sino-Soviet rupture had not yet intensified, so this honor did not disqualify Du Bois to the Chinese.

After that gratifying stop in Moscow, despite the injunction in their new U.S. passports that these were "not valid for travel to or in communist controlled portions of China[,] Korea [and] Viet-Nam[,] or to or in areas of Albania [and] Hungary," the Du Boises left on February 9 for the People's Republic. Because the Korean War, described officially as a "police action," had never (and still has not) been officially settled, as Du Bois observed in his *Autobiography*, the United States and China remained in conflict during his journey, and he risked being jailed for "trading with the enemy." Indeed, during their world tour the couple's home at 31 Grace Court in Brooklyn was ransacked for incriminating evidence. But Du Bois felt that he would like to revisit China "because it is a land of colored people," echoing his sentiment over the hospitality he had received in Japan. In addition, since the Chinese government had already invited him in 1956 to come celebrate the 250th birthday of Benjamin Franklin, the trip was an overdue pleasure. Du Bois was pleased that the new invitation came from Guo Moruo and Madam Sun Yat-sen, vice chair of the National People's Congress Standing Committee. Thus, "this risk I thought it my duty to take," as Du Bois put in his *Autobiography*.[80]

When the couple arrived in China, border officials asked if they wanted to keep the visit quiet to avoid irritating the U.S. State Department. Du Bois responded that his wife and he were honored to be invited to China and that the officials could let the whole world know. While his words received rapid and universal approval in China, the *New York Times* commented that Du Bois had no authorization to visit there. The FBI took note and prepared to cancel the couple's passports upon their return to the United States.[81]

When the Du Boises arrived in Beijing on February 14, 1959, the Chinese rolled out the red carpet for the travelers. The *People's Daily* described an array of dignitaries greeting the couple, demonstrating the CCP's emphasis on

FIGURE 1.4. W. E. B. and Shirley Graham Du Bois
arrive in Beijing from Moscow, February 14, 1959.
*Courtesy of W. E. B. Du Bois Papers, mums312-i0740, Special Collections
and University Archives, University of Massachusetts Amherst Libraries.*

the intellectual, artistic, and ethnic importance of their guests. These official
greeters included Ding Xilin (Ting Shih-ling), a noted playwright and scientist and vice chair of the CPACRFC; Ji Chaoding (Chi Ch'ao-ting), a brilliant
America-educated economist who had joined the Communist Party USA
and the CCP in 1926 and was now an executive member of the CPACRFC;
Bauer Khan, a Uighur and the vice chair of the China Peace Council; and Lao
She, author of the famous novel *Rickshaw Boy* and vice chair of the China
National Association of Writers (fig. 1.4). Over the next eight weeks, Chinese organizations feted the couple. Among the highlights, the Du Boises
shared a toast with China's top leadership, including Chair of the State Liu
Shaoqi, Vice Chair of the State Dong Biwu, Premier Zhou Enlai, CCP general secretary Deng Xiaoping, head of the People's Congress Zhu De, and
their wives (fig. 1.5). The CPACRFC and the China Peace Council held a welcoming banquet on February 18. There Lao She sang Beijing opera for the
guests. The Du Boises responded with a spontaneous, vigorous duet of the
African American spiritual "Down by the Riverside," sometimes known as
"Ain't Gonna Study War No More" (fig. 1.6).[82]

After a private dinner at his residence for the Du Boises the previous
night and the grand birthday speech, Premier Zhou Enlai hosted a birth-

FIGURE 1.5. W. E. B. and Shirley Graham Du Bois share a toast with China's top leadership in February 1959. *From left to right in the front row*: Dong Biwu (second); Zhou Enlai (third); Du Bois (fifth); Liu Shaoqi (sixth); Zhu De (eighth); Zhou's wife, Deng Yingchao (ninth); Liu's wife, Wang Guangmei (tenth); Graham Du Bois (eleventh); and Deng Xiaoping (sixteenth). *Courtesy of W. E. B. Du Bois Papers, mums312-i0706, Special Collections and University Archives, University of Massachusetts Amherst Libraries.*

day banquet for the aged scholar at the upstairs hall of the Beijing Hotel, which served overseas Chinese and foreign dignitaries exclusively (figs. 1.7 and 1.8). Zhou's cosmopolitanism always impressed foreign guests. Du Bois boasted in his *Autobiography* that he "dined twice with . . . the tireless Prime Minister of this nation of 680 million souls." Zhou brought a birthday cake and a bowl of "long-life" peaches to the nonagenarian and wished him longevity. In his opening speech, Guo Moruo hailed the support the Du Boises had given to the Chinese liberation movement. Lao She, noted writer Bingxin, and other Chinese scholars and artists presented a copy of the Chinese translation of *In Battle for Peace*, brightly colored congratulatory calligraphy scrolls, and a statue of the longevity god, which glowed in the light of giant red candles. The Du Boises transported the gifts across the globe and prominently displayed them in their homes in Brooklyn and then Accra, Ghana. Some objects appeared in the photographs of Ghana's national leader Kwame Nkrumah and his wife congratulating Du Bois on his ninety-fifth birthday. Folksingers and children serenaded the couple with traditional Chinese music and dance and two "Negro folk songs sung in Chinese." Glasses clinked and the honored guests chatted breezily with Chinese friends around them throughout the happily noisy evening. Zhang Qian conversed with Graham Du Bois at the banquet, while her husband Chen Yi, the minister of foreign affairs, listened attentively, as shown in the documentary on the Du Boises' visit. Madam Sun Yat-sen telegrammed her warm congratulations. An interview with Du Bois on the front page of the *People's*

W. E. B. and Shirley Graham Du Bois

FIGURE 1.6. W. E. B. and Shirley Graham Du Bois sing
"Down by the Riverside," sometimes known as "Ain't Gonna Study
War No More." In the middle is Ding Xilin, vice chair of the CPACRFC.
*Courtesy of W. E. B. Du Bois Papers, mums312-i0688, Special Collections
and University Archives, University of Massachusetts Amherst Libraries.*

Daily detailed his accomplishments and highlighted his support for China.
Bingxin, who had learned of Du Bois during her student years at Wellesley
College from 1923 to 1926, exclaimed, "Only four decades later, in the capital of the new China, I meet this Black American writer, poet, and fighter!
I am enormously excited and honored!" She described how the sight of "the
dignified but funny, kind, steady, brown-skinned gentleman who appeared
only around sixty years old" conjured up her memory of injustice suffered
by African Americans at Wellesley.[83]

The Du Boises expanded their African contacts during their visit to Beijing. His sporadic message on unity between Africa and China and broader
Asia became more systematic, as intensely expressed by three major public
speeches on Africa delivered during this trip. Kwame Nkrumah said that
Du Bois had been "a real friend and father to me," since they grew closer
at the Fifth Pan-African Congress in Manchester in 1945. At the dawn of
Ghana independence, Du Bois published an essay in the *National Guardian,* a progressive weekly, to tell "The Saga of Nkrumah." However, relationship between the two soon turned subtle. Du Bois recalled in his *Autobiography* that although he missed Nkrumah's inauguration because he had been
stripped of his passport, "I ventured to advise" him. He sounded alarm over
the attempts of U.S. business to influence the leader of the newly independent African nation. Nkrumah was invited to the United States in 1958 and

FIGURE 1.7. W. E. B. Du Bois meets Premier Zhou Enlai at Zhou's home, with Ji Chaoding's half-brother Ji Chaozhu serving as interpreter. *Courtesy of W. E. B. Du Bois Papers, mums312-i0729, Special Collections and University Archives, University of Massachusetts Amherst Libraries.*

"treated as never a Negro had been treated by the government," Du Bois wrote. "I saw Mr. Nkrumah briefly. He was most cordial and I expected soon to be invited to the Sixth Pan-African Congress in Accra."[84]

When the long-awaited invitation finally arrived in Tashkent, where Du Bois had delivered his first speech on Africa, he noted that it was "not from Nkrumah nor for a Pan-African congress" but from a new "All-Africa Congress" (the Accra Conference of African States) to be held in December 1958. In this shift, Du Bois quickly detected a gesture of the newly risen "educated groups of Africans" rejecting "American Negro leadership of the African peoples," which he accepted as only "natural." Although that initial invitation "said nothing about my expenses," the offer soon came with "a cordial note." By then, Du Bois was recovering from his illness in a prestigious sanitarium near Moscow after his long travels, obviously too frail to attend the conference. Graham Du Bois stepped in "as a guest of the Soviet Embassy." Du Bois proudly noted that his wife "was shown rare courtesy" as the only non-African allowed to address the assembly, and that her reading of his speech "Africa Awake!" was "greeted with applause."

In the speech, Du Bois asked rhetorically, "Which way shall Africa go?" Toward capitalism, or toward socialism? He called on Africans to practice "sacrifice and self-denial of temporary advantages—automobiles, refrigerators, and Paris gowns" to avoid "prolong[ing] fatal colonial imperial-

W. E. B. and Shirley Graham Du Bois

FIGURE 1.8. W. E. B. Du Bois's ninety-first birthday banquet at the Beijing Hotel. *From left to right*: Guo Moruo, unknown, Zhou Enlai, Du Bois, Graham Du Bois, Zhang Qian, and Chen Yi. *Courtesy of W. E. B. Du Bois Papers, mums312-i0726, Special Collections and University Archives, University of Massachusetts Amherst Libraries.*

ism" with costly capital from Western powers. He argued that, "with infinite sacrifice," the Soviet Union and China were "pouring out . . . blood and tears" to spare smaller but "rapidly growing" capital without "bonds." Du Bois urged the masses in Africa to comparison-shop and make the obvious sensible choice. Echoing his upcoming birthday speech in Beijing, Du Bois concluded,

> Africa, mother of men. Your nearest friends and neighbors are the colored people of China and India, the rest of Asia, the Middle East and the sea isles, once close bound to the heart of Africa and now long severed by the greed of Europe. Your bond is no mere color of skin but the deeper experience of wage-slavery and contempt. So too, your bond with the white world is closest to those like the Union of Soviet Socialist Republics, who support and defend China and help the slaves of Tibet and India, and not those who exploit the Middle East, the West Indies, and South America. "Awake, awake, put on thy strength, O Zion"; . . . Africa awake, put on the beautiful robes of Pan-African socialism. You have nothing to lose but your chains! You have a continent to regain! You have freedom and human dignity to attain![85]

In Beijing, the Du Boises renewed their connection with Ghana by meeting its representatives, who would enable Du Bois's long-delayed visit to their country. On the second anniversary of Ghanaian independence,

FIGURE 1.9. W. E. B. Du Bois with two Ghanaian guests and
Chinese hosts including Mao Dun *(third from right)*, Ding Xilin
(third from left), and Xia Yan *(second from left)* in Beijing, March 6, 1959.
*Courtesy of W. E. B. Du Bois Papers, mums312-i0683, Special Collections
and University Archives, University of Massachusetts Amherst Libraries.*

China's Afro-Asian Solidarity Committee welcomed visitors from Ghana:
the secretary-general of the Preparatory Committee for the forthcoming Pan-African Conference, who also served as the editing consultant of
Ghana's *Pan-African Century Magazine,* and the magazine's publisher. The
Du Boises were invited to a gathering of Chinese and Ghanaians, where
Mao Dun welcomed all, characterizing Ghana's independence as a "significant victory in the African people's struggle for national independence and
freedom." Mao Dun stated that the Chinese people "harbor great sympathy
and support for the people of Africa's struggle to kick the imperialists out of
Africa," a line consonant with Du Bois's long-held beliefs that people of color
should unite against white aggressors. Du Bois delivered an energetic speech
in which he declared that, while he had been born in the United States, his
ancestors were from Africa. As he had never been to Ghana, it was a "very
meaningful" event for him to meet friends from Ghana in the new China. He
wished the Ghanaian people happiness and prosperity and ended his speech
by shouting, "Long Live Africa!" (fig. 1.9).[86] Beyond the ideological symme-
try, this was a consequential meeting of Ghanaians and the Du Boises. Soon
the couple would move to Accra, take Ghanaian citizenship, and establish
their lives there. Du Bois would be buried in Ghana.

For now, China was their temporary home. Having made their fealty

W. E. B. and Shirley Graham Du Bois

clear to their hosts, they traveled first class by railway, boat, plane, and auto-mobile over 5,000 miles throughout Chinese cities, including Beijing, Shang-hai, Nanjing, Wuhan, Chengdu, Kunming, and Guangzhou (Canton), at each stop hosted by governors and other top officials. The journey was carefully "managed" by Tang Mingzhao, vice chair of the China Peace Council, director of the Department of Liaison with Anglophone Countries, and future under-secretary of the United Nations (1972–79). Du Bois refreshed his impression of Beijing in his *Autobiography*: "We remember Peking; a city of six million; its hard workers, its building and re-building; that great avenue which passes the former Forbidden City, and is as wide as Central Park; the bicycles and pedicycles, the carts and barrows. There was the university where I lectured on Africa, and a college of the 50 or more races of China (Central Ethnicities University). We looked out from our hotel window at the workers. They all wore raincoats beneath the drizzle. We saw the planning of a nation and a sys-tem of work rising over the entrails of a dead empire." He recorded himself instructing kindergarten students visiting the Forbidden City: "Your fathers built this, but did not enjoy it; but now it is yours; preserve it."[87]

After taking a thirty-hour overnight sleeper train from Beijing, the Du Boises arrived in Shanghai, where the documentary recorded the couple scanning the Bund from a balcony. "In 1936 I came to China and stayed for a week," the film quotes Du Bois. "Now I have come again with more knowl-edge. I know the existence of China is of tremendous importance not only to our own people but to the entire world." With his wife, Du Bois finally visited the home of Madam Sun. In the documentary, while the hostess somewhat shyly engages Graham Du Bois in close conversation, Du Bois chimes in occasionally, listens, and smokes. He is also filmed speaking at the Shanghai Foreign Languages University, and the couple is shown laying a wreath at the tomb of Lu Xun (fig. 1.10).[88]

On March 14, the couple received the highest validation of their impor-tance when Mao Zedong hosted them at a luncheon banquet at the Chair-man's summer residence in Wuhan. Also present was Anna Louise Strong, one of the three U.S. journalists (with Agnes Smedley and Edgar Snow) most revered by the CCP for promoting the party abroad (figs. 1.11 and 1.12). Mao had used Strong to promulgate his famous paper tiger thesis—that imperi-alists were superficially powerful but naturally would become overextended and then collapse. Graham Du Bois recalled that Strong talked incessantly. Over a python steak lunch, whose warm atmosphere the documentary on the Du Boises' visit captured, the Du Boises spoke with the Chairman for four hours about issues concerning African Americans. Du Bois had a pri-

FIGURE 1.10. W. E. B. and Shirley Graham Du Bois
lay a wreath at Lu Xun's tomb in Shanghai in 1959.
*Courtesy of W. E. B. Du Bois Papers, mums312-i0667, Special Collections
and University Archives, University of Massachusetts Amherst Libraries.*

vate walk in the garden with Mao, after which the Chairman gave him a
book of his poems (fig. 1.13).[89] That evening Strong created a transcript of
the event, which was not published until 1985, fifteen years after her death.
Strong noted that this was the first time that Mao met with any other U.S.
citizens since 1949. She recalled that Chinese officials kept the visitors in
the dark as to whether or where they would meet the Chairman, until they

FIGURE 1.11. W. E. B. and Shirley Graham Du Bois with
Chairman Mao Zedong at the latter's villa in Wuhan, March 14, 1959.
*Courtesy of W. E. B. Du Bois Papers, mums312-i0692, Special Collections
and University Archives, University of Massachusetts Amherst Libraries.*

saw him walking down the steps. After a few disarming jokes about relative
ages and skin color, Mao expressed his wish to travel to the United States
someday as a tourist, swim in the Mississippi River, watch President Dwight
Eisenhower play golf, and visit Secretary of State John Foster Dulles in the
hospital. Du Bois responded that Dulles might suffer a stroke if Mao suddenly appeared. The chairman said that that was far from his desire, since
Dulles was so useful as a foil for the PRC, due to his anticommunism and use
of militarism to suppress global freedom.

Observing Du Bois's dismay and skepticism, Mao explained that Dulles
helped the masses understand imperialism and capitalism, and taught the
Chinese how to avoid the brink of war in conflicts over Taiwan. Du Bois
asked if Mao recommended that he vote for Dulles, a dry joke that made Mao
admit that he would never do that himself. Du Bois responded that African
Americans in the United States faced annihilation because of Dulles's policies and actions. Mao replied that he had lost many family members in revolution and war, and that the bourgeoisie would be exterminated long before
the 18 million African Americans. "Dulles," Mao reassured Du Bois, "is doing

FIGURE 1.12. W. E. B. and Shirley Graham Du Bois with Chairman Mao Zedong, Anna Louise Strong (*third from left*), Tang Mingzhao (*second from left*), Ding Xinglin (*second from right*), and others at Mao's villa in Wuhan, March 14, 1959. *Courtesy of W. E. B. Du Bois Papers, mums312-i0678, Special Collections and University Archives, University of Massachusetts Amherst Libraries.*

all he can to exterminate himself. That is why I appreciate him so much." Mao suggested that the problem was worship of power, which affected both white and Black Americans. Du Bois replied that income rather than fear and power admiration limited African Americans. The two then discussed how the power of superstition affected decisions of the masses. Strong and Mao talked about communes, the need for steel production in China, and anxieties about a World War III. Mao declared that China did not want war, but talk of war curbed imperialist agendas. He concluded that at the age of sixty-six, he still hoped to live to see the end of imperialism. At least from Strong's perspective, Du Bois, and not his wife, was the guest of honor.[90] Graham Du Bois would have to learn about China from others besides Chairman Mao. Although Du Bois did not mention the backyard steel furnaces that were transforming China's landscape, he marveled at "the bridge that had been miraculously thrown across the Yangtze" and shook hands with welcoming workers in a "great steel mills" that hinted at China's industrial achievement. In their "little hotel adorned with flowering cabbages," the couple received "a colored American prisoner of war" who had chosen to stay in China happily "with his wife and baby" rather than return to the United States.[91]

The Du Boises then departed by boat up the Yangzi River to Chong-

W. E. B. and Shirley Graham Du Bois

FIGURE 1.13. W. E. B. Du Bois and Chairman
Mao Zedong in Mao's garden in Wuhan, March 14, 1959.
*Courtesy of W. E. B. Du Bois Papers, mums312-i0741, Special Collections
and University Archives, University of Massachusetts Amherst Libraries.*

qing and Chengdu, where they visited a commune of 60,000 members and
climbed mountains to see the famous ancient Dujiangyan irrigation system
initially constructed during the Warring States. At the summit, which boasted
a "glorious temple" (commemorating the Tang dynasty poet Du Fu), they
watched "four rivers roll down from the Himalayas, out of Tibet into the
Yangtze." While the Du Boises lingered at the border between Sichuan and

Tibet, the Tibetan Uprising erupted, on which De Bois commented in his *Autobiography*: "The landholders and slave drivers and the religious fanatics revolted against the Chinese, and failed as they deserved to. Tibet has belonged to China for centuries. The Communists linked the two by roads and began reforms in landholding, schools and trade, which now move quickly." Then the Du Boises flew to Kunming, where ethnic students, including Tibetans, danced and sang welcome. At Guangzhou, an impressive "marble commercial building" recently opened for international trades renewed Du Bois's vision of China as a rising world factory. He imagined it producing high-quality but cheaper consumer goods such as "silk and woolen clothing, watches, clocks, radios and television sets, looms, machinery and lamps, shoes and hats, pottery and dishes." In a completely different context decades later, this vision would materialize.

Du Bois expressed profound appreciation of the "universal goodwill and love, such as we never expected," that he and his wife had received in the PRC, in contrast to the "insult and discrimination on account of our race and color" that "all our lives have been liable to." He called this trip "the most fascinating eight weeks of travel and sight-seeing I have ever experienced," even above his multiple visits to the Soviet Union. Du Bois exclaimed romantically, "I have travelled widely on this earth since my first trip to Europe 67 years ago . . . but I have never seen a nation which so amazed and touched me as China in 1959. . . . Oh beautiful, patient, self-sacrificing China, despised and unforgettable, victorious and forgiving, crucified and risen from the dead." The allegedly unprecedented "vast and glorious a miracle as China" convinced Du Bois "how splendidly and surely the world could be led by the working class; even if at times they wavered and made vast mistakes."[92]

However, the Du Boises' visit contained much of the "arranged reality" that the CCP and other communist governments created for distinguished political tourists. The banquets and testimonials were ego massages for Du Bois; the private meetings with Zhou and Mao were elite techniques of hospitality. Du Bois had to be impressed with both men's status as scholars and statesmen. But they weren't the only visible Chinese intellectuals. After decades of his own marginality in the United States, Du Bois met intellectuals who seemed well integrated into government policies, taken seriously by political figures, and generally well treated, if they had survived the 1957 anti-rightist campaign.[93]

The Du Boises, in the words of David Levering Lewis, moved about China "in their ceremonial cocoon [knowing] absolutely nothing about the catastrophe of the Great Leap Forward." The couple joined other foreign

W. E. B. and Shirley Graham Du Bois

intellectuals who seemed oblivious to mass starvation.[94] In fairness, one must recall that the worst effects of the Great Leap Forward had yet to hit the Chinese people; they were still two years from coming to pass. Even so, as in his earlier comments about the Japanese occupation of China, Du Bois was willing to accept oppression if its aims fit his conception of the future. In a manner strikingly similar to his account of his 1936 trip to Manchukuo, Du Bois highlighted the wide range of places he visited, from villages, communes, parks, restaurants, to homes of the high and the low, and the diverse crowds they had mingled with, including national leaders, minority groups, "the workers, the factory hands, the farmers and laborers, scrubwomen and servants." Echoing Du Bois's impression of Manchukuo, the couple saw only cheerful crowds working busily in revolutionary unity. As Du Bois put it in his autobiography, "Always I saw a happy people; people with faith that need no church or priest, and who laugh gaily [in theaters] when Monkey King overthrows the angels." Theatrical scenes like this one, based on the classical Ming dynasty fiction *The Journey to the West*, deeply impressed the Du Boises, who were treated to opera in every town and city.[95]

Though one may view the visit to China as managed and the Du Boises as naive, there were benefits, including an expanded cultural awareness, particularly for Graham Du Bois. She claimed to have been transformed by the visit to a country she admitted that she had known little about. Her only previous encounters with Chinese in the United States were in "Chinese restaurants or laundries and those Chinese I knew were either American-born or from Hong Kong or Taiwan."[96] She was aware, despite her friendship with Huang Hua, a noted Chinese diplomat and graduate of Yenching University, that Orientalism still affected her thinking. At times, Graham Du Bois performed the role of an enthusiastic tourist, declaring China a lovely place and describing Chairman Mao's "fairy-like lakeside villa." She expressed enthusiasm about the sights in China, while overlooking the terrible famine that wracked the land. Gerald Horne has pointed out that Graham Du Bois was repeating her husband's arguments three decades earlier, though this time the CCP took the role of the heroic movement while racist America became the villain. The trip reaffirmed her socialist vision and made her strongly sympathetic to the Beijing government.[97]

IMMEDIATE AFTERMATH OF THE MILESTONE TRIP

Shortly after the Du Boises left China for Moscow on April 6, their hosts bestowed lasting gifts by publishing more translations of their books. Graham

Du Bois's biographies of Robeson and Carver had been in print in China for ten years. Now the volume on Carver was released in Hong Kong, and her biography of Frederick Douglass came out in a Chinese translation with the prestigious People's Literature Publishing House. This was China's introduction to Douglass.[98] Du Bois's *In Battle for Peace* had been released to Chinese readers in the heat of the Korean War. Mirroring what Japan did for Du Bois in the 1930s, the new tribute for him was the first Chinese translation of his most famous book, *The Souls of Black Folk*, under the title *Heiren de linghun*. Du Bois contributed a brief foreword to the Chinese edition and added the introduction written for the 1953 Blue Heron Press edition, which had incorporated changes made since the original printing in 1903 and eliminated references that might be regarded as anti-Semitic.[99]

The *People's Daily* printed a lengthy review, "The Voice from the Heart of Black People," which detailed the official view of the classic's virtues and noted a few faults. The reviewer, Huang Xinxi, using a standard to evaluate literature long established by leftist critics, praised the collection's enduring "deep realistic meaning." Citing Du Bois's brilliant synthesis of Civil War history, Huang argued that the book revealed that Blacks had not obtained real liberation. Evoking Mao's ideology of the revolutionary quality of the peasantry, Huang praised Du Bois's true revolutionary character for opposing the capitulationism of Booker T. Washington. Arguing that the liberation of Black Americans was incomplete and, by implication, that they needed to learn from the revolutionary Chinese peasantry, Huang articulated how landless Blacks had thrown off slavery's shackles but had become entrapped by capitalists, a message sure to resonate with Maoist intellectuals. Huang emphasized how racial discrimination had adversely affected Black intellectuals, something Du Bois, repeatedly denied major faculty positions at white universities despite his enormous education, could appreciate. Huang advised that through Du Bois's writings, the Chinese people could learn how racial discrimination had limited, oppressed, and destroyed Black Americans. Huang also praised Du Bois's account of the loss of his son, a chapter from *The Souls of Black Folk* that so impressed the Chinese that the Commercial Press, the nation's most prestigious imprint, published it as a separate pamphlet the following year.[100]

Huang ended with some mild criticism of the book. As it was written at the beginning of the twentieth century, Du Bois, as the author noted himself in the foreword to the Chinese translation, "was not a socialist and did not know much about communism." Therefore, Huang submitted, the book inevitably had limitations and some incorrect views, which did not represent the later thoughts of the author. For instance, the book argued that education could overcome racial prejudices and liberate Blacks, and that a Black small-scale agricultural economy could prevent capitalist crimes. Huang noted that Du Bois had won the Lenin Peace Prize as recognition for his contribution to the cause of world peace. All this, Huang concluded, demonstrated that the Black liberation movement was marching forward, as was Du Bois, in concert with the CCP. Huang's reduction of one of the most important works of twentieth-century American literature to the level of CCP ideological standards was reminiscent of Zhou Enlai's unwillingness to compromise at the Bandung Conference in 1955. The party had its position, and all works of art or diplomacy had to bend to it. At the same time, Huang's review expressed commonality between the Black and Chinese peasantry and sympathized with their shared racial oppression. Huang also called Du Bois's book a major intellectual achievement from whose example Chinese writers could learn.[101]

In his foreword, written expressly for the Chinese version and translated anonymously, Du Bois acknowledged two problems with his famous text. The first was his lack of understanding of the significance of psychology for the Black masses, a topic he had just discussed with Mao, and the long revolution necessary to help them. The second, Du Bois admitted, was that he had little understanding of the importance of Karl Marx and Marxist theory in 1903. Du Bois had hinted at such a need in *Dusk of Dawn*.[102] Now he made his admiration for Marx explicit. The color line became less important than class consciousness, a key change that allowed greater unity for the common struggle of African Americans and their Chinese comrades. Du Bois had doubtless been moving in this direction anyway, but the influence of his wife and their experiences in China cannot be underestimated. In his *Autobiography*, Du Bois explained the limitation of his elite education in teaching Marxism. He reiterated that "Negro citizens" had to embrace socialism and communism, since "above all nations," the Soviet Union and China "fight the very color bar which we try to get rid of."[103]

The Souls of Black Folk was not the first American classic to have dramatic influence in China. Huang's emphasis on the revolutionary aspects of *Souls* resonated in new Chinese reactions to Harriet Beecher Stowe's *Uncle Tom's Cabin* (1852), which enjoyed a revival of interest in the early 1960s. Sun Weishi, the Soviet-trained goddaughter of Premier Zhou, directed a play based on it in 1961. Chinese communists argued that Uncle Tom's Christian consciousness had betrayed him. Now, they contended that Du Bois had awakened a new understanding of Black resistance.[104]

Chinese approval of violent Black resistance highlighted the translation and publication of a lesser-known book by Du Bois, *John Brown* (*Yuehan Bulang*), in 1959. Tian Han, a noted writer and lyricist of "March of the Volunteers" ("Chee Lai!"), the signature piece for the cooperation between Liu Liangmo and Paul Robeson, and now a high-level government official, reviewed the book in the *People's Daily*. Tian hailed Du Bois's history of John Brown's insurrection at Harper's Ferry, Virginia, in 1859. He quoted Brown's words that became as familiar to Chinese students as to Americans: "I, John Brown, am now quite certain that the crimes of this guilty land will never be purged away but with blood." For Tian, the question was how to instill Brown's consciousness in that of Uncle Tom, the lead character of Stowe's famous novel. In short, Tian wondered how to transfer violent revolutionary leadership into the minds and hearts of both Chinese and Black masses. Du Bois's work on John Brown showed the way. Near the end of the Cultural Revolution, the Workers' Theory Group of the Beijing Micro-electronics Factory would reissue the piece with the People's Publishing House.[105] World Affairs Press translated Du Bois's prospectus for his never-completed *Encyclopedia Africana* in 1964 for "internal circulation." The Shanghai Writers' Publishing House released a Chinese version of his "Black Flame" Trilogy (*The Ordeal of Mansart, Mansart Builds a School,* and *Worlds of Color*) two years later.[106]

As the Chinese marveled at his past productions, Du Bois poured out new writings. He continued to expose the Chinese to ideas of Afro-Asian unity. While touring the country, Du Bois published "Our Visit to China" in the popular *China Pictorial*, accompanied by four photographs highlighting the climax of their visit—meeting with Mao and Zhou, making the epic speech, and receiving birthday scrolls. After sketching his and his wife's family backgrounds, which demonstrated their entitlement to U.S. citizenship, Du Bois traced the history of African Americans' struggle against slavery and now "colonial imperialism," to which he believed rising socialism in the Soviet Union and China posed "a fatal threat." Du Bois affirmed that the mission of their trip was to reveal "the truth about Communism" to the "mass of American Negroes," since U.S. citizens' right to travel was limited and available knowledge on socialism was distorted.[107] He declared later in his *Autobiography*, "Let *Life* lie about communes; and the State Department shed crocodile tears over ancestral tombs. Let Hong Kong wire its lies abroad. Let 'Divine Slavery' persist in Tibet until China kills it. The truth is there and I saw it."[108]

Profoundly moved by the sympathy and welcome during his extended

FIGURE 1.14. Guo Moruo, a high-level intellectual official, proposes a toast to W. E. B. Du Bois at his ninety-first birthday banquet. *China Reconstructs* 8 (June 1959): 25.

visit to China, Du Bois penned a lengthy poem "I Sing to China," which he dedicated to Guo Moruo, on International Labor Day in Moscow. Published in *China Reconstructs*, it is illustrated by a photograph of the two scholars clicking glasses at Du Bois's birthday banquet (fig. 1.14). Echoing the passionate grand opening of his birthday speech, the poem starts by applauding brotherhood and kinship based on color:

> Hail, dark brethren of mine,
> Hail and farewell! I die,
> As you are born again, bursting new with life.
> Kith you are of mine, and kin.
> That Sun which burned my fathers ebony,
> Rolled your limbs in gold,
> And made us both, cousins to the stars!

It then portrayed the dire situation shared by both African and Chinese Americans back home:

> Hail, China!
> I go, I leave, I hasten home
> Where Dulles' brink can punish a nigger,
> For greeting a chink!

My country, 'tis of thee,
Rich land of slavery, of thee
I cannot sing.

After narratives weaving China's long history, its recent colonial humiliation, waves of revolutions, and the CCP victory, Du Bois frankly admitted how he was "bought" by the warm reception he had just received:

You carry Gold, but not the Gold
Of banks and war-lords

But the fine Gold of human hearts
Whose price can never fall!
Which is scarce only as it is not used
Spend your Gold, China, scatter it and throw it abroad

Buy all mankind as you have bought me
Bought me and bound me and made me
Forever and forever yours!

He concluded by saluting China's mighty landscapes while issuing commands:

Thunder your lightnings
From the Great Wall to Himalayas

. . . .

Shout, China!
Roar, Rock, roll River;
Sing, Sun and Moon and Sea!
Move Mountain, Lake and Land,
Exalt Mankind, Inspire!
For out of the East again, comes Salvation!
Leading all prophets of the Dead —
Osiris, Buddha, Christ and Mahmoud
Interning their ashes, cherishing their Good;
China save the World! Arise, China![109]

SPREADING THE MESSAGE HOME AND BEYOND

As their hosts surely intended, W. E. B. and Shirley Graham Du Bois took their lessons home. Upon returning from the trip to the United States by

W. E. B. and Shirley Graham Du Bois

way of Sweden and England, Du Bois wrote to William M. Brewer, editor of the *Journal of Negro History* and a critic of communism, "I have just returned from living eight months behind the iron curtain. My whole attitude toward life has been changed."[110]

The Du Boises launched a tour along the Pacific Coast and the Midwest, speaking enthusiastically about China, in late 1959. "Even more astonishing than the Soviet Union," Du Bois declared before the Afro-American Heritage Association in Chicago, "is China." Echoing Great Leap Forward slogans, he forecast that "sooner than any nation today it is likely to achieve complete Communism." In a nod to his infamous observations about China in 1936, Du Bois recalled that China was then "under the heel of Europe and America." Now it was completely revolutionized and "the white masters were gone," satisfying his anticolonial views. He urged African Americans to visit socialist societies and study socialism. Among those inspired was the writer Truman Capote, who contacted Du Bois for advice on a possible trip to China in the winter. In a speech at the University of Wisconsin, Du Bois renewed his blasting of U.S. policy toward China, calling it our "most unforgivable deed today." Signaling a new historical approach, he contended that Chinese in America had been treated worse than Italians or even Blacks. "Lazy and jolly Negroes" infuriated slave owners by their passive resistance, but capitalist masters were pleased by "Chinese coolies [who] worked like dumb, driven cattle," he observed. Chinese Communists would not have found that characterization accurate, but they would have acknowledged Du Bois's next point, that Americans had supported the "murderous traitor," Chiang Kai-shek, until the Communists drove him into the sea, "where he still squats on an island, protected by our money and guns." Graham Du Bois gave a lecture titled "Women of the Far East" at the Women's Peace and Unity Club in Indiana. The Du Boises also spoke of their trip at the Third Baptist Church in San Francisco and the First Unitarian Church in Los Angeles.[111]

Du Bois published an article on his tour of China in the *National Guardian*, with the sentiments further elaborated in his *Autobiography*. He praised the Chinese for overcoming class differences to build an egalitarian society and for exorcising the great fears that haunt the Western worker: loss of work, no health insurance, anxieties about accidents, and lack of vacation time. While Americans scrimp, save, steal, gamble, and even murder for such necessities, he noted, the Chinese workers, male and female, "sit high above these fears and laugh with joy." Yes, Du Bois acknowledged, "China is no utopia. Fifth Avenue has better shops where the rich can buy and the whores parade. Detroit has more and better cars. The best American housing outstrips the Chinese, and Chinese women are not nearly as well dressed as the guests of the Waldorf-Astoria. But the Chinese worker is happy," and envy and class-hatred were disappearing in China. Thus, he believed China "follows its leaders and sings: 'O, Mourner, get up off your knees.'" People were encouraged to write poetry, once considered solely the province of the elite, to lift revolutionary morale.[112] Evidently, Du Bois was not aware of or was willing to overlook that only a small percentage of workers in state-owned enterprises enjoyed such privileges at the expense of millions of farmers within a newly constructed rigid hierarchy.

As they journeyed around China, the Du Boises had focused on improved conditions for women. Doubtless influenced by his wife, Du Bois next reported that, above all, "the women of China are becoming free. They wear pants so that they can walk, climb and dig; and climb and dig they do. They are not dressed simply for sex indulgence or beauty parades. They occupy positions from ministers of state to locomotive engineers, lawyers, doctors, clerks, and laborers."[113] State feminism had pushed women into traditionally male-dominated domains. As for African Americans in World War II, access to modern machinery in workplaces symbolized liberation and equality for women in Maoist China. Du Bois recalled watching in astonishment as "a crane which moved a hundred tons loomed above" in "one of the greatest steelworks of the world" in Wuhan and commenting to his wife, "'My God, Shirley, look up there!' Alone in the engine room sat a girl with ribbon braids, running the vast machine." Du Bois added, "You won't believe this, because you never saw anything like it; and if the State Department has its way, you never will." During the Great Leap Forward, such women were promoted as "iron girls" by the Chinese state. Guided by his wife, Du Bois now looked for such examples of women's liberation. Referring to the short-lived government policy centralizing childcare and meal preparation, he acclaimed that Chinese women were escaping "household drudgery" and that motherhood was easy with free prenatal care, wage and job security, nursery school, and kindergarten. Overall, as Du Bois saw it, Chinese women "are strong and healthy and beautiful not simply of leg and false bosom, but of brain, bran, and rich emotion."[114]

In his 1959 poem "I Sing to China," Du Bois paid his ultimate tribute to Chinese women, focusing on their motherhood:

To school, to school, Golden baby, China doll.
Kowtow, all Sons of Heaven

W. E. B. and Shirley Graham Du Bois

To the Daughters of Destiny!
Mothers of Men.
To the women of China
Pregnant with the fairest Future
Man ever knew![115]

As the couple left China, Graham Du Bois's interpreter, (Pei) Kwang-li, beamed with pride as she said that her next job would be laying bricks for the new People's Hall. The CCP carefully chose translators who could read the emotional desires of their guests in addition to interpreting their conversations. Certainly, Kwang-li did a good job with Graham Du Bois. According to the *People's Daily*, at the farewell banquet held by the China Peace Council and the CPACRFC, Graham Du Bois was emotional and chatty. She said poetically, "The China I see is so beautiful. Her children and women, and all the others are so happy. China is a great country."[116]

Graham Du Bois published an article with *Dagong Bao* (*Ta Kung Pao*, *L'Impartial*) in Hong Kong on September 20, 1959, which was soon reprinted in the *People's Daily*: "Today, I have seen the People's Republic. I would like to announce to all the Black sisters in the United States, West Indies, and Africa, that there is a new phenomenon in the world now that could inspire your heart and fill it with hopes. The once oppressed, discriminated, and contemptuously treated colored people now got rid of the oppressors, imperialists and slave owners. They have created world records in human relationships, agriculture, industry, construction and overall development."[117] Inspired by the achievements of state feminism in China, Du Bois sent a deeply emotional "Greetings to Women" the same year to the journal of the Women's Democratic Federation, based in Berlin. In his 1916 speech before the Civitas Club at Women's Clubhouse in Brooklyn, Du Bois had urged his white audiences to "take into account the women of China, of India, and of Africa" and Black American women "when you settle the problem of the status of women." Now, echoing his wife, he evidently considered the advancement of Chinese women to be way ahead of their white sisters.[118]

During the early years of their marriage, Graham Du Bois had taken a secondary role to her famous husband. In China, she guarded Du Bois's diet and general health. When she returned to the United States, Graham Du Bois declared herself a "new-born woman" and proclaimed that her husband "supported everything I did, even if I wasn't there when he needed me." Chinese women had told her that she was wasting time washing dishes when she should be writing, playing music, and teaching. Touched by state feminism there, she quickly hired a housekeeper upon her return to the United States, became editor of *Freedomways* magazine, and dived into politics.[119]

In an indication of her growing importance, Chinese media attention shifted gradually to Graham Du Bois. In 1961, she told a *People's Daily* reporter at the Afro-Asian Women's Conference in Accra, Ghana, that the "days visiting China were among the best days of my life," that many lively and fresh things about China attracted her, and that she hoped to return soon. Graham Du Bois added that she and her husband missed the Chinese people and would never forget their friendship. The reporter concluded that these were the words of a "typical" American woman.[120] Attention reverted back momentarily to Du Bois with the announcement on October 1, 1961, that at the age of ninety-three he had applied for membership in the Communist Party USA. The Du Boises then immediately departed to live in Accra, Ghana. There he planned, with the support of the government, to finish his long-delayed *Encyclopedia Africana*. Ensconced in the most exclusive neighborhood in Accra, the couple soon received a pilgrimage of guests, including, frequently, Huang Hua, now the Chinese ambassador to Ghana. For readers in China, Bingxin translated Du Bois's "Ghana Calls-A Poem," which had been published in *Freedomways*. The Du Boises then renounced their U.S. citizenship. This extraordinary move, made out of frustration and anger, gave symbolic importance to Ghana, their new country. Identifying with an African nation was consistent with the Du Boises' worldview. Though the FBI dismissed Ghana's importance for Du Bois and seemed not to worry about the Chinese ambassador, it kept tabs on the couple.[121] At the same time, China embraced his adopted nationality and its current press refers to Du Bois as an American Ghanaian. Du Bois and Graham Du Bois looked east to China for inspiration. The Chinese returned their gaze.

The *People's Daily* took Du Bois's conversion to communism seriously. Yuan Ying, a writer whose work was standard in middle- and high-school textbooks, rhapsodized in the newspaper about Du Bois's party membership. Yuan recalled Du Bois's speech at Beijing University as an inspiration. He then sent best wishes across the "strong waves of the Pacific. We salute you, respectful comrade Du Bois." Li Zhun, a noted scholar, sent a poem to Du Bois that was published in the *People's Daily*, affirming that joining the party had rejuvenated Du Bois: "You are ninety-three years old, and I am thirty-three years old; your age triples mine. But I feel that you are just as

FIGURE 1.15. W. E. B. and Shirley Graham Du Bois with Guo Moruo, 1962.
*Courtesy of W. E. B. Du Bois Papers, mums312-i0701, Special Collections
and University Archives, University of Massachusetts Amherst Libraries.*

young, young as a newborn. Youth is the sister of the truth. Dear comrade Du
Bois: Truth is ours, hope is ours, and tomorrow is ours." The Du Boises sent
telegrams of gratitude for China's opposition to the U.S. laws that sought
to imprison communists. Guo Moruo invited the couple to come back to
China, and they quickly accepted (fig. 1.15).[122]

The Du Boises returned to China on September 29, 1962, to celebrate
the thirteenth anniversary of the PRC's founding. The ironies of the previous visit returned. While regular Chinese starved, the Du Boises met once
more with Mao Zedong and Zhou Enlai and assumed a place of honor in
the reviewing stand at Tian'anmen Square, becoming the first Westerners
to take part in this enormous annual celebration (fig. 1.16). Premier Zhou
held a grand reception for National Day, which was attended by guests from
all over the world, including the Du Boises (fig. 1.17). Their names and pictures next to the top leadership graced the front page of the *People's Daily*
for days during the grand celebration.[123] Bingxin recalled her memorable reunion with the Du Boises at a farewell banquet held in a cozy dining hall on

FIGURE 1.16. W. E. B. and Shirley Graham Du Bois watch the parade celebrating the thirteenth anniversary of the People's Republic of China's founding on the balcony of the Tian'anmen Podium, October 1, 1962. To their right are China's top leadership: Deng Xiaoping, Zhou Enlai, Mao Zedong, and Liu Shaoqi. *Courtesy of W. E. B. Du Bois Papers, mums312-i0670, Special Collections and University Archives, University of Massachusetts Amherst Libraries.*

a chilly winter night after the couple rested in China for a few months. She noted that, despite two recent prostate surgeries in London, "the ninety-four-year-old warrior was still surprisingly chatty, humorous, and enjoyed a good appetite." Du Bois mentioned to the Chinese writer of his love of Chinese food, Beijing, and everything about the new China. He also noted that in his *Encyclopedia Africana*, he intended to restore the truth about Africa that had been distorted by white writers.[124]

The visit was the last W. E. B. Du Bois made to China. The world mourned his death on August 27, 1963, in Ghana, on the very morning of the historic civil rights march on Washington, D.C. In Beijing, an audience of 10,000 stood for three minutes of silence in mourning for Du Bois. Mao, Zhou, Chen Yi, Madam Sun, Guo Moruo, and numerous individuals and institutes, including Beijing University, sent telegrams and letters of condolence to Graham Du Bois. Mao's telegram, published in the *People's Daily*, read, "Madam Du Bois, I received the news of Dr. Du Bois's passing with

W. E. B. and Shirley Graham Du Bois

FIGURE 1.17. W. E. B. and Shirley Graham Du Bois and other foreign guests with Mao Zedong, Liu Shaoqi, and Zhu De on National Day in 1962. *Courtesy of W. E. B. Du Bois Papers, mums312-i0697, Special Collections and University Archives, University of Massachusetts Amherst Libraries.*

profound sadness and would like to express my condolences to you. Dr. Du Bois was a giant of our time. His brave struggles for the liberation of Blacks and humankind, extraordinary academic achievements, and genuine friendship toward China, will forever stay in the memory of our people. August 29, 1963."[125] Graham Du Bois replied to Zhou's telegram: "Dr. Du Bois witnessed the rise of African Americans against the unbearable conditions in the United States during life and their marching steps will continue to resonate in his ears after death." After Mao publicly declared support for the struggles of African Americans, Graham Du Bois issued a statement through a reporter for the New China News Agency in Accra: "Never a leader of a strong country issued such a call to the world. On behalf of myself and my late husband, I would like to express our appreciation to Chairman Mao, the great leader and friend of humanity." Guo Moruo published a passionate poem of imagined dialogues with the late Du Bois in the *People's Daily*. Bingxin's lengthy memorial piece repeatedly hailed Du Bois "a giant Black star!" She summarized his impressive academic, writing, and political careers and promised that his legacies would be carried on by the colored world, "resonating across forests, fields, rivers, lakes to Africa and other continents, like the loud tom-tom." The piece concluded, "Forever, Dr. Du Bois!"[126] Abbreviated versions of Du Bois's *Autobiography* were released in China, the Soviet Union, and the German Democratic Republic in their respective languages between 1964 and 1965, before it was published in New York in 1968.

THE TWILIGHT YEARS

The CCP's lauding of Du Bois stood in sharp contrast to its condemnation of the nonviolent philosophy of Martin Luther King Jr. Early on, the party praised King for his leadership in the civil rights movement. King had little to say about China, though he expressed support, in a private letter, for its inclusion in the United Nations.[127] Despite this small nod, by 1965 the *People's Daily* coverage of King had turned sour. Robert Williams, author of *Negroes with Guns* (1962) and the exiled Black American nationalist living in Beijing after years in Havana, declared, "American Blacks deeply believe in the truth of Chairman Mao's declaration and their struggles are taking the authentic revolutionary route," despite the efforts of right-wing leaders of some Black organizations, including King. Williams derided King for coming to Los Angeles during the riots to help white racists persuade Blacks to end their violent struggle.[128] Shortly thereafter, the *People's Daily* referred to King as an Uncle Tom and a "traitor who was the mask of [U.S. president Lyndon] Johnson and spokesman for the Nazi Los Angeles police chief, William Parker." The *Daily* castigated King's philosophy of nonviolence and referred to him repeatedly as a "running dog of counterrevolutionaries," who slandered armed Black resistance. After King's assassination in 1968, the newspaper quoted Robert Williams as saying that the pastor believed in nonviolence but was murdered by imperialist and racist violence. Chairman Mao taught that if you do not beat down the counterrevolutionaries, they would never stay down. During the heyday of the Cultural Revolution, the *People's Daily* invoked about sixty times the "irony" that King advocated nonviolence but died violently, as a countereducation case, showing the world's oppressed masses that they must pursue violent struggle.[129]

Joining Williams in support of the CCP was Shirley Graham Du Bois. In the aftermath of her husband's death, she tilted sharply toward China. In Ghana, Huang Hua cultivated her favor and ensured her creature comforts. She arranged a meeting between Malcolm X and Kwame Nkrumah. When Graham Du Bois was forced to leave Ghana following a military coup in 1967, she moved to Cairo, Egypt. There, as Vaughn Rasberry has pointed out,

Graham Du Bois developed her concepts of social modernity for the Third World. Ultimately, she spent most of her time in China, which was undergoing the violent turmoil of the Cultural Revolution. She chose the Chinese version of communism over the Soviet variety. She visited China in 1967 on the fourth anniversary of her husband's death, taking an appointment with the Permanent Bureau of Afro-Asian Writers.[130] As her biographer relates, there she had an exceptional meeting with Premier Zhou. One U.S. expatriate recalled that Zhou summoned Graham Du Bois to his office in the middle of the night. She was astonished to see the suave leader's face tense and anxious. He told her that he was worried that the Chinese Revolution might "go down to defeat in the Cultural Revolution. But it's O.K. You'll have your own revolution in Africa and you'll develop your own Mao Zedong."[131] It was an amazing admission to a foreigner and a testament to how deeply Chinese leaders trusted her.

Graham Du Bois had earned that respect through her devotion to the Chinese Revolution. Her diary from 1967 reveals painstaking notes on the history of the CCP. She offered assiduous commentary on visits to the Shanghai Industrial Exhibition, emphasizing the construction of heavy machinery, electronics, toys and athletic equipment, arts and crafts, as her husband had noted in Guangzhou in 1959. In these and subsequent entries on visits to communes, Graham Du Bois always credited Chairman Mao's leadership. In one section, she described how Mao had transformed the Shanghai Conservatory of Music. She moved around China, mingling with crowds in the streets, spending days on communes, and traveling with the army and Red Guards. Her diaries reveal that she had limited access to Red Guard condemnations of traitors to the CCP.[132] Although she considered the Cultural Revolution a "breath of fresh air," Graham Du Bois had to have noticed when Red Guards attacked her old friend, Guo Moruo. Two of his sons committed suicide after being persecuted. Unlike her Chinese friends, Graham Du Bois was free to roam the world, but she always returned to China. After spending some time in the Bahamas and Cairo, she returned to Beijing in February 1968. There she befriended Robert Williams and Gora Ebrahim, a representative of the Pan Africanist Congress of South Africa. She joined with other African Americans in China in admiring Mao's militancy about race in the United States and supported moves to supply African Americans with guns to fight oppression.[133] Using today's standards, one may criticize Graham Du Bois for her unquestioning acceptance of Mao and the Cultural Revolution, but at the time her actions indicated commitment to the international revolution and to China. In that light, she toiled even more intensely than the fabled China Hands (U.S. diplomats of the 1930s and 1940s), to understand China.[134]

Despite her strong support for the Cultural Revolution and though the event left her dumbfounded, Graham Du Bois bent her convictions to support Mao when the Chairman invited Richard Nixon to Beijing in 1972. Her reaction to this seismic shift in policy was to find common ground with the Chinese, which she had been doing since her first arrival in 1959. In 1970, following considerable negotiations, she was able to return temporarily to her native United States. There she told an audience at a Yale University conference on African women that they should not worry about their sisters in Africa, North Vietnam, or China, as they are "more liberated than you are."[135] Graham Du Bois crisscrossed the world in the early 1970s. She sold her husband's papers to the University of Massachusetts Amherst for a sum that allowed her a comfortable living. But age caught up with her. As her health deteriorated and lung cancer set in, she was advised to slow down. Ignoring this advice, she continued to write, made a short trip to London, and even began to criticize China's foreign policy. But now China was her home, though it was thousands of miles from her family. In 1974, she produced a film, *Women of the New China*, in celebration of the twenty-fifth anniversary of the PRC's founding. Two years later she joined her Chinese comrades in mourning the deaths of Zhou Enlai and Mao Zedong.[136]

Shirley Graham Du Bois died on March 27, 1977, and was buried in the Babaoshan Cemetery for Revolutionary Heroes in Beijing. The dignitaries present at her funeral service reflected the leadership of the Cultural Revolution. They included the vice premier, Cheng Yonggui, an illiterate farmer whose Dazhai Commune was held up as an example of Maoist selflessness and productivity, and Deng Yingchao, Zhou's widow. The CCP chair, Hua Guofeng, sent a memorial wreath, as did the embassies of Tanzania, Ghana, and Zambia.[137] The death of Graham Du Bois, fourteen years after that of her fabled husband, did not end their influence.

For diplomatic and economic reasons, China continued to maintain a large presence in Africa, which the Du Boises helped to foster. While Zhou Enlai's speech at the Bandung Conference in 1955 signaled China's racial alliance with Africa and Asia, W. E. B. Du Bois's preeminent reputation and endorsement meant a great deal to the CCP. China's outreach to Africa through diplomatic exchanges, aid, and propaganda soon peaked.[138] Du Bois's philosophy of Pan-Africanism explicitly extended to Pan-Asianism in the last five years of his life. Shirley Graham Du Bois greatly enabled that transition through her consistent social and political involvement in China. The state media's intense coverage of their visits indicated the breadth of the affection that CCP officials had for the couple and how they in turn influenced Chinese political attitudes toward Africa and African Americans.

The next chapter shifts to the reciprocal fascination of Paul Robeson and China. The great singer never visited China, but his impact was sizable. China in turn provided Robeson with support and inspiration in his times of trial.

Arise! Ye Who Refuse
to Be Bond Slaves!

Paul Robeson, "the Black King of Songs"

In November 1940, Paul Robeson received a phone call, perhaps from the noted Chinese writer Lin Yutang, asking him to meet a recent arrival from China: Liu Liangmo. Within half an hour, Robeson was in the caller's apartment. Liu recalled Robeson "beaming over me with his friendly smile and his giant hands firmly holding mine." They became fast friends. When Robeson inquired about the mass singing movement that Liu had initiated in China, Liu related the backstory behind the new genre of Chinese fighting and folk songs he had helped to invent for war mobilization, singing some examples. Robeson's favorite was "Chee Lai!" or "March of the Volunteers," because, as he explained, "Arise, Ye who refuse to be bond slaves!" expressed the determination of the world's oppressed, including Chinese and Blacks, to struggle for liberation. Listening intently to Liu's rendition of the song, Robeson wrote down some notes, and left with a copy.[1]

Robeson and Liu met at a propitious time. Robeson was one of the most popular singers and actors in the United States and amplified his fame with the recording "Ballad for Americans," which became a national sensation after a live radio broadcast on November 5, 1939. At the same time, Robeson's politics had tilted to the left. The FBI maintained a growing file on him. Robeson's interest in China was not new; he had been studying the Chinese language and Chinese philosophy for several years. He was well known to the Chinese people. Liu had heard of Robeson's travels to Spain to sing songs to encourage the embattled defenders of the Spanish Republic. Aware that Robeson often sang freedom songs of all countries in their original language, Liu had brought copies of Chinese fighting and folk songs to the United States, hoping that Robeson might perform them. Several weeks later, on a starry night, Liu attended an outdoor Robeson concert at Levisohn Stadium of the City College of New York. Robeson sang many Black spirituals and songs of national battles against fascism; then he announced, "I am going to sing a Chinese fighting song tonight in honor of the Chinese people, and that song is 'Chee Lai!'" Robeson, Liu recalled, sang in perfect Chinese; the audience demanded an encore.[2]

Robeson reprised this song in his numerous concerts in North America and Europe, sometimes amid entangled racial and ideological controversies. He sang it when the Washington Committee for Aid to China invited him to headline an event to raise money for United China Relief in 1941. The event had taken on additional political significance after the Daughters of the American Revolution (DAR) refused to rent out Constitution Hall because of his race. The DAR had apparently learned little from the scandal two years earlier when it refused access to Marian Anderson, only to have Eleanor Roosevelt resign from the organization and then arrange Anderson's historic concert on the steps of the Lincoln Memorial. The Committee for Aid to China found a new venue, Uline Auditorium. Even then, significant controversies arose over segregated seating and the division of the proceeds. The committee was also anxious about sponsoring the event with the National Negro Congress, which was suspected of communist connections. Eventually most of the committee resigned, ostensibly because Uline Auditorium refused to guarantee that it would not segregate in the future; under the surface was the fear of contamination with communism.[3]

Chinese intellectuals in the United States kept tabs on this controversy as it played out. In her memorial piece for W. E. B. Du Bois, the noted writer Bingxin recalled her encounter with a member of the DAR while staying at the National Women's Club in Washington, D.C. After Bingxin mentioned the "startling Jim Crow streetcars," the other woman, with clenched teeth and a red face, passionately defended the practice, citing African Americans' lack of "human intelligence and feelings." Shocked by this "mad-dog . . . daughter of revolution," Bingxin wrote that she heard "the striking voice of Paul Robeson singing at our school—'nobody knows the trouble I've seen'—suddenly ringing in my ears."[4] Liu, his former colleague in China's mass singing movement Chen Yiming, and the future vice president of the China Society for People's Friendship Studies Chen Xiuxia (both then Columbia University students) fondly remembered the excitement of hearing Robeson sing "Chee Lai!" in both Chinese and English for thousands of Americans at Union Square in Washington, D.C., in 1942 and Madison Square Garden in New York City in 1948. At the Union Square concert, Robeson stood shoulder to shoulder with Liu and performers of the Chinese People's Chorus, which Liu had organized in New York City's Chinatown. Robeson also sang this song, along with a Spanish fighting song and a Jewish song popular in Warsaw under German occupation, for Alexander Pushkin's 150th anniversary tribute in Moscow in 1949. The considerate Robeson sent royalties to the lyric author Tian Han, who forwarded part of them to the surviving mother and brother of the composer Nie Er in Yunnan Province.[5]

In November 1941, with the cooperation of the China Aid Council (under United China Relief), a conduit organized by Madam Sun Yat-sen's China Defense League, Robeson, Liu, and the Chinese People's Chorus recorded an album of Chinese fighting and folk songs for Keynote Records titled *Chee Lai! Songs of New China* (fig. 2.1). They intended the record to be played on radio stations and in homes around the United States. The chorus had asked Liu to approach Robeson about making such an album and the singer agreed readily. Liu saw such collaboration as "a strong token of solidarity between the Chinese and the Negro People." The album included such songs as "Chee Lai!," "Work as One," "Fengyang," "Chinese Farmers' Song," "Chinese Soldiers' Song," "Riding the Dragon," and "Song of the Guerrillas." Robeson sang "Chee Lai!" and the third, fifth, and sixth songs, after repeated careful rehearsals, while Liu and the chorus performed the others. Robeson's liner notes read: "Chee Lai! (Arise!) is on the lips of millions of Chinese today, a sort of unofficial anthem, I am told, typifying the unconquerable spirit of this people. It is a pleasure and a privilege to sing both this song of modern composition and the old folk songs to which a nation in struggle has put new words." Madam Sun's liner notes praised Robeson, "the voice of the people of all lands," and "our own Liu Liang-mo, who has taught a nation of soldiers, guerrillas, farmers, and road builders to sing while they toil and fight." She hoped that the album of songs "that blend the harmonies of East and West [would] be another bond between free peoples." Lin Yutang was involved in recording the album and contributed an accompanying booklet, and his liner notes exclaimed that "China is finding her voice." The *New York Times* lauded it as one of the year's best and noted that profits went to the China Relief Fund; the *Philadelphia Inquirer* applauded its "tonic glimpses of a heroic people." Local newspapers advertised it among eight "Allied War Songs of Special Merit." The album quickly became popular across the United States.[6]

Dagong bao, then printed in exile in Guilin, noted its wide reception

FIGURE 2.1. Cover of the album *Chee Lai!* recorded by Paul Robeson, Liu Liangmo, and the Chinese People's Chorus for Keynote Records in 1941. *Author's collection.*

throughout the Americas. In response to demand from Western customers, Chinese restaurants in New York City and Chicago reportedly ordered the full set of six records, priced at $2.75, to play during dinner. Following Robeson's lead, Kenneth Spencer, another noted African American baritone, adopted some songs from the collection to his repertoire. Liu subsequently published a slim collection of Chinese "folk-songs and fighting songs," with arrangements by musician Evelyn Modoi. Hollywood eventually adopted "Chee Lai!" The U.S. Army Air Force Orchestra played the tune at the start and conclusion of the film *Why We Fight: The Battle of China* (1944), directed by the famed Frank Capra and produced by the State Department.[7]

In recent years, Robeson and Liu's collaboration and friendship have received scholarly attention. Richard Jean So has imaginatively configured their connection as an example of "pentatonic democracy" and has shown the similarities in structure and message of the African American and Chinese songs which the two friends collaborated on and sang. Such universality, however, extended well beyond their art into the realm of politics, which was always foremost for both men.[8]

Nevertheless, Robeson's ties with China were frequently off the radar of even the FBI during his lifetime, and they have received insufficient study given Robeson's profound affection for China, a nation he never visited. More attention has been given to Robeson's adoration of the Soviet Union. He famously remarked in 1949, "I am truly happy that I am able to travel from time to time to the USSR—the country I love above all. I always have been, I am now and will always be a loyal friend of the Soviet Union."[9] "Chee Lai!" was by no means the sole connection between Robeson and the Chinese people. This chapter rediscovers and unpacks Robeson's faith in the cultural and political kinship between China (and Asia) and Africa, his enthusiasm for China's resistance against Japan, his long-term alliance with the leftist Chinese artists who sojourned abroad, and his eventual embrace of the Chinese Communist Party (CCP) and the People's Republic of China (PRC).

ARTICULATING THE AFFINITY BETWEEN AFRICA, CHINA, AND ASIA

Paul Robeson's eventual ties with China built on a profound intellectual and emotional foundation. Long before W. E. B. Du Bois's comments on the revolutions in China and their positive impact on lifting the colored world, his subsequent full endorsement of a Sino-African alliance, and Mao Zedong's development of the Third World theory that binds the destinies of former colonies in Asia, Africa, and Latin America, Robeson consistently articulated the linkage between African and Chinese civilizations.

Echoing Langston Hughes and other Harlem Renaissance artists, Robeson drew power and strength from the concept of "primitive" Africa as an "unpolluted" alternative to the corrupted European model. Since the 1920s, Robeson had claimed that "the only true artistic contributions of America are Negro in origin" and called on African Americans to culturally "return to the primitive soil" of Africa. He considered his "discovery" of the "pure" "original" folklores of West Africa a "home-coming" that penetrated to the core of African culture. To counter negative stereotypes associated with perceived African "primitivism," Robeson stressed that African civilizations were as significant, distinctive, and venerable as that of China, and he sought to illustrate their linguistic, philosophical, and artistic kinship. In addition to "identical" historical handicrafts and "comparable" harvest dances, he noted that the similarly monosyllabic and tone-oriented African languages and Chinese could be rendered "perfectly" into each other. Sharing the often-despised "primitive" African way of thinking in concrete symbols, China had produced philosophical giants such as Confucius, Mencius, and Lao-tze. Robeson urged Black students to find a spiritual father in Confucius in Beijing, rather than wrestling vainly with Plato at Oxford. Du Bois had similarly cited these Chinese philosophers as he debunked scientific racism or the popular Orientalist pseudo-Confucianism of Charlie Chen. Robeson suggested that the "rich" and "beautiful" pentatonic system shared by Hebrew and Chinese folk music had been commonly used before the better-known diatonic seven-tone system of modern European music. Robeson announced in London in 1933 that he would perform Asian folk songs he understood rather than German opera alien to him.[10]

Robeson's narrative of comparative cultures fit into contemporary global discourse during the interwar period. Mahatma Gandhi and Western intellectual dissenters contrasted Asian and Western civilizations by opposing their spirituality and religion against Western rationalism and technology. Robeson insisted that the "primitive" nature of African civilizations was actually the source of their sophistication and distinctive contributions. Although science and technology enabled the Europeans to conquer nature and colonize the world, their machines ultimately brought misery, he observed. Thus, the "Negroes and the great Eastern races" were destined to teach the West to balance spirituality and rationality. Echoing the Confucian scholar-officials of China's self-strengthening movement in the late nineteenth century, Robeson insisted that culture, the "essential," had to be inherited and internal, while technology could be borrowed and remain external. "The Negro," he wrote, "will remain sterile until he recognizes his cultural affinity with the East" and "sticks to their shared emotional capacity" of "terrific power." The *North-China Daily News* quoted Robeson: "Everyone has heard of Chinese art. Who has ever heard of Chinese science? The Chinese, before they built a house, even in these days, want to know that the wind and the tides of the water are favorable! Theirs is not a 'rational' culture. It is a culture of emotion." For Robeson, this cultural kinship necessitated political alliance. At the gatherings of the NAACP (1934) and the League of Colored Peoples in London (1935), Robeson declared that the future of Africa was connected with China and called for Africans and Chinese to solve their common problems as colonies, sketching the outline of a partnership that Du Bois and Mao Zedong would elaborate decades later.[11]

Yet in the 1930s, Robeson and Du Bois disagreed about the hostilities between China and Japan. Robeson consistently denounced Japanese aggression and was active on committees and in events to aid China, while Du Bois endorsed Japan as preferable conquers to the West. In 1936, when Du Bois articulated this view during his trip to East Asia, Robeson exclaimed "Manchuria—yellow Japanese making war on yellow Chinese!" He was thus refuting an absolute color line and the notion of war between the races. He acknowledged the "silent Chinese [volunteers] who fire their rifles at Italians and Germans" on antifascist fronts in Europe, while China fought against the Japanese "who profane[ed] Nanking." As soon as the war broke out in Europe, Robeson insisted upon treating China and Europe as a united "international fight for democracy [of the equally oppressed Blacks, Chinese, and Jews] and against Fascism." From 1941 on, he connected race and class issues. The world's fundamental problem, as Robeson saw it, was that "a few landlords owned all the land and told the peasants, as they tell the Negroes in the South, they must remain in slavery."[12]

COLLABORATION WITH PEARL S. BUCK

Paul Robeson sought to learn more about China from one of the most prominent U.S. Sinologists, Pearl S. Buck, by whom W. E. B. Du Bois was similarly inspired. Judging by the correspondence between their families, the Nobel laureate took pains to reach out to the star. Their friendship started with Robeson's diligent effort to study the Chinese language. During an evening conversation in early 1942, he mentioned to Buck's husband, Richard Walsh, head of the John Day Company and editor of *Asia* magazine, his desire to replace his lost copy of *The Student's Four Thousand Tzu and General Pocket Dictionary* by William Edward Soothill. After trying four bookstores in New York City without success, Buck's assistant earnestly assured Robeson that a copy could be found for him soon. She mentioned that she had greatly enjoyed Robeson singing Chinese songs on his *Keep 'Em Rolling* program.[13]

The Walshes were anxious to nurture family bonds. After spending some time together in early 1943, Robeson sent photographs of his family's daily activities in their Connecticut house. The Walshes proposed reciprocal hospitality at each other's country homes and extended a warm invitation, promising to "make a great effort to fetch" the guests from the train, but the plan seemed to fall through. Buck telegrammed her "warmest good wishes" and highest acclaim ("You are one of the world's greatest and best, and I am proud that we are fellow-Americans") for Robeson's much celebrated forty-seventh birthday in 1945. The congratulatory words were returned due to a wartime rule against telegramming congratulations. Determined to send "what I really wanted to say," Buck forwarded her message through Max Yergan, the cofounder of the Afro-American Council, "earnestly" hoping they could reach Robeson before his birthday.[14]

Ultimately, Robeson's relationship with Buck remained formal and professional, as indicated by full-name salutations, signatures, and the reserved tone of their correspondence, yet constructive. In addition to sharing a forum at the Manhattan Center, Buck ensured that Robeson spoke and sang at several race-themed meetings that her East and West Association sponsored between 1943 and 1944. She strove to convince the singer that a meeting on the peoples of Africa "would not be complete" without him; and the importance of a town hall meeting on Korea, Japan's long-term colony, was "beyond the Korean people." Buck prepared a "fragile glass recording" and sheet music of the Korean folk song "Arirang Hill" and the national anthem "Aikookka," offering to find someone to help with the Korean words. Suspecting that his manager "has ulterior motives in not wanting to get this song into Mr. Robeson's hands," Buck managed to reach him through Yergan. Robeson would recall his contribution to the meeting in the heat of the Korean War, arguing that it was "ridiculous to even imagine these two peoples [Koreans and Chinese] embarking on predatory war to conquer other peoples."[15] On March 12, 1944, along with Mayor Fiorello La Guardia, Robeson spoke and sang at the Sun Yat-sen tribute dinner organized by Buck at the Metropolitan Opera House in New York City. The professional cooperation between Robeson and Buck in that year was capped by MGM's adaption of *Dragon Seed*, her novel about China's resistance against Japan, starring Katherine Hepburn and featuring Robeson's version of "Chee Lai!" as the theme song.[16]

A couple of months after the atomic bombing of Hiroshima and Nagasaki, Buck forwarded to Robeson a John Day Company manuscript, "The Bomb That Fell on America." Believing that the text, "a dramatic poetic treatment of what the atomic bomb means and a moving appeal to the soul of America," had a role to play in the world peace movement, she "earnestly" urged Robeson to read an abbreviated version on a national radio program that she would arrange for. Slightly embarrassed, Buck withdrew her request shortly afterward, having learned that the author intended to dedicate the piece to the Moral Rearmament Movement and that John Day had abandoned the project.[17]

Among the few white women who made a place for herself in nonwhite communities in this era, Buck's cross-race endeavors often met gendered responses. While Robeson was lukewarm toward Buck's outreach, his wife, Eslanda, in her pursuit of an independent career as a writer and lecturer, eagerly cultivated a productive personal and professional relationship with the famous author. They frequently interacted as family friends. Eslanda wrote Buck in the summer of 1944, "This seems to be a Walsh day. I have to answer both your son's letter, and your husband's, all of which came some time ago!" She proudly shared detailed information about her own son. Soon even her mother, Eslanda C. Goode, felt comfortable enough to send Buck a six-page, tightly written letter, complaining about household issues and disagreements over rearing Paul Jr. Buck politely expressed her sympathy and assured Goode that Walsh and herself "think very highly indeed of Pauli and . . . have been following his career in college with much interest." In 1946, Buck sent some John Day books that Goode had requested from her nursing home, including *Tell the People: Talks with James Yen about the Mass Education Movement*, wishing her better health.[18]

The Walshes sometimes attempted to reach Robeson through his more accessible wife. Walsh wrote to Eslanda that he and Buck had acquired tickets "with much effort" and saw Robeson in *Othello* on November 30, 1943. They were "quite swept away by its magnificence and especially by the tremendous effect of your husband's presence, his voice and his acting." Walsh then mailed Eslanda a collection of the "best" Chinese folk songs "for the Western public," translated by a young Chinese friend of theirs and with musical arrangements by Buck, hoping Robeson would sing some of them in theaters. Buck wrote to Eslanda in 1945 inviting the Robesons to sponsor an African booklet and sending some materials on China and Russia. Eslanda responded that she had no money but would ask her husband when he was home. Buck promised to send the manuscript, "if he is the least bit interested."[19]

Considering Eslanda a "very clear headed, forceful, direct person" without "race bias" or "bitterness" and confident in her ability to secure funds, Buck in 1944 joined her ambitious campaign to improve the status of African Americans through federal laws. Eslanda dived into speeches at schools, churches, and women's clubs to stir public political action. She frequently sent her lecture notes and speech invitations to the Walshes seeking comments and reported her exciting interactions with eager audiences. When

Eslanda wrote to Benjamin Davis Jr., the New York City councilman and communist, about her endeavors to win federal guarantees of civil rights, he praised her "independent contributions to the people's movement in this country." In 1947, Robeson launched a campaign to outlaw lynching and the poll tax and restore the Fair Employment Practices Committee, an initiative his biographer Martin Duberman credited to Eslanda. Eslanda and Buck's shared activism on racial relations took printed form in their 1949 book *American Argument*. In 1944, Buck had sponsored Eslanda's membership in the Authors' League of America, hoping to promote the latter's play *Goodbye Uncle Tom* in theaters. The John Day Company published Eslanda's *African Journey* in 1945.[20]

Eslanda connected Buck with her circle of African American women activists. In 1945, she invited Buck to the seventieth birthday party of Mary McLeod Bethune, founder and president of the National Council of Negro Women, celebrating her accomplishments in Black advancement, "interracial goodwill and social welfare." Buck declined the invitation but telegrammed acclaiming Bethune as the "proof of what one person can do, with inspiration and determination." Buck then contributed a guest editorial, "The Wisdom and the Power," to the council's quarterly, the *Aframerican Woman's Journal*. Bethune called the piece "sublime. Only a Pearl Buck could have penned these powerful words."[21]

FRIENDSHIP WITH THE SOJOURNING
LEFTIST CHINESE ARTISTS

In addition to maintaining a friendship with Pearl S. Buck, white America's chief interpreter of China, the Robesons regularly interacted with Chinese themselves. Besides Liu Liangmo, among the Chinese sojourners Robeson befriended were the actress, writer, and activist Wang Yung; Mei Lanfang, "the King of Beijing Opera"; and Madam Sun Yat-sen. Their mutual attraction lay in both artistic achievements and leftist politics. Mirroring Liu's endeavors during World War II, Wang Yung, as the leading lady and scripter of Chinese street plays, brought the new genre adapted for wartime mobilization into global circulation, twice performing at the White House in 1943 and 1945. Impressed by Wang's work and media coverage of her, Robeson requested that Buck, Wang's collaborator and sponsor, introduce them in New York City in 1942. Several decades later, Wang's husband, Xie Hegeng, recalled how the two artists talked frequently, traded compliments, and autographed albums and records to each other. Robeson taught Wang to sing

"Joe Hill" and "Ol' Man River," which she would reenact at the celebrations of her own wedding and at Christmas in 1965, the last one before the Cultural Revolution engulfed her. In return, Wang helped Robeson to improve his Chinese pronunciation and the rhythms of Chinese songs. Matching his effusive comments about the Soviet Union, Robeson reportedly told Wang, "China is a great country. Your Madam Sun Yat-sen has invited me to visit and perform. When you teach me these songs, I hear the heart beating of the Chinese people and see their unyielding struggles against Japanese fascists, which will certainly lead to ultimate victory."[22]

Robeson met Mei Lanfang in 1935 through mutual friends, including Anna May Wong (黄柳霜), the noted Chinese American actress, the critic and novelist Carl Van Vechten, and his wife, Fania Marinoff. Though neither set foot in Africa or China until the mid-1930s, Hollywood had both Robeson and Wong perform a racialized "Blackness/Africanness" and "Chineseness" in their screen roles. Caught in the same dilemma, their friendship offered an avenue for mutual support. Mei arrived in London in May 1935, after a highly successful three weeks of appearances with China's "Movie Queen" Hu Die (Butterfly Wu) in Moscow and Leningrad. Wong was in the midst of one of her many London visits. Robeson was there acting in *Stevedore*, a play about Black-white labor unity that had been produced in New York City in 1934. Wong took a snapshot of Robeson and Mei outside the Claridge's Hotel (fig. 2.2). Marinoff, who ordinarily was uncomfortable with Robeson, took a snapshot of the three famous actors. Joining them in another photograph were the American-trained Chinese dramatists Xiong Shiyi (Hsiung Shih-I) and Yu Shangyuan (Yui Shang-Yuen) (fig. 2.3). Yu, who had helped to launch China's national drama movement in the late 1920s, accompanied Mei to study theaters in Europe. Xiong was producing his Beijing-opera-based modern play *Lady Precious Stream* (*Wang Baochuan*), which had more than 400 performances in London from November 1934 to October 1935. After being picked up by theaters in Berlin, Amsterdam, and Shanghai, *Lady Precious Stream* came to Broadway in 1936. Eleanor Roosevelt and her children watched and met Xiong and the actors.[23]

After Mei watched Robeson in *Stevedore* at the Embassy Theater, the two internationally famous artists became fast friends, exchanging souvenirs along with views on singing, performance, and the cultural affinity and shared political destiny between Africa and China. "The King of Beijing Opera" cherished gifts from the Robesons throughout multiple periods of political chaos and relocation. One was an autographed photograph of Robeson singing "Ol' Man River" in *Show Boat*, with Eslanda's note on the back explain-

FIGURE 2.2. "The Black King of Songs" Paul Robeson and
"the King of Beijing Opera" Mei Lanfang in London in 1935. The famous
Chinese American actress Anna May Wong took the picture.
*Photographs of Prominent African Americans, box 16, folder 169, Beinecke
Rare Book and Manuscript Library, Yale University Library, JWJ MSS 76.*

ing that his part was the boatman Joe in the 1928 London production. Mei's
son Shaowu later recalled that, as a child, he asked his father who was this
Black man wearing ragged clothes in this photograph kept under glass on
the desk in his parents' bedroom. Mei responded, "Never look down upon
him. He is a world-famous singer and his name is Robeson!" The second was
Eslanda's biography of her husband. Next to Mei's special bookplate on the
inside cover, the Robesons inscribed in June 1935, "To Mei Lanfang, with sincere and profound admiration. We hope to see you and your great art again
in your motherland." In the early 1950s, Mei passed the book to Shaowu to
be cherished. During the Cultural Revolution, when ownership of publications in foreign languages became dangerous, Shaowu preserved the book by
wrapping it carefully and hiding it among trash. Shaowu's biography of his
father devotes a long chapter to the friendship between Robeson and Mei.[24]

    After Mei returned to China, Robeson retained ties with leftist forces

FIGURE 2.3. Paul and Eslanda Robeson with Anna May Wong,
Mei Lanfang (*second from right*), Xiong Shiyi (*third from right*),
and Yu Shangyuan (*first on right*) in London in 1935.
*Photographs of Prominent African Americans, box 16, folder 169, Beinecke
Rare Book and Manuscript Library, Yale University Library, JWJ MSS 76.*

there. Robeson never met Madam Sun, but he transmitted to her a flux of
speeches, writings, and recordings. She was among the nineteen Chinese
representatives selected for the International Anti-aggression Conference
in London in 1938. Unable to attend due to her pressing work setting up
the China Defense League in Hong Kong, she telegrammed the conference,
calling for "promoting world peace, and penalizing those invaders." The experienced diplomat Wellington Koo (Gu Weijun), who made a speech calling for a boycott of Japanese goods, ably represented her. Robeson spoke as
well, and strongly condemned the Japanese invasion at a special meeting of
the conference supporting China's resistance. Koo certainly reported Robeson's words to Madam Sun. Soon Robeson was invited to serve as an honorary chair of the China Defense League.[25]

Robeson sustained consistent contact with Madam Sun throughout
World War II and after. In addition to their cooperation on the *Chee Lai!*
album, there were other indirect interactions. Drawing parallels between
Africa and China at the Sun Yat-sen tribute dinner in 1944, Robeson reiterated that both had long glorious cultures and that now each suffered from
the "exploitation and oppression of aliens who spat upon their cultures and
spread abroad the poison of racial hate and intolerance." He remarked, how-

Paul Robeson

ever, that China, now considered a world leader as the Allied Powers united to defeat Japan, was poised to claim all stolen territories and renounce the "offensive" extraterritoriality privileges enjoyed by multiple colonial forces, after the United States repealed the "humiliating" Chinese Exclusion Act. Evidently, Robeson connected discrimination endured by racial minorities in the United States to colonialism suffered by people in their ancestral lands. Madam Sun, unable to attend, broadcast on national radio a "splendid" eight-minute speech from China's wartime capital, Chongqing, stating that Chinese revolutionaries drew inspiration from the American struggle for independence from England. The recorded speech by Sun Yat-sen's son Sun Ke (Fo), which Pearl S. Buck considered "surprisingly good," was also played at the meeting.[26]

In February 1943, when Madam Chiang Kai-shek was making her triumphant visits to the White House, Madam Sun entertained Spencer Kennard, affiliated with the International Peace Hospitals, and his wife with a dinner at her home in Chongqing. Asked what they could do for her, Madam Sun expressed her desire to escape the "immediate anxieties and living conditions of free China" to rest and recuperate, not to speak, for a few months in the atmosphere of her American college days. As soon as they returned to the United States the following summer, the Kennards approached Eleanor Roosevelt and others to arrange Madam Sun's visit. The first lady suggested that a powerful organization should request such an invitation through the State Department. Accordingly, supported by Buck's East and West Association, Mrs. Edward C. Carter, president of the China Aid Council, contacted the director of the Far Eastern Division of the State Department. Carter argued that Madam Sun, as president of the China Defense League, "could bring an interpretation of China to all whom she meets in this country which would help in our future relationships." However, the division kicked the ball to the Chinese embassy, which neither Buck nor Carter felt comfortable approaching. When Carter turned back to the State Department, insisting that Madam Sun would not consider leaving China in wartime out of pride, it demanded a formal written request from her. Sensing that Madam Sun would not want to publicly request such a privilege, Kennard, Carter, and Buck decided to wait for a better occasion for inviting Madam Sun to arise "naturally."[27]

After this diplomatic soccer match, it was Robeson who finally came through. On behalf of the National Peace Commission and other organizations, he invited Madam Sun in July 1946 to visit and deliver a speech on China at a mass gathering in New York City's Madison Square Garden. Madam Sun declined with regret: "How much I wish my plan to visit the United States could be materialized right now!" The Chinese authorities would not issue her a passport. More important, Madam Sun refused to leave her disaster-stricken motherland during a worsening political crisis and civil war. "When children risk death," she wrote, "mother should not leave home." In 1948, Robeson joined Jawaharlal Nehru, his sister Vijaya Lakshmi Pandit, British Sinologist Joseph Needham, Guo Moruo, and Mao Dun, among the thirteen sponsors of China Welfare Fund that Madam Sun established in Shanghai, to replace the China Defense League. Appreciative of and impressed with Robeson, Madam Sun cherished the *Chee Lai!* album and preserved it in her Shanghai house for the rest of her life.[28]

AN ALLIANCE WITH THE CHINESE COMMUNIST PARTY AND THE PEOPLE'S REPUBLIC OF CHINA

Paul Robeson's and his wife's long contacts with left-wing Chinese led to their alliance with the CCP and the PRC during the transition from World War II into the Cold War. While Robeson and W. E. B. Du Bois were hardly alone in condemning the Nationalists and embracing the Communists, their attitude was unusual among African American leaders, who generally favored the Nationalists. Robeson and the PRC lent each other unyielding support during their most dramatic and trying moments as an individual artist and a nation — the Peekskill Riots overlapped with the rough birth of the new China, and his passport issue with the Korean War. Like Du Bois, Robeson framed his campaign to halt U.S. intervention in China's civil war and the Korean War within the international peace movement.

As early as the 1944 Sun Yat-sen tribute dinner, Robeson argued that "the picture of China's internal conflict as the Kuomintang vs. the Chinese Communist is . . . false," because the true fight was between the "Chinese people and a small reactionary clique" in the Nationalist Party. Thus, China was fighting with one hand tied behind its back, while the clique was denying financial, military, or economic aid for the valiant efforts by "Communist-led Eighth Route and New Fourth Armies" to fight and mobilize the people for national defense, and even blockading and hunting them down. He applauded the Communist leaders' "frank declaration" that they would maintain national unity, freedom, and democracy. "The three-year's blockade against the Chinese guerrilla forces must be lifted," Robeson demanded. "The entire might and strength of China's 400 million must be united."[29] He denounced U.S. support of Chiang Kai-shek at the 1945 World Peace Conference as well as at several public gatherings he organized with the American National Peace Commission in 1946. The CCP noted such activities by Robeson with appreciation. The Xinhua News Agency, still located in Yan'an, reported one of the gatherings in San Francisco, to which Madam Sun telegrammed her well wishes. At the prestigious Spingarn award ceremony in 1945, which, Martin Duberman notes, "marked both the apex of his public acclaim and the onset of his fall from official grace," Robeson pronounced that "the people of Asia, China and India want to realize promises [of decolonization] made to them."[30]

Robeson quickly adopted the CCP's narrative that the forthcoming "new China" would sharply depart from the thousands of years of "old China." The "forces of liberation" were bringing millions of Chinese "freedom such as they have never known throughout the course of their long history," he announced. He compared the sense of freedom and dignity he felt during his first visit to the Soviet Union in 1934 and his concert tour in Jamaica and Trinidad in 1948 to "what a Jew must feel when first he goes to Israel, what a Chinese must feel on entering areas of his country that now are free."[31] Echoing Du Bois, Robeson eagerly predicted that the establishment of the PRC would elevate the colored world. His May 11, 1949, statement to explain his much-distorted speech at the International Congress for Peace in Paris announced that the creation of the "gallant China" would be "world-shattering," ensuring that "all men can be free and equal." He challenged "the mighty Blacks" to follow China's step at a London gathering protesting racism in South Africa and a Welcome Home Rally sponsored by the Council on African Affairs (CAA) in New York City in 1949.[32]

Among the numerous things Robeson found laudable about the CCP's victory was the adoption of "Chee Lai!" as China's national anthem. At the Preparatory Assembly for the First National People's Political Consultative Conference in Beijing in July 1949, a national anthem committee was formed. Premier Zhou Enlai said that he personally liked "March of the Volunteers," but the masses should be consulted. After China's state media and overseas and Hong Kong newspapers announced a massive competition for the lyrics, the committee received 694 pieces. At the First National People's Political Consultative Conference, Zhou's view prevailed. Liu Liangmo, freshly returned from the United States, argued for the song's global popularity. "March of the Volunteers," instead of the national anthem of the Republic of China, had been performed at all China-related gatherings and celebrations. To support the point, architect Liang Sicheng (a son of the noted scholar and reformer Liang Qichao) recounted an anecdote of hearing an American youth whistling the tone on the street. The noted painter Xu Beihong echoed that "Volunteers," which had awoken millions during the War of Resistance, would continue to inspire future fighting spirit. The meeting concluded with Mao Zedong and Zhou Enlai leading the singing of the new national anthem.[33]

To celebrate the announcement of the PRC's establishment on October 1, 1949, Robeson sang "Chee Lai!" on the streets of Harlem. He famously telegrammed Mao Zedong to congratulate the new regime: "We celebrate the birth of the People's Republic of China, because it is a great force in the struggles for world peace and human freedom. Chairman of the Council on African Affairs, Paul Robeson." The contents of the telegram were immediately published in the *People's Daily* and *Xinhua Telegram*, and would be featured in other publications on Robeson in China in the 1950s.[34] To further signal his solidarity with the PRC, using musical notes from Madam Sun with her inscription, Robeson performed portions of the *Yellow River Cantata* to celebrate the United Nations Day on October 24 and with the Toronto Jewish Folk Choir at Massey Hall in Toronto in December 1949. The cantata was created by the lyricist Guang Weiran and the musician Xian Xinghai in Yan'an. Liu Liangmo had brought the sheet music to the United States, and a university in the New York region performed it in English in 1941.[35]

Eslanda Robeson's 1949 visit affirmed the alliance between the Robesons and the PRC. Readers of Shanghai English-language newspapers were familiar with her writing career. The *Shanghai Times* favorably reviewed her biography of her husband in 1930, and the *China Press* reported that *African Journey* was banned in South Africa in 1946. Eslanda and her traveling companion, Ada Jackson, a Brooklyn-based American Labor Party activist, arrived in Beijing from the Soviet Union to attend the First Asian Women's Congress (December 10–16, 1949), the first major international conference held in the PRC. The meeting was originally scheduled to be in India in October 1948, but Jawaharlal Nehru's government had forced its relocation. Eslanda and Jackson were, according to the *Amsterdam News*, the first African American women to visit the PRC. Eslanda joined a few other delegates to deliver speeches at the meeting and toured Shanghai, Nanjing, and Jinan afterward. She announced the end of colonialism but warned against inaugurating "a native regime as dictatorial as their foreign masters were," a warning soon echoed by W. E. B. Du Bois in his high-profile speeches on Africa. Furthermore, she noted how the women of Madagascar and the Ivory Coast had united to resist French and British colonial rule, as exemplified by sit-down strikes to rescue their husbands from prison. Eslanda reported that the Chinese greeted her and fellow delegates at airports and train stations with singing and dancing, before arranging for them to speak at mass meetings. Madam Sun, whose long congratulatory letter had been read at the conference, invited Eslanda to lunch at her residence in Shanghai, where they spoke at length about world politics and China's revolutionary changes, especially the status of women. The hospitality China extended to Eslanda foreshadowed the reception of W. E. B. and Shirley Graham Du Bois there a decade later. Eslanda and Jackson headed home from Tianjin on December 26.[36]

Inundated with requests to speak about the new China, Eslanda held a press conference in New York City on January 23, 1950, and toured the country addressing churches, women's conferences, and African American societies, including her sorority sisters. The Du Boises would similarly serve as messengers to the American public following their visit to China. To her American audiences, Eslanda applauded land reform as "the greatest thing," because it allegedly granted all Chinese citizens, women and men, equal access to a home, school, and job. "Women are people. People are citizens. Citizens are equal," Eslanda was reportedly told. She dismissed the allegation that the PRC government was being manipulated by the Soviets and stressed its stability, its burning desire for peace behind the so-called Iron Curtain, and the importance of the United States establishing friendship and trading with the new regime. She mentioned that her sympathetic Chinese hosts had often asked her about the abuse Blacks suffered in the so-called democratic United States. Like the Du Boises, Eslanda retained public and private contacts with CCP officials at a time when the United States had suspended any official relations with the PRC. The Chinese media followed her work on behalf of the PRC. The *People's Daily* reported her speech at the women's gathering for peace in Amsterdam in 1950 and her shared actions with Shirley Graham Du Bois at the All-Africa Congress in Ghana.[37]

Paul Robeson joined his wife in further celebrations of the PRC. He enthusiastically wrote a lengthy article, "Happy Birthday, New China," to mark the third anniversary of the PRC's founding. Robeson explained that, lacking the opportunity to visit China as his wife had done, he had reached out to its compatriots by continuously studying their language and singing their songs. He invited his fans to join the 475 million Chinese in celebration of their true freedom. Invoking the metaphor popularized by Pearl S. Buck's famous novel, Robeson exclaimed that China's "good earth" and "all its riches" belonged to the Chinese people for the first time. "No more drivers' lash for them—oh no, they're in the driver's seat now." Robeson romantically imagined that the colored world could view the rising China as a "new star of the East . . . pointing the way out from imperialist enslavement to independence and equality. China has shown the way." Citing the Sino-African affinity that he had been urging for decades, Robeson declared, "With China free and Africa rising against the rule of White Supremacy, I look forward to a new flowering of those two great ancient cultures, bringing to all mankind new riches in the arts and science."[38] Du Bois would elaborate on Robeson's metaphor and sentiment one decade later.

When the nascent PRC regime confronted the United States, a superpower with nuclear weapons, during the Korean War, Robeson joined Du Bois to declare his unyielding support for China. Robeson exclaimed in his birthday letter to the new China, "Yes, China is a power for peace as it is for liberation." The communist regimes' mutual support would be the "great truth" in their shared journey to freedom. "Backed by their mighty Soviet ally," Chinese workers and farmers could "look Mr. Big Western imperialist dead in the eye and say. . . . 'Better not mess with us!'" Thus, it was only logical for the Chinese volunteers to come to "the aid of the heroic Korean people," Robeson insisted. He firmly believed that China's involvement in the Korean War was essential to defend hard-earned "freedom, dignity, and security" on behalf of millions in Asia. He condemned U.S. manipulation of the United Nations for "imperialist" purposes — calling U.S. foreign policy "unforgivable trickery . . . quite comparable to the taking of Texas from Mexico, the rape of Cuba, the Philippines, Puerto Rico and Hawaii." As the war progressed, Robeson's tone grew even more forceful. He condemned "today's would-be Hitlers" in the United States (under the banner of Confederate flags!), who still despised the "475 million Chinese people" as "hordes" of "coolies" and "gooks." This, he explained, was why they refused to make an "honorable" peace, and chose to threaten them with the atomic bomb instead. He credited "American peace sentiment" with stopping President Truman from using this ultimate weapon of mass destruction and forcing the recall of Douglas MacArthur.[39]

The Shanghai Municipal Department of Education organized a seminar in November 1950 for thirteen students who had "overcome various obstacles to return from the United States to the motherland." The students cited Robeson's example frequently, noting his tours across the United States singing and promoting peace despite government surveillance, efforts they said illustrated the rise of a global peace movement against U.S. involvement in the war.[40] The People's Daily cited a national poll in the United States showing majority support for ending the Korean War immediately and credited Robeson and Du Bois with influencing this trend in public opinion. Robeson's speech at the Civil Rights Congress and his joint statement with Du Bois on behalf of the Council of African Affairs in 1950 demanded U.S. withdrawal from Korea. Supporting the Korean cease-fire proposal by Jacob Malik, the Soviet representative to the United Nations, Robeson led the American Peace Crusade to deliver a petition at UN headquarters in August 1951. He joined other noted figures in calling for a peace conference in Washington, D.C., and presenting a letter to the newly elected president Eisenhower demanding an immediate truce. In 1952, Robeson reiterated the demand at the meeting of the National Council of American-Soviet Friendship in New York City, which marked the thirty-fifth anniversary of the Bolshevik Revolution and the nineteenth anniversary of U.S.-Soviet relations. He announced again unambiguously in his 1953 open letter to Jackie Robinson, the baseball star whom Robeson had helped integrate the game several years before, "I was and am for an immediate cease-fire in Korea and for peace."[41]

The *People's Daily* noted that while the truce was negotiated, in his *Pravda* letter mourning Stalin's death, Robeson echoed Du Bois, reiterating that the PRC served as the model for millions to beat colonialism. He affectionately proclaimed, "You, young Soviet citizens, whom I so deeply admire; you brave youth of new China; young Korean patriots and fighters for independence throughout Asia, the future of the world is well placed in your hands." The paper also reported that, between 1953 and 1955, at gatherings at the Peace Arch (located at the Western extremity of the Canadian-U.S. border) and on Union Square in New York City for International Labor Day, Robeson repeatedly congratulated China for its victorious struggle for peace on behalf of Asia and affirmed, "I stretch my hand" to the new regime. As late as 1958, publications in China commemorating Robeson's sixtieth birthday still highlighted that he had loudly and passionately declared, "No invasion of Korea!"[42]

Robeson was not speaking only to the Chinese throughout the Korean War. He strove to articulate the conflict's immediate relevance to Blacks around the world. Three days after the war broke out, he delivered a speech at a major rally sponsored by the Civil Rights Congress at the Madison Square Garden in New York City. The CAA released its transcript under the title "Robeson Denounces Korean Intervention." A strong, modern new China liberated from the "same financial robbers who have waxed fat on our father's cotton-field labor" was destined to fight for "our full emancipation," Robeson reasoned. He warned that unless the United States was stopped in

Asia, "Africa would be next in line" and African American youth would be drafted to "put down these brave African peoples!" At the 1953 Convention of the National Negro Labor Council in Chicago, he demanded to know how sacrificing the lives of Black youth to shoot down Chinese would "help us get our freedom." He continued to fuse race and class perspectives: "What business a Black lad from a Mississippi or Georgia share-cropping farm has in Asia shooting down the yellow or brown son of an impoverished rice-farmer?" Robeson highlighted the plight of African American soldiers in the war, pointing out that in neither the Chinese nor the North Korean army were minority soldiers with darker skin or speaking different languages mass court-martialed, set apart to do the menial labor, or sacrificed while lighter-skinned units retreated. He recounted how a young Black soldier, with "eyes blazed in remembering the bomb-blackened villages" in Korea, came to his table in a Harlem restaurant, urging him to speak on behalf of most Americans and demand peace.[43]

Robeson urged African Americans to appreciate China's involvement in the war as self-defense against MacArthur and Truman's attempt to bring "Jim Crow" to East Asia. Explaining "the old China" through the prism of African American racial experiences, he made the otherwise remote country familiar and relevant. With widespread hunger and poverty, China was a "Jim Crow country [as indicated by its segregated treaty ports], just like our country," Robeson explained. He credited Sun Yat-sen and, particularly, Mao Zedong for ending "Jim Crow" and the "big plantation system that was starving the Chinese to death." Thus, symbolically, "Never again in China will any Englishman or American kick around a Chinese rickshaw driver, or put up a sign on a building to keep Chinese out." Robeson invited African Americans to imagine the scenario: "Slaveholders' army should suddenly attack Cuba or Mexico" in order to restore "hunger and Jim Crow" on the big plantations that had been taken over by former slaves. Obviously, "our folks" would "help the Cubans and Mexicans stop the slaveholders there," a straightforward analogy to the Korean War.[44]

Throughout the PRC's ordeals, Robeson joined Du Bois's efforts to win its international acceptance as the "authentic" China. The Committee for a Democratic Far Eastern Policy, in which both Du Bois and Robeson were active, launched a public campaign in 1949 to recognize the new regime. Countering the rhetoric of the House Un-American Activities Committee, Robeson declared as early as February, "I am a friend of the new China, not of a revived fascist Japan. I, too, am American." Under Robeson's leadership, the above-discussed public statement of the Council of African Affairs and the American Peace Crusade petition to the United Nations demanded that the PRC be granted "its rightful seat in the United Nations." Robeson insisted that this must be part of the arrangements to end the Korean War and the foundation of U.S. diplomacy, denouncing opposition to it as a "white supremacist trick." He reiterated his position in his recording played at the Second Soviet Congress of Writers in 1954, which the *People's Daily* lauded. The daily quoted one of his *Pravda* articles, "American people know that the Chiang Kai-shek gang on Taiwan Island is just a bunch of hooligans and bandits, who absolutely cannot represent the Chinese people."[45]

CHINA SPEAKS OUT ABOUT THE PEEKSKILL RIOTS, ROBESON'S PASSPORT, AND OTHER ISSUES

Paul Robeson's devotion to and affection for the PRC were reciprocated. By the time of the CCP triumph in 1949, he had become enshrined as a fearless and reliable friend of China, which staunchly defended him during his own trials. Chinese media celebrated Robeson as a heroic "peace soldier" and lauded his joint efforts with Du Bois and representatives of China in the world peace movement. On April 20, Robeson famously told the International Congress for Peace in Paris that it was "unthinkable that American Negroes would go to war on behalf of those who have oppressed us for generations against the Soviet Union." That statement quickly brought him massive condemnation, including from Walter White, head of the NAACP, and Jackie Robinson.[46] W. E. B. Du Bois stood firmly on Robeson's side, as he recalled in his *Autobiography* (fig. 2.4):

> Robeson said that his people wanted Peace and "would never fight
> the Soviet Union." I joined with the thousands in wild acclaim. This,
> for America, was his crime. He might hate anybody. He might join
> in murder around the world. But for him to declare that he loved
> the Soviet Union and would not join in war against it — that was
> the highest crime that the United States recognized. . . . Yet has Paul
> Robeson kept his soul and stood his ground. Still he loves and honors
> the Soviet Union. Still he has hope for America. Still he asserts his
> faith in God.[47]

Joining Du Bois in Robeson's defense was the CCP. At the very moment when Robeson delivered that speech, Mao Zedong and Zhu De ordered the People's Liberation Army to cross the Yangtze River, launching the final blow against the Nationalist government. With CCP control imminent, the main-

FIGURE 2.4. W. E. B. Du Bois and Paul Robeson at the
International Congress for Peace in Paris, April 20, 1949.
*Courtesy of W. E. B. Du Bois Papers, mums312-i0485, Special Collections
and University Archives, University of Massachusetts Amherst Libraries.*

stream media in Shanghai was shifting. Echoing the *People's Daily*, the *Shanghai Daily*, arguably the most widely circulated newspaper in the Republic of China, reported Robeson's speech, noting the standing ovation it received from the 2,000 attendees, and his election, along with Du Bois, to the leadership of the International Congress for Peace. The paper's coverage mirrored Du Bois's vivid observations:

> The Salle Pleyel was packed to the high, many-balconied ceiling
> with delegates from sixty countries representing the whole world.
> Paul Robeson entered and the whole audience, around twenty five
> hundred, rose and cheered in all human tongues. I doubt if any other
> person on earth could have elicited such [a] spontaneous tribute.
> It was a many-sided outburst to a magnificent voice; . . . to a son of
> Black slaves, a coworker not with wealthy and titled snobs but with
> laborers of all climes and colors. We had men of stature and renown
> at that gathering: Joliot-Curie and Aragon, Nenni and Picasso,

Bernal, Zilliacus and Fadeev; none of these received so tumultuous a tribute. The program was interrupted and Robeson ascended the podium. His great voice rose in song—song of Black slaves, song of white slaves, songs of Russia and France. Then among the few words of a short speech, Robeson said: "The Black folk of America will never fight against the Soviet Union!" The applause swept up to the skies.[48]

The *People's Daily* quickly condemned Robinson in Robeson's defense and applauded Robeson's "anti-imperialism, antiwarmonger, and antiracist" speeches and songs at the International Congress for Peace and his concerts across Europe. The daily reported that the Chinese colleagues of Robeson and Du Bois on the standing committee of the World Peace Council in Paris were Guo Moruo, economist Ma Yinchu, writer Emi Sao (Xiao San), and vice chair of the National Workers Union Liu Ningyi. On his way home from the congress, Guo Moruo stopped in Prague to receive an honorary doctoral degree at Charles University, an honor similarly granted to Du Bois a decade later.[49]

The China Peace Council, with Guo Moruo, Tian Han, the noted writer and vice minister of culture Xia Yan, Emi Sao, Liu Ningyi, and Robeson's old friends Madam Sun, Mei Lanfang, and Liu Liangmo on its executive committee, formed in Beijing the second day after the establishment of the PRC. The Chinese translation of Shirley Graham Du Bois's biography of Robeson included a photograph of him before his passport revocation at the 1950 London Peace Congress with Liu Ningyi, now vice chair of the China Peace Council, Alexander Korneichuck of the Soviet Union, Gabriel d'Arboussier of Africa, and J. D. Bernal of Great Britain. Liu delivered a speech at the congress in which he said imperialists were digging their own graves and noted he was the first Chinese person visiting London with a PRC passport. The *People's Daily* reported that Robeson's new Chinese colleagues on the World Peace Council included Guo and Ulaan Hüü (of Mongolian ethnicity), Madam Sun, and Wu Yaozong (Wu Yao Tsung) of the National Y. The *Daily* reported that along with James G. Endicott of Canada and representatives of Chile and North Korea, Robeson was named a vice chair (Guo was already serving) of the Asia and Pacific Rim Peace Council led by Madam Sun during its 1952 conference in Beijing. Learning from a visiting Soviet journalist how deeply he was missed at the conference, as reported in the Chinese press, Robeson stated romantically, "If my heart could be transformed into a bird, I will let it soar freely to China afar, conveying all my words to the great Chinese people. Their liberation has proved that truth could overcome falsehood!" Noting that the conference called for "peace . . . to be won by the peace-loving peoples in unity," Robeson concluded, "Let us take their out-stretched hand. Let us win that peace."[50]

The official Chinese media mentioned a play performed in Moscow's Pushkin Theater lauding Robeson as the "Peace Soldier" and hailed his selection as recipient of the 1950 International Peace Prize for his series *Songs of Peace*, which included "Chee Lai!," and of the 1952 Stalin Peace Prize. In his "Thoughts on Winning the Stalin Peace Prize," Robeson noted that, among his numerous recognitions in the fields of sports, the arts, and the struggle for peace and the rights of Blacks and laborers, this award was special and truly international with its judges from diverse backgrounds, including Guo Moruo. He urged the peace movement in the United States to connect with the Beijing and Vienna Peace Congresses. The *People's Daily* described the details of the award ceremony at New York's Theresa Hotel, translated the speech of noted Soviet writer Ilya Ehrenburg praising Robeson's bravery and determination against war, and covered Robeson's press conference on the event. It commented that Robeson's name had been turned into a banner to inspire millions of oppressed Blacks and anti-imperialist righteous Americans against war hysteria and police terror.[51]

The Peekskill Riots of August 1949 were the most significant and ugliest sign that the United States had turned against Robeson because of his politics. As the news of the riots rolled around the world, the PRC state media reported angrily and in detail the abuse Robeson suffered. Organized by the American Civil Rights Association, thousands gathered peacefully in the town of Peekskill, forty-one miles north of New York City, for Robeson's concert on August 27. As the *People's Daily* and *Xinhua Telegram* reported, concert-goers were met by thousands of "fascists and hooligans organized by counterrevolutionary veterans groups," who launched a massive surprise attack, beating the audience with stones, sticks, and other weapons, over-turning numerous vehicles, and setting the theater on fire. The mob burned a cross, in KKK style. The state media informed Chinese readers that, a few hours before the concert, the New York City branch of the American Labor Party, concerned by the public threats from the veterans groups, had telephoned New York State authorities requesting police protection. However, the state police only arrived several hours after the mob concluded its three-hour riots, in which at least thirteen people were injured, two critically. The police made no arrests. Robeson barely escaped lynching. China's state media quoted Robeson as saying that the attacks were part of a coordinated "national terror" campaign against Blacks and progressive leaders by the few who owned 60 percent of American wealth, controlled the government, and backed the veterans groups.[52]

Robeson, supported by Benjamin Davis Jr., conducted a second concert before several thousand spectators and guarded by a volunteer security force on September 4. Once again, thugs attacked Robeson's fans as they departed after the concert, actions that the Chinese press denounced as fascist. Citing United Press, the *Xinhua Telegram* reported that "data from hospitals indicated that 138 people were injured, many mobs were in military uniforms, and the very few arrested criminals, including the son of a local police chief, were released immediately on bonds ranging from $35 to $500." The magazine *New Music* printed a "special column for the Robeson Incident" to report the riots in detail. Articles described the outpouring of protest against "crimes" at the riots and petitions sent to President Truman and New York governor Thomas Dewey. Chinese journalists for the state media expressed the nation's profound affection for Robeson and novelist Howard Fast, who had introduced the singer at the concert. Robeson's humble background and his undying support for China were emphasized to indicate his correct proletarian politics. A writer named Jingye described crowding around a radio with twenty or so friends to listen to Robeson sang "Chee Lai!," feeling "unspeakable happiness that filled my soul" and "love from the bottom of my heart for this brave soldier battling for world peace and democracy." The attacks on Robeson at Peekskill instantly turned Jingye's happiness to "hatred" toward the U.S. counterrevolutionaries.[53]

China's state media followed closely how Robeson answered the "fascist challenge" and his defiant response to the Peekskill Riots. The *Xinhua Telegram* reported that thousands of progressive figures, with African American veterans in the majority, warmly welcomed Robeson at a mass gathering divided into two sessions due to the difficulty of renting space in Chicago. Robeson was quoted calling for Black youth to "stand up for our people's rights, and to march forward, chest out, for equality and dignity." The *People's Daily* reported that, with Henry Wallace and New York Labor Party congressman Vito Marcantonio, Robeson helped to organize the American Union Peace Congress in Chicago. The *New China Monthly* reported that Robeson summarized his working conditions following the Peekskill Riots: "86 out of 89 of my concerts were cancelled, because I supported Henry A. Wallace's presidential campaign and insisted on interpreting songs in my own spirit. Many businessmen refused to sell my albums fearing the destructive power of my songs." The periodical approved Robeson's decision to perform for the alternative wide audience of laboring people who otherwise could not afford the high price set by concert hall bosses, charging admission equivalent to the value of bus tickets or giving them for free. It described the singer's brief but lively introductions to each song at his Moscow concert, so that the audience could understand its progressive nature. Commenting that "Joe Hill" narrated the tale of a heroic martyr in the U.S. workers' movement, Robeson invited the audience to repeat after him: "Joe is dead, but he is still alive, in the hearts of workers, at American workers' picket lines, and among the ranks of the Communist leaders in New York." The article reported that Robeson's interpretation of "Joe Hill" for the laboring Americans led to his censorship by U.S. and Canadian authorities.[54]

The China Federation of Literary and Artistic Circles (CFLAC) and the China National Association of Musicians issued a joint public letter to console Robeson, "a sincere friend of the Soviet and Chinese peoples," and express "our extraordinary wrath and firm protest against the crimes of American fascist bandits attacking the concerts of 'the Black King of Songs.'" The letter read, "Robeson's 'singing is a weapon of social meaning' [quote of Robeson]. The masses in China who deeply love and respect Robeson are especially moved by his internationalist spirit, as demonstrated by his ability to sing revolutionary songs in Russian, Chinese, and Spanish. . . . We send our brotherly consolations to Robeson from the East afar, and warmly welcome him to liberated China."[55]

Corresponding to Robeson's public celebration of the grand opening of the PRC, the *People's Daily* honored him with the diplomat Yao Niangeng's statement that people in Moscow had heard the "genius" singer and progressive political activist at concerts and on the radio in June 1949, celebrating the triumph and free speech Robeson enjoyed in the "democratic" world. The newspaper followed with details of the Chinese workers' delegates to the Soviet Union encountering Robeson back then. In the dining hall of the International Hotel facing the Kremlin, the Chinese delegates noticed that a serious Black man with an "endearing and honest dark face and thick lips" returned their gazes warmly. Introduced by Liu Ningyi, Robeson joined them quickly and, to thunderous applause, announced his "great pleasure to meet representatives of the victorious working class of the new China." They toasted to "Chairman Mao's health" and sang "March of the Volunteers." The Chinese delegates attended his concert at Gorky Park, part of an enthusiastic audience of 30,000. The *Daily* commented, "Robeson could sing freely in the Soviet Union, but he suffered mob attacks in his own country. We had exclaimed, 'Robeson, come to sing in the free new China!'"[56]

Yet soon after the new China was forced to confront the challenge of the

Korean War, Robeson suffered another personal blow. One month after he first spoke out against U.S. involvement in the war on June 28, 1950, the State Department demanded that Robeson hand in his passport, which he refused to do. In August, in response to FBI demands, the State Department voided Paul Robeson's passport and informed customs agents that they were "to endeavor to prevent his departure from the United States" should he attempt to leave. Eslanda could visit China, but her husband could not.[57]

Robeson kept accepting international invitations, even though there was little hope that he could attend, in order to keep his passport issue alive. For example, he noted that as he wrote "Happy Birthday, New China!," the Asia and Pacific Rim Peace Conference was underway. He trusted that the peoples of the region could help to "tear down the barriers to world trade and to free cultural exchange and friendship of all peoples." Such barriers had prevented him from visiting China, despite repeated invitations from Guo Moruo. He emphasized that the denial of his passport was "especially bitter in this case," because of his deep concern for the world peace movement and his long-felt "close kinship with the Chinese people."[58]

During the 1950s, the CCP repeatedly expressed outrage over the U.S. government's treatment of Robeson, made much of this denial, a violation of the Universal Declaration of Human Rights, which guaranteed freedom of travel and communication, and tied the passport issue to many other political causes in Robeson's life. Yuan Shuipai, editor of the literary section of the *People's Daily*, reported that a "Dirty Rat" represented the United States as a speaker at the Second World Peace Congress in Warsaw on November 19, 1950, while Robeson was unable to attend. Nonetheless, his recorded speech and singing of "Chee Lai!" received thunderous applause. The newspaper condemned the U.S. State Department's refusal of Robeson and his son's passports to attend the meeting as the "arrogant behavior of a police state." Other articles attributed the cancellation of Robeson's passport to his demand that the United States publicize the secrets of the atomic bomb, or his campaign for a national vote to end the Korean War. One instance argued that if Harriet Beecher Stowe were alive, the U.S. government would ban the publication of *Uncle Tom's Cabin* and deny her a passport.[59] In 1955, in a public letter to the *Nation*, Madam Sun denounced the cancellation of Robeson's passport and disputed that association with her would qualify the singer as a traitor. She argued that, like Nehru and President Roosevelt's mother, Anna, Robeson had worked with the China Defense League solely to provide medical and other services to China while it was under Japanese attack and later in a civil war "stoked by foreign forces."[60]

The *People's Daily* relayed Robeson's "wrathful denunciation of the U.S. government's political and economic persecutions" with a correspondent of *Black Forum* in 1957. It quoted Robeson as saying, "I have been confined seven years without a trial. . . . I am not allowed to perform as an artist, by which I am deprived of the rights of a full human being." The Chinese public learned that "people cannot hear Robeson anymore. Hosts of major concerts pretend that he does not exist, officials lock up city halls upon hints of his planned presence at public gatherings, Hollywood is too scared to touch him, and those who had followed him closely for autographs step aside to give way to the FBI investigators." The *People's Daily* detailed the financial persecution that Robeson suffered as a result of his forced cultural and political exile, as calculated by the singer himself: "From 1950 on, his income from concert tours dropped to around $2,000 from $14,000 in 1947. He would have starved without the $30,000 earned from his 1949 tour in Britain, donations from several Black churches, and sale of his Connecticut house. He was not even allowed to enjoy the Stalin Peace Prize of $25,000, since the government insisted on taxing it as 'earnings for service' to the Soviet Union, unlike the Nobel Peace Prize."[61] The paper reported that Robeson's appeal for a passport was denied again by a federal court on August 16, 1955, because he firmly rejected the State Department's "unreasonable requests of no speech abroad and denial of Communist membership under oath." Quoting the *Daily Mirror*, the *People's Daily* contended that the State Department denied Robeson's application again to sabotage his scheduled singing appearance on a British TV station on April 6, 1958. It reminded the Chinese readers that the reactionaries had prevented Robeson from going abroad or performing domestically since 1950.[62]

China's state media emphasized optimistically that Robeson would stick to his principles, growing stronger with clearer political views and more refined artistic cultivation, despite the menace of poverty and other hardship. In early 1958, the *People's Daily* featured an article by the Soviet writer Vadim Kozevnikov detailing his visit to Robeson's "small and plain" apartment in Harlem. The visitor reported that, although his temples were turning silver in his forced eight-year confinement, Robeson spoke with determination and pride: "I never feel lonely, because one who devotes his whole life to unite tens of millions to defend peace would not feel so." Gazing at his telephone set and fondling the receiver with affection, Robeson continued with excitement, "I am called frequently. When anonymous people from various countries call me, my heart is warmed!" Hearing his son confiding to the visitor that threats from New York reinforcing "American spirit" came through the same phone, Robeson interrupted, "No! Those are just noise from tire-some mosquitos and worms, not the voice of the American people." He con-cluded passionately, "I deeply believe in the power of reason, justice, truth and peace to overcome the dark force." In their letters saluting Robeson's sixtieth birthday, Qian Junrui, Robeson's personal friend and China's vice minister of culture, affirmed, "It is not you but a small bunch of worms and mice — leading invaders and war smugglers that are isolated in this world." Xia Yan exclaimed, "Oppression, persecution, and endless smearing could not shake in the least the courage of Robeson, who proudly stands high like pine and chrysanthemum in snow," a metaphor used for Du Bois as well.[63]

Chinese officials and media echoed Robeson's defiance, celebrating how his voice broke through the U.S. government's blockade to reach the world using advanced communication technology. In a 1957 interview with the (London) *Daily Worker*, Robeson recounted how the previous year he had bypassed the imprisonment by singing over transatlantic cable to a concert at London's St. Pancreas Hall. His voice was broadcast and amplified under the personal supervision of the head of the British communications system. "It was as though I were on the stage in London myself, and the whole affair was such a success that the *Manchester Guardian* said, 'Never has the U.S. State Department looked sillier.'" Quoting Kozevnikov, the *People's Daily* reported that, with a lasting smile and shining eyes, Robeson revealed that British peace supporters had recorded the concert. "Even I myself am jeal-ous of my own voice, because I wish to travel along with my songs to meet the listeners."[64]

The paper reported that Robeson's recorded speeches and songs were continuously heard at the Second, Third, and Fifth International Youth Con-ferences in Budapest (1949), Bucharest (1953), and Warsaw (1955), respec-tively, and the executive committee meeting of the World Peace Council in 1954. In Warsaw, youth from China, the Soviet Union, Britain, France, and the United States listened to his poetic speech and resonant songs, includ-ing Beethoven's "Ode to Joy." Along with Du Bois and Anna Louis Strong, Robeson spoke at the mass gathering in New York celebrating the fortieth anniversary of the 1917 Bolshevik Revolution, urging friendly relations be-tween the two super powers. Xia Yan noted that the speech was broadcast to the Soviet People on television. Since tractors cultivating virgin farmland be-came symbols of socialist superiority to the delinquent capitalist consumer culture represented by race cars, Robeson's virtual interactions with young Soviet tractor drivers reclaiming farmland in the wilderness of Kazakhstan were repeatedly celebrated. According to the *People's Daily*, a state farm in the Soviet Union granted Robeson honorary membership and named its broadest road after him. Residents along that road called Robeson for New Year 1957, telling him that they had brought his records to the prairie to hear his songs as soon as the first tent was up. After reporting the fruits of their labor, the callers asked Robeson to convey Soviet youth's friendship to their American counterparts. Eslanda joined the conversation; the appreciative Robeson sang over the phone a few passionate songs that were broadcast on radio. In their birthday letters, mentioned above, Xia and Qian noted romantically that "only those low and stupid could believe they could suffocate" Robeson's grand voice, "with its wings." They celebrated that the world could still hear his "songs like spring thunder, the battle hymns of our time," defying the oppression of "McCarthyism, the KKK, and those like Dulles."[65]

The *People's Daily* remained optimistic about Robeson's ultimate victory in the passport battle. It reported that the Communist Party USA called on progressive Americans to struggle for civil rights, including the right to travel, citing Robeson's case. Charlie Chaplin telegrammed from Switzerland condemning the U.S. government for treating Rockwell Kent and Robeson, artists of world reputation, as "paroled criminals" with its "evil and dangerous" passport policy. Noted literary and artistic figures formed the National "Let Paul Robeson Sing" Committee in Great Britain, demanding that the U.S. State Department issue Robeson a passport. The *Daily* published a passionate poem, "Epitaph of McCarthy," ridiculing the "sealing of Robeson's mouth" as among McCarthy's "deeds."[66]

A HEROIC MODEL FOR THE CHINESE PEOPLE IN THE 1950S

The relationship between Robeson and the PRC transformed beyond mutual support through such testy issues and moments. Similar to what we saw with W. E. B. Du Bois, while friends in his China circle ran afoul of China's new regime, Robeson's reputation reached its peak in the 1950s. Pearl S. Buck, Lin Yutang, and Anna May Wong, notables who had rubbed shoulders with the political and cultural elites in the Republic of China, fell out of favor. In her biography of Robeson, Shirley Graham Du Bois noted that Wong brought "greetings and appreciation from China" to Robeson's forty-sixth birthday celebration hosted by the CAA at the Seventeenth Regiment Armory in New York City. By the time Graham Du Bois's book was translated into Chinese in 1950, Wong had become such a nonentity that her name was rendered as an unrecognizable Wang Mei Anna (王梅安娜). Buck and Lin did not

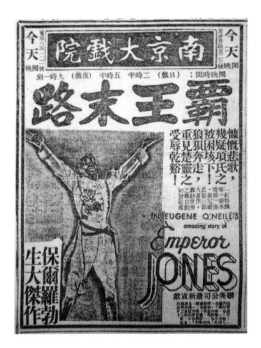

FIGURE 2.5. An advertisement for the film *Emperor Jones* that invokes the memory of the tragic Chinese historical hero Xiang Yu. *Shenbao*, March 25, 1934.

share the Robesons' enthusiasm for the PRC. In *American Argument*, Buck and Eslanda presented opposing views on the new China. Lin resettled in Taiwan and was attacked as "reactionary" throughout the Maoist years. In contrast, Robeson, propelled by Liu Liangmo, became for the Chinese the embodiment of African American revolutionary culture, particularly in his presentation of "racial music and songs, which are a source of national pride for many Americans."[67]

The mainstream media in the Republic of China rarely covered Black celebrities, as W. E. B. Du Bois's experience would confirm, but it made an exception for Robeson, due to his global fame. *Emperor Jones* opened in Shanghai at the Nanjing Theater on March 25, 1934, and continued at the Paris Theater until the following November. Invoking the tragic Chinese historical hero Xiang Yu, who inspired the famous Beijing opera program and later the motion picture *Farewell, My Concubine*, *Emperor Jones* was translated as *End of the King* (*Bawang moluo*). The *Shanghai Daily* prominently published an advertisement promoting the film as a "Lifetime Masterpiece by Paul Robeson," with a couplet summarizing Xiang Yu's defeat (fig. 2.5). The highly popular women's magazine *Linglong* and the *China Press* lauded Robeson's performance as "to perfection" and the film as one of the top ten released in 1933. *Maodun Monthly* featured a grand still of the "famous Black

FIGURE 2.6. Still of Paul Robeson in *Emperor Jones*. *Maodun yuekan* 3, no. 2 (1934).

actor" starring in the film, its caption noting that China's leading dramatist, Hong Shen, and film director, Gu Zhongyi, had translated Eugene O'Neill's script (fig. 2.6). The *Shanghai Times* reported that Robeson won the English Amateur Film Award Best Performance of 1935 and that its producer, London Film Productions, won the annual gold medal from the Institute of Amateur Cinematographers. However, Robeson's singing and acting ultimately put him in the denigrated category of musicians and entertainers in which the "primitive" stereotype was reinforced and celebrated. For example, *Dagong bao* (Shanghai) enthusiastically reported the impressive box office achievements of *Sanders of the River* (translated as "War in Africa") at the Nanjing Theater in 1935 and Guanglu Theater in 1936, thanks to the "startling performance of its protagonist, Paul." But it described the film as about "internal atrocities among Blacks" and commented that "although Nina [McKinney] was made up to appear Black, her beauty could not be disguised." The *Shanghai Daily* advertisement for the movie at the Mingxing Theater adopted a similar racist tone. *Show Boat* and *King Solomon's Mines*, a British adventure film starring Robeson, opened at Metropol and Cathay Theaters on September 10, 1936, and April 7, 1938, respectively, which the Chinese-language press did not mention.[68]

Meanwhile, the sympathetic Shanghai English-language newspapers reported the "cruel" racial discrimination Robeson suffered in life and career, his aspirations for racial equality, and his alliance with the Soviet Union. The *Shanghai Times* observed that some London journalists created the "unfortunate and ridiculous uproar" when Robeson was announced to appear in *Othello*, opposite a white actress. The daily was indignant that "the 'yellow' press jumped on the announcement for a front-page racket and worked it to death." It praised the resilient Robeson for adhering to the task and earning the "unanimous applause of Britain's greatest dramatic critiques." Those newspapers highlighted Robeson's extraordinary artistic, intellectual, and athletic capabilities, but their readership was limited.[69]

Robeson's enthusiasm for Chinese civilization, his friendship with leftist Chinese cultural and political celebrities, and his activism on behalf of China's resistance failed to earn him respectability and recognition from conservative Chinese. From 1940 to 1945, *China at War*, a semi-official English monthly published by the China Information Publishing Company from Chongqing and Hong Kong and distributed globally, ran Lin Yutang's article "Music Bolsters Morale," an advertisement for the songbook *China's Patriots Sing*, and news items to introduce China's mass singing movement and songs of resistance. Its omission of "March of the Volunteers" and the album *Chee Lai!*, which was endorsed by Madam Sun Yat-sen and Lin, was conspicuous.[70]

The leftist origins of "March of the Volunteers" were partially to blame. Tian Han and Nie Er, then both underground communists, initially produced the piece as the theme song of the resistance film *Heroic Sons and Daughters* (*Fengyun ernü*, 1935) by the leftist Denton Studio, of which Wang Yung was then an employee. Its music combined elements of the "Internationale" and "La Marseillaise" with Chinese folk music. After the *Denton Pictorial* published the song in May, it was recorded and became an instant hit ahead of the movie's July release. However, the studio was soon shut down by the Nationalist government. Both Agnes Smedley and Israel Epstein recalled that the song was officially banned in China before the full-scale war broke out. According to Epstein, on the sixth anniversary of the Mukden Incident, the radio station in China's capital broadcast the song for the first time.[71] Meanwhile, Robeson's racial image as a Black entertainer was probably a concern.

In contrast, encouraged to accept Robeson as a model to inspire, the masses in the PRC found themselves bombarded with Robeson biographies, information about his singing and acting, and celebrations of his birthdays. In addition to the intensive coverage of Robeson in state media, PRC pub-

FIGURE 2.7. A sample page from the biographical children's cartoon series, titled "Today's Hero: Black Singer Robeson." The caption on the top left reads: "He gets along very well with Chinese friends in the United States." Paul Robeson says, "I salute the democratic revolution in China." *Xin ertong banyue kan* 23, no. 2 (1949): 44.

lishers kept up a steady pace of materials on and by Robeson from the moment of the regime shift in 1949 through the 1950s. He had been first introduced as "the Black King of Songs," an all-around talent, and a collaborator of Liu Liangmo in some Shanghai journals in 1946, after a reporter listened to him singing "Chee Lai!" for a CAA meeting at Max Yergan's home. In 1949 "the Black King of Songs" was quickly promoted as a "hero" for the oppressed masses, through Liu Liangmo's widely circulated article "People's Singer Robeson" and subsequent biographical essays and cartoon series in children's magazines (fig. 2.7).[72]

The CCP's embrace of Robeson as a "brave singer and peace soldier" expanded with a translation of his biography by Shirley Graham Du Bois, another favored African American. Prefatory material included a copy of his congratulatory telegram to Mao and poetry extolling the singer for "paving roads" and "building bridges" for the masses. There were stills from Robeson's 1944 New York production of *Othello*, realistic drawings of him singing at Peekskill, cartoons of "American counterrevolutionaries" silencing him by Soviet artist L. Brodaty, photographs with Russian children in New York City celebrating the Stalingrad festival, and other images indicating his international credentials and support for China. The translator noted that the book was released at the ideal moment, given the recent outbreak of the Korean War. It was thus deeply meaningful to introduce Robeson as a brave and determined peace solider who denounced the United States for its involvement in the war. This praise of his principled stance stood in contrast to descriptions of the "betrayal" by the Progressive Party's Henry Wallace, whose neutral position entailed declaring both the Soviet Union and the United States to be threats to world peace. Convinced that Robeson's activities as a leader of the world peace movement after the initial release of Graham Du Bois's book would be critically important to Chinese readers, the editor compiled 131 pages of appendices of Chinese and Soviet newspaper articles by and about Robeson. Above all, the translator lauded Robeson as an internationalist who "embodied the perfect marriage between art and politics."[73]

The following year, editor Zhu Mo abbreviated Graham Du Bois's book as part of a biography series for fifth- to eighth-graders and workers and farmers with equivalent education (fig. 2.8). Lu Xun, Ivan Vladimirovich Michurin, Ivan Petrovich Pavlov, Marie Curie, Ho Chi Minh, Kim Il-Sung, as well as domestic military heroes and model workers had been similarly honored. The series intended to use these role models to instill new socialist values such as internationalism, bravery, discipline, and patriotism. The CCP clearly promoted Robeson as a solid cultural and political example for China's youth.[74]

In 1956 a forty-three-page compilation of Robeson's "Black spirituals" appeared in Chinese. Released by the China National Central Symphony, the booklet has extensive musical annotation and a preface by Robeson borrowed from a 1949 publication.[75] Jazz was now despised for its associations with the Black and Filipino musicians active in the nightclub scenes of the colonial Republic of China; and religion was rejected as spiritual opiate. In his piece published in the *People's Daily* to commemorate Robeson's sixtieth birthday, musician Zhao Feng credited Robeson for rescuing "Black spiritu-

新少年傳記叢書

羅伯遜傳

朱　沫編著

上海童聯書店發行

太平洋出版社

FIGURE 2.8. The cover of an abbreviated biography of
Paul Robeson, part of a series intended to instill new socialist
morality into adolescents through role models.
Author's collection.

als" from religious hymns and "loud and messy jazz." Zhao explained that, influenced by "Black spirituals," jazz had initially shared characteristics of ancient African music—flexibility, simplicity, and spontaneity. However, "thoroughly commercialized in capitalist United States, jazz has deteriorated into pornographic, abnormal, and crazy stuff" that no longer has anything to do with "Black spirituals." Robeson's talents aside, the party's position on jazz was antiquated and isolated, especially when Black jazz musicians Louis Armstrong and Dizzy Gillespie were touring the world for the U.S. government and exciting audiences in Europe, Africa, India, and Southeast Asia.[76] An article titled "To Learn from Robeson" in the magazine *People's Music* re-narrated Liu Liangmo's detailed description of Robeson's dynamic interactions with his audiences at outdoor concerts. It called on Chinese singers to follow the master's humble connection to the masses, broadening their appeal and stepping out of their elegant concert halls. Soon Robeson was bizarrely promoted as a model to serve the masses with basic skills rather than selfishly pursing lofty professional achievement, a trend that peaked during the Cultural Revolution as experts were attacked as useless "stinking old ninth," invoking the low social status of Confucius scholars during Mongol's Yuan dynasty.[77]

Print media was not the only means for spreading Robeson's name in China. After the PRC established a diplomatic relationship with the Great Britain in 1954 and gradually resumed cultural exchanges, British movies were made available to Chinese audiences. *Proud Valley* (1939) was mentioned in China by the *North-China Daily News* under the title *David Goliath*, the name of Robeson's character, a foreign miner in Wales Valley. The film was translated into Chinese around 1956. The Chinese press generally had harsh criticism for Hollywood and European films. However, with his highly popular singing and performance, the muscular and bare-chested image of Robeson in the movie provided a model of masculinity for socialist citizens. "The naked manhood of Paul Robeson," of which "some white folk are frightened," as Du Bois previously noted, had profoundly inspired China. As early as 1933, Nie Er had impersonated an African miner in the film *The Glory of Motherhood*. Nie proudly distributed to friends autographed stills of himself, half-naked and painted dark, imitating Robeson.[78] Featuring Robeson's still from the movie, the *People's Daily* remarked that Chinese audiences celebrated Robeson's sixty-first birthday by watching *Proud Valley*. The audiences, overwhelmed by the tragic fates of the miners of South Wales, reportedly left the theater silently in the twilight as if in a funeral parade. While China kicked off the disastrous Great Leap Forward, the film critic quoted data from the *New York Times* to demonstrate the advantage of socialism over the "man-eating" capitalist world plagued by unemployment, poverty, and disease.[79]

Robeson's athletic body was also employed to highlight the distinction between "abnormal" and corrupt commercialized professional sports in both capitalist countries and the colonial treaty ports of "the old China," on the one hand, and socialist sports for the well-being of the citizenry and the nation, on the other. Zhu Mo justified Robeson's brief career as a professional athlete with the image of a good family man "pressured by heavier obligations after his marriage." He applauded Robeson for comprehending that the capitalist owners ran their stadiums and teams like stores, exploiting athletes and putting their lives at risk for profits. Zhu noted that while some shrewd businessmen attempted to lure Robeson into highly racialized and controversial professional boxing by promising him the title "King of Boxing" and great wealth, Robeson flatly refused. That was a sharp turn from the recent treatment of Joe Louis, the actual "World Champion of Boxing," by the media in the Republic of China. Extending admiration of Jessie Owen's athletic prowess, the *Shanghai Daily* serialized Louis's biography and featured the news of his retirement up to early 1949, calling attention to his earning power as the fabled "Brown Bomber," who made nearly $4 million during his twelve-year career.[80]

Anniversaries were another means of promoting Robeson as a friend of the revolution and lamenting his absence from China. When the Chinese marked major literary events, such as the combined celebration of the 100th and the 350th anniversaries, respectively, of the publication of Walt Whitman's *Leaves of Grass* and Miguel de Cervantes's *Don Quixote de la Mancha* at the Capital Theater in Beijing in 1955, Robeson's inability to attend due to his passport troubles was underscored. Mao Dun, then vice chair of CFLAC, and the China National Association of Writers, read Robeson's congratulatory telegram in front of American and Spanish guests. The presence of the "progressive Black American" Aubrey Pankey, who had recently relocated to the German Democratic Republic to escape the persecution of McCarthyism, somewhat made up for Robeson's absence at the celebration. Pankey's article "The People's Poet Whitman" appeared in the *People's Daily*. As the first American artist traveled to the PRC, the singer, accompanied by Maria Knotkova, a pianist and professor at the Prague Conservatory, conducted an intensive concert tour across major cities.[81]

China fervently joined the world (with the important exception of the United States) in a celebration of Robeson's sixtieth birthday in 1958. Preceding the grand celebration of Du Bois's ninety-first birthday, the event was marked both as a state and family event. The China Peace Council, the Chinese People's Association for Cultural Relations with Foreign Countries (CPACRFC), CFLAC, and the China National Association of Musicians organized a birthday gala with 1,000 guests in Beijing. Guo Moruo was host, and Zhao Feng, Qian Junrui, and Liu Liangmo, now executive committee member of the China National Democratic Youth League, made laudatory speeches. The meeting approved the collective congratulatory telegram to Robeson and read individual ones by Guo, CPACRFC president Chu Tunan, Qian, and leaders of the China National Association of Musicians including Lü Ji, Ma Sicong, and He Lüting. Among the numerous renowned figures publishing affectionate letters and poems in the state media to salute Robeson were Emi Sao, Xia Yan, and Qian. Xia noted that although Robeson's birthday in his motherland was shadowed under dark clouds, his heart would be warmed by paeans arriving in New York City from Moscow, Beijing, Delhi, Rome, and London. Xia wrote, "Across the Pacific, we wish you eternal youth and longevity. Your songs inspire an instant sense of grandeur and solemnity in me, someone who knows little about music." "Chee Lai!" and Robeson's rendition of "John Brown's Body," which "represents truth, beauty, and kindness," were Xia's favorites. Xia described Brown's proud and dignified words before his death, which Karl Marx called the "greatest event in the world." His praise of Robeson's performance of the song was soon followed by the much-celebrated translation of Du Bois's book *John Brown*. Qian echoed Xia's sentiment and wished that Robeson would live for "ten thousand years," an imperial expression normally reserved for Mao Zedong in contemporary China. He lamented that Robeson's promise to him in Prague in 1949 to "come next year — first the Philippines, then China," had not materialized yet.[82]

In response, Robeson penned a letter of greeting to the Chinese people and enclosed a family photograph, as well as his freshly self-published memoir titled *Here I Stand*. He concluded the letter, "We deeply appreciate the brave leaders and people of China as a whole for your contribution to socialism and peace. I wish to reach your soil soon to show respect. It would be a day of true happiness." The book was promptly translated into Chinese by the Foreign Affairs Press (fig. 2.9). A reader reported in the mass circulation magazine *Reading* (*Dushu*) that the book brought "a strong, unyielding warrior right in front of my eyes."[83]

Other publications marked Robeson's birthday. The Beijing Music Publishing House issued a booklet titled *Paul Robeson* for general readers that

FIGURE 2.9. The cover of the Chinese translation of
Paul Robeson's self-published memoir *Here I Stand*.
Author's collection.

included biographical materials, his essay "Songs of the Black Race," versions of his favorite songs, and his "quotations" highlighting his determination to struggle on behalf of oppressed races and classes (fig. 2.10). As essential truths uttered by immortalized domestic and international heroes to inspire, the "quotations" signaled Robeson's ultimate model status. The booklet acknowledged his ability in the Chinese language, his unyielding support for China's war of resistance, and the pleasure he took in China's grand socialist construction. It exclaimed, "How enormously we miss this outstanding people's singer and how much we yearn to hear his voice and see him in person!" Both the Chinese version of *Here I Stand* and this music pamphlet prominently featured Robeson's letter and his family photograph, whose English caption simply mentioned names, while the Chinese version detailed his family structure, with Robeson a venerable patriarch. A similar book, *Collections of Songs Sung by Paul Robeson*, was released by the Shanghai Music Publishing House, with assistance from the Liaoning Association of Musicians. The majority of the songs of high "political and artistic values" were translated from a 1957 version released by the Soviet Music Publishing House. In addition to "Chee Lai!," "Song of Peace" (Soviet Union), "Oh, No, John" (England), and sixteen Black spirituals, it featured a brand new "Song of Peace" created by Yuan Shuipai and composer Zhou Weisi especially for Robeson's birthday. The song concludes, "When the spring breeze blows over the good earth, even the prisons in heaven and hell will open wide!"[84]

Mao Zedong's 1939 eulogy "In Memory of Norman Bethune" would soon become one of the mandatory "Old Three Classics" for Chinese citizens, thereby elevating the Canadian doctor to an icon of internationalism during the Cultural Revolution. Robeson served a similar purpose. Publicity materials promoting him as a heroic model emphasized his love of and appeals to various races and nationalities. "Robeson is not only a patriot caring for the fate of Blacks and his motherland, but also an internationalist supporting all the oppressed nations' struggles for liberation." A poem dedicated to the "Negro Brother" Robeson by Nazim Kikmet, the imprisoned patriotic poet of Turkey, was featured among the appendices of the Chinese translation of Graham Du Bois's biography of him. Mexican artist Leopold Theodore Montesquieu's woodcut of Robeson breaking chains, with a dove near his chest, widely circulated in the Chinese press. It inspired Jack Chen's cartoon illustrating Du Bois's birthday speech.[85]

Robeson's international appeal was underlined by his race and class. Defined as "the Black King of Songs," his color was prominently highlighted. The *People's Daily* exclaimed, "As long as we have Robeson, Black music's

音乐出版社

保罗·罗伯逊

FIGURE 2.10. The cover of the booklet *Paul Robeson*,
featuring the drawing of him singing at Peekskill.
Author's collection.

contribution to world culture is self-explanatory." Covers of all the imprints on Robeson were dominated by a dark background indicating his race, into which his face blurred, with Chinese characters in blood red symbolizing his leftism. Graham Du Bois's *Paul Robeson: Citizen of the World*, which highlights his internationalism but neutralizes his race, was translated as *Black Singer Robeson*. In his passionate poetry narrating the Peekskill riots in the *People's Daily*, Yuan Shuipai wrote, "Robeson's dark face shines, and Robeson's songs ring."[86] The precedent for integrating the singer's physical features into discussions of his art and politics was set by a 1928 *Shanghai Times / London Daily Express* essay, the earliest coverage of Robeson in China. The author, James Douglas, reported how Robeson's "magical genius" in creating "the soul of people in bondage" captivated his audiences at the Drury Lane Theater in London. Robeson, he wrote romantically with affection, "is not quite black or quite white. His skin is a mellow ivory. His features are negroid, but they are so plastic that they shape every shade of feeling and imagination. His lips and his eyes change with every tone of dramatic vision in his voice. There were seconds when his face was alight and aflame with seership. We saw the rapt mysticism gathering in intensity until it reached the height of the mood and then it slowly faded like a sunset, and he locked the door on it with a tightened, tense mouth."[87]

Zhu Mo added extra materials in his abbreviated biography of Robeson to familiarize his readers with the Black race and counter Chinese racial prejudice. Assuming that lighter skin was preferable, he explained, "The skin tones of Blacks range from light to dark brown, rather than dark as soot at the bottom of cooking pots as we would imagine. It is their puffy kinky hair, especially for males, that distinguishes Blacks from other races. For the convenience of maintenance, males shave their head and females wear braids."[88] In contrast, Chinese media did not mention Du Bois's physical features, probably due to his light skin and mixed ancestry.

The color dimension of Robeson as a model for China's and the world's "revolutionary" community entailed complex twists. Various biographical pieces in Chinese highlighted how Robeson articulated his experience of being treated for the first time as a full human being no longer exposed to racial prejudice when he traveled to the Soviet Union in 1934. Although they noted that Robeson's Black friends in the Soviet Union were well-educated professionals, such as doctors and engineers, Chinese sources echoed the Soviet authorities' silence on the African heritage of the highly popular Russian poet Alexander Pushkin. Even so, Robeson prominently cited the poet to exemplify the advancement his people enjoyed in the Soviet Union. In his famous speech at the International Congress for Peace in Paris, Robeson mentioned that he was among the guests of honor to commemorate the 150th birthday of the "great Russian Negro poet" and "our proud world possession" in the Soviet Union. "Could I find a monument to Pushkin in a public square of Birmingham or Atlanta or Memphis, as one stands in the center of Moscow?" he asked. "No. One perhaps to Goethe, but not to the dark-skinned Pushkin."[89]

Chinese publications repeatedly adapted as one of Robeson's most memorable experiences Graham Du Bois's story of him watching a popular play titled *The Negro Boy and the Monkey* at the Children's Theater in Moscow. Set in an African jungle, the play features a group of Black children who select as their leader a boy who could "run best, jump best, and sing best," who evidently resembles Robeson. The boy moves to Moscow, rising to a leadership role in a chocolate factory under the guidance of his Soviet comrades. The protagonist and his monkey, whom he rescues from an abusive capitalist circus manager, return to the jungle. The play concludes with the boy's speech: "These presents are from the children of Moscow to the children of the dark forest. For the Moscow children wish every child in all the world, be his color white, red, yellow, or Black, be his race what it may and be his language what it may, to enjoy the same full richness of life as Moscow children now enjoy." Robeson was observed being moved to tears by the play's theme of racial inclusion. However, neither Graham Du Bois nor the Chinese translators noted Moscow's patronizing gesture toward "dark Africa," which it stereotypically represented through a jungle and a monkey or ape, as in the Hollywood hits *Tarzan* and *King Kong*.[90]

Childlike Blacks, jungle and simian imagery, and other exotic metaphors for "primitivism" frequently appeared in publications for children in 1949, when the Chinese press generally increased friendly coverage of Blacks. As late as 2018, a program during the highly popular annual Spring Festival gala on China Central TV attempted to showcase African love for China's investment in medicine and railroads as "one family," with marriage between an African woman and a Chinese man teased at but not materialized. The gala unambiguously featured the cliché jungles, apes, and comical blackface figures in shabby costumes.[91] Amid many appeals to African and Chinese unity, W. E. B. Du Bois urged in his 1959 poem "I Sing to China":

Reach down, O mighty People,
With your clenched left fist,

Grip the hands of Black Folk!
Hold fast the men from whom this world was born:

That great-brained Ape
Who stood erect and talked to his fellows
Who planted seed and first boiled Iron
And civilized a World.

. . . .

Help her, China!
Help her, Dark People, who half-shared her slavery;
Who know the depths of her sorrow and humiliation;
Help her, not in charity,

But in glorious resurrection of that day to be,
When the Black Man lives again
And sings the Song of the Ages![92]

The TV gala would far exceed Du Bois's expectations.

While U.S. authorities launched campaigns to purge "un-American" activities based on ideology, the Chinese state defined two Americas from a class perspective, one for the "vicious, despicable, and wily American imperialists — millionaires on Wall Street actively preparing to launch a great massacre in a World War III," and the other for the "broad American laboring people." Mao Zedong had telegrammed on the thirtieth anniversary of the Communist Party USA in 1949, "America's future belongs to you, the American people, not the American counterrevolutionaries." The letter by CFLAC and the China National Association of Musicians to console Robeson over the Peekskill Riots stressed, "We have always separated the counterrevolutionary government from the American people."[93]

Robeson was cast as the symbol of world proletarian solidarity in the 1954 German Democratic Republic documentary *Song of the Rivers* (*Lied der Ströme*). Directed by Joris Ivens and shot with transcontinental collaboration, the film focuses on the shared destinies and hope of workers across the world, as represented by the Volga, Mississippi, Nile, Yangtze, Amazon, and Ganges Rivers. China instantly embraced the documentary, and the Shanghai Film Studio translated it into Chinese. To salute Robeson on his sixtieth birthday, the magazine *Cinema Arts* featured an essay on Robeson's recollections of making the documentary. "Across time and space, Robeson's songs are true to the hearts of laborers," exclaimed an article in the *People's Daily*. "We love and respect you, first of all out of class instinct!"[94]

Although they recounted Robeson's extraordinary achievements as a singer, actor, athlete, and lawyer with political commitment, all the biographical information also highlighted his slave family background and poverty, his early menial jobs, and the harsh race and class oppression that he suffered. Chinese citizens were called on to imitate his drive, diligence, and determination to confront any adversary and achieve the impossible. "However hard the American government and fascists try to silence Robeson and suppress his extraordinary artistic achievements; the broad masses' righteous indignation only soars daily! The counterrevolutionaries called Robeson's singing 'explosive.' Indeed, it blasts away Morgan, Rockefeller, and all other financial oligarchs; the counterrevolutionaries called Robeson's songs 'red.' Indeed, they are dyed by the blood of tens of thousands of victimized Black brothers."[95] The PRC's successful confrontation of the strongest imperialist power in the Korean War, after a century of colonial humiliation, boosted national confidence and contributed to the myth of formidable human determination. This new worldview helped to bring on the Great Leap Forward. As a leading figure who supported China in the war, Robeson personified this iron will, which was allegedly unique to the working class and its vanguard, the communist parties.

TRANSITIONS DURING THE GREAT LEAP FORWARD

The U.S. State Department was forced to restore Robeson's passport in June 1958, granting him the same legal victory enjoyed by the Du Boises. Sharing Du Bois's joy as "a released prisoner," Robeson immediately traveled to Europe, although he still could not visit China due to the travel restrictions on U.S. passports, which the Du Boises defiantly violated, at heavy cost. Returning from the World Youth Festival in Vienna and en route to Budapest in August 1959, Robeson delivered a speech and conducted an interview with the Hungarian Telegraph Office. This led the State Department to consider invalidating his hard-won passport. Since he was technically in transition in Budapest, the government decided to delay action against him, pending whether his intended visit to China materialized. Thus Robeson did not join the Du Boises there.[96]

While the Du Boises' high-profile trips created thunder during China's disastrous Great Leap Forward, the *People's Daily* continued to highlight the brutal oppression suffered by Robeson. Meanwhile, his affection toward the nation and his reunion with Chinese delegates in London were prominently presented to paint a rosy picture of socialist construction.

Covering Robeson's "silence-breaking" concerts on the eve of his passport victory, the *People's Daily* reported that his performance at the Oakland,
California, city hall in February 1958 instilled such panic among counterrevolutionaries that a self-proclaimed leader of the West Nationalist Crusade threatened to keep Robeson offstage by force. The newspaper lauded
Robeson's Carnegie Hall concert in May as "songs shattering the censorship." He paid tribute to the supportive Chinese people by inserting Chinese folk songs, including the classic "Over That Faraway Place," adapted
from a Kazak folk tune by "the King of Folk Songs," Wang Luobing. As soon
as his passport was restored, the singer left for more concerts in Europe. He
thanked the British people, whose "outspokenness on the question of China
had greatly strengthened the sane forces in the United States."[97] The *People's
Daily* celebrated Robeson's freedom to travel as a triumph of justice, peace,
and democracy. Between 1958 and 1960, the newspaper followed his whereabouts, plans for screen roles, and new international folk songs in his concert
programs in Moscow, at the Seventh World Festival of Youth and Students in
Vienna, and the thirtieth anniversary celebration of the *Daily Worker* at the
Royal Albert Hall. It reported that he reprised "Over That Faraway Place" at
the British Peace Council gathering in London in June 1958.[98]

The *People's Daily* hailed the fact that Robeson "sang for the new China's
tenth birthday" at a concert organized by the Sino-British Friendship Association at London's Prince Theater on October 4, 1959. "This is no ordinary
performance, because 'the Black King of Songs' poured profound friendship
into his baritone voice to salute the Chinese people galloping on the road of
socialist construction," exclaimed the *Daily*. It reported that while Robeson
had sung "Fengyang" and "March of the Volunteers" to narrate the people's
suffering and struggle in the dark "old China," he performed romantic folk
songs, including "Over That Faraway Place" and "Riding the Dragon," which
had been included on the *Chee Lai!* album, to reflect the optimism and happiness in the new China. Eslanda attended a reception at the PRC Office of
the Chargé d'Affaires at 49 Portland Place, which coordinated the ceremony
presenting a gift from W. E. B. Du Bois (a bust of himself) "to the Chinese
people as a sign of deep friendship and sympathy." The Robesons joined
9,000 people attending the first Chinese Film Festival in London organized
by Jay Leyda, Sylvia Si-lan Chen's husband, on behalf of the British Academy
of Film in 1960. Robeson commented that, unlike American films, Chinese
cinema reflected the feeling of the people. A review article in the (London)
Daily Worker echoed his sentiment and recommended Chinese films.[99]

The *People's Daily* detailed Robeson and his wife's interactions with the

China Song and Dance Troupe at the Adelphi Theater and in Chinese restaurants. He was introduced as a "great and loyal friend of 600 million Chinese," to thunderous applause, handshakes, hugs, and exchanges of gifts, before he sang an old Chinese folk song. "I have heard and read a lot about Chinese theater," the newspaper quoted Robeson, "but I never expected it to be so unbelievably beautiful and touching, with music, dance, and acting coherently synthesized. . . . I hope I will see you again soon in your and also my lovely China." He further elaborated on the Sino-African musical lineage, noting that the rhythm of the two-string instrument (*erhu*), with five musical scales, was similar to Hebrew and African music familiar to him. Robeson resumed early ties with Chinese theater through leftist artists, although his friends were then under attack or marginalized in China.[100]

During offstage informal and intimate interactions, Robeson conversed with Chinese delegates and correspondents of the *People's Daily* in English, Chinese, and Russian on Chinese festivals, Beijing opera, Confucius, and Sino-African linguistic and philosophical affinity. Robeson confided that he had been keeping up with his Chinese by learning a few new characters, listening to Chinese records of songs and dialogue, writing a few lines of calligraphy daily, and maintaining a sizable library of books in Chinese. He learned to pronounce and write his name in Chinese from his Chinese companions. They were impressed by the great singer's "genius" linguistic skills and observed that each page of his worn Chinese textbook was jotted with heavy notes. After listening to Robeson sing at mass gatherings on Trafalgar Square and for the tenth anniversary of the PRC's founding in 1959, Pan Fei, a *People's Daily* correspondent, requested an interview. He was soon chatting with Robeson in his "spacious but somewhat rundown apartment," while Eslanda made coffee and snacks for the guest.[101]

Until 1961, the PRC held up Robeson as a genuine Black revolutionary and contrasted him with such perceived sellouts as Martin Luther King Jr. and Ralph Bunche, the UN undersecretary-general and Nobel Peace Prize laureate. Reviewing a film biography of Bunche, Yuan Xianlu, an editor of the *People's Daily*, dismissed it as U.S. government propaganda aimed at the new African nations. Heaping contempt on Bunche, the author claimed that the diplomat enjoyed a "smooth climb up" the ranks of government offices. He compared Bunche's methods to those Robeson revealed in *Here I Stand*. Robeson cited the (New York) *Amsterdam News*: "Our government has long employed Black intellectuals, performers, ministers, and others . . . to show their fat, bulky, and decorated faces, as living proof that everyone is equal and free in an America without racial boundaries. . . . This kind of baseless global propaganda campaign has not achieved its goal, because facts speak louder than empty words." The Chinese critic doubted that the result would be different when propaganda experts in Washington, D.C., promoted Bunche. Yuan derided Bunche's accomplishments in Palestine and Africa as "eagerly selling American neocolonialism" and ridiculed his obsequious behavior when confronted with racism in his own town over use of a tennis court.[102] The *People's Daily* did not mention that James Hicks, editor of the *Amsterdam News*, destroyed photograph negatives of Robeson and Bunche shaking hands at the 1948 New Year's assembly in the Renaissance Ballroom of Harlem to avoid hurting Bunche's political career. Back then, Bunche was first favorably covered as a significant Black politician by the *Shanghai Daily*, which was coming under the influence of the CCP.[103] The official line on Bunche shifted according to political dynamics, as Robeson himself soon experienced.

THE ABRUPT SILENCE ON ROBESON (1962–76)

Suddenly, in 1962, the state media and publishers in PRC fell silent on Robeson, whose seventieth birthday slipped by without notice in China. The September 6, 1963, editorial in the *People's Daily* titled "The Origin and Development of the Differences between the Leadership of the CPSU and Ourselves" marked the open split between the CCP and the CPSU. Among the various disagreements between the two parties, the piece highlighted Nikita Khrushchev's policy of "peaceful coexistence" with the United States, which the CCP had been portraying as the top imperialist villain in its new narrative of the international order since the Korean War. Throughout and after the war, Robeson had been advocating "peaceful coexistence," which he defined as "living in peace and friendship with another kind of society." At a 1954 meeting of the National Negro Labor Council, echoing Du Bois, Robeson articulated that the U.S. government "must like the politics" of and trade with China, the "Eastern European democracies," and the Soviet Union, in order to "fortify our economy against depression." Thus, instead of "walking the streets in search of work," American workers "could be making the tractors, farm implements, tools and structural steel which New China needs and is ready to buy." The attempt by McCarthy and the China Lobby to "starve" the CCP government and restore Chiang Kai-shek "as an American puppet on the mainland" by embargoing China was failing, Robeson observed, because

China's trade and economy were constantly expanding and opening to other Western nations.[104] However, Robeson's position was caught in between the shifting dynamics among the transpacific triangular powers, now falling on the wrong side of the PRC.

Nikita Khrushchev's secret speech at the Twentieth Congress of the CPSU in 1956 caused an earthquake in the communist bloc, and his visit to the United States in 1959 accelerated the Sino-Soviet split. While remaining silent on the speech, Robeson exclaimed that Khrushchev's trip "certainly rocked the land and many others to their foundations." He trusted that the "Americans saw for themselves, day after day on television, in person, the dynamic, humane, warm personality" of the Soviet leader, who "clearly . . . works in the interest of peace and abundance for his own people and for all of human kind."[105] Following the open Sino-Soviet split and the U.S. media's wide speculation on Robeson's disillusion with communism, the Chinese press promoted and celebrated the Black Panther Party and Robert Williams as the true Black revolutionaries, a view for which Graham Du Bois adjusted her previous position on peace to embrace and one that reached its peak during the Cultural Revolution. In 1964, the Beijing Music Publishing House issued *American Negroes Want Freedom*, a collection of songs of alternative flavor created by Lü Ji and Guang Weiran. Departing from the refined lyrics of Robeson's songs, they narrated "centuries of hatred seething in the awakening hearts of the oppressed Blacks" and "the marching tunes of the liberating forces ringing in the eighteen-level imperialist hell."[106]

Despite Chinese inattention, Robeson still harbored dreams of visiting the PRC, which his friends encouraged. Between his 1959 and 1962 trips to China, Du Bois wrote to Robeson on January 5, 1961:

Dear Paul: I do not often offer advice, but here is an exception.
I have heard of your hesitation as to your next step. My advice is [to] go to China and make a tour of from three to six months. Consult the Chinese Chargé d'Affaires in London about arrangements. Write the American Ambassador and say that you have promised not to visit any country with which the United States has no diplomatic relations; but upon reflection you cannot keep this promise which you now think was extracted unfairly. On return from China arrange for a three month trip to Africa. By that time Kennedy will be president. Apply to him for a renewal of your passport. If he refuses, take out citizenship in a European or African country. Our love to you and Essie. Sincerely, W. E. B. Du Bois[107]

Anna Louise Strong agreed with Du Bois, writing from Beijing in 1966, "I personally have always felt that Paul's trouble [in health] had a deep psycho-somatic cause in the shock and trauma he suffered from the Sino-Soviet split. . . . Paul had a very deep love and devotion both for the USSR and for China's revolution and . . . consequently the split must have been especially hard for him, since his devotions have always been through passionate allegiance rather than through theory." Urging Robeson to come to Beijing so that he could be surrounded by love and recover soon, but uncertain about the official attitude, Strong "made inquiries" and learned Robeson would be "extremely welcome." By this time, however, Robeson was too sick to make such a journey.[108]

BACK IN FAVOR AFTER 1976

In a sign that Robeson had returned to the pantheon of Chinese heroes after the Cultural Revolution, the *People's Daily* reported in 1978 that the United Nations held a memorial ceremony to mark his eightieth birthday.[109] Robeson's son Paul Jr. and his Jewish wife, Marilyn Greenberg (whom the Chinese press noted was "a white woman"), visited China in 1980. Madam Sun Yat-sen received them at her Beijing residence. Overwhelmed by Zhou Enlai's death, she had not learned of Robeson's death in 1976 promptly. Finally getting a chance to commemorate her great friend, she said to Paul Jr., "The Chinese people hold profound affection toward your whole family. Many, including myself, treasure your father's records." Paul Jr. presented a tape of eighteen songs including "Chee Lai!," "Ol' Man River," and "Joe Hill," and a list he had compiled especially for Madam Sun. She kept the gifts in her bedroom until her death. Robeson had asked his son to forward a copy of the *Chee Lai!* album to his old associate Liu Liangmo. Paul Jr. told Yuan Xianlu, "To me, an African American, the ethnic issue remains fundamental, and I judge a social and political system according to its treatment of the ethnic/racial minorities." Following a four-week trip to the Xinjiang Uyghur Autonomous Region, he offered "constructive criticism" on improving China's ethnic policies. He concluded, "China's growth into a powerful socialist country is extremely important to the Third World. . . . I proudly declare that I was, am, and will forever be a friend of China." At gatherings of the Washington, D.C., branches of the Sino-American Friendship Association and the Chinese American Association for the thirty-second anniversary of the PRC's founding, Paul Jr. recalled his recent visit to China, urging the U.S. government to cease selling weapons to Taiwan.[110]

There were tributes to Robeson on the tenth anniversary of his death in China, including Pan Fei's article on his personal encounters with Robeson. Pan highlighted Robeson's deeds on behalf of China and remarked that even the noble title "Black King of Songs" was insufficient to capture his worth as an artist and "a warrior for truth and justice." Pan concluded, "As a sincere friend of the Chinese people, the glorious image of Paul Robeson will remain in our memory, forever and ever."[111]

Meanwhile, Robeson's life and work were reintroduced to younger generations in China after his memory faded over two decades of omission. A new biography, *Paul Robeson: The Life and Times of a Free Black Man*, was translated into Chinese with the title *Black King of Songs Robeson*.[112] A 1980 pamphlet *American Popular Songs* and a 1991 *Collection of Negro Folk Songs Sung by Paul Robeson*, released by the People's Music Publishing House included songs with lyrics in both English and Chinese and simplified musical notes accessible to the general public and secondary school students. These publications and recordings used the term *popular* not in the sense of Top 10, but rather in that of labor-themed "people's songs."[113] Robeson's singing sustained followers in China as American folk singers came to sing his most famous hits. Kevil Maynor conducted such a concert at the Sun Yat-sen Park in Beijing in 1999 to mark the 100th anniversary of Robeson's birth. Under the title "To Answer or Not to Answer," the concert program printed Robeson's famous response to the question of whether he was a communist during his June 12, 1956, hearing before the House Un-American Activities Committee, demonstrating the ultimate wit and courage of an artist entangled with fascism, McCarthyism, and communism.[114] "Ol' Man River" continues to fascinate the Chinese. A reporter for the *People's Daily* recounted in 1981 that as the Black chair of the Sino-American Friendship Association drove her along the Mississippi River, "suddenly, rang in my ears the resonant voice of Robeson: Ol' Man River, Ol' Man River, He don't say nothing, he must know something; Ol' Man River, he just keeps rolling along." That sentiment was echoed two decades later by a popular essayist, who recalled how his eyes widened at the sudden appearance of a blue street sign, "Paul Robeson Street," during an evening stroll while visiting Princeton. He wrote, "My memory flashed back to the 1950s when I, then a sixth grader, first heard Robeson's 'Ol' Man River' on a neighbor's radio, deeply touched." The British film *Song of Freedom* (1936), starring Robeson, was translated into Chinese in 2006.[115]

Although Paul Robeson never visited China, his songs, words, and deeds traveled to a very receptive audience there. The Chinese regarded Paul and Eslanda Robeson as cherished friends. For a time, ideological conflict pushed him into the shadows, but he reemerged as a hero there and remains so into the present. One powerful reason for Robeson's overall positive reception in China was his deep friendship with Liu Liangmo, who is the subject of the next chapter.

3

Transpacific Mass Singing, Journalism, and Christian Activism

Liu Liangmo

In February 1941, the noted Chinese writer Lin Yutang published a laudatory article in *Asia* magazine about Liu Liangmo (刘良模 ca. 1909–88), a little-known diaspora musician, prolific journalist, public speaker, and Christian activist. Richard Walsh, the editor of the magazine, then sold a condensed version of the article to *Reader's Digest*, one of the most widely read periodicals in the United States, with nearly 1.5 million subscribers. A few months later *Time* magazine, the nation's leading weekly, included a brief biographical sketch of Liu. Much as Americans had become fascinated by China, such coverage of a previously unknown immigrant was unusual. Liu would later become somewhat of a household name in the United States after the Japanese attack on Pearl Harbor, the onset of the Pacific War, and the subsequent Sino-American alliance. For now, Lin's story recounted Liu's discovery and application of mass singing to China's patriotic war effort against Japan and gave the history of "Chee Lai!" or "March of the Volunteers." Lin appended the lyrics of several fighting songs from Liu's repertoire, including "Song of the Guerrillas":

> We are all raised up in this land
> Every inch of it belongs to us
> Whosoever dares to take it from us
> We will fight them to the end![1]

By kicking off all of the coverage that followed, Lin was responsible for introducing Liu to both the American public in general and Paul Robeson in particular.

Five feet and seven inches tall, Liu had a handsome face with a strong nose, a trim athletic figure, and, judging by his archived performances on U.S. radio stations, a beautiful, soothing voice. He usually dressed in either conservative Western business suits or Chinese scholar's robes and possessed a confident, congenial personality. Fluent in Shanghai dialect, Cantonese, Mandarin, and English, he was well informed on politics and religion and published prolifically on diverse topics in both Chinese and English throughout his career. His primary fame for Americans came from his reputation as "the man who largely coaxed the Chinese into mass singing" of powerful songs of national resistance "with a single voice," as applauded by *Time* magazine.[2] Both the Nationalist and Communist militaries endorsed and adopted his methods, and Liu clung to a delicately balanced independence to maintain his Baptist missionary zeal and Chinese nationalist fervor. Given that his sponsors in China were leading communist or left-wing figures, it is reasonable to suppose that Liu was sympathetic to the party's aims.[3]

After arriving in the United States in 1940 and adjusting to his new life, Liu soon revealed other skills. He toured the country, gave hundreds of speeches, sang and recorded Chinese fighting and folk songs, and published innumerable articles in scores of American periodicals. Upon returning to the People's Republic of China in 1949, he carved out a political career as a high-level government official while maintaining his Baptist faith, no easy task in the atheist communist state. Liu vigorously promoted the Three-Self (self-governance, self-support, and self-propagation) Reform Movement (renamed the Three-Self Patriotic Movement in 1954), which helped to bring Chinese Christianity into line with the ideology of the new regime, and rode smoothly on waves of radical political campaigns.

Apart from some fine, brief coverage by Mark Gallicchio, Him Mark Lai, Joseph Tse-Hei Lee, and Richard Jean So, scholarship on Liu is scant. Mass singing, his major contribution to Chinese culture, has received little attention. Andrew F. Jones has studied Shanghai popular music in the 1930s, focusing on the frequently blurred boundaries between jazz-influenced yellow (decadent/pornographic) music and leftist music. Such vocalizing was individual and consumer-oriented.[4] Examining Liu's transpacific career and impact, which synthesized radical Chinese nationalism, missionary Christianity, cross-race collaborations, and modern popular culture, this chapter looks to Liu's popularization and translation of Chinese militarist and folk music through cooperation with Paul Robeson to show the complexities of transpacific colonial modernity.

Liu Liangmo's early life both set the stage for his launch of the mass singing movement and prepared him for his later stays in the United States. His biography matches the American myth of the self-made man, a quality that would endear him to many white middle-class Americans. He was born in poverty, with an older brother, Liu Liangtza, in Zhenhai County (now Ningbo), Zhejiang Province, between November 11, 1908, and November 9, 1909, to Liu Chia-foo (Kai Toh) and Koo Shu Cheng. His father, an atheist merchant and customs officer in Chen Chao Han, died when Liu was only eighteen months old. His mother, a Buddhist, labored to put her two sons through school before Liu became a scholarship student at the Baptist Minqiang Academy in Shanghai and the Middle School Affiliated to the University of Shanghai from 1922 to 1928. He was active in the student union and contributed essays to the school journal, *Shanghai Tide*, and other periodicals. He won second place in an national essay competition, held by Ma Yinchu, then a professor at Beijing University, on fighting opium addiction.[5]

Liu attended the University of Shanghai from 1928 to 1932. His family finances worsened. His brother's failed investment in film used up all their savings and left them 3,000–4,000 yuan in debt, which was followed by the untimely death of his sister-in-law. The resourceful Liu persevered, scraping together his 120 yuan annual tuition and fees with a one-time scholarship, student loans, part-time jobs in the library and telephone booth for 0.15 to 0.2 yuan per hour, tutoring in math and English, and occasional royalties from journal essays and editing work. He borrowed classmates' textbooks and had to work carefully around their schedules. Nevertheless, Liu thrived as a protégé of Liu Zhan'en. In classical Chinese, he vividly described the president's inaugural ceremony amid the wave of Chinese replacing foreign leadership in Christian institutions following the Northern Expedition. Liu converted to Christianity under the influence of the new leader. He matured into a prolific writer, contributing hundreds of articles in the *University of Shanghai Weekly*, including his humor column "Radio Station," and national periodicals. He won the fourth place in the Third National Essay Competition on the familiar topic resisting opium addiction. Liu found time to translate a book titled *Methods of Study* by an American academic. He became an articulate public speaker, competing in several national speech contests on contemporary political issues and winning second place in a contest judged by Liu Zhan'en and senior Nationalist Party member Pan Gongzhan. Liu met Chen Weijiang (ca. 1911–95), a fellow student from Nanjing, and married her on July 21, 1934, in Guling, Jiangxi Province.[6] After earning a bachelor's degree in sociology with honors, Liu first worked as a social worker. His experience in the left YMCA movement instilled in him a radical egalitarianism far exceeding that preached by the Social Gospel. Liu began regular work for the Shanghai YMCA, a branch that augmented the famous institution's Christian-inflected emphasis on health and hygiene with instruction on workers' issues, especially education, and advocated strong resistance against Japan. Its secretary, Wu Yaozong, was aligned with the CCP; after becoming secretary-general of the China National YMCA in 1935, he declared that China needed socialism to remedy its corrupt social system. Liu joined Wu on a special YMCA commission on youth and social reconstruction to endorse a revolutionary Christianity. He replaced Wu as the secretary of the Shanghai YMCA and served as the student secretary at the national YMCA from 1932 to 1949.[7]

Liu's fusion of Baptist missionary evangelicalism and Christian musical performance soon found a way to satisfy Chinese patriotic and military needs through mass singing. Chinese intellectuals historically despised singing, relegating it to professional actors in theaters, singsong girls in brothels, and storytellers, stevedores, knife-grinders, food peddlers, professional mourners, rickshaw pullers, and cobblers in public spaces. Mass choruses were unknown in China. Inspired by an American book, *Music Unites People*, that espoused the use of community song, Liu began teaching mass singing to improve wartime morale and promote national unity. The role of public singing rapidly transformed. Liu started with a chorus of more than ninety people, mostly young clerks at nearby banks, post offices, and shops, and cleaning women, at the North Sichuan Road YMCA in late 1934. Within weeks, Liu expanded the People's Choral Societies around Shanghai. Between 1935 and 1936, he traveled to Jinan, Beiping, Baoding, Ding County of Hebei Province, Taiyuan, Kaifeng, Hong Kong, Guangzhou, Shantou, Wuhan, Yuezhou, Changsha, Jiujiang, and Nanchang to popularize the format. The National YMCA helped to organize more choral societies in Nanjing, Xiamen, Fuzhou, Yantai, and Chengdu by 1937.[8]

Collaborating with leftist/communist composers, Liu's mass singing movement quickly inspired the creation of a new genre—songs of resistance that transformed folk songs and adapted militarized tunes suitable for collective singing with easy-to-memorize lyrics based upon a set of standard nationalist themes. The mass singing movement had to overcome a lack of proper songs, since the highly popular yellow music, routinely performed solo by a female in a high pitch, evidently did not suit. Ever creative,

Liu spontaneously compiled a song, "Saving China," by inserting the lyrics "Save, save, save China" to the simple tune of the lullaby "Row, Row, Row Your Boat," which his chorus group mastered in half an hour. Soon musicians such as Xian Xinghai, Ren Guang, Lü Ji, He Lüting, Shu Mo, Wang Luobing, and Nie Er, whom Liu would remember as "the father of the new music in China," created similar songs to fill the gap. Based in the remote Xikang (today's Qinghai) Province, Wang would emerge as the legendary "King of Folk Songs," whose classics Robeson reprised. "March of the Volunteers," acclaimed as "the war anthem of a struggle for freedom," pushed the genre to its peak. Many songs appeared on the soundtracks of contemporary leftist films, enhancing their accessibility and popularity. Successfully melding traditional melodies and martial music and adapting patriotic themes, the marriage of mass singing and the new popular political musical genre pushed aside yellow music as China's dominant musical paradigm for the rest of the century.[9]

Liu quickly extended the mass singing movement to military use. In early 1937, he traveled to Suiyuan (part of today's Inner Mongolia) to work with the warlord Fu Zuoyi's army, following Fu's recent military triumph against the Japanese at Bailingmiao, a border town near the Great Wall. According to one legendary story, Liu taught a song to 10,000 soldiers within forty minutes during a sand storm by instructing the lyrics first to twenty-odd soldiers and then placing them strategically in the ranks. Liu returned through Datong and Taiyuan, teaching mass singing to both the military and civilians under another warlord, Yan Xishan, and soon visited Tianjin for a similar mission.[10] Liu's immediate impact spread beyond the military to China's elite families. Ji Chaozhu (Chi Ch'ao-chu), Ji Chaoding's half-brother, recalled singing the newly learned "March of the Volunteers" with another brother, Chaoli, at the top of their lungs to lift their spirits during the family's long walks from their Japanese-occupied hometown of Fenyang, Shanxi Province, to Wuhan in 1937.[11] Liu organized several mass singing concerts in Shanghai to raise funds for war efforts in Inner Mongolia and refugee relief. In addition to donating around thirty yuan, eager female workers took unpaid leave to perform, dressing in purple cotton *qipao* (a style of dress popular in the 1930s and 1940s) and standing neatly in rows onstage. To amplify the message of civilian-military alliances, Liu placed photographs that he took at the Suiyuan front in several periodicals, including the *Young Companion Pictorial*, allegedly the most popular glamor magazine in the Republic of China.[12]

On July 7, Liu witnessed the Japanese attack on the Marco Polo Bridge, kicking off a full-scale war on China. Soon, assigned by the YMCA's Commission to Serve the Military, with the quiet agreement of the Nationalist government, Liu left his pregnant wife behind to join other urban professionals, such as artists and intellectuals in mobile theaters, to support soldiers in the front lines. He and his followers traveled from Suzhou, Zhenjiang, Nanjing, Xuzhou, Fuzhou, Xiamen (to attend the Sun Yat-sen Memorial Week at Xiamen University), Zhengzhou, Kaifeng, Wuhan, Changsha, and Guilin to Zhejiang Province between 1937 and 1940. They walked and took whatever transportation available, slept on floors and in open fields, and sometimes went days without food or water, singing "March of the Volunteers" to lift their spirits along the way. They viewed their work among the masses and soldiers as sacred, and their lice as badges of honor. Realizing their proximity to death by bombing, bullets, or disease, they pledged to "view death as inevitable to serve the military with determination." They taught songs of resistance and organized a mass singing chorus whenever possible. In the renowned writer Xiao Hong's novel *Ma Bole*, from Nanjing to Wuhan, refugees from all walks of life and soldiers marching toward the front lines sing songs of resistance, reflecting the impact of Liu's team. Liu and his followers also focused on serving the wounded soldiers, whose lack of care plagued the Nationalist army, and promoting civilian-military alliances. Liu believed that, in addition to physical care, the military, especially the wounded men, needed cultural food for their mental health and morale. He complicated the nationalist message by arguing that soldiers were "armed physically but not mentally." The tools Liu's team used to enrich the soldiers' knowledge and arm their minds were a truckload of record players, records, radios, pictures, and chess games worth 5,000 yuan, donated by the supporting public in Shanghai.[13]

On New Year's Eve 1938, they left Wuhan for Changsha, which hosted as many as 70,000 wounded soldiers, and clashed with and harassed civilians, causing resentment and plunging the city into chaos. Local officials responded with force, conducting daily executions of troublesome soldiers, while Liu tried to tackle social problems with persuasion. He broadcast his approach from the Changsha Municipal Radio Station on January 2, immediately after he reached the city. He coauthored with the noted cartoonist Lu Shaofei a cartoon series on civilian-military alliances for the *National Mobilization Pictorial*. Still, in one incident, Liu mobilized civilians to return to their businesses and serve the military's needs. His work was instantly wasted, as a soldier refused to pay for his food, punched a restaurant owner, and quickly dispersed the civilians once again. Liu and his followers established choral groups among the wounded men and distributed candies and cigarettes raised from Hong Kong and Chinese Americans, which greatly pleased the soldiers. Respect and care were gradually reciprocated. When Liu organized the locals to bring letters and gifts, including Moon Festival cakes, to the soldiers, they agreed that the gifts should be auctioned off to raise funds for refugees streaming into the city, in addition to donating 700 yuan saved from their food allowances. To help civilians shake off their traditional prejudice against soldiers, Liu enthusiastically reported how wounded soldiers demonstrated their creative talents by building theater stages, performing plays and songs of resistance, and exhibiting their calligraphy, paintings, essays, bulletins, crafts, and even bullets from their bodies. He helped publish some of the soldiers' essays and penned flattering sketches of individual soldiers. Though Liu's work in Changsha was highly successful, after ten months it was rudely interrupted. To impede the approaching Japanese, the Nationalist army set a major fire in November without warning, scorching the city. Liu's team barely escaped.[14]

Meanwhile, the CCP recognized the potential of Liu's mass singing program. As Zhou Enlai commented, "Many hot-blooded youths, with backpacks, singing the songs of resistance, marched to Yan'an."[15] In December, Liu's team moved into Jinhua, Anji, Meixi, Xindeng, and Hangzhou in west Zhejiang, guerrilla areas controlled by the Communist New Fourth Army. There they helped set up medical facilities, organized transport systems, and instructed the public on sanitation. Agnes Smedley recalled that when Dr. Loo Chih-teh of the International Red Cross Committee established respite stations for wounded soldiers and malnourished refugees, "I went off immediately to the Chinese Y.M.C.A. in search of a young Christian war-worker, Liu Liang-mo. Mr. Liu listened and then returned with me to Red Cross headquarters. Within a week, he and a group of young Y.M.C.A. men and women had taken over many stations on the route to the front. I delivered to Liu Liang-mo many huge crates of prunes and raisins which had arrived from America. These had been nine months on the way and half of them were spoiled. The flat roof of the Y.M.C.A. was soon blanked with prunes drying in the sun."[16] Liu demonstrated his skills in morale uplift, fundraising, and organization, all of which would be highly useful in the United States later on. Local press across the Pacific lauded the role of mass singing under his leadership in China's resistance.[17]

In bringing mass singing to the battlefield, Liu simultaneously expanded the movement. He released three books: *Collection of Songs for the Youth*, *ABC of Mass Singing*, and *Roaring Voice of the Nation*. They collected lyrics and accompanying simplified scores of rousing songs. He published several articles on techniques to teach and conduct mass singing.[18] Liu proposed a new category called "song-drama" (*juge*), a hybrid of a song of resistance, street play, and pictures, as a powerful wartime propaganda tool to reach the illiterate masses through both visual and audio means. Liu believed that the simple dialogue and familiar lyrics of song-drama helped actors to memorize their parts easily, and enabled convenient on- and offstage interaction with the audience singing theme songs between acts, thus adding life to otherwise dull mass singing. Liu sought to integrate forms of traditional local theaters favored by the masses. He published a script, *The Huang Village*, a simple family melodrama adapted from a Bengbeng opera in Henan Province. Backed by guerrilla forces and the volunteer army, the play's protagonist was a shrewd young woman who heroically killed the Japanese after they attempted to prey upon her sexually. The play was staged in Zhengzhou and adapted into Shaoxing opera in Jinhua.[19]

Liu also used his talents as a journalist to relate the progress of the mass singing movement and to convey both the suffering and resilience of the nation. Concerned that omission of news about Japanese aggressions in the Chinese press left "400 million compatriots" in the dark, in 1935 Liu took up the mission to "enable the blind to see." He edited the resistance-themed periodical *Messages* from 1932 to 1936 and published hundreds of articles. Some appeared in the format of correspondence with Zou Tao-fen, a noted journalist and editor of several resistance-themed journals, and Qian Junrui, a journalist and a future cultural official in the People's Republic of China (PRC) who would befriend Du Bois and Robeson. Liu compiled some pieces with sensitive material from Shanghai English-language journals such as the *Shanghai Evening Post and Mercury* and *Miller's Review*, which were exempt from censorship by Chinese authorities. Liu also wrote two books on his experiences on the front lines. His article "Japanese Planes and Chinese Children" told the story of a little girl who had lost one arm and her siblings and parents to Japanese bombs. Liu noted that the piece came to be taught in schools and was translated into many foreign languages. It was also anthologized in *The Battles in Shanghai*, along with works by Guo Moruo, Xia Yan, the noted female soldier Xie Bingying, and journalist Fan Changjiang, and interviews with top Nationalist generals. In the wake of the Nanjing massacre, his articles passionately called for the use of mass singing's inspiring power and efficient organization to turn the Chinese masses from mercilessly butchered "pigs" and "lambs" into "iron soldiers." Liu insisted that the key to China's ultimate victory was national unity built on a united front between the Nationalist Party and the CCP — though this alliance faced many difficulties because of Nationalist sabotage and problems with military-civilian cooperation.[20]

As Japan's aggression intensified, Liu employed his skills as a photographer to show children and landscapes under attack, civilians supporting wounded soldiers, and farmers working hard to support the "protracted war." Some appeared next to a photograph showing Madam Chiang Kai-shek consoling wounded soldiers, taken by the famous H. S. "Newsreel" Wong (王海升 or 王小亭), then Far Eastern correspondent for the International Newsreel Corporation of New York. Liu managed to place more photographs in the prestigious *Young Companion Pictorial*, portraying him leading a 1937 mass singing meeting of 3,000 in Fuzhou and the guerrilla forces near Hangzhou in 1939.[21]

Despite his devotion and heroism on the front lines, Liu had a falling out with the Nationalist government over suspicions of his Communist sympathies. He recalled decades later that the "Nationalist counterrevolutionaries, who faked resistance and really attacked the CCP," tried to suppress his efforts and threatened his life. He was detained in Ningbo by the Nationalist government for two months between July and October 1939. Once released, the undeterred Liu lingered in Fuyang to establish a bathhouse and club for wounded soldiers, soliciting donations of magazines and a radio from Shanghai around Christmastime. Soon he decided to leave for the United States, accepting invitations from the American Bureau for Medical Aid to China and the China Aid Council, both tied to Madam Sun Yat-sen.[22] Wu Yaozong and Zhou Enlai helped obtain permission for Liu's journey to the United States. Wu, Zhou, and Liu met in Wuhan in 1938 after Wu, a Columbia University graduate, had returned from further study at Union Theological Seminary in New York City. Liu saw Zhou again in Jinhua, right before the Nationalist government detained him (fig. 3.1). Madam Sun's and Zhou's involvement suggests that high-level Chinese authorities were aware of Liu's itinerary.[23] Liu had sojourned in the United States before.

A BRIEF YET EVENTFUL JOURNEY TO
THE UNITED STATES IN 1936

Amid his efforts to promote mass singing in China, Liu Liangmo had made a quick trip across the Pacific in 1936. Accompanied by six other delegates from Ginling and Yenching Universities and Beijing Union Medical College, he traveled to Mills College in Oakland, California, to represent the Shanghai YMCA at the Pan-Pacific Conference of the World's Student Christian

Federation, held from August 23 to September 2. With a nonimmigrant visa issued by the U.S. consulate-general in Shanghai and $100 in his pocket, Liu joined his delegation in third-class aboard the S.S. *President Lincoln*, which sailed from Shanghai on August 2 and arrived in San Francisco on the 19th (fig. 3.2).[24]

Ever prolific, Liu published three articles in the Shanghai magazine *Woman's Life* to chronicle his trip. He discussed the dynamics between Cantonese seamen and overseas Chinese students, who mass sang songs of resistance to overcome seasickness. Liu witnessed superior levels of industrialization and efficiency in Kobe and Yokohama, as Du Bois would experience a few months later. In Hawaii, he had mixed feelings at his first sight of U.S. soil. While impressed with the beautiful landscape, the mixed races, and the robust physiques of indigenous Hawaiians, he was sympathetic to their suffering under colonial oppression and poverty. Liu observed that Japanese, who represented 65 percent of the residents of Honolulu, posed a serious security concern for the United States.[25]

Liu's trip soon took a darker turn. His essays published in Chinese women's magazines detailed the differential treatments by race and class

AMERICAN CONSULATE-GENERAL

SHANGHAI, CHINA, ~~Kiangsu~~ July 30, 1936.

PRECIS OF INVESTIGATION.

Name: LIU, Liang-mo   (劉良模)
Nationality: Chinese
Class: Traveler.
Passport Visa No.:   74/1936-7

Section 6 certificate issued by the   Bureau of Public Safety
at Shanghai, China,   on July 1, 1936.

Visa granted by this Consulate General on   July 28, 1936.
under Section 3 (2)of the Act of   1924.

Applicant's birthplace: Shanghai, China.
Date of Birth by western reckoning: November 11, 1908.
Applicant's family (ages by Chinese reckoning): Wife, Chen Wei Giang, 26;
   residing in Shanghai.

Standing of applicant: Was graduated from the University of Shanghai,
   in 1932 with B.A. degree. For the past four years he has been
   secretary, National Committee, Y.M.C.A., Shanghai.

Purpose of travel: To attend the Conference of the World Student
   Christian Federation to be held at Mills College, Oakland, Calif.

Applicant's reference: O. R. Magill, 19 Rue La Salle, Chicago.

Consular investigation and remarks: Examination has been made of the
   applicant who has presented a letter from S. C. Leung, General
   Secretary of the National Committee of the Y.M.C.A., Shanghai;
   a letter from H. A. Wibur, Special Secretary of the International
   Committee of the Y.M.C.A. of the U.S. and Canada; both recommending him highly and vouching for the purpose and temporary
   nature of his visit to the United States.

Intended departure:

Steamship: PRESIDENT ~~McKINLEY~~ LINCOLN
Sailing date: August ~~XXIX~~ 2, 1936
Port of entry: ~~Seattle, Wash.~~ San Francisco

C. E. Gauss,
American Consul General.

811.11- Liu, L.M.
HDP/Mf

PHOTOGRAPH ATTACHED
AMERICAN
CONSULAR SERVICE

Note—This form to be used only in the cases of Chinese merchants and travelers proceeding to the U.S. or P.I.

6-36

FIGURE 3.2. A visa Liu Liangmo obtained from the U.S.
consulate-general in Shanghai to visit the United States in 1936.
*"Liu Liangmo," file 36590/7-4, box 3429, shelf 3300E, group
85, Immigration and Naturalization Service, San Francisco
District Office, National Archives at San Francisco.*

at the Angel Island immigration station and his own unpleasant detention. "Only non-white third-class passengers" had to make the trip there, which initially seemed a predictable nuisance for Liu. He reported, "We talked and laughed on the ferry toward the world-famous demon's cave, whose notoriety could not dampen the courage of youths like us." After men and women were stripped bare and closely examined by the surgeons from the U.S. Public Health Service, they were sent to the Immigration and Naturalization Service (INS), "whose staff were polite but would not release us." Liu continued. "Then an officer walked in and instructed: 'All can go, but these two,' pointing toward me and Yuan Jialiu [Luke Yuan Chia-liu, a grandson of the warlord Yuan Shikai]." Liu and Yuan were detained overnight in a room with 140 people. "Like ants in a hot pan, we do not know why we have been detained, and for how long." In the hellish and isolated conditions, Liu heard terrifying stories of long-detained Chinese immigrants and copied some of the sad Chinese-language poems inscribed on the wall. He noted the INS's hierarchical treatment of the detainees, with the Chinese, the only group deprived of bedding, at the bottom. Liu and Yuan's problem turned out to be minor. Their medical certificate maliciously exaggerated that they were "afflicted with DEFECTIVE VISION–Class B, which may affect ability to earn a living." A hearing was held to confirm that their eyesight was normal with glasses, then they were released. Liu kept his promise to other Chinese detainees, immediately reporting to the Chinese embassy what he had witnessed at Angel Island. The embassy replied that it had proceeded to address the issue.[26]

Liu's ordeal at Angel Island was not an isolated incident. He bitterly commented that, because the Chinese were considered a "colored race," one Americans perceived to be dirty and diseased, all Chinese travelers had to obtain a health certificate to "keep from contaminating the noble whites." Since even discolored fingers or toenails could lead to disqualification, doctors would sometimes humiliate the traveler by burning the affected spot with an electric needle. He snorted, "When white lords, even with syphilis, arrive in China, they are free to land and spread such contagious diseases to we Chinese. No one dares to make a sound." He attributed such unfairness to China's status as a semicolony and commented that the ultimate solution was for the 400 million Chinese to unite with progressive Americans and break the giant oppressive chain binding weak and small nations.[27]

Harsh treatment by the INS did not dampen his enjoyment of the conference. In his article published in *Messages*, Liu highlighted the diversity of the 150 conference attendees in skin color, age, credentials, denomination, and belief. He wrote, "Behind a dark face is the Negro Problem [in English in the original] in the United States; behind an Indian face, the issue of national independence; . . . behind a Chinese or Japanese face, the life-and-death struggles of a nation." Liu described how the Chinese delegation "dropped a bomb" by calmingly reporting the nation's resistance against Japan during the preceding five years, which made the conference chair "anxious as if sitting on needles." Overall, the conference had positive results. Liu observed that heated but sincere debates within the spirit of Christianity led to communication and understanding, even between Japanese and Chinese delegates.[28] There was one final insult. While his return ship delayed its departure from September 4 to 10, the INS mistakenly claimed that Liu failed to reboard. Confirming he had indeed departed, the agency wired to Shanghai, "asking that upon the arrival of the *President Hoover*, Liu Liangmo be taken before the American Consul for identification." The FBI would later insist that Liu had been deported.[29]

RETURNING TO THE UNITED STATES (1940–49)

Liu's second journey to the United States, in 1940, was much smoother. According to the records of the U.S. State Department, he obtained a travel certificate from the commissioner of customs at Shanghai and a nonquota immigrant student visa from the U.S. consul general in late August. Such a visa required a letter of admission from an American school, bonds to ensure one would not depend on public funds in the United States, and "ten dollars (180 yuan!)," Liu gasped. With his fare paid by his employer, the National Committee of the YMCA, he departed from Shanghai aboard the *Princess Marguerite* on September 8 and landed in Seattle on the 24th without incident. This time he could afford the $200 fare for second-class passage, twice the cost of third-class, thus escaping the harsh race- and class-based immigration ordeal at the U.S. border.[30]

Liu was admitted for a year to study theology at the School of Orientals at the Baptist Crozer Theological Seminary in Upland, a suburb of Chester near Philadelphia, which Martin Luther King Jr. would attend from 1948 to 1951. Liu studied at the institute with a scholarship granted on the basis of his work with the YMCA in China. Due to the steep currency exchange rate (16–20 yuan to $1), the minimum funds for the "hollow reputation of studying in the United States" was 10,000 yuan, for which many Chinese students sold chunks of their ancestral land or accumulated sizable debt, according to Liu. He attended Crozer for three full semesters from September 1940

Liu Liangmo

to June 1941 and simultaneously took classes at the University of Pennsylvania. Crozer offered a liberal, interracial, intellectually stimulating atmosphere. Whether in classes, during private faculty mentoring, or in fervent dormitory discussions, Liu learned of the tenets of Gandhian nonviolence and of the critical debates about the Social Gospel, now sullied by capitalist economic exploitations and the collusion of government. Crozer professors taught that true Christian eschatology was in the historic triumph of political democracy and socialism. While not explicitly Marxist, Crozer's pedagogy indicated that class struggle and dialectical materialism were more convincing than the instability of capitalism. Anticipating that he would soon receive an Oriental Certificate, Liu booked passage back to war-torn China in September 1942.[31]

An unexpected opportunity would delay his return for seven years. Probably facilitated by Madam Sun Yat-sen, United China Relief (UCR), which had been recently formed by seven leading China aid groups, drafted Liu as a traveling lecturer and entertainer based in New York City on its special staff on September 1, 1941. UCR's executive director, Bettis A. Garside, a skilled diplomat and fundraiser, was a former Presbyterian missionary who spoke Mandarin. He had taught at Cheeloo (Qilu) University in Jinan, Shandong Province, and held administrative positions to promote Christianity in China. The UCR Board of Directors included Pearl S. Buck; *Time* magazine publisher Henry Luce and his wife, Claire Booth Luce; politician Wendell Willkie; film producer David O. Selznick; millionaire John D. Rockefeller; Col. Theodore Roosevelt, the eldest son of former president Theodore Roosevelt; and Robert G. Sproul, president of the University of Michigan. While UCR was primarily associated with the Republican Party, which Franklin D. Roosevelt had defeated in three consecutive presidential elections, Eleanor Roosevelt was closely involved. She and Garside assiduously strove to avoid partisan political identification. UCR sought to raise relief funds for China and to educate Americans. Liu was a perfect candidate to provide this service.[32]

Liu canceled his passage, left school, and moved into the McBurney YMCA at 215 West 23rd Street. A fellow resident would describe Liu to the FBI as "quiet and uncommunicative" in 1945. Probably alarmed by such unwanted attention, Liu had taken up residence at Apartment 2B, 211 West 88th Street, in November 1944 and remained there until his departure for China in 1949. Liu would recall rejections by numerous landlords due to his ethnicity. Such discrimination made him sympathetic to Blacks in their segregation to Harlem, the "worst district in New York City with higher prices for inferior housing." His uncharacteristically reserved style with his neighbors (he could be voluble and engaging when he chose) indicated that Liu was carefully protecting himself in the treacherous political environment.[33]

Liu was right to be wary. In crossing the Pacific, he did not escape political controversy. His brief alliance with the Chinese military, especially the Communist New Fourth Army, triggered strong interest from U.S. authorities. The FBI, the War Department, and the Chester and New York City Police Departments coordinated vigilant surveillance of his whereabouts and activities from February 10, 1941 to September 1956. A few months after his arrival, while national magazines printed laudatory stories about Liu, the FBI opened a file on him.[34]

Initially, the authorities could find little at fault with Liu. The Chester Police Department provided a report to the Philadelphia FBI office on October 5, 1941, which contained "no derogatory information and definitely disputes any allegation of Communist activities on his part." James H. Franklin, president of Crozer, offered unreserved support for Liu in his confidential interview with the police. He swore that Liu had been "very thoroughly investigated before being furnished with his scholarship," and that Liu had "absolutely no affiliation with the Communist Party in China." Instead, he worked with Chiang's Nationalist Army "in the capacity equivalent to that of an army chaplain in the United States Army." Franklin cited Liu's acquaintance with China's ambassador Wei Daoming and Lin Yutang's widely circulated article on Liu. However, those recommendations failed to quell the authorities' suspicions. The Philadelphia District Intelligence Office of the War Department reported to its Military Intelligence Office in Washington, D.C., in January 1943 that Liu, a "Chinese solder and singer," had just discussed China's struggle and World War II at the Tom Paine Forum, "the Communist Workers School," in Philadelphia. The Washington, D.C., office forwarded the information to FBI director J. Edgar Hoover in May. Meanwhile, in March, Wallace S. Wharton, commander of the U.S. Navy Reserve, had sent a memorandum to the FBI on behalf of Admiral H. C. Train, director of naval intelligence, requesting more information on Liu's background and activities.[35]

Hoover acted quickly. He delivered a summary of Liu's activities to Train through a special messenger, and forwarded Wharton's memorandum to the FBI's New York City office in April, demanding a comprehensive investigation. Hoover instructed, "This inquiry should, of course, be handled discreetly in view of Liu's connections with Chinese relief organizations and other causes which relate to the Allied war effort." The FBI contacted its confidential informant Timothy Holmes, a Black former Communist Party leader, the following March about Liu's alleged communist affiliation. Though Holmes failed to provide anything incriminating about Liu, Hoover grew annoyed at the New York office's silence and followed up sternly. "You are instructed to immediately submit a report in this case," he wrote, demanding a report in less than three months. Startled, on the same day, the New York office supplied an eight-page report on Liu's background and speaking engagements collected from media coverage, confidential informants in the Chinese community, the New York City Police Department, and UCR director Bettis A. Garside. The report stressed that Liu lectured and sang for various communist front meetings and was "generally considered a Communist among the Chinese and follows both the Chinese and American Communist Party lines." It promised to confirm such accusations through ongoing investigation.[36]

Hoover reached out to the FBI's Philadelphia office to dig out Liu's detailed biographic information from Crozer, the YMCA board in Chester, and the INS. The FBI noted that, in his alien registration with the INS, Liu stated that he had no military service, which contradicted Franklin's statement. Despite his "alien status," Liu registered for the Selective Service with the local board of the YMCA in Chester. In early 1945, Mrs. Lawrence Green, secretary of the dean at Crozer, would add to the discrepancies by praising to the FBI Liu's legendary service in the Chinese army as the famous originator of community singing. The New York Police Department alleged that Liu had lectured and sung the song of the Communist Eighth Route Army, which he believed superior to other Chinese armies due to its "political instruction," at the Madison Square Garden meeting sponsored by the American Council on Soviet Relations in 1942. The FBI concluded, as "the originator of China's mass singing movement," Liu had "traveled over that country in 1937 with some two hundred assistants teaching soldiers [of the Communist Units of the Chinese army] marching songs and developing new lyrics."[37]

Under such a veil of suspicion, Liu had to navigate the slippery terrain of transpacific politics and ideology with caution, courage, and charm. Back in 1934, in a striking moment of self-reflection, he had contributed an essay to *Woman's Voice* on the benefits of collegiality and friendship with people of diverse ages, genders, nationalities, and geographic origins. Liu's affability proved essential to creating networks that enabled the spread of mass singing and ultimately enhanced his political survival across the Pacific.[38]

While Liu spent nearly a decade in the United States, there was little ostensible evidence that he planned to stay, although China's turbulent political and war situation could have forced such a decision. Both UCR, his principal employer, and the INS regarded him as a visitor. Without the Chinese Exclusion Act and its racialized barriers, an educated, cosmopolitan, and congenial man, Liu would have exemplified an ideal immigrant, highly compatible with his American peers. He proved attractive to distinctive constituencies in the wartime United States. The three major strands of Liu's work and influence revolved around the single purpose of urging assistance to China. His multiple messages crossed boundaries of race and class as he became one of the most popular speakers in the United States.[39]

INITIAL OUTREACH TO AFRICAN AMERICANS

Liu's initial narrative was directed at African Americans, bridging a gap between Chinese and left-wing African American nationalism. It distinguished him from the many Chinese celebrities and intellectuals who came across the Pacific at that time to win support for their country in its struggle against Japanese brutality. Echoing Du Bois and Paul Robeson on the Sino-Black lineage, Liu declared at the Detroit YMCA in 1941 that "the Chinese have much in common with the American Negro." As we saw in chapter 2, Liu cultivated a warm collegiality with Black leaders, especially the famed singer and actor Robeson. After their initial meeting, Liu followed up by writing to Robeson and offering his services as a Chinese language teacher. Following their successful cooperation, Robeson accelerated his Chinese language lessons and began carrying around the *Three-Character Introductory Reader*, as the FBI reported. Liu recalled that, whenever possible, Robeson took the book out of his briefcase to discuss the structure, meaning, and pronunciation of Chinese characters with him. Liu was impressed with how carefully Robeson made sure he understood and correctly pronounced each character of the lyrics so as to master the spirit of Chinese songs.[40]

Family interests intersected with politics. Liu frequently visited Camp Wo-Chi-Ca, a communist interracial summer camp for workers' children near Hackettstown, New Jersey, which Paul Robeson Jr. attended between 1942 and 1948. So did Liu's son after he was brought to the United States by his mother in 1945. Although Robeson was featured in all of the camp's advertising materials, Liu was also a notable figure there. Liu taught one counselor, Naomi Field Basuk, Russian and Chinese songs and instructed mass singing of fighting songs and Chinese-language phonetics to the campers, as illustrated in the camp's brochure. He led the American Youth Chorus, sponsored by the camp, in a songfest featuring "Chee Lai!" at Union Square in New York City to raise funds for UCR. He brought along his good friend Kumar Goshal, a noted Indian American journalist, to educate the campers on China's and India's struggles for freedom. The campers put on a play in which a Black boy played a Chinese seaman, who introduce China's resistance against Japan to the Indian people. Liu announced that the campers of diverse races modeled living as "citizens of the world."[41]

Robeson was hardly the only Black luminary at Wo-Chi-Ca. There, Liu met among the staff such important African American artists as Charles Alston; Elizabeth Catlett and her husband, Charles White; Ernest Crichtlow; dancer Pearl Primus; poet Gwendolyn Bennett; and actor Canada Lee. Langston Hughes often stopped by the camp, as did prominent left-wing white intellectuals and artists. Liu encountered fabled folk singers such as Woody Guthrie and Pete Seeger, as well as the novelist Howard Fast. Benefit dinners in New York City for the camp provided opportunities for Liu to engage with Black notables such as W. E. B. Du Bois, Duke Ellington, and Jacob Lawrence. Not everyone approved of such mingling. Convinced that Robeson was a communist operative and suspecting Liu's own communist leanings, the FBI monitored these gatherings closely.[42]

Whatever the government spies thought, Robeson regarded contact with Liu as a major opportunity to expand the vision of the Council on African Affairs (CAA), which the singer had helped found in 1937 and chaired for most of its existence as a principal donor. The CAA's leftish position was tolerated by the U.S. government during the war. The two friends appeared together publicly at large rallies to cheer the African American war effort, starting with entertaining 6,000 people at Uline Arena in Washington, D.C., in 1941. John P. Davis, a former editor of the Crisis and national secretary of the National Negro Congress, made a speech at the rally. A week later, they all spoke at the Lincoln University Conference organized by Davis on the status of the Negro, along with Walter White; Adam Clayton Powell, the prominent Black minister and New York City council member; Channing Tobias of the national YMCA; novelist Henrietta Buckmaster; historian Herbert Agar; and Krishnalal Shridharan, Jawaharlal Nehru's representative to the United States. Robeson and Liu joined others in delivering platform addresses at the 1942 National Conference of the YMCAs, discussing "The Stake of the Darker Races in the War." In his musical revue It's All Yours, Robeson described Liu as a Chinese singer of guerrilla songs.[43]

Although sympathetic to China's resistance to Japan, Americans knew little about China's specific plight or about groups such as the American Bureau for Medical Aid to China that had been transferring medicine and other materials to the Chinese Army Medical Service, the National Health Institute, the Red Cross of China, and the National Medical Colleges through Madam Sun. Liu and Robeson often appeared together to promote these causes. In July 1941, they spoke at a gathering at Madison Square Garden in New York City, under the auspices of the American Council on Soviet Relations, and at a meeting of the American Youth Congress (AYC) in Philadelphia, urging the United States to provide aid to the Soviet Union and stop sending supplies to Japan, an issue Liu raised often. Liu was collaborating closely with the AYC, an organization associated with Eleanor Roosevelt. He had received tremendous applause when delivering "hearty greetings from Chinese youth who are fighting courageously on the front lines against the Japanese and against appeasers, traitors, and fifth columnists within China" at the AYC's Town Hall Meeting of Youth in Washington, D.C., in February. AYC chair Jack McMichael joined Liu in singing a Chinese song of resistance. Soon the AYC released a pamphlet, *Young China*, coauthored by Liu and Helen Simon, director of the American Youth Fellowship Campaign. The FBI noted that Liu corresponded from Crozer with Simon, an alleged member of the Communist Party USA, while she was obtaining a divorce in Reno, Nevada, that year. One evocative image reproduced in Robeson Jr.'s biography of his father and in a memorial anthology for Liu in Chinese shows Robeson, Liu, and seven other Chinese Americans at a "Stars for China" war relief benefit in Philadelphia in 1941 (fig. 3.3).[44]

Among Liu's most significant accomplishments was his weekly column "China Speaks!" which ran for 123 weeks in the *Pittsburgh Courier* between September 12, 1942 and April 14, 1945. The *Courier* was the nation's largest Black newspaper, to which W. E. B. Du Bois had similarly contributed his weekly column "A Forum of Fact and Opinion" from 1936 to 1938. At the Lincoln University Conference, Liu had met P. L. Prattis, the paper's new publisher, who likely hired him. The *Courier*'s subscriptions climbed to more than a quarter million, with an actual readership three times that size, in the early 1940s. It was the first time an American newspaper had invited a Chinese writer to contribute a column, as Liu would proudly point out in 1949 in the *Guangming Daily*, a leading official newspaper oriented toward intellectuals in the PRC. Getting such a column was indeed a coup for Liu, who reinforced his various messages in the columns with public speeches. The Black American leadership, encompassing President Roosevelt's "Negro Cabinet," the NAACP, church figures, politicians, and the expansive Black press, all endorsed a new internationalism where Liu could find attentive listeners.[45]

FIGURE 3.3. Liu Liangmo, Paul Robeson, and other Chinese at
the "Stars for China" war relief benefit at Philadelphia in 1941.
Liu Liangmo xiansheng jinian wenji.

The *Courier* strove for a strong internationalist bent. It also featured columns by Kumar Goshal and Trinidadian journalist George Padmore commenting on their ancestral countries. Liu's "China Speaks!" appeared right next to Goshal's "As an Indian Sees It," with the two columns frequently complementing each other, taking on similar topics. Liu's essays connected Chinese and Indian struggles for independence with African American concerns over racial oppression. As early as 1935, to inspire his Chinese compatriots, Liu had described Mahatma Gandhi's awakening to Indian nationalism as being a result of the brutal racism he had personally suffered. After Gandhi called on the British to "quit India" in 1942, Liu unambiguously voiced his support for India's cause at the National YMCA Conference for Secretaries and Laymen in Bordentown, New Jersey, and the Free India Rally in Manhattan Center of New York City under the auspices of the CAA. He opened his speech at the Free India Rally with Lincoln's famous statement that the world "cannot endure ... half slave and half free," and he concluded by dedicating "Chee Lai!" to the Indian people on China's behalf, as meticulously recorded by the FBI.[46]

Liu's columns linked the burning issues facing Chinese Americans and African Americans, such as the poll tax, the Chinese Exclusion Act, Jim

Crow laws, and the lynching of African Americans, urging their abolition. He was particularly appalled by the segregation of the American YMCA and YWCA, calling these policies "affronts to Christianity." Liu stated bluntly, "Treat negroes as human beings and there won't be any race problem here." The *Daily Worker* reported that he spoke at a rally in the Golden Gate Ballroom at Harlem sponsored by the Negro Labor Victory Committee, the lefty *Negro Quarterly*, and actor Orson Wells in 1942, protesting the lynching of three Blacks in Mississippi. His columns argued that African American support for abolition of the Chinese Exclusion Act and China's national aspirations would help them win rights at home. When the act was finally repealed in December 1943, Liu immediately urged abolishing the poll tax, which prevented African Americans in many southern states from voting. He connected homegrown fascism with appeasement of the Nazis and was sharply critical of essayist George Schuyler for referring to China as a weak nation.[47]

Liu expanded his joint efforts with Robeson, lauding African American war service in his journalism, augmented through talks and songs at Black churches and schools. In 1942, along with Earl Robinson and Josh White, he contributed to "folk ditties, workers' chants, war songs . . . against Nazi art" presented at the Town Hall in New York City under the auspices of the Negro Publication Society of America. According to the *New York Times*, the "lively program" contended that "men fight for their liberty with songs on their tongues as well as with guns, tanks and planes." In 1943, representing the China YMCA, Liu attended the Eastern Seaboard Conference of the National Negro Congress, along with prominent speakers, including Adam Clayton Powell, New York congressman Vito Marcantonio, and Max Yergan, president of the congress. Liu led a panel discussion on "the Negro and the Moor," pleading for African Americans' full participation in the global struggle against Nazism, and co-led with Kumar Goshal another panel on "the colonial peoples in the war."[48]

Liu's columns denounced discrimination suffered by Chinese, African, and Native Americans in the U.S. military. He wrote about the discriminatory treatment of 20,000 Chinese seamen as "colonial coolies" on British and Dutch ships and detailed the abuse some of them suffered in New York Harbor in 1942. Introduced as a collaborator of Robeson's in the preparation of Chinese songs, Liu delivered a passionate speech at a rally organized by the Japanese-American Committee for Democracy at the Hotel Diplomat in New York City, relating to the Chinese sailors. The sailors were given only half pay and refused shore leave, while their peers took leave with full pay after their ship docked. When two of their representatives voiced their grievances, the captain brutally murdered one of them. Liu concluded the story with the acclamation "We will demand justice" and a Chinese song that repeated, "We are brothers." Shortly afterward, Liu and New York City councilman Benjamin Davis Jr. attended a tribute to Black servicemen sponsored by the National Council of Negro Youth and the New York State Conference of Negro Youth. Liu's speech condemned Jim Crow in the military and pledged that Chinese and Blacks would "fight for freedom and equality regardless of race, creed, or color."[49]

Liu's columns connected the racial oppression suffered by African and Chinese Americans with U.S. neglect of China's war efforts, bitterly complaining about the paucity of supplies to beleaguered China, and beseeched the Allies to open a second front in the Asia-Pacific. At the Free India rally and the Warehouse Workers Union's rally at Astor Place in New York City in 1942, he noted that African Americans contributed most of the funds raised by UCR. Liu conveyed this support to his readers in China with an anecdote from his speaking tour. Overhearing Liu's conversation with a friend in a restaurant on the plight of China, a Black maid emerged from the kitchen to donate a half dollar, equivalent to the cost of one day's food for her family. Concerned that China was not receiving equal treatment during the global conflict, Liu repeated demands that the nation be a part of the Atlantic Charter to improve its postwar status. He translated an "Anthem of the Allies" composed by Soviet musician Dmitri Shostakovitch, which enthusiastically forecast liberation for all oppressed nations. In 1943, with simplified musical notation, it appeared in several Chinese periodicals, including *Revolutionary Youth*, a magazine published in Shangrao, Jiangxi Province, a longtime CCP base.[50]

Asked why he cared so deeply about Black issues, Liu replied that any progressive Chinese would feel the same. He reasoned, "The Chinese here are mostly ignorant about the mistreatment of Negroes and I believe it is my duty to teach people about the wrongs they may be ignorant of." Liu translated and published *Courier* news items and columns on "Chinese Anti-Negro Discrimination" in *China Daily News* (*Meizhou huaqiao ribao*) and the *Chinese Journal* (*Meizhou ribao*), two of the largest Chinese-language newspapers in the United States.[51] Liu's emphasis on African Americans was important, coming at a time when W. E. B. Du Bois and ordinary citizens voiced sympathy for Japanese goals in Asia, believing their race would benefit from a Japanese victory.

Liu's race advocacy intensified U.S. authorities' scrutiny of him. Wallace S. Wharton's memorandum to the FBI emphasized that Liu was "a newspaper columnist, contributing to the Negro press," and was "very race conscious."[52] The Bureau reviewed Liu's writings as part of its general scrutiny of the nation's Black newspapers, which reached about 75 percent of African Americans in one form or another, as noted by the watchful military police. FBI agents routinely visited the *Pittsburgh Courier* to complain about articles the government felt were damaging to the war effort, such as Liu's pieces focusing on racism on military bases. Federal prosecutors dismissed such concerns as more individual opinion than newspaper policy. The FBI was not the only government agency surveilling African American newspapers. Attorney General Francis Biddle's office was actively censoring and prosecuting disloyal commentary. The U.S. Post Office halted mail of newspapers it regarded as subversive, or redacted them so much that a Cuban distributor for the *Courier* complained that he had received little more than the newspaper's masthead. Only skilled negotiation by John Sengstacke, the publisher of the *Chicago Defender*, kept Biddle from ordering multiple indictments of African American journalists.[53] It is safe to say that whatever Liu published, especially in the *Courier*, was scrutinized by unsympathetic white government agents.

All the while, Liu's evolving positions about Chinese politics in his columns and speeches further fanned the suspicion of his alleged communist ties. Initially he highly praised the Nationalist government, its leader Chiang Kai-shek and his wife, although he tempered this with tributes to Sun Yat-sen and especially his leftist widow.[54] As World War II drew closer to its end, attacks on the Nationalists became routine. Liu used his U.S. freedom of speech to decry its absence in China. He blasted one-man rule, abetted by stagnation, inflation, and censorship, and urged the Chinese people to demand democracy. He applauded the book by journalists Theodore White and Annalee Jacoby, *Thunder out of China*, which attacked the Nationalist government's suppression of free speech, its "reign of terror," and its secret police forces and arbitrary arrests. The Nationalist Party, Liu wrote, had "a membership of 1 percent of the Chinese people, but appoints itself the boss of China." He contended that the Chinese, like Blacks, would maintain the struggle "till democracy is really won, and no one is going to stop us." Liu praised the Communist forces for engaging nearly half of the Japanese occupying China with only one-fifth of the fighters and no aid from the Nationalists. Calling the lack of an alliance between the two parties "obstinate," and "prolonging the war," Liu urged them to negotiate. Not surprisingly, Liu

FIGURE 3.4. Liu Liangmo welcomes Col. John Stilwell, brother of Lt. Gen. Joseph W. Stilwell, at UCR headquarters in New York City in 1942. *Box 89, folder 13, UCRA.*

and Robeson's descriptions of Nationalist-Communist conflicts had much in common.[55]

Liu had sided with Lt. Gen. Joseph W. Stilwell, the commander of U.S. forces in China, Burma, and India, in Stilwell's unsuccessful struggle with Chiang Kai-shek, who demanded Stilwell's recall, saying he would work with any U.S. general except "Vinegar Joe." Between April and May 1942, Liu twice was the guest speaker at UCR meetings at the home of Col. John Stilwell, brother of General Stilwell and chair of the Yonkers branch of the YMCA and Yonkers Appeal for UCR. Liu praised the general and vowed that China and the United States would continue to fight together in Burma though heavily outnumbered. The *New York Times* featured a photograph of the two shaking hands, with Liu, as an "official lecturer," welcoming Stilwell at UCR headquarters in New York City (fig. 3.4). Although China's Nationalist government would have approved officially of such praise, secretly Chiang was conspiring against Stilwell with Claire Chennault, the U.S. general's top aide. After Chiang and Stilwell became enemies, Liu's *Courier* column called Stilwell a "most sturdy friend of China" and argued that President Franklin D. Roosevelt and Stilwell were for democracy in China, not tyranny. He maintained close contact with Stilwell's brother in Yonkers, even after the general's recall in October 1944.[56]

As we will see later, in subsequent columns, Liu, probably wary of being publicly identified as a communist, walked back his harsh criticism of Chiang, blaming the Nationalist Party rather than Chiang personally for Japanese advances. One of the burning issues in China in 1945 was the possibility of a coalition government between the Nationalists and the Communists. In January, Liu praised Chiang for promising the Chinese people a constitutional government and a People's Congress now, rather than after the war. Liu called this a "huge step towards true democracy," though he qualified his optimism in later columns. The maneuver did not seem to help, since, according to Liu, his column was abruptly canceled thanks to the "Nationalist spy" Chen Zhimai, who was employed in the Chinese embassy, at the peak of allegations of his communist affiliation. P. L. Prattis announced that the *Courier* wished to tell the story about the disappearance of Liu's column, but "we can't."[57]

During his column's more than two-year run, Liu articulated a combination of internationalism with a Chinese twist on the African American Double V wartime campaign. He connected discrimination against and the struggle for rights by African and Chinese Americans. In his coverage of the plight of Chinese seamen and Black factory workers, Liu showed concerns for ordinary individuals alongside global affairs. His prolific writings for a Black audience indicated how he strongly valued their support and identified with their aspirations and resistance to discrimination. He demonstrated his own evolving political ideals and independent politics through his initial support and later harsh criticism of Chiang's government. All this occurred while he was feverishly organizing Chinese American musicians and touring the United States talking to white middle-class groups, a testament to his energy and adept juggling of complex ideological concerns.

NAVIGATING THE CONTENTIOUS
CHINESE AMERICAN COMMUNITY

Liu's collaboration with Chinese Americans was less visible than his extraordinary outreach to African Americans. He probably made a conscious choice to keep a low profile within the dangerously contentious Chinese community, which intimately mirrored the complex political landscape in China. While highly educated and respected elites aligned with the Nationalists, laundry and restaurant workers, the bulk of local Chinese American laborers, shifted to the left. Naval Commander Wallace S. Wharton believed Liu was a sponsor of the leftist China Defense Corps in New York City. Similarly, in his initial request for an investigation into Liu, J. Edgar Hoover called for attention to "the possible influence he might have over the Chinese groups in this country," considering Liu's "apparent pronounced Communist sympathies and connections." Wary of the treacherous situation, Liu kept his distance from Chinese American community leaders. With confidential informants eagerly reporting him to the FBI, sometimes making malicious exaggerations, Liu's caution could never be enough.[58]

Among the FBI informants were Chih Meng, then director of the China Institute; C. L. Shia, director of the Chinese Ministry of Information at 30 Rockefeller Plaza; and Shia's assistant Lin Lin, all well placed in the Chinese community of New York City. Meng, who was a friend of Liu Zhan'en, Liu Liangmo's mentor at the University of Shanghai, and Liu were certainly not strangers. They spoke together in Carmel, New York, on two occasions in the summer of 1941, raising $600 for UCR. In a joint interview with the FBI in March 1944, Shia and Lin emphasized that all Chinese circles on both sides of the Pacific, including the Chongqing government, regarded Liu as a communist. They asserted that Liu followed the line of the CCP, which he viewed as the true heir of Sun Yat-sen, and called the Chongqing government and Chiang Kai-shek "reactionary and Fascist." Lin insisted that Liu allied with communists in New York City, observing that, except for members of the Chinese Hand Laundry Alliance, Liu's associations there were not usually Chinese but communist-inclined Americans such as his close friend Paul Robeson and many labor union leaders. She complained that a Chinese translation of the Soviet national anthem replaced the Chinese national anthem in a songbook Liu had compiled. Lin cited a 1942 conversation with Liu during summer vacation in Silver Bay, New York, to prove the point. Those assertions correlated the private conversation reported to the FBI in June 1941 by an anonymous informant intimately familiar with China's situation and trusted by Liu. Liu allegedly confided that he had been "an active political worker for the CCP" and his life was endangered while detained by the "reactionary forces." He allegedly commented, "The good force, the CCP, was working very hard to liberate the Chinese people," but it had made a critical error by embracing the united front with Chiang. That was the opposite of what Liu had been advocating in China. The informant insisted that Liu's official connections with the Chinese army were through the Communist units.[59]

Liu had a complex relationship with prominent figures introducing China to the West. While sailing across the Pacific in 1940, Liu read Lin Yutang's *My Country and My People* and Pearl S. Buck's *East Wind, West Wind* to "find out whether the two acclaimed authorities presented China accurately or not." He determined that they did not and wrote that the two famous authors "presented the dying old China," catering to "foreigners'" taste and "making a fortune." While attributing Lin's fault to "the perspective of a petit bourgeois," Liu harshly criticized Buck's racial perspective as that of "a clever daughter of an imperialist country." He argued that her preface to Lin's *My Country and My People* attempted to "clear foreigners' responsibility for the troubles in China" with "distorted and poisonous" analysis. He exclaimed sarcastically, "Such a clever 'foreign' girl!" Liu was particularly disgusted by Buck's "importing fake antiques" through detailed descriptions of bound feet, concubinage, and sex. He observed that she was obsessed with capturing conflicts between the new and old in China, "materials of the May Fourth period," which were "at least twenty years behind our time." Liu vowed to take on the task of presenting "the new China, exemplified by its fighting masses and youth."[60]

Fortunately, Lin Yutang seemed to have missed the piece, and it did not hinder the initial close collaboration between the two men. Ultimately, however, their divergent positions in Chinese politics caught up with them. In his final columns in the *Pittsburgh Courier*, Liu highlighted negative reviews of Lin's new book, *The Vigil of a Nation*, in the *New York Times* and the *New York Post*. He ridiculed his old patron as an "example of a liberal who has become a reactionary," citing his fawning report on Chiang Kai-shek and "very malicious attitude toward the Communist." For Liu, Lin should be ignored as a defeatist. Once deemed the "Republican Chinaman," and the principal Chinese literary celebrity in America, Lin's apolitical position was no longer sufficient, and Liu's article hastened his fall from fame.[61]

Condescension between Liu and Buck was mutual. On one occasion, Buck dismissed Liu as "a little Christian worker whose family name is Liu." Sharing the stage numerous times as UCR associates did not seem to improve their relationship. After attending the Sixth Nobel Anniversary dinner chaired by Buck on December 10, 1946, Liu wrote to congratulate her for a "fair and excellent speech" and requested a copy, which Buck gently declined, saying she had "no manuscript copy . . . as I spoke from notes." Also present at the dinner was W. E. B. Du Bois, who had a more cordial relationship with Buck. He followed up with a note thanking her for letting him "say a word. . . . I trust that stressing my pet peeve was not altogether out of place." Buck wrote back, "Of course I was only happy that you came . . . and that you closed the meeting as you did." Status mattered among elite intellectuals. At the same time, Buck remained wary of male Chinese intellectuals, whose critiques of her tended to be harsh.[62]

Liu Liangmo had ambitious plans to work with average Chinese Americans. Freshly arrived in the United States and traveling on the transcontinental train from San Francisco to New York City, he had written about "overseas Chinese" for his readers in China. He criticized their obsession with gambling and urged more parental attention to children's education, rather than rushing teenagers into business. Liu contended, "Our overseas Chinese are using eighteenth-century methods to conduct business in the twentieth century." Clearly there was much to be done.[63] He strove to teach the community to sing patriotic songs. His outreach soon produced a significant cultural artifact—the Chinese People's Chorus that he had organized among young employees of printing shops and restaurants and members of the Chinese Hand Laundry Alliance. This leftist organization was established in 1933 to protect the rights of thousands of Chinese laundry workers in Chinatown when New York City passed a burdensome tax aimed at them. According to Liu's liner notes for the *Chee Lai!* album, the voices of the chorus "are entirely untrained; but this is a real people's chorus—the voice of the Chinese people." Every Saturday afternoon in the early 1940s, Liu and the chorus practiced Chinese songs of resistance. His influence can be discerned in Lin Yutang's novel about New York City's Chinatown life. At a Moon Festival during World War II, the novel's chief characters decide to visit an amusement park, where they encounter about 1,000 other Chinese Americans gathered around a fountain under a huge Chinese national flag, while a band plays the national anthem. A Chinese woman with a rich contralto voice sings "Chee Lai!," as men, women, and children lift their voices and march to the martial tune. Later at a meeting, an American star (based on Robeson) sings the same song. There had never been anything like this before in Chinatown.[64]

In addition to using the Chinese People's Chorus on the *Chee Lai!* album, Liu performed in public with the group on several occasions. He led the chorus singing "Chee Lai!" on the UCR "China, March On" radio broadcast on CBS on March 24, 1941. Two days later, they reenacted the song at the UCR First Aid China Dinner in New York City, which aimed to raise $5 million. Among the 2,000 famous American and Chinese attendees were Pearl S. Buck; Wendell Willkie; Hu Shi, the Chinese ambassador to the United States; Yu Tsune-chi (Yu Junjie), consul general in New York City; and aviatrix and actress Ya-ching Lee (formerly Li Dandan). Along with the notables' speeches from their dinner tables, a performance by Liu and the chorus was broadcast across the United States. A Chinese American girl student choir entertained the guests with mass singing. Facilitated by Liu, numerous glamorous photographs of the event graced pages of the *Young Companion Pictorial*. Liu and the chorus performed at the Brooklyn Museum and in Central Park in the autumn of 1943. The following year, they joined African Americans including the Hall Johnson Choir, pianists Mary Lou Williams and Teddy Wilson, singer Aubrey Pankey (Liu would help to arrange his 1955 concert in Shanghai), dancer Pearl Primus, and activist Max Yergan to celebrate "I Am an American Day," a folk festival sponsored by the George Washington Carver School in New York City.[65]

Liu interacted with other educated leftist Chinese close to the laundry workers, including Ji Chaoding's family and Ji's fellow underground CCP member Tang Mingzhao. The American-born Tang and his family would return to China in 1950, and Tang would manage W. E. B and Shirley Graham Du Bois's visit in 1959. Ji had shepherded the household of his father, Ji Gongquan (Chi Kung-chuan), then war refugees, across the Pacific to a six-floor walkup apartment at 225 East 10th Street in New York City in 1937. The elder Ji, a Japanese-educated esteemed lawyer and official, and Tang also worked closely with the Chinese Hand Laundry Alliance. With Tang as CCP representative and Ji as editor-in-chief, they launched the influential Chinese-language newspaper *China Daily News* in Chinatown on the third anniversary of Japan launching the full-scale war against China. Echoing Liu's concern over the network of Nationalist spies, Ji Gongquan warned his young son against setting foot in Chinatown. "Too many eyes and ears. . . . And no place for a kid. There are hardly any women and children there. All men, and some of them no good." The Ji family only trusted and socialized with like-minded Chinese such as Tang and Liu.[66]

Meanwhile, Liu was profoundly concerned with issues affecting Chinese Americans as a whole, as indicated by his *Courier* columns addressing the Chinese Exclusion Act. An Edward R. Lewis published a letter supporting the act in the *New York Times* on June 25, 1943. "If this immigration question were a two-way question. . . . Does anyone believe that the Japanese or the Chinese would permit white common laborers, white farm laborers and mechanics to enter their countries?" Liu quickly corrected Lewis's ignorance, pointing out in his June 30 letter to the *Times* that Americans had been living and working freely in China over the past century. He contrasted the racist law with the current war against absurd theories such as Hitler's concept of the "master race." Liu concluded his letter by quoting the newspaper's recent editorial: "The continuance of excluding the Chinese in this country is a matter 'hurting China, helping Japan.'"[67]

LECTURE CIRCUITS FOR THE WHITE MIDDLE CLASS

If his collaboration with ordinary Chinese Americans was less visible nationally, Liu's far more successful work with white Americans was widely trumpeted. Within the first year of his arrival, Liu's debut article for the American public, "The New Year at the Front," appeared in *Asia*, and he had breakout performances on national radio programs, while also delivering talks locally. Accompanying Lin Yutang's piece that introduced him, Liu's article recalled events in a little village in the war zone around Nanjing, Shanghai, and Hangzhou. He described how he sought a method to "mobilize the people" there for "our resistance in a progressive way." On New Year's Day, soldiers and civilians filled the village with elaborate lanterns and scrolls subtly linked to the resistance. At the beginning of the parade, the villagers presented the commander with a homemade national flag. The grocer displayed a huge tortoise lantern, with a strip issuing from the lantern's mouth saying, "I am Wang Ching-wei," a sarcastic curse hurled at the treasonous leader of the collaboration government in Nanjing. Liu's favorite lantern depicted a rotating horse, with figures of Chinese guerrilla fighters and Japanese soldiers cleverly cut out from cardboard and colored paper, the Chinese chasing the Japanese. A dragon lantern led the mile-long procession of soldiers and villagers singing patriotic songs with such vigor that "the gigantic roars almost shook the mountains around us." Liu proclaimed, "Look, the ancient Dragon of the Far East is now soaring and fighting and about to throw all its strength against the aggressor." The article revealed Liu's talent for marrying folk traditions with patriotic themes, organization, and his combined evangelical and nationalist beliefs.[68]

Liu joined Ambassador Hu Shi, in singing "Chee Lai!" and Republican China's national anthem, "San Min Chu I" (Three People's Principles) at China Week in Baltimore, sponsored by various Chinese welfare groups. The *Baltimore Sun* exclaimed, "Little Man, Big Voice, Keep China Singing."[69] Liu began appearing at the Brooklyn Museum and on WQXR, the radio station of the *New York Times*, giving concerts of Chinese martial music, offering music lessons, and playing "a set of Shanghai recordings." He gave historical commentary that "old Chinese music was weak and wailing tunes, but now the music is militant and strong-sounding," a sentiment similarly expressed in Liu's liner notes to the *Chee Lai!* album. He participated in more UCR events.

FIGURE 3.5. Local newspapers often used this image of Liu Liangmo in coverage of his lecture tours. *Green Bay (WI) Press-Gazette*, October 11, 1943.

Liu and J. K. Lee, a Columbia University student of opera and former faculty member at Beijing University, performed for "Chinese Culture Day," which was hosted by Sigmund Spaeth, the "Tune Detective" on WOR-AM, in co-operation with UCR. Liu's performances, marked by easy switching between Mandarin and English, clear diction, and concise presentation, must have further impressed UCR, which offered him a contract. UCR paid Liu a living wage of $45 per week, which rose steadily over the next few years to $75 in 1944, and a high of $80, plus travel expenses, in 1947. This affiliation would help his standing soar among white Americans.[70]

UCR advertised Liu as having "travelled more than 100,000 miles to tell the thrilling story of China's fight to audiences in almost every state."[71] Tracing his tours covered by hundreds of articles in national and local news-papers confirms that this figure was not an exaggeration (fig. 3.5). This wide coverage reinforced Liu's fame among Americans, and some of the papers refreshed their memories of him decades later. At large gatherings, he shared the stage with some of the most powerful names in Sino-American relations. In July 1941 at Madison Square Garden, among his fellow speakers at a mass rally sponsored by the American Council on Soviet Relations were President Roosevelt, Secretary of State Cordell Hull, Vice President Henry Wallace, and labor leader William Green. That October, Liu returned to Madison Square Garden for another major rally before 18,000 people, leading a thousand-person chorus singing "Chee Lai!" to accompany speeches by Willkie, columnist Walter Lippmann, New York City mayor Fiorello La Guardia, UCR Board of Directors chair and New Jersey governor Charles Edison, and Hu Shi.[72] At the above-mentioned Hotel Diplomat rally in 1942, Liu shared the stage with Pearl S. Buck, Roger Baldwin, Pierre Cot, Adam Clayton Powell, Kurt Rosenfield, and Shiro Tahahiza. At a big gathering with representatives from various nations in Woodstock, New York, he urged the world to abolish "hate, mistrust, and suspicion." The FBI observed that Liu often praised the Soviet Union on those occasions. He credited the Communist state with providing 65 percent of foreign aid to China, a point he would reiterate at the American-Soviet Friendship Congress in 1942. The speakers at the Hotel Diplomat rally allegedly reminded the audience that Russia was "a great democracy" and Stalin "a true leader of the people," while attacking the Axis. The FBI learned of the meeting leaflets "advertising Russian films and a Russian restaurant." In addition to the injustice suffered by Chinese seamen, Liu discussed his service with the Chinese army and articulated his "definite knowledge that an undercurrent [antiwar] movement" existed in the Japanese army.[73]

Liu did not always agree with the big names he encountered. Only having recently arrived on U.S. soil, he had derided President Roosevelt to his readers in China for Roosevelt's insufficient efforts to improve domestic employment and for his passivity toward Japan and Germany. Liu had no more confidence in Wendell Willkie, the Republican candidate for president in 1940. In a 1944 statement that was sure to cause controversy, Liu joined the NAACP, the American Civil Liberties Union, and the Socialist Party in decrying the blanket discrimination announced by La Guardia that restricted Japanese Americans from locating in the New York metropolitan area. Liu spoke as an individual but was identified as a speaker for UCR. Newspapers from Japanese American internment camps reported his courageous and reasoned protest, quoting him as saying, "The Chinese people do not hate the Japanese people. We regard the Japanese people [to be] the victims of the same evil under which we are suffering." Sharing Liu's position, Robeson was popular among Japanese Americans and sang several times for them from 1942 to 1944.[74]

More often, Liu promoted China to the white middle class at churches of all denominations, synagogues, schools, colleges, and children's camps, as well as in Rotary Clubs, women's societies, and socialites' homes, raising from $400 to $600 for each occasion. He spoke about mass singing, the

YMCA's relief work, Chinese society and the war, and Sino-American ties, sometimes sang songs, and commented at screenings of war propaganda films. Accounts of his talks describe Liu as always well prepared and pleasant in demeanor. Attendance ranged from 50 people at Rotary Clubs to 900 to 1,500 at high schools. He reached broader audiences by conducting several radio broadcasts in each of the states he visited. UCR also distributed recordings of speeches by Liu, along with ones by Pearl S. Buck and Wendell Willkie.[75]

Initially, Liu toured Manhattan; Brooklyn; Long Island; Bordentown, New Jersey; Peekskill; Rochester; and other towns near New York City, between the summers of 1941 and 1942. At one of his speeches in Brooklyn, Liu said he hoped to help raise $1.75 million in New York City out of UCR's $7 million goal. He returned often to Yonkers and Carmel. The Chinese American writer Helena Kuo (Guo Jingqiu), who would translate Lao She's work during his visit in the 1940s; Lowell Thomas, an NBC radio broadcaster and a writer; and H. R. Ekins, former manager of United Press bureaus in Honolulu, Manila, Shanghai, and Beiping, and editor and publisher of the *Schenectady (NY) Union-Star*, joined Liu as guest speakers. Liu occasionally ventured beyond the New York region to Florida and midwestern cities such as Chicago, Minneapolis, and St. Louis, as well as small towns in Iowa and Indiana.[76]

Between 1942 and 1943, Liu expanded his visits in New York State, ranging as far as Albany, Richfield Springs, Cooperstown, and into western New York, while he continued frequent appearances at local and national conventions in New York City and New Jersey. He joined Anna May Wong and Beatrice Fung-Oye, a Chinese American blues and swing singer, for a China Day Celebration at the Brooklyn Shore Army and Navy Center, kicking off a series of UN festivals for service men to honor nations fighting the Axis. The FBI noted that he spoke at a gathering sponsored by the city's Teacher's Union at the Washington Irving Auditorium, raising a plaque honoring union members serving in the army, and a meeting organized by the Japanese Committee for Democracy to commemorate Pearl Harbor. Liu expanded his radio broadcast in New York City, appearing with Lin Yutang, actor Ronald Young, and a Czechoslovakian quartet at stations such as WNEW, WABC, and WNYC.[77]

As public interest in Liu increased, UCR sent him farther afield. He zigzagged back and forth through Michigan, Ohio, Illinois, Iowa, Indiana, Pennsylvania, Delaware, and North Carolina (including a visit to Duke University), Wisconsin, Virginia, and Rhode Island. At a typical meeting of the People's Forum in York, Pennsylvania, in March 1943, Liu urged that "equal treatment [must] be given all people of the world — Black, white[,] or brown, and the smaller and weaker peoples of Asia, including Korea, Malaya, Dutch East Indies, and India be given the right to govern themselves." He retold anecdotes that Madam Chiang Kai-shek had related to her Chinese audience in New York City and concluded the speech singing "Chee Lai!" Liu sang at a UCR dinner in Philadelphia honoring Y. C. Yang, president of Soochow University and a member of the Rotary Club. The FBI spotted Liu at a reception for a Soviet woman sniper at the Hotel Baltimore.[78]

Despite this surveillance, UCR kept Liu moving at a faster and faster pace. He spoke at the Women's Club in Germantown near Philadelphia on January 11, 1944, and left on an express train for Providence, Rhode Island, to attend an event at the Moses Brown School the following morning. He took another train to the Boston area for talks with students at Milton Academy and St. Mark's School that afternoon, before returning to New York City for more engagements. Liu toured North Carolina for ten days the following month, giving as many as four talks a day. On a typical day as February 26, he began a speech in Smithfield, drove thirty miles to events at schools and clubs in Raleigh for the remainder of the day, and visited three elementary schools the following morning. After his return, UCR dispatched him on a three-day tour to Columbus, Ohio, and South Bend, Indiana, and back to Benton Harbor, Michigan, in April.[79]

Liu spent the rest of the spring and summer of 1944 around the East Coast, visiting Troy, Kingston, Niagara Falls, and Auburn, New York, several times, which suggests receptive audiences and fundraising success. He represented China at a concert, "Times Square — 60 Hours from Anywhere," that presented music, drama, and dance of various nations. He recorded seven songs with the Catskill Folk Festival at Camp Woodland, which are now preserved in the Library of Congress. Liu also traveled to mostly small towns in Pennsylvania, New Jersey, Maryland, Kentucky, and Connecticut. He attended the Maryland Federation of Music Clubs convention in Hagerstown. John V. A. MacMurray, former U.S. minister to China, introduced him at a gathering in Baltimore. In the fall he traveled from Pasadena, Los Angeles, San Francisco, to Berkeley, Salt Lake City and its environs, and Colorado before stopping in Grinnell, Iowa (home of Grinnell College), and other small towns in that state. Liu also found time to visit the Webster Baptist Church in Rochester and lead the Regional Conference of the State Council of Churches in Niagara Falls and Cortland, New York. The winter brought him to Catasauqua and Allentown, Pennsylvania, and Wayne State

University in Detroit. There was no sign that Liu was slowing down in 1945, as he continued to Florida, Mississippi, Virginia, Massachusetts, New York, Iowa, Minnesota, California, Utah, Pennsylvania, and Delaware.[80]

Audiences of various professions and locations across the nation testified to Liu's popularity, as UCR publicity materials recorded. Representative testimonials include the following: "Enlightening and very timely" (Maj. Hugh L. Roberts, Oriental Officer, U.S. Army, Grand Central Palace, New York City); "Mr. Liu did an excellent job and universally his work was received with enthusiasm. Definite words of appreciation and praise came following each presentation. I feel quite confident that United China Relief has received a tremendous boost" (James C. Vynalek, Community and War Fund of Metropolitan Chicago); "We consider you as the most outstanding speaker yet presented in six years of brilliant programs offered by the National Farm Institute" (Kirk Fox, National Farm Institute, Des Moines, Iowa); "I don't know when I have heard a more refreshing or appealing talk" (Louis D. Newton, *Atlanta Constitution*); "Scholarly, logical, eloquent, sincere, impassioned and tremendously effective" (Leonard P. Stewart, Walnut Hills High School, Cincinnati, Ohio); "He lived up to the high expectations which we had entertained for his return visit" (John Mayher, Phillips Exeter Academy, Exeter, New Hampshire).[81] Liu's YMCA background and Baptist theology created powerful organizational and spiritual connections with his white Christian audiences. No other Chinese could match his vast and deep experience with American leaders and private citizens across broad spectrums of race, class, and gender through talks, song festivals, dinner conversation, and worship.

Liu seemed to enjoy a particular rapport with female audiences. He had always taken pride in putting women at ease by treating them as equals. Influenced by his own strong wife, Chen Weijiang, and by Liu Wang Liming, the American-educated wife of Liu Zhan'en and a pioneering celebrity feminist and suffragist, Liu paid close attention to modern gender issues. He frequently contributed to leading women's magazines, including the biweekly *Woman's Voice* published by Liu Wang Liming in the 1930s. Most of these writings and translations ventured into contemporary controversies of sex, love, and marriage such as modern husbandhood. Liu commented on the love triangles that led to the suicide of the famous actress Ruan Lingyu and another murder case that dominated the tabloids in Shanghai, blaming such tragedies on loose sexual morality. Sympathetic to the female victims, Liu advocated mutual respect, self-control, and caution with respect to extramarital physical intimacy, to which both men and women readers responded eagerly, debating the meaning of gender equality. In addition to coauthoring some of these articles, Chen Weijiang, then a journalist for *Woman's Voice*, also wrote similar sociological pieces on her own. With Japan's invasion intensifying, the couple's articles shifted to women's role in the resistance. Criticizing the Three K (die Küche, die Kirche, die Kinder) movement in Nazi Germany, Chen penned and translated a series of articles and poems, including Rudyard Kipling's poem "If—," to encourage women to empower themselves for political and military roles.[82]

Liu and Chen had reached across the Pacific to the first lady of the United States to seek inspiration for Chinese women. They translated Eleanor Roosevelt's book *It's Up to the Women* into Chinese. An advertisement boasted that the book was "a treasure box of wisdom for modern women and a must-read for female students."[83] Now Liu strove to link the concerns of white American women with their Chinese counterparts. For instance, discussing the new Chinese fashion trend stressing athletic beauty, Liu voiced support for the movement among American women to forego silk stockings and boycott Japanese goods generally. At Hunter College in 1941, he declared, "American women will be glad to lose silk stockings, like Chinese beauties have done for years, going around barelegged, and the men will appreciate it too."[84]

Such outward presentation hid Liu's struggles during this most tumultuous decade in the Asia-Pacific region, since his popularity did not allow him to navigate the murky political and ideological waters any less cautiously. Acutely aware of suspicions triggered by Liu's association with the military in China, UCR strove to reframe it. Its 1944 promotion flyer, "Former Chinese Army Morale Officer," re-narrated Liu's work with Chinese civilians and soldiers in Changsha and the guerrilla areas. UCR's copy exaggerated reality, claiming that "Generalissimo Chiang Kai-shek recognized the value of Liu's work and ordered him to bolster the army's fighting morale by teaching them to sing" and outlining his advanced education credentials in both China and the United States. Accordingly, local media, which tended to repeat such boilerplate, frequently (and erroneously) called him "Dr." and a direct underling of Chiang. The flyer also cited Madam Sun Yat-sen's liner notes to the album *Chee Lai!* as evidence of Liu's accomplishments.[85]

Despite these protective UCR gestures, it seemed that Liu's lectures on the situation in China and his associates at rallies were coming under closer scrutiny than his activities with African American and Chinese American audiences. When every meeting took on political importance, minor missteps treading the fine political line could lead to controversies. At one of his earlier talks in Yonkers, New York, Liu announced that the Japanese army had placed a $5,000 bounty on his life.[86] The FBI alleged that Liu stated at a gathering in New York City that he was a political worker in China, declaring, "I am glad I am a Communist and an antifascist," a public affirmation of Communist Party membership that the cautious Liu would never have made at this time. In 1944, when Liu's speech schedule was the most intense, a student journalist at Rutgers University reported that Liu had made a number of disparaging remarks about the Nationalist government at a celebration of China's National Day. To the U.S. government, UCR, and the major media, Chiang's was the legitimate government of China. The controversy exploded when the *New York Times, New York Post,* and even some local newspapers picked up the story, creating a potentially dangerous situation for Liu. Asked by Garside for clarification, Liu wrote back regretting any "embarrassment" for UCR and contending that the articles were distortions. Explaining that his speech was extemporaneous and that he thus had no notes for it, Liu contended that he did not favor or disfavor any political group but sought a democratic and unified China, a stance with which he expected his American sponsors would concur. He emphasized that his hosts at Rutgers had received his speech warmly and, apparently, he had made many friends for China that night.[87]

Liu had personal reasons to clear up any suspicions stemming from his Rutgers speech. Just before that furor, Liu had appealed to UCR to sponsor his wife and their son to leave China for the United States. When Liu left for the battlefield following the outbreak of full-scale war, his family, including his parents, had remained at House 105, Lane 1462, Avenue Edward VII, in a modest area in Shanghai also called Yangjingbang. His wife worked as an editorial secretary of the YWCA and translated *Toward a World Christian Fellowship* by Kenneth Scott Latourette, an American historian of East Asia and world Christianity, into Chinese for extra income. Reflecting her leftist politics, Chen had also translated *Red Bread: Collectivization in a Russian Village* by Maurice Hindus and articles on the complicated geopolitics that the Soviet Union faced. She gave birth to their son Kang (Kong, meaning "resistance") on November 16, 1937, amid Japan's full-scale attacks on Shanghai and Nanjing.[88] After moving her family to the International Settlement, Chen joined a group of women, including Xu Guangping, in making gas masks and uniforms for the Chinese army, and she planned clandestine political activities under the guise of social occasions. In an affidavit for the Chester YMCA on August 2, 1941, Liu stated that Chen Weijiang, then unemployed, was experiencing wartime hardships caused by food profiteering. He also claimed as a dependent his brother, who was receiving $30 weekly from him through the YMCA. The impossible situation in Shanghai following the Japanese attack on Pearl Harbor forced Chen and four other women to take their children on a three-month walk to Chongqing, with a wheelbarrow but little food. They slept on the ground. Unaware of Liu's whereabouts, Chen then traveled to Xi'an searching for him. She returned to Chongqing to edit *Woman's New Life*, a publication of the New Life Movement led by Madam Chiang, and taught history and Chinese language at a girl's high school.[89]

Liu explained to one of the UCR officers that his wife could only get permission to leave if a U.S. organization invited her. Liu asked UCR to extend such an invitation, noting that his wife would assume the travel expenses. UCR agreed, enabling Chen and Kong to join Liu in early 1945. Upon their arrival in the United States, mother and son immediately visited Consul General Yu Tsune-chi, attending a small ceremony to present two scrolls of appreciation to the Flying Tigers, a group of American volunteers in the Chinese air force. The media portrayed how Kong, perched on the lap of a Flying Tigers general, discussed their time back in Chongqing as "two old China Hands."[90] UCR soon hired Chen as a lecturer at $40 per week. Her first talks were auspicious. She appeared with Eleanor Roosevelt in a series of UCR lectures at Vassar College and several high schools in the Poughkeepsie, New York, area. After accompanying her husband on some of his speaking and performance trips, Chen began to tour New York, New Jersey, and Pennsylvania on her own in late 1945. She described to her audiences her dramatic experiences in Shanghai and Chongqing and, at a women's club, stressed that "this is a man's world, and women must fight for their rights."[91]

Serious problems lay ahead for the Lius, resulting largely from the fast-shifting sands of transpacific politics. As the relationship between the Nationalists and Communists in China worsened at the close of World War II, the Marxist left among Chinese Americans withdrew its active support for UCR, the Lius' employer. Meanwhile, UCR had to mind new trends in U.S. domestic politics, which had swung to the right. The House Un-American Activities Committee became a full-time standing congressional committee in 1944 and was determined to ferret out any left-wingers, American or foreign. While Nationalist China was clearly an ally of the United States, such ties did not extend to Chinese Communists.

In this context, Liu's comments on the situation in China came under closer scrutiny. His harsh criticism of the Nationalists in his *Pittsburgh Courier* columns brought him political difficulties. Around the same time as the Rutgers incident, the FBI surveillance finally surfaced — its New York office contacted UCR director Bettis Garside three times between March 1944 and February 1945. In the first interview, Garside provided comprehensive information on Liu that was available in UCR records, including his address and phone number. Garside emphasized that UCR "has a high regard for the ability and performance of Liu." "Given an opportunity to elaborate on possible Communist tendencies of Liu" by the FBI agents, Garside coolly stated, "Liu did not refuse a lecture before any group, Communist dominated or otherwise," since "the primary purpose of . . . UCR was to obtain aid for China rather than to engage in any political activity." He assured the FBI that Liu had been "warned to be very careful not to bring up any controversial matter when lecturing and singing before any organization." Garside admitted that he had received several complaints from scattered sources on the topics of Liu's lectures and songs, but he did not elaborate on the nature of the complaints. When the FBI returned the third time, Garside "could furnish no information reflecting that Liu belonged to or was sympathetic to any Communist organizations." He stated that, although "Liu's duties were to address groups on the problems of China, which in itself is a difficult assignment in view of the political ramifications in that country," he had been "very successful in avoiding political questions in his speeches." Garside noted that UCR's investigation had cleared Liu in the Rutgers incident; it was someone in the audience, not Liu, who remarked during the question and answer session that "China too has its concentration camps." UCR considered Liu "a sincere patriot of China" who was "anxious" to return and resume his work with the YMCA there.[92]

Confronted by the accusations of Communist Party membership, even though he was defended by UCR, the stung and anxious Liu penned a letter to Garside from his hotel room in Washington, D.C., dated October 22, 1944. In it, he declared, "I am not a member of the Chinese Communist Party. I belong to no political party. I am a Christian. I sincerely believe in the Fatherhood of God and the Brotherhood of Man." He hoped that democracy close to Christian principles would take shape in the government of China and contribute to a positive Sino-American relationship. Liu's statement, ringing with sincerity, convinced the UCR leadership that he was "vigorously opposed to the ideology and political organization of Communism," an appraisal that would protect him in the future. Liu did not seem to be duplicitous. For instance, in 1943, the heartfelt practical guidance he drafted for new missionaries to China testified to his devotion as a Christian. Though sympathetic to Communist Party goals, as long as they helped create a strong, independent China, Liu operated on the fault lines between U.S. and Chinese politics.[93]

There are few indications that the FBI accusations hurt Liu with UCR. Around the time of his third FBI interview, Garside joined Liu in singing "Chinese Soldiers' Song" on WNYC. Memos from Edward Ballin, who handled Liu's travel schedule, indicate a constant stream of speeches in New York City, upstate New York, New Jersey, and Pennsylvania even after the war. Liu remained forthright about his concerns with Sino-American relations, urging the United States to withdraw its troops from China's civil war, and China's future in building a democracy. Liu was also requested to critique American democracy and the weaknesses in American society. He was encouraged to attend events for families. Sponsors of a children's party at the New York Public Library asked Liu to bring his son to a "Book Treasures" event. Liu and his wife spoke at the National Doll and Toy Collectors Club at the Hotel Pennsylvania.[94] Liu continued to popularize Chinese music, though his concerts now elicited different commentary. In May 1946, he appeared at the second "Hootenanny" presented by the People's Songs Inc. at Town Hall in New York City. Its program was composed of American and Australian military songs, African American spirituals, work songs, blues, and Scottish, Irish, Jewish, and Chinese folk melodies devoted to freedom. Participating with Liu were Pete Seeger, Josh White, and several left-wing folk singers. Such associations, considered innocent during the war, now troubled Liu's status. He then instructed on mass singing at Syracuse University.[95]

As U.S. politics veered more sharply to the right, UCR, attentive to accusations that Liu's politics were communist, decided to monitor his activities. In 1946, the right-wing *New York World-Telegram* castigated an organization called Win the Peace that had criticized the U.S. government's growing animosity toward the Soviet Union.[96] When the Win the Peace Committee of the Lower East Side announced that Liu would speak on "China's Problems Today" at Corlear's Hook Stadium in New York City, UCR sent an undercover agent named Eric J. Cudd to monitor his speech. Cudd submitted a report of the rally along with his comments on a list of the national Win the Peace groups. He dismissed one large group, labeled as "Reds and Pinks," that included Robeson, Benjamin Davis Jr., Canada Lee, Congress of Industrial Organizations executive secretary Saul Mills, and author Carl Van Doren, as "window dressing." According to Cudd, the rally initially attracted about 1,500 people, before a heavy rain drove away all but 100, who huddled under a tent. Hiding in the bleachers, Cudd sat through speakers from the American Labor and Communist Parties and the local congressman, before Liu's one-minute, relatively anodyne comment followed by singing "Chee Lai!" But he did say that it was "up to the American people to stop the war in China, for it is the embryonic beginning of the Third World War." Then, unannounced in the program, Chen Weijiang came to the podium and spoke words far more radical than her husband's. She claimed that "reactionaries in China started the civil war—which they have no chance of winning—with the avowed purpose of crushing the Communists." She blasted that U.S. "troops helped transport Nationalist troops to the fighting zones. . . . American grenades were used to kill Chinese people." She challenged the American people to stop their government's actions, in a test of democracy. Cudd submitted his report to a UCR staff member, who noted that neither Liu nor Chen was identified as "representing . . . UCR" and forwarded the document to Garside.[97]

Garside responded with a policy memo two months later, lauding Liu for his "remarkably fine" job explaining China to Americans over the last five years. He stressed the necessity to protect both Liu and UCR by avoiding situations in which "he may lay himself and the organization open to attack for publicly taking a left-wing position." Garside acknowledged the serious gap in UCR guidelines about what speakers could say at partisan meetings but insisted that UCR had been carefully planning not only Liu's itinerary but also his speech topics.[98] Garside claimed that left-wing groups often sought to affiliate with UCR but were invariably rebuffed by its nonpartisan nature. However, he observed that American journalists in China, returned soldiers, and recent visitors like Liu tend to be more critical of the Nationalist government. Thus, while UCR could not take a side in the Chinese civil war, avoiding left-wing commentators would severely limit its speakers, alienate an important constituency, and open it to charges of being a tool of the Chinese government's propaganda agency. Referring to past incidents in which Liu had been too critical of the Nationalist government, Garside defended him by noting that Consul General Yu Tsune-chi had "a friendly talk with him" and cleared up matters satisfactorily. Thus, Garside concluded that Liu's beliefs had been fully vetted several years before and UCR had decided he was anticommunist. As for Chen, Garside wrote, she was kept off political subjects, "so her view in these matters has not been much of a factor." With that, he dropped the matter.[99]

Maintaining legal immigrant status, like seeking financial support, posed the ultimate test for Chinese sojourners in the United States like Liu. Tracing

Liu's immigration footprints, which was not always straightforward due to confusion over the romanization of his name and his birth date, was the FBI's top concern. The Bureau searched tirelessly for any lapse in his legal status with various INS offices throughout his stay. In J. Edgar Hoover's initial request to investigate Liu thoroughly, he focused on the circumstances of his entry and stay. Soon, the FBI learned of his 1936 visit and the circumstances of his 1940 entry. Its second communication with Garside in the fall of 1944 focused exclusively on Liu's immigration status. The UCR director pledged complete ignorance of Liu's "naturalization," but he guaranteed that Liu had "complied with all requirements." While immigration struggles had disastrous consequences for Sylvia Si-lan Chen, as we will see in the next chapter, Liu was fortunate to maintain his legal status. Sponsored by Crozer, his initial visa had been extended to August 6, 1943. Working with UCR brought Liu personal support beyond his family's admission to the United States. On July 3, the INS office in Philadelphia transformed his student visa to visitor status, contingent on his employment with UCR and valid for a year. The INS's New York office later extended this visa for another year.[100]

When further extensions became less than routine at the end of the war, Liu maintained a powerful ally in Bettis A. Garside. Writing to Joseph Spengler, chief of the Entry and Departure Section of the Justice Department and INS between late 1945 and early 1946, Garside praised Liu for providing "extremely valuable service both to China and to America as an interpreter to the American people of present day China" on behalf of UCR. Garside's lobbying on behalf of Liu proved successful. After the INS reviewed Liu's status and extended his visa to August 2, 1946, Liu applied to go back to China with an option to return. The agency extended his visa to March 1 and again to October 1947, allowing time for Liu to obtain a "valid passport" from China to replace the one-page student certificate he had been using as his identity card.[101]

According to the regulations of China's Ministries of Education and Finance, students who studied subjects not of immediate use to war needs for three or more years with study permits "should at once return to China. No remittance permit will be granted them in case of further delay on their part."[102] Thus, obtaining a passport was not simply a routine process for Liu. To push the Chinese government to issue one, Garside had UCR Board of Directors chair Charles Edison write P. H. Chang, the Chinese consul general in Los Angeles. Edison called Liu a patriot, praised his work with "all age-groups, children, young people, adults," and affirmed UCR's need for his further services. Liu wrote happily a letter of appreciation to Garside, asking for a copy of Edison's letter and highlighted his personal connection with UCR. Liu mentioned that his wife's grandfather, Admiral C. P. Sah (Sa Zhenbing), a naval officer who fought in the first Sino-Japanese War, knew the Luce family. He provided the eighty-nine-year-old Sah's address in Fuzhou so the old acquaintances could get in touch. Garside himself sent Chang a letter detailing Liu's work with UCR to back up Edison's request for help. In responses to Edison and Garside, Chang stated that he had assigned his deputy, T. J. Liu, to take care of Liu immediately.[103] The process did not seem to go smoothly. According to Liu's grandson, as a maneuver against the INS's attempt to deport the family following the cancellation of their passports by the Nationalist government, Tang Mingzhao advised the Lius to have another child. Kangjian (whose name meant "resistance" and "reconstruction"), was born on April 9, 1947, an instant U.S. citizen, thus allowing the parents residency as caretakers.[104]

Despite these efforts, Liu's career with UCR ultimately ended for mundane reasons. On January 2, 1948, Garside wrote that the agency could no longer fund his speeches due to a drastic drop in income during the previous year. He offered to pay Liu's salary to the end of the month and invited him to discuss the severance in person. Garside was apologetic about laying off his top Chinese speaker but argued that the organization was being reduced to a skeleton force for the foreseeable future. Liu had spoken on contemporary China and the world for the Citizens Committee of Upper West Side at the Hotel Beacon, Flatbush-Topkins Congregational Church in New York City, the Pennsylvania College for Women, and the Bellefield Presbyterian Church in Pittsburgh, and had traveled to Council Bluffs, Iowa; Cincinnati, Ohio; St. Paul, Minnesota; and Utah in 1947. In Salt Lake City, he warned that Winston Churchill's "Iron Curtain" speech would harm the chance for the coalition government to succeed in China. He returned to WEVD to speak for *U.N. Evening.* He gave talks at several colleges for the World Student Service Fund between February and May 1949 to raise funds for Chinese and other distressed students, but his speaking career in the United States appeared to be over.[105]

BACK TO THE PEOPLE'S REPUBLIC OF CHINA

Facing the threat of deportation, and invited to attend the First National People's Political Consultative Conference (NPPCC) and the Grand Opening of the PRC by Zhou Enlai, Liu Liangmo and his family departed New York City for China on August 1, 1949. Sharing the rostrum at Tian'anmen

Square with the core of the CCP, Liu witnessed Mao Zedong announcing the birth of the PRC two months later.[106]

Liu's return to China was auspicious. The adoption of "March of the Volunteers" as national anthem and his close relationship with Paul Robeson gave him immense stature. He regarded the Communist victory as an accomplishment of the anti-Japanese and civil wars by countless Chinese youth singing, "Arise, Ye Who Refuse to Be Bond Slaves!," the opening lines of "March of the Volunteers."[107] Liu's departure did not mean his FBI files closed. Learning that Liu had flew to Hong Kong and then returned to ~Flown~ Shanghai, the Bureau was mystified at how he had slipped away without a required INS permit to depart. After carefully confirming that he was the same person who had toured the United States over the past decade, the FBI updated its files on Liu, continuously watching his whereabouts, particularly trips abroad, and frequently linking his activities to those of Robeson.[108]

With the political agility that he had demonstrated in navigating the slippery transpacific political and ideological terrain, Liu was able to balance his Christianity with influence at the highest levels of the PRC government and survive decades of social and political upheaval. He functioned as a high-ranking and prolific cultural official representing the religious circles. Serving as chief of staff of the China National Y and head of its Service Division for decades, Liu was the fourth-leading figure of the religious circles, beneath only Wu Yaozong, Liu's old YMCA colleague and now head of the Y's Publishing Division, and leaders of Buddhism and Islam. In that capacity, Liu remained active in various democratic parties and the NPPCC. In early 1949, before the establishment of the PRC and while Liu was still in the United States, he had been elected an alternate member of the National Democratic Youth League, and he became its executive member in 1958. He alternatively served as an alternate member, executive member, and consultant of the national committees of the China Democratic League from 1949 until his death in 1988. During the same period, following his membership of the preparatory committee for organizing the central government, Liu served as an executive committee member of the third and a standing committee member of the fourth, fifth, and sixth NPPCC. He was also a vice chair of the Shanghai Municipal People's Political Consultative Conference in 1981 and 1983.[109]

Journalism remained key to Liu's visibility and influence. The *People's Daily* featured his writing ninety-six times from 1950 to 1984, twice carrying his lengthy speeches in full, which illustrated how highly the top leadership of the PRC regarded his efforts in official capacities. He churned out numerous articles for the nation's leading newspapers, including the *People's Daily*, *Guangming Daily*, and the *Liberation Daily* published by the Shanghai municipal government. He penned forty-six articles in the high-profile Christian magazine *Heavenly Wind* from 1959 to 1961. Madam Chiang Kai-shek and the U.S. ambassador to China, John Leighton Stuart, had contributed to the magazine soon after it was founded in 1947. Wu Yaozong and Liu quickly transformed it into a powerful tool to bring Christianity under the CCP's heel.[110] At the birth of the PRC, Liu poured out his enthusiasm for the new regime by writing or editing four books for the series "Study in the New Time," released by the National Y Publishing House in 1950. They were manuals for studying new key political concepts such as new democracy, the united front, the NPPCC provisional constitution and laws on organizing the central government, and, most important, Mao Zedong Thought, a phrase that Liu helped to coin.[111]

While involvement in China's civil war and the Korean War transformed the United States from China's ally to its worst enemy, Liu was valued as a credible expert commentator with profound connections to the American soul who could help redefine the narrative, while enhancing the PRC's awareness of African Americans. Immediately upon returning, barely recovered from jet lag, Liu attended a seminar for social workers to discuss the U.S. State Department white paper "United States Relations with China" and meetings of Beiping and Tianjin press and religious representatives of the NPPCC between August and September 1949. He announced being "extremely happy to see the motherland's pending liberation, and the sun of freedom will shine soon." Liu testified that U.S. imperialism, oppressor of progressive Christians and laboring people, was just a paper tiger facing a looming catastrophic economic depression.[112]

While China was officially closing off to the West, Liu published nine essays in *Guangming Daily*, *Liberation Daily*, and *World Affairs*, published by the Ministry of Foreign Affairs, between September 7 and October 21, 1949, to offer his firsthand insights on the United States. The National Y Publishing House immediately anthologized the essays as *My Impression of the United States* in early 1950. *China Daily News* in New York City's Chinatown, whose coverage and tone now were not far from the official newspapers in the PRC, featured these pieces in the summer to inform overseas Chinese. Consistent with the government narrative dividing the United States into its good and evil components, in these widely circulated pieces, Liu continued the race-based approaches that his work in the United States had adopted. Writing of white America, he had harsh words for the "ruling imperialists,"

China's real enemy, while he hailed the power of U.S. "progressive forces." He reserved sympathy for Chinese Americans and African Americans, and had fond words particularly for Paul Robeson.

Liu waxed optimistic about American revolutionary traditions as represented by Thomas Jefferson, Abraham Lincoln, and Thomas Paine. He traced their lineage up to the contemporary "progressive forces" represented by the Progressive Party of "bourgeois and petit bourgeois" and the Communist Party USA and the Labor Party of "proletarians." Liu believed that Harry S. Truman had stolen the 1948 presidential election from Henry Wallace by hijacking the popular leftist platforms, even though Wallace's Progressive Party played a negligible role in the general election. The FBI noted that the New China News Agency in Hong Kong quoted Liu as condemning Truman for "blasphemous utterances." Liu took part in the official mourning for a beloved American radical figure, Agnes Smedley. Along with Mao Dun, Emi Sao, and Ding Ling, Liu helped to organize her funeral and contributed to a memorial anthology.[113]

Liu repeated the analogy linking "fascist America" to "a setting sun," doomed to imminent economic collapse, in contrast to "the New China" as "a rising sun," a metaphor employed by both W. E. B. Du Bois and Mao Zedong in their articulation of the world order. Echoing Du Bois and Robeson, Liu believed the economic blockade against the Soviet Union, Eastern Europe, and China harmed the U.S. economy. He detailed the anticommunist hysteria and corruption of the House Un-American Activities Committee led by imperialist "mad men." Liu illustrated how the "monopoly capitalists" terrorized "the American people" with anticommunist lies and manipulated them through the powerful media, citing the case of a protest on September 4, 1949. Nineteen organizations of Chinese Americans in New York City met at Columbia University's Teachers College to protest Chiang Kai-shek's use of U.S. planes to bomb civilians in Shanghai. Organizers of the meeting distributed a letter of protest to the U.S. government and various news agencies. To Liu's chagrin, the media remained silent about the atrocities in Shanghai and instead enthusiastically promoted the story of a U.S. veteran's family adopting an orphan girl from Guangzhou. All the movie theaters in New York City included that story in their news reels. Liu commented that such "skilled propaganda" left Americans puzzled at China's hatred of U.S. imperialists.[114]

Such controversies quickly set Liu at odds with the Chinese American community. Liu noted that ten New York City restaurateurs originally from Guangdong Province joined the U.S. media's celebration of the adoption of the Guangzhou orphan by the veteran's family, throwing a huge banquet, and presenting a banner of gratitude. He attributed the complex political situation among "our overseas Chinese compatriots" to a "very few hooligans identifying with the American and Chiang governments," the narrow attachment to native places, and vulnerability to media manipulation. Highlighting the "insults" suffered by overseas Chinese, Liu disputed the opening statement in the 1949 U.S. State Department white paper on China that the United States had always been a friend of China. He vividly portrayed the harsh treatment of Chinese immigrants under the Chinese Exclusion Act, recounting his own ordeal at Angel Island in 1936 and how the INS, "like hooligans," extorted Chinese. He condemned restrictions against Chinese female immigrants as "the most inhuman part" of the act, reporting that he had seen few women or children in the Chinatowns of New York City and San Francisco until recently. Liu noted with indignation that segregation in housing forced a Chinese friend, then a professor at the University of Southern California, to live in a ghetto.[115]

With Liu's previous efforts speaking to white Americans having lost their value, he foregrounded the revolutionary credentials and intellectual capacity of African Americans. Giving his Chinese readers a strong sense of racial antagonism in the United States, Liu connected anti-Chinese bias with discrimination against African Americans. He recalled how in Wallace's presidential campaign, a white senator was arrested for entering a gathering at a Black church, and he detailed similar racial segregation against Blacks that he witnessed in the South. He noted that job discrimination restricted Black women to work as domestic servants and men to menial labor, as exemplified by college graduates serving as porters at train stations in New York City. He was appalled that Black veterans, who had contributed to the antiracist war and now demanded domestic democracy and freedom, faced a revived KKK, kidnapping, and lynching. Introducing racial solidarity into Chinese politics, Liu contended that, as fellow oppressed, African Americans, an integral element of their country's revolutionary force, were eager to learn about Chinese people's struggles for democracy and liberation. He elaborated how his collaboration with the *Pittsburgh Courier* met such needs. To counter Chinese prejudice viewing Blacks as racially inferior, Liu pioneered in hailing the greatness and achievement of African Americans. In his *Pittsburgh Courier* columns, Liu had lauded poet Margaret Walker, effusively credited Marian Anderson and Robeson for their contributions to China relief, and referred to Frederick Douglass and George Washington Carver as role models for young Chinese. He had stated that the Chinese people had great empathy for African Americans and proudly announced that Lee Te-Chi had translated Richard Wright's best-selling novel *Native Son* into Chinese. Now, he introduced Douglass and Carver to Chinese readers, arranged for the translation of the scientist's biography by Shirley Graham Du Bois, and declared that the best American dancers and athletes were Black. He condemned the "shameless American rulers" for their propaganda that "Blacks are the most stupid race!"[116]

Liu focused much of his praise on Robeson. He wrote a major article lauding the "People's Singer" as being esteemed by the whole world, months before the establishment of the PRC and Eslanda Robeson's visit there, and helped alter the narrative on the singer within China from that of an exotic entertainer to a heroic role model for Chinese citizens. Liu recounted his first meeting with Robeson and their subsequent recording of "Chee Lai!" with affection. Linking the Peekskill riots to "Chiang's hooligan tricks," he proclaimed Robeson to be "the most courageous and progressive warrior in the United States." He helped publish the Chinese translation of Shirley Graham Du Bois's biography of Robeson and added his article as an appendix. In this and his many ensuing publications on Robeson over the next decade, Liu reiterated the singer's greatness in using his voice to struggle for Black and other oppressed people around the world against U.S. imperialism. Liu continued to remind the Chinese of Robeson's outstretched hands at the peak of the Cold War, organized the singer's sixtieth birthday celebration, and welcomed W. E. B. and Shirley Graham Du Bois on their own accounts and as friends of Robeson in 1959.[117]

Liu put his heart into advocating for China's interests in the Korean War. With the nuclear bomb assuming enormous psychological power, he led religious circles in issuing public statements condemning the United States for refusing to ban this weapon of mass destruction.[118] With CCP approval, Liu joined Du Bois and Robeson in the international peace movement against the war. Representing the East China and Shanghai branch of the China Peace Council, he attended the 1950 Second World Peace Congress in Warsaw, from which the *People's Daily* prominently noted Robeson's absence. Liu made speeches on the "glorious achievements" of the congress at the branch's welcome-home gathering, the Beijing YMCA, Ginling University, and a meeting in Shanghai to commemorate the February 29 Uprising against Chiang in Taiwan. These occasions sought to raise funds and materials and to inspire letters from the masses in support of China's volunteer army. Echoing his efforts to serve the military during the war of resistance, Liu tirelessly promoted movies and writing that saluted the volunteer army as the "Most Lovable People." Some of these materials were later included in secondary school textbooks. Liu attended the World Peace Congress and the Asia and Pacific Rim Peace Conference in 1952, as well as the Australian Assembly of Peace in Sydney in 1956, as the FBI noted in its final report on Liu. He remained a leader of the China Peace Council until 1965.[119]

Much of Liu's energy was also directed toward remaking China's Christianity, which was "caught in severe ideological clashes between Christianity associated with declining capitalism and the world socialist revolution driven by Marxist materialism," as Wu Yaozong contended in his introduction to Liu's book *My Impression of the United States*. For the survival of Christianity in China, Liu focused his efforts on the Three-Self Reform Movement, a state-controlled mass campaign designed to sever Protestant churches in China from Western missionary efforts and to bring them into line with party ideology. The party could thus claim inclusiveness while constructing a loyal and obedient theology.[120]

In July 1950, Liu and Wu led forty prominent religious figures in issuing a statement, "Ways for Chinese Christians to Contribute to Constructing the New China," calling on Christians and churches around the nation to cut ties with foreign imperialists and enforce the Three-Self Reform Movement. The statement was widely circulated in newspapers across China, capped by an approving editorial, "The Patriotic Movement of Christian Figures," in the *People's Daily*. During the Korean War, the U.S. government declared it would take over public and private Chinese properties in the United States, halt currency exchange, and eliminate U.S. stipends for institutes in China. The Chinese government immediately retaliated with similar measures, determined to "settle issues with cultural, educational, charity, and religious organizations receiving American stipends." Liu joined other religious leaders in hammering out another statement on January 3, 1951, warmly supporting such official moves, including the government takeover of church assets.[121]

Liu strove to justify the Three-Self Reform Movement by editing a book illustrating how Christianity had served as a cultural tool for U.S. imperialists to invade China. In his review of an exhibition on this theme in Ginling University, he condemned how U.S. professors such as John Lossing Buck, former husband of Pearl S. Buck, had helped their government to survey and rob silver from China and guided the U.S. Air Force in photographing China's terrain. Liu disapproved of the fact that all previous documents at Ginling, a missionary school, were in English, although a similar arrangement at his alma mater, the University of Shanghai, had enabled his fluency in English. He castigated the "colonial curriculum" at Ginling, whose history textbooks included "the British-American propagandist [Rudyard] Kipling's 'white man's burden' theme, which designated whites to 'civilize' such 'backward' nations as China and India." Another English-language textbook featured "American fascist Charles Lindbergh's famous transatlantic flight," and domestic economy courses focused on training female students to "Americanize their marital life."[122]

Liu's actions quickly brought him to greater prominence. He was appointed to the Religious Bureau inside the Culture and Education Division of the central government and to the twenty-five-member China Christian "Resisting America and Supporting Korea" Three-Self Reform Movement Committee. Liu consolidated his demands for religious "reform" by drafting "The Joint Statement by Various Christian Churches and Groups in China," which the *People's Daily* printed in full on April 25, 1951. It called on Christians to fully support the central government's decision for the Three-Self Reform Movement, actively participate in "resisting America and supporting Korea," and support other contemporary official policies such as land reform and suppressing the counterrevolutionaries.[123] Liu's numerous articles in *Heavenly Wind* reinforced the above points and urged churches to link Christianity with patriotism, as exemplified by Jesus himself. Resorting to a familiar tool, Liu composed "Song of the Three-Self Reform Movement," whose lyrics included, "Arise! Christians across China! Churches in China, hurry, study hard."[124]

Liu began to flush out resisters ruthlessly. Along with Wu Yaozong and other prominent Christian leaders, he published articles in the *People's Daily* and *Liberation Daily* between March and April 1951 to "reveal crimes of bad elements among Christians" and to condemn a U.S. agent, Gu Ren'en. Joseph Tse-Hei Lee has ably demonstrated how Liu used psychological intimidation to tame Christian leaders. He orchestrated meetings at which members, using rehearsed lines and expressions, denounced Western theologians and missionaries as imperialists and U.S. intelligence agents. He published articles in *Heavenly Wind* to popularize such techniques to run "accusation meetings." Relatives spoke out against the theologians in accusation sessions and publicly humiliated them. Although there was some underground resistance, most people quickly renounced Christianity in favor of communism.[125]

Liu soon escalated his harsh actions, purging those under attack while publishing muscular statements defending every radical political campaign. This somewhat tarnished his legacy. Official condemnation of the so-called Hu Feng counterrevolutionary group in 1955 was a prelude to the antirightist campaign. Liu chimed in vigorously. Reviewing materials about Hu, scholar and writer, and his associates in the *People's Daily*, Liu concluded that this "dangerous wolf in sheep's clothing" and his hangers-on were "American and Chiang spies, counterrevolutionary officials, Trotskyites, and traitors." Liu's own résumé could have made him a perfect target for attack as an "American spy." Probably acutely sensing his own vulnerability, Liu eagerly demonstrated his loyalty. He even called Hu subhuman for referring to his former friend, the late Lu Xun, as a "dead man." He snorted, "Hu Feng elements are fed by the people, clothed by the people, but they dare to 'hate the society.' You demons, we hate you more! We would never allow you to smear our lovely motherland! We people across the nation, who deeply appreciate the government and Chairman Mao, will root out all the sinister ones like you."[126]

Liu loudly beat the drum for the Great Leap Forward. The *People's Daily* carried his long speech made at the third NPPCC on April 6, 1960. He revived the concept of Mao Zedong Thought vigorously, claiming that once it was mastered by the masses, its power could surpass that of the atomic bomb. He exclaimed that technological innovation enabled China to "ride on the back of the dragon to soar in the sky." Liu also offered rare self-criticism to inspire others. He claimed that the training seminar "To Make Bourgeois Individualism Stink," under the auspices of Shanghai Municipal People's Political Consultative Conference, had helped him to discover the disease in his soul: "I overestimated my own role during the war of resistance. . . . After liberation, although I understood the historical trend of socialism replacing capitalism, the demon in me played its tricks when facing concrete issues. I had doubted the feasibility of the Great Leap Forward. When the People's Communes emerged, I had worried about my own housing and the quality of food in the public cafeterias." Liu pledged his determination to serve as a tiny cog in the motherland's great communist cause. He declared that "we bourgeois intellectuals" had to accept the socialist path and the CCP's leadership. Liu concluded his speech, "Long live the CCP! Long live Chairman Mao!" In his writings and at other meetings of the NPPCC, Liu invariably reiterated his full adherence to Mao Zedong Thought, his determination to reform his bourgeois worldview, and his complete support for the Great Leap Forward.[127]

Of course, Liu testified without reservation to the "miracles" achieved during the Great Leap Forward. For a week in 1956, he and Wu Yaozong led a Shanghai delegation on a tour of Anhui, a province historically suffering from "drought nine years out of ten," as portrayed by the song "Fengyang."

Liu eagerly described a collective farm, hydropower from a new dam on the Hui River, and comfortable mines, which contrasted with their dangerous and dirty counterparts in the United States and "the old China," speaking volumes about socialist superiority. The *People's Daily* reported that Liu joined another delegation to Anhui in August 1958 to inspect and confirm a new record output of 16,909.6 *jin* (0.5 kilograms) in dry grains harvested on 1.042 *mu* (less than 0.165 acre) of land on an experimental farm. In 1961, when the famine hit hard, Liu and other members of the Shanghai Municipal People's Political Consultative Conference inspected the Xuxing People's Commune in the nearby Jiading County. Liu again exaggerated the productivity and happiness of the farmers, who enjoyed their household electronics, theaters, and a hospital.

Although Liu's observations echoed those expressed by the Du Boises, they reflected anything but naivete. Obviously aware of food shortages, he underscored that commune members ate the "best-quality rice," which the visitors tasted. Adding to the irony, the *People's Daily* broadcast a piece of advice from Liu and his two colleagues to citizens across the nation: avoid washing rice too hard to save grain. "Put the rice in a basket," they instructed, "remove unwanted material, then soak in water to stir gently. The rice will thus remain nutritious and clean."[128]

While busy riding on the Great Leap Forward wagon, Liu was able to return to his intellectual roots. Along with Guo Moruo, Liu Ningyi, Ji Chaoding, and Bingxin, he led China's delegation to the Afro-Asian Peoples' Solidarity Conference in Cairo in December 1957.[129] During the Du Boises' historic visit in 1959, Liu published a laudatory article about the scholar for *Heavenly Wind*. He quoted the *Soviet Encyclopedia* in referring to Du Bois as the "founder of African American literature." Liu detailed Du Bois's cosmopolitan development, from his studies in Germany in the 1890s to his founding of the *Crisis* in 1913. He summarized Du Bois's contributions to the world peace movement and brave struggles against the U.S. government, highlighting how Du Bois "challenged U.S. invasions of Korea and opposed Chiang Kai-shek's government in Taiwan." Liu concluded that Chinese Christians should salute Du Bois as, like Robeson, a tough and determined fighter for peace and democracy on behalf of people of color in Africa and elsewhere, and celebrate his life and recent ninety-first birthday.[130]

Liu extended his mandate to purify culture by aligning official ideology to music criticism, joining the mass campaign to sweep away the "vulgar and ugly yellow music." While sheet music for "yellow" songs popular since the 1930s, now even including Wang Luobing's romance-oriented folk songs, was trashed, new scores with colorful imagery to promote mass singing of revolutionary songs began flourishing around the nation in 1957. Thousands of choruses mushroomed in army barracks, factories, the countryside, offices, and schools. Liu called for advancing red music through grassroots-level mass singing. The *People's Daily* reported that Liu, "acclaimed veteran leader of mass singing during the war of resistance," led a mass singing concert featuring both amateur and professional singers in Shanghai in 1963. More than 4,000 people sang songs praising the Great Leap Forward and new landscapes in socialist China, in addition to old revolutionary songs.[131] Thus Liu's technique of mass singing for war mobilization was transformed into a powerful propaganda tool for the People's Liberation Army and waves of mass campaigns.

As the cult of personality during the Cultural Revolution transformed Mao Zedong Thought into a household phrase, Liu's 1950 *Manual for Studying Mao Zedong Thought* was reprinted in 1971, as radicalism was in full swing. The devoted Christian who had spent a decade in the United States was nevertheless surviving the political tornado unscathed. That was indeed extraordinary, testimony to his shrewd political maneuvers and skills of self-preservation. He even managed to maintain some visibility. As vice chair of the Returned Overseas Chinese Association, Liu, as reported by the *People's Daily*, condemned the 1966 anti-Chinese movement in Indonesia as part of the anticommunist conspiracy by U.S. imperialists. He also participated into ceremonial events such as seeing off foreign visitors at airports and attending birth and death anniversary commemorations in honor of Sun Yat-sen.[132]

Liu reemerged as a proponent of Christianity in the post-Mao era, recreating a historical missionary connection with the United States. Morris Salz and other former campers from Camp Wo-Chi-Ca visited him in Shanghai in 1977. The old friends recalled summer days in the 1940s and sang "Chee Lai!" together. U.S. newspapers quickly interpreted the reappearance of religious leaders such as Liu in China's state media as a sign of increased religious freedom and a return to normalcy.[133] Liu kept up his commentaries on the importance of music in politics. At the Shanghai Municipal People's Congress and Political Consultative Conference in 1981, he strongly advocated exposing young people in elementary and secondary schools to revolutionary mass singing, so that red songs could beat back the reemerging yellow music, just as the songs of resistance had done.[134]

Liu Liangmo died with honor in Shanghai in 1988. His saga serves as an example of how highly educated and politicized Chinese negotiated their own beliefs within the shifting transpacific ideologies of the twentieth century. Liu's ability to navigate treacherous political waters enabled him to have an illustrious career in both the Republic of China and the United States during World War II. He contributed to China's war efforts with creativity and devotion, encouraged Chinese Americans, offered strong support to African Americans, and was an effective ambassador for China to middle-class white America. Sharing mutual dreams of equality, Liu worked extensively with African Americans and experienced their social activism firsthand. The lessons he learned in the complex racial and ideological scenes of the United States enabled him to survive, as an avowed Christian, an even more rigid system later in the PRC. Liu primarily served the new regime as its go-between with Protestant churches and managing their new theologies in accordance with party lines. He managed to become a practiced cultural interpreter of the United States and sustained support for African Americans, particularly the Robesons and the Du Boises. Matching his success was much harder for a woman sojourner, as the next chapter, on Sylvia Si-lan Chen, demonstrates.

4

Choreographing Ethnicity, War, and Revolution around the Globe

Sylvia Si-lan Chen Leyda

"Si-lan, I found a delicate, flowerlike girl, beautiful in a reedy, golden-skinned sort of way, in her long, tight, high-necked Chinese dresses with a little slit at the side showing a very pretty leg. Si-lan was the girl I was in love with that winter [1932–33]," wrote Langston Hughes.[1] The U.S. Immigration and Naturalization Service "translated" the writer's lively portrait of Si-lan in 1950 as "Height: 5′ 11″ [mistaken, she was 5 feet tall]; Weight: 100 Pounds; Hair: Black; Eyes: Dark Brown; Brown Complexion, Mole on Upper lip, Left."[2] Paul Robeson fondly remembered meeting Si-lan and her siblings, though he primarily recalled her brother Jack:

> In Moscow, some years ago [1934] I met three young Chinese, a fellow named Jack Chen and his two sisters. Jack was a newspaperman, one of his sisters was a motion picture technician and the other was a dancer. . . . Jack was a slight chap, medium height and soft-spoken. He spoke beautiful English. He came to my concerts and we sat around many nights and talked of China and its future. This was in 1936 and '37. Later I met him in London and we often appeared there for China Relief. It was an interesting experience to see and meet a Chinese who was part Negro and felt close to both his people. I believe he is now back in China — the new China — helping to build a better life for his countrymen.[3]

Sylvia Si-lan Chen (陈茜 [锡, 西] 兰, ca. 1905–96), and her three artist-journalist siblings captured the fanciful gazes and imaginations of two African American cultural giants of the twentieth century. The siblings were brothers Percy (Pei-shih 丕士, nicknamed P. J., 1901–89) and Bernard (I-wan, 依范, nicknamed Jack, 1908–95) and a sister, Yolanda (Iolanda, Yu-lan, 幼[郁]兰, 1913–2006). The three eldest children were born in Port of Spain, Trinidad, British West Indies, and Yolanda in London to Eugene Bernard Chen (Chen Youren, Chen Yu-jen 陈友仁), the would-be minister of foreign affairs of the Republic of China, and Alphonsine Agatha Ganteaume, a French Creole (fig. 4.1). The Chens' Chinese, African, and French heritages afforded them a host of complex racial and political experiences as they crossed the globe.[4]

This chapter traces Si-lan's life, career, and cosmopolitan family, which did so much to shape her story. Earlier in Si-lan's life, African American dance was barely recognized as serious art. Dance in China was limited to the physical education curriculum, commercialized social dance at cabarets and nightclubs, and coarse imitation of Western dances by overly sensual song and dance troupes. Si-lan emerged as the first "modern Chinese/ Soviet dancer-choreographer" with an international reputation. Similar to her better-known African American dance contemporaries Katherine Dunham and Pearl Primus, Si-lan fused classical dance with African and African American folk cultures. Like Primus, she was profoundly political and viewed the cultures that she visited and lived in with an almost anthropological eye. Whereas Dunham and Primus drew largely from African American and African cultures, Si-lan took cues from unique and diverse interpretive styles from the Caribbean, the Soviet Union (particularly Central Asia), and China's folk tradition and contemporary war and revolutions. She shared the background, career, and vision of her cousin Dai Ailian. Also born in Trinidad, Dai spent much of her life in China and was acclaimed "the mother of China's modern dance." Only Chen, a true globe-trotter, invented her own choreography combining all these styles.[5] While privileged to push geographic, gender, and racial boundaries during the turbulent years of the twentieth century, Si-lan negotiated racial ambiguity and was often caught by crushing ideological, political, and bureaucratic obstacles.

BRITISH EMPIRE, BLACK FAMILY, AND CHINA

Si-lan's paternal grandfather, Joseph Guixin Chen, and grandmother, Marie Liang, were Hakka immigrants from Guangdong Province. Joseph, who had lost a leg as a bodyguard for the East King Yang Xiuqing during the apocalyptic Taiping Rebellion, took refuge in the West Indies as an indentured laborer

FIGURE 4.1. Si-lan Chen, holding a Black doll, with her mother Alphonsine
Agatha Ganteaume and younger brother, Jack, at Port of Spain in 1908.
*Box 33, folder 17, Jay and Si-lan Chen Leyda Papers and Photographs,
Elmer Holmes Bobst Library, New York University.*

in 1870. Si-lan's maternal grandfather, Admiral Ganteaume, was a French nobleman who fled to the West Indies after Napoleon's defeat and established a plantation there. Her Black maternal grandmother, Goring, was enslaved to Ganteaume. She later purchased her freedom but continued to work in his household as a kitchen servant. The fact that Goring was Alphonsine's mother was not publicly recognized. After Eugene and Alphonsine's marriage in 1899, and with the assistance of her father, Eugene launched his career as a leading barrister.[6]

After their ancestors had reached the West Indies from three different continents, surviving waves of war and revolution, the Chens scattered around the world. Affluent and mobile within the British Empire, the family, including the Black grandmother, settled comfortably at 11 Clifton Hill in the St. John's Wood neighborhood of London in 1910 for the children's education. Si-lan attended Stedman's Academy on Great Windmill Street in Soho for training in "classic ballet, tap, acting, and singing."[7] Content with her "own particular mixture," she recalled not being aware of racial or national identities. When people, including Queen Alexandra, whom she met at a charity bazaar at the Albert Hall, were puzzled by her origin, this "unfamiliar island" of Trinidad, or even by "West Indian," "it never occurred to me say 'Chinese.'" Reflecting the racial ambiguities she faced throughout her career, Si-lan played marginal, nonwhite roles, including Topsy in *Uncle Tom's Cabin* in the Stedman's Academy production. However, racial prejudices rudely announced themselves soon enough. Elite girls' boarding schools rejected her as a "colonial girl," before she was finally admitted to the Upper Chine School in Shanklin, on the Isle of Wight, as one of its two nonwhite girls (the other was Indian) out of forty students, in 1918. There she excelled in dance. The family moved back to a luxurious house "beautiful enough to fit all our dreams" in Trinidad in 1925, so that Percy could follow in his father's steps and practice law there.[8]

Meanwhile, Eugene was adventuring in China, which remained foreign and distant to the rest of the family. After settling his family in London, he took the Trans-Siberian Railway, on which most figures discussed in this book would travel, to Beijing in 1911. Surviving a jail sentence imposed by the pro-Japanese premier Duan Qirui, Eugene joined the Chinese delegation to the 1919 Versailles Peace Conference as secretary and publicity agent of Sun Yat-sen. There, he might have crossed paths with Du Bois. Eugene was soon promoted to be the Nationalist Party's foreign adviser and minister in charge of publicity and public relations.[9]

Why did Eugene set his political career and family life on separate continents? Langston Hughes powerfully explored the complex relationship between a white father and his mixed child in his play *Mulatto*. The dynamics between Eugene and his mixed children and wife were no less complicated. Eugene refused to grant his wife's request to join him in Guangzhou in 1922. Even in multiracial Trinidad, his unconventional marriage to a Creole had already triggered a storm of protest from his family and the Chinese community. In China, he found a brutally racially charged political setting that his wife never imagined. Eugene drafted the "Declarations of the First Congress of the Nationalist Party," which controversially advocated unity with the Soviet Union and the Chinese Communist Party, in 1924. It triggered an explosion of resentment over his rapid rise inside the party. The most venomous attacks were rumors smearing him as "a bastard with slave blood" from a "loose" Creole mother. Although it was Eugene's wife, not he, who had a Black parent, these slurs challenged his racial and moral qualifications to serve in the Chinese government. Eugene's "darker skin, characteristic of Cantonese," made the rumors somewhat credible, and his complex family situation prevented him from responding publicly and forcefully. Further complicating matters was the fact that his father indeed had a daughter with a mixed-blood mistress, whom his attackers purposely confused with his mother. And Eugene himself had twin daughters, only one year younger than Percy, with a French Creole mistress. Interpreting Eugene's style based on his racial background, the *New York Times* claimed that "he isn't quintessentially Chinese. Three fourths, or seven-eighths, or perhaps fifteen-sixteenths is Chinese; the rest is Trinidadian, West Indian." Ever cautious, Eugene decided against displaying his mixed-race wife and children and Black mother-in-law in China. According to Jack's widow, Chen Yuan-tsung, Eugene's racially motivated calculation "dramatically traumatized the young Jack."[10]

In 1926, after his status in China stabilized with his appointment as minister of foreign affairs, Eugene finally invited the family to join him. His wife, Alphonsine, fell ill with cancer and soon died. Si-lan and Percy, who had taken Yolanda's passage to escape his marriage to Carmen Maillard, arrived in Guangzhou following a luxurious itinerary through Europe, while Jack remained in London to study law. Yolanda had to stay behind until Eugene, who was unpleasantly surprised to see Percy, sent for her.[11]

AT CHINA'S CROSSROADS: THE NORTHERN EXPEDITION (1926–27)

Six days after landing in Guangzhou, Si-lan joined the Chinese Revolutionary Government for a three-month journey to Wuhan. Then she made a brief

Sylvia Si-lan Chen Leyda

trip to Shanghai to greet her younger siblings in March 1927.[12] This brief proximity to the political center in China's dramatic Northern Expedition, which W. E. B. Du Bois monitored closely across the Pacific, profoundly shaped Si-lan and her siblings.

At the peak of Eugene's political career, the Chen children inevitably rose into the global media spotlight, while details on their mother and maternal grandmother remained missing. British and U.S. media inflated Si-lan's education and style: "Fresh from an American college for women, Miss Sylvia Chen wears the latest Paris fashion with true Western grace. She entered Hankow with her father, clad in well-cut riding breeches, to the great discomposure of the local Chinese dignitaries." Si-lan would reveal that her "glorious riding habit" was actually "the overnight creation of our Canton tailor." Newspapers across the United States exaggerated how she had become "her father's right hand 'man'" and a "Chinese Joan of Arc." The *Lincoln (N.C.) Herald* featured her article on "China Affairs" along with a piece by Madam Sun Yat-sen, dubbing them "two of the most prominent women in China."[13]

Glamour and prestige could not overcome the racist undertones that followed the Chens. Naturally, there was competition within Sun Yat-sen's inner circle between Eugene and Chiang Kai-shek and the family of soon-to-be First Lady May-ling Soong. As a sensitive teenager, Si-lan quickly detected the "antagonism" in the Soongs' treatment of Eugene, which was typical of the way "native Chinese [behaved] toward Chinese born and married outside of China," and even worse toward a Black woman (the Soongs' own American education notwithstanding). Si-lan's suspicions were confirmed when she was invited to Soong's Shanghai house for dinner. Since Si-lan appeared an "English-trained flapper girl" in her "1926 dress," "probably . . . a little short," Soong wondered aloud whether she herself should wear leg-revealing European clothes. After subtly calling attention to their choices of wardrobes, Soong revealed her true point: "'Wouldn't you really prefer to be whole Chinese?' she asked in a tone guaranteed to invite confidences. This was a question I had never thought about. I replied that I was quite happy being myself, thank you. Dinner was not a very gay affair." Eugene was concerned with the innocence and vulnerability of his daughter, who was probably perceived as sexually available. On the train from Guangzhou to Wuhan, Eugene repeatedly and not-so-subtly interrupted when May-ling's brother, T. V. Soong, took a seat beside her "to talk about less political subjects."[14] Those incidents hinted at official attitudes toward Blacks.

Si-lan began to adjust her racial consciousness. Under the influence of

Eugene, she identified with the Chinese while distancing herself from the British Empire. Previously, she wrote, "I was willing to find the Chinese enormously interesting, but only as a quaint and foreign race." Now, "I began to feel proud of my Chinese ancestry for the first time in my life, and I started to look at the Chinese around me not from the outside but from among them." Witnessing British colonial brutalities in China accelerated the shift of her self-identification. Just as Du Bois and Langston Hughes would quickly note "Jim Crow" behaviors against Chinese on China's soil, Si-lan recalled her shock "that a people could be so brutally excluded from a part of their own land." In reactions echoed by Du Bois later, she was particularly "unprepared for the signs of Chinese servitude to foreigners in Shanghai's International Settlement. The Coolies never looked in your face."[15]

Eugene's historic triumph reclaiming the British concessions in Hankou (part of Wuhan) and Jiujiang through the 1927 Chen-O'Malley Agreement boosted Chinese national pride and bolstered Si-lan's new patriotism.[16] The impossible breakthrough in China's confrontation with the stronger colonial powers permanently cemented Eugene's reputation as the "iron-wristed revolutionary diplomat." Prestigious periodicals including *Eastern Miscellany* and *Shanghai Daily* carried statements made by Eugene and his British opponents in full to inform the public of their rigorous negotiations. *Young Companion Pictorial* featured six photographs by H. S. "Newsreel" Wong. They portrayed "Chen Youren, the Key Figure in negotiating the Hankou Incident," and scenes of conflict between the passionate Chinese masses and the armed British force. Biographical pieces described Eugene as "armed with knowledge in English literature beyond regular college graduates and possessing an ideology closer to Thomas Jefferson than communism." The *New York Times* labeled him "China's scorching tongue."[17]

Si-lan and her sister contributed to the nationalist revolution through service to the hospital for the soldiers wounded in the Northern Expedition and started to grasp some Chinese culture. They braved a three-hour-long Chinese fairy tale film and started to tackle the language barrier by mastering around 500 Chinese characters. Their study would be abruptly cut short.[18]

THE SOVIET DECADE (1927–36): MATURING INTO A "SOCIALLY DIRECTED PANTOMIME"

After the Wuhan government collapsed, life in China became dangerous for anyone suspected of leftism. The marriage of May-ling Soong and Chiang Kai-shek on December 1, 1927, signaled the thorough defeat of leftist forces. The Chens left China in two groups. Si-lan, her father and sister, and Madam Sun Yat-sen escaped from Shanghai to Vladivostok by boat, before taking the Trans-Siberian Railway to Moscow, while her brothers and Anna Louise Strong accompanied the Comintern adviser Mikhail Borodin to drive through the Gobi Desert. Despite their rumored romance, Eugene went into exile in Paris, taking up residence at the Gallic Hôtel, 288 rue de Vaugirard, and Madam Sun returned to China through Berlin.

With the Soviet Commissariat for Foreign Affairs, Eugene arranged for his children to settle down in Moscow. He stayed in frequent touch with them and sent them monthly allowances through his oldest son, Percy, according to the Chinese custom, until the early 1930s. Unhappy with the way Percy handled the funds, Si-lan sought Eugene's intervention in 1931. However, the situation did not improve. Langston Hughes noted the following summer, "A Chen family row was going on. . . . A great deal of disagreement with what this 'just due' was occurred every month, so the three younger Chens were angry with Percy most of the time." Gradually, Jack took over as the chaperone, "a very useful and necessary household utensil," as he declared himself, and helped her sisters to grow financially independent of Eugene.[19]

The Chen siblings matured into journalists and artists over the following decade. Percy worked as a foreign reporter for the All-Union Society for Cultural Relations with Foreign Countries (VOKS). After a brief stint in Berlin, he returned to Moscow to work for General Motors while serving as an officer in the Red Guard and a director of the Shum Chun Rural Welfare Center. In Hankou, Jack had been a cartoonist, illustrating editorial ideas for the *People's Tribune* (*Minbao*), a newspaper that Eugene had set up as one of the foremost voices criticizing British imperialism. He enrolled in the Moscow Arts Institute and became a political cartoonist for the city's only English-language newspaper, the *Moscow Daily News*, edited by Borodin and cofounded by Strong. Jack was promoted to assistant editor by 1930. Both brothers also served as correspondents for various periodicals in China. After studying in London for a few years, Yolanda enrolled in a cinematography class at the Moscow State Film Institute in the spring of 1930.[20]

Si-lan jump-started her career through formal training at the prestigious Bolshoi Ballet School, Vera Maya's Isadora Duncan School, and the Lunacharsky Theatrical Technicum, an unofficial subsidiary of the Bolshoi. She was employed by GOMETZ, "the government concert bureau that paid artists an agreed sum for each performance as well as supplying transportation and lodgings," for fifty-four concerts over three-month summer tours.

The official employment afforded her gradual financial independence and a steady pianist. The bureau deployed her to the Caucasus (1930), Crimea (1931), Ukraine and the Volga region (1932), and the Don Basin, Soviet Central Asia, and Tbilisi, Georgia (1933), dancing in theaters, factories, and collective farms.[21]

Si-lan's growth as a professional dancer-choreographer entailed major domestic and international performances. Her debut, a solo concert at the Isadora Duncan School in Moscow for an audience of 100 in 1928, was a great success. Encouraged, she delivered a powerful performance at the concert of Kasyan Goleizovsky, the legendary impresario of the Moscow Chamber Ballet and a frequent contributor to the Bolshoi Theater, the following year. With inflated ambition and VOKS sponsorship, Si-lan gave a solo concert composed by Goleizovsky at the Moscow Conservatory in early 1930. Spreading news from London, the Los Angeles Times exclaimed that "the premiere ballerina . . . is receiving a tremendous ovation. Her work is essentially classic, contrasting sharply with the more stylized dancers of the London stage." However, Soviet critics contended that the performance was a disaster, poisoned by bourgeois ideology. The unyielding Si-lan managed a comeback concert with a recalibrated class angle at the same location exactly a year later. Established, she gave concerts at the Kamerny Theater in 1932 and the Vakhtangov Theater in 1933, for which Jack designed costumes, and his pregnant wife, Lucy Flaxman, and Yolanda participated in group dances. Si-lan's growing reputation landed invitations to perform at the Det Nye Theater in Oslo in 1934, the Royal Swedish Academy of Music in Stockholm, and the Finnish Opera in 1935, billed as a Chinese dancer fresh out of the Soviet Union.[22]

While redefining their national and racial identity during their brushes with pivotal events in modern Chinese history, the Chen siblings initiated their lifelong alignment with the left, which was further cemented in the Soviet Union. They arrived at a time when political orthodoxy was becoming paramount over revolutionary ethics. By 1928, Stalin's rise had created a cultural revolution in which workers could confront older specialists in the arts. As even the Bolshoi Ballet became a center of Soviet culture, there were calls for greater worker influence on dance.[23] The Soviet authorities began tightening their control over the arts and judging sexuality in terms of socialist morality in the late 1920s, leading to intensifying attacks on the eroticism in the work of artists such as Kasyan Goleizovsky and photographer Alexander Grinberg. The dancing pose of the scarcely clad Si-lan and other seminaked women in Grinberg's photographs were labeled as pornographic

FIGURE 4.2. The "decadent"
dancing pose of Si-lan Chen
captured by photographer
Alexander Grinberg in
Moscow in the late 1920s.

(fig. 4.2). For Si-lan, the 1930 concert proved to be a turning point. Goleizov-sky's choreography for her concert renewed his typical erotic theme through the struggle between a woman and a dominant man. Scorching reviews de-nounced her dancing as pornography, lending her talent to "this decadent and bourgeois ballet master," and having "nothing to offer the proletariat." Si-lan would admit that the "avalanche" of criticism put her career at grim crossroads.[24]

Burdened by suicidal thoughts, Si-lan turned to her family for succor. She wrote to Eugene for advice on whether she should return to China or tour Europe. Her absent father appeared to be growing more distant and ap-parently did not grasp her plight. Eugene congratulated her on her concert triumphs, supported her wish to break away from Goleizovsky, and encour-aged her to "wisely" consider the criticism in order to "please" her audiences. Most important, he emphatically double-underscored his advice for her to stay put so as to "consolidate your position" in Moscow as her base. "Tour the principal cities of the U.S.S.R. and devote the proceeds of the tour, less expenses, to some proper public purpose in consultation with either VOKS or the Foreign Office."[25]

Jack offered key assistance with the ideological framework of Si-lan's de-veloping aesthetic. He penned several lengthy letters during her 1931 summer tour, assuring her that "we'll work it out" and urging her to abandon the bourgeois perspective represented by Goleizovsky and adopt a proletarian one. Jack unambiguously insisted that Si-lan should regard her work as cultural "propaganda" and forget about "commercialism," because money would "roll in just the same" with her "bigger, brighter, and better dancing" for the masses. Si-lan shared with Eugene her new understanding of dance as "a propaganda medium," but he shrewdly cautioned against using the term *propaganda*. Unlike bourgeois dance oriented toward "grace, beauty, and mimicry," such as ballet or Duncan-inspired modern dance, Jack wrote, proletarian themes required movements drawn from the masses' real-life activities and emotions. Thus, "you must learn to move powerfully, get out of your head the idea of creating 'beauty,' it is surprising that at this date you still have that fetishism in tow."[26] Jack's criticism of "beauty"-making as bourgeois would be echoed by Chinese critiques of Langston Hughes's poems. Determined to deepen her education in political economy and Marxist theory and thus enable her to create a realistic choreography for the proletariat, Si-lan studied at the Eastern Academy for two terms.[27] The academy taught Marxism-Leninism and colonial theory to hundreds of students from the Soviet Caucasus and Central Asia, Asia, Africa, and the Americas from 1921 to 1938. Among its alumni were Ho Chi Minh, Nazim Hikmet, Jomo Kenyatta, William L. Patterson, and Rattan Singh.

Si-lan found her niche by inventing a brand of ethnic choreography based on real-life issues facing people in China and African Americans as well as on folk materials from China and Soviet Asia. Collaborating with Jack, a rising artist using cartoons as a powerful weapon to reach the masses amid China's war and revolution, she created a choreographic style that shared characteristics with cartoons, including satire, brevity, and straightforwardness. Jack's involvement was best illustrated in *Militarist: Dance for Revolutionary Carnival Demonstration*, Si-lan's first attempt to shift her choreography from bourgeois eroticism to proletarian realism. She would credit the "naive" program with rescuing her sanity and career at a critical moment.

Jack provided the idea, inspired by an ancient Chinese play featuring a fiery warlord that he had recorded in Mongolia during his journey to the Soviet Union. He also designed the costumes, which "combined elements from [a] modern military uniform with [a] Beijing opera head piece, long beard, and the loose belt." Inserting the "Internationale" to symbolize the strength of the masses, Si-lan showed how the "militarist ran, panic-stricken, around the stage as though the whole Chinese people were chasing him," concluding with a backward somersault that landed him flat on his face. "The whole composition was as direct and as unsubtle as a caricature poster," Si-lan would write. Her other compositions "concentrating on simple cartoons or emotional miniatures" included *Angel of Peace, Brown Shirt, National Anthems,* and *Sweet Sue,* satirizing the Geneva Conference, the Nazis, various national attitudes, and sports, respectively. They overlapped with the content of some of Jack's cartoons and writings. He continued to design costumes, provide detailed critique of Si-lan's performances, and advise her on concert programs. Her other caricatured compositions included a moralizing lecture on "the yellow menace" and "a gentle song by a Pekinese about his rich mistress's vagaries and brainlessness."[28]

Si-lan's brief trips to Shanghai provided inspiration as well as the locale for some of the classics in her repertoire. *Shanghai Park,* focusing on a legendary sign that barred Chinese and dogs, addressed the exclusion of Chinese from public facilities that she had witnessed in Guangzhou, Wuhan, and Shanghai. Her miniature ballets *Shanghai Sketches,* composed of solos less than two minutes long, sought to provide "glimpses of typical characters that a sympathetic and satirical eye might encounter in Shanghai" and to show "sympathy to the underdogs." They included "Rickshaw," from the puller's perspective; "Empty Bowl," addressing "the common Chinese note of hunger"; "Waiter," whose title character was servile but contemptuous of well-to-do diners; and "Returned Student," whose "nose tilted at the moon" in "dark China." Her opinion of overseas Chinese students was shared by Pearl S. Buck and Paul Robeson, who similarly criticized such "foreign Chinese" for being shamed of their chaotic and weak motherland. Si-lan choreographed themes of the Chinese Revolution, with *Red Spear* on the Communist guerrilla fighters and *Defeat but Final Victory* on the Northern Expedition.[29]

Images of Harlem also captured Si-lan's imagination. She came across the Charleston dance in London and was thrilled by the "amazing wriggling" of Josephine Baker in Paris theaters. In Moscow, the Chen siblings sought out the community of African American students, performers, and celebrities such as Robeson, Hughes, and Marian Anderson. Si-lan and her soon-to-be husband Jay Leyda met Robeson and his wife in the National Hotel in the winter of 1934. She later recalled that Robeson, initially "unsure of the new surroundings" and "the genuineness of the Soviet welcome," "went rambling off on an endless comparison of Chinese and African sculpture." She wrote to Hughes,

Moscow was quite thrilled by the arrival of Paul Robeson. I think he is a swell person, completely unspoiled and sincere. He loves Moscow and intends to return in April indefinitely. His wife is not all pleased by this decision. She is materialist and afraid he will lose his bourgeois public, but forgets he will gain the respect of the proletariat, probably be twice as interesting for the bourgeois in consequence. He will sing in closed evenings, and made a big impression. . . . How is your play getting on? It would be swell if you have a part for Paul Robeson in it.[30]

Si-lan composed a dance interpreting the lyrics of "Ol' Man River" by imitating the movements of Black laborers pulling their feet out of the heavy black mud along the Mississippi. Jack praised her enlisting audiences' sympathy "on the side of the Negro, particularly when he makes a move to fight for his freedom." She attempted her first tragedy, titled *Lynch*, reflecting racial brutality suffered by African Americans.[31]

Inspired by the gender egalitarianism of Marxist theory and the role models of strong leftist women such as Madams Sun Yat-sen, Borodin, and Alexandra Kollontain (then Soviet ambassador to Norway and the first female governing cabinet member in the world), Si-lan was ever conscious of the struggles of women. In 1934, after hearing from Agnes Smedley about the heroic deeds of the leftist female writer Ding Ling, whose execution by the Nationalist government for "dangerous thoughts" was falsely reported, the "terribly indignant" Si-lan composed a memorial program, titled *Ding Ling*. She would recall that Leyda liked the piece best for "its dramatic pantomime . . . its storytelling and audience involvement" and include a pose of herself dancing it in her autobiography. Si-lan applauded the Young Communist League members who forcefully persuaded women in Soviet Asia to burn their heavy horsehair veils, which she viewed as the "most symbolic fragment of the dark past" and women's servitude, comparable to the practice of foot-binding in China. Meanwhile, she embraced tradition and folk culture. The clothing of Uzbek women, composed of a colorful flowing gown and "headdress of smooth black plaits topped by a fascinating embroidered skullcap," became Si-lan's signature costume. She adapted their "pure" dance with styles gracefully stylizing women's work movements for her long-term repertoire.[32]

Due to language barriers, Soviet artists employed simple audio means to satisfy Soviet curiosity about China triggered by the alliance of the Chinese Revolution and the Comintern. By similarly presenting China to the Soviet masses through visual means, Si-lan found her place in the Soviet world of

Sylvia Si-lan Chen Leyda

arts as the "first modern Chinese/Soviet dancer." She wrote contentedly to Hughes in the summer of 1934, "I am going to dance lots about China. The more I live here, the more I want to propagandize through my dancing the need for revolution in China." Now completely identifying with proletarian realism, Si-lan boasted, "I never had to submit my new dances to any kind of censorship, and no one interfered with my work." She was proud that her contemporary Chinese subjects of satire found a perfect rapport with her working-class audiences.[33]

THE NEAR-FATAL "HOMECOMING": THE 1935 TRIP TO SHANGHAI

Coming of age in the Soviet Union as guests, the Chen siblings longed to return to China, a nation they had just had a glimpse of but regarded as home. The ties they perceived, however, were shadowed by their father's complex political career while Japan's aggression loomed large. Eugene returned to Shanghai on February 6, 1931. The media quickly noted how the former "bright vigorous young man" had "aged considerably, with conspicuous gray hair," during his three-year exile. It speculated as to the political significance of Eugene's return. M. Z. T. Tyau, director of the Intelligence Department at the Ministry of Foreign Affairs, personally delivered an invitation from Wang Zhengting, the minister, to a prompt reception in Eugene's honor, which turned out to be one of "the most brilliant social functions in diplomatic circles." Eugene and Sun Yat-sen's son Sun Ke soon met the Nationalist leaders Chiang Kai-shek and Hu Hanmin.[34]

Eugene and Guangzhou mayor Liu Jiwen traveled to Japan to meet Prime Minister Baron Shidehara during the summer. As Eugene later explained to the National Congress of the Nationalist Party, the trip was to learn Japan's ultimate intention in China in order to determine whether compromise was feasible. Soon after Japan took over Manchuria, Eugene joined the "senior clique" led by Sun and Hu in Guangzhou in a standoff against the nonresistant Nanjing government.[35] After the conflict was solved through a coalition government, Eugene returned to Nanjing as minister of foreign affairs in January 1932. Following Japanese attacks on Shanghai on the 28th, he forcefully advocated severing all diplomatic relations with the enemy. Leftist media such as the *Independent Weekly* and *Citizens' Forum* applauded his courage in sharing the position of "the broad laboring classes." They feared that Chiang's rejection of Eugene's policy, "backed by the capitalists, imperialists and shameless intellectuals," would lead the nation "galloping" toward "destruction." Thus, "several hundred million 'yellow slaves' would emerge in East Asia, comparable to the plight of the Black slaves in America." Chiang forced Chen to resign overnight and arranged for him to "tour Europe for a year." The defiant Eugene helped to establish the rebellious People's Revolutionary Government in Fuzhou, associated with the rural communist forces there, in 1933. The Fuzhou government was suppressed in a few weeks, bringing an end to Eugene's official political career.[36]

Eugene continued to adventure in China's political scenes, however, now accompanied by Georgette Chang (Zhang Liying, 1906–93), the French-born fourth daughter of the senior Nationalist Party member Zhang Jingjiang (Chang Ching-kiang), whom he had married in Paris in 1930. In contrast to the invisibility of his first wife of mixed race, Chang was praised as "a perfect linguist," and she accompanied Eugene everywhere, both as his interpreter and to reinforce his Chineseness. *Young Companion Pictorial* featured Chang on its cover and included candid photographs by "Newsreel" Wong of the couple dancing at a charity ball hosted by the Women's Association as well as symbolically working together in front of a desk in Japan. The photograph of Chang leading her girlfriends to the front lines to console soldiers under Japanese attack appeared in the *Shanghai Daily Pictorial*, along with battle scenes in Shanghai, to signal her husband's strong position of resistance.[37]

Eugene's new marriage proved insufficient to shield him from renewed personal attacks. Continuing to underscore his shortcomings in the Chinese language, the media commented on how the marriage made his life more extravagant. Worse, newspapers for political opponents, such as the semi-official *Central Daily*, accused the "mysterious" Eugene of traveling to Japan and secretly meeting the Japanese consul in a Hong Kong hotel room to negotiate compromise and sell out China. It compared Eugene's alleged misdeeds with a "concubine leisurely writing love letters to and flirting with her neighbors." Questioning Eugene's loyalty to the nation in sexualized terms reinforced venomous attacks on his national and racial identity. Under the label "amorous story," the media vaguely described his mother as a "native of the Caribbean" or a "pure American woman." The *Central Daily* and *Overseas Chinese Weekly* led the charge: "Born and brought up in a barbaric Negro place, Chen Youren was a stranger to our national language and the ancestors' culture." The newspapers accompanied these attacks with a powerful superstitious hint: "How could Chen, not a member of the yellow race, serve as a major official and dominate our national affairs? Did the heaven send him down to bring disaster to the Chinese race?" They urged that "compa-

Sylvia Si-lan Chen Leyda

triots ... always remember" that the national crisis had been brought by the "demon" Chen, warning that he was conspiring with Japan to "shatter China into pieces."[38]

Such smears were soon extended to his children. The *Shanghai Weekly* "revealed" that Eugene's first wife was a Black woman whom he had rescued from a hysterical "white American man mounted on a white horse one summer evening near a river." He took his daughter, who "resembled her mother," to the riverbank to mourn after his wife's death. These invented details coincided with the plot of Georgii Eduardovich Grebner's original Russian script for the planned-but-never-produced film "Black and White," for which Langston Hughes was recruited to Moscow as a scriptwriter. The gossip magazine *Truthful Words* reported that, although it "dared not share the numerous rumors about his special family and background," it was "definitely a fact" that Eugene's four grown children from his first marriage were living in the Soviet Union.[39]

These attacks resonated as far away as Moscow, where the Chen siblings felt their effects. Eugene assured Si-lan that his record refuted the constant lies that he had betrayed his country. Meanwhile, the magazine *Communist International* and newspapers such as *Yefimov* in Moscow accused Eugene of selling out to China's bankers and militarists and Japan by joining the Nanjing government. Si-lan would recall angrily defending before her classmates in the Eastern Academy her father's true intention to incorporate the CCP into a strong coalition government and resist Japan. After Hughes mentioned reading about Eugene daily in the United States, Si-lan vented with him about Vincent Sheean's attacks on Eugene, allegedly as revenge for a personal feud back in Wuhan, in his *Personal History* (1935). "He even had to lie about the pater's origin as though that makes any difference to the man as a person." Hughes responded, "I know he must be a pretty nice fellow, or you wouldn't be such a nice girl." Si-lan would write in her autobiography, "I was boiling mad. How dare he [Sheean] twist historical episodes and characters to fit his personal likes and dislikes?"[40]

Si-lan explained her deferred China trip to Hughes, "Now with my papa playing politics there, it's hardly likely that I shall be received in Shanghai." Between 1930 and 1931, Eugene consistently warned his children of the danger of coming to China directly from Moscow, especially without his presence there, although he was proud that "the Chinese" in Si-lan "is now coming out decisively." Catching wind that their father was on his way back to China, the Chen brothers rushed to Hong Kong in 1931, but Eugene ordered them back to Moscow immediately due to his "extremely precari-

FIGURE 4.3. The biography page of Si-lan Chen's Chinese passport obtained from the Chinese consulate in Berlin, November 23, 1932. *Box 28, folder 3, Jay and Si-lan Chen Leyda Papers and Photographs, Elmer Holmes Bobst Library, New York University.*

ous" situation.[41] He even advised that they be extra cautious in their correspondence, instructing Si-lan to insert letters inside an envelope addressed to "Mr. John Smith c/o Messrs. A. Tack & Co 26 Des Voeux Road Central, Hong Kong" and to mail them from Berlin or London, rather than Moscow. Legally affirming her identity as a Chinese, Si-lan obtained a passport as the "female student" Chen Xuelan (陈雪兰) from the Chinese consulate in Berlin on November 23, 1932, for travel in Europe (fig. 4.3).[42]

While Eugene faded from China's political scene, the Chen siblings maintained their presence in the popular press there, which updated the Chinese public on their marital status and career developments in the Soviet Union. As a correspondent for the *Moscow Daily News* and a colleague of the noted journalist Ge Gongzhen (K. C. Koh) stationed in the Soviet Union for *Dagong bao* (Shanghai), Percy and his new bride, Musya (Mucia) Lukina, were presented as "celebrities in the Soviet Union."[43] The most popular press covered Si-lan extensively. Facilitated by Ge, *Young Companion Pictorial* fea-

Sylvia Si-lan Chen Leyda

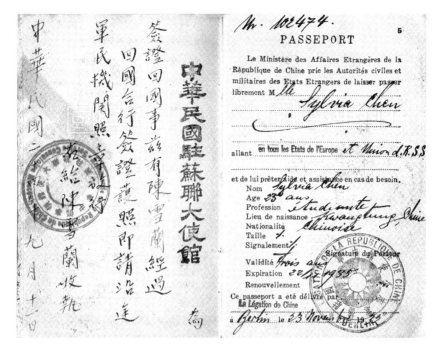

FIGURE 4.4. Si-lan Chen's visa to visit China obtained from
the Chinese embassy in Moscow, September 11, 1935.
*Box 28, folder 3, Jay and Si-lan Chen Leyda Papers and Photographs,
Elmer Holmes Bobst Library, New York University.*

tured her twice, a rare frequency, between 1933 and 1934. She was celebrated
as an accomplished dancer famous in the Soviet Union and Europe, and
photographs of "a daughter of the former minister of foreign affairs" striking Turkestan and Uzbek dance poses glowed in the columns "Personages in
the Public Eye" and "Society Figures." Si-lan shared these pages with powerful politicians such as Sun Ke, Feng Yuxiang, Wang Jingwei, and Wu Zhihui.
Reporting on her major concerts in the Soviet Union and Europe and stints
in Soviet cinema, the Chinese press, including *Linglong*, announced that
"the noted dancer who blends Western robust beauty and oriental gentility"
would soon "present her unique and refined choreography in front of her
compatriots" in major theaters across China. The *Shanghai Evening Post &
Mercury* featured Jack's articles on Soviet art, including ballet.[44]

Finally, Si-lan indicated to Hughes in the summer of 1935, "My papa
is not in China, so there is nothing to stop me" (fig. 4.4). She boarded the
Trans-Siberian Railway and then a boat, finally arriving in Shanghai on Oc-

tober 15 along with some Chinese diplomats, according to the *Shanghai Daily*. She would recall feeling "awfully alone, and . . . a little scared," rather than "thrilled" as she had expected. In fact, she needed to convalesce. She was diagnosed with cancer and underwent major surgery at the Shanghai Red Cross hospital, which was supported by the Rockefeller Foundation. Released on November 6, Si-lan settled in a boarding house in the French Concession, where she soon found herself in constant quarrels with her "imperialist" fellow boarders. Unable to give concerts as planned, she focused on collecting materials for the forthcoming 1936 International Dance Festival in Moscow.[45] Si-lan dismissed as useless the "tremendous" stadium, gymnasium, and open-air swimming pool that the Nationalist government constructed for the National Games to promote national pride and symbolize modernization. However, she was "enchanted" by the "dance pattern" of the "miraculous" movements in the Chinese boxing exercises, swordplay, and traditional theater. Mei Lanfang, whom she had met along with Butterfly Wu the previous winter in Moscow, happened to be performing in Shanghai. The actor invited Si-lan to his home for tea and sent an instructor to teach her movements of the classical theater. Meanwhile, both Si-lan and Mei had the chance to watch their friend Robeson in *Emperor Jones* and *Sanders of the River* at theaters. Si-lan would proudly write to Hughes two weeks after her return to Moscow, "Mei Lanfang helped . . . and I ought to do a quite interesting program." A portrait of Mei and a copy of the book *Mei Lanfang and Chinese Drama* inscribed to Si-lan are preserved in her papers.[46]

Si-lan had lunch at Madam Sun's home at 29 rue Molière (today's Sun Yat-sen Memorial House at 7 Xiangshan Road) in the French Concession on November 26. She found Madam Sun "practically a prisoner, watched both by the Japanese and by government agents," and keeping two huge police dogs for protection. She would recall that Madam Sun exclaimed, "Why Sylvia, you used to be such a frivolous and silly girl. Now you seem to be thinking!" She proposed that Si-lan remain in China and open a school of dance, for which Madam Sun was "all ready" to raise funds. "We parted feeling that in each other we had found an ally, for we believe in the same things." The following day, Si-lan wrote to her family in Moscow, expressing her enthusiasm about Madam Sun. She urged her siblings that they "must come and work. And Jack, you'd be surprised to know how familiar people here are with your cartoons." Si-lan's letter also revealed a surprise: "Mrs. Sun thinks that the Pater came over because his new father-in-law is sick, and his coming has no political significance. This father-in-law (our grandfather-in-law!) is in Shanghai so maybe I'll see our fond parent soon."[47]

Although Si-lan was enthusiastic about a family reunion in China, Eugene had grown distant, probably because of his new marriage. Despite his daughter's life-threatening hospitalization, Eugene did not see her in Shanghai. She had first heard of her father's new amour, a "most beautiful Chinese girl ... studying painting" in Paris, from Yolanda, after the latter returned to Moscow, having traveled from London through Paris in 1930. Eugene only confirmed his marriage after Si-lan read about it in the newspapers and inquired. He was most enthusiastic about his new wife: "Our marriage is a love-match and naturally, has no political significance. Georgette is about your age and a shade shorter than you. Petite, lovely but full of character and will force. She is regarded in art circles here as a young painter of great promise. ... I am very very happy."[48] It seemed Eugene's new marriage stimulated his children to grow up and form their own families. In January 1931, Si-lan hastily married Mikhail Mikhailovich, a Soviet film director she had met on the train back to Moscow in the previous summer, "for no better reason than that he insisted upon it." They never lived together during the three-month-long "miserable" union, which ended in divorce on March 2. Mikhailovich's mental illness that strained the marriage finally engulfed him — he hung himself the following spring.[49] The communication between father and children had become so infrequent that Eugene was not updated on the most important milestones in his children's lives. In his November 17, 1931, letter to Si-lan, he urged, "You must write me more regularly and tell Yone [Yolanda] to do the same. We must keep in touch. I did not know that you were married to Miguel — is he that fine looking chap who danced with you sometimes at the concert given at your first dancing school? I hope you will be more careful in your next matrimonial venture: one's body is a bit sacred — particularly a woman's — and it is not well to suffer it to be touched by coarse hands."[50] Fast forward to 1936: when Si-lan traveled to Paris to see Leyda off to the United States, she "suddenly remembered that father and his new wife might be in Paris." She rushed to the Chinese embassy to find Eugene's address, but he and his wife had left for a trip a week earlier.[51]

Si-lan did see Percy and his wife, who had settled in Shanghai in early 1935, on November 14, one week after her release from the hospital. "I was glad that he had phoned. I was lonely and ill, and although I could never forget the quarrel we had had, I suppose that blood is thicker," she would recall. Si-lan updated her family in Moscow: "Well, P. J. arrived just before lunch, shook hands politely and we had a talk, not heart to heart, you may be sure, but polite. He took me to their flat, on the edge of the Chinese district, for Tiffin, and I was very glad to see Musya." It seemed that Percy did not mention their father's presence in Shanghai (possibly he was unaware), but he introduced Si-lan to his social circle, including American journalist Bernadine Fritz and Lin Yutang, who, inspired by Eugene, had served as secretary of the Ministry of Foreign Affairs in the Wuhan government. As the only woman at a lunch with "a group of Chinese gentlemen," Si-lan enjoyed a long argument with Lin on "emancipation for women." Arranged by Fritz, her scheduled dance recital as "China's sole exponent of the modern dance" at the International Arts Theater was replaced by her debut lecture on "real freedom for women" under state feminism in the Soviet Union. Si-lan had to be rescued from her only public appearance from attacks by "all the White Russians in Shanghai." She returned to Moscow by the same route in January 1936, promising to return in the fall for concert tours.[52]

The political atmosphere was shifting rapidly. The domestic purges began to affect foreign residents and specialists, who faced a choice of leaving or adopting Soviet citizenship. Si-lan remained sympathetic to the policy, writing in her autobiography, "Too much espionage and far too many employers were hidden beneath the immunity of a foreign passport. A period of wars seemed near, and one country was not going to take any chances." However, her family further dispersed over the summer, shortly before W. E. B. Du Bois's visit to the Soviet Union and East Asia. Si-lan extended her Chinese passport on August 15, 1936, with the Commissioner of Public Safety of the City Government of Greater Shanghai for another year. In the same month, both Si-lan and Jack obtained new passports from the British consul in Moscow (fig. 4.5). Encouraged by the good news about the reception of his art in China, Jack immediately left for Shanghai. He was warmly received at the harbor by the leading artists Zhang Guangyu and Ye Qianyu, future husband of Dai Ailian.[53]

Si-lan remarried Jay Leyda, a union that eventually took her back to the hemisphere of her birth (fig. 4.6). He had arrived in Moscow from New York in the fall semester of 1933 to study with Sergei Eisenstein at the Moscow State Film Institute and started to work as a correspondent for *Theater Arts Monthly* the following year. Leyda was soon introduced to Si-lan by her sister, Yolanda, a fellow film student. In July 1936, he departed for New York City en route to Paris to collect films for his new employer, the Museum of Modern Art (MoMA) Film Library, where he would work as an assistant film curator. She followed him there after several months of struggle with immigration obstacles.[54]

Sylvia Si-lan Chen Leyda

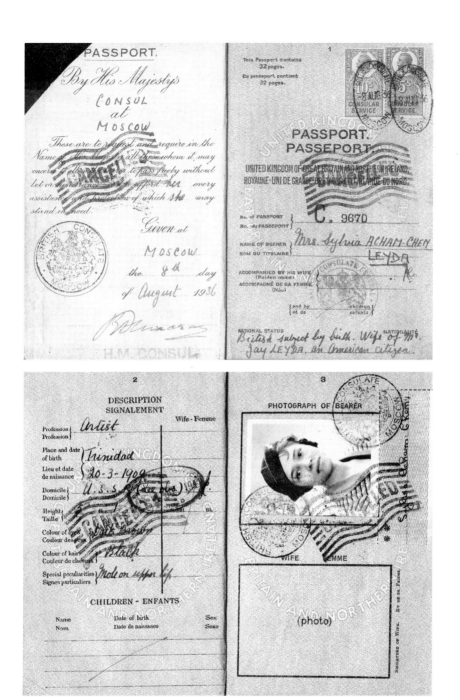

FIGURE 4.5. Pages from Si-lan Chen's British passport obtained
from the British consulate in Moscow, August 8, 1936.
*Box 28, folder 3, Jay and Si-lan Chen Leyda Papers and Photographs,
Elmer Holmes Bobst Library, New York University.*

FIGURE 4.6. Si-lan Chen and her husband, Jay Leyda.
Box 33, folder 17, Jay and Si-lan Chen Leyda Papers and Photographs,
Elmer Holmes Bobst Library, New York University.

Expecting to make a home in the United States with her American husband, Si-lan did not suspect that the Immigration and Naturalization Service (INS) would regard her as only a visitor over the next four decades. The double burdens of her race and leftist background forced her to live under heavy shadows cast by the powerful INS and FBI. After she parted from Leyda in Paris, wrapped up their lives in Moscow, and toured Oslo, Si-lan arrived in London to apply for a visa to the United States, overwhelmed by the sense of drifting.[55] She had been casually curious of racial issues in the United States but insisted that only class mattered. Her romantic correspondence with Langston Hughes occasionally touched on the issue of identity, although they quickly laughed it off as "politics." She responded to his brief exile from Carmel, California, due to attacks from right-wingers in 1934: "So fascism has got you, I notice. Aren't Negroes supposed to be Americans in a fascist regime — or are they left without a nationality — why are you people living in a capitalist country so crazy about nationality. It is not a bit important, only your class viewpoint is important. Of course, I know why capitalists stress nationality, but you all should know better — Oh, excuse me I was talking politics!"

She portrayed herself as living in a different world, telling Hughes of "an ideal holiday spent in the Yusupov Palace, the family home of the baron who killed Rasputin. It's only in the USSR that I could have had such a marvelous time for nothing — remarkable place!"[56]

Now, she was forced to depart the "remarkable place" for the "capitalist country," whose harsh racial politics would be remote no longer. Feeling extremely lonely and uncertain packing up her Moscow home for good, she wrote to Hughes on August 16, 1936, hoping to maintain their friendship while breaking the news of her marriage:

> The most disturbing, the lights have gone out, I am finishing this
> in the dark. It's raining and I'm very lonely — Jay left for Paris about
> a month ago — and now I can't even write to you. Please note
> Yolanda's address as I don't know where I'm going to be. . . . I'm
> awfully nervous about coming to America. My husband being white,
> I colored might cause a lot of embarrassment. Don't you think?
> Please look out for me & come & see me. I don't know anyone there,
> except you & the Ellis. So, I'm going to feel mighty lonely I guess.
> Let's hear from you in a hurry. As ever, Sylvia.[57]

There were early warnings about race in Europe. Encountering a Fascist Party member in Norway, she wondered in her letter to Leyda on September 18, "What will happen to me in America with all those prejudices against foreigners and Orientals and Negroes? I hear today that the biggest paper here has refused to print anything about me, because I spent too much time in the Soviet Union!"[58]

Although Hughes would marvel at the one-drop rule through the voice of Jessie Simple, the character he created, Si-lan and he had jokingly discussed the flexibility or uncertainty of Chen's ethnic and racial identity in their correspondence. "It's powerful. . . . That one drop of Negro blood — because just one drop of Black blood makes a man colored. One drop — you are a Negro! Now, why is that? Why is Negro blood so much more powerful than any other kind of blood in the world? If a man has Irish blood in him, people will say, 'he's *part* Irish.' If he has just a small bit of colored blood in him, Bam! — 'He's a Negro!' Not, 'He's *part* Negro.' No, be it ever so little, if that blood is black, 'He's a Negro!'"[59]

It seemed that Hughes had trusted that the "Negro blood" in Si-lan did not possess such defining or contaminating power. She wrote to him in 1934 that Seki Sano, a former director of the famous Tsukiji Theater in Tokyo, suggested she dance about Japan after he observed her "dance a lot of Chinese modern life." She continued, "I'm going to dance a lot about Japanese fascism. Convenient, isn't it, to be able to change one's nationality so easily. Chinese, Japanese, West Indian, Negro, you like me least as the latter, don't you? But my politics don't change, am always for the oppressed races or in the light against imperialism — oh, dear, he is going to laugh at me for talking politics." Hughes soon responded, "Are you going to dance in the Dance Festival? When is it to be? And will you be Chinese-Japanese-Negro-Uzbek or Anti-Fascist? I don't care which, and we're too far apart to talk politics — as you put it." Si-lan inquired in 1936, "What shall I come [to the United States] as [?] Chinese, Negro, Soviet — take your choice." Hughes advised, "Come as Chinese, I'd say. (Or do you know any Chinese dances by now?) The critics will probably compare you to both Mei Lan Fang and Anna Mae [May] Wong — so look out! They're the only two Chinese artists we know much about in this home of the brave."[60]

U.S. law would never allow Si-lan such flexibility, classifying her instead by the most restrictive Chinese heritage, although she had lived in China for only a few months. At the U.S. consulate in London, she learned that she was subject to the Chinese Exclusion Act, of which she heard for the first time, and was refused a visa. Si-lan had to settle down at 24 Bedford Place before moving to the cheaper YWCA at Flat D, 15 Fairfax Road, Hampstead. Across the Atlantic, from December 1936 to February 1937 she and Leyda frantically petitioned for a waiver of the act based on her British and his U.S. citizenship.[61] A lengthy INS "Office Memorandum," dated February 2 and riddled with legal jargon, explained why Si-lan could only be admitted as a visitor. It stated that she was "born in Trinidad of Chinese parents," omitting her non-Chinese heritage, dismissed Leyda as a "dolichocephalic" (a person with a relatively long skull), and underscored they were married "in Moscow." Citing *Ewing Yuen v. Johnson*, in which the judge ruled that the Chinese Exclusion Act applied to "'every Chinese person' whether Chinese subject or subject of any other sovereignty," the memorandum determined that Si-lan's British citizenship could not shield her from the act. It also speculated that the decision by the consul in London was based on the case *Chang Chan v. Nagle*, in which the court unanimously ruled that marriage to "an American citizen, born in the United States, of Chinese parents" would not affect the application of the act. Although Leyda was not born of Chinese parents, the memorandum concurred with the consul nonetheless. Immigration law had been amended to admit "the Chinese wife of an American citizen who was married prior to May 26, 1924," which, as the memorandum put, "of course" did not apply to the Leydas' marriage "consummated in 1936." Thus, Si-lan was deemed "an alien ineligible to citizenship" under the Chinese Exclusion Act and could only be admitted into the United States as a "nonquota immigrant," which referred to returning legal immigrants, academic and religious professionals and their families, and students. The memorandum concluded that she obviously did not fall in those "definitely specified and narrowly restricted classes."

While the door to the United States was almost slammed shut in Si-lan's face, the memorandum nevertheless left open a crack for her. "The only basis upon which Chen would be entitled to enter the United States" was Section 265 of Title 8 of the United States Code, in accordance with Article 2 of the Treaty of Commerce and Navigation with China (November 7, 1880). Both provided that "every Chinese person, other than a laborer," was entitled to visit "as teachers, students, merchants, or from curiosity." Thus, Si-lan was qualified as a "teacher" or "student" (of dancing) or as one who seeks to enter "from curiosity." The memorandum noted that Si-lan was not required to post a bond, which was to ensure a temporary visitor would not become an immigrant or "nonquota immigrant." This was not an open-ended permit and she was expected to depart after "completing a reasonable visit."[62]

As the "half-Chinese wife of an American citizen," Si-lan was finally granted a visa on February 17 to "visit" her husband for six months — "the first blow to my illusion of American sentimentality." She sailed from Southampton on the SS *Europa*, "the first and fastest liner available," on February 20 and arrived in New York Harbor on the 25th. Her autobiography confused the date as Valentine's Day, but there was nothing romantic about her arrival. The Statue of Liberty was invisible in a heavy snow, she recalled, and "all the childhood legends of Ellis Island attacked me" while she waited among a dozen passengers whose birth or races were scrutinized and who were forced to wear humiliating labels around their necks. (Given Liu Liangmo's detention at Angel Island only a few months earlier, Si-lan's fear was not just paranoia.) Shaken by the immigration ordeal, Leyda was not taking any chances. He had arranged for the Rockefeller Foundation to send a letter to Byron H. Uhl, district director of Ellis Island. The document pledged that the foundation had granted an annual stipend of $2,500 for Leyda to study at the MoMA Film Library, which was adequate to support the couple, and that Si-lan, as a tourist, possessed a return ticket to England. Armed with a copy of the letter and a customs pass, Leyda "claimed" his wife after the immigration officer warned her against working in the country. The Leydas soon moved from 485 Madison Avenue to 441 East 92nd Street. In the 1940 U.S. Population Census, the Assembly District 16 in Manhattan unambiguously registered Si-lan's "Race" and "Ethnicity" as "Chinese," consistent with INS practice.[63]

Still, Si-lan's husband's home was legally not hers. Each time she completed her six-month "visit," immigration law required her to repeat the process of leaving and reapplying for entrance. After she applied for two consecutive six-month "visits," a hearing "before six rather grim gentlemen" in Washington, D.C., extended her visa to February 25, 1938. She traveled to Mexico on September 9, obtained another visitor's visa in Mexico City, and returned through Laredo, Texas, on October 22. After her visa was extended multiple times, Si-lan's next trip was around the West Indies from November 1940 to August 1941. She obtained a new visitor's visa in Hampton, Bermuda. Ironically, as a "visitor," she needed to provide a "permanent residency" abroad on her visa applications, which she alternately listed as 24 Upper Bedford Place, the YWCA at 15 Fairfax Road, Hampstead, in London, or her former sister-in-law's residence at 4 Murray Street, Port of Spain, Trinidad. In Port of Spain, she publicly socialized with the rebellious British heiress Nancy Cunard, whose giant anthology *The Negro* had been banned, while both were under official surveillance.[64]

These crippling immigration legal battles not only caused stress and uncertainty but, more important, deprived Si-lan of financial independence. Under the watchful eyes of the FBI and INS, whose documents described her as "dancer, actress, housewife," she had to be extremely careful to avoid the appearance of earning money, since she was ineligible for paid work as a "visitor." The Leydas had each symbolically paid half of the two-ruble fee for their marriage license, she would recall, "thus establishing our economic independence of each other." Now, she had to depend on him.[65] Adding to the financial stress, Si-lan and Yolanda financially supported Jack's wife and child in Moscow while he struggled as an independent artist in the upheaval of the war. While Si-lan pushed uphill against the INS, Jack was stranded at 415 rue Cardinal Mercier in Shanghai's French Concession for the first half of 1937, facing mysterious obstacles to obtain a visa back to Moscow. Madam Sun saved the day when he was down to five dollars. Si-lan informed Jack in her letter, "Luce [Lucy] needs money again." The Leydas helped to peddle Jack's work, including satirical items on Chiang Kai-shek, to the *Nation*, the *Republic*, and the *American Mercury*, "exclusive" photographs taken in Southern Yangtze and Yan'an to *Life* and *Asia* magazines, and a photograph of *New York Times* correspondent Tillman Durdin at the front lines in China to the newspaper. The fund was to pay what he owed the Leydas and reserve around $500 for his plan to bring his family to China by way of London and the United States before the following spring.[66]

To comply with INS regulations, Si-lan had to work as a volunteer, donating her performances for charitable causes. Meanwhile, like all Chinese immigrants during the era of the Chinese Exclusion Act, she had been given a registration number and fingerprinted upon admission, practices that were extended to all immigrants during the war. Liu Liangmo complained that U.S. authorities continued these insulting methods, which implied that new arrivals were criminals, four years after the end of the war.[67]

Nevertheless, under the Chinese name Si-lan (so far never officially used) to highlight her patriotism, she fit smoothly into the world of modern dance, where she had been known. The U.S. media had been following her career in the Soviet Union. The prestigious theatrical weekly *Variety* and numerous local newspapers hailed her as part of "Russia's Revolution of the Dance" between 1929 and 1930. The *Brooklyn Daily Eagle* and *Daily Worker* acclaimed her as one of the two "representatives of modern dance of the Soviet Union" at the 1936 International Dance Festival in Moscow, to which several American dancers, including Martha Graham, were invited. The New School for Social Research invited her to speak on Soviet arts in May 1937.[68]

Si-lan showcased her dance-choreography at two events sponsored by

FIGURE 4.7. A newspaper clipping anticipating Si-lan Chen's debut concert in New York City in 1938. The photograph shows Chen, in her signature gown adapted from the traditional clothing of Uzbek women, admiring a cartoon drawn by her brother Jack. *Box 30, folder 9, Jay and Si-lan Chen Leyda Papers and Photographs, Elmer Holmes Bobst Library, New York University.*

the American Friends of the Chinese People, a branch of the Friends of China controlled by German Comintern agent Willi Muenzenberg. First, she performed a new dance on national liberation for A Night of China's Culture, an event at the Brooklyn Academy of Music chaired by Maxwell Stewart, associate editor of the *Nation*, on November 26. Old family friend Lin Yutang and Tao Heng-chih (Xingzhi), noted initiator of the mass education movement, spoke at this event. Then Si-lan gave a successful debut concert in the Windsor Theater on 48th Street on January 30, 1938, which the *Daily Worker* lauded as the first formal Broadway recital by a Chinese artist since Mei Lanfang. The ticket prices ranged modestly from $0.83 to $2.20. The publicity materials advertised her "American Premiere of Dances from Modern China and U.S.S.R." She presented her new social satire *Landlord on a Horse* with a theater whip from Shanghai, a contrasting pair of women's portraits, *Peach-Blossom Lady* and *Boat-Girl*, in addition to *Shanghai Sketches, Chinese Student-Dedication*, and two Turk and Uzbek folk dances. Si-lan invited Anna Sokolow, Martha Graham's student whom she had first met in Moscow in 1934, as her guest artist, hoping "her serious dances gave a needed weight to my partially lighthearted program" (fig. 4.7).[69]

Critics hailed her art for "combin[ing] the delicacy of the traditional Chinese with the vigor of West civilization." John Martin of the *New York*

Sylvia Si-lan Chen Leyda

Times wrote that most of her numbers were "the merest wisps, over almost before they are well begun." He nevertheless detected "a sharp and keen sense of comedy" and "a convincing dramatic strength," and he recognized her "unpretentious program," "definite talents," and potential. He attributed her "crisp and smart" movement to "the characteristic clarity and precision of her race." The overall success of her debut gave her the confidence "that I could dance anywhere now." Si-lan was struck by the comment that distinguished her "genuine Chinese dancing" from "examples of the pseudo-Orientalism and false exoticism," realizing that she was entering the contentious site to present the "authentic" China.[70]

With her new visibility, Si-lan was invited to speak at an antisilk parade organized by the Brooklyn Women's Committee for the Boycott of Japanese goods, a cause that Liu Liangmo would support as well. Her fellow speakers included representatives from the American Friends of the Chinese People, the Progressive Women's Council, and the Daughters of the American Revolution. She also addressed members of the American League for Peace and Democracy at Hempstead, New York, urging aid for China.[71]

When the China Aid Council sought to expand across the country, Si-lan proposed the experiment of dance tours and built up a schedule of thirty-two concerts in diverse communities across the United States and Canada within two months. However, it does not appear that the tour took her to Canada, probably due to her immigration status. The publicity materials still highlighted that she was the "daughter of the former Chinese Foreign Minister." Si-lan kicked off her tours with concerts for the Medical Bureau to Aid Spanish Democracy and the American Committee for Chinese War Orphans at the former Scottish Rite Temple in Philadelphia and the Guild Theater in New York City (with Lily Mehlman), respectively, between February and March 1939. The visual artist Man Ray captured Si-lan in action onstage at the Guild Theater. John Martin praised Si-lan for "prov[ing] herself once again to be a spirited and delightful little dancer," noting that her *Uzbek Dance* "literally stopped the show." Then, accompanied by a Filipino pianist, Si-lan zigzagged between the East Coast and the Midwest for a couple of months. After touring Massachusetts, she arrived in Rochester, sponsored by the American League for Peace and Democracy. There, she performed and spoke at the Central YMCA, East High School, and the radio station WSAY. She then danced at Odeon Arthur Jordon Conservatory of Music in Indianapolis, the University of Cincinnati, and the YMCA in Kingston, New York. The American League for Peace and Democracy brought Si-lan back to Baltimore, where her recital was supplemented by a speech by Lin

SI-LAN CHEN
and DANCE GROUP

DANCES OF
U.S.S.R., CHINA
and WEST INDIES

Guest Artist

OLGA
COELHO

SONGS OF BRAZIL

Barbara Morgan

BARBIZON PLAZA THEATRE

APRIL TWENTY-THIRD 9 P.M.

RUSSIAN WAR RELIEF BENEFIT

TICKETS: $2.20, 1.65, 1.10, on sale at the Barbizon Plaza Theatre, 6th Ave. and 58th Street, and Russian War Relief, 535 Fifth Avenue.

Sally Copeland
Russian War Relief
535 Fifth Ave., New York City
   I am enclosing $........ for .... tickets to the Si-lan Chen Dance Recital.
Name ....
Address ....
   Make checks payable to Sally Copeland, Russian War Relief, 535 Fifth Avenue, New York.

FIGURE 4.8. Si-lan Chen's dance program, featuring a photograph from her number *Ding Ling*, performed at the Barbizon Plaza in New York City in 1942. *Box 30, folder 6, Jay and Si-lan Chen Leyda Papers and Photographs, Elmer Holmes Bobst Library, New York University.*

Mousheng, an author and research assistant of China Institute. She then visited Allentown, Pennsylvania, performing for the women's club and Allen Delphian chapter.[72]

Si-lan danced at a Chinese shadow play benefit at the Hotel Ambassador, a tea and musical party at Hampshire House, and the World's Fair, all in New York City, as well as a Chinese garden party at Yonkers, New York, for the benefit of the American Bureau of Medical Aid to China between 1939 and 1940. Col. Theodore Roosevelt, head of the United Council for Civilian Relief in China, Consul General Yu Tsune-chi, Vice Consul Cheng Pao-cheng, and Lin Yutang's family were among those present at the Hampshire House event. Along with a new composition by Earl Robinson, her choreography was featured at the American Music Festival at Mecca Temple in New York City for the benefit of the Dorothy Parker Spanish Children's Relief Fund. She also performed for the Russian War Relief funds at the Barbizon Plaza in 1942 (fig. 4.8). Meanwhile, Si-lan remained active with the American Dance Association, participating in its numerous recitals at the Doris

Sylvia Si-lan Chen Leyda

Humphrey Studio and the Guild Theater in New York City between 1938 and 1940.[73]

Si-lan found her American audiences "a sympathetic people." As China's national crisis worsened, resistance replaced themes of class and revolution in her choreography. In an interview with the *New York Post*, she insisted, "without pretense or excuse, [that] her dance will be propaganda, just like the powerful drawing of her brother," to arouse China's spirit of resistance. Si-lan's publicity materials prominently featured the photograph of her new signature dance pose, holding a sword with a determined look and angular movements in a loose, dark martial arts costume (fig. 4.9). To her repertoire, she added new compositions including *Nanjing under Occupation* and *In Conquered Nanjing*, memorials to the Nanjing massacre, and *Death from the Skies*, on contemporary war scenes in China. John Martin called these numbers "effective rather than moving." She composed the new dances at a summer camp at Allaben Acres, New York, where she worked as a counselor. "After the Marco Polo Bridge Incident, our summer camp and mountain lake suddenly seemed as close as a suburb of Peiping," she would recall. "My fumbling and hesitating compositions gained point, and I began the best dances of China that I had ever done." The martial movements that Si-lan had absorbed from a soldier's sword exercise in Hankou and Beijing opera entered her compositions.[74]

Si-lan had had no trouble integrating traditional ethnic dances of Soviet Central Asia into her choreography. Now she was determined to break down Orientalist stereotypes by performing "authentic modern" China, as opposed to traditional theater, although her publicity materials exaggerated in saying that she was a pupil of Mei Lanfang. The tension between presenting new and catering to the audiences' familiarity with the old rooted deep. She had attributed her disastrous 1930 concert in Moscow partly to the challenge of connecting with an audience that had been misguided by publicity, "expecting to see Tang Figurines come to life on the stage." Her choreography now consciously maintained modern looks and themes. Intrigued by her success using American dance techniques to transform Chinese folk material into programs presenting modern China, Si-lan attempted to modernize the indigenous dances of ethnic minorities and invent new realistic ballets in the Soviet Union. In her unsuccessful 1944 application to the INS for a reentry visa that would allow her to visit the USSR, she stated these intentions.[75]

Si-lan tapped into a high-level intellectual and artistic community in her endeavors to seek understanding, sympathy, and financial aid by per-

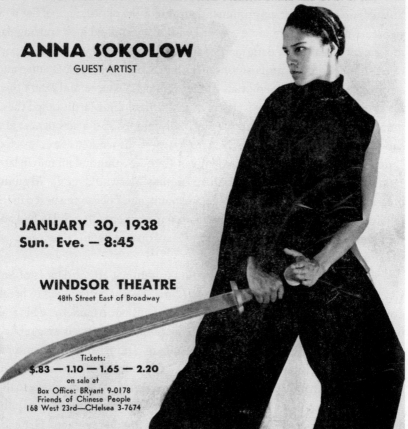

FIGURE 4.9. Si-lan Chen's signature militant dance pose.
*Box 30, folder 6, Jay and Si-lan Chen Leyda Papers and Photographs,
Elmer Holmes Bobst Library, New York University.*

forming an "authentic modern" China to entertain and inform ordinary Americans from diverse communities. Chinese American journalist Helena Kuo and Ayako Ishigaki, a Japanese American feminist and peace activist who had reported for the progressive *New Masses* and *China Today*, joined Si-lan's national tours.[76] Her pioneering approach inspired other intellectuals and artists of Chinese ancestry, including Liu Liangmo, Wang Yung, and the aviatrixes Ya-ching Lee, Hilda Yank Sing Yen (颜雅清), and Jessie Zheng to launch their own tours. Si-lan joined Lee and singer Jen Kung Li, a graduate of the University of Nanjing and the Julliard School of Music, to appear at United China Relief's fourth Red Feather Night in Philadelphia in 1942. Si-lan's solid reputation in the American dance community was demonstrated at the 1940 Dance Archives reception at the MoMA. She attended as the "Chinese Dancer," along with "Hindu Dancer" Ragini Devi, "Leading Spanish Dancer" La Argentinita, "Star of Ballet Russe" Alexandra Danilova, and Martha Graham.[77]

During her trips abroad for immigration purposes, Si-lan performed for the Chinese Red Cross at the Palace of Fine Arts in Mexico and toured Port of Spain; Bridgetown, Barbados; Georgetown, Guyana; and Bermuda for the Win the War Association, turning over the proceeds from a concert in Bermuda to the China Aid Fund. While approaching local Chinese in Georgetown for a benefit concert on behalf of the Chinese Red Cross, she encountered complex identity politics. The wealthy "British" Chinese merchants' attitude hindered other Chinese from working on behalf of China publicly, as Si-lan observed.[78]

Si-lan maintained her connection with the African American community, especially with Langston Hughes. She wrote to him in 1942, "I'm really quite grown up now—at last! And finally discovered the marvelous dance of my African ancestors." She composed movements to jazz and blues, which she had tentatively started in Moscow, turning what had seemed "so sexy" into tragedy and protest, as she reflected in her autobiography. One such program, *Southern Blues*, is adapted from a poem by Hughes. African American blues singer Huddie Ledbetter (better known as "Lead Belly") frequently performed the song at Si-lan's concerts. The African American press featured Si-lan as a "young Chinese dancer." She lent her talent to multiracial functions, where she encountered Liu Liangmo. She joined Duke Ellington and dozens of other performers at a party to celebrate the first birthday of the Friends of the Abraham Lincoln Brigade for U.S. servicemen fighting in Spain in 1938. The *Crisis* promoted a joint recital by Si-lan and the pianist William D. Allen sponsored by the China Aid Council and the Negro Committee for Spanish Refugee Relief at the High School of Music and Art in New York City in 1939. The paper detailed comprehensively her family and career background, highlighting her accomplishments amid wars and exiles, and somewhat exaggerated in reporting that she had "danced often for the Chinese army in Hankow." She danced at a New York Theater Arts Committee venue in Philadelphia to raise funds for the Committee for People's Rights in 1940. She shared the stage with Ethel Waters, Bill Robinson, Helen Hayes, John Garfield, and other entertainers at the "Night of Nights for China" sponsored by the China Aid Council at the Central Theater of Radio City in New York City. She joined Liu, Canada Lee, Josh White, Earl Robinson, the boogie-woogie pianists of Café Society Downtown, and other "Broadway-ites" in appearing at a "Stars for China" benefit sponsored by the American Friends of the Chinese People at Town Hall in 1941. Oscar-winning actor Luise Rainer performed a chapter from Pearl S. Buck's *The Good Earth* on both occasions. Similarly identifying with the African American community, Jay Leyda now described his birth place in Ohio as "where Paul Lawrence Dunbar was born."[79]

ON THE MARGINS OF HOLLYWOOD (1941–47)

The Leydas survived the turbulent post–Pearl Harbor and postwar years in Hollywood. With the repeal of the Chinese Exclusion Act on December 17, 1943, the significance of Si-lan's race faded. However, her past and present radical politics continued to pose a formidable obstacle as the Cold War intensified.

The Leydas appeared on the radar of the FBI, whose New York office first forwarded a file on Jay Leyda titled "The New Lander, espionage" to its Washington, D.C., headquarters on July 3, 1940. Mysteriously, he lost his job at the MoMA around the same time, and the imminent prospect of his being drafted added to uncertainty for the couple. Fortunately, studio work in Hollywood opened up to Soviet and China themes following U.S. involvement in the war. After Leyda was hired by Warner Brothers for the film *Mission to Moscow*, the couple settled into a cramped apartment at 6227 1/4 De Longpre Avenue in Hollywood, where they would live from August 1941 to April 1947. Since Si-lan's return from the West Indies to New York City aboard the S. S. *Evangeline* on August 14, 1941, her six-month "visit" was extended a few times (fig. 4.10). Fearing that she would not be allowed to continue to "visit" once he joined the military and the marriage would be torn apart permanently, Leyda desperately petitioned to defer his draft. The FBI

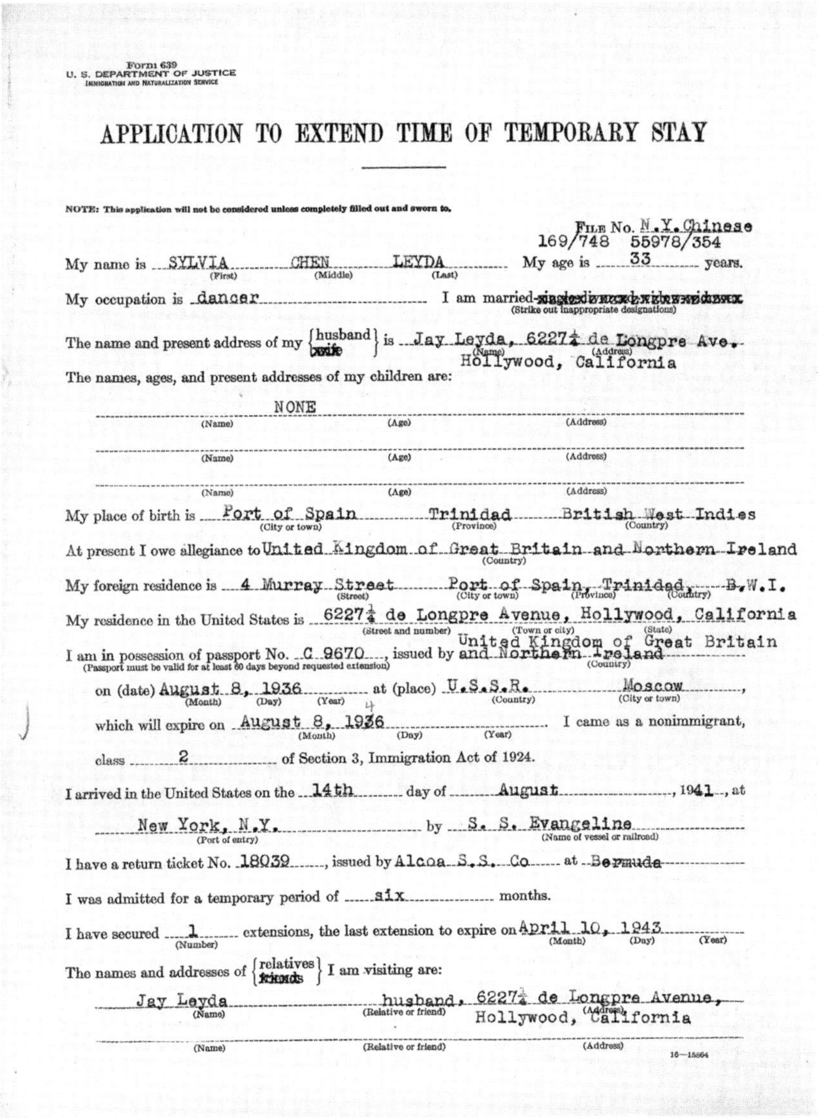

Form 639
U. S. DEPARTMENT OF JUSTICE
IMMIGRATION AND NATURALIZATION SERVICE

APPLICATION TO EXTEND TIME OF TEMPORARY STAY

NOTE: This application will not be considered unless completely filled out and sworn to.

FILE No. N.Y.Chinese
169/748 55978/354

My name is SYLVIA   CHEN   LEYDA   My age is 33 years.
        (First)   (Middle)   (Last)

My occupation is dancer   I am married-single,widowed,divorced
(Strike out inappropriate designations)

The name and present address of my {husband/wife} is Jay Leyda, 6227¼ de Longpre Ave.,
                                                        (Name)   (Address)
                                        Hollywood, California

The names, ages, and present addresses of my children are:

NONE
        (Name)   (Age)   (Address)

        (Name)   (Age)   (Address)

        (Name)   (Age)   (Address)

My place of birth is Port of Spain   Trinidad   British West Indies
                     (City or town)   (Province)   (Country)

At present I owe allegiance to United Kingdom of Great Britain and Northern Ireland
                               (Country)

My foreign residence is 4 Murray Street   Port of Spain, Trinidad,   B.W.I.
                        (Street)   (City or town) (Province) (Country)

My residence in the United States is 6227¼ de Longpre Avenue, Hollywood, California
                                     (Street and number)   (Town or city)   (State)

I am in possession of passport No. C 9670, issued by United Kingdom of Great Britain
(Passport must be valid for at least 60 days beyond requested extension)   and Northern Ireland
                                                                           (Country)

on (date) August 8, 1936   at (place) U.S.S.R.   Moscow   ,
          (Month) (Day) (Year) 4   (Country)   (City or town)

which will expire on August 8, 1936   I came as a nonimmigrant,
                     (Month) (Day) (Year)

class 2   of Section 3, Immigration Act of 1924.

I arrived in the United States on the 14th day of August , 1941 , at

New York, N.Y.   by S. S. Evangeline
(Port of entry)   (Name of vessel or railroad)

I have a return ticket No. 18032, issued by Alcoa S.S. Co at Bermuda

I was admitted for a temporary period of six months.

I have secured 1 extensions, the last extension to expire on April 10, 1943
               (Number)   (Month) (Day) (Year)

The names and addresses of {relatives/friends} I am visiting are:

Jay Leyda   husband, 6227¼ de Longpre Avenue,
(Name)   (Relative or friend)   (Address)
            Hollywood, California

(Name)   (Relative or friend)   (Address)

16—15864

FIGURE 4.10. One of Si-lan Chen's application forms for extending her "visit" in the United States. Note that she had to present a return ticket, in this case to Bermuda. *Box 29, folder 5, Leyda Papers and Photographs, Elmer Holmes Bobst Library, New York University.*

alleged that Si-lan had declared that Leyda would risk jail to resist the draft and that she would divorce him if he ended up in the military. Still, he joined the U.S. Army Tank Corps at Fort Knox in late 1943 and was honorably discharged in 1944 after contracting pneumonia.[80]

It turned out that Leyda's service actually helped to alleviate Si-lan's precarious immigrant status. While confirming her ineligibility for paid work with the INS, the Selective Service authorities learned that the "present practice" was to allow any "visitor" to be employed. Accordingly, she notes in her autobiography that she had to find employment to augment Leyda's salary as a private in the military. Si-lan continued to work with African American artists. Her "debut in Hollywood" was a joint dance concert with Archie Savage, a pioneer in modern African American dance, at the Assistance League Playhouse in 1943. The *Los Angeles Times* reported that "the diminutive Eurasian's . . . sinuous body ate up the space of the little Playhouse stage like a panther." Captivated by Si-lan's performance, the Allied Arts League invited her to their meeting, to answer questions about the Soviet Union. Collaborating with African American composer William Grant Still, a close friend of Hughes; the Negro male Quartette; and Russian dancer Olga Cantu, she danced at the Redland Society Bowl and the Ebell Theater in Los Angeles between 1943 and 1945, sometimes to West Indian music at some of the concerts. In 1945 in Hollywood, she shared the stage with Earl Robinson, Huddie Ledbetter, the Abraham Lincoln Brigade Chorus, and other artists at a folk musical based on the front-line songs of the United Nations and named after the new song by Robinson and lyricist E. Y. Harburg, "We're in the Same Boat, Brother."[81]

Si-lan's first film role was the "rice Christian" in *Keys of the Kingdom* (1944) by 20th Century Fox. Her profound loathing of the Nationalist government led her to side with Hollywood over the former's campaign to purge films that insulted China or the Chinese. In her autobiography, she would laud *Keys* "as the first large-scale Chinese subject filmed in Hollywood without the official sanction and veto power of the Chinese government. Their interference with MGM's *The Good Earth* had taught the studios a lesson. In spite of pressure from Chungking, we relied on a young Jesuit priest, Father Albert O'Hara, to keep us reasonably accurate and authentic. Gregory Peck needed no coaching. I relied largely on walking and moving in a Chinese manner to draw attention away from my less-sure words. The finished film ran into no trouble in China." Ultimately, like other nonwhite talents, Si-lan was frustrated during her brief stint in Hollywood by the "distinct contrast between the responsible technicians and the often irresponsible contents of the films." She complained to her husband how director John M. Stahl attempted to "show me what he thought was a Chinese character. Oh dear shades of Chin Chin Chinaman, subservient is what he wants." She vowed to resist, "I won't be a wilted lotus blossom to fit into any director's perception of what a Chinese person is like." Among Si-lan's costars was H. T. Hsiang, a writer and actor from China whose trouble with the INS had landed him in the Ellis Island immigration station from November 1940 to July 1941. In a phone call, Hsiang supported her in her conflict with Stahl regarding the authority to present "authentic" Chineseness.[82]

The rest of Si-lan's Hollywood credits were for dancing and choreography. Her second job was providing a ballet background for another 20th Century Fox production, *Anna and the King of Siam* (1946), based on Margaret Landon's bestseller on her missionary experience in Thailand. Si-lan would recall that she had "thoroughly enjoyed" composing the Siamese ballet by "stitching together passages" from all the recordings of Siamese and Balinese music available at the Fox music department. However, her first on-screen choreography was almost invisible. After seeing *Anna* with Percy's son Brian in New York City, Hughes wrote to Si-lan in 1946, "I saw your name on the program, but the dance sequence came on and off so quickly that I could not tell where you were. (Damn the cutting room!) but Brian swears he saw you." She responded graciously, "I was awfully pleased . . . even if you did not see me." The film was advertised in the *Shanghai Daily* among "ten notable motion pictures." Si-lan staged several dance moments in *Slave Girl* (1947), a Universal Studios vehicle for Yvonne De Carlo. She was frustrated that "the directors and the writers never bothered to pin down the date or place — vaguely exotic (and in color), perhaps North Africa." Meanwhile, the clichéd Hollywood portrayal of colonial space as timeless enabled her to "fantasize" freely. "Made up with lots of extra wrinkles," she auditioned for the role that eventually went to Tilly Losch in *Duel in the Sun*. She played the only Chinese role in *South Sea Sinner* (1950) with Universal Studios, which was panned in the *New York Times*.[83] Si-lan last appeared on the silver screen as an uncredited old woman in the anticommunist *Peking Express* (Paramount, 1951), the first Hollywood film set in the People's Republic of China.

SI-LAN AND JACK'S PARALLEL WARTIME ENDEAVORS

In 1942, President Roosevelt and T. V. Soong, China's minister of foreign affairs, attended a ceremony to issue a five-cent stamp commemorating the Sino-American alliance. The first U.S. stamp ever featuring a foreign language, it bears a map of China covered by Chinese characters for the slogan "Fight the War and Build the Country," under the portraits of Abraham Lincoln and Sun Yat-sen. Accompanying a photograph of this occasion, the Black newspaper *People's Voice*, edited by Adam Clayton Powell, published an article lauding the Chen siblings' mixed heritage and their contributions to the war from the "four corners of the earth."[84]

Si-lan's contribution to China's resistance was inspired by her family's transpacific endeavors, especially Jack's. Immediately after her debut concert in the United States, Jack wrote that he was "anxious to hear about" it. He offered strong views on class as usual, insisting that "modern dance must necessarily be at first mainly of a realistic pantomimic nature." Si-lan sought his advice on Buddy Ebsen, Imogene Coca, and other dancers performing in her Broadway concert. Jack helped to connect Si-lan's work directly with China. He requested that she forward some illustrations for a book about Isadora Duncan, translated by a friend of his, through the Shanghai address of Yao Xinnong, China's premier poet and an associate of the late Lu Xun.[85] Si-lan's wartime endeavors on behalf of China were acknowledged there. Citing Havas News in New York, *Woman's Literature* and the *China Press* reported on her 1939 fundraising concert for war orphans in China, commenting that "the daughter of the former minister of foreign affairs" gained fame in the United States as a "Chinese dancer."[86]

Si-lan's concert tours to win sympathy for disaster-stricken yet modern (new) China were matched by Jack's transcontinental exhibitions of realistic cartoons by young artists in China working under his mentorship. Their art broke away from traditional paintings of landscapes and flowers to highlight the motherland's suffering and militant resistance, a sentiment shared by Liu Liangmo. While trapped in Shanghai, Jack emerged as a leading cartoonist, as he rightfully claimed in his letter to Si-lan. Among his numerous publications was a series on the world journey of a character called "Little Chen," a Chinese peasant boy. While censorship and widespread kidnapping gradually closed all the magazines he worked for, Jack started to publish long political essays in local English papers and the magazine *Voice of China*. He hoped to "break into the American press seriously," after he published two articles in *Asia* and a drawing in the *New Masses*.[87]

Jack's ordeal with the Soviet bureaucracy finally ended with a visa in June 1937. He returned to Moscow with his long-packed trunk full of artwork for overseas exhibitions, as encouraged by Sun Ke. Then he traveled to London, where he was involved with several left-wing societies, including the China Campaign Committee and China Relief Commission, to promote support for China's resistance. He connected with Paul Robeson under the FBI's watchful eyes. At a Trafalgar Square mass rally organized by the China Relief Commission, Jack spoke on Japanese brutality against China following Robeson's singing of "Chee Lai!." His cartoon exhibition toured Oxford, Cambridge, Dundee, Glasgow, Edinburgh, and Swansea under his newly official Chinese name, Chen I-wan, sharing Si-lan's patriotic gesture. His success convinced the American Friends of the Chinese People, which was working closely with Si-lan, to sponsor the exhibition at American Contemporary Art galleries in New York City, the Boston area (including Harvard University), Detroit, Chicago, Los Angeles, San Francisco, and Berkeley. The *New York Times* and *Life* magazine featured drawings from the exhibition and gave enthusiastic reviews. Jack had arrived with the exhibition on December 16, 1937, in New York City, where he told the INS that, as an artist and journalist by profession, he was supported by his father and earnings from painting and drawing. He stayed with the Leydas and allegedly solicited assistance from several organizations for the China Campaign Committee, according to the FBI, and left San Francisco on April 8, 1938, for Hong Kong. After meeting Eugene, who had returned there from Paris to serve the wartime government, Jack adventured to Yan'an in the summer, anticipating a "world wide scoop!" as Edgar Snow and Agnes Smedley did a year earlier. Jack wrote to Si-lan, promising to send her music for a *yangge* (crop sprout) dances that he collected there; he reported seeing the "reds work regularly" in Shanghai, considering them his "main inspiration." With recently acquired art for a new show, he returned to Hong Kong, aiming to raise funds and equipment for an "art-propaganda school on the Lines of the Lu Hsun Art Institute" in South China.[88]

As fellow pioneers in redefining wartime popular arts for the illiterate and in overcoming language barriers through visual means, both Si-lan and Jack strove to present the proper "Chineseness" and promote militarism. He introduced and defined the cartoon movement and provided theoretical guidance to young cartoonists in China by publishing critical essays in the Chinese and Western press and lecturing at the International Arts Theater. In "China's Militant Cartoons," which appeared in *Asia*, Jack called for reason, healthy spirit, and "good taste" in militarism. Despite the extreme Japanese brutality, Chinese artists must reject promoting hatred, and stick to fighting for justice, Jack urged. Noting hundreds of hands saluting Chiang in "Hitler fascist style" in a drawing, Jack commented, "That is too bad! We should salute our leader with a tight fist for the united front." He insisted, "The best art is the best propaganda. . . . While the world is gazing at our anti-

Japanese, anti-fascist struggles with urgency and sympathy, we must prove that we are superior to the invaders in every aspect." Both siblings were careful to present the right "looks" of the Chinese patriots. Sensitive to racial stereotypes in media abroad, Jack called for attention to detail in presenting Chinese physical features. For instance, considering a street cartoon at Hankou, he was concerned that a Chinese soldier "with eyes and mouth wide open, teeth completely exposed, and a particularly flat nose" looked "like a clown." Jack emphasized, "We must select the model of brave soldiers with caution to symbolize the Chinese nation as a whole." [89]

Consistent with Si-lan's voluntary service on behalf of China, Jack highlighted cartoonists' poverty and sacrifice. They were former or part-time students, journalists, teachers, commercial artists, and clerks, scraping along, "and yet—making cartoon history." Si-lan's ethnic dance and Jack's indigenous cartoon movement shared an undercurrent of sexuality. While her dance signified female exoticism, Jack pointed out that Chinese cartoons were "most essentially a man's art, which indulges in what is best described as 'Elizabethan coarseness'" and eroticism under influence of such magazines as the American *Esquire*, but "with an element of quite Chinese abandon." [90]

CONFRONTING THE WAR AS A FAMILY

As the war became a global conflagration, other members of the Chen family were forced to fend for themselves. Promised that he would get a visa to Moscow if he applied in London, Jack traveled to the British capital in late 1938, but his frantic efforts proved fruitless. He waited in vain for the arrangements to return to China that Percy had promised. They lost touch after Hong Kong was evacuated, and Percy left for Chongqing to join the Nationalist government. Forced out of his brief service in the Chinese government, Eugene had returned to London. He was able to avoid military service as a skilled metal worker making aircraft, an obligation from which a major news agency interested in hiring him as a news editor attempted to arrange his release in 1941. [91]

Eugene wrote sympathetically about Leyda's unemployment but hinted that he could not help as before: "I know what no job means, darn it, though I must say I never lived so well as I did then on my debts. . . . Which I am still paying off now. Another five pounds will see me clear though, thank heaven." He reported that he and his wife were "doing rather well," but their trouble was with margarine coupons rather than money. With unusual political foresight, Jack predicted in 1940 that the war would last about five

Sylvia Si-lan Chen Leyda

years and Leyda would be drafted in a year or two. He analyzed Si-lan's options for surviving the war in the United States, the Soviet Union, or Canada but warned, "Do not go for heaven's sake back to Trinidad." Eugene echoed strongly, "Glad to . . . know you are safely back from the wild West Indies," which "are not for us." The hearts of Jack and Eugene were in the troubled ancestral home. Jack proposed China as an "excellent" alternative that would add new meaning to Si-lan's dance career, despite "material discomfort." He suggested that if she could get some of Yolanda's $1,000 draft in Shanghai, he would join her in New York, then they could sail to Chongqing together by way of Burma before war broke out in the Pacific. Eugene looked forward to the future in his letter to the Leydas: "So dear children, until after the war, we meet in China."[92]

The rapid progress of the war forced the Chens to make radical adjustments. By August 1940, the Blitz had forced Jack to evacuate with his English Jewish girlfriend Betty Miriam Aaronson to Evesham, Worcestershire. While remaining active in the local art scene through his own art studio, he was hired later that year as staff cartoonist for the (London) *Daily Worker*, which was soon shut down. According to the FBI, he helped to found a *Daily Worker* Defense League, which denounced the government for depriving the newspaper employees of a livelihood. He then started to work as a radio correspondent for TASS, the Soviet news agency. In his letter to the Leydas, Eugene announced that Jack had "made quite a name for himself as a British proletarian artist." Jack continued to send his new work to the Leydas for placement in the United States.[93]

After Jack divorced Flaxman, married Aaronson, and had another son, Chenny (Chenni) I-Wan (一文), in 1941, his new family moved to North Wales. On order from Eugene, Si-lan served as the difficult messenger during the breakup. Eugene wrote to the Leydas on August 17, 1941, "Jack earnestly asks you to write to Lucy and Yone and break the news" that he "has got married to Betty and they are having a baby sometime next year. . . . He wants Lucy to end their engagement, *finally*. . . . I think that you should write to them air mail *immediately*, you or Jay." Eugene argued that the long separation and slim prospect of Jack's return to the Soviet Union justified the change. Eugene shared Jack's indignation over Lucy Flaxman's alleged sabotage of Jack's attempts to get a visa back to Moscow. He mentioned a "rather peculiar letter" to Jack in which Flaxman declared they were obligated to "choose definitely which country they belonged to" and her choice was to stay "where she was a 'good patriot.'" Eugene continued, "Worse, she announced that for 'personal' and 'political' reasons she was not going to do anything to help him get over." He instructed Si-lan to "tell Yone also to look after Denny [Jack and Flaxman's son] until further arrangements can be made." Delaying the difficult task for several months, probably until Chenny was born, Si-lan forwarded Jack's request to Flaxman, who had evacuated with her "very sick" son, her parents, and a maid to the village of Orda, in the Urals, in early 1942. Echoing Eugene, Si-lan largely blamed Flaxman for the "terrible mess." Heartbroken, Flaxman vented to Si-lan about Jack's consistent callousness but agreed to obtain the divorce when she could make it to Moscow.[94]

The war eventually delivered a major blow to the Chens — Eugene died in Shanghai of a heart ailment on May 20, 1944, after three years' house arrest by the Japanese. His passion and ambition had not allowed him to settle into the forced retirement in London. On the reverse side of his 1941 letter to the Leydas, Eugene jotted a quick note: "Percy! I got a grandiloquent letter from him saying that he had fixed everything up with all the ministers and governments who would get me out to China." Accordingly, Eugene wrote letters and even went to see Quo Tai Chi, then minister of foreign affairs, but heard from nobody for several months. Frustrated and humiliated, he vented against Percy: "Typical of the man. Don't know where he is, but heard he had gone to Chunking." Still, he wished for the safety of Percy's family under heavy bombing. Next to Eugene's note, someone jotted, "The old man is in Hong Kong."[95]

Si-lan's autobiography noted that Eugene lived in Hong Kong following the Pearl Harbor attack. While he took a "roving ambassadorial appointment" and prepared to visit the United States in that capacity, the Japanese took over the city. He was detained along with his longtime friend and diplomat Weiching Williams Yen in the Gloucester Hotel and then transferred to Dongcheng Hotel in Shanghai in the spring of 1942. Eugene fearlessly resisted Japanese pressure to join Wang Jingwei's collaborationist government, and his voice resonated through Chinese press. He called on the Chinese to protest the imprisonment of Mahatma Gandhi, whom he acclaimed as a "symbol of Asian struggles for revival, self-determination, and freedom from imperialist political oppression and economic exploitations." An essay in *Politics Monthly* attempted to connect Eugene with Wang Jing-wei by falsely stating that the latter arranged his 1931 trip to Japan to improve Sino-Japanese relations. Eugene unambiguously rejected the claim: "Wang was not in a position to do that." While the Japanese cited Sun Yat-sen's Pan-Asianism, Eugene reportedly responded, "Sun's Greater East Asia was among equals. We could only talk about peaceful cooperation after your

Sylvia Si-lan Chen Leyda

military withdraws completely from China, including Manchuria!" Si-lan would recall that the last words Eugene's children heard from him came through a reporter's story, in which Eugene denounced as "a pack of lies" the rumor circulated by the Japanese War Office that he had consented to join Wang's collaborationist government.[96]

Soon after Eugene's death, the so-called number one cultural traitor, Chen Binghe of the collaborationist *Shanghai Daily*, directed Eugene's secretary, Li Weichen, to publish a lengthy "Report on Mr. Chen Youren" in *Politics Monthly*. Li first "refuted the rumor" that Eugene's death was "abnormal." He reminded "compatriots" that Eugene was a sixty-nine-year-old man (he was actually sixty-five), despite "his youthful progressive energy." Li blamed the cold Eugene caught due to the lack of heat during his transition from Hong Kong to Shanghai for his rapidly declining health, detailing his subsequent physical condition by months, days, and then hours.[97]

Li's piece included the alleged full text of Eugene's will, which Li claimed to translate from English into Chinese. The key sentences read,

> This is my last will. All my current and future estates and personal belongs of any category be bequeathed to my wife. I solemnly state: Only my wife can use my name or speak for me; Only my wife can make statements regarding my name and reputation; My wife has the full authority to dispose of my body in any manner she considers proper, including cremating and spreading my ashes in China's major rivers or the sea. I declare: I am pure Chinese with both my parents originally from Guangdong Province; I wish to alert the public that, from all those not of pure Chinese blood, male or female, I absolutely sever ties and do not recognize any as family or relatives. If anyone dare to dispute them, I hereby entrust my wife to sustain my own wishes. If my wife takes any action or pursues any lawsuit, I sincerely ask all my friends, Chinese or other compatriots of the yellow race, to support my wife. November 26, 1942, in Shanghai.

Li acknowledged that this will was of a "totally different nature" from the one Eugene had orally communicated to him in a Hong Kong hotel, but he saw no reason to release the previous one.[98]

Shockingly, the racist shadow that Eugene had faced was pushed to extremes, while he allegedly disowned his mixed children in pursuit of his own pure Chineseness. Eugene had indeed been growing increasingly distant from his children since his latest marriage. His only wartime correspondence to the Leydas was a reply to Si-lan's letter almost one year later, mainly to assign her the task of facilitating Jack's divorce. He used the address of the Chinese consulate in London, rather than his own, and signed formally as "Bernard."[99] Still, it is hard to believe that was his wish. Anxious to counter the rumor that Eugene had entrusted others to carry out his political beliefs, Li Weichen claimed that Georgette Chang authorized him, as a friend and colleague of Eugene's for seven years, to write his "report." Li warned those operating in Eugene's name to heed the will. He stressed that Eugene's "determination" to disown any family or relatives "not of pure Chinese blood" was well known among his friends, since he had repeatedly made such unambiguous declarations in his correspondence. Li specified that when "a relative of such category" misused his name in political activities six years earlier, Eugene wrote to relevant military and political authorities and published a public statement in Hong Kong's *South China Morning Post* to clarify his position. The alleged offender was probably Percy, who then served as Sun Ke's assistant at the Legislative Yuan in Chongqing. Unaware or undeterred by Li's intimidation, Percy claimed in his autobiography that in his political career he had mostly carried out his father's vision.[100]

According to Li, Eugene stressed his being "pure Chinese" because he had acutely suffered from the smear that he was "mixed" due to his poor command of the Chinese language. Initiated by his political opponents in China, such attacks were worst and most frequent in British press when Eugene led the Chinese nation to diplomatic victory. Probably fooled by the Chiangs' Australian adviser William Henry Donald, according to Li, even John Gunther included this "senseless mean smear" in his influential book *Inside Asia* (1939). Li cited Eugene's ninety-year-old mother as living proof of his parental ties to Guangdong Province. He affirmed that the role of Eugene's father in the Taiping Rebellion showed his "hot blood was not only of pure Chinese, but also of passionate nationalists and revolutionaries." Reviewing Eugene's career from "a rich capitalist gentleman to a modern Chinese revolutionary," Li returned to an old anecdote. When offered release from the prison of the Manchurian warlord Zhang Zuolin on the condition that he acknowledge his British citizenship, Eugene had reportedly replied without hesitation: "Shoot me, I am Chinese."[101] However, the rumor of Eugene's mixed heritage was so deep-seated that Paul Robeson wrote in 1951 that the father of the Chen siblings was "part Chinese and part Negro."[102]

It is unlikely that the Chen children were ever aware of Li's piece, according to Chen Yuen-tsung, partly due to the language barrier. Si-lan learned of her father's death through English media. However, she was not spared political controversy even after his death. Si-lan would recall being disturbed

Sylvia Si-lan Chen Leyda

by an anonymous "vituperative" obituary notice published in the *New York Times*, which soon featured a rewritten piece without the open hostility, to her relief.[103] Si-lan and her siblings would have been heartened by the post-war Chinese media's tributes to the courage and strength of the "legendary" diplomat during his imprisonment by the Japanese.[104]

SURVIVING THE EARLY COLD WAR

The close of the war brought one bit of good news to Si-lan: she was finally granted permanent residency in the United States in Los Angeles on April 24, 1946, and applied for U.S. citizenship on January 14, 1949. Jack advised that the sooner Si-lan was naturalized, the better, warning, "Don't prejudice it by any unwise action. . . . A U.S. citizen able and willing to work for real international peace will be very worthwhile." It seemed that the United States would finally become her home after nearly two decades as a "visitor." However, the increasing anticommunist hysteria and the long arm of the Nationalist government posed more formidable obstacles. Alarmed by the State Department's cancellation of passports, including those of some of their friends in Hollywood and of Du Bois and Robeson, Si-lan abandoned her application for U.S. citizenship, retaining her British passport, which she had validated on August 8, 1946, in Bermuda.[105] The FBI files on the Leydas, with data from media coverage, her extensive INS files, and reports from FBI agents and domestic and foreign informants on their daily activities, had been growing rapidly.

Reminiscent of the treatment of Liu Liangmo, the War Department forwarded a memorandum detailing the couple's activities to the FBI on February 21, 1942, before Leyda was drafted. Two months later, J. Edgar Hoover instructed the New York office to conduct a "thorough" and "immediate investigation" of them. The Bureau's surveillance followed them to Hollywood, as its New York office twice forwarded reports on Si-lan to its counterpart in Los Angeles on March 10, 1943, and January 10, 1944. The latter followed up with lengthy reports on her on February 24, 1944, and April 19, 1950. The focus was on her involvement with alleged communists and communist-front organizations, which the FBI legally referred to as "coming within the Purview of Executive Order 9835," as declared by the U.S. attorney general. Such reports provided a glimpse of Si-lan's political activism on behalf of the Soviet Union during the war and the CCP postwar. The FBI believed that the Leydas served on the committee to transform the American Polish League into the Southern California branch of the

National Council of American-Soviet Friendship. Si-lan allegedly served on the executive board for the council's Los Angeles branch, as reported by the *Daily People's World*, the alleged "Communist news organ of the West Coast," and its program committee to organize a rally in late 1943. She was allegedly scheduled to dance for the 1944 Lenin Memorial Rally under the auspices of the Los Angeles County Communist Party, but failed to appear. Si-lan's 1944 application to visit the Soviet Union must have aroused further suspicions. At the INS's demand, she detailed her relatives and acquaintances in the Soviet Union, including Mikhail Borodin; Sergei Eisenstein; Lisa Mukusei, wife of the former vice consul in Los Angeles; and Anna Louise Strong, who "knew me in Hankou, Moscow, and New York." The FBI followed the Leydas' interaction with Joris Ivens, "a dutiful Communist who plied back and forth between Holland and the Soviet Union in the early 1930s . . . an instructor in revolutionary literature in Moscow." Si-lan credited Ivens's film *Four Hundred Millions* for the inspiration to present an "authentic" China to her American audiences through dance tours. In 1945, the Leydas allegedly served on the advisory board of the American-Russian Club of Los Angeles, a nonprofit organization enabling U.S. citizens of Russian descent to provide medical and other relief supplies to the Soviet people. Even their receipt of a copy of "Call to a Conference to Strengthen American Soviet Relations" in 1950 was recorded by the FBI. Si-lan had also been spotted attending a lecture by Vice President Henry Wallace in 1944 and talking to performer Sue Remos, an alleged Communist Party member, onstage.[106]

The FBI quickly picked up on Si-lan's activism during China's civil war and the Korean War, similar to its surveillance of W. E. B. Du Bois and Paul Robeson. She reportedly attended general meetings and the 1949 executive meeting of the Congress of American Women and was elected cochair of its Cultural Committee. She was spotted speaking about the peace movement in China at the congress's International Women's Day gathering and joining the picket line organized by its Los Angeles chapter in front of the local Republican Party headquarters to demonstrate "for peace." The Congress of American Women cosponsored a mass farewell gathering for Charlotta Bass, editor and publisher of the *California Eagle*, before her scheduled departure on November 28 to join Eslanda Robeson and others in Beijing for the First Asian Women's Congress. The FBI noted that, at the gathering, Si-lan enthusiastically served as mistress of ceremonies, spoke, and performed. The *California Eagle* reported that she shared the stage with Earl Robinson at a holiday celebration for the Southern California Labor School, and that she taught weekend classes on children's dance and on China, as confirmed by an FBI informant, a female student attending the school.[107]

The 1948 report of the Senate Fact-Finding Committee on Un-American Activities for the State of California listed Si-lan among the sponsors of the China Conference Arrangements Committee in Los Angeles, which allegedly pressured the U.S. government to withdraw military support for Chiang Kai-shek. She was also allegedly active in the Committee for a Democratic Far Eastern Policy (CDFEP). The FBI noted that she was introduced as "one of the world's greatest dancers and the daughter of Eugene Chen, former minister of Sun Yat-sen," at several events sponsored by the CDFEP to raise awareness of China issues between 1949 and 1951. A 1950 event to "Celebrate China's '1776'" and to "Salute the Greatest People's Liberation of Today" featured Si-lan's performance along with Eslanda Robeson's "first eye-witness report" on women's liberation, land reform, trade unions, and food and the standard of living in the People's Republic of China (PRC). Among the event's sponsors were the CDFEP, then actor Ronald Reagan, and his first wife, Jane Wyman. Si-lan reportedly spoke at the "Chinese dinner" at the Grandview Gardens Restaurant for the CDFEP to launch a "nation-wide campaign for trade recognition and friendship for the PRC." The FBI traced the phone number used for the dinner reservation to her through the telephone directory. At the 1951 forum sponsored by the CDFEP, Si-lan allegedly quoted extensively from Mao Zedong's speech at a forum for artists, stressing that only socialist revolution could rid the world of discrimination. The FBI concluded in its 1944 report, however, that Si-lan was fundamentally harmless: "In view of subject's alien status it would appear that she is ineligible for membership in the Communist Party, U.S.A." The Bureau closed her case on April 19, 1950. Meanwhile, informants supplied the FBI with alleged details of Jay Leyda's Communist Party membership.[108]

The Bureau's interest in Si-lan was suddenly rekindled by "a confidential foreign source which conducts intelligence." Judging by its mostly precise and extremely detailed data on the Chen clan—their aliases (including family nicknames), births, citizenship documents, marriages, residences, employment, travel, contacts, and political activities, the source was almost certainly the Chinese Nationalist government. Despite the persistent rumors of Eugene's mixed heritage, the source conceded his "Chinese descent." However, the source portrayed him as a criminal, who fled from "his creditors and imprisonment" in Trinidad in 1910 and was "imprisoned by the [Chinese] government for allegedly spreading false rumors and attacking government policies" in 1917. Above all, the source highlighted the Chen family's affiliation with the Soviet Union, accusing Eugene of "receiving a large weekly stipend from Russia" and declaring "a willingness to join the Russian Communist Party, and . . . take over the Chinese section of the Comintern." It stated that Mikhail Borodin guided the Chen children's career in the Soviet Union. "Jack's cartoons in *The Moscow Daily News* were primarily focused on the exploitation of colonial peoples by 'imperialist' countries." Si-lan was "heralded as one of the foremost exponents of the Russian dance" and "an ardent admirer of the Russian way of life." Yolanda was "enthusiastic about Russia and about the Communist triumph in China as the solution to China's problems." The source detailed Percy's and Jack's activities and how their speeches "violently attacked the Kuomintang government and alleged intervention of the U.S. in China" but supported the CCP.[109]

The FBI and INS immediately escalated their surveillance of the Leydas and started to create difficulties for them. The FBI's Los Angeles office reopened Si-lan's case, starting a lengthy report on January 27, 1951, to synthesize information, which swelled into forty-four pages by May 20, 1952. The document categorized available data into "personal history," "family connections," and "connections with subversive organizations." It even searched her credit and criminal records. "A foreign confidential source" (likely Japanese authorities) advised the FBI that Si-lan "was arrested for picketing the Japanese consulate in NYC in protest of the Japanese invasion of China" in 1938, but the FBI found no record on her with the New York Police Department. Prominently listed among Si-lan's contacts was Anna Louise Strong, who the FBI alleged had "openly espoused" for the Soviet Union for years before being deported on subversion charges in 1949. The list of "subversive organizations" grew from the above-discussed six to eleven, adding the American Russian Institute (ARI); the Hollywood Arts, Sciences, and Professional Council (HASPC); the Independent Progressive Party (IPP) in Los Angeles County; the American Committee for Protection of Foreign Born; and the Southern California Peace Council (SCPC).

It seemed that Si-lan's professional and political activities continued to be entangled with these organizations. FBI agents followed her to HASPC gatherings, claiming she advocated ending the Korean War and defiantly "stated that she did not care if FBI agents were in the audience, she was going to speak her 'bit' anyhow." As the main speaker at the Commonwealth Club of the IPP in early 1950, Si-lan reportedly stated that the Marshall Plan was helping the Chinese Nationalists instead of the Communist soldiers, who did not loot or rape as the U.S. media complained. She was spotted at the

Southern California Peace Conference to promote the Stockholm Peace Declaration, coordinating Du Bois's efforts. At the "Peace on Earth" rally jointly sponsored by the SCPC and the Los Angeles Labor Peace Committee later that year, she reportedly made a brief speech on how the People's Republic of China was for the benefit of the people instead of profit, and on U.S. soldiers' brutality against women and children in Korea, before reading a poem by Mao Zedong. An FBI informant in Hollywood maintained that Si-lan was a "red-hot radical whose position is perfectly clear," although he had no proof that she was a registered Communist Party member.[110]

In a letter to Leyda, Si-lan explained that while the FBI, the State Department, the Chinese consul, and some "reactionary club women and the agents of UCLA" tried to prevent her from dancing at a UN show, she held her ground lest her enemies be convinced that she was an undercover agent for the PRC. In her notes for a lecture preserved in her papers, Si-lan celebrated China for driving away its colonial masters and Chiang Kai-shek. She concluded that "each of us has to find his citizenship in the world through his own best abilities. Only then we will find ourselves standing alongside those other citizens of the world who believe in the future of the Asiatic countries."[111]

Si-lan paid for her defiance. The INS repeatedly confronted her with tricky questions on paper and in person, putting her under enormous pressure to make affidavits. During one interview in 1942, she denied that she was a member of any club or political party and affirmed her belief in democracy and national independence. She declared that the only organization she had ever joined was the then-dissolved American Dance Association and that Leyda belonged to the American Labor Party. Si-lan intended to participate in the 1951 International Folk Dance Festival held in Italy, France, and the Scandinavian countries as a member of Irwin Parnes's Crossroads of the World dance group based in Hollywood, for six months to a year. Following an in-person interview regarding her application for a reentry permit for the proposed lengthy trip, the INS called her back for a transcribed and sworn "questions and answers" session in February. The INS's detailed reminders of her past activities forced Si-lan to "think" that she had had memberships in the American Association of the United Nations, the Screen Actors Guild in Hollywood, and the YWCA, attended performances of the Actors Laboratory, and danced for other organizations. Pressured whether she had been "in any way associated with" a list of groups "designated by the Attorney General as Communist organizations," Si-lan recalled that she had danced for and spoke on dance in the Soviet Union and on the contemporary "attitude of culture" in China at meetings of the ARI and the CDFEP. She conceded that the Congress of American Women had sponsored a concert of hers at the Wilshire-Ebell Theater about four years earlier. The FBI noted that her statement was "in contradiction to" information "furnished" by informants.[112]

Si-lan then left for New York City and scheduled a departure for Europe on April 12. The Leydas had sublet their Hollywood apartment to Gertrude Binder, a roommate of Agnes Smedley in Shanghai between 1929 and 1930, as the tenant herself revealed to the FBI. Prodded by the FBI, as indicated in the April 25 report from its Los Angeles office to J. Edgar Hoover, the INS soon denied Si-lan's application "on the grounds that her reentry would be prejudicial to the interests of the US," because she "is, or has been, affiliated with the Communist Party." She retained attorney Tats Kushida, the Southern California regional director of the Japanese American Citizens League dedicated to combatting anti-Japanese American legislation, to appeal the denial. Kushida appeared at the INS office in Los Angeles in May 1951, demanding the permit on her behalf, of course, to no avail.[113]

Persecution by the FBI and INS forced the Leydas into internal exile, roaming around the United States on the verge of homelessness. They moved ten times from Hollywood, to New York City, to Cambridge, Massachusetts, from 1947 to 1951, under close observation by the FBI in cooperation with the U.S. Post Office. Adapting to such adverse settings, the couple continued.to pursue their careers with determination. Since neither was able to obtain studio work anymore by 1950, they relocated to the East Coast and Leyda changed his profession to research in nineteenth-century American literature. His published work on Herman Melville helped him secure two Guggenheim fellowships to work on Emily Dickinson from 1948 to 1952. His books on these topics were later chosen for the White House library.[114] Si-lan remained active at the Choreographers' Workshop in New York City. In 1954, the Leydas were invited to the Yaddo colony, a prestigious retreat for artists and writers near Saratoga Springs, New York. In 1956, they moved to Washington, D.C., where he worked on the Dickinson book and she taught dance in public schools.[115] The persecution and drifting seemed to wear them down. In between his research trips, Leyda wrote to Si-lan of his wish to "find some more money right away," deliberating whether he "dare use" a royalty check, "which is really Eisenstein's." While donating a box of materials to the Melville Society Cultural Center, Walter E. Bezanson, a fellow Melville scholar and good friend of Leyda, wrote in an accompanying note dated April 5, 2006:

Jay Leyda left this box of notes and letters with me years ago. He and his exotic wife, Si-lan, stayed with us overnight several times. We had a large old home, and at the time Jay and Si-lan seemed to have no "place" other than the beat up car in which they arrived. Jay asked if he might leave this box with me. He never re-claimed it. . . . It seems appropriate for this miscellany from the time when Jay was working on *The Melville Log* to come to rest with the society. It's merely a fragment from his incredibly productive and slightly mysterious life. He was a dear friend. — Walter[116]

While Si-lan was confined in the United States amid this uncertainty, her siblings resumed their globetrotting, which enabled a family reunion for the first time in a decade under close surveillance of the above-discussed "foreign source" and the FBI. In 1946, Jack and Yolanda, now an acclaimed cinematographer and producer working for the Moscow Children's Studio, returned to China, where the media fondly reported on them as children of the late legendary diplomat. Chinese and Western reporters gathered at the International Hotel to interview Yolanda, the "only cinema entrepreneur of China," although she traveled with a Soviet passport. The Shanghai artistic circles and some bankers urged her to set up a studio to make films "introducing authentic Chinese lives to overseas audiences," starting with one on Sun Yat-sen and Eugene. The "foreign source" informed the FBI that Jack had been briefed by the Communist Party of Great Britain, which he and his wife had joined between 1940 and 1941, before he arrived in China. There, he allegedly joined the China Democratic League, in which Liu Liangmo would soon be active. Consistent with his publications stressing that the CCP leaders were actually pro-British and did not "wish to embark on any action that would embarrass authorities in Hong Kong," Jack's mission was reportedly to promote "trade between China and Great Britain and China and Russia." He wrote to Si-lan after revisiting Yan'an and returned to London the following year to set up a branch of the New China News Agency there, which would be the first overseas CCP news agency, to voice its perspective on the civil war. He also became a special correspondent for the *Shanghai Evening Post & Mercury*. Jack requested that the Leydas deposit $40 in an account at National City Bank in New York City to renew the *China Weekly Review* for his work at the News Agency. He instructed, if the Leydas did not have the cash, they should seek help from Israel Epstein of the CDFEP at 111 West 42nd Street.[117]

Percy and his wife established temporary residence at 100 West 96th

Street, New York City, in 1947. He toured the United States delivering lectures, tried to enlist prominent Americans' support for the China Democratic League, and became cochair of the Liberal Democratic Action Committee of China, as the FBI noted. Yolanda arrived in San Francisco from Shanghai on April 7. After spending several weeks in Los Angeles and touring Paramount Studios, arranged by the Academy of Motion Picture Arts and Sciences, she and the Leydas moved briefly to Percy's vacant apartment. Yolanda sailed on June 10 for London. Despite her long-standing desire to visit Jack, Si-lan did not go due to ongoing immigration concerns. With Jack's assistance, Yolanda toured the cinematic world in London, meeting Lawrence Olivier on the *Hamlet* set, Jean Renoir, and Vivien Leigh. Returning to Odessa, Yolanda worked on a script for the Sun Yat-sen film, tentatively titled "Three Songs about Lenin."[118] She and her husband collaborated most notably on *Romeo and Juliet* in 1955 and on several parts of *War and Peace*, which won the Oscar in 1969 for Best Foreign-Language Film.[119]

Jack's marital life took a tragic turn during the following few years. He filed for divorce "on the grounds of her desertion," before he located his wife in a mental asylum, where she was being treated for schizophrenia and tuberculosis in early 1949. Her family had kept her medical condition a secret. The divorce case ended with his wife's death on August 3 after four years of separation. Preparing for the worst, Jack entrusted the care of his son, Chenny, to Si-lan when necessary. He updated her on his two life insurance policies worth £530, and his savings, house, and other properties worth £500, in addition to the upcoming inheritance of £2,000–3,000 from his former father-in-law. Si-lan did her best to care for the bereaved father and son by sending food and clothing. Some of her parcels disappeared and others arrived opened. Nearly every chocolate in a box she sent "had been pushed in with someone's thumb," Jack wrote. "I suppose they were looking for diamonds this time."[120]

EXILES ABROAD AND THE END (1957–96)

Jack was anxious to realize his dream of settling down in China and returning to the Lu Xun Art Academy as a director and lecturer. His work at the New China News Agency left little time for his "real job," the painting and drawing, which were "really getting somewhere now if only I could get back to my source material," he confided to Si-lan. Although pressured to stay, Jack was determined to leave for China by late 1950. He was romantically enthusiastic, "Things are going fine in China! New Republic, new government! Victory!" Jack had proposed that his sisters and their spouses all join him in the Art Academy. Now that the authorities in China assigned him to work for the *Peking Review*, he had to give up his career as an artist.[121]

Still, Jack forwarded an invitation for Si-lan to help with the "new China's dance." Their cousin Dai Ailian, who had been appointed director of the newly formed Central Dance Ensemble and Beijing Dance Academy, added her urging to Jack's. Dai first learned dance from Si-lan in Trinidad and followed in her footsteps to study in London in 1930. While struggling in London to obtain her visa to the United States, Si-lan enjoyed a reunion with Dai. She wrote to Leyda on December 28, 1936, "Yesterday I went to see some Chinese cousins who were living here — do you remember my telling you about one who dances? She is really quite a good dancer, and a very nice girl, too, and we had lots of fun recalling all the theatrical productions that mother and I organized in Trinidad." Dai went to China through Hong Kong, where Percy saw her through, in 1940. Soon she married Ye Qianyu, in a ceremony presided by Madam Sun Yat-sen. Jack wrote to Si-lan of Dai's move, "She never did a wiser thing.... I understand everything went very nicely." At the 1951 forum sponsored by the CDFEP, Si-lan mentioned proudly that her cousin was developing a "people's dance" in China. She was excited that her own China-themed composition employing classical, modern, and ethnic techniques would be appreciated and developed in China. She was also "intensely curious" to see Beijing, "the center of new China's dance world."[122]

The Leydas started their two-decade-long exile abroad with Leyda's employment at the Cinémathèque Française in Paris in 1957. After their visas to China came through, they reached Beijing in May 1959, soon after the Du Boises. Si-lan would recall the atmosphere of their arrival: "Though I am only half Chinese, I was welcomed back to the 'homeland,' an 'overseas Chinese back where she belongs.'" Happily, in this case, "one drop" of Chinese blood was sufficient to make one Chinese. Si-lan observed that her father's memory was "silently respected and his children are regarded with tolerance and sympathy." Leyda first helped to establish the Chinese Film Archives and arranged the first Chinese film festival in London. Si-lan composed dances at the Beijing Dance Academy, now comfortably employing "the grant pheasant feathers worn by heroic warriors in Peking opera." Anna May Wong had adopted the object for her costumes, but Si-lan had carefully avoided it to maintain the "modern looks" of her choreography in the United States. Echoing Robeson, her "biggest surprise was the transformation of the Congo music into Chinese theater music — an exact translation of every sound that had first attracted me, even the moaning Pygmies."[123]

Si-lan soon ran afoul of the controlling state. Highlighting the distinction between "the new China" and "the old China," the official narrative stressed, to her discomfort, that there was no ballet dancing in China before 1949. The truth was, in addition to the Isadora Duncan group's 1927 visit in Shanghai and Hankou, which Si-lan witnessed, the white Russian immigrants frequently associated with prostitution taught ballet classes and staged performances, sensually known as "thigh dance," in Shanghai and Harbin. Now, under the newly translated romantic name *balei*, grand programs were copied from Soviet state institutes; Si-lan's cartoon-style sketches were marginal in such a stately order. She complained that she "nearly drowned" in the ever-repeating *Swan Lake* at the Beijing Dance Academy: "My first decision was to keep whatever small dances I composed as far as possible from the giant swan!" She would publish an illustrated essay on the theme in *Dance Magazine* more than a decade later. Central Dance Ensemble uncritically imitated the "blonde heroine and Oriental villainess" in *The Fountain of Bakhchisarai*. Yet it also adopted the Soviet patronizing attitude toward the folk dance tradition of ethnic minorities, which the ensemble considered too "raw and direct" and had to be cleansed and disciplined for the music hall. When China and the Soviet Union drifted apart, a synthetic Chinese classical ballet replaced the Western classical one in the Third World. "The thought of endless Nigerian or Chilean productions of *The Magic Lotus Lantern* [based on Chinese mythology] seemed a more horrible prospect for dance creativity in those places than *Swan Lake* seemed to me at first in Peking."[124]

Si-lan had expected that the "Chinese dances" she had composed abroad would be accepted. "Since I am part Chinese and lived all my life among Caucasian people, I thought that the struggle I had to wage in order to dance would mean something to a Chinese audience." However, she quickly found that the realistic style and "Western" background in her choreography, which had represented "authentic" China in the United States, were now anathema. One short ballet originally composed amid the peace movement during the Korean War was particularly criticized, since China had shifted toward advocating violent struggles. In this, Si-lan was receiving a treatment that mirrored the one China gave Robeson's peace advocacy. She persevered with a new dance, *Hutong*, based on children's games in Beijing's alleyways. Among the select audience for its performances at the Nationalities Palace in 1962 were the Du Boises. Noting that their eagerness to commend this original ballet surprised the authorities, Si-lan resumed her hope to help "create ballets of and for modern China." Soon, she turned down an invitation to join the "collective" army project *The Red Detachment of Women*, which evolved into one of the eight model plays sponsored by

Sylvia Si-lan Chen Leyda

Madam Mao Zedong during the Cultural Revolution. The trial of the Gang of Four revealed that Madam Mao's interest in ballet began in 1963, the year Si-lan produced *Hutong*.[125]

U.S. persecution, on the one hand, and harassment by an idealized regime, on the other, took their toll. While Leyda was away, a nervous breakdown sent Si-lan to the First Mental Clinic at Anding Hospital in Beijing. In an undated, hasty note to Leyda, Jack explained that "worry about you and work, difficulty of adjusting are the causes." Apologizing for not having looked after her better, Jack wrote Leyda that "your presence will help crucially."[126] The political crackdown and the open Sino-Soviet split made life "impossible for an independent choreographer." In 1964, the couple left for East Berlin, where Leyda took a job at the Staatliches Film Archive. His five-year stint in China led to an impressive monograph on Chinese cinema, *Dianying: Electric Shadows*. Before their departure, the Leydas and Jack's wife, Chen Yuan-tsung, and son, Chen Jeh, visited the newly erected memorial grave for Eugene at the Babaoshan Cemetery for Revolutionary Heroes, where Shirley Graham Du Bois would be buried as well.[127]

The Leydas' departure was wise. As the Cultural Revolution unfolded, a photograph was exhibited capturing Si-lan demonstrating dance poses at a seminar organized by the Dance Research Institute to welcome her arrival in China. The handwritten caption reads, "Allow the British Chinese modern dancer to perform, spreading poisonous Western bourgeois dance elements in great volume" (fig. 4.11).[128] In 1967, Madam Mao named Dai Ailian for investigation, opening up the dancer's life to relentless persecution and public humiliation. Dai was eventually sent to a farm to tend livestock; after returning home she was forced to darn ballet shoes for twenty days and nights without being allowed to sleep.[129]

During their five years in East Berlin, the Leydas visited the Soviet Union several times. Si-lan started to carry a Trinidad and Tobago passport after the new nation gained independence in 1962. They returned to the United States when Leyda took a job as a teaching fellow at the Ezra Stiles College of Yale University from 1969 to 1970, during which Si-lan's application for a reentry permit to visit her family abroad was turned down. Leyda would recall, "This was refused with such hints of deportation (and no effective support from the university) that we both had nervous breakdowns." The Leydas were forced to move to Toronto, where he worked as an adjunct professor of Fine Arts and she taught dance at York University, before he was recruited as Gottesman Professor of Cinema Studies of the School of the Arts at New York University in 1974.[130]

一九五九年舞研会为欢迎英籍华人现代派舞蹈
家陈西兰组织了座谈会. 让陈西兰表述大量散布西
方资产阶级舞蹈毒素.

FIGURE 4.11. A photograph exhibited during the Cultural Revolution,
accusing Si-lan Chen of "spreading poisonous Western dance elements."
Original photograph from the personal collection of Sheng Jie.
*Digital image provided by Emily Wilcox and the Pioneers of Chinese Dance Digital
Collection, Asia Library, University of Michigan. Reproduced with permission.*

Immediately, New York University retained Samuel Paige of the law
firm Paige & Paige to handle Si-lan's application for an immigrant visa at the
U.S. consulate general in Toronto. Paige's "persistent" efforts proved equally
"fruitless," and her case was transferred to the consulate general in Montreal.
In a letter to Paige, dated November 9, 1976, the consulate there informed
him of "a preliminary finding of ineligibility . . . based upon her past affiliation with Communist front organizations." It advised Si-lan to wait "for an
extended period" in Canada, so that a formal interview in Montreal, essential for a final determination, could be arranged. Using the Freedom of Infor-

Sylvia Si-lan Chen Leyda

mation Act, Paige sought from the FBI documents that determined Si-lan's "ineligibility." The Bureau replied in January 1977 that the "request has been assigned number 37,712," and it would take several months to be processed. Leyda then pleaded with his congressman, Edward I. Koch, to intervene, complaining that Si-lan's treatment by the INS over four decades "can only be described as a constant harassment." She was first refused an immigration visa due to the Chinese Exclusion Act, he explained, and later "we have been allowed only to imagine the reasons for this discrimination." Leyda wrote that Si-lan's "alien" status had prevented her from all domestic political activities, including voting, and she had never belonged to any political party. He suspected that "her father's being a well-known antagonist of Chiang Kai-shek could have encouraged Chinese officials in this country (especially during the war) to invent accusations against her." His suspicion was proved by the above-analyzed FBI files, which the Leydas would receive and deposit in their papers.[131]

Fortunately, Si-lan's family offered unyielding support and experience in jumping endless immigration hurdles. Surviving the Cultural Revolution, Jack and his family, except Chenny, escaped to the United States by way of Hong Kong in 1972. Jack wrote to the Leydas detailing his family's 1977 INS interview in Buffalo for permanent residency. Si-lan was then going through the final round of her immigration ordeal. Jack wrote that for the crucial question "Were you ever a member of any organization?" he always answered, "Yes, but my views are no longer compatible with membership in such organizations." He was optimistic about his application because the immigrant officer spoke of "when" rather than "if" he received his permanent residency. During the following decade, Jack authored several books on China and Chinese Americans and attempted a biography of Eugene. Now, he was content with the "American dream" his family was building together, which he asked his wife to model by standing near their house and car in a photograph he took.[132]

In 1984, Si-lan's autobiography, which she had worked on and off for almost four decades, was published under the title *Footnote to History*, but it remains virtually unread. The union of the Leydas that survived so much hardship ended with Jay's death in 1988. Si-lan spent her last years with Jack's family. Jack died in 1995 and Si-lan on March 8, 1996, in Contra Costa, California.[133] Of the figures considered so far in this book, all of whom left powerful marks on the countries they visited, Sylvia Si-lan Chen and her family were the worldliest. Only Langston Hughes, the subject of the next chapter, was as cosmopolitan as Chen.

5

Roar, China!

Langston Hughes, Poet Laureate of the Negro Race

Roar, China!
Roar, old lion of the East!
. . . .
Even the yellow men came
To take what the white men
Hadn't already taken.
The yellow men dropped bombs on Chapei.
The yellow men called you the same names
The white men did:
Dog! Dog! Dog!
Coolie dog!
Red! . . . Lousy red!
Red coolie dog!
. . . . . .
Laugh—and roar, China! Time to spit fire!
Open your mouth, old dragon of the East.
To swallow up the gunboats in the Yangtse!
Swallow up the foreign planes in your sky!
. . . .
Break the chains of the East,
    Little coolie boy!
Break the chains of the East,
    Red generals!
Break the chains of the East,
    Child slaves in the factories!

Smash the iron gates of the Concessions!
Smash the pious doors of the missionary houses!
Smash the revolving doors of the Jim Crow Y.M.C.A.S.
Crush the enemies of land and bread and freedom!
    Stand up and roar, China!
    You know what you want!
    The only way to get it is
To take it!
Roar, China![1]

On August 29, 1937, less than two months after Japan launched the full-scale war on China, Langston Hughes (1902–76) passionately penned this poem in embattled Madrid, calling for China's resistance. The poem was integral to the global circulation of the "Roar, China!" theme, a phenomenon that testified to transnational anticolonialist solidarity.[2]

Soviet futurist poet and playwright Sergei Tretiakov had first authored a poem titled "Roar, China!" around 1924, while teaching Russian in Beijing. He soon transformed it into a play prophetically predicting the 1926 Wanxian Incident, in which the British military massacred hundreds of Chinese civilians. The Tsukiji Theater in Tokyo performed it briefly from August 31 to September 4, 1929, before the authorities, concerned with the anti-imperialist passion the play roused among the audiences, particularly Chinese students, shut it down.

Across the Pacific, Theater Guild's production of *Roar, China!* made history on Broadway, as reported by hundreds of newspaper articles. It ran seventy-two performances at the Martin Beck Theater from October to December 1930. Chinese critics were amazed that the play, with two American merchants as the colonial villains, was staged in the imperialist country. They were excited by its first primarily Asian cast on Broadway, with "members of both races" performing "the complicated struggles between yellow proletariats and white capitalists." The *New York Times* echoed that, unprecedently, sixty-six "Chinese characters are played by Chinamen" recruited through the Chinese Benevolent and Dramatic Association. The cast included T. C. Wang, a chemical engineer who secured leave from his Guggenheim fellowship to play a thespian; writer H. T. Hsiang, who would become a colleague of Sylvia Si-lan Chen in Hollywood; You Wing Woo, a magician in vaudeville; journalists Don Su and Y. Y. Hsu; and Ji Chaoding. They put aside their political differences as followers of both the Nationalist and Communist Parties to join the production as a patriotic duty. The

English speakers patiently interpreted the director's instructions for the ten players who did not understand English, "sometimes in several dialects. . . . Patriotism conquered all."

Since the play was set on a British gunboat, Lord Chamberlain banned it at the Cambridge Festival Theater; the Unnamed Society managed to stage it in Manchester in November 1931. The play was also performed in Berlin, Vienna, and Frankfurt. Nikolai Bukharin, a prominent revolutionary theorist and then a close ally of Joseph Stalin, contended that the global productions of *Roar, China!* represented a genuine historical process in which throngs of workers become revolutionaries.[3]

Si-lan Chen's family watched the play as directed by the acclaimed Vsevolod Emilevich Meyerhold and met the playwright during their early exile in Moscow. There, probably through Chen, Hughes met Tretiakov in 1932. Hughes recalled that Tretiakov gave him "an enormous poster, showing a gigantic Chinese coolie breaking his chains, and . . . a copy of *Roar, China!* inscribed in English." He observed that the "very political minded" Tretiakov was "interested and excited" about the Scottsboro case (nine Black boys from Alabama falsely accused of raping two white women in 1931) and Black issues. The playwright and his wife were "dynamic, talkative people and outgoing hosts, with a spick-and-span apartment, modern and bright." The couple saw him off at the Moscow train station when he departed for East Asia in June 1933.[4]

Since the Soviet Union regarded China as a key revolutionary ally, increased curiosity made China frequent front-page news there in the 1920s. However, China was mostly presented in the haze of Orientalism and "revolutionary realism," as exemplified when *The Red Poppy* premiered in the Bolshoi Theater on October 23, 1927. Major political leaders had instructed senior artists to create this first ballad on the revolutionary theme to welcome the Wuhan delegation, including the Chen family and Madam Sun Yat-sen. Although the Soviet Union intended it to symbolize a common commitment to proletarian revolution and Sino-Soviet friendship, Chinese including senior CCP member Chen Boda and the Chens were horrified at how *The Red Poppy* portrayed China. Even at the crossroads of her career in 1930, Si-lan declined the leading role in it offered by the Bolshoi Theater.[5]

Tretiakov's work was exceptionally popular in China, where his poetry and plays were translated multiple times. Prominent political and cultural figures, including both Nationalist leader Hu Hanmin and Communist writer Zheng Boqi applauded his play *Roar, China!* as a true reflection of life in China and the Chinese people's suffering at the hands of imperialist powers.

It was staged under China's shifting political contexts throughout the 1930s and 1940s. At the Nationalist revolutionary base Guangzhou, Ouyang Yu-qian led the Theater Research Institute to perform it in Cantonese at the Nationalist Party headquarters, the police club, and the Whampoo Military Academy in 1930. The *New York Times* commented that "all the roles were taken by natives." Soon, Ying Yunwei directed the Shanghai Stage Society (Xiju xieshe) in a production of *Roar, China!* at the Hung King Theater in the French Concession to mark the second anniversary of the Mukden Incident. The press widely celebrated this as an epic moment in the history of China's modern drama. *Theater* magazine released a special issue, and the *Young Companion Pictorial* featured an article by Zheng and numerous photographs of the production to commemorate the milestone (fig. 5.1). Numerous reviewers, including Hong Shen, commented on the production's political significance, settings, and acting; the affordability of tickets (ranging from 0.5 to 1 yuan) for the laborers; and the passion of the audiences. Two members of the League of Nations' investigation commission in Manchuria watched the performance and released their sympathetic messages to China in *Theater*. Mei Lanfang paid tribute to the author of *Roar, China!* and Sergei Eisenstein during his 1935 tour in the Soviet Union, as captured by a photograph of the three masters published in the *Beijing Morning Pictorial*.[6]

Mounting pressures from Japan led to the censorship of *Roar, China!* Ying, then dean of the National Theatrical Academy, was to reenact the play with his students at the Capital World Theater in Nanjing in 1936, but the Nationalist government stymied it. Zheng Boqi and other critics were indignant that the play had run in imperialist countries and in foreign concessions in Shanghai but was forbidden in China's own capital. Little did they know that the attitudes of colonial authorities in Shanghai were shifting as well. Sponsored by Zhang Shankun, owner of the Xinhua Studio, Shanghai Amateur Troupe recruited the most popular stars, including Wang Yung and the future Madam Mao Zedong, to increase the appeal of *Roar, China!* and overcome rising political obstacles. Yet the troupe's scheduled performances at the Carlton Theater in the International Settlement was banned by the British authorities. Ironically, fitting into Japan's Pan-Asianism against white colonizers, the play gained new steam under Japanese occupation. The China Anti-British-and-America Association staged it at the Grand Theater in Shanghai in 1942. That was followed by performances at the Dahua Theater in Nanjing (sponsored by Wang Jingwei's Department of Propaganda), and then in Suzhou and Beiping the following year. Reviews highlighted "friendly neighbor" Japan's aid in China's resistance against British

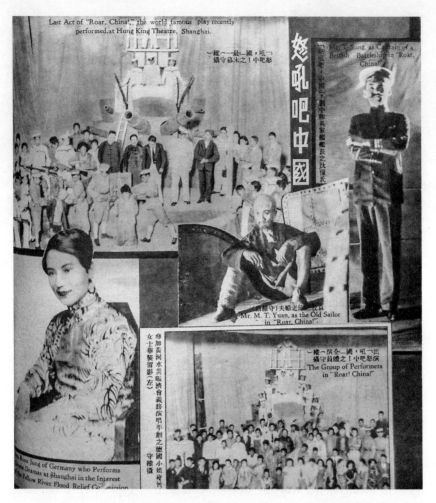

FIGURE 5.1. The *Young Companion Pictorial* celebrates the staging of the play *Roar, China!* in Shanghai on the second anniversary of the Mukden Incident. *Young Companion Pictorial* 81 (October 1933).

and American aggressions in "East Asia." As late as the summer of 1949, the Cinematic and Theater Association attempted to put on the play for the triumphant Communist army.[7]

Tian Han penned a lengthy review of the global staging of Tretiakov's play and adapted it into a film script titled *Roar, China!* The play also influenced print art and literature in China. Catering to fascination over its sophisticated stage designs, the covers of numerous popular periodicals featured photographs or colorful drawings of the gunboat-dominated settings at metropolises across the world. Chinese artists transformed the "Roar, China!"

Langston Hughes

theme into traditional paintings and woodcut prints, a rising art form for wartime mobilization. Poets attempted verses titled "Roar, China!," whose indignation and sentiments would be echoed by Hughes's version.[8]

The feelings Hughes expressed in "Roar, China!" about China's glories, ancient history, recent humiliation, the rise of the Chinese Communist Party, and the imperative for China to "roar" at this critical historical moment were taken up by W. E. B. Du Bois in his 1959 poem "I Sing to China." Echoing Du Bois's call, "Africa, Arise! Face the Rising Sun" from the East, China's East Is Red Dance Troupe presented a full-length dance drama, *Congo River Is Roaring*, in 1965, with the cast wearing "blackfaces," commemorating the Congo crisis amid decolonization and the Cold War. The "roar" to resist colonialism reverberated in different contexts.[9]

Hughes's contribution to the "Roar, China!" theme was not accidental. He was the first African American celebrity in China. There, his formidable intellectual reputation was foregrounded over stereotypical images of "primitive" athletic and trivial musical personas and the commercialized exoticism of Blacks in advertisements. Hughes's journey to Moscow and Japan is well known, but his connection with China has been insufficiently studied. Donald C. Dickinson's *A Bio-bibliography of Langston Hughes* includes Hughes's works in various languages but omits those in Chinese.[10] This chapter explores the unique roles Hughes played connecting the liberation campaigns of African Americans and the Chinese by addressing his interaction with overseas Chinese communities, his romance with Si-lan Chen, his 1933 journey to China as the first Black writer-intellectual, his extensive writings about China, and the reception of his work in shifting ideological contexts.

AFFINITIES WITH THE OVERSEAS CHINESE COMMUNITIES IN THE 1920S

While W. E. B. Du Bois and Paul Robeson sought inspiration from famous Chinese sages and Robeson formed an alliance with elite Chinese sojourners at the peak of his fame, Langston Hughes's humble background led to early affiliation with overseas Chinese and their Chinatowns, where he found that Jim Crow was mostly absent. He recalled, attending Columbia University in 1921, that his only friend was a similarly excluded student from China named "Chun," who was likely Chiu Chun, a Quinghua College graduate who earned a master's degree from Columbia University in 1923. The "small Mandarin vocabulary" Hughes acquired and the Chinese-sounding pseudonym "Langhu" or "Lang-Hu" that he used to publish four poems in the *Columbia*

Daily Spectator indicated a bond between the two racial outsiders. Hughes would likely have been familiar with the Columbia University Chinese Students Club, which the Chinese consulate in New York City had helped to found in 1908. He might have crossed paths with the scores of other Chinese students, including Chih Meng, Liu Zhan'en, and P. C. Chang, a rising star in China's transpacific modern drama movement and a would-be diplomat and human rights activist. In the summer of 1927, while working as a sailor on a ship sailing from New York City to Havana, a journey on which he was the "only 'colored' colored person," he wrote to Carl Van Vechten, his private adviser, that his "good friends" were the Chinese cooks on the ship.[11]

Readers in China had a glimpse of Hughes's talent through his short poem "Sea Charm" published in the *China Press* in 1925. Yet China remained remote in Hughes's imagination, as indicated by his recommending the gardens at Versailles as "worth coming from China to see" to writer Harold Jackman. To satisfy his curiosity about China, Hughes frequented New York City's Chinatown under the guidance of Chun, and then sought out other Chinatowns during his global journeys as a sailor. Havana's "marvelous Chinatown" left a lasting impression when Hughes visited it with his cook friends. He wrote to Van Vechten, and Claude McKay, and later recalled in his autobiography his amazement at the sight of thousands of Chinese immigrants, including his friends' cousins, packed like sardines in a tin at night on straw mats on tired shelves in warehouse-like boarding places, waiting for a chance to be smuggled to New Orleans or New York. Hughes watched herds of such immigrants crowded in a brothel, gazing silently for hours at the Cuban prostitutes.[12]

Food strengthened Hughes's alliances with the overseas Chinese communities. He shared with his cook friends the meals they prepared for themselves on the ship, "usually fish and herbs and rice," and "some very good food" in Havana's Chinatown. The friendship symbolized by Chinese food and drink extended to Van Vechten, for whom Hughes bought "a jar of Chinese whiskey," flavored with lichee nuts and stored in brown clay jugs, to "make grand cocktails."[13] At places without a Chinatown, the omnipresent Chinese restaurants were among the few public places serving African Americans. During his brief exile in Reno, Nevada, in 1934, Hughes wrote to Si-lan there were "no public spaces where Negroes could eat other than two cheap Chinese restaurants" in this "very prejudiced town."[14]

It seemed that Hughes was mostly oblivious to the treacherous political and ideological cross-currents that Chinese Americans, and sojourners like Liu Liangmo, experienced in Chinatowns, but he was probably not immune to the subtle racial dynamics there. As late as 1943, Lily Ho Quon, head of the Chinese Women's Service Club in Los Angeles, wrote to Pearl S. Buck, as a family friend, asking "what the Chinese can do for better understanding among Americans." Buck responded with her concern that "some" Chinese in the United States had "adopted, for commercial reasons [referring to restaurants and laundries], prejudices against Negroes." She strongly urged China to "keep her own high traditions of the worth of the individual human being whatever his color" and hold "no race prejudice." Buck insisted that maintaining that alleged "finest" Chinese quality would enhance race relations in the United States.[15]

Brotherhood with the equally oppressed overseas Chinese fed Hughes's budding writing career. In 1929, he complained that literary and commercial magazines rarely accepted stories of "Negro themes," which were considered exotic, "in a class with Chinese or East Indian features." During his second trip to Havana in 1930, Hughes met Rigino Redroso (1896–83), a "Chinese-Negro" poet who worked in an iron foundry and wrote "grand radical poems and Chinese revolutionary stuff and mystical sonnets." Enthusiastic to spread this voice marrying Black and Chinese elements, he translated some of Redroso's revolutionary poems and helped to publish one titled "Alarm Clock" in *Quarterly*, a New York–based poetry journal. Hughes penned a poem "Merry Christmas," connecting anticolonial struggles in China, India, Africa, Haiti, and Cuba.[16] Soon more international opportunities came Hughes's way.

ENCOUNTERING THE CHINESE CIRCLES IN MOSCOW

Langston Hughes joined twenty-one other African Americans, including Dorothy West and Louise Thompson, in June 1932 on a mission to produce a motion picture, to be titled "Black and White," on U.S. race relations with Mezhrabpofil'm (International Workers Relief Film) in Moscow. Although the film was never made, the journey brought Hughes closer to China.[17]

Intensely interested in issues of ethnicity and race, Hughes engaged the community of Soviet artists concerned about China. He also familiarized himself with China's struggle as a semicolony, an essential theme of his radical creation during and beyond his stay in the Soviet Union. In addition to Tretiakov's *Roar, China!*, he was impressed by Soviet works such as the film *My Motherland*, on clashes between the Soviet Red Army and Chinese troops in Manchuria. Hughes contended that this "most beautiful film," illustrating "the Soviet way of teaching friendship between peoples of varying colors and races," deserved to be seen by the world. He recounted one scene vividly:

A young Russian soldier, "fists doubled ... begins to curse those slant-eyed bastards who have killed his comrade. Quietly, an officer goes toward the body, draws back the sheets so that the Russian boy may see the still, brown face there, and says simply, 'Our comrade's eyes are slant eyes, too.'"[18]

Hughes was attracted to the expatriate artistic community in Moscow, where he met Chinese writers, including Emi Sao, representing China's leftist literary circles.[19] Far more important was Hughes's romantic encounter with Si-lan Chen, the most visible and best known of Hughes's heterosexual relationships. His biographer Arnold Rampersad was puzzled by "the absence of love letters" in Hughes's file: "We have a paucity of love letters to women, and none to men, if Hughes ever wrote any of those." Among the "few mildly romantic letters to or about women," those to "Si-lan Chen [Leyda]" were notable. Kate A. Baldwin has highlighted Hughes's oblique sexual desire in his description of Uzbek boy folk dancers, but the writer's correspondence with Chen was straightforward in its expressions of love. To his friends Prentiss Taylor and Van Vechten and in his autobiography, Hughes repeatedly wrote that the "pretty Chinese dancer" was then his girlfriend.[20]

After learning of the arrival of the African American film group, Chen's sister Yolanda, who together with her husband, Alexander Shura Shelenkov, was employed by Mezhrabpofil'm, invited Si-lan to visit Hughes at the Grand Hotel to learn about Harlem entertainment. "After we had introduced ourselves, Langston was charming, listening very seriously to our naive questions," Si-lan recalled. It seemed that a relationship developed quickly. "Si-lan Chen ... had been a writer's delight in Moscow, serving me tea and cakes in her lovely room overlooking the Bolshoi Square on snowy afternoons," Hughes would recall. While spending memorable times together, she gave a "little cap" that he would cherish for years to come.[21] His several poems preserved in her archives testified their romance. A poetic note read, "Sorry I missed Neilson and my cigarettes last night — and you tonight. Better luck next time." Chen included "the only poem of his written especially for me" in her autobiography (see fig. 5.2):

To Sylvia Chen,

I am so sad
Over half a kiss —
That with half a pencil
I write this

Langston[22]

Langston Hughes

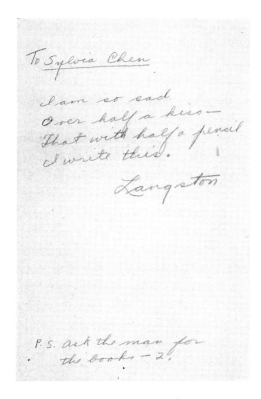

FIGURE 5.2. A poem that
Langston Hughes dedicated to
Sylvia Chen in Moscow in 1933.
*Box 29, folder 4, Jay and
Si-lan Chen Leyda Papers and
Photographs, Elmer Holmes Bobst
Library, New York University.*

Hughes explained their separation: "But she was going away in a long tour of the Soviet Union to dance, and shortly before I left Moscow, she departed." This was curiously consistent with Hughes's treatment of women in his stories. The poet and scholar James Emanuel observed, "Most of them, if main characters, are looking for love in an ultimately satisfying way, but somebody or something is making it hard for them to pin love down, even when it is a non-physical, non-sexual love in the sense of simply being appreciated, maybe even understood."[23] Chen attempted her own verses to express feelings including love, self-consciously and jokingly inviting him to select the "choicest":

> Like birds in flight we passed on our way,
> we spent together a glorious day
> But we had to part, what for I don't know
> Because I liked you—I liked you so![24]

From late 1933 until Chen's departure from Moscow for the United States in August 1936, they exchanged scores of love letters filled with intimate phrases. In a typical letter from Hughes, he referred to an Ethel Waters song, "Loving You the Way I Do," and then asked, "Will you kiss me next time or not? Heh! You better!" He signed the letter "Love and kisses. xxxxxx These are the kisses xxxxxx Lang." However, emotionally unavailable, Hughes refused to write about his life and thoughts beyond such quick expressions of desire. To her open and frequent communications, his responses were usually guarded and sporadic, with empty flirting letters, cards, telegrams, or books. Hurt and frustrated, Chen repeatedly urged him to write back, threatening to stop writing to him if he continued to act like a "ghost," and chiding him for being "sketchy and superfluous." She complained, "You treat me, and most people whom I saw you with over here so artificially," blaming his nature, habit, or "maybe protection from sentiment." The non-committal Hughes typically evaded her confrontation with empty affection: "The reason I don't like to write letters to you is because it makes me want to see you too much. . . . But I do miss you—lots more than you miss me, I guess—and I want you, Sylvia baby, more than anyone else in the world, believe it or not. I love you. . . . Please, dear kid, believe what I say about how much I like you. If you want me to say it *over and over* and *more and more*, just act like you don't believe it in the next letter you write me." She gave up, but retorted nevertheless, "Flirting around being amiable . . . don't you think you had me fooled, no sir, I know you—and, I may add, being frank as usual, like you in spite of knowing you!"[25]

They often fantasized a reunion, while Chen pondered the uncertain meaning of being together. She invited Hughes to attend her 1934 concerts at Oslo and Moscow, where he might attend a writers' conference and take in her performance at the theater festival. She wondered, "And if you come over there, then what—we'd live together, maybe a day, a week, I go east and you go west. That's all—I guess we'd have a good time while together, I suppose that's as much as one can demand from this life of ours." He declined her invitation yet countered with fantasy travel proposals, which she laughed off: "I want to be with you, Langston, not necessarily as a wife, but just to be with you." Chen observed, "There has not been one negro representative" at the writer's conference; "aren't you sorry you didn't come?"[26] Hughes kept passionately inviting her over to the United States, as a joke. He wrote in early 1934, "Come on over this way, will you?" Then he telegrammed, "Sylvia, baby, I would love you and keep you all the time, if you came to stay with me." Soon he sent another one, "Come over here this is serious I love you." Chen was confused and slightly insulted. "Do you really think that I take you seriously now—of course I don't. . . . I do not quite know what line I should take. I was really awfully glad to receive it. I even thought for a second you meant it. I wish you had, Langston dear." Chen repeatedly threatened to come to the United States, which Hughes refused to believe. "Darling Kid, you know what would happen if you came over here? I would take you and keep you forever, that's what would happen. And even if you didn't come over here and I ever found you anywhere else in the world—I'd keep you, too. So you see, I love you!"[27]

Chen needed a real-life companion, much more than occasional letters from Hughes. As the ultimate revenge, in her August 16, 1936, letter, the last before she headed for the United States, she casually broke the news of her marriage to Jay Leyda: "I don't remember whether I ever wrote telling you about my American husband, yes, I got tired of waiting for you to propose, so got myself a consort. Maybe you'd like to get on my waiting list for future consideration. I'm an awfully good wife, although I say it as shouldn't. No fooling, I am very happy when we are together." Thus, for real, "I'll be coming to the States." Chen first mentioned Leyda to Hughes in December 1934. After "quite objectively" dismissing Hughes's article in the *Theater Arts Monthly* he had sent her, she asked, "Did you notice an article in the same issue about Lishler, written by Jay Leyda, I mention this because he's a good friend of mine. What did you think of the article?" In 1935, she invited Hughes to stay in her "wonderful" new residence at Apartment 590, Bolshoi Pirogovskyi 51, with two spacious rooms overlooking the Moscow River, if his Guggenheim fellowship took him there, without revealing that she shared the apartment with her new husband. The disillusioned Hughes responded to the breaking news with a "very angry" letter, which, Chen would recall, she immediately tore to pieces. Perhaps still upset over Chen's marriage to Leyda, Hughes mentioned her only briefly in his autobiography, noting that he had been in love with her that year in Moscow, but he said little of their torrid correspondence.[28] The Hungarian Jewish writer Arthur Koestler, one of Hughes's travel companions in Soviet Central Asia, echoed Chen's complaint about Hughes. He noted Hughes's "impenetrable, elusive remoteness which warded off all undue familiarity." Hughes explained that such aloofness had to do with race, but an additional reason was probably his sexuality.[29]

Hughes is widely speculated to have been gay, an orientation that Chen did not suspect.[30] Rather, she attributed his passivity to possible involvement with other women. Hughes indeed appeared to be involved in a love triangle, while his colleagues in the movie set found new sexual freedom across color and gender lines, despite tightened controls over sexuality in the contemporary Soviet Union. Photographs apparently revealed Hughes and Dorothy West as a couple in New York Harbor as they boarded the SS *Europa* for Moscow in 1932. The pair posed, half embracing, on the ship stairs; and West leaned on Hughes in a group photograph. They remained intimate in Moscow, as revealed by more photographs and West's letters to Hughes, repeatedly fantasizing about being "mother of your four children." Hughes somehow managed to keep both women in the dark over his romantic dalliances. West's letters to her mother suggest that she spent much time with Hughes, mentioning that he took her to visit Chen's residence, where they also met Yolanda and her husband. She wrote of Chen, "She is one of the better-known dancers here. She belongs to the new school of the dance, of course, and is thought very clever. She is half Chinese and half West Indian Negro. Her feature is somewhat Negroid. But her hair is beautiful and slightly curly! She has nothing of the American Negro in her and talks with a heavy English accent. . . . [We] danced and drank tea and ate cake and candy. It was a pleasant evening, because Sylvia was interesting, although she shows off a little."[31] Chen wrote to Hughes in early 1934, "I suppose one of your New Year duties is to write to all your girl 'friends' who are scattered over the world, and tell them you remember them. I see I happen to fall into this category—how flattering." Anticipating his disappearance to Mexico, she wrote, "My dear Langston, where for the silence. Have the bells gotten you or just the Mexican gals?"[32]

The distinction in their class backgrounds—his drifting childhood in a dysfunctional family and lifelong struggles with poverty, on the one hand, and her highly privileged upbringing, on the other—made profound understanding and connection difficult. The rare occasions that Hughes mentioned his family to her were to identify his location. He explained his presence in Mexico after his father's death in 1934 and his deferred trip to Spain due to his mother's fatal illness. His father had disinherited him and his mother bombarded him with desperate letters about her near homelessness and serious health issues. Chen barely acknowledged or showed much sympathy, writing, "I believe you're just rumbling in Mexico and having a hell of a good time—how I envy you, Langston"; and "Gee wasn't I sorry that your skip to Spain had to be postponed."[33]

Yet the romance confirmed their shared radicalism, racial identity, and interest in revolutionary China, despite the fact that they frequently joked about not talking politics amid discussions of race and ideology. Hughes inscribed to Chen a copy of his radical poem "Goodbye Christ" to mark the peak of their intimacy in Moscow on March 29, 1933. She opened her above-mentioned verses,

To Langston:

Revolutionary greetings I sent
And best of luck.

From Sylvia Chen[34]

She shared the details of her concerts and travels, eager to boast of her "success" and the "sensation" she had stirred. Hughes responded by sending dance programs, a dance book by Vaslav Nijinsky, and the magazine *Dance Observer* featuring an article on him, often without adding any accompanying words. Despite her urging that he update her on his writing, the guarded Hughes did not even reveal the news of his Guggenheim fellowship, which Chen learned from a mutual friend. However, aware of her passion for class, he did share most enthusiastically his essay "The Vigilantes Knock at My Door," in which he condemned the right-wing politics in Carmel, California, urging Chen to read for details. He enclosed a sample newspaper article to provide her a glimpse of the press attacks on him and "others of our John Reed Club members." Hughes explained somewhat apologetically that one of his plays on Harlem, which had been "quite a hit" in Cleveland in 1936, was "pure comedy and hasn't much class angle, but a little at least is there." He boasted about his speech against war and fascism before a large audience at the U.S. Congress after the New Year.[35]

Hughes forwarded to Chen his newly released collection of short stories *The Ways of White Folks* (1934). She claimed to be "proud and happy" for the success of the book and reported that everyone she lent the copy to "has praised it to the skies." With little experience then of American race issues, Chen soon lost track of the book, despite her promise to read it cover to cover in "quieter moments." However, they were conscious of their shared racial identity. Their flirtatious correspondence reached the level of joking about having a child. Chen wrote, "I've decided to have a baby also. But it must be brown. Unfortunately, all prospective papas are fair, so I've turned down all offers—any more offers!" Hughes responded, "What nationality would our baby be anyhow? Just so he or she is Anti-Fascist!" Mentioning that a former member of the movie group who had remained in the Soviet Union was now married with a one-year-old child, Hughes imagined, "Ours would be dancing by this time, wouldn't it?" Chen shot back, "What do you mean 'ours,' no one even thought of babies, except how not to have one." She explained that striving to be a better dancer had prevented her from having children.[36] Chen never conceived a child, probably not by choice but rather as an after-effect of her life-threatening surgery in Shanghai in 1935.

The only piece of his work that Hughes discussed in relative detail was his play *Mulatto*, about the mixed child of a white plantation owner and his Black slave. Hughes was acutely aware that Chen's mother was a French Creole, thus his and Chen's ancestry shared the racial narrative in the play. He wrote to her in the summer of 1936 that he had finished the play five or six years before and later revised it into a poem and then a short story, both titled "Father and Son" and included in *The Ways of White Folks. Mulatto* had been running on Broadway since the previous October. Uncharacteristically, Hughes revealed his feelings about it: "Although in its present version it's one of the worst plays ever known to the theater. It was a poetic tragedy as I wrote it, but when they got through changing it around, it turned out to be a melodrama with a big M. However, there is a public for such plays, and this one is now going into its ninth month, and probably will still be there when you get over to visit us in the autumn." It seemed the theme was touching a nerve for Chen now. Anxious about her future in the United States, she half-jokingly invited him to write a play or ballet for her.[37]

It is unclear whether Eugene Chen, whose mixed family caused controversy in China, was aware of this love affair involving a Black man and one of his children, and, if so, how he reacted. In any case, the Chen family and China remained a constant topic of conversation between Hughes and Chen. Hughes recalled memorable times in Chen's cozy room in Moscow, with her "telling me dramatic tales of the Chinese Revolution and the family flight over the Gobi Desert into Turkestan when the counterrevolution took over." Hughes stayed with his friends Walt and Rose Carmon for one month in the winter of 1932 at the apartment they shared with Jack Chen's family. Responding to Hughes's greetings to and inquiries about her siblings, Chen updated their whereabouts, families, and careers. They talked most frequently about her father. To his friends and in *I Wonder*, Hughes introduced the Chen siblings as the children of "Eugene Chen, the former Trinidad merchant who had given his early savings to the founding of the Republic and had been Minister of Foreign Relations under Dr. Sun [Yat-sen]."[38]

Hughes's encounter with the Chinese community in Moscow fanned his ongoing interest in China and propelled him into the leftist circles in Shanghai, for which Agnes Smedley served as a catalyst. She arrived in Moscow in May 1933, right before Hughes's departure, in a temporary exile from political dangers in Shanghai stemming from her espionage activities. Smedley had interacted with Hughes earlier, after he sent her a copy of his novel *Not without Laughter*. She felt a kinship with Hughes, regarding him as a little brother in politics, according to her biographer. Chen soon wrote to update Hughes of "gruesome conversations" about China with Smedley.[39]

PIONEERING ADVENTURE IN SHANGHAI IN 1933

Langston Hughes arrived in China after the collapse of the planned film "Black and White" in 1933. Among the several former cast members who discussed going home through China, only Hughes remained committed to the trip, partially motivated by the news that the singer and composer Nora Holt was living in Shanghai.[40] Hughes planned to take the Trans-Siberian Railway from Moscow to Shanghai, by way of Beiping, before continuing on to Japan. However, intensified Japanese military action in Manchuria had cut the Chinese Eastern Railway line. Without the Yasuichi Hikida network that would bless Du Bois's trip four years later, Hughes had to adjust his route. He toured Kyoto and Tokyo for a few weeks, then visited Shanghai and returned to Tokyo.[41]

Hughes quickly made his position about the color line and Japan's aggression in China clear. It was exactly opposite W. E. B. Du Bois's stance. He was invited to deliver a speech at a monthly luncheon of the prestigious Pan Pacific Club during his first trip to Tokyo. Hughes praised the absence of Jim Crow in Japan that enabled him to dine publicly beside a white fellow American (the wife of a U.S. consular official), an act prohibited in her hometown of St. Louis. He applauded Japan for maintaining its sovereignty as "the only non-colonial nation in the Far East . . . without the unwelcome intrusion of the imperialist powers of the West who brought the color line to Africa and Asia." However, he urged Japan to avoid "the old mistakes of the West," attempting to "take over other people's lands or make colonials of others." He imagined "how wonderful . . . it would be if all the colonies and color lines in the world were wiped out."[42]

Yet, in contrast to Du Bois's naive observation that there was no racial prejudice in the Japanese Empire, Hughes quickly detected the racial hierarchy in Japan's Pan-Asianism. "Both the Japanese and the Koreans were colored races, but I saw quite clearly color made no difference in the use of race as a technique of hurting and humiliating a group not one's own." He reported that Koreans received racial tags in negative Japanese press coverage exactly as Black Americans did in the U.S. white press, and "the Japanese were quicker to slap a Chinese coolie than the white colonial overlords" in Shanghai. Unlike the hospitality that the Japanese authorities would extend to Du Bois, Hughes's second visit to Tokyo ended with police harassment and deportation as a persona non grata. He would marvel, "I, a colored man, had lately been all around the world, but only in Japan, a colored country, had I been subjected to police interrogation and told to go home and not return again." Following Hughes's departure, the Japanese police released a fabricated "interview" with him that was quickly picked up by the Japanese press, including the *Nichi*. According to this falsification, Hughes had declared that "Japan was the destined savior of the darker races of the world, the leader of Asia, and a great stabilizing force in those areas of backward China where the armies of the Rising Sun were spreading culture." Hughes distanced himself from this coverage, though Du Bois would apply similar rhetoric to the People's Republic of China (PRC) decades later. The Japanese continued to keep tabs on his travels — in August, Hughes arrived in Honolulu, where an FBI agent alerted by the Japanese authorities was waiting for him, as he would recall.[43]

Before that, Hughes had adventured to "incredible" Shanghai, becoming the first Black American intellectual to ever step on Chinese soil. Immediately, he encountered the complexities of race, body, hygiene, disease, and prejudice as they were entangled with simple daily needs such as finding food and lodging in the segregated treaty port. Pampered by the Japanese authorities, Du Bois would stay at the luxurious Cathay Hotel on the Bund and not have to confront similar inconveniences. Hughes settled down in a "little Chinese-owned but European-style hotel in the International Settlement" with reasonable rates, a clean room, but no restaurant. He was aware that the "white" YMCA and leading hotels excluded "Asiatic or Negro guests. The British and French clubs, of course, excluded Orientals." Warned about both color lines in public places and unclean food in Shanghai, Hughes found filling his stomach a complex task. Stepping from the hotel door into the busy "dusty" street on a steamy summer afternoon, he would recall, the first thing he did was to consume two pieces of "reddest of red-hearted watermelon" from an "uncovered cart," with the vendor "shooing flies away with a paper fan." Other foreigners in Shanghai were startled by his "very dangerous" practice of eating watermelon, any fresh fruit, or green salads before the food was "first washed in some sort of antiseptic solution."

Hughes heard that "unscrupulous vendors" dragged the watermelons in rope nets behind their junks for miles in the filthy Yangtze River, polluted by the dead bodies of hundreds of stillborn babies. "The melons would soak up this water and thus weigh more," enabling market vendors to sell them for higher prices. Ignoring such warnings, riddled with racial stereotypes of

Chinese as diseased and dirty, that white communities circulated widely and Liu Liangmo would soon be forced to confront, Hughes "kept right on eating watermelon the whole time I was in Shanghai." He wrote defiantly, "Even if they were dirty, they were sweet. The Chinese had been eating watermelon for centuries — and millions were living."[44]

Food and diet carry profound racial, religious, and political meanings. It was not accidental that Hughes recalled in such detail his eating the "dangerous" watermelon on dusty Shanghai streets. While "food Chinese style" had affirmed his earlier friendship with overseas Chinese, Hughes's watermelon anecdote signaled his identification with the Chinese masses and racial solidarity between African Americans and Chinese. He frequently used the fruit to refer to the interplay between racial stereotypes and racial pride. Hughes described how he and Zora Neale Hurston had bonded in the American South in 1927: "Right off we went to eat some fried fish and watermelon." In a letter to Carl Van Vechten, Hurston indicated that consuming the jar of "Chinese whiskey," which Hughes had initially bought for Van Vechten in Cuba, further consolidated the two African American writers' friendship.[45] Similarly, Simple, a character Hughes created later, repeatedly declares that he is proud to enjoy watermelons "with a deep red heart and coal-black seeds," even "before the Queen of England," advising watermelon lovers not to "pass" as otherwise. Another character of Hughes's, Tempy in *Not without Laughter*, does exactly that in hopes of imitating middle-class whites.[46]

Hughes found "the Chinese in Shanghai a very jolly people, much like colored folks at home," an observation Liu Liangmo would echo later. He felt he belonged with the Chinese as fellow "colored people" in segregated Shanghai. "[Against warnings by] Occidentals not to go outside the International Settlements alone at night nor wander too far even by day into the Chinese districts of Shanghai, I did so many times just to see what would happen. Nothing happened . . . just as I never had ill effects from eating Shanghai watermelon." Hughes lingered freely at Nantou, Zabei, and Hongkou in the Chinese quarters beyond "the barbed-wire fences and patrolled gates of the International sectors." He concluded that the warnings were perhaps valid only for "white foreigners — not much liked by the Shanghai masses in spite of years of missionary charities." Their "impudence . . . in drawing a color line against the Chinese in China itself," as well as other colonial power wielded by the Westerners and Japanese, appalled Hughes. Du Bois would soon express similar outrage, but without the indignation against Japan. Hughes observed that soldiers of various nations, including U.S. marines, filled Shanghai "like an armed camp." Sikhs, Annamites (Vietnamese), and Japanese policed and patrolled the British, French, and Japanese sections, respectively. He witnessed the British Sikh police raiding a student meeting at the Chinese YMCA, in which Liu Liangmo was active, for harboring "radicals."[47]

Often-told stories about abused rickshaw pullers in Shanghai served as clichéd symbols of China's colonial humiliation—yet the ways people responded to seeing these workers in the flesh revealed much. Du Bois's observations were remote and cold. He remembered his personal experience of being carried by Chinese coolies to the Great Wall as part of his lofty narratives of China's grand sites and history. Si-lan Chen's story about the awakening of her Chinese identity centered on her physical and verbal defense of the rickshaw pullers. Hughes felt an even more personal sense of connection and profound sympathy with the coolies, be they rickshaw pullers or other downtrodden workers, which further embodied his identification with the oppressed Chinese.

While planning his journey, Hughes had written to Prentiss Taylor to explain the necessity for fundraising, "because I might not be able to master a rickshaw before hunger gets me."[48] Sure enough, his magical debut in Shanghai happened on a rickshaw.

> I reached the international city of Shanghai in July, with the sun beating down on the Bund, the harbor full of Chinese junks, foreign liners and warships from all over the world. It was hot as blazes. I did not know a soul in the city. But hardly had I climbed into a rickshaw than I saw riding in another along the Bund a Negro who looked exactly like a Harlemite. I stood up in my rickshaw and yelled, "Hey, man!" he stood up in his rickshaw and yelled, "What ya sayin'?" we passed each other in the crowded street, and I never saw him again.[49]

Although white foreigners warned Hughes against trusting rickshaw boys beyond the concessions, he frequently hired them to navigate the Chinese sectors. "The rickshaw men waited patiently for me if I chose to descend from their cabs and walk around in the teeming odd-smelling exotic streets or go into the shops." Hughes would report, "The rickshaw boys ran faster in Shanghai than they did anywhere else in the Orient," because of the well-known abuse from "the Germans or the English or the French" as well as the "Chinese warlord or banker."[50]

Guided by two liberal white American women working for the Shanghai YWCA, Hughes visited a large gated textile factory, where "indentured" (sold) child labor labored under conditions of enslavement. He portrayed these conditions with an indignation echoed in the movie *Roar of Women*, starring Wang Yung, and in Xia Yan's novella "Indentured Laborers." "This I found hard to believe of a modern city in the twentieth-century world," Hughes wrote. "These youngsters spent the whole of their youth here like prisoners — their only crime the misfortune of having been born." Facilitated by Harold Isaacs, Smedley's associate, a CCP collaborator, and active member of the international communist network, Hughes deplored the plight of the factory children in *Shanghai Evening Post & Mercury*. He announced, "I don't think Shanghai is a very nice place" from the perspective of the oppressed Chinese workers. Hughes witnessed "all sorts of vices and corruptions," such as omnipresent child and adult prostitution, crude begging, indifference to violence and brutal death, and counterfeiting even in everyday transactions.

What Hughes experienced during his epic visit to Shanghai rings in his poem "Roar, China!" His indignation over China's suffering reinforced his passion for its resistance, with Japan as the main enemy, while China's humiliation triggered Du Bois's contempt for the Nationalists and his praise for the Japanese invaders as saviors of Asia. Hughes observed the Japanese poised to take over with increased numbers of barbed-wire barricades and military personnel stalking the city, and saw buildings destroyed by Japanese air raids on Zabei. His hope that, along with the rural communists, the abused coolies would rise as the dominant force in China's resistance echoed the passions of his friends Smedley Isaacs and Si-lan Chen.[51]

STIRRING THE CULTURAL CIRCLES IN SHANGHAI

Langston Hughes's stance on Japan ensured that leftist Shanghai literary circles would receive him warmly. In *I Wonder* he writes, "A group of Chinese journalists and writers gave a luncheon for me before I left Shanghai, and I met there the young man engaged in translating my novel — *Not Without Laughter*, into Chinese."[52] The prestigious literary journals *Les Contemporains* and *Literature*, the Chinese and Foreign News Bureau, some commercial magazines, and a few other literary groups invited Hughes, accompanied by Harold Isaacs, to a question and answer session over refreshments at the News Bureau on the afternoon of July 13. Among the attendees were editors Du Heng for *Les Contemporains*, Fu Donghua for *Literature*, Lou Shiyi for Tianma Press, and Bao Kehua and Ming Yaowu for the Chinese and Foreign News Bureau. Yao Ke, a close friend of Lu Xun and Edgar Snow, served as interpreter. *Les Contemporains*, *Literature*, *Photography*, and *Modern Press* featured photographs capturing scenes at the gathering honoring Hughes, whom the caption introduced as a "revolutionary Black writer and contributor to *New Masses*" (fig. 5.3).[53]

Under the pen name Wu Shi, Fu Donghua published an essay in *Literature* in which he strove to translate as "accurately as news coverage" Hughes's answers to the five questions posed by his hosts about his personal experiences of Soviet culture and African American literature. The opening question was on the impact of the Second Five-Year Plan on culture in the Soviet Union. Hughes confirmed the excitement of the Soviet masses over the shift in priorities from heavy manufacturing to light industry. Without engaging in lofty theory, he noted the plain fact that, with increased paper production, official restrictions on publication had been lifted.

Hughes was invited to articulate the "theory and practice of so-called socialist realism and revolutionary romanticism, which supposedly co-existed harmoniously in current Soviet literature and arts." He acknowledged the limits of his knowledge of Soviet literary theory due to the language barrier, but he suggested that screenwriters inserted "elements on emotions" into otherwise "too serious" revolutionary themes to interest the audiences, which probably exemplified so-called revolutionary romanticism.

Hughes had much to say about "the contemporary Soviet cinema." Citing his involvement with "Black and White," which had intended to portray Blacks realistically on plantations in the American South, he pointed out the sharp contrast with American cinema, which rarely focused on Blacks, particularly the harsh reality of their lives under the dual oppression of capitalism and racism. Dark chapters such as lynching, which Fu defined for his readers as "private punishment of alleged Black rapists and other offenders by whites, an extremely brutal form of racial abuse," could never be shown on-screen. Hughes's sentiment echoed the statement by a New York fundraising committee for "Black and White." He recommended *Heart of Dixie* and *Hallelujah* as the only worthwhile films on oppressed Blacks. He compared the shocking working conditions of child labor he had witnessed in Shanghai factories the previous day with those of Blacks in the American South. He praised the new play *Introduction*, "by the playwright of *Roar, China!*," which recounted how a German engineer came to realize that workers in China and Germany were similarly mistreated. According to Hughes, it was "the best script lately produced in the Soviet Union." He added that the play had been "most successfully staged" by Meyerhold.

The session continued with a question about "the general condition of American Black literature." Hughes commented that talented but commer-

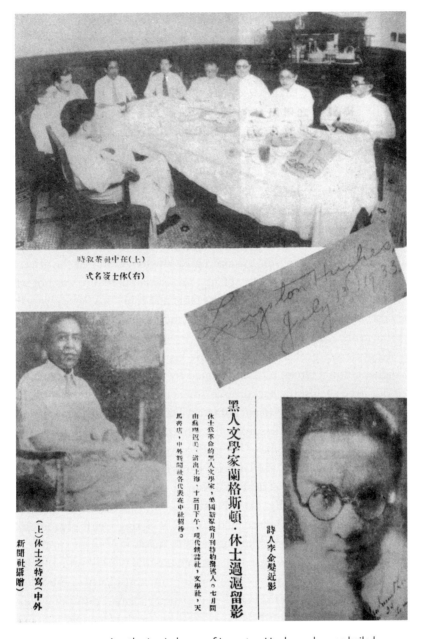

時敍茶社中在(上)
式名簽士休(右)

黑人文學家蘭格斯頓・休士過滬留影

休士代表革命的黑人文學家，美國新羣衆月刊特約撰述人。七月間
由蘇聯返美，道出上海，十三日下午，現代雜誌社，文學社，天
馬書店，中外新聞社各代表在中社招待。

(上)休士之特寫(中外
新聞社贈)

詩人李金髮近影

FIGURE 5.3. A gathering in honor of Langston Hughes, who was hailed
as a "revolutionary Black writer," at the Chinese and Foreign News Bureau
in Shanghai, July 13, 1933, and Hughes's portraits taken on the occasion.
Other attendees were Harold Isaacs (on Hughes's right side), Hong
Shen, Yao Ke, Du Heng, Fu Donghua, Lou Shiyi, Bao Kehua, Ming Yaowu,
Zheng Zhenfeng, Huang Yuan, and Shi Zecun. These images appeared
in multiple publications in Shanghai. *Wenxue* 1, no. 2 (1933): 1.

cialized authors had filled the market with shallow products during the past decade. "Those authors could not represent Blacks as a whole," he said, "just as one Chinese [Jiang Kanghu] criticized that *The Good Earth* could not represent Chinese as a whole in the *New York Times*." Hughes recommended *Home to Harlem* by Claude McKay and *The Fire in the Flint* by Walter White as the best works reflecting the struggles of Blacks. He also criticized these writers, however: "With financial gains from their successful books, these promising authors abandoned their obligations to the poor masses and pursued a life of leisure instead." Taking Hughes's recommendation seriously, *Literature* soon translated a chapter from White's novel, noting the author's contribution to antilynching by passing as white, and promised to feature McKay's work soon.

The final question was on "the development of proletarian literature under American capitalism." According to Hughes, although the government did not exercise strict censorship, proletarian literature was not well developed in the United States—Mike Gold and John Dos Passos were the only authors of international importance, and the modest *New Masses* was the sole proletarian publication.[54]

Hughes was probably unaware that his visit stirred controversies in Shanghai cultural circles already plagued by race and class acrimony. His visit occurred against the backdrop of others by foreign intellectual celebrities. China had received William Somerset Maugham in 1919, John Dewey in 1919–21, Bertrand Russell in 1920, and Rabindranath Tagore in 1924 and 1928. In 1933, in addition to Hughes, George Bernard Shaw and the French writers Paul Vaillant-Couturier and Maurice Dekobra visited in February, September, and November, respectively. Lu Xun observed, "Now, foreign writers visit China almost annually, inevitably stirring some tiny waves." Shaw's visit was widely covered by Chinese media, some attacking him for "promoting communism." "No one is willing or dares to mention Vaillant-Couturier," who was attending the Far Eastern Conference of the World Anti-imperialist War Committee as a member of the French Communist Party's central committee and chief editor of the party's newspaper. Vaillant-Couturier was also an underground Comintern operative, a fact Lu Xun might not have known. When a Chinese reporter inquired about Dekobra's "opinion on Japan invading China" at a tea party cohosted by the Sino-French literary and artistic circles and the Shanghai media, he responded, "Such a solemn question is beyond a novelist." Inquired of his "impression of China," he responded, "China's fine cuisine and beautiful women are the most notable." Dekobra similarly engaged the government officials and intellectuals who warmly received him in Nanjing and Beiping. Echoing the *Shanghai Daily*, Lu Xun commented, "Attempting to steer clear of politics and controversies, Mr. Dekobra unexpectedly earned the reputation of a 'foreign literary hooligan' for praising food and women."[55]

Hughes's visit further thrust race to the foreground. In his summary of the luncheon, Fu Donghua prominently noted Hughes's racial background. The definition of "Blackness" varies across the world. It seemed that the Chinese, like the Africans Hughes encountered as a sailor, were not used to the U.S. "one drop rule" and were slightly puzzled by how Hughes's mixed ancestry inflected his racial identity. "The Africans looked at me and would not believe I was a Negro," Hughes wrote. In vain, he protested that he was not white, but he was told, "You are not Black either." Similarly, Fu wrote that Hughes did not fit the stereotype of Blacks at the bottom of the racial hierarchy as imagined by the Chinese public and media, thus subtly raising Hughes's image to that of one more civilized: "The Hughes we saw was only a bit darker, without a protruding lower jaw, particularly thick lips, exposing scarlet gums, or face angled at seventy degrees. With manner and behavior not far from that of a white gentleman, he does not appear as terrifying as revolutionary authors imagined by the general public."[56] Fu's approach presaged the apologetic explanation of Blackness that Robeson's Chinese biographer would deploy two decades later, though the much lighter-skinned Du Bois escaped such scrutiny.

In Tokyo, Hughes had been "warmly welcomed as the first Negro writer" to visit the New English Literature Association, to whose journal he soon contributed twenty-one poems, and the Tsukiji Theater. Since Seki Sano had written from Moscow about his arrival, Hughes would recall, he was greeted by the actors "with open arms" backstage after a performance, "as if Eugene O'Neill or George Bernard Shaw had walked into the theater." Little did Hughes know that his treatment was directly contrasted with that of Shaw in China. Shaw, who shared Hughes's leftist politics, had just visited China five months earlier. Fu complained that the "American Black author" was unfairly snubbed by Shanghai's cultural circles, in contrast to the "splashes" made by Shaw. He explained that "we" organized the luncheon to help balance the welcomes the two writers had received, which were as different as "night and day."[57]

One of the highlights of Shaw's visit had been a widely publicized luncheon that the China Civil Rights League hosted in his honor at Madam Sun Yat-sen's residence on February 17. Guests included political and cultural celebrities such as Agnes Smedley, Harold Isaacs, Lin Yutang, Yang Xingfo,

Cai Yuanpei, and Lu Xun, who recorded the occasion in his diary. Two photographs of the group were immediately published in the daily *Morning News*.[58] Lu Xun had submitted a letter and an essay "Bidding Farewell to Shaw" to the *Shanghai Daily* two days before the luncheon and published "Gawking at Shaw and 'Those Gawking at Shaw'" in *Les Contemporains* immediately after. He and Qu Qiubai, a senior Communist Party member, pulled together the anthology *Bernard Shaw in Shanghai* and had it released within forty days. In the preface to this "unprecedented book," Lu Xun wrote, "We the editors collect, analyze, and compare almost all the praise, criticism, and insults directed toward Shaw by numerous periodicals. The goal is to demonstrate how Shaw served as a flat mirror, in which those who usually appear with normal facial features in convex mirrors finally showed their truly distorted ones." He challenged "Shanghai newspapers' hatred of Shaw" and declared his obligation to support Shaw's hurling a "grenade" toward "slave-cultivating education" in China. In the summer immediately following Shaw's and Hughes's visits, in a series of essays published in the *Shanghai Daily*, Lu Xun discussed the frustrating "slave" characteristics of his compatriots, being indifferent, passive, and sacrificing dignity for "a bit tip."[59]

Hughes received few such plaudits. On his behalf, Fu Donghua protested:

> There were no ladies or gentlemen welcoming him at the port
> [Madam Sun and Smedley had greeted Shaw on his ocean liner].
> Nor could his name be found in the dailies. Naturally, Shaw as a
> celebrity deserved receptions by our celebrities, which even enabled
> Mr. Lu Xun and Dr. Mei Lanfang [who do not normally get along]
> the rare chance to cross paths. Hughes does not fit in the mold of
> celebrities as perceived by our celebrities, besides the taboo of his
> skin color. If we are not certain that yellow skin is genuinely superior
> to a Black one, this fighter who has been howling and struggling for
> the oppressed races deserves a bit of our attention.[60]

In fact, Hughes mingled with the same leftist figures who had welcomed Shaw, almost certainly through introductions by Si-lan Chen and Smedley. At Madam Sun's house, Hughes would recall, he had dinner — "a traditional Chinese banquet with intriguing dishes from bird's nest soup to 'thousand-year-old' eggs." She inquired about "news of the Chen children in Moscow." Hughes later used this episode to make a brief mention of Chen in *I Wonder*. He found Madam Sun "as lovely to look at as her pictures, with jet-black hair, soft luminous eyes and a complexion of delicate amber." Speaking "beautiful

English . . . she was a relaxing and delightful woman with whom to talk." It seemed that the good impression was mutual. Smedley reported to Hughes, "I gave your love to Mrs. S. She was delighted. She spoke of you with enthusiasm."[61] Hughes wrote to Chen that he'd had a "swell" time in Tokyo and Shanghai, meeting people who remembered her as "both brilliant and beautiful!!" He also noted, however, that in these cities "all the radicals [were] scared of their lives." He would soon follow Chen's trip to Shanghai through correspondence, mutual friends in New York, and coverage by *Variety*. She updated him on her own visit to Madam Sun, who "was awfully nice to me. She's a great woman and entirely on the side of the Chinese masses. Am most enthusiastic about her and want to work with her when I return to China via America." Hughes suggested, "Next time we see each other, let's stop going to China—unless we go together."[62]

Hughes would recall "at a private gathering [at Harold Isaacs's residence] one evening I met the elderly Lu Hsin [Xun], then under a cloud for his 'dangerous thoughts,' but nevertheless one of the most revered writers and scholars in China." Lu Xun did not record the occasion in his diary. Threatened by an arrest warrant from the Nationalist government for his involvement in the China Civil Rights League, he had sought refuge in the bookstore owned by his Japanese friend Kanzo Uchiyama in early 1930. Nevertheless, in his July 29, 1933, letter to *Literature*, Lu Xun refuted Fu Donghua's "masterpiece associating me with Mei Lanfang." Announcing that he had never received an invitation to the luncheon honoring Hughes, Lu Xun was indignant over the accusation that he was looking down on Blacks: "I trust that I am not such a snobbish lowlife! . . . Wu Shi, which is apparently a pen name, must be a celebrity himself, since no non-celebrity could have been allowed to receive Hughes." When Lu Xun demanded that *Literature* reveal the true identity of the writer, it quickly named Fu and printed his and the journal's apologies. However, the controversies did not stop there. A *Central Daily* essay attacked Lu Xun, whose "forced excuse" was irrelevant to his having cowardly missed the gathering to avoid political danger. It announced, "Seeing Hughes had to be secretive, while seeing Shaw was glamourous and public." The essay dismissed the conflicts between Fu and Lu as ugly power struggles within the leftist literary circle, calling Fu a former gambling addict who was striving to replace Lu as an icon.[63]

The *Shanghai Daily* reported that Hughes was staying with Harold Isaacs. Hughes published an essay titled "From Moscow to Shanghai" in *China Forum* that was "designed to inform local Chinese and influence international opinion on matters of importance to the Chinese Communists." He detailed how the office of Isaacs, editor of the journal, had been destroyed by Nationalist gangs. Intimidated by the McCarthy hysteria, Hughes would purge details on his interactions with Isaacs from the draft of his 1956 autobiography *I Wonder*. Instead, he would simply mention socializing with Isaacs among Western journalists who told him "hair-raising" stories about the semicolonial "multi-racial city."[64]

Even back in Shanghai, Hughes's experiences were much lower key, without celebrity guests or the presence of reporters, probably partially due to security concerns triggered by his Soviet connections, his recent high-profile trip in Japan, and his proximity to activists in the international communist movement. Caution seemed wise. According to Hughes, his Japanese interrogator asked, "In Shanghai last week when you dined at the Lotus Flower Café with two Chinese newspapermen known as Ah Wong and Lee Ching Way, did Ah Wong ask you about Si Bong Chai in Moscow? . . . Since in Shanghai you met Harold Isaacs, I know he gave you copies of the *China Forum*." Chinese media, including the *Shanghai Daily*, *Literature*, and the *China Press*, reported Hughes's deportation after he had been accused of carrying messages between the Communist Party of the Soviet Union and "red elements" in Japan. Isaacs's vacation there immediately attracted suspicion from the Japanese authorities.[65] While sick in a Shanghai hospital with "heart & ulcerated stomach" caused by her nerve-wracking espionage activities, Smedley wrote to Hughes on October 31, 1934. In addition to a review copy of *The Ways of White Folks*, she requested "an account of your Tokyo examination, and including the lying reports they published about you afterwards. Both charge that you admitted you were an 'agent' and that you approved Manchukuo and Japanese conquest in China. I need this very much out here to publish." Smedley instructed that Hughes only put her initials on an inside envelope mailed to her confidential address at "Mr. Raudall Gould, Apart 5, 297 Ave. Pétain [today's Hengshan Road], Shanghai."[66]

However, Lu Xun's public defense of Hughes was just as forceful, if not more so, than his support for Shaw's criticism of China. Shao Xunmei, a liberal poet, publisher, and future lover of the *New Yorker* writer Emily Hahn (who authored the book *The Soong Sisters* through Shao's connections), published a sixteen-page overview of modern American poetry in *Les Contemporains* in 1934. He categorized leading white poets into styles of country, urbanism, lyricism, imagism, modernism, and internationalism/cosmopolitanism. Shao inserted a couple of sentences at the very end: "There is sensational jazz poetry by Black poets such as [Vachel] Lindsay [who was actually white] and Langston Hughes, who focus on Black issues. However, I believe poetry of their style cannot reach beyond America, at least not beyond the Anglophone circle. Theirs are just wriggling little creatures at the foot of internationalist/cosmopolitanist poetry, but with their own life."[67] Lu Xun responded, "Poet Shao, while praising white poets, put down Black ones in his essay. . . . Although I am comparable to Black slaves in the eyes of rich and noble Chinese and their hangers-on, my voice has traveled around, a fact they loathe the most. As a matter of fact, Blacks' poetry has also reached beyond 'the Anglophone circle,' something the American millionaires, their sons-in-law, and their hangers-on could do nothing about."[68]

A common theme in Lu Xun's defense of Hughes and Shaw was "slave/slavery" and his humorous yet indignant defiance against it. Lu's rebuke notably connected class in China with race in the United States, identifying rich and powerful Chinese with privileged whites and the rest of Chinese with Blacks as fellow oppressed "slaves." He half-jokingly claimed a "slave" background based on his birth in Manchu's Qing dynasty in contrast to those born as "masters" in the Republic of China. Shao's wealth, which Lu (under various pen names) ridiculed repeatedly as acquired by being the "son-in-law" of one of the richest families in Shanghai, identified him with (white) "American millionaires." Comparing such "inglorious tactics of sudden rise [up the social ladder]" to "worshiping Shanghai gangster leaders as godfathers," Lu called into question Shao's masculinity, respectability, judgment, and literary accomplishments. One of Lu Xun's *Shanghai Daily* essays, published soon after Hughes's departure, read, "In order to climb on the forum of literature, a rich wife with inheritance . . . is essential, since the dowry could be used as literary capital to print one's own mediocre work, oblivious to ridicule. . . . Once fame multiplied tenfold, the pleased wife would at least shoot a glance at him amid her mahjong games." Lu Xun asserted that "becoming the son-in-law of a rich family" was not for "a genuine, capable, and ambitious man who depends on his brain and physical prowess as an alternative [to sexuality]."[69]

While it is difficult to speculate on the private conversations between the two writers, their writings shared common views of race and class hierarchy, as seen from their vividly described personal experiences in theaters and in confrontations with white people. Lu Xun further pursued the racial dynamics behind the Dekobra episode: "While cinema and literature hit the wall in Western Europe, some so-called writers have to search for 'grotesque' and 'erotic' [in English in the original] stuff catering to their customers. Thus, the purpose of their adventures goes beyond bow or banquet offered by the locals. They respond to silly questions with jokes, because the truth is that they do not care about that sort of stuff." Calling Dekobra "oily headed" and of a "French version of the Saturday School [a popular literary style of cliché romance]," Lu was suspicious of his itinerary, which included "China, the South Pacific, and South America." He warned Chinese that their "honor" being portrayed "along with the other 'indigenous'" in such white authors' work would multiply due to market demand. He concluded with characteristic sarcasm, "There is nothing we can do about our small flat nose — far less grand than the ones of Europeans. However, the least we can do is to watch movies just like them. Bored with detective, romance, war stories, and comedies, there are *King Kong, Jungle Savages,* or *Adventure in Africa* promoting beasts and primitivism, decorated with primitive curves of primitive women. If we sort of love to watch those, evidently, we are willing to accept their ridicule, after all 'sex' is quite important to philistines."[70] Lu Xun would probably have been horrified that such stereotypical narratives of Black primitivism would endure in the PRC.

Lu Xun explored race and class scenarios in theater in another *Shanghai Daily* essay published after Hughes's visit. He recounted how his childhood friends from rural backgrounds ("destined to hold the hoes") watched historical plays about generals fighting for territory and romances between ladies and gentlemen, acutely aware of the distance between them and what was presented onstage. The on- and offstage class hierarchy in his home village theater was complicated by race in the modern movie theaters of Shanghai. "I have long become a 'Chinese of lower class [*xiadeng huaren*],'" Lu wrote. "On-screen, white soldiers fight, white lords make fortunes, white ladies get married, and white heroes have adventures; along with white and rich audiences upstairs, Chinese of middle and lower classes downstairs admire, are terrified, and are moved, but conscious that the stories are way beyond their reality."

Similar scenes had marked Hughes's life across the Pacific. "I used to fall in love with movie stars when I was a young boy, and you know I could not get near no movie star, they being white and way up on the screen and me in a Jim Crow balcony down in Virginia." Hughes further affirmed his race and class solidarity by enjoying Shanghai's noisy and chaotic traditional theater frequented by the Chinese masses, in sharp contrast to "such playhouses as the Kabuki with high social, artistic and governmental status" in Japan. He wrote appreciatively, "Sometimes the whole audience would be quiet, listening to a brief bit of famous thousand-year-old poetry, but eating sunflower seed and calling for hot towels again as soon as the Chinese 'to be or not to be' was over."

Lu Xun illustrated the connection between the "servant/slave" Chinese and Blacks in such settings. Back to his home village theater, "the farmer audiences accustomed to serving rich families" managed to identify with one figure onstage—a loyal, honest, and chivalrous old servant who took the place of his master, a wrongly condemned high official, to receive "the penalty of law." "His tragic yet grand gestures and singing genuinely touched their hearts." Similarly, while white heroes explored Africa on-screen, there always were loyal Black servants to guide, serve, struggle, and die, so that the master could return safely. The hero would turn solemn during his return adventure, remembering the dead servant whose dark face flashed on-screen as memory. "Most of the yellow-faced audiences turn solemn as well in the dim light—they are moved." Since "Chinese, like Blacks, cannot marry princes of major nations in Euro-Asia, films such as *Amorous History of Yao Mountain* on Han Chinese 'civilizing' the ethnic Yao by marrying its princess began to emerge as a substitute."[71]

Both Hughes and Lu Xun addressed the self-consciousness of their races facing the whites. Lu was not impressed with "a new characteristic of Chinese developed since the May Fourth Movement—asking visiting famous or rich foreigners their impression of China." He cited such awkward exchanges between inquisitive Chinese students and journalists and Russell, Shaw, and Prince Carl Christian of Sweden, in addition to Dekobra. Lu Xun observed, "The truth is that Russell and Shaw were not wily or mean as accused. Imagine that a foreigner tosses the question back, 'What is your impression of your own China?' The essay would be hard to write."[72] The sensitivity of Chinese intellectuals and the public regarding whites' view of their race and country was shared by African Americans. Hughes convincingly explained the phenomenon: "They had seen their race laughed at and caricatured so often in stories . . . maligned and abused so often in books . . . made a servant or clown always in the movies, and forever defeated on the Broadway stage." Thus, they craved a "clean," "cultured," "polished," and "good" image.[73] Evidently not concerned that Hughes might be racially superior, the attendees at the luncheon in his honor were not anxious to pry into his "impression of China."

Soon Hughes became a yardstick by which to measure the racial and gender hierarchy of visiting foreign literary figures. A Manchurian author named Mu Mutian wrote, with black humor, how, as a refugee in Shanghai (the Oriental Paris), he felt somewhat inspired when Ivan Bunin, a Russian exiled in Paris, won the 1933 Nobel Prize in Literature. "It seems that the Nobel Prize committee finally gave some consideration to the politically marginalized." Mu declared with irony, "After Black writers get their chance, Manchurian ones should finally have their turn." However, "while no Black authors, even Hughes, were ever awarded the prize, we refugees from Manchuria better not hold our breath."[74] When Lili Körber, a lesser-known leftist Austrian writer, visited Beiping and Shanghai in 1934, *New Yulin* magazine and two other literary agencies held the sole banquet in her honor. Only five people showed up and "lots of food was wasted," which surprised Lu Xun. Missing the occasion due to illness, he published his translation of Körber's poems, somewhat making up for the embarrassment. Writer Xu Maoyong, who published an essay in the *Shanghai Daily* and corresponded with Lu Xun on the "unprecedented cool reception" afforded Körber, subtly attributed it to gender. "It is natural for the famous Bernard Shaw to stir waves everywhere. Even the Black writer Hughes and [light-weight] Maurice Dekobra, the French Zhang Henshui, were not neglected."[75] The leftist cultural circles, which lost Lu Xun on October 19, 1936, remained silent on W. E. B. Du Bois's visit. He contacted some leading Chinese intellectuals, who happened to be Hughes's fellow alumni at Columbia University, but that did not fare well. Hughes recorded no attempt to reach out to that elite circle affiliated with the Nationalist government, probably due to his miserable memory of his student days at the university and, more important, his recent alliances with the Left.[76]

RADICAL WRITINGS CIRCULATED ACROSS
THE PACIFIC IN THE 1930S

Langston Hughes's radical writings, inspired by his journey to the Soviet Union and China, won little support in the United States. Carl Van Vechten and Blanche Knopf, two key figures in Hughes's publishing career, strongly disapproved of his new style. On March 1, 1933, he mailed the *Good Morning, Revolution* manuscript from Moscow to Knopf and wrote to Van Vechten, declaring that the collection contained "the best of the proletarian poems I've been doing the last two years." The Soviet State Publishing House of Artistic Literature had just released the Russian version of the book, following translations of *Not without Laughter* and his Scottsboro poetry in 1932. Hughes assured Van Vechten that the poems had been well received at his previous readings in the United States and by expert criticism in the Soviet Union. Aware of the controversies such writings had stirred even among African Americans, he acknowledged that "some of them have been talked about quite a lot in the States." Hughes insisted, "I think this book represents pretty well the younger Negro mind today, and will be quite as timely as was my *Weary Blues* six years ago — since everything seems to be moving left at home." He added that he was mailing another manuscript, tentatively titled "Dark People of the Soviets," to Knopf. Publishers in the Soviet Union, which continued to embrace Hughes with numerous translations of his work, released the book the following year under the title *A Negro Looks at Soviet Central Asia.*[77]

After consulting with each other to exchange their views, Knopf and Van Vechten each expressed their disapproval to Hughes separately. Knopf advised, "I think that you have become much too important than this poetry is and that the publication of such a book now would tend to hurt your name rather than help it."[78] Van Vechten echoed her criticisms: "As usual about your work I am going to be frank with you and tell you I don't like *Good Morning, Revolution* (except in spots) at all." He suggested that the "lyric side" of these revolutionary poems was so weak that Hughes would be "shamed" of them in ten years. He had "no quarrel with your linking the American Negro with Communism. It even seems a little ironic to me to ask a capitalist publisher to publish a book which is so very revolutionary and so little poetic in tone." Hurt, Hughes wrote back sternly to Knopf, "I would appreciate very much your releasing the book so that I might turn it over to the International Publishers or some others who cater to a workers' public and who will distribute it through workers' bookshops, unions, etc. throughout the country." He refuted Van Vechten, "[Your disapproval] is merely my taste against yours, and means nothing as everyone has a right to his own likings, I guess. . . . And if Knopf's do not care to do it, they have a perfect right to refuse. One must admit that their clientele hardly consists of workers and peasants, so I could understand how they might feel." Hughes and Van Vechten debated Hughes's new poem "Advertisement for Opening of the Waldorf-Astoria" to illustrate their contending views on capitalism. Van Vechten questioned, "Why attack the Waldorf? This hotel employs more people than it serves" and was then the cheapest. Hughes disagreed, "At the time that I wrote the poem it was one of the best American symbols of too much as against too little. I believe that you yourself told me that the dining room was so crowded that the first week folks wouldn't get in to eat $10.00 dinners. And not many blocks away the bread lines I saw were so long that other folks couldn't reach the soup kitchens for a plate of free and watery soup."[79]

Hughes revised and resubmitted the manuscript to Knopf under the new title *A New Song* in March 1934. He updated Van Vechten: "I know you *don't* like them, but I *do* like them, and have been reading them with loud acclaim, even before the conservative Y.M. & Y.W.C.A. groups out here. At least, they would be timely if published soon, I believe." Van Vechten remained unconvinced: "In looking over your volume of poems again I find I like them even less than I did last year. In fact, I find them lacking in any of the elementary requisites of a work of art . . . better propaganda for the Negro." Hughes informed Van Vechten in October, "My proletarian poems will not come out in a book after all. My agent thought it best not to try to place them now, so they rest in peace." Eventually, the International Workers Order sponsored a printing of 15,000 copies of the book at fifteen cents apiece in 1938.[80]

Simultaneously, measured by the opposite standard of "revolutionary realism," which would be applied to Du Bois's work in the 1950s, Hughes's reputation peaked across the Pacific Ocean. His brief but eventful visit profoundly connected him to China, especially Shanghai, as indicated by his frequent references to the city in his correspondence. He was accumulating a growing collection of Chinese books, although he could not read the language as Robeson did. Planning to move his terminally ill mother from Cleveland to New York City in 1936, he instructed her to pack the materials. She wrote, "What do you mean by Chinese, you meant [books in the] bath room etc. Yes, I'll bring your books, Chinese, Russian, Yiddish, &ct."[81] While Americans puzzled over his radical turn, the impressed Chinese lauded him as "the established revolutionary artist," enthusiastically reviewing and translating his works in journals of Qinghua, Fudan, Yenching, and Beijing Universities, the nation's top institutes of higher learning, and popular periodicals, throughout the 1930s. It was the very first time a Black author received such an honor, triggering strong interest in African American literature among the leftist cultural circles and academia in China.

Drawing information from Hughes's personal statement in *New Masses* and an essay on him in *International Literature*, a left-wing journal published in English, French, German, and Russian, Fu's above-discussed piece overlapped with Zheng Linkuan's lengthy review essay in *Qinghua Weekly*. They introduced Hughes's life story, highlighting his various menial jobs, his drifting inside and outside the United States, and his family association with John Brown. Both acclaimed him "an extraordinary genius," "the only established Black poet," and "forever a vanguard fighter against petit bourgeois and bourgeois literature." For Chinese reviewers, Hughes's greatest achievements were protest poems such as "Good Morning, Revolution," "Goodbye Christ," "A New Song," and "Scottsboro Limited," the very verses dismissed by Van Vechten and Knopf. Du Bois had famously written in the opening of

The Souls of Black Folk, "Between me and the other world there is ever an un-asked question: ... How does it feel to be a problem? ... I answer seldom a word." Fu and Zheng believed that the value of these Hughes poems lay in their confrontation of realistic issues and demonstration of the path to solv-ing the "Negro problem" through "xxist [Marxist] revolutionary struggles." Zheng applauded Hughes for reaching out to "the most backward among American working classes—southerners harboring profound racial preju-dices" for class unity across racial lines, as indicated by his poem "Open Let-ter to the South." The reviewer called Hughes's work the "marching tunes" and "most powerful weapon" for the proletarian revolution. Enthusiastic about Hughes's political activism, Zheng even declared the writer "an active member of the X [Communist] Party USA."[82]

Critiquing Hughes's major works, Fu and Zheng evaluated the writer's "several transformative stages" in the process of overcoming the "petit bour-geois radicalism that trapped his contemporary Black writers." Translating the famous excerpt from Hughes's 1926 essay "The Negro Artist and the Racial Mountain," the reviewers strove to demonstrate how Hughes had initially defended such "bourgeois aestheticism" as beauty-making: "We younger Negro artists who create now intend to express our individual dark-skinned selves without fear or shame. If white people are pleased we are glad. If they are not, it doesn't matter. We know we are beautiful. And ugly too. The tom-tom cries and the tom-tom laughs. If colored people are pleased we are glad. If they are not, their displeasure doesn't matter either. We build our temples for tomorrow, strong as we know how, and we stand on top of the mountain, free within ourselves." Zheng argued that Hughes's fellow "vanguards of the Black [Harlem] Renaissance" Claude McKay and Coun-tee Cullen, though highly regarded by senior critic Alain Locke and "Black intellectuals of the past," such as James Weldon Johnson, W. E. B. Du Bois, and Charles W. Chesnutt, made the mistake of neglecting social criticism. Consequently, their "extremely empty and pale arts catered to the stinky taste of American capitalists," encouraged by ill-intended white critics. That was probably the only mention of Du Bois in the Chinese-language press of the Republic of China.[83]

The Weary Blues had "propelled Hughes to the rank of first-rate Ameri-can poets," allowed Fu and Zheng, but its lyrical poems only "demonstrate the beauty of Black skin to the world with paramount pride, completely ne-glecting racial oppression" and class distinctions. Both cited the following verses from "My People" to stress their points:

The night is beautiful,
So the faces of my people.
The stars are beautiful,
So the eyes of my people.

Zheng translated "I, Too" to further illustrate how the poet pronounced Blacks' equal rights as U.S. citizens within the framework of "They'll see how beautiful I am" and capitalism. He criticized Hughes's metaphors "I'll be at the table" or being ordered to "Eat in the kitchen" as "characteristic of Black culture represented by Harlem restaurants and jazz. . . . Such exotic Harlem tradition could not reflect the life of poor Black laboring masses." The reviewers diagnosed Hughes as falling for the romantic illusion that "racial inequality would disappear once whites recognize the beauty of Blacks and extend their kind hands." The inevitable "clashes with the harsh reality" led to his sense of "isolation in the cruel icy prison of capitalism" and "strong suicidal tone and desperation," as exemplified in "Afraid":

We cry among the skyscrapers
As our ancestors
Cried among the palms in Africa
Because we are alone,
It is night,
And we're afraid.

According to Zheng, with "his dream of a better future murky and his protest abstract," Hughes drew on the "ancient unpolluted African spirit to counter American capitalist culture void of tradition."[84]

The reviewers detected a "fundamental transformation" with *Fine Clothes to the Jew*, because it brought the working class into Black literature and treated the "laboring masses as the core of the Negro problem." The poet "seems not good at verses above eight lines," Zheng observed, but his short ones with "strong rhythm, tight and intense structures" resembled "a cute dew," as exemplified by "Mulatto" and "Cat and Saxophone." He translated excerpts from "Elevator Boy" and "Porter" to illustrate Hughes's maturing spirit of resistance and sharpened facility for caricature. Citing Hughes's poems on prostitutes, which "best demonstrate the omnipresent horrifying racial oppression in 'democratic' America," Zheng argued that *Fine Clothes* had more depth than *Weary Blues*. While the former explored economic roots, pointing out that "low wages of Blacks have driven their women to delinquency," the latter only portrayed how these fallen women tarnished Harlem streets under a glorious sunset.[85]

Fu and Zheng regarded *Not without Laughter* as a breakthrough in Hughes's career, Black literature, and even modern American literature, for finally integrating race and class issues. Grasping the reality of a Black working-class family with "genius," they declared, Hughes outgrew the "dreamy" Harlem tradition and became a mature realistic writer. The reviewers reduced the novel to "the transformation of slave psychology" harbored by the characters Hager and Annjee, who loyally serve whites, to the rising "rebellious mentality" of the protagonists Sandy and Harriet. They interpreted "the self-important Black petit bourgeois Tempy" as evidence of class stratification among Blacks. By insisting that "Blacks could be completely liberated through revolution against capitalism, the root of racial inequality," Hughes overcame the shortcomings of his previous work — "passive obedience and pleading," as the reviewers saw it. Yet they regretted that Hughes still took "education and the cultivation of Black creativity, culture, and talent" as the route to solving the "Negro problem."[86] Controversies over the role of education in racial uplift for African Americans similarly raged amid class struggles during China's Cultural Revolution.

The reviewers celebrated Hughes's revolutionary poems "Call to Creation" and "Our Spring," which they translated in full, as the qualifiers for his ultimate establishment as a "revolutionary artist." They were relieved that Hughes, in "Call to Creation," finally rejected the "futile beauty-makers":

> Listen!
> All you beauty-makers,
> Give up beauty for a moment.
> Look at harshness, look at pain,
> Look at life again.
>
> . . . .
>
> Listen!
> Futile beauty-makers —
> Work for a while with the pattern-breakers!
> Come for a march with the new-world-makers:
> Let beauty be!

More important, they enthusiastically lauded Hughes's linking violent class struggles in China, India, and Africa:

Look at starving China dying.
Hear the rumble in the East:

. . . .

In India with folded arms,
In China with the guns,
In Africa with bitter smile —

. . . .

Free! To be Free!⁸⁷

"Our Spring" turned out to be the favorite of Chinese intellectuals across the political spectrum. Translations by Fu Donghua, Yang Cunren, and others appeared soon after Hughes's visit. Fu applauded Hughes's newly "gained confidence and optimism after hearing the rumble in the East and clearly seeing the route to salvation":

You can't stop all of us —
Kill Vanzetti in Boston and Huang Ping rises
In China.
We're like those rivers
That fill with the melted snow in spring
And flood the land in all directions.
        Our Spring has come.

. . . .

And you will be washed away — ⁸⁸

Zheng offered recommendations for how Hughes might continue on the "revolutionary path." He was concerned that Hughes was "still at a dangerous stage of being obsessed with formula-like rhetoric," as exemplified by the "undistinguishable seven children" in "Scottsboro" symbolizing the working class. He believed that such a flaw was common among early-stage revolutionary writers, citing the German poet Johannes Robert Becher as an example. Critiquing internationalism "unnaturally cleansed any national/racial flavors" in Hughes's recent work, Zheng urged the writer to combine "national/racial form and socialist content," since his "top priority is to help solve problems facing the Black masses from a class perspective." Zheng directed Hughes to the Soviet futurist poet Vladimir Mayakovsky (1893–1930) as the model balancing abstract revolutionary symbols with specific individual features. Zheng's critiques paraphrased Lydia Filatova's article on Hughes published in *International Literature* (though he did not mention her by name). Soviet critics like Filatova had enshrined Mayakovsky as the standard-bearer for Soviet art's development of "the socialist-in-content, national-in-form culture" and "a model for minority writers." In fact, Hughes actively participated in expanding the futurist poet's inclusive, cross-cultural writing, including translating Mayakovsky's two "Afro-Cuban" poems, "Black and White" and "Syphilis," which remained unpublished during Hughes's lifetime. The second poem shared Liu Liangmo's indignation over sexualized and gendered colonial power, as reflected in the common narrative of white men spreading "syphilis" to indigenous women. Due to either ignorance or neglect of Hughes's contributions on this front, Zheng's prescription that Hughes attend to Mayakovsky rang hollow and presumptuous.[89]

Nor was Zheng finished. Picking up on the Marxist line that "religion is the opiate of the masses," Zheng harshly criticized Hughes's "antireligion" attitude as "far from straightforward and thorough," expressing his disapproval of poems with religious and mythical overtones in *Fine Clothes, Dream Seekers and Other Poems* and *Dear Lovely Death*. Zheng singled out *Popo and Fifina*, "co-authored with the Black capitalist writer Arna Bontemps," as "the darkest stain and great shame in Hughes's literary career." By presenting the romantic life of scarcely clad indigenous inhabitants of a wonder island, where the ocean provides fish along with beautiful fairies and nature solves all social problems, the "fairytale" concealed conflicts in reality and, according to Zheng, dimmed Black children's spirit of struggle. He professed disbelief that some readers were misled that "such a happy island does exist — it is Haiti, where white devils actually brutally oppress the natives!" as revealed by Hughes's own short story "People without Shoes." Fu translated the piece and published it in the same issue of *Literature* that featured his review essay. Zheng was appalled: "Hughes even practiced religion, pleaded with God, and praised angels with white wings, while the ruling class employed religion to numb Blacks, the most superstitious race in the United States. Thousands of priests daily instill such poisonous thoughts as 'non-resistance' and 'turning the other cheek' deeply in the hearts of Blacks, hindering all revolutionary thoughts." Aunt Hager in *Not without Laughter* vividly reflected "the psychology of the religious working Blacks — obedient and tame." Fortunately, Hughes presented this character as one "of the past," Zheng wrote. Since Hughes had recently "bid farewell to religion and ordered Christ away," Zheng continued, there was reason to "hope that we will never see this devil again in his future work." He concluded paternalistically, "Despite remnants from the past, Hughes fundamentally desires revolution. It seems that he is quietly pleased with his rising as the first Black revolutionary poet."

. . . A writer defines himself through continuous struggle. Now Hughes is learning."[90]

Among critics and translators in China, Hughes's Blackness became the focus of increasing attention. Writer Zhao Jiabi included Hughes in his 1933 series introducing world-class twentieth-century writers at the *Central Daily*. Zhao asserted that "Hughes's visit attracted major attention not because he was the leading poet of Black skin but because he represented the new trend of modern American literature as the first realistic Black writer." Zhao attributed the writer's serendipitous encounter with Vachel Lindsay to his fame and awards that "have brought glory to the Black race," and he encouraged readers to seek out Hughes's recent publications in *New Masses* and *International Literature*. A year later, the *Central Daily* published another essay almost identical to Zhao's, but "authored" by a Jin Ge, who claimed to introduce Hughes's "greatness beyond his Blackness" to educate the public who "tend to look down on Blacks." Another author paraphrased Zhao's essay for the journal *Chinese Students* and added that *Not without Laughter* had already been translated into several languages, "shining on the literature forum for the glory of Blacks." The odd phenomenon of plagiarism indicated Hughes's popularity. Writer Ye Junjian's 1935 essay introduced "Black Poets in the Americas," identifying Hughes, Claude McKay, and Countee Cullen as a new trend in world literature where they countered stereotypes of "uncivilized" Blacks. Similar to woman authors, whose gender was often flagged by the prefix "Miss," Hughes's race/color was invariably identified by the prefix "(American) Black."[91]

Chinese cultural circles remained intrigued by Hughes's experiences in the Soviet Union, noting his travels, his publications there, his interactions with local writers, and his book project on ethnic groups in Central Asia.[92] His lengthy essay "Moscow and Me," in which Hughes extolled the Soviet Union as being without Jim Crow, praise soon strongly echoed by Robeson and similar to Du Bois's admiration for the Japanese Empire, appeared in *International Literature*. It was translated into Chinese multiple times in 1934. The essay detailed the comfortable living conditions afforded Hughes as a Black writer who was honored with membership in the Revolutionary Writers' Association and whose work was sought after and paid for in a racially harmonious society. It countered warnings about the scarcity of consumer goods, thought control, and political persecution. Hughes noted plays sympathetic to Blacks at the Children's Theater, including one about the happy life of an African immigrant girl, similarly experienced by Paul Robeson as recorded in Shirley Graham Du Bois's biography of him. Consistent with sentiments he expressed during the luncheon in Shanghai, Hughes disputed complaints by his colleagues on the "Black and White" film project and the conspiracy theory over its collapse. He praised the social mission of Soviet cinema as superior to that of profit-driven Hollywood. The essay also detailed his trip to Central Asia.[93]

The young translator of *Not without Laughter* whom Hughes met in Shanghai was Zhu Xiuxia (1907–86), then a member of the Left-Wing Writers' League, an editor of the monthly *Modern Culture*, and a frequent contributor to *Linglong*. Zhu later abandoned leftism and served as an alternate member of the Central Supervision Committee of the Nationalist government. Lu Xun corresponded with him often around the time Hughes visited, probably on the translation project.[94] With Zhu and (Xia) Zhengnong (future husband of Mao Zedong's widowed sister-in-law) credited as cotranslators, the novel was serialized to launch the magazine *Literature and Art* (*Wenyi*) in October 1933. In his introduction, Zhu drew readers' attention to the fact that the "American Black writer" had just visited China, Fu Donghua's review essay, and the thunder the novel had created in Black and American literature.[95] It was released in book form in 1936 by the Young Companion Publishing House at the modest price of 0.65 yuan. Featuring a portrait of the author, an advertisement for the book in the *Shanghai Daily* announced that "Langston Hughes possesses the most progressive thoughts and most refined technique among Black writers" and called it a milestone hailed by the critics. In 1936 and 1938, Hughes's mother informed him of the arrival in Cleveland of copies from Shanghai, commenting, "It is the most comical looking book, with your picture on the back or front."[96]

Qinghua Weekly introduced Hughes's new story collection *The Ways of White Folks*, translated as *Tricks of Whites*. It allegedly revealed his "profound hatred" of white discrimination against and cultural appropriation of the colored, and Black elites' attempt to cozy up with the oppressors, reminiscent of "the dynamics between the imperialists and us." One reader who read the book in the United States, heeding Carl Van Vechten's recommendation, found its new relevance in Shanghai. He urged that the book be translated into Chinese to break down blind belief in white superiority. Translations of several short stories from this collection and poems from *Weary Blues* and *Fine Clothes*, "full of race and class sentiments," appeared in numerous periodicals and in a pioneering anthology of African American literature between 1933 and 1935.[97]

Hughes's trip to embattled Spain sparked renewed interest in his work as China suffered conflicts of its own between 1936 and 1937. Curiously, it seemed that his epic poem "Roar, China!" went scarcely noticed. Among the new translations of his work were the poem "Madrid" and the short stories "Laughter in Madrid" and "Air Raid on Barcelona." The translators of multiple versions of these pieces inevitably noted that Hughes "had recently served in the Spanish Republican army for six months." Yao Ke translated "One Christmas Eve."[98] Zhu Xiuxia translated Hughes's short story "Gift of Sandy" for the anthology *Famous Short Stories of Weak/Oppressed Nations*.[99] Mayakovsky translated Hughes's English translations of two revolutionary poems, "Ashore at Havana" and "Leave China!," by Rigino Redroso. They were then translated from Russian into Chinese. Here, I translate "Leave China!" back to English:

> Hurl the world bandits out of the Great Wall!
> We are to help all those enslaved to fight,
> Prepare and issue orders,
> We are with you, China!
> Leave China!
> Workers, attack the bandits under the cover of dark,
> Your slogan roars like rockets:
> Leave China![100]

Poems like these permitted Black-Chinese internationalism to circulate from Havana to Harlem, Moscow, and Shanghai.

TRANSFORMATION DURING THE TUMULTUOUS 1940S

During World War II, Hughes strongly endorsed the Double V campaign—victory over Hitler abroad and victory over Jim Crow at home. Meanwhile, the rise of anticommunist hysteria forced him to repudiate his radicalism. Works on religious themes now became a lightning rod. Aimee Semple McPherson, founder of the evangelical International Church of the Foursquare Gospel in California, launched a protest campaign against the author's blasphemous works. Whereas other figures in this book stood unyieldingly against such interference, it seems that Hughes's chronically precarious finances made him vulnerable. Concerned that enraged evangelists threatened to disrupt his future lecture opportunities, a major source of his meager livelihood, Hughes issued a statement retracting the radicalism of his youthful past.[101]

Hughes made every effort to clear himself of allegations of communist association and sever ties with leftist organizations. In his letter to Carl Van Vechten, Hughes commented on Winston Churchill's June 22, 1941, speech advocating cooperation between the "free world" and the Soviet Union, which Germany had just invaded: "I do declare! All of which will no doubt make the Communist Party change its line again. Strange bedfellows! . . . Will the Red Cross start sponsoring Sacks For The Soviets as well as Bundles for Britain? I'm glad I'm a lyric poet. It might be interesting to search for new rhymes for moon and June as the old ones have been worn out." He lamented aloofly in another letter, "How awful it would be if Communism, Fascism, and Democracy all became the one and the same."[102] Hughes repudiated his earlier passion for China and the Spanish Republic, and he struggled to put the past behind him.

Yet Hughes's past affiliations kept resurfacing. In late 1947, he was alarmed to receive a copy of the *Negro Year Book* published by Tuskegee Institute in Alabama, which listed him along with A. Philip Randolph, Angelo Herndon, and Richard Wright as eminent African American writers who had deserted the Communist Party. He asked that the "error" be "corrected immediately," anxiously contending, "I have never been a member of the Communist Party. . . . The FBI gave complete clearance." The following year, Hughes pleaded with Horace Mann Bond, the first African American president of his alma mater, Lincoln University, "Certainly you can state categorically that I am not now and have never been a member of the Communist Party" in response to all such inquires. Eager to convince Bond, he resorted to religion: "[An] atheist or a good party-liner would hardly have permitted the publication of a group of religious poems, 'Feet O' Jesus,' in my book, *The Dream Keeper*, that appeared the very year I was in the Soviet Union; or the publication of a song based on the same poem, 'At the Feet of Jesus,' in 1947."[103] In early 1948, Eslanda Robeson alerted Hughes that Henry J. Taylor "went to town against you." On his radio program *Taylor Talks*, sponsored by General Motors, Taylor, with his "so incensed," "vicious" voice, detailed how Hughes had been prevented from speaking at a Chicago school and read lines from Hughes's poem "Good Morning, Revolution" and another "one about Marx being like God." Eslanda warned, "Take it easy, stay out of jail" during the hysteria.[104]

It was unlikely that Hughes joined W. E. B. Du Bois, Shirley Graham, and Paul Robeson at the Cultural and Scientific Conference for World Peace in 1949. Oddly, his name appeared forty-four times in the House Un-American Activities Committee's review of the conference. The document ranked the alleged sponsors of the conference according to the number of communist front organizations they were allegedly affiliated with. It listed Hughes among the top four, with alleged membership in seventy-one to eighty such "subversive" organizations. Hughes was probably unaware of this document, but he was conscious of the danger. As late as 1952, seeing his name on the membership list of the National Council of American-Soviet Friendship, an affiliation with which he had long intended to let lapse, Hughes wrote to its executive director, "Regretfully I must resign."[105]

As Hughes disowned "Goodbye Christ," a key poem commemorating his radicalism and love affair with Si-lan Chen in Moscow, he withdrew from her. He concluded his account of their relationship with a wistful air in his autobiography, "The next time I saw Si-lan she was married, living in Hollywood, and directing the dances for *Anna and the King of Siam*."[106] Yet there was more to their story than he let on.

The erstwhile lovers stayed in touch during the decade following her migration to the United States, mostly through occasional postcards. The old dynamics continued. Chen warmly reached out, always including her phone number and the sign-off "Love, Sylvia," while Hughes remained evasive as ever, now formally signing his correspondence "Sincerely, Langston." Still rattled by her immigration ordeal and nervous about meeting her husband's friends at the upcoming housewarming party, Chen invited Hughes, her "only friend" in the United States, asking him to "phone or write" at once.[107] Hughes promised to phone upon returning to New York City from Cleveland around March 10, 1937. "It will be swell to see you again, and to meet your new husband." Probably eagerly waiting for the phone to ring that day, Chen dropped a few sharp lines the following day: "Langston! Why haven't you phoned? . . . Hope you're ashamed of yourself." Still, she reiterated the invitation to the party and requested that they also meet in advance. When Hughes did not acknowledge her communications, Chen chided him: "I can hardly believe that you came to New York and did not even ring me up. . . . I also want to go to Harlem with you so I'm putting that off until you come." She reached out again in early 1938, "Jack is here. We're looking forward to seeing you." Once again, Hughes remained silent. Chen sent a postcard from Mexico months later, "Dearest Lang, I dreamt about you last night. Hence the PC."[108]

Hughes and Chen mainly communicated about professional matters. Hughes mostly managed to avoid Chen while living in the same city. He telegrammed his "very best wishes and splash salute" for her debut concert.

After his collection of radical poems was finally published, Hughes inscribed a copy, "To Si-lan Chen—with 10 stars out of Harlem for her dancing shore." Both were scheduled to appear at the *Daily Worker* staff party on November 5, 1938, as fellow entertainers, with Hughes contributing his Harlem Suitcase Theater and Chen "oriental dances." It seemed that more opportunities arose for them to meet in person. During one of her trips back to New York City from Hollywood, Si-lan wrote to her husband, "I will be seeing Langston. Did I tell you how impressed [with my performance] he was? I hope that perhaps he will know someone who'd sponsor a concert for me."[109]

Their communications then ebbed to a trickle. Chen sent a note after she had attended one of Hughes's lectures without approaching him. Hughes forwarded her a copy of the poem "The Negro Speaks of Rivers," which he mass-distributed to mark the twentieth anniversary of his writing career. He mentioned Leyda's publications occasionally and always remembered to send greetings to him to guard against any hint of a lingering romantic connection.[110]

Though Hughes and Van Vechten were closely associated with the circle of Black dancers in New York City, Hughes never engaged Chen's repeated request to connect her to the American dance world and to a publisher for her autobiography. Formerly a dance critic for the *New York Times*, Van Vechten wrote to Hughes about making his first public speech, along with Alain Locke, at the launch of the Negro Dance Theater in October 1942. Hughes mentioned to Van Vechten that Maudelle Bass, the African American dancer and Diego Rivera model, was living at his house after returning from Mexico in 1949.[111] Van Vechten began his career as a photographer taking portraits of Anna May Wong. He shot numerous stunning photographs of "the great belles of China" who had adventured to the United States on behalf of China relief, including Loh Tsei, the "Chinese Joan of Arc"; Maimai Sze (daughter of diplomat Shi Zhaoji, also known as Alfred Sao-ke Sze); and Chen's old family friends Hilda Yen and Ya-ching Lee. The photographer wrote to Gertrude Stein and Alice Toklas that he held "a Chinese luncheon party (with a few Spaniards!) at the Algonquin" for Yen, attended by Lin Yutang and his wife. Van Vechten explained that Yen "began to learn [aviation] in Italy and then they thought she was learning too much and stopped her."[112] Hughes did not introduce Chen to this inner circle probably because Van Vechten had rejected her along with Hughes's radicalism. In the above-mentioned letter first discussing the manuscript *Good Morning, Revolution*, Hughes introduced Chen as his girlfriend. Van Vechten did not acknowledge her, simply writing, "You seem to be having a perfect time." While Van Vechten and Knopf dismissed Hughes's radical work, Chen remained enthusiastic about "Turkestan and other Soviet topics" that he had started to work on when they were together. Soon, Van Vechten was setting up his cousin Mary Blanchard and Hughes as lovers.[113]

While reading Hughes's autobiography *The Big Sea* in 1942, Chen first asked Hughes to read her own manuscript, teasing, "Shall I include you in my book?" Undiscouraged by his silence but humbled by a fresh rejection by her husband's publisher, Harcourt Brace, she wrote again inquiring about the possibility of publishing with Knopf. Hughes wrote back a couple of months later from Yaddo, where he had been invited as the first Black resident, instructing her to send the manuscript to his Harlem address at 634 St. Nicolas Avenue. Apparently nothing came of this exchange. Si-lan forwarded the manuscript to Jack in 1943 for criticism. He quickly advised that she should refrain from open criticism of the Chiangs, and that "the personal touches about P. J. must go after all he is now working in Chungking and the thing would damn him." She also sent the manuscript to Pearl S. Buck, who had a working relationship with the Chen brothers, in 1945. The Nobel laureate allowed, "It is true that your mixed heritage, fascinating in itself, could make a good book." However, she was not confident that the manuscript, "a wholly personal record" of someone "not famous enough, or notorious enough," would attract readers.[114]

After being turned down by numerous publishers, who consistently recommended she rewrite the "otherwise interesting materials," the persistent Chen wrote to Hughes in 1946. "Would you still like to read my manuscript?" she asked. Hughes agreed again. She expressed her frustration that she "got nothing" with her manuscript while attempting to demonstrate through her own life experience that "it was not one's nationality but socialism [that] mattered," which Hughes could hardly echo now. Soon after the manuscript reached him, Chen wrote that she "became very self-conscious about what I had said about you. I do hope it was nothing that you would object to — you have my permission to rewrite that page if it does not please you!" Again, Hughes avoided reading the "beautiful looking manuscript," because her nephew Brian "happened to drop by the very day it came and immediately carried it off to read himself."[115]

Hughes and Chen's last surviving correspondence was her 1948 note sent to the Clark Hotel in Los Angeles, where he stayed. She invited him to a family dinner before a film to which Hughes contributed narration. It repeated her chronic complaint, "Dear Lang, You did not call back! . . . Please *phone* and let me know."[116] Hughes had inserted Chen's name in his 1947 children's poem "Little Song," which celebrates diversity:

Carmencita loves Patrick.
Patrick loves Si Lan Chen.
Xenophon loves Mary Jane.
Hildegarde loves Ben.[117]

Chen reserved three paragraphs for Hughes in her autobiography, calling him "a very good friend" whose "integrity and art" she admired more "each time we met." She recounted some anecdotes in Moscow illustrating his poetic innocence.[118] It seemed that with their relationship now ended, they never wrote each other for the rest of their lives.

However, Hughes's interest in and connection with China survived his political transformation and disaffection from Chen. He continued to offer gifts from Chinatowns to maintain friendship, sending Maxim Lieber "a Chinese puzzle" in 1941. He refreshed his friendship with Agnes Smedley at Yaddo the following summer. Hughes reported to friends that Smedley, who "didn't use up all her energy in China," organized programs for kids on vacation there, recruiting him to read poetry.[119] Hughes wrote more about China's struggle. His 1940 poem "Song of the Refugee Road" questioned, "Will the world listen to my appeal? From China where the war gods thunder and roar." He routinely commented on China in his columns for the *Chicago Defender*. He recalled scenes he witnessed in Shanghai, such as numerous "whites only" signs, sadly familiar to African Americans, and bamboo cane factories where young children labored so that wealthy white capitalists could enjoy walking sticks.[120] Hughes articulated the Asian ramifications of the Double V campaign. He revised "Our Spring" under the title "The Underground: Antifascists of the Occupied Countries of Europe and Asia," connecting the struggles "from Norway to Slovakia, Manchuria to Greece." His pamphlet *Jim Crow's Last Stand* associated the battle of African Americans in Harlem with global resistance against racial segregation: "India, and China and Harlem, too / Have made up their minds Jim Crow is out on his tail." At the end of the war, Hughes predicted that China would "control her own rivers and her own ports" but wondered if African Americans would share the freedoms earned by Black soldiers:

I've driven back the Germans and the Japs
From Burma to the Rhine

. . . .

Italians, Chinese, Danes are liberated

. . . .

Will I still be ill-fated
Because I am Black?"[121]

Despite his fear of being associated with communism, Hughes took a stand in China's civil war. In one of his first articles in the *Chicago Defender*, he echoed Du Bois, recalling the racial segregation he had personally experienced in Shanghai as "Jim Crow" and dismissing Chiang Kai-shek as a "Chinese Uncle Tom." Hughes argued that the rise of the CCP had much meaning for African Americans due to a shared experience of discrimination. On the eve of the CCP victory, he wrote to Melvin B. Tolson, "I like your poem, *African China*, immensely. In fact, I think it is one of the best things of yours that I have seen." Hughes made some revisions and published the piece in *Voices*.[122]

In China, Hughes, as a prized writer of color, grew more popular in diverse political circles in the competing discourses of Pan-Asianism. His work highlighting the oppression people of color suffered in the hands of whites fit into Japan's propaganda portraying itself as the leader in Asia's resistance against white colonialism, despite Hughes's unpleasant encounters with the Japanese authorities. Chinese translations of his work widely appeared in Japan's two puppet states in the early 1940s. In occupied Shanghai, the fabled female CCP secret agent and writer Guan Lu translated "Slave on the Block" misleadingly as "Slave on the Boxing Platform" and "A Good Job Gone" as "Mr. Lloyd and Pauline: Love Story between a White Man and a Black Girl" for *Shanghai Woman*, and "Home" for another journal. Another female writer, Bai Ying, also translated "A Good Job Gone" for the legendary *Magazine*, which had featured a comprehensive biographical piece on Hughes and was then promoting Eileen Chang into rapid fame. A Zhang Youlan translated several other short stories from *The Ways of White Folks*, including "Father and Son," for the magazine *Constitutional Politics Monthly*, which would be important for Eugene Chen in his final years.[123]

In Manchukuo, Hughes's poems "To a Negro Girl," "I, Too," and "Indentured Labor," along with Claude McKay's "Spring in New Hampshire" and "If" and Frances E. Harper's "To Women," were included as "supplementary" in the *Selection of Modern Poetry*. The editor explained that since these "Black poets" were not as famous, their pieces might provide just an alternative flavor, hopefully "not spoiling readers' appetite." While other authors, including Alexander Pushkin (whose African heritage was generally deempha-

FIGURE 5.4. 1942 woodcut
portraits commemorate Langston
Hughes and Rabindranath Tagore
as global poets of color.
Shi chuangzuo (Guilin) 15 (1942): 2.

sized in the Soviet Union and Asia), were categorized by nationality and
introduced with a brief biography, the Black poets were defined by their skin
color without any biographical information. Consistent with Shao Xunmei's
treatment of Black poetry a decade earlier, this gesture signaled the implicit
racial hierarchy in Japan's colonial endeavors. The editor boasted that the
book was "a seed" sowed in the desert-like literary forum in Manchukuo and
credited support from the literary circles in Osaka. Multiple translations of
"Professor" appeared in Shanghai journals and the monthly *Literature and
Arts*, based in Jilin Province of Manchuria.[124]

Exiled leftist cultural circles soon promoted Hughes as an idol equal to
Rabindranath Tagore in his capacity to inspire the masses. A woodcut print
featured their portraits as global poets of color on the same page in *Writing
Poetry*, a journal founded in 1941 in Guilin, one of the wartime cultural cen-
ters (fig. 5.4). In Chongqing, Yuan Shuipai, then an underground communist poet, translated "The Colored Soldier" and "The Negro Mother" for the
Literature Monthly. At the end of the war, *Not without Laughter* was reissued
under the title *Black Harriet*. In his new introduction, Zhu Xiuxia optimisti-

cally argued that, while lessons from war brutality would inspire world peace and racial equality, republication of the first Chinese translation of a novel on Blacks was quite meaningful. He again highlighted Hughes's journey to the Soviet Union and China.[125]

Between 1946 and 1948, translations of Hughes's poems, including "Freedom Train," appeared in journals across the nation, some of them in multiple versions. Yuan Shuipai translated "Homesick Blues," "Brass Spittoons," "Song for a Dark Girl," and "Stalingrad: 1942" to celebrate Hughes's forty-fifth birthday. In the brief biography, Yuan lauded Hughes as "the most renowned poet of the Black race," whose work captured "the soul and pain of the oppressed nations."[126]

DURING THE LONG POST-1949 DECADES

Langston Hughes retreated further from radicalism to safeguard his writing career and meager livelihood as a "literary sharecropper," as he called himself, from the intensifying harassment of McCarthyism in the 1950s. In 1952, "reactionary whites" forced the cancellation of his fundraising event for a local Black school with the Business and Professional Women's Club of Fort Worth, Texas. He soon noted that interracial engagements by prominent figures such as Pearl S. Buck, Lillian Smith, and the presidents of Atlanta University and Morehouse College suffered the same fate. Since Black speakers could not secure engagements with "the vast arena of white women's clubs," to which Liu Liangmo had enjoyed full access, Hughes's income came largely from lecturing in African American educational institutions in the South. Heavy dependence on the already meager grants made them vulnerable to pressure from state boards or local politicians to screen speakers according to the U.S. attorney general's list of subversive organizations.[127]

In 1953, Hughes was called to testify before the House Un-American Activities Committee, a hearing that was televised across the nation, although even the FBI admitted that he had never been a communist. In contrast to Paul Robeson's defiance telling the committee, "You are the un-Americans, and you ought to be ashamed of yourselves" three years later, Hughes declared that a "complete reorientation of my thinking and emotional feelings occurred roughly four or five years ago." However, he did not name or denounce any of his former leftist associates, passing the ultimate test of virtue during the anticommunist hysteria. Probably shaken by the experience, Hughes self-censored more diligently. He even deliberated whether to send the FBI a "copy of the transcript of my testimony for their files with a brief covering note." He was anxious to advise J. Edgar Hoover, who had reportedly referred to "Goodbye Christ" in a speech, "that this no longer represents my views in any way."[128]

Hughes's gestures of submission led to a rift with other prominent African American intellectuals. When W. E. B. Du Bois requested Hughes's input for organizing a colonial conference in early 1945, Hughes declined: "I do not belong to any organizations which I feel would be helpful to you." In 1950, Paul Robeson invited Hughes to preorder a book (for $10, costly at the time) to support its author, John Howard Lawson, one of the Hollywood Ten who had been jailed for defying the House Un-American Activities Committee. The following year, Robeson, Lawson, and Shirley Graham urged Hughes to attend a meeting they had organized to defend V. J. Jerome, a Marxist scholar who had been indicted for conspiring to overthrow the U.S. government. Between 1951 and 1952, Du Bois solicited Hughes to join him as initiating signers for two petitions: One was to pardon W. A. Hunton, who was jailed for refusing to reveal contributors to the fund that the Civil Rights Congress in New York used to bail those convicted as communist leaders; the other one objected to the U.S. government policy on "colonial and subject peoples, especially in Africa." There are no records indicating that Hughes ever responded to such calls for leftist activism.[129]

Furthermore, Hughes "deliberately" omitted W. E. B. Du Bois and Paul Robeson, then under assault by McCarthyism and banished by the mainstream media, in the new editions of his children's books *Famous American Negros* (1954) and *Famous Negro Music Makers* (1955). In 1956, probably hoping to make peace privately, Hughes wrote to Du Bois, whom he had always respected, "Dear Dr. Du Bois, I have just read again your *Souls of Black Folk*—for perhaps the tenth time—the first time having been some forty years ago when I was a child in Kansas. Its beauty and passion and power are as moving and as meaningful as ever." Still, Du Bois publicly criticized his deletion of Robeson from the books. At Robeson's sixtieth birthday, Du Bois defended the singer's speech at the International Congress for Peace in Paris and condemned the persecutions of him that followed: "And above all, his own people, American Negroes, joined in hounding one of their greatest artists—not all, but even men like Langston Hughes, who wrote of Negro musicians and deliberately omitted Robeson's name—Robeson who more than any living man has spread the pure Negro folk song over the civilized world."[130]

Amid the turmoil, Hughes maintained his association with China in a mostly nonpolitical fashion. Responding to a 1952 appeal to help Chinese students stranded due to the change in regimes, Hughes contacted the China Institute to offer his support. It assigned him a student born in the United States and "whose parents own big shops in San Francisco! And his uncle edits one of New York's Chinese dailies," as he complained to Van Vechten. In his short story on the twisted, violent love affairs of two circus performers, Hughes named the protagonist "Mysterious Madam Shanghai," although she had nothing to do with the city.[131] After Maoist China became largely inaccessible (though the Du Boises and the Robesons managed to maintain contact), Hughes replaced it with Hong Kong in his writing. In his Simple stories, the protagonist imagines himself living in a global village, losing money on the "Chinese lottery," and drinking in a "Chinese bar" there, before riding ten minutes in a rocket plane back to Harlem to take an aspirin.[132]

While continuing to associate African Americans' fight for freedom with China, Hughes carefully avoided the theme of class struggle. In his *Chicago Defender* column, echoing Paul Robeson and W. E. B. Du Bois, he highlighted the relevance of the 1949 CCP victory to "Negroes" and "people of color all around the world."[133] His 1951 poem "Consider Me" articulated a Sino–African American alliance for racial justice:

> Black,
> Caught in a crack
> That splits the world in two
> From China
> By Way of Arkansas
> To Lenox Avenue.

Hughes's 1957 poem "In Explanation of Our Times" took a similar approach:

> Dixie to Singapore, Cape Town to Hong Kong
> The Misters won't call lots of other folks Mister
>
> . . . .
>
> George Sallie Coolie Boy gets tired sometimes
> So all over the World today
> Folks with not even Mister in front of their names
> Are raring up and talking Back
> to those called Mister
> From Harlem past Hong Kong talking back.[134]

Hughes remained confident of the PRC's power. Recognizing domestic and international challenges the regime was facing, Hughes's unpublished poem "China," penned on August 26, 1963, reframed the metaphor in his 1937 poem "Roar, China!":

> And so the old lion
> Lift it [*sic*] mighty head
> And roars within the cage
> in which it is confined
> and looks out on a narrow world
> But is not blind.[135]

Hughes's suppressed inspiration drawn from the CCP resurfaced in his fury at the brutal racial violence African Americans suffered. In "Birmingham Sunday," his eulogy to the four black girls killed in the bombing of the Sixteenth Street Baptist Church in Birmingham, Alabama, on Sunday, September 15, 1963, Hughes connected his rage with the one once felt by oppressed China:

> And bloodied Sunday dresses
> Torn to shreds by dynamite
> That China made aeons ago —
> Did not know
> That what China made
> Before China was ever Red at all
>
> . . . .
>
> Four tiny little girls
>
> . . . .
>
> In little graves today await
> The dynamite that might ignite
> The fuse of centuries of Dragon Kings[136]

The girls might never know China, but Hughes subtly made their martyrdom also about the communist revolution in China.

While the official press in China applauded Robeson and Du Bois as defiant peace fighters at the peak of McCarthyism and the Korean War, it remained silent on Hughes's public renunciation of his radical past, instead fixing its gaze at the writer of the 1930s as if he were preserved in a time capsule. His classic poems "The Negro Speaks of Rivers," "Brass Spittoons," "Song for a Dark Girl," "Let America Be America Again," and "I, Too" dominated two versions of *Selection of Poetry by Blacks* (1952 and 1957) (fig. 5.5). Similarly, his short stories "Home," "Father and Son," and "A Friday Morning" stood out in two versions of *Selection of Short Stories by Blacks* (1955 and 1957) with

FIGURE 5.5. Cover of *Selection of Poetry by Blacks* published by the Writers' Publishing House in Beijing in 1957. The muscular image of the Black farmer was adapted from a 1953 charcoal painting titled *Harvest Talk* by African American artist Charles White, a friend of Paul Robeson. *Author's collection.*

almost identical contents. Since the volumes were translated from anthologies published in the Soviet Union and the German Democratic Republic, they were presented within a shared Cold War paradigm.[137]

Echoing the pronouncements of 1930s leftist cultural circles, the translators and editors of the 1950s lauded Hughes as "the most renowned," "genius Black poet, essayist, and critic" and "the excellent representative of Black proletarian literature as a realistic writer." They framed Hughes's earlier work as integral to the contemporary peace movement, which was propelling Blacks' long struggle toward "the path of democracy and socialism." While Hughes distanced himself from Robeson across the Pacific, Chinese translators and editors strove to connect the two. Following lengthy quotes from Robeson's speech at the peace conference in New York City on mobilizing more Americans to join the peace movement, one translator commented, "Among voices of the progressive American writers devoting their lives to peace, freedom, and democracy, we hear Hughes's."[138]

The biographical information on Hughes in these volumes repeated the stories synthesized by leftist intellectuals before 1949, highlighting his various menial jobs and his drifting. His early creation was criticized as "politically and ideologically immature and naive," under the influence of bourgeois nationalism and aestheticism. The translators applauded Hughes's shift to proletarian internationalism, crediting the influence of the 1917 Bolshevik Revolution, his adventures in the Soviet Union, China, and the Spanish Republic, and his active participation in antifascist struggles. They appraised, "The healthy and progressive ones are the mainstream of his works." His poems of the late 1930s and early 1940s, "full of passionate revolutionary spirit," served as "roaring marching tunes for a once-trampled people now galloping toward liberation." They lauded his "revolutionary poetry," citing "How about It Dixie?" "Ballads of Lenin," and "Ballad of the Spanish Civil Guard." They described *Not without Laughter*, translated as *Chilling Laughter*, as autobiographical. The translators mentioned dramatic recitations of "The Negro Mother" and the poetry collections *Dear Lovely Death* and *The Dream Keeper* for the first time in China. They alerted readers of some of Hughes's recent works, including *A New Song, Shakespeare in Harlem, Fields of Wonder, The Big Sea*, and *Simple Speaks His Mind*.[139]

"Father and Son" and "Home" from *The Ways of White Folks*, now translated as *Brutalities by Whites*, were particularly employed to reveal the "unbearable . . . terror in the South—the barbaric fortress of racial discrimination." The translators summarized the plot of "Father and Son" as the mixed-race son "stands up for his human rights and martyrs himself at the brutal hands of his exploitive and despotic plantation-owner father." They argued that the short story reflects the father's "shamelessness and lewdness, abusing Black women at will, mistreating Black servants, and torturing his 'mixed-race' son to death without hesitation just to avoid being calling 'father.'" They called on readers to pay "special attention" to this piece as "a strong voice of the fighting American proletariat and unity between white and Black masses." Meanwhile, the translators frowned on the author's lack of criticism of the protagonist's "innocent belief that Blacks in the American North enjoy 'privileges.'" "Home" portrays "the barbaric lynching of a gifted Black musician by a mad mob, just because he dares to talk to a white woman on the street," the translators summarized. They argued that the two volumes of short stories fit in the trend set by Black communist Angelo Herndon's autobiography *Let Me Live* (1937) to focus on "unyielding struggles for the people's freedom and happiness."[140]

While mainland China generally neglected Hughes during the more radical 1960s and 1970s, Bingxin translated Ghanaian poet Matei Markwei's "Life in Our Village" from Hughes's edited anthology, *An African Treasury*, in 1962. Meanwhile, persecuted citizens found private inspirations from Hughes's work. A reader suffering from the "family background" theory during the Cultural Revolution recalled the powerful emotion aroused by Hughes's poem "Words Like Freedom." Taiwan paid tribute by including his poems "Merry-Go-Around" and "Brass Spittoons" in an anthology by Black writers. Celebrating him as an "award-winning professional writer," the Taiwanese translators described his global travels as glamourous and mistakenly inflated his academic credentials — teaching at Columbia University in 1921 and earning a doctoral degree in 1929. This was a far cry from Hughes's proletarian image presented in China's leftist tradition.[141]

Memories of Hughes, who had passed away in 1967, were refreshed during the post-Mao decades. *The Big Sea* and *Something in Common and Other Short Stories* were translated into Chinese in 1986 and 1988, respectively. The translator of *Something*, Luo Xingqun, confessed that she had sometimes lost heart for the project, "uncertain whether works by Blacks would be well received by [Chinese] readers." In his foreword, Zou Jiang, a professor of literature at Southwest Normal University who had translated hundreds of Hughes's poems, highly recommended "Father and Son" as the "most powerful." He traced the various formats that Hughes had attempted with the miscegenation theme. The collection pioneered in introducing Hughes's work on themes beyond racial conflict. Avoiding the offensive stereotypical image, Luo subtly translated *Fine Clothes to the Jew* as *Fine Clothes to Pawn*

Shop Owners. Zou commented, "These diverse themes reflect the author's profound concern for humanity."[142]

Luo's short biography of Hughes as "the first professional Black writer" was the most comprehensive ever available to Chinese readers. She highlighted the family's antislavery tradition, which had been surprisingly omitted by the previous Chinese reviewers and translators seeking out Hughes's revolutionary credentials. Luo mentioned the deeds of his maternal grandmother's former husband as a colleague of John Brown and how "his paternal grandfather devoted thirty years to abolition." She detailed Hughes's close relationship with his maternal grandmother, "who, armed with a certificate of freedom, was never a slave . . . often held Hughes on her laps to tell stories of Black heroes." Luo introduced Hughes's cold father, whom the author "hated," with sympathy: "Working day and night, he could not support his family due to brutal racism, since he was treated as a Black despite his mixed blood." Among Chinese reviewers and translators, Luo first addressed Hughes's sexuality and marital status, portraying him as asexual: "Never married, Hughes hung a picture of his girlfriend, with whom he maintained a platonic relationship, in his bedroom." She attributed the unique situation to "his deeply hidden special psychology of self-protection against women. Since Hughes had spent his childhood with his grandmother, mother, even mother's girlfriends, his consciousness trusted that women, instead of men, dominate in life." Luo detailed Hughes's poverty and suffering from "countless" instances of racial discrimination, but praised his open mind toward whites, quoting Hughes, "From very early on, I learned not to hate all whites." She first reported Hughes's association with his patron, the philanthropist Charlotte Mason, which, ill fit for the leftist revolutionary narrative, had been consistently suppressed. Probably unaware that Hughes's conflicts with Mason's other Black protégés Zora Neale Hurston and Alain Locke had contributed to the end of their relationship, Luo fully accepted Hughes's explanation: "She demanded that gifted Black artists discover 'primitive innocence' and 'exotic beauty' among Blacks and 'leave politics to whites.' Hughes rejected her tight control in his quest for independence, while his work was growing more and more political in the early 1930s. He resumed his dependence on royalties as a professional writer living on the edge of poverty, despite his fame." Luo wrote that Hughes's poem "Roar, China!" was inspired by his encounters with the revered Madam Sun Yat-sen and Lu Xun and by the knowledge he acquired in Shanghai of "the deep crisis and hope of China."[143] A Sino–African American linkage from an earlier era continued to resonate through the evolving political contexts of succeeding decades.

Epilogue

The five extraordinary people whose lives and work have been the subject of the preceding chapters had an extensive and lasting impact on Sino–African American relations. While it is beyond the scope of this book to delineate fully and precisely how these strands of influence have persisted into recent decades, some general observations can be made about their impact.

Though the United States has never fully reckoned with the reception of W. E. B. and Shirley Graham Du Bois in China, their visits not only were important for the Du Boises personally but also helped shape future geopolitical developments. W. E. B. Du Bois's experiences in China added a crucial class dimension to his famous dictum regarding the color line. By vouching for alliances between postcolonial states in Africa and the People's Republic of China (PRC), the Du Boises arguably helped pave the way for China's massive intervention into Africa in the twenty-first century.[1]

Paul Robeson continues to be remembered as a loyal friend to China. He is celebrated for globalizing China's national anthem, for his songs that set hearts stirring across the Pacific, and for his contributions to the Chinese nation's liberation and to the friendship between the peoples of China and the United States. While the Du Boises' primary impact was political, Robeson's legacy in China has extended from politics to the arts.

Even though China's economic system now blends communism and capitalism, both the Du Boises and Robeson occupy a special place in the nation's heart. China Society for People's Friendship Studies, headed by Huang Hua, the Chinese People's Association for Friendship with Foreign Countries, and the Chinese Commission of the International Science and Peace Week, organized the "Tribute to the 125th Birthday of Dr. Du Bois, an

Old Friend of the Chinese People and Famous African American Scholar," in Beijing on October 12, 1993. The tribute announced the founding of the China Du Bois Research Center. President Jiang Zemin forwarded a congratulatory letter wishing that "the great spirit and cause of Dr. Du Bois shine forever!" Among the 170 attendees were Graham Du Bois's son David Du Bois, who had traveled to China as a delegate of the Young Progressives of America in 1950 and studied at Beijing University around 1959; diplomats from Africa; Israel Epstein; Gong Pusheng; and faculty members of Beijing University and the China Academy of Social Sciences. The tribute played Robeson's records and featured Black folk songs performed by professors from Central Conservatory of Music.[2]

The Research Center of Soong Qingling (Soong Chingling, Madam Sun Yat-sen) Foundation, China Society for People's Friendship Studies, Beijing Foreign Languages University, *China Daily*, and the Foreign Languages Education and Research Publishing House organized the tribute for Robeson's 110th birthday at the former residence of Madam Sun in Beijing on April 9, 2008. Fifty people, including officials, professors, artists, Madam Sun's friends, and journalists attended the event. Paul Jr. sent a letter from New York City on behalf of his family. "A firm and dear friend of the Chinese people during your epic struggles against imperialism, [my father] courageously opposed Fascism and colonialism. It is fitting that this tribute from the people of China marks the 110th anniversary of Paul Robeson's birth." The tribute concluded with the attendees singing Robeson's classic "Joe Hill." His "Chee Lai!" was played in the Grand Hall of the People's Congress in Beijing during the Nie Er Music Week in 2009 and integrated into the "Hundred Years of Songs" program on the Music Channel of China Central TV in 2012, narrating the resilience of the nation.[3]

Liu Liangmo proved to be a model for Chinese engagement with African Americans and with Americans generally. Cosmopolitan, well educated, and comfortable in a wide variety of transpacific political and racial settings, he advocated effectively for China, Chinese Americans, and African Americans. His outreach shaped his writings and talks, which would remain unparalleled for decades and belie commonplace beliefs about racial animosity between the two peoples. Liu promoted the legacies of Du Bois and Robeson, helping to keep their words and songs before the Chinese people. Popularizing "Chee Lai!" around the globe through collaboration with Robeson and pushing its adoption as the national anthem of the People's Republic China was perhaps his greatest individual legacy. His performance as a Christian speaker, musician, and journalist in the Republic of China and the United

States transitioned into his remarkable ability to juggle faith and radical ideology in the PRC. Contemporary Christianity in China is more Pentecostal than Liu would have liked, but all denominations have to follow the path he blazed blending Christian witness with the political realities of a communist state.[4] Mass singing remains the Chinese Communist Party's hallmark cultural vehicle.

Sylvia Si-lan Chen's life and career made her experience political tumult in numerous countries across several continents. She left her mark as a dancer wherever she lived, contributing her unique combination of Afro-Creole, European, Chinese, and other Asian folk and classical dance forms. Her artistic breadth was arguably wider than that of any other Black or Chinese dancer.[5]

Langston Hughes's writings are hailed as classics in the United States and endure in China as well. Entering the twenty-first century, the Chinese remain fascinated by Hughes's masterpieces. "Father and Son" was released in book form by the prestigious Shanghai Classics Publishing House in 2008. Since 2009, the Ministry of Education has included a translation of "The Negro Speaks of Rivers" in the approved textbook of Chinese language and literature mandated for ninth graders across the nation to teach the "condensed history of the Black race." Hughes's work thus continues to boast an enormous readership in China comparable only to that enjoyed by figures as prominent as Mao Zedong and Lu Xun.[6] Recent waves of translations of and scholarship on Hughes's works are appearing in publications from the most prestigious academic presses to obscure journals of various types.[7]

Just as the five figures' political and cultural legacies persist in spite of the dramatic changes that followed their deaths, their lives were also marked by narratives of survival. Du Bois, Robeson, and Hughes were major American talents during the long Jim Crow era when their careers and lives were always vulnerable to racist discrimination and deadly violence. Liu and Chen navigated incessant political and social upheavals and wars. The most tragic story is that of Robeson. Passionate, committed, and politically innocent, he soared to great heights as a popular artistic hero but fell from international prominence into an eventual mental breakdown. After Eslanda Robeson's passing in 1965, he endured lonely final years until his own death in 1976.

W. E. B. Du Bois, Shirley Graham Du Bois, Sylvia Si-lan Chen, and her husband, Jay Leyda, were accomplished left-wing intellectuals and artists who suffered from bureaucratic oppression. The Du Boises' passports were canceled for years, while the Leydas were ensnarled in racialized interpretations of her status as the wife of a U.S. citizen. The Du Boises command a profound legacy today, but throughout their lives they were often marginalized, even within the civil rights movement and certainly in the academic world. For the Leydas and Du Boises alike, exile proved the only solution. Harassment by the U.S. Immigration and Naturalization Service and the Federal Bureau of Investigation drove the Leydas into homelessness, statelessness, and extreme psychological strain. These obstacles curtailed Chen's artistic achievements, and she had to find security in her husband's academic career.

The survival tactics followed by Liu Liangmo and Langston Hughes were the most successful. Caught between the rivalries between the Nationalist and Communist forces while promoting mass singing of songs of resistance, Liu skipped to the United States. After an illustrious career promoting China in the 1940s, he slipped back to China, beyond the clutches of the FBI and INS. In the PRC, Liu managed to sustain a high political profile while protecting to some extent his Christian faith. He served as a premier interpreter of American life and culture, particularly with respect to race, and survived numerous radical political campaigns unscathed by closely following the official line. Hughes, in turn, abandoned his left-wing idealism and joined the movement to interpret folk-based African American culture pioneered by Zora Neale Hurston and Sterling Brown. Like Liu, Hughes successfully sustained his career in extremist political contexts.

These five citizens of the world interacted with one another in a variety of ways, at times collaborating and contributing to historic alliances, at other times falling in and out of love. Together, their lives stand as powerful counters to narratives that foreground racism and alienation. Their lives offer a view into the power and potential of Black internationalism and Sino–African American collaboration. "Arise, Africa!" and "Roar, China!" as articulated by Du Bois and Hughes, respectively, match the shared struggles of a nation and a nation-within-a-nation. Their power and promise resonate to this day.

Notes

ABBREVIATIONS

JSCL Jay and Si-lan Chen Leyda Papers and Photographs, Elmer Holmes Bobst Library, New York University

LHP Langston Hughes Papers, Beinecke Rare Book and Manuscript Library, Yale University Library, New Haven, Conn.

LHP-HL Langston Hughes Papers (1932–34), Huntington Library, Manuscript Department, San Marino, Calif.

NYT *New York Times*

PSBH Archives of the Pearl S. Buck House, 520 Dublin Road, Perkasie, Pa.

RR *Renmin ribao*

SGDBP Shirley Graham Du Bois Papers, Arthur and Elizabeth Schlesinger Library, Radcliffe Institute for Advanced Study, Harvard University, Cambridge, Mass.

UCRA United China Relief Archives, Seeley G. Mudd Manuscript Library, Princeton University, Princeton, N.J.

WDBP W. E. B. Du Bois Papers, Special Collections and University Archives, University of Massachusetts Amherst Libraries, Amherst, Mass.

INTRODUCTION

1. Benedict Anderson, quoted and discussed in Perry, *May We Forever Stand*, 39. Robeson, Liu Liangmo, and the Chinese People's Chorus, *Chee Lai!*; Robeson and Keynote Orchestra and Chorus, *Anthem of the U.S.S.R.* Paul Robeson's brother Benjamin C. was pastor at Mother Zion from 1936 to 1963. The church's civil rights orientation attracted Paul and, among many others, Langston Hughes and W. E. B. Du Bois. Wandering through Harlem streets, these titanic African American figures encountered friendly Chinese merchants, laundrymen, and restaurant workers, who were well integrated into the community. For Chinese in Harlem, see Ottley, *New World A-Coming*, 51.

2. Lin Yutang, *My Country and My People.*

3. Chang, *Fateful Ties*; Xu Guoqi, *Chinese and Americans*; Pomfret, *Beautiful Country*;

Hsu, *Dreaming of Gold*; Bandele, *Black Star*; Edwards, *Practice of Diaspora*; Makalani, *In the Cause of Freedom*; Meriwether, *Proudly We Can Be Africans*; Singh, *Black Is a Country*; West, Martin, and Wilkins, *From Toussaint to Tupac*; "AHR Conversations: Black Internationalism."

4. Gallicchio, *African American Encounter*; So, *Transpacific Community*; Frazier, *East Is Black*; Taketani, *Black Pacific Narrative*; Mullen, *Afro-Orientalism*; Ho and Mullen, *Afro Asia*; Plummer, *Rising Wind*; Kelley, "But a Local Phase." The Fairbank Center for Chinese Studies at Harvard University has created a useful website covering scholarship on Sino–African American interactions: https://medium.com/fairbank-center/teaching-china-through-Black-history-30e3cdc32f03.

5. Cheng, *Citizens of Asian America*; Huang Yunte, *Inseparable*; Huang Yunte, *Charlie Chan*; Hsu, *Floating Chinaman*.

6. Lovell, *Maoism*.

7. For a good account of the relationship between Du Bois and Robeson, see Balaji, *Professor and Pupil*. Blain, *Set the World on Fire*.

8. Hughes, *Big Sea*; Hughes, *I Wonder as I Wander*.

9. *Shidai manhua* 29 (August 1936): covers; "Yangmei tuqi de Heiren," *Linglong* 2, no. 63 (1932): 622; Gao Yunxiang, *Sporting Gender*, 219; Lewis, *W. E. B. Du Bois*, 403.

10. Lin Shu and Wei Yi, *Heinu yutian lu*, 5. The play remained influential during China's 1911 Revolution and in Shanghai in the 1920s. It was performed in Ruijin, the capital of the Jiangxi Soviet, in 1932 to inform the Chinese masses about oppression of Blacks by capitalists. Tian Han, "Tan *Heinu hen*," *RR*, July 12, 1961. In her essay commemorating W. E. B. Du Bois, the renowned writer Bingxin testified to the impact of *Uncle Tom's Cabin* on Chinese readers. She recalled, after her uncle told her bedtime stories from the book, that the "inhuman cruelty" suffered by American Blacks made her "toss and turn, clenching my tear-soaked handkerchief." Bingxin, "Dao Duboyisi Boshi," 9.

11. Blain, *Set the World on Fire*; Rasberry, *Race and the Totalitarian Century*.

12. Greenbaum Wolf & Ernst Office Memorandum, Reinhardt to Ernst, re: "Letter from Jay Leyda," February 2, 1937, box 29, folder 5, JSCL; Yung, *Chinese Exclusion Act and Angel Island*; Bay, *Traveling Black*.

13. Gilroy, *Darker than Blue*, 175–76; Appiah, *Cosmopolitanism*.

14. There are no records or indications that they received royalties from publication of their work in Chinese; anecdotal evidence indicates that they did not. Works of Du Bois, Robeson, and Hughes were released as "tributes" rather than commercial translations during the Maoist years, when royalties were largely abolished and Chinese professional writers and artists received salaries instead.

CHAPTER 1

1. Du Bois was introduced at the gathering by Zhou Peiyuan, vice chancellor of Beijing University and a noted physicist. "Beida shisheng jihui qinghe Duboyisi Boshi shouchen," *Beijing Daxue xuebao* 1 (1959): 38; photograph mums312-i0698, WDBP. "Duboyisi xiang Feizhou renmin fachu zhaohuan: Feizhou, zhanqilai! Mianxiang shengqi de taiyang! Heise dalu keyi cong Zhongguo dedao zuiduo de youyi he tongqing" and "Jiushi gaoling you fendou," *RR*, February 24, 1959; W. E. B. Du Bois, "China and Africa," *Peking Review*, March 3, 1959, 11–13. The speech has been reprinted in the posthumously published Du Bois, *Autobiography*, 405–8. It is anthologized under the title "Hail Humankind!," in Foner,

W. E. B. Du Bois Speaks, 1920–1963, 316–21; and most recently in Mullen and Watson, W. E. B. Du Bois on Asia, 196–201. For the documentary Welcome, Dr. William E. B. Du Bois!, see https://credo.library.umass.edu/view/full/mums312-b246-i002.

2. "Du Bois, 91, Lauds China," NYT, March 5, 1959.

3. Horne, Black and Red, 212–18; Lewis, W. E. B. Du Bois, 554, 559–60; Du Bois, Autobiography, 11–12.

4. Brazinsky, Winning the Third World, 4–9, 150–52; Friedman, Shadow Cold War, 10–11.

5. Waldo McNutt to Du Bois, February 13, 1939; Du Bois to McNutt, February 25, 1939, WDBP; Aptheker, Correspondence of W. E. B. Du Bois, 184–85.

6. Lewis, W. E. B. Du Bois, 559–63.

7. Mullen, Afro-Orientalism, 1–43, esp. 30; Kelley and Esch, "Black Like Mao"; Ho, "Inspiration of Mao," 155–65; Frazier, "Assault of the Monkey King."

8. Horne points out that Alice Walker and Maya Angelou, among others, dismissed Shirley Graham Du Bois and her work. Horne, Race Woman.

9. Graham Du Bois, His Day Is Marching On, 275–87.

10. Du Bois, Dusk of Dawn, 59; "Address to the Nations of the World," in Foner, W. E. B. Du Bois Speaks, 1890–1919, 124–27; Du Bois to Madam Song, July 6, 1958, WDBP, http://www.library.umass.edu/spcoll/dubois/?cat_54.

11. Works by W. E. B. Du Bois: Autobiography, 142–43; "The Evolution of the Race Problem"; "World War and the Color Line," Crisis, November 1914, 28–30.

12. Works by W. E. B. Du Bois: "World War and the Color Line," Crisis, November 1914, 28–30; "The African Roots of War"; "The Conversation of Races," in Foner, W. E. B. Du Bois Speaks, 1890–1919, 73–85; "The Evolution of the Race Problem"; "On Being Black," New Republic, February 18, 1920, 338–41; "Liberia and Rubber," New Republic, November 18, 1925, 326–29; "As the Crow Flies," Crisis, June 1931, 188; March 1931, 80; "The Winds of Time," Chicago Defender, March 13, 1948; New York Age, November 20, 1935; "Shall the Negro Be Encouraged to Seek Cultural Equality?," in Foner, W. E. B. Du Bois Speaks, 1920–1963, 47–54.

13. W. E. B. Du Bois, "Opinion: Race Pride," Crisis, January 1920, 105.

14. Works by W. E. B. Du Bois: "China" (editorial), Crisis, February 1912, 156; "The African Roots of War"; "World War and the Color Line," Crisis, November 1914, 28–30; "The Black Soldier," Crisis, June 1918, 60.

15. Du Bois, "The Pan-African Movement"; Chicago Tribune, January 19, 1919; Meriwether, Proudly We Can Be Africans, 21.

16. Works by W. E. B. Du Bois: "Opinion," Crisis, June 1922, 55–60; "The Wide Wide World," Crisis, March 1927, 3; "The Pan-African Congresses," Crisis, October 1927, 263–64; "As the Crow Flies," Crisis, August 1927, 183; February 1928, 39; July 1929, 223; December 1930, 404; September 1929, 41; August 1930, 257.

17. Du Bois, "Evolution of the Race Problem."

18. Fukuzawa, "Disassociating Asia," 353. Works by W. E. B. Du Bois: "World War and the Color Line," Crisis, November 1914, 28–30; "The World Problem of the Color Line, Manchester (N.H.)," Leader (Manchester, N.H.), November 6, 1914; "The African Roots of War"; "The Battle of Europe," Crisis, September 1916, 216–17.

19. Works by W. E. B. Du Bois: "The Pan-African Movement"; "Opinion," Crisis, February 1922, 151–55; April 1922, 247–52; "Editorial: Japan," Crisis, January 1918, 114.

20. Works by W. E. B. Du Bois: "As the Crow Files," Crisis, June 1927, 111; September 1929, 293; October 1930, 329; December 1930, 404; "World War and the Color Line," Crisis,

November 1914, 28–30; "The Pan-African Congresses," *Crisis*, October 1927, 263–64; "The Wide Wide World," *Crisis*, May 1927, 75; "The Browsing Reader," *Crisis*, July 1927, 159–60.

21. Works by W. E. B. Du Bois: "A Forum of Fact and Opinion," *Pittsburgh Courier*, September 25, 1937; "Prospect of a World without Race Conflict."

22. Meng, *China Speaks*; "Paul Chih Meng, 90, Headed China Institute," *NYT*, February 7, 1990; Meng, *Chinese American Understanding*, 162–64; Kiyoshi Karl Kawakami, *Japan Speaks on the Sino-Japanese Crisis* (New York: Macmillan, 1932). I purchased a copy of *China Speaks* carrying the stamp of the South Manchuria Railway Company at a used bookstore in Upstate New York.

23. Works by W. E. B. Du Bois: "The Program of Peace in Manchuria," *Amsterdam News*, November 18, 1931; "As the Crow Flies," *Crisis*, December 1931, 412; April 1932, 116; May 1933, 101.

24. W. E. B. Du Bois, "Postscript: Listen, Japan and China," *Crisis*, January 1933, 20. Lewis, *W. E. B. Du Bois*, 391.

25. W. E. B Du Bois, "As the Crow Flies," *Crisis*, August 1932, 246; February 1934, 31.

26. Works by W. E. B. Du Bois: "The Program of Peace in Manchuria," *Amsterdam News*, November 18, 1931; "Postscript," *Crisis*, March 1932, 93–94; "As the Crow Flies," *Crisis*, April 1932, 116; "Again Japan," *National News*, March 10, 1932; "A Forum of Fact and Opinion," *Pittsburgh Courier*, February 29, 1936. In his 1952 speech "The Negro and the Warsaw Ghetto," Du Bois would articulate that the "Jewish problem" gave him "a real and more complete understanding of the Negro problem," realizing that the race problem "cut across lines of color and physique and belief and status." Foner, *W. E. B. Du Bois Speaks, 1920–1963*, 250–55.

27. Works by W. E. B. Du Bois: "Postscript: Listen, Japan and China," *Crisis*, January 1933, 20; "As the Crow Flies," *Crisis*, November 1933, 245.

28. W. E. B. Du Bois, "Postscript: Japan and Ethiopia," *Crisis*, December 1933, 293.

29. *Pittsburgh Courier*, March 28, 1936. Lewis, *W. E. B. Du Bois*, 389, 565.

30. As a cover, Hikida worked as a cook for a prominent white family in Bedford Hills, New York City, and performed clerical services in the Japanese consulate. Lewis, *W. E. B. Du Bois*, 390–93, 409–10, 565. Hikida mentioned that his network similarly facilitated Helen Keller's reception in Japan. At a home dinner, he introduced Du Bois to some officials of the South Manchuria Railway Company, whose global network, in collaboration with Japanese diplomats and officials, would help smoothly coordinate Du Bois's trip. Hikida to Du Bois, June 19, 1935, March [date unknown], April 15, 24, May 20, October 15, 1936; Du Bois to Hikida, June 1, July 9, September 10, 1935, May 12, 1936; Kumazawa (Foreign Section of Manchukuo State Railways) to Du Bois, July 29, September 9, 19, November 5 (the railway tickets), 20, 1936; photographs of the railway tickets, mums312-b081-i124/i125; all in WDBP. Works by W. E. B. Du Bois: "A Forum of Fact and Opinion," "Yosuke Matsuoka," "Conference," and "Japanese Colonialism," *Pittsburgh Courier*, February 13, 1937; *Darkwater*. *Shanghai Times*, November 30, 1936.

31. W. E. B. Du Bois, "Forum of Fact and Opinion," *Pittsburgh Courier*, February 13, 1937.

32. W. E. B. Du Bois, "Japanese Colonialism," *Pittsburgh Courier*, February 13, 1937.

33. Du Bois, *Autobiography*, 45.

34. Du Bois to Chih Meng, December 16, 1935, May 15, 1936; Meng to Du Bois, December 18, 1935, May 19, September 10, 1936; Liu Zhan'en to *Crisis*, March 5, 1930; Du Bois to Liu, May 12, 1930; Liu visiting card, Liu to Du Bois, December 2, 1936; Poeliu Dai to Du Bois, November 27, 1936; all in WDBP. Taketani, *Black Pacific Narrative*, 166. Works

by W. E. B. Du Bois: "Normal US-China Relations"; "A Forum of Fact and Opinion," *Pittsburgh Courier*, February 27, 1937; *Autobiography*, 45–46. Lewis, *W. E. B. Du Bois*, 413. After graduating from Nankai University, Liu Zhan'en earned a doctoral degree from Columbia University in 1922, and Chih Meng earned a master's degree in 1924. *Columbia University Alumni Register 1754–1931*, 528, 594, https://babel.hathitrust.org/cgi/pt?id=uc1 .b4525470&view=1up&seq=9; Meng, *Chinese American Understanding*, 53–61, 105–7, 145.

35. Works by W. E. B. Du Bois: "A Forum of Fact and Opinion," *Pittsburgh Courier*, February 27, March 6, 1937; "Normal US-China Relations"; *Autobiography*, 45–46.

36. Works by W. E. B. Du Bois: "A Forum of Fact and Opinion," *Pittsburgh Courier*, February 27, March 6, 1937; "Normal US-China Relations"; *Autobiography*, 45–46.

37. Du Bois to Madam Song, July 6, 1958, WBDP.

38. Works by W. E. B. Du Bois: "A Forum of Fact and Opinion," *Pittsburgh Courier*, February 20, 1937; "Normal US-China Relations"; *Autobiography*, 44–45. Lewis, *W. E. B. Du Bois*, 412.

39. Works by W. E. B. Du Bois: "Japan," *Pittsburgh Courier*, February 22, 1936; "A Forum of Fact and Opinion," *Pittsburgh Courier*, March 13, 20, 27, 1937. Photographs mums312-i0461/i0446/i0447/i0449/i0450/i0459/i0460/i0540/i0459/i0461; newspaper clippings mums312-b078-i387/i388; Hikida visiting card introducing Du Bois to a scholar at Honganji University; all in WDBP. *Tōkyō nichinichi shinbun*, August 12, 1936; *Asahi shinbun*, August 13, 1936; Lewis, *W. E. B. Du Bois*, 415–18.

40. Works by W. E. B. Du Bois, "A Forum of Fact and Opinion," *Pittsburgh Courier*, October 23, 1937; "As the Crow Flies," *Amsterdam News*, November 4, 1939. Interviews with Du Bois, *New York Post*, January 27, 1937; *Staats-Zeitung und Herold*, January 29, 1937; Waldo McNutt to Du Bois, February 13, 1939; Du Bois to McNutt, February 25, 1939; both in WDBP; Aptheker, *Correspondence of W. E. B. Du Bois*, 184–85.

41. Du Bois to Chih Meng, September 19, 1938; correspondence between Talitha Gerlach on behalf of China Welfare Appeal Inc. and Du Bois from January 12, 1949, to September 14, 1951; Madam Song to Gerlach, September 12, 1949; Du Bois to Madam Song, July 6, 1958; all in WBDP.

42. I searched major databases of 1930s periodicals in the Shanghai Municipal Library, the China National Library (Beijing), the Nankai University Library, and the Beijing University Library for any coverage of Du Bois's visit. Only the English-language *Shanghai Times* mentioned that the "noted negro sociologist of the United States" was taking the trip from Germany, via Siberia and Manchukuo, to Tokyo. *Shanghai Times*, November 30, 1936.

43. Works by W. E. B. Du Bois: "A Forum of Fact and Opinion," *Pittsburgh Courier*, March 27, September 25, 1937; "A Chronicle of Race Relations, 1939," *Phylon* 1, no. 1 (1940): 90–97; 1, no. 2 (1940): 175–92; 1, no. 3 (1940): 270–88; 3, no. 4 (1942): 417–34; 4, no. 1 (1943): 73–84; 4, no. 3 (1943): 270–89; 4, no. 4 (1943): 362–87; "As the Crow Flies," *Amsterdam News*, December 14, 1940, August 9, 30, 1941, January 24, 1942; "Prospect of a World without Race Conflict."

44. Works by W. E. B. Du Bois: "A Chronicle of Race Relations," *Phylon* 2, no. 4 (1941): 388–406; 3, no. 4 (1942): 417–34; "As the Crow Flies," *Amsterdam News*, December 23, 1939, February 24, March 30, 1940, January 24, 31, 1942.

45. Works by W. E. B. Du Bois: "As the Crow Flies," *Amsterdam News*, June 10, 26, 1944; "A Chronicle of Race Relations," *Phylon* 2, no. 2 (1941): 172–93; 3, no. 1 (1942): 66–86; 3, no. 3 (1942): 320–34; 4, no. 3 (1943): 270–89.

46. Gallicchio, *African American Encounter*, 76–84, 184–85; Plummer, *Rising Wind*, 69–72, 119; "Du Bois Says Stick to Education," *Fisk News*, February 1941, 5.

47. Works by W. E. B. Du Bois: *Color and Democracy*, 17; "The Winds of Time," *Chicago Defender*, August 14, 1945.

48. Works by W. E. B. Du Bois: "The Winds of Time," *Chicago Defender*, August 25, September 15, 1945; "As the Crow Flies," *Amsterdam News*, August 12, 1944; "Prospect of a World without Race Conflict."

49. Works by W. E. B. Du Bois: "As the Crow Flies," *Amsterdam News*, January 16, 1943; "The Winds of Time," *Chicago Defender*, September 15, December 29, 1945, January 12, 1946.

50. Works by W. E. B. Du Bois: "As the Crow Flies," *Amsterdam News*, March 25, 1944; *Color and Democracy*, 17; "The Negro and Imperialism," in Foner, *W. E. B. Du Bois Speaks, 1920–1963*, 150–60.

51. Du Bois, *Autobiography*, 31; Rasberry, *Race and the Totalitarian Century*, 155.

52. Graham, *Paul Robeson*.

53. Works by W. E. B. Du Bois: "A Forum of Fact and Opinion," *Pittsburgh Courier*, March 27, 1937; "As the Crow Flies," *Amsterdam News*, November 18, 1939, April 1, August 12, 1944; "Prospect of a World without Race Conflict."

54. W. E. B. Du Bois, "As the Crow Flies," *Amsterdam News*, April 8, 1944. Ironically, although Du Bois did not know, Chiang and Mao were similar in their fervent anti-imperialism and even in their support for Indian independence. Taylor, *Generalissimo*; Stowe, *They Shall Not Sleep*.

55. Madam Chiang declared in the speech, "I met the crews of your air bases. There I found first-generation Germans, Italians, Frenchmen, Poles, Czechoslovakians, and other nationals. Some of them had accents so thick that, if such a thing were possible, one could not cut them with a butter knife. But there they were—all Americans, all devoted to the same ideals. . . . This increased my belief and faith that devotion to common principles eliminates differences in race, and that identity of ideals is the strongest possible solvent of racial dissimilarities." Madam Chiang address to the U.S. Congress, February 18, 1943, https://archive.org/details/MadameChiangToCongress.

56. Works by W. E. B. Bois: "A Chronicle of Race Relations," *Phylon* 4, no. 2 (1943): 164–80; "The Winds of Time," *Chicago Defender*, June 2, 1945; "Prospect of a World without Race Conflict."

57. Works by W. E. B. Du Bois: "The Winds of Time," *Chicago Defender*, January 10, 1948; "As the Crow Flies," *Chicago Globe*, May 13, 1950; "Normal US-China Relations." *NYT*, August 10, 1948. Yu Minsheng, "Guanghui de shiye."

58. Works by W. E. B. Du Bois: "As the Crow Flies," *Chicago Globe*, May 6, June 24, July 8, July 22, August 5, September 23, 1950; "Normal US-China Relations."

59. "I Take My Stand," in Foner, *W. E. B. Du Bois Speaks, 1920–1963*, 242–49. Works by W. E. B. Du Bois: "We Cry Aloud," *National Guardian*, July 10, 1952; "Insist on Peace. Now, Forever," *Peace Reporter* (New York), September/October 1953, 1–2.

60. Mullen, *Un-American*, 144–501.

61. Works by W. E. B. Du Bois: "Cold War Hysteria," *National Guardian*, June 11, 1956; "Normal US-China Relations."

62. Works by W. E. B. Du Bois: "Opinion: The Negro and Radical Thought," *Crisis*, July 1921, 102–4; "Black and White Workers," *Crisis*, March 1928, in Moon, *Emerging Thought*, 274–76; "A Decent World for All," *March of Labor*, March 1954, 20–23; "Opinion," *Crisis*,

April 1923, 247–51; "The Pan-African Congresses," *Crisis*, October 1927, 263–64; "The African Roots of War"; "We Must Know the Truth," in Foner, *W. E. B. Du Bois Speaks, 1920–1963*, 222–27; "Prospect of a World without Race Conflict."

63. Works by W. E. B. Du Bois: "The American Negro in My Time," *United Asia*, March 1953, 155–59; "Pan-Africanism: A Mission in My Life," *United Asia*, March 1955, 23–28; "Negroes and the Crisis of Capitalism in the United States," *Monthly Review*, April 1953, 478–85; "The Negro and Socialism," in Foner, *W. E. B. Du Bois Speaks, 1920–1963*, 297–311.

64. "Mei ershiba zhou Heiren he bairen daibiao jihui," *RR*, February 19, 1949.

65. "Meiguo zhuming Heiren xuezhe, Shijie Heping Lishihui lishi, Duboyisi Boshi he furen dao Jing," *RR*, February 14, 1959; Rasberry, *Race and the Totalitarian Century*, 188; Brady, *Making the Foreign Serve China*, 92.

66. Du Bois, *Autobiography*, 349; W. E. B. Du Bois, "Freedom's Road for Oppressed Peoples," *Daily Worker* (New York), April 17, 1949; John McCarten, "All Together, Please," *New Yorker*, April 2, 1949; House Un-American Activities Committee, "Review of the Scientific and Cultural Conference for World Peace," Washington, D.C., April 19, 1949, 6, 12; Bosworth, *Marlon Brando*, 80.

67. *RR*, April 18, 20, 21, 22, 24, 30, May 4, 13, 19, 26, 27, 28, 1949; Yu Minsheng, "Guanghui de shiye."

68. Yu Minsheng, "Guanghui de shiye."

69. "Text of the Acheson Statement," *NYT*, July 13, 14, 1950; Walter H. Waggoner, "Acheson Derides Soviet 'Peace' Bids," *NYT*, July 13, 1950; Du Bois, *Autobiography*, 358, 373–77, 388; Yu Minsheng, "Guanghui de shiye"; "A Call to Courage," *National Guardian*, October 3, 1951.

70. Du Bois, *In Battle for Peace*, 160; Wei Ai Bojiate Duboyisi, *Wei heping er zhan*; "Shoudu gejie longzhong jihui qingzhu shijie heping yundong shi zhounian," *RR*, April 20, 1959. Gerlach to Du Bois, December 12, 1952, August 15, 1954, November 16, 1955; Du Bois to Gerlach, October 29, 1952, March 5, October 15, 1954; all in WDBP. Arthur Miller and his wife, Inge Morath, interviewed Gerlach during their 1978 trip to China, finding that "she could not bring herself to an even implicit rejection of the past decade's insanities." Morath and Miller, *Chinese Encounters*, 107–8; Yu Minsheng, "Guanghui de shiye."

71. "Wo Duiwaiwenxie he Heda sheyan," *RR*, February 18, 1959; Yu Minsheng, "Guanghui de shiye."

72. Lewis, *W. E. B. Du Bois*, 547–48; Horne, *Race Woman*, 30–31, 121–23, 134.

73. Geleimu and Lisike, *Heiren kexue jia Qiaozhi Huashengdun Kafo'er zhuan*; Graham and Lipscomb, *Dr. George Washington Carver, Scientist*; Gelanmu, *Heiren geshou Luoboxun*.

74. "Wo Duiwanwenxie he Heda sheyan," *RR*, February 18, 1959; Yu Minsheng, "Guanghui de shiye"; Higbee, "A Letter from W. E. B. Du Bois to His Daughter Yolanda"; Du Bois, *Autobiography*, 399–404.

75. Baldwin, *Beyond the Color Line*, 166; Carby, *Race Men*, 10.

76. Frank Dikotter does not mention the Du Boises' visit. Dikotter, *Mao's Great Famine*.

77. Burke, *Decolonization*, 20–25, 33–34; Wright, *Color Curtain*; Plummer, *Rising Wind*, 247–50; Singh, *Black Is a Country*, 175; W. E. B. Du Bois, "Spotlight on Africa," *New Africa*, January 1955; Roth, *P. C. Chang and the Universal Declaration of Human Rights*.

78. Larkin, *China and Africa*, 41–48.

79. Du Bois did not receive the prize until 1960 at a reception at the Soviet embassy in Washington, D.C. "W. E. B. Du Bois," FBI files, 100-99729, part 4: 37–40, part 5: 42–48. Lewis, *W. E. B. Du Bois*, 559–63; Duberman, *Paul Robeson*, 473; Graham Du Bois, *His*

Day Is Marching On, 269–70; Du Bois to Abbott Simon, January 27, 1959, in Aptheker, *Correspondence of W. E. B. Du Bois*, 434. Higbee, "A Letter from W. E. B. Du Bois to His Daughter Yolanda"; photographs mums312-i0663/i0649; all in WDBP. Du Bois saw Khrushchev again at a party the Soviet leader hosted during his visit to the United Nations in New York in 1960. *NYT*, January 21, 1959, October 5, 1960.

80. The Chinese translation of Du Bois's message at the event, which celebrated Franklin, and Pierre and Marie Curie, was distributed to all the attendees, and the original English version was published in the biweekly *People's China*. Photographs mums312-b291-i006/i007/i008/i011/i013; Talitha Gerlach to Du Bois, December 16, 1956; Du Bois's passport; all in WDBP; *NYT*, February 14, 1959; Du Bois, *Autobiography*, 28, 47; Horne, *Race Woman*, 159; Yu Minsheng, "Guanghui de shiye"; Zheng Xiaozhen, "Song Qingling Fu Weiyuanzhang jiejian Duboyisi," *RR*, April 21, 1959.

81. Graham Du Bois, *His Day Is Marching On*, 277; "Du Bois, 91, Lauds China," *NYT*, March 5, 1959; "W. E. B. Du Bois," FBI files, 100-99729, part 5: 63.

82. "Meiguo zhuming Heiren xuezhe, Shijie Heping Lishihui lishi, Duboyisi Boshi he furen dao Jing," *RR*, February 14, 1959; "Wo Duiwaiwenxie he Heda sheyan," *RR*, February 18, 1959; photograph mums312-i0732, WDBP.

83. "Zhou Zongli jiejian Duboyisi Boshi," *RR*, February 23, 1959; "Jiushi gaoling you fendou," *RR*, February 24, 1959; Yu Minsheng, "Guanghui de shiye"; Bingxin, "Dao Duboyisi Boshi"; "Birthday Party in Peking," *Peking Review*, March 3, 1959; Du Bois, *Autobiography*, 47–48; photographs mums312-i0521/i0754/i0782/i0848; Soong Chingling on behalf of the China Welfare Institute, telegram for Du Bois's birthday, 1959; all in WDBP.

84. Kwame Nkrumah, "Tribute to W. E. B. Du Bois," in Foner, *W. E. B. Du Bois Speaks, 1920–1963*, 327–28; Du Bois, "The Pan-African Movement"; "The Saga of Nkrumah," *National Guardian*, July 3, 1956.

85. The full text of the speech is in *National Guardian*, December 22, 1958; Du Bois, *Autobiography*, 399–404; and Foner, *W. E. B. Du Bois Speaks, 1920–1963*, 312–15.

86. "Shoudu huanying Jiana pengyou jihui shang bingzhu tongsheng zhichu," *RR*, March 7, 1959.

87. Du Bois, *Autobiography*, 47, 51; Graham Du Bois, *His Day Is Marching On*, 262.

88. Du Bois, *Autobiography*, 47–49; Graham Du Bois, *His Day Is Marching On*, 288–95. For travel, see also "W. E. B. Du Bois," FBI files, 100-99729, part 4: 32–36; photographs mums312-i0694/i0675/i0682, WDBP.

89. "Mao Zhuxi jiejian Duboyisi he Sitelang," *RR*, March 14, 1959; Du Bois, *Autobiography*, 47–48.

90. Strong and Keyssar, "Anna Louise Strong," 494–95.

91. Du Bois, *Autobiography*, 49.

92. Du Bois, "The Vast Miracle of China Today"; Du Bois, *Autobiography*, 47, 49, 53, 306; "Duboyisi fu Chongqing fangwen," *RR*, March 15, 1959. The Du Boises visiting a commune in Chengdu in 1959, photograph mums312-i0725-001, WDBP.

93. Brady, *Making the Foreign Serve China*, 97–98; Hollander, *Political Pilgrims*, 343.

94. Lewis, *W. E. B. Du Bois*, 563; Baldwin, *Beyond the Color Line*, 175; Brady, *Making the Foreign Serve China*, 116.

95. Du Bois, "The Vast Miracle of China Today"; Du Bois, *Autobiography*, 47–49.

96. Graham Du Bois, *His Day Is Marching On*, 266.

97. Horne, *Race Woman*, 158.

98. Geleihanmu, *Congqian you ge nuli*; Geleimu, *Heiren kexue jia Kafo*; Graham, *There Was Once a Slave*; Du Bois, *Autobiography*, 47.

99. Duboyisi, *Heiren de linghun*. For the history of changes to *The Souls of Black Folk*, see http://www.loa.org/volume._39&section_notes (accessed April 30, 2012). Lewis, *W. E. B. Du Bois*, 393.

100. Huang Xinxi, "Heiren de xinsheng—du *Heiren de linghun*," *RR*, May 19, 1959; Duboyisi, *Yuehan de guilai*.

101. Huang Xinxi, "Heiren de xinsheng—du *Heiren de linghun*," *RR*, May 19, 1959; Duboyisi, *Heiren de linghun*.

102. Duboyisi, *Heiren de linghun*, preface; Du Bois, *Dusk of Dawn*, 143–44, 151.

103. Du Bois, *Autobiography*, 142, 168, 289, 305, 338.

104. Tian Han, "Tan *Heinu hen*," *RR*, July 12, 1961; Xia Yan, *Lan xun jiumeng lu*, 96, 159–61.

105. Duboyisi, *Yuehan Bulang*; Tian Han, "Tan *Heinu hen*," *RR*, July 12, 1961.

106. Duboyisi, *Mengsa de kaoyan, Mengsa ban xuexiao, Youse renzhong de shijie*; Duboyisi, *Feizhou*.

107. W. E. B. Du Bois, "Our Visit to China," *China Pictorial*, March 20, 1959, 4–5.

108. Du Bois, *Autobiography*, 52–53.

109. Du Bois, "I Sing to China." Du Bois had been receiving the magazine *China Reconstructs* free since 1951 in exchange for criticism and suggestions. Lu Ping to Du Bois, December 15, 1951, March 21, 1953, February 15, 1954, WDBP.

110. Du Bois to Brewer, August 6, 1959; and Brewer to Du Bois, December 30, 1959; both in WDBP.

111. W. E. B. Du Bois, "Socialism Today," eight-page unnumbered pamphlet, in Aptheker, *Pamphlets and Leaflets by W. E. B. Du Bois*, 342–47. Flyers for speeches by the Du Boises; Truman Capote to Du Bois, October 20, 1959; Du Bois to Capote, December 2, 1959; all in WDBP.

112. Du Bois, "The Vast Miracle of China Today."

113. Shirley Graham Du Bois, "Travel Diary, China, 1959," SGDBP; Graham Du Bois, *His Day Is Marching On*, 294.

114. Du Bois, "The Vast Miracle of China Today"; Du Bois, *Autobiography*, 51–53.

115. Du Bois, "I Sing to China."

116. Shirley Graham Du Bois, "Travel Diary, China, 1959," SGDBP; "Zai wo Duiwaiwenxie he Heda de yanhui shang," *RR*, April 21, 1959.

117. "Baiwen buru yijian, shishi shengyu xiongbian," *RR*, January 4, 1960.

118. Du Bois, "Greetings to Women," *Women of the Whole World* 7 (1959): 24; "Dr. Du Bois Talks to Civitas about Recognition for Negro," *Brooklyn (N.Y.) Daily Eagle*, March 30, 1916.

119. Horne, *Race Woman*, 158.

120. Lin Hai, "Ya Fei funü tuanjie zai fandi de qizhi xia—ji Ya Fei funü huiyi," *RR*, February 12, 1961.

121. Lewis, *W. E. B. Du Bois*, 567–68; W. E. B. Du Bois, "Ghana Calls-A Poem," *Freedomways* 2, no. 1 (Winter 1962): 71–74; Weilian Aidehua Bogehade Duboyisi, "Jiana zai zhaohuan," trans. by Bingxin, *Shijie wenxue*, September 1963.

122. Yuan Ying, "Sui han ranhou zhi songbai zhi hou dian," *RR*, December 1, 1961; Li

Zhun, "Zhi Duboyisi," *RR*, December 1, 1961; "Beijing Shi, Hebei Sheng . . . ," *RR*, January 18, 1962; "Meiguo zhuming Heiren xuezhe Duboyisi fufu dian xie . . . ," *RR*, January 21, 1962; "Duboyisi Boshi fufu dao Jing," *RR*, September 29, 1962.

123. "Woguo lingdaoren he gejie renshi," *RR*, October 1, 1962; "Sanbai duo wei waibing," *RR*, October 1, 1962; "Wushi wan ren reqing huahu," *RR*, October 2, 1962; "Mao Zhuxi Liu Zhuxi," *RR*, October 2, 1962; "Zhou Enlai Zongli he furen Deng Yingchao jiejian he yanqing Duboyisi fufu," *RR*, November 3, 1962.

124. Bingxin, "Dao Duboyisi Boshi."

125. Mao Zedong, "Dian yan Duboyisi Boshi shishi," *RR*, August 30, 1963; telegrams of consolation, WDBP; Horne, *Race Woman*, 356.

126. "Fandui Mei diguozhuyi," *RR*, October 11, 1963; Guo Moruo, "He Duboyisi Boshi wenda," *RR*, September 8, 1963; Bingxin, "Dao Duboyisi Boshi."

127. Example entries: "Fandui zhongzu qishi," *RR*, March 24, 1960; "Ruci 'ziyou shijie,'" *RR*, May 24, 1961; "Dui zhongzu qishi de tiaozhan," *RR*, June 29, 1961; "Meiguo shi 'gongkai kongbu de wangguo,'" *RR*, October 7, 1961; "Meiguo Heiren jizhe Weilian Yuedi," *RR*, July 22, 1961; Leshan, "Ruchi 'pingdeng quanli,'" *RR*, August 21, 1962; Leshan, "Bominghan zaji," *RR*, May 29, 1963; Leshan, "'Duli Xuanyan,' 'Xianfa,'" *RR*, June 6, 1963; Leshan, "Kennidi xiongdi yu Meiguo Heiren," *RR*, August 12, 1963; "Meiguo Heiren fandui zhongzu qishi," *RR*, May 9, 1963; "Meiguo Heiren shiwei," *RR*, May 10, 1963; "Shenshou zhongzu nuyi," *RR*, August 5, 1964.

128. "Luobote Weilian shuo Meiguo Heiren shenxin Mao Zhuxi shengming zhichu de zhenli," *RR*, August 20, 1965; Weilian, *Daiqiang de Heiren*.

129. Example entries: "Meiguo jinbu laogongdang," *RR*, August 31, 1965; "Caiqu baoli shouduan," *RR*, July 12, 1967; "Ditelü shi Heiren . . . ," *RR*, July 28, 1967; "'Feibaoli zhuyi' de pochan," *RR*, August 1, 1967; "Dasui 'Feibaoli zhuyi' jiasuo," *RR*, August 8, 1967; "Diguozhuyi de chong'er." *RR*, October 31, 1967; Xiang Donghui, "Beimei dipingxian shang de xin shiwu," *RR*, March 28, 1966. For Mao's statement on King's death and the need for armed struggle, see "Zhongguo Gongchandang Zhongyang Weiyuanhui Zhuxi Mao Zedong tongzhi zhichi Meiguo Heiren kangbao douzheng de shengming," *RR*, April 17, 1968, or Ho and Mullen, *Afro Asia*, 94–96.

130. "Luobote Weilian he Duboyisi Furen relie huanhu Mao Zhuxi," *RR*, April 18, 1968; "Duboyisi Furen ganxie Mao Zhuxi," *RR*, January 15, 1964; "Zhou Zongli Chen Fu Zongli jiejian Duboyisi Furen," *RR*, January 16, 1964; "Kawengda Zongtun li Jing fangwen," *RR*, June 26, 1967; Marable, *Malcolm X*, 317; Rasberry, *Race and the Totalitarian Century*, 241–48, 269–304.

131. Horne, *Race Woman*, 230–33. For a photograph of Graham Du Bois, Zhou Enlai, and others in 1967, see Shi Yanhua, "Zhou Enlai zhidao waishi fanyi gongzuo," May 27, 2017, Renmin wang, http://dangshi.people.com.cn/n1/2017/0527/c85037-29303971.html (accessed March 20, 2021).

132. "China Diary, 1967," SGDBP; photographs mums312-b291-i125/i074/i067/i092, WDBP.

133. Horne, *Race Woman*, 163; Tyson, *Radio Free Dixie*.

134. Spence, *To Change China*.

135. Horne, *Race Woman*, 238; Thomas A. Johnson, "Yale Conference Studies Role of Black Women," *NYT*, December 14, 1970.

136. Horne, *Race Woman*, 261–62. A copy of the film is available at the New York Public Library. "Speeches and Press Clipping for Chou En Lai and Mao Tsedong," SGDBP.

137. Horne, *Race Woman*, 16; "Obituary of Shirley Graham Du Bois," *NYT*, April 5, 1977; "Shirley Graham Du Bois Dies in China," *Black Scholar* 8, no. 7 (May 1977): 12.

138. Lovell, *Maoism*, 189–90; Snow, *Star Raft*, 74, 106, 120.

CHAPTER 2

1. Liu Liangmo later simply recalled the caller as "a friend," probably because Lin Yutang was politically condemned in the People's Republic of China. Works by Liu Liangmo: "Renmin geshou Luoboxun"; "Luoboxun yu 'Yiyongjun jinxing qu'"; "Wei zhandou de Zhongguo renmin gechang," *RR*, April 9, 1958; "Zhongguo kangzhan gequ zai Meiguo." Robeson, *Undiscovered Paul Robeson*, 25.

2. Works by Liu Liangmo: "Renmin geshou Luoboxun"; "Luoboxun yu 'Yiyongjun jinxing qu'"; "Wei zhandou de Zhongguo renmin gechang," *RR*, April 9, 1958; "Zhongguo kangzhan gequ zai Meiguo."

3. Duberman, *Paul Robeson*, 236–52; Robeson, *Undiscovered Paul Robeson*, 25–27.

4. Bingxin, "Dao Duboyisi Boshi."

5. "Paul Robeson in Moscow to Honor Pushkin," *Shanghai Evening Post & Mercury*, June 6, 1949. Works by Liu Liangmo: "Renmin geshou Luoboxun"; "Luoboxun yu 'Yiyongjun jinxing qu.'" Works by Chen Yiming: "Gesheng jili aiguo qing"; "Huainian Liu Liangmo xiansheng," *Tianfeng* 9 (1998): 40–41. "Baoluo Luoboxun danchen 110 zhounian jinianhui zai Jing juxing," China Net, http://www.sclf.org/sclf/zjsql/zx/200804/t20080 410_6860.htm (accessed March 13, 2021). Bai Ruixue, "Xian wei renzhi de guoge gushi," *Zhengyi bao*, July 17, 1944; Suolu duofu ni kefu (Soviet Union), "Luoboxun."

6. Robeson, Liu Liangmo, and the Chinese People's Chorus, "Chee Lai!," *Chicago Tribune*, September 21, 1941; *NYT*, November 30, December 28, 1941; Howard Taylor, "Songs of China at War Offered by Paul Robeson," *Philadelphia Inquirer*, December 14, 1941; *Pittsburgh Courier*, September 12, 1942; *Argus-Leader* (Sioux Falls, S.D.), November 28, 1943; *Miami (Fla.) Daily News*, September 30, 1945.

7. "Wo kangzhan gequ fengxing xin dalu," *Dagong bao* (Guilin), April 23, 1942; Liu and Modoi, *China Sings*; *Why We Fight: The Battle of China*, http://www.imdb.com/title/tto 184254/?ref_=nv_sr_6 (accessed September 27, 2018).

8. So, *Transpacific Community*, 81–94. Epstein, *Woman in World History*, includes a half-page image of Robeson and the *Chee Lai!* album. Robeson's biographers have paid scant attention to his friendship with Liu or his Chinese ties, perhaps regarding it as marginal. Martin Duberman, though noting that Robeson praised the Chinese people in his writings of the 1930s, does not mention his wartime efforts with Liu. Duberman, *Paul Robeson*, 174–75, 188, 201–2, 254, 466. Robeson, *Undiscovered Paul Robeson*, gives a single mention on page 25; see also 163–64. Boyle and Bunie, *Paul Robeson*, makes no mention of China.

9. "'I Love Above All, Russia,' Robeson Says," *Baltimore Afro-American*, June 25, 1949; "Paul Robeson Loves USSR People the Most," *North-China Daily News*, June 21, 1949.

10. Works by Paul Robeson: "An Actor's Wanderings and Hopes," *Messenger*, October 1924, 32; "Reflections on O'Neill's Plays," *Opportunity*, December 1924, 368–70; "The Culture of the Negro," *Spectator* (London), June 15, 1934, 916–17; "I Want to Be African"; "Negroes—Don't Ape the Whites," *Daily Herald* (London), January 5, 1935; "Never Again Can Colonialism Be What It Was," *New Africa*, March 1945, in Foner, *Paul Robeson Speaks*, 160; "How I Discovered Africa," *Freedom*, June 1953; "Greetings to Bandung," *Freedom*,

April 1955; "Songs of My People," *Sovietskaia muzka* (Soviet Music) 7 (July 1949): 100–104, trans. by Paul A. Russo, in Foner, *Paul Robeson Speaks*, 211–17; "A Word about African Language," *Spotlight on Africa*, February 1955, 3–5, in Foner, *Paul Robeson Speaks*, 396–98; "Primitives," *New Statesman and Nation*, August 8, 1936, 190–92; "The Related Sounds of Music," *Daily World* (Aberdeen, Wash.), April 7, 1973, in Foner, *Paul Robeson Speaks*, 443–48. "Robeson Spurns Music He 'Doesn't Understand,'" *New York World-Telegram*, August 30, 1933; "Interview in *PM* and Paul Robeson's Reply," *PM*, September 12, 15, 1943; J. C. O'Flaherty, "An Exclusive Interview with Paul Robeson," *West African Review* 7, no. 107 (August 1936): 12–13; George Matthews, "My Aim — Get British and U.S. People Together," *Daily Worker* (London), May 5, 1959; Julia Dorn, "I Breathe Freely," *New Theater* (Moscow), July 1935, in Foner, *Paul Robeson Speaks*, 100–102; "Paul Robeson Decides to Go Back to Africa," *China Press*, January 8, 1935; "Paul Robeson, Famous Negro, 'Going Back to Africa,'" *Shanghai Times*, January 8, 1935. On Charlie Chen, see Huang Yunte, *Charlie Chan*.

11. Works by Paul Robeson: "I Want Negro Culture," *London News Chronicle*, May 30, 1935; "I Want to Be African"; "The Culture of the Negro," *Spectator* (London), June 15, 1934, 916–17; "Negroes — Don't Ape the Whites," *Daily Herald* (London), January 5, 1935. "Negro Enthusiast's Hope," *North-China Daily News*, August 19, 1934; "Fate of the Negro Peoples Bound up with the East Not the West," *North-China Daily News*, January 14, 1935; "Paul Robeson on His People," *North-China Daily News*, May 30, 1935.

12. Works by Paul Robeson: "Greetings to Bandung," *Freedom*, April 1955; "Speech at the Third National Convention of the National Maritime Union of America," *Proceedings* (Cleveland, Ohio), 1941, 56–57, in Foner, *Paul Robeson Speaks*, 137–39; "Speech at International Fur and Leather Workers Union Convention," *Proceedings*, 1948, 201–4, in Foner, *Paul Robeson Speaks*, 183–88. "Robeson Visions an Africa Free of Rule by Europeans," *New York Herald Tribune*, January 12, 1936; Nicolás Guillén, "Paul Robeson in Spain," *Mediodía* (Havana), 1938, trans. by Katheryn Silver, *Daily World* (Aberdeen, Wash.), July 25, 1976; Gordon, "A Great Negro Artist"; Julia Dorn, "Paul Robeson Told Me," *TAC* (Theater Arts Committee), July/August 1939, 23, in Foner, *Paul Robeson Speaks*, 130–32; Gelanmu, *Heiren geshou Luoboxun*, 1–2, 221–22.

13. In addition to providing detailed information on eleven similar books and dictionaries available, Buck's assistant recommended that Robeson contact George A. Kennedy of Yale University for his materials, which were widely used in colleges and universities. Soothill, *The Student's . . . General Pocket Dictionary*; Constance Wade to Robeson, March 30, 1942, Paul Robeson Alpha Files, the East and West Association, group 5, series 1, box 3, PSBH.

14. Walsh to the Robesons, January 8, Walsh Correspondence, 1943, group 1, series 2, box 22; telegram from Buck to Robeson, April 13; Buck to Yergan, April 14, Buck Correspondence, 1944, group 1, series 2, boxes 15, 20; all in PSBH.

15. Walsh sent Robeson a John Day Company book, *American Counterpoint*, with an introduction by Buck to keep in touch. Walsh to Robeson, September 10, Walsh Correspondence, 1943; Buck to Robeson, April 20, 1942, March 22, 1943; Buck to Smith, April 23, 1942; Mrs. James E. Hughes to Robeson, April 24, 1942; all in Paul Robeson Alpha Files, the East and West Association, group 5, series 1, box 3, PSBH. Paul Robeson, "Conversation about the New China," *Freedom*, May 1951.

16. Afterward, Buck telegrammed the speakers at the dinner to express her deep appreciation while hectically enlisting donations, including $85 from Peggy and Edgar

Snow, to help cover the deficit of the meeting. La Guardia to Buck, February 29; Buck to La Guardia, March 3; Buck to Peggy Snow, April 20; Peggy Snow to Buck, May 6; "Sun Yat-sen Day" materials; all in Buck Correspondence, 1944, PSBH. During her 1943 lecture tour on China in the Deep South, the overly enthusiastic Agnes Smedley presented Buck's address to the "most intelligent and attentive" students in a scarcely funded Black school in Lafayette, Louisiana, because they had just studied Buck's novel *Dragon Seed*. She asked Buck to respond to forthcoming student letters "personally" and send proper literature on Asia at her own expense. Buck to Smedley, March 10 and December 30; Smedley to Buck, December 15, Buck Correspondence, 1943, group 1, series 2, box 14, PSBH.

17. Buck to Robeson, November 6, 9, and 12, 1945, Buck Correspondence, 1945, group 1, series 2, box 23, PSBH.

18. For similar dynamics with white women entering the Black community, see Kaplan, *Miss Anne in Harlem*, 61–62. Eslanda to Buck, July 17, Buck Correspondence, 1944; Buck to Goode, January 7, 1945, September 27, 1946; Goode to Buck, December 27, 1946, Buck Correspondence, 1946; all in group 1, series 2, box 27, PSBH.

19. Walsh to Eslanda, December 6, Walsh Correspondence, 1943; Eslanda to Buck, July 6; Buck to Eslanda, July 14, Buck Correspondence, 1945, PSBH. Buck probably did not realize the tensions between the Robesons at the peak of his fame. In a lengthy letter to her husband in December 1946, Eslanda complained about her stretched finances under the control of his longtime manager and attorney Bob Rockmore. Robeson then agreed to provide $200 weekly for the household and her personal allowance. Duberman, *Paul Robeson*, 292–94, 313–15, 322.

20. Walsh to Eslanda, November 19, Walsh Correspondence, 1943; Buck to Sillcox, July 24 and August 4; Sillcox to Buck, July 27 and September 16; Buck to Smith, June 3; Buck to Eslanda, July 21 and 22; Eslanda to Buck, June 7, July 17 and 27, Buck Correspondence, 1944; Buck to Eslanda, July 14, Buck Correspondence, 1945; all in PSBH. Duberman, *Paul Robeson*, 292–94, 322; Robeson, *African Journey*; Buck and Robeson, *American Argument*. They started to write the book in late 1945, after Buck and Jawaharlal Nehru's sister Vijaya Lakshmi Pandit coauthored a piece on India for *Voice of India*, May 1945. "Paul Robeson Heads Drive to End Lynching," *China Press*, September 15, 1946; "Paul Rebeson Sees Truman on Lynching," *Shanghai Evening Post & Mercury*, September 24, 1946; "Paul Robeson Pickets White House," *North-China Daily News*, June 4, 1948.

21. Eslanda to Buck, July 12; Buck to Eslanda, July 17, Buck Correspondence, 1945; Buck to Bethune, March 1 and April 12; Bethune to Buck, April 9, Buck Correspondence, 1946; all in PSBH.

22. Li Runxin, *Jiebai de mingxing Wang Ying*, 295; Sun Ruizhen and Zou Jin, *Malaiya qingren*, 291, 462; Li Guowen, "Baoluo Luoboxun de Zhongguo qingyuan," *Jinri Zhongguo* 5 (2008): 48–49; Wang Xueqi, "Dianying xiju mingxing Wang Ying he Heiren Gewang Luoboxun de youyi jiaowang," China Society for People's Friendship Studies, http://www.cspfs.com.cn/speechbyWangXuexin.html (accessed November 14, 2014).

23. Paul Robeson, Photographs of Prominent African Americans, box 16, folder 169, Beinecke Rare Book and Manuscript Library, Yale University Library, JWJ MSS 76; Hodges, *Anna May Wong*, 91, 134, 150; *London Morning Post*, May 20, 1930; "Lady Precious Stream," *North-China Daily News*, November 26, 1939; Zheng Da, "Bailaohui Zhongguo xiju daoyan di yi ren." Xiong's programs were later transformed into monologues by the Chinese American actress Soo Yong and performed across the United States. Gao Yunxiang, "Soo Yong"; Yeh, *Happy Hsiungs*.

24. Mei Baojiu, "Mei Lanfang de liang jian zhengui jinian ping," *Hunan wenshi* 6 (2001); Mei Shaowu, *Wode fuqin Mei Lanfang*, 984, 88–94; Scott, *Mei Lan-Fang*, 118–19.

25. He Dazhang, "Ta changchu le renlei de xinsheng," *Guangming ribao*, April 17, 2008.

26. Robeson, "China: Promise of a New World"; Soong Chingling, *Struggle for New China*, 177–79. "Sun Yat-sen Day" materials, Buck Correspondence, 1944, PSBH.

27. Kennard to Carter, June 26, July 26; Kennard to Buck, August 4; Price to Buck, June 30 and August 3; Carter to Buck, July 26; Carter to Grew, July 26; Buck to Price, August 7, Buck Correspondence, 1944, and Buck Correspondence, Kennard, J. S., group 1, series 2, box 18; all in PSBH.

28. He Dazhang, *Yi ge zhenshi de Song Qingling*, 148–56; "Sponsors of the China Welfare Fund, Shanghai"; Madam Sun to Du Bois, December 14, 1948; both in WDBP.

29. Robeson, "China: Promise of a New World."

30. Gelanmu, *Heiren geshou Luoboxun*, 255, 394–96; He Dazhang, *Yi ge zhenshi de Song Qingling*, 148–56; *RR*, October 1, 1949; "Jiujinshan juxing Zhongguo Yuandong huiyi," *RR*, October 22, 1946; Duberman, *Paul Robeson*, 300–301.

31. Works by Paul Robeson: "Freedom in Their Own Land," *National Guardian*, December 20, 1948; "Racialism in South Africa," speech at Protest Meeting, Friends' House, London, March 25, 1949, in Foner, *Paul Robeson Speaks*, 194–97.

32. "Paris Peace Conference," news release of Council on African Affairs, in Foner, *Paul Robeson Speaks*, 197–200. Works by Paul Robeson: "For Freedom and Peace," speech at Welcome Home Rally, New York City, June 19, 1949, in Foner, *Paul Robeson Speaks*, 201–11; an abridged version, titled "I'm Looking for Freedom," was published in the *Worker* (New York), July 3, 1949. "My Answer," *New York Age*, August 6, 13, 20, and September 3, 17, 1949; "Negro Artist Looks Ahead," *Masses & Mainstream*, January 1952, 7–14.

33. Zhirun, "Liu Liangmo zai Meiguo jiao Heiren Gewang chang 'Yiyongjun jinxing qu'"; Li Zhuang, "Ji Renmin Zhengxie di liu tian dahui," *RR*, September 28, 1949. The national anthem suffered during China's political upheavals: the music, but not the lyrics, were played during the Cultural Revolution, when lyricist Tian Han was persecuted. It was replaced from 1978 to 1982. Wu Beiguan, "Jidu cangsang hua guoge," *RR*, March 31, 2004.

34. "Luoboxun dian Mao Zhuxi zhihe," *Xinhuashe dianxun gao*, October 16, 1949, 294; "Shijie geguo renmin jixu lai dian," *RR*, October 18, 1949; Gelanmu, *Heiren geshou Luoboxun*, 1; *Baoluo Luoboxun*, 24–26; Zhu Shengjun and Lin Caibing, *Baoluo Luoboxun yanchang gequ ji*, 3–5; He Dazhang, "Ta changchu le renlei de xinsheng," *Guangming ribao*, April 17, 2008.

35. Du Yingzi, "Huanghe dahechang," *RR*, May 21, 1999; Chen Lian, "Huanghe," *RR*, December 16, 1989; Reiter Ester, "Secular *Yiddishkait*," *Labour/Le Travail* 49 (Spring 2002): 132; Epstein, *My China Eye*, 234–35; Lü Qiqing and Zhao Le, "Gesheng zhong de kangzhan chuanqi," China National Radio, http://gscq.cnr.cn/gbgx/20150921/t20 150921_519921389_4.shtml (accessed February 25, 2021).

36. Ransby, *Eslanda*, 197–205; "Mr. Paul Robeson," *Shanghai Times*, July 16, 1930; "Mrs. Paul Robeson's Book to Be Banned by S. African Gov't," *China Press*, October 23, 1946. Baisheng, "Xiang diguo zhuyi zhe shiwei," *RR*, December 11, 1949; "Song Qingling Fu Zhuxi," *RR*, December 14, 1949; "Yazhou Funü Daibiao Huiyi shang," *RR*, December 18, 1949; "Jing shi gejie siwan ren jihui," *RR*, December 19, 1949; "Yazhou Fudaihui geguo daibiao laibing zai Hu," *RR*, December 30, 1949; Deng Yingchao, "Yazhou Funü Daibiao Huiyi de gaikuang ji shouhuo," *RR*, January 17, 1950; Yu Minsheng, "Guanghui de shiye."

37. *California Eagle*, March 23, 1950; "He jing funü jihui haozhao baowei heping," *RR*, January 21, 1950; "Heiren gesheng Luoboxun furen you Hua fan Mei," *Meizhou huaqiao ribao*, January 25, 1940.

38. Buck, *Good Earth*; Robeson, "Happy Birthday, New China!"

39. Works by Paul Robeson: "Thoughts on Winning the Stalin Peace Prize," *Freedom*, January 1953; "To You Beloved Comrade," *New World Review*, April 1953, 11–13; "Negro History," *Freedom*, February 1951; "National Union of Marine Cooks and Stewards Convention," *Freedom*, June 1951; "Unity for Peace," *Masses & Mainstream*, August 1951, 21–24; "Happy Birthday, New China!"

40. "Liu Mei guiguo tongxue zai Hu zuotan," *RR*, November 18, 1950; "Kangyi Meiguo qinlüe Chaoxian," *RR*, July 27, 1950.

41. "Meiguo Heping Shizijun zhi shu Lianheguo," *RR*, August 11, 1951; "Meiguo renmin guangfan zhankai yundong," *RR*, December 13, 1952; "Robeson Denounces Korean Intervention," in Foner, *Paul Robeson Speaks*, 252–53. Works by Robeson: "A Letter to Warren Austin, U.S. Delegate to the UN," *Freedom*, July 1951; "Which Side Are We On?," *Freedom*, January 1952; "Southern Negro Youth," *Freedom*, October 1951; "Toward a Democratic Earth We Helped to Build," speech at convention of National Negro Labor Council, Cincinnati, Ohio, October 27, 1951, *Daily World* (Aberdeen, Wash.), April 8, 1976, in Foner, *Paul Robeson Speaks*, 289–93; "Speech to Youth," speech at First National Convention of Labor Youth League, November 24, 1950, in Foner, *Paul Robeson Speaks*, 254–59; "Greetings to World Youth Festival in Berlin," *Freedom*, September 1951; "Africa Calls—Will You Help?," *Freedom*, May 1953; "Land of Love and Happiness," *New World Review*, December 1952, 3–4, in Foner, *Paul Robeson Speaks*, 328–30; "An Open Letter to Jackie Robinson," *Freedom*, April 1953 (Robeson addressed major league baseball owners in 1946, demanding that "the bars against Negros in baseball be dropped"); "Thoughts on Winning the Stalin Peace Prize," *Freedom*, January 1953.

42. "Quan shijie renmin aidao Sidalin," *RR*, March 12, 1953; "Daonian Sidalin," *RR*, March 18, 1953; "Ziben zhuyi guojia laodong renmin . . . ," *RR*, May 4, 1954; "Geguo renmin qingzhu 'Wuyi,'" *RR*, May 2, 1955; "Meiguo mingliu duoren fabiao xuanyan," *RR*, February 28, 1952; Fei Kerefunikefu (Soviet Union), "Women de pengyou Luoboxun," *RR*, January 13, 1958; Zhu Shengjun and Lin Caibing, *Baoluo Luoboxun yanchang gequ ji*. "Paul Robeson Speaks! International Peace Arch, Blaine, Washington State, May 18, 1952," https://www .youtube.com/watch?v=VLCndkx1e1o; "Speech at the Peace Bridge Arch," August 16, 1953, in Foner, *Paul Robeson Speaks*, 363–66.

43. Works by Paul Robeson: "The Road to Real Emancipation," *Freedom*, January 1951; "Playing Catch-Up," *Freedom*, 1953; "Conversation about the New China," *Freedom*, May 1951; "Robeson Denounces Korean Intervention," in Foner, *Paul Robeson Speaks*, 252–53; "Happy Birthday, New China!"

44. Paul Robeson, "Conversation about the New China," *Freedom*, May 1951.

45. Works by Paul Robeson: "I, Too, Am American," *Reynolds News* (London), February 27, 1949, in Foner, *Paul Robeson Speaks*, 191–93; "Here's My Story," *Freedom*, November, 1950; "Negro History," *Freedom*, February 1951; "A Letter to Warren Austin, U.S. Delegate to the UN," *Freedom*, July 1951; "Which Side Are We On?," *Freedom*, January 1952; "Conversation about the New China," *Freedom*, May 1951; "Perspectives on the Struggle for Peace in the United States in 1954," *Pravda*, January 2, 1954, in Foner, *Paul Robeson Speaks*, 372–75. "Meiguo Heping Shizijun zhi shu Lianheguo," *RR*, August 11, 1951; "Di

Er Ci Quan Su Zuojia Daibiao Dahui," *RR*, December 27, 1954; "Jianjue fandui Meiguo ganshe Zhongguo neizheng," *RR*, February 2, 1955. Materials from and on the Committee for a Democratic Far Eastern Policy, WDBP.

46. Robeson, *Undiscovered Paul Robeson*, 160; "Symposium: Paul Robeson Right or Wrong?" and "Paul Robeson, Right or Wrong? — Right, Says W. E. B. Du Bois," *Negro Digest*, March 1950, 8, 10–14; "[Jackie Robinson] Says Singer Paul Robeson Plain Silly," *North-China Daily News*, July 21, 1949.

47. Du Bois, *Autobiography*, 396–97.

48. In the late 1940s, Shanghai English-language newspapers expanded their coverage on Robeson's political activism for racial justice and the world peace movement and against the emergent McCarthyism fanned by the Mundt-Nixon Communist Control Bill. The *North-China Daily News* described his defiance against the Senate Judiciary Committee on May 31, 1948: "Mr. Robeson gestured violently when he declared he would not say whether he was an American communist because the question was an 'invasion of my right to secret ballot.'" "Paul Robeson Declines to Answer," *North-China Daily News*, June 2, 1948; *North-China Daily News*, December 8, 1938, June 23, 1946, October 21, 1947, June 15 and 22, July 27, November 28, 1949; *China Press*, February 18 and 27, April 21, May 12, 1947; *Shanghai Evening Post & Mercury*, November 20, 1946, June 1 and 4, 1948; "Luobosheng yanshuo" and "Bali Heping Dahui tongguo jueyi," *Shenbao*, April 22, 1949; "Su Bao Ying Mei Fa Jia zhuguo daibiao," *Shenbao*, April 24, 1949. The *Shanghai Daily* also followed Robeson at the congress of the Communist Party in Czechoslovakia in May 1949. "Jie Gongdang dahui jiemu," *Shenbao*, May 27, 1949; Du Bois, *Autobiography*, 396–97.

49. "Jie jing Chalishi Daxue zeng Guo Moruo mingyu boshi xuewei," *RR*, April 29, 1949; Ma Fantuo (Yuan Shuipai), "Wei Bali Heping Dahui zuo," *RR*, April 29, 1949; "Heiren Gewang wei Bolan gongren gechang," *RR*, June 5, 1949; September 1, 1949; "Luoboxun," *RR*, April 1950; "Shijie Baowei Heping Weiyuanhui," *RR*, November 27, 1950.

50. "Zhongguo Baowei Heping Dahui Fu Zhuxi Liu Ningyi," *Meizhou huaqiao ribao*, June 19, 1950; "Song Qingling, Guo Moruo, Lin Boqu," *RR*, October 3, 1949; Gelanmu, *Heiren geshou Luoboxun*, 1–2; "Zouxiang Shijie Renmin Heping Dahui," *RR*, November 23, 1952; "Yazhou Ji Taipingyang Quyu Heping Huiyi bimu," *RR*, October 16, 1952; "Yazhou Ji Taipingyang Quyu Heping Huiyi . . . ," *RR*, October 13, 1952; *Baoluo Luoboxun*, 24–26; Zhu Shengjun and Lin Caibing, *Baoluo Luoboxun yanchang gequ ji*, 3–5.

51. Zhang Tiexian, "Baowei heping yundong zhong," *RR*, April 1, 1951; *RR*, December 22, 1952; "Sidalin Guoji Heping Jiangjin," *RR*, December 23, 1952; "Luoboxun xuanbu jieshou Sidalin Guoji Heping Jiangjin," *RR*, December 27, 1952; "Zai Sidalin Guoji Heping Jiangjin . . . ," *RR*, February 1, 1953; "Luoboxun zai Niuyue jieshou . . . ," *RR*, September 27, 1953; *Baoluo Luoboxun*, 26–27; Paul Robeson, "Thoughts on Winning the Stalin Peace Prize," *Freedom*, January 1953.

52. "Meidi zongrong faxisi da guimo xingxiong . . . ," *RR*, September 1, 1949; "Mei faxisi fenzi xiji Luoboxun yinyue hui," *Xinhuashe dianxun gao*, August 30, 1949, 419; "Renmin yinyue jia Luoboxun shijian zhuanye," *Xin yinyue* 8, no. 4 (1949): 36–37.

53. "Mei faxisi fenzi dui Luoboxun yinyue hui . . . ," *Xinhuashe dianxun gao*, September 7, 1949, 106–7; "Mei ren jixu kangyi Luoboxun shijian" and "Mei ge tuanti kangyi Mei faxisi fenzi," *Xinhuashe dianxun gao*, September 1949, 141; "Niuyue Zhou jingcha canjia gongji Luoboxun," *Xinhuashe dianxun gao*, September 10, 1949, 160; "Baoli zhixi buliao renmin de gesheng" and "Zhu Luoboxun geng yonggan di gaochang," *RR*, September 8, 1949; Jingye,

"Wo tingdao le Luoboxun," *RR*, October 6, 1949; Suolu duofu ni kefu (Soviet Union), "Luoboxun"; "Renmin yinyue jia Luoboxun shijian zhuanye," *Xin yinyue* 8, no. 4 (1949): 36–37.

54. "Heiren Gewang Luoboxun" and "Haiyao dao gedi qu gechang," *RR*, September 4, 1949; "Quan Mei Zhigong Heping Dahui . . . ," *RR*, October 6, 1949; "Zhijiage liang qunzhong dahui huanying Luoboxun," *Xinhuashe dianxun gao*, September 28, 1949, 410; Suolu duofu ni kefu (Soviet Union), "Luoboxun."

55. "Quanguo Wenlian he Yinxie dian wei Luoboxun bing xiang Mei kangyi," *Xinhuashe dianxun gao*, September 7, 1949, 95; "Weiwen Luoboxun," *Xinhua yuebao* 1, no. 1 (1949): 309.

56. Yao Niangeng, "Luoboxun zai Mosike," *RR*, October 1, 1949; Zhou Ming, "Zai Mosike kanjian Luoboxun," *RR*, October 12, 1949; "Paul Robeson Makes Big Hit in USSR," *North-China Daily News*, June 17, 1949.

57. *North-China Daily News*, November 5, 1949; "Paul Robeson Deprived of Passport," *North-China Daily News*, August 6, 1950; "Czeches Hit Move Against Paul Robeson," *North-China Daily News*, August 8, 1950; Foner, *Paul Robeson Speaks 1920–1963*, 39; Duberman, *Paul Robeson*, 388–90.

58. "Mei zhuming gechang jia Luoboxun . . . ," *RR*, March 25, 1957; Robeson, "Happy Birthday, New China!"

59. "Mei zhengfu ju fu huzhao," *RR*, November 16, 1950; Yuan Shuipai, "Yi zhi angzhang de laoshu," *RR*, December 24, 1950; "Zouxiang Shijie Renmin Heping Dahui," *RR*, November 23, 1952; "Meiguo dangju dui heping zhuzhi . . . ," *RR*, August 19, 1955; Pu Xiao, "Wei shenmo bu gei Luoboxun huzhao," *Renmin yinyue* 7 (1956): 29; Yao Pingfang, "Jiaru Situo Furen jintian hai huozhe," *RR*, December 26, 1956; *RR*, June 21, 1957. "Heping de gesheng suo bu zhu," *RR*, June 29, 1958.

60. Americans who had been associated with Madam Sun were accused of being traitors during the Senate hearing of journalist John W. Powell, a former editor of *Miller's Review* in Shanghai, and his wife, Sylvia. The couple was tried for sedition in 1959 for his report that the Chinese government believed the United States employed biological weapons in the Korean War. "Song Qingling gei Meiguo 'Minzu' zhoukan de gongkai xing," *RR*, May 20, 1955; Margalit Fox, "John W. Powell, 89, Dies," *NYT*, December 17, 2008.

61. "Luoboxun fennu de kongsu," *RR*, November 12, 1957. Robeson won the fight to avoid paying $9,655 in federal income tax on the Stalin Peace Prize, which in 1959 the Internal Revenue Service eventually recognized as similar to Nobel and Pulitzer Prizes. Foner, *Paul Robeson Speaks 1920–1963*, 43.

62. "Meiguo dangju dui heping zuzhi . . . ," *RR*, August 19, 1955; "Mei gechang jia buneng chuguo yanchang," *RR*, January 24, 1958.

63. Fei Kerefunikefu (Soviet Union), "Women de pengyou Luoboxun," *RR*, January 13, 1958; Qian Junrui, "Weida de geshou he zhanshi," *RR*, April 9, 1958; Xia Yan, "Cangsong aoju, jinzhu gutong," *RR*, April 9, 1958; *Baoluo Luoboxun*, 26–27.

64. David Ordway, "Paul Robeson Sings to 10,000 on the West Coast," *Daily Worker* (London), August 15, 1957; Fei Kerefunikefu (Soviet Union), "Women de pengyou Luoboxun," *RR*, January 13, 1958.

65. Robeson had given a concert at the Club of Stalingrad Tractor Works in June 1949. *Shanghai Evening Post & Mercury*, June 14, 1949. "Geguo qingnian relie zhichi . . . ," *RR*, July 26, 1953; "Shijie Heping Lishihui huiyi bimu," *RR*, May 31, 1954; "Shijie Heping Lishihui

jixu juxing huiyi," *RR*, November 24, 1954; "Zai Di Wu Jie Shijie Qingnian Lianhuanjie shang," *RR*, August 8 and 12, 1955; Feng Zhidan, "Qingnian ren jue bu rongxu zai shiyong yuanzi wuqi," *RR*, August 9, 1955; "Mei Su Youhao Xiehui," *RR*, November 20, 1955; "Niuyue juxing qingzhu Shiyue Geming," *RR*, November 12, 1957; Xia Yan, "Cangsong aoju, jinzhu gutong," *RR*, April 9, 1958; "Message to Youth Festival in Budapest" (broadcast by Radio Moscow), *Daily Worker* (New York), August 23, 1949; "Meiguo 'tiemu' dang bu zhu renmin de youqing," *RR*, December 29, 1956; Fei Kerefunikefu (Soviet Union), "Women de pengyou Luoboxun," *RR*, January 13, 1958; Qian Junrui, "Weida de geshou he zhanshi," *RR*, April 9, 1958.

66. "Meiguo Gongchandang quanguo huiyi," *RR*, August 20, 1955; "Zhuobielin chize Meiguo zhengfu," *RR*, October 27, 1955; Chi Bei'ou, "Ni Maikaxi de muzhiming," *RR*, May 11, 1957; *RR*, June 21, 1957; London Robeson Committee, "Britain Says: Let Robeson Sing," WDBP.

67. Graham, *Paul Robeson*, 208, 255; Buck and Robeson, *American Argument*; Xie Qihuang, "Tantan Heiren dui Meizhou wenhua de gongxian," *RR*, December 17, 1963; Luoboxun, "Heiren minzu de gequ," in Gelanmu, *Heiren geshou Luoboxun*, 346, 364.

68. *Shenbao*, March 25, 1934, November 13 and 14, 1935, March 6 and 7, 1939; *Linglong* 128 (1934): 185; *Maodun yuekan* 3, no. 2 (1934); "Feizhou zhanzheng," *Dagong bao* (Shanghai), February 8, 1936; *Linglong* 135, no. 54 (1934): 632. "Paul Robeson Acts, Sings in Nanking Film" and "The Preview," *China Press*, March 25, 1934; "'Sanders of the River' to Open Today," *China Press*, October 4, 1935; "Paul Robeson Wins English Amateur Film Award," *Shanghai Times*, February 2, 1936; "Highlights of 'Show Boat' Revealed in Tale of Picture" and "Old Man River," *China Press*, September 10, 1936; "Paul Robeson Stars in New Cathay Film," *China Press*, April 8, 1938.

69. James Douglas, "A Negro Genius in London," *Shanghai Times*, September 8, 1928; "Paul Robeson Fought a Bitter Fight," *Shanghai Times*, March 20, 1934; "Negroes Today in United States," *Shanghai Times*, August 5, 1935; *Shanghai Times*, April 27, 1933, May 16, 1937; *North-China Daily News*, December 4, 1929, March 12, 1930, November 29, 1936; "Mr. Paul Robeson as Othello," *North-China Daily News*, June 14, 1936; "London Cinema Chronicle: The Problem of Paul Robeson," *North-China Daily News*, November 1, 1936; "Paul Robeson Bound for Russia to Act," *China Press*, May 2, 1933; "Paul Robeson Leaves Moscow," *China Press*, December 27, 1934.

70. Example entries: *China at War*, April 1941, 82; "Western Music in Chongqing," *China at War*, July 1941, 71–72; Lin Yutang, "Music Bolsters Morale," *China at War*, July 1941, 97; "China's Patriots Sing," *China at War*, January 1941, 97.

71. Tian Han hastily set down the lyrics of "Chee Lai!" on a piece of foil cigarette wrapper and passed them to Xia Yan before his arrest by the Nationalist government. Xia copied the lyrics, blurred by tea stains, for Nie Er, who soon took political refuge in Japan, planning to study in the Soviet Union and Europe. Nie mailed the musical notes back to China shortly before his premature death. Cong Xue, "'Yiyongjun jinxing qu' dansheng," *RR*, December 17, 1982, and *Jiefang ribao*, December 9, 1982; "'Yiyong jun jinxing qu,'" *Diantong huabao*, May 16, 1935; Price, *Lives of Agnes Smedley*, 299; Epstein, *My China Eye*, 77.

72. Zhirun, "Liu Liangmo zai Meiguo jiao Heiren Gewang chang 'Yiyongjun jinxing qu'"; "Heiren Gewang Luobosheng," *Yiwen zhi* 1, no. 7 (1946): 72; Liu Liangmo, "Renmin geshou Luoboxun"; "Heiren Gewang Luoboxun," *Meizhou huaqiao ribao*, January 19, 1950; Yi Qing, "Yi ge wei renmin dazhong gechang de Heiren Gewang Luoboxun," *Xiao penyou*

966 (1949): 15–16; Lin Xin, "Cong Heiren Gewang xiangqi," *Xinya* (Kaifeng) 1 (1949): 22–23; "Jinri de yingxiong," *Xin ertong banyue kan* 23, no. 2 (1949): 44–48.

73. Gelanmu, *Heiren geshou Luoboxun*, 1–2, 353–58, 353–484.

74. Zhu Mo, *Luoboxun zhuan*, 1–2, 31–34.

75. Luoboxun and Li Shishao, *Baoluo Luoboxun yanchang de Heiren minge*.

76. Yang Changxi, "Heiren yinyue zhong de minzu xing," *Zhongyan ribao*, November 22, 1931; Zhao Feng, "Luoboxun he Heiren minge," *RR*, April 9, 1958; Von Eschen, *Satchmo Blows Up the World*.

77. Gong Qi, "Xiang Baoluo Luoboxun xuexi," *Renmin yinyue* 5 (1958): 29.

78. "Paul Robeson at Work," *North-China Daily News*, November 26, 1939; W. E. B. Du Bois, "As the Crow Flies," *Crisis*, July 1930, 221; Zhou Boxun, "Nie Er yu dianying gequ," *Dianying huabao* 6 (1980); Mao Dun, "Meiguo dianying he Sulian dianying de bijiao," *RR*, October 30, 1949; "Dianying xiaodu yundong," *Xinhua yuebao* 1, no. 1 (1949): 310; "Zhongguo dianying zai Lundun shoudao haoping," *RR*, September 6, 1960. *Thief of Bagdad* (aka *Treasure Box in the Lunar Palace*) was another British film well-received in China in 1958. "Yingguo pian *Bageda qiezei*," *RR*, May 3, 1958; Xing Zuwen, "Yingguo dianying zai Zhongguo, 1929–1984," *Dazhong dianying* 9 (1984): 30–31.

79. Li Ling, "Jiao'ao de shangu," *RR*, April 9, 1959; Dancheng, "Bu jinjin shi tongji," *RR*, May 10, 1959.

80. Zhu Mo, *Luoboxun zhuan*, 18–19; "Shijie quanwang 'Heise Hongzhaji' Qiao Luyi tuixiu," *Shenbao*, March 2, 1948; "Qiao Luyi zizhuan," trans. by Cang Long, *Shenbao*, March 5 and 8, 1949.

81. The CPACRFC published a pamphlet of Chinese translations of songs performed by Pankey and an overview of the African American musical tradition. *Yinyue hui*; Aobulei Panji, "Renmin de shiren Huiteman," *RR*, November 27, 1955; *RR*, November, 20, 27, and 30, 1955; *Jiefang ribao*, December 12, 13, and 15, 1955; *Guangming ribao*, November 18, 1955; *Hangzhou ribao*, February 23, 1955; "Pankey in New China," *Pittsburgh Courier*, January 7, 1956. Waldo Frank, William Faulkner, Pearl S. Buck, Karl Thunberg, and Samuel Heron were also invited to this literary event. *RR*, September 21, 1955; "*Caoye ji* chuban yibai zhounian, *Tang Jikede* chuban sanbai wushi zhounian," *RR*, November 26, 1955.

82. Qian Junrui, "Weida de geshou he zhanshi," *RR*, April 9, 1958; Xia Yan, "Cangsong aoju, jinzhu gutong," *RR*, April 9, 1958; Liu Liangmo, "Wei zhandou de Zhongguo renmin gechang," *RR*, April 9, 1958; Yuan Shuipai, "Xifang tiankong yi ke xing," *RR*, April 9, 1958; Li Ling, "Luoboxun ai chang naxie ge," *RR*, April 9, 1958; "Yingyong de heping geshou Luoboxun," *RR*, April 9, 1958; "Meiguo he geguo jinbu renshi qingzhu . . . ," *RR*, April 9, 1958; "Mosike juxing wanhui qingzhu . . . ," *RR*, April 10, 1958; "Rang heping gesheng xiangbian," *RR*, April 10, 1958; "Zhu heping zhanshi Luoboxun bai nian changshou!," *RR*, April 10, 1958; Zhao Feng, "Heping zhanshi, yishu dashi . . . ," *Renmin yinyue* 4 (1958): 2–5; "Luoboxun de gesheng shi chong bu po da bu duan de," *Renmin yinyue* 4 (1958): 2.

83. "Baolun Luoboxun zai liushi shouchen gei woguo renmin de yi feng xin," *Renmin yinyue* 4 (1958): 4; "Luoboxun xiang woguo renmin zhiyi," *RR*, April 20, 1959; "Meiguo geshou xiang Zhongguo geshou zhiyi," *RR*, July 17, 1958; Robeson, *Here I Stand*; Luoboxun, *Wo jiu zhanzai zhe'er*; Zhu Shengjun and Lin Caibing, *Baoluo Luoboxun yanchang gequ ji*, 3–5; Zhu Ziqi, "Nin zhongxia le xiwang," *RR*, March 3, 1983; Bao Jun, "Du Luoboxun de *Wo jiu zhanzai zhe'er*," *Dushu* 10 (1959).

84. *Baoluo Luoboxun*; Zhu Shengjun and Lin Caibing, *Baoluo Luoboxun yanchang gequ ji*.

85. Gelanmu, *Heiren geshou Luoboxun*, 2, 400; *Baoluo Luoboxun*, 24–26, 44.
Montesquieu's artistic achievements and his winning the 1952 International Peace Award
were featured in China's state media. "Moxige yishu jia Liaoboduo Mengdesi he tade
'tongsu guohua she,'" *RR*, August 31, 1953; "Moxige banhua," *Meishu* 3 (1956): 31; Ma Ke,
"Kan Moxige de banhua yishu," *Meishu* 4 (1956): 41–43.

86. Ma Fantuo (Yuan Shuipai), "Meiyou gechang ziyou," *RR*, September 15, 1949; Qian
Junrui, "Weida de geshou he zhanshi," *RR*, April 9, 1958; Xie Qihuang, "Tantan Heiren dui
Meizhou wenhua de gongxian," *RR*, December 17, 1963; Luoboxun, "Heiren minzu de
gequ," in Gelanmu, *Heiren geshou Luoboxun*, 364.

87. James Douglas, "A Negro Genius in London," *London Daily Express*, July 5, 1928, and
Shanghai Times, September 8, 1928.

88. Zhu Mo, *Luoboxun zhuan*, 1–2.

89. Julia Dorn, "I Breathe Freely," *New Theater* (Moscow), July 1935, in Foner, *Paul
Robeson Speaks*, 100–102; "Paris Peace Conference," news release of Council on African
Affaris, in Foner, *Paul Robeson Speaks*, 197–200; Graham Du Bois, *His Day Is Marching
On*, 225–26; Zhu Mo, *Luoboxun zhuan*, 31–34. Emi Sao was invited to Moscow, and Guo
Moruo led the Beiping cultural circle to celebrate Pushkin's 150th birthday. Among the
People's Daily articles, only Ge Baoquan's mentioned the Russian poet's Black heritage.
"Ping wenyi jie Guo Moruo deng mingri jinian Puxijin danchen," *RR*, June 5, 1949;
Ge Baoquan, "Weida de Eluosi shiren," *RR*, June 6, 1949; Guo Kangke, "Renmin de
Puxijin," *RR*, June 6, 1949; "Puxinjin baiwushi," *RR*, June 8, 1949; "Gechang renmin tiancai
Puxijin," *RR*, June 20, 1949; "Eluosi renmin de Puxijin," *RR*, June 21, 1949.

90. Graham, *Paul Robeson*, 225–26; Zhu Mo, *Luoboxun zhuan*, 31–34.

91. *Ertong zhishi* 34 (1949): 25; China Central TV, Lunar New Year Gala 2018, https://
www.youtube.com/watch?v=FeRi86DcfyA (accessed March 1, 2018); "Blackfaces"
reemerged at the opening dance segment featuring Africa in the 2021 Spring Festival gala
on China Central TV; Adam Taylor, "Chinese State Media's New Year Gala Once Again
Features 'blackfaces' in Segment Depicting Africa," *Washington Post*, February 12, 2021.
China Central TV, Lunar New Year Gala 2021, https://www.youtube.com/watch?v=MZ
8MpS6tLcY (accessed February 12, 2021).

92. Du Bois, "I Sing to China."

93. "Quanguo Wenlian he Yinxie dian wei Luoboxun bing xiang Mei kangyi," *Xinhuashe
dianxun gao*, September 7, 1949, 95.

94. Qian Junrui, "Weida de geshou he zhanshi," *RR*, April 9, 1958; Yijun, "Qiujin bu liao
de heping gesheng," *Dianying yishu* 6 (1958): 79–80.

95. Yao Niangeng, "Luoboxun zai Mosike," *RR*, October 1, 1949; *Baoluo Luoboxun*,
24–26; Zhu Mo, *Luoboxun zhuan*, 1–2; Suolu duofu ni kefu (Soviet Union), "Luoboxun";
Yang Xuechun, "Weida de heping geshou," *Shijie zhishi* 3 (February 5, 1953).

96. Duberman, *Paul Robeson*, 480; Du Bois, *Autobiography*, 11–12.

97. "Luoboxun yinhang gaoge," *RR*, February 12, 1958; "Luoboxun de gesheng guan bu
zhu," *RR*, February 9, 1958; "Chongpo jinling de gesheng," *RR*, May 12, 1958; Zhang Wei,
"Yi 'Zaina yaoyuan di defang'"; *Baoluo Luoboxun*, 26–27; George Matthews, "My Aim —
Get British and U.S. People Together," *Daily Worker* (London), May 5, 1959.

98. "Chongpo jinling de gesheng," *RR*, May 12, 1958; "Heping de gesheng suo bu zhu,"
RR, June 29, 1958; "Heping gechang jia Luobuxun," *RR*, July 15, 1958; "Luoboxun zai
Mosike," *RR*, August 19, 1958; "Baoluo Luoboxin canjia quan Fei . . . ," *RR*, December 9,
1958; "Fandui hezi wuqi," *RR*, June 30, 1959; "Heping liliang tuanjie yizhi," *RR*, August 3,

1959; "Ying Gong qingzhu *Gongren ribao,*" *RR,* March 15, 1960; "Yingguo gongren jieji zhongshi . . . ," *RR,* July 11, 1960; Robeson, *Undiscovered Paul Robeson,* 275; *Baoluo Luoboxun,* 26–27.

99. Su Lan, "Wei xin Zhongguo gechang," *RR,* October 6, 1959; "Zhongguo dianying jie zai Lundun kaimu," *RR,* August 25, 1960; "Zhongguo dianying zai Lundun shoudao haoping," *RR,* September 6, 1960; "Jay Leyda: A Brief History." Huan Hsiang to Du Bois, November 2, 1959, September 27, October 10 and 21, 1960; Du Bois to Huan Hsiang, November 9, 1959, April 6, 1960; Huan Hsiang to Graham Du Bois, May 30, 1960; all in WDBP.

100. "Luoboxun li Su qu Lundun," *RR,* September 17, 1958; "Luoboxun di Lundun," *RR,* July 13, 1958; *RR,* July 12, 1958.

101. Pan Fei, "Huainian Baolun Luoboxun," *RR,* January 26, 1986, and *Yinyue shijie* 10 (1986); "Zhongguo daibiaotuan xiyin jiabing," *RR,* August 4, 1959; Su Lan, "Wei xin Zhongguo gechang," *RR,* October 6, 1959.

102. Yuan Xianlu, "Guanggao he jiaocai," *RR,* April 16, 1961.

103. Foner, *Paul Robeson Speaks,* 36; "Lianheguo ling Pengqie Boshi," *Shenbao,* September 19, 1948; "Heiren yangmei tuqi," *Shenbao,* March 16, 1949; "Pengxie keneng bei ren Mei zhuli guowuqing," *Shenbao,* April 27, 1949; "Pengqie wei Heiren huyu," *Shengbao,* May 20, 1949.

104. "Su Gong lingdao tong women fenqi de youlai he fazhan," *RR,* September 6, 1963. Works by Paul Robeson: "Negro History," *Freedom,* February 1951; "Unity for Peace," *Masses & Mainstream,* August 1951, 21–24; *Masses & Mainstream,* January 1952, 7–14; "Thoughts on Winning the Stalin Peace Prize," *Freedom,* January 1953; "The 'Big Truth' Is the Answer to the 'Big Lie' of McCarthy," *Freedom,* January 1954; "Fight We Must," speech at the National Negro Labor Council meeting, New York City, September 25, 1954, in Dent and Robeson, *Paul Robeson, Tributes, Selected Writings,* and in Foner, *Paul Robeson Speaks,* 381–86.

105. Paul Robeson, "Come and See for Yourself," *Moscow News,* February 24, 1960, in Foner, *Paul Robeson Speaks,* 463–64; Duberman, *Paul Robeson,* 437.

106. *Meiguo Heiren yao ziyou*; Foner, *Paul Robeson Speaks,* 44; Xiang Yansheng, "Meiguo Heiren Gewang Luoboxun yu 'Yiyongjun jinxing qu.'"

107. Aptheker, *Correspondence of W. E. B. Du Bois,* 435.

108. Anna Louise Strong to Steve Fritchman, September 20, 1966, Paul and Eslanda Goode Robeson Archives, Moorland-Spingarn Research Center, Manuscript Division, Howard University, Washington, D.C.; Duberman, *Paul Robeson,* 540–41, 760n5.

109. "Lianheguo jinian Meiguo Heiren geshou Luoboxun," *RR,* April 17, 1978.

110. He Dazhang, *Yi ge zhenshi de Song Qingling,* 148–56; He Dazhang, "Ta changchu le renlei de xinsheng," *Guangming ribao,* April 17, 2008; Chen Yiming, "Gesheng jili aiguo qing"; "Song Qingling huijian Xiao Baoluo Luoboxun he furen," *RR,* May 16, 1980; "Mei Zhong Youxie quan Mei Huaren Xiehui," *RR,* October 5, 1981; Yuan Xianlu, "Baolu Luoboxun fuzi he Zhongguo," *RR,* November 21, 1981.

111. Pan Fei, "Huainian Baolun Luoboxun," *RR,* January 26, 1986, and *Yinyue shijie* 10 (1986).

112. Hanmi'erdun, *Heiren Gewang Luoboxun*; Hamilton, *Paul Robeson.*

113. *Meiguo mingge xuan*; Li Shizhao, *Baoluo Luoboxun yanchang de Heiren minge.*

114. Sun Yanyan, "Kaiwen Meinuo xianyan Baoluo Luoboxun gequ," *RR,* December 10, 1999; Shao Yanxiang and Fang Cheng, "Huida he bu huida"; "Investigation of the Unauthorized Use of United States Passports—Part 3," *Hearings before the Committee on*

Un-American Activities, Eighty-Fourth Congress, Second Session, June 12, 1956, Washington D.C., 4492–4510, in Foner, *Paul Robeson Speaks*, 413–36; "Testimony of Paul Robeson before the House Committee on Un-American Activities, June 12, 1956," YouTube, https://www.youtube.com/watch?v=VhnCrHZkgNk.

115. Zhang Yan, "Meiguo nanbu xing," *RR*, May 2, 1981; Xiao Fuxing, "Laorenhe jingjing liutang dao jintian," *Renwu* 6 (2011): 80–82; "Baoluo Luoboxun de zuji," *Renwu* 6 (2011): 83; *Ziyou zhi ge* (Chengdu: Emei dianying zhipianchang, 2006).

CHAPTER 3

1. Lin Yutang, "Singing Patriots of China." For *Reader's Digest* circulation, see http://www.rda.com/rda-timeline.

2. *Time*, June 16, 1941; "What They Say about Liu Liangmo," advertising statement, n.d. (ca. 1944), UCRA; Liu Liangmo and Simon, *Young China*.

3. Zhang Gaofeng, "Daonian Liu Liangmo xiansheng," in *Liu Liangmo xiansheng jinian wenji*, 401–2; "Liu Liangmo," FBI files, NY 100-47820.

4. Gallicchio, *African American Encounter*, 161, 164–65, 175–79, 199; Lai, *Chinese American Transnational Politics*, 93, 109–10, 128, 138; So, *Transpacific Community*; Jones, *Yellow Music*; Lee, "Co-optation and Its Discontents."

5. Liu was allegedly born on November 11, 1908, or September 6, 9, or November 6, 9, 1909. Mixing the lunar and solar calendars likely contributed to such confusion, which was common for those born in China before official record keeping was strictly enforced. "Liu Liangmo," FBI files, NY 100-47820, and Bureau files 100-201676–1/5/6/8/10; "Liu Liangmo," file 36590/7-4, box 3429, shelf 3300E, group 85, INS, San Francisco District Office, National Archives at San Francisco. Works by Liu Liangmo: *Shaonian* 14, no. 5 (1924): 125–27; *Huchao* 1 (1928): 10–12, 37; "Judu shi quanti renmin de zeren," *Judu yuekan* 19 (March 1928): 29.

6. Lu Xun also noted the inauguration of Liu Zhan'en, who would be assassinated by the Japanese in 1938. Yingang (Luxun), "Jiebao yi ban"; Li Hanru, "Yi Hujiang gu xiaozhang Liu Boshi," *Tianfeng*, April 10, 1948. Works by Liu Liangmo: "Huansong Wei Xiaochang li Hu ji," *Huchao* 1, no. 2 (1928): 44–45; *Shenghuo zhoukan* 4, no. 40 (1929): 456–57; *Minguo ribao*, August 1, 1929, July 7 and 11, December 2 and 4, 1931; *Xinghua* 28, no. 48 (1931): 5–6; *Xuesheng zazhi* 16, no. 6 (1929): 53–58; *Dasheng zhoukan* 1, no. 7 (1933): 130–31; "Wo yi Zenyang xiuxue de dongji," *Changcheng* 3, no. 1 (1935): 18–19; *Fujian daobao* 2, no. 1 (1939): 12–13 (offering advice on a career as a journalist); "Aiguo jiaoyu jia Liu Zhan'en Boshi," *Shehui kexue* 8 (1983): 64–66; "Wuxian diantai," *Huda zhoukan*, 1928–32. Claude C. Crawford, *Methods of Study* (Moscow, Idaho, 1926); Kelaofu, *Zenyang xiuxue*, trans. by Liu Liangmo (Shanghai: Changcheng shuju, 1933); *Xiandai qingnian* (Beiping) 3, no. 2, (1936): 27–28. *Shibao*, January 13, 1930; *Judu yuekan* 52 (1932): 1. Chen Weijiang, "Songbie," *Huda zhoukan* 17, no. 14 (1928): 56.

7. Liu Liangmo, "Yi kang Ri jiuwang geyong yundong," *Renmin yinyue* 6 (1980): 16–20, 26; Lou Weihong, "Liu Liangmo yu kang Ri qunzhong geyong huodong," *Shiji*, October 15, 2005; Zhao Puchu, "Zai Wu Yaozong Xiansheng shishi shi zhounian . . . ," *Fayin* 11 (1989): 29–30; Lai, *Chinese American Transnational Politics*, 93; Reilly, "Wu Yaozong and the YMCA." Young activists such as Rewi Alley formed Marxist study groups within the Shanghai YMCA. Rewi later led the wartime Chinese Industrial Cooperative Association (INDUSCO) movement with Ida Pruitt, a self-acclaimed cultural mediator born to and

raised by Christian missionaries in China, and Edgar and Helen Snow. The INDUSCO papers are in the Rare Book and Manuscript Library, Columbia University, MS#0644.

8. *Xianggang qingnian* 3, no. 23 (1935): 193. Example works by Liu Liangmo: *Xiaoxi* 6, no. 3 (1933): 2–11; 7, no. 2 (1934): 2–8; 7, no. 7 (1934): 48–49, 60; 8, no. 3 (1935): 51–52; 8, no. 8 (1935): 71; 8, no. 9 (1935): 49; 8, no. 10 (1935): 51; 9, no. 3 (1936): 52; 9, no. 10 (1936): 34–40; 10, no. 3/4 (1937): 16–19; *Tonggong* 132 (1934): 21–28; 147 (1935): 59; 158 (1937): 11–13; *Changcheng* 2, no. 4 (1935): 79–80; 2, no. 5 (1935): 100; 2, no. 10 (1935): 195; 2, no. 11 (1935): 214–15; 3, no. 1 (1935): 18–19; 3, no. 2 (1935): 22–24; 3, no. 3 (1935): 42–44; 3, no. 4 (1935): 67; 3, no. 5 (1935): 82–84; 3, no. 6 (1935): 112–13; 3, no. 7 (1936): 2–3; 3, no. 8 (1936): 22–23, 35; 3, no. 9 (1936): 44–46; *Shanghai qingnian* 35, no. 34 (1935): 5–7; *Guangzhou qingnian* 22, no. 45 (1935): 159–60; "Shanghai kang Ri jiuwang de geyong yundong." Sun Shen, "Kangzhan shiqi de qunzhong geyong yundong," *RR*, September 2, 1985.

9. Example songs: *Zhonghua zhoukan*, October 16, 1937; "Jiu Zhongguo," *Xiao pengyou* 719 (1936): 11; "Da Riben ge," *Shige* 31 (1937): 8. Works by Liu Liangmo: "Shanghai kang Ri jiuwang de geyong yundong"; "Xikang zaji," *Huanian* 1, no. 26 (1932): 15–16; "Qilai! Buyuan zuo nuli de renmen," *Renmin yinyue* 12 (1984): 37–38. Qu Wei, "Jinian xin yinyue de kailu xianfeng—Nie Er tongzhi," *RR*, July 17, 1949; Dai Penghai, "Zhongguo yinyue shi shang de fengbei," *RR*, September 17, 1991; Lin Yongwu, "Weida renming geshou Xian Xinghai," *Tianfeng*, October 22, 1949. China Central TV, "Salute to Classics: Wang Luobing," https://www.youtube.com/watch?v=6Rky-2kP240 (accessed February 2, 2019). Liner notes, Robeson, Liu Liangmo, and the Chinese People's Chorus, *Chee Lai!*

10. "Liu Liangmo Press Release," n.d. (ca. 1942), UCRA. Salz, "Thunder of 10,000 Voices." Works by Liu Liangmo: "Yi jiu san liu nian jiefang nian," *Changcheng* 3, no. 7 (1936): 2–3; "Suiyuan de dazhong geyong," *Xiaoxi* 10, no. 5 (1937); Suiyuan de minzhong liliang. "Liu Liangmo zai qianxian . . . ," *Tiebao*, April 24, 1937.

11. Ji Chaozhu served as a top interpreter for Mao Zedong and Zhao Enlai, as ambassador to the United Kingdom (1987–91), and as undersecretary-general of the United Nations (1991–96). Ji Chaozhu, *Man on Mao's Right*, 10.

12. *Guansheng* 1, no. 12 (1937): 103; "Liu Liangmo jun zai benhui jiao changge shengkuang," *Tianjin qingnian* 127 (1937): 1–2; *Liangyou* 127 (1937): 52; *Laosao yuekan* (Tianjin) 1, no. 5 (1937): 19; "Kangdi qianxian minzhong de wuli," *Dongfang huabao* 34, no. 8 (1937): 3. Sun Shen, "Kangzhan shiqi de qunzhong geyong yundong."

13. On the YMCA's Commission to Serve the Military, see *Tonggong* 158 (1937): 14–17, 27–39; *Libao*, August 23 and 30, 1937. Works by Liu Liangmo: "Zai guofang de zui qianxian—Beiping," *Zhoubao* 1, no. 3 (1937): 86–88; "Suzhou He xunli," *Dikang sanri kan* 7 (1937): 8; *Dikang sanri kan* 23 (1937): 5; *Guomin zhoukan* 1, no. 12 (1937): 270; *Libao*, October 3 and September 24, 1937; *Kangzhan sanri kan* 17 (1937): 7; 31 (1937): 2–3; 53 (1938): 6; 66 (1938): 12; 6, no. 9 (1938): 5–6; 81 (1938): 5–7; "Qianxian zhanshi de wenhua shenghuo," *Dushu* 1, no. 3 (1937): 172–74; *Xiada xiaokan* 1, no. 8 (1937): 4; *Dafeng* (jinhua) 73 (1938): 3–4; 89/90 (1939): 29–31; 92 (1939): 14–16; *Zhejiang chao* 44 (1939): 810–11; *Shiba ge yue zai qianfang*, 1–41. Yan Xu, *The Soldier Image and State-Building in Modern China*, 84–88; Xiao Hong, *Mo Bole*, chaps. 50 and 51, https://www.haoshuya.com/11/5517/397478.html#headid (accessed April 9, 2021).

14. Works by Liu Liangmo: *Shiba ge yue zai qianfang*, 42–63; "Ji Shanghai qingnian," *Yibao zhoukan* 1, no. 26 (1938): 328–29, and *Liansheng* 3 (1939): 2–3; "Zenyang zuzhi junren fuwu tuan," *Quanmin kangzhan sanri kan* 1, no. 29 (1938): 140–42; "Junren fuwu zai Hunan," *Xin Hunan xunkan* 1, no. 2 (1938): 21–22; "Kangzhan qijian de jiaoge gongzuo,"

Xin Hunan xunkan 1, 3 (1938): 32; "Tongjun jinxing qu," *Tuanxun* (Changsha), November 16, 1938; "Fuwu junren yundong," *Xiehui xiaoxi* 1, no. 1 (1938): 46–48, and *Kangzhan sanri kan* 37 (1938): 9; "Pang Qingquan," *Daobao*, October 27, 1938; "Jieshao yi wei qingnian zhanshi," *Quanmin kangzhan sanri kan* 45 (1938): 10; "Zuo tankeche de nengshou," *Xuesheng zazhi* 1 (1938): 139–41. Liu Liangmo and Lu Shaofei, "Kangzhan changshi manhua."

15. Dai Penghai, "Zhongguo yinyue shi shang de fengbei."

16. Yinyu, "Liu Liangmo xiansheng yanjiang zhuiji," *Beilei* 1 (1939): 30; Tao (Zou Taofen), "Guanyu Liu Liangmo xiansheng de xiaoxi," *Quanmin kangzhan zhoukan* 102 (1939): 1532. Works by Liu Liangmo: "Hangzhou qulai," *Quanmin kangzhan zhoukan* 87 (1939): 1276–78; *Jinhua dongnan zhanxian* 1 (1939); "Ban nian lai zai youji qu," *Shehui ribao*, March 23, 1940. "Liu Liangmo Press Release," n.d. (ca. 1942), UCRA; Smedley, *Battle Hymn of China*, 224.

17. *Santa Fe New Mexican*, January 15, 1938; *Abilene (Tex.) Reporter-News*, January 16, 1938; *Lansing (Mich.) State Journal*, November 17, 1938; *Daily Missoulian* (Mont.), January 25, 1938.

18. Works by Liu Liangmo: *Qingnian ge ji; Minzhong geyong abc; Minzu husheng;* "Changge jianpu shang de jihao," *Honglu* 1, no. 5 (1936): 110; "Zenyang zhidao dazhong changge," *Shenghuo jiaoyu* 3, no. 10 (1936): 409–10; "Kangzhan qi zhong de geyong gongzuo dagang," *Dikang sanri kan* 29 (1937): 9–10; "Zenyang Chang? Zenyang jiao?" *Zixiu daxue* 1, no. 3 (1937): 40–42; "Zhanshi jiaoyu zhong zhi geyong jie de dongyuan," *Zhanshi jiaoyu* 2 (1937): 7; "Zenyang zhihui changge," *Zhange* (Shaoxing) 1 (1939): 11–16.

19. Works by Liu Liangmo: "Xuanchuan de xin gongju — juge," *Quanmin kangzhan sanri kan* 11 (1938): 130–31; *Shiba ge yue zai qianfang*, 36–41; *Huangjia Zhuang*.

20. Works by Liu Liangmo: *Zhanshi de junren fuwu; Shiba ge yue zai qianfang*. Example essays by Liu Liangmo: "Zhong Ri guanxi zuijin zhi jinzhan," *Xiaoxi* 8, no. 9 (1935): 10–15; "Xiang duzhe gaobie," *Xiaoxi* 9, no. 6 (1936): 9; "Jieshao jizhong shubao," *Xiaoxi* 9, no. 4 (1936): 21–23; "Riben feiji he Zhongguo xiaohai"; *Changcheng* 3, no. 8 (1936): 22–23; "Guanyu junren fuwu," *Kanzhan sanri kan* 46 (1938): 11 (a letter from Liu to Qian Junrui); *Kangzhan sanri kan* 46 (1938): 11; 66 (1938): 12; 69 (1938): 5–6; 81 (1938): 5–7; 85 (1938): 5–6; *Qingnian dazhong* 1, no. 7/8 (1939): 5–6; 2, no. 3 (1939): 129–30; *Guomin gonglun* (Hankou) 2, no. 3 (1939): 129–30; "Liangnian lai Zhongguo zhi geyong yundong," *Kangzhan yuebao* 8 (1939): 33–36; "Junmin hezuo de guanjian," *Quanmin kangzhan sanri kan* 53 (1939): 731–32, and *Gongyu banyue kan* 8 (1939): 8.

21. Works by Liu Liangmo: "Zenyang sheying," *Nüduo* 23, no. 1/2 (July 1934): 25–29; "Yingyou lai yin," *Aikefa yingkan* 1, no. 8 (1939): 16. Photographs by Liu Liangmo: *Keda zazhi* 4, no. 7 (1933): 15; *Da Shanghai tuhua zazhi* 1 (1934): 16; *Nü qingnian yuekan* 14, no. 9 (1935): 1; 15, no. 1 (1936): 1; 15, no. 2 (1936): 1; 15, no. 4 (1936): 1; *Kangzhan huakan* 6 (1937): 7; *Zhanshi huakan* 2, no. 10 (1937): 2; 3, no. 18 (1937): 12–13; *Kangzhan huabao* 7 (1937): 7; 9 (1937): 6; 10, (1937): 2; *Sheying huabao* 13, no. 9 (1937): 2; *Liangyou* 124 (1937): 12; 145 (1939): 16.

22. Liu Liangmo, "Yi kang Ri jiuwang geyong yundong," *Renmin yinyue* 6 (1980): 16–20, 26; "Kang Ri jiuwang geyong yundong shiliao," and Luo Guanzong, "Yi Liangmo," both in *Liu Liangmo xiansheng jinian wenji*, 61–62, 397; *China at War*, December 1940, 14–16, April 1941, 62–63; Ding Ke and Fen Yuan, "Tianxia wuren bu shi Liu," *Lianhe shibao*, August 28, 2009; "Jinhua nuhou le," *Yibao zhoukan* 1, no. 26 (1938): 330; *Kangjian fukan*, December 11,

1938; Tao (Zou Taofen), "Guanyu Liu Liangmo Xiansheng de xiaoxi," *Quanmin kangzhan zhoukan* 102 (1939): 1532; *Liansheng* 2, no. 3 (1939): 1; "Liu Liangmo Xiansheng cong Fuyang laixin," *Liansheng* 2, no. 4 (1939): 7; *Tonggong* 187 (1940): 20.

23. Zhang Biyu, "Cong Guilin dao Jinhua he Loujiata," in *Liu Liangmo xiansheng jinian wenji*, 82; Reilly, "Wu Yaozong and the YMCA," 286. Wu Yaozong earned a master's degree from Columbia University in 1927. *Columbia University Alumni Register, 1754–1931*, 976, https://babel.hathitrust.org/cgi/pt?id=uc1.b4525470&view=1up&seq=9.

24. For a photograph of the delegation, see *Xiaoxi* 9, no. 9 (1936): 18. "Liu Liangmo," FBI files, NY 100-47820, PH 100-29204; "Liu Liangmo," file 36590/7-4, box 3429, shelf 3300E, group 85, INS, San Francisco District Office, National Archives at San Francisco. Liu Liangmo, "Fu Mei Zhongguo daibiaotuan riji," *Funü shenghuo* 3, no. 4 (1936): 23–24; 3, no. 6 (1936): 12–14.

25. Works by Liu Liangmo: "Fu Mei Zhongguo daibiaotuan riji," *Funü shenghuo* 3, no. 4 (1936): 23–24; 3, no. 6 (1936): 12–14; "Tanxiangshan de Hei'an mian," *Funü shenghuo* 3, no. 8 (1936): 14–16.

26. Yuan, a future famous physicist, was to study at the University of California, Berkeley. "Liu Liangmo," FBI files, NY 100-47820, PH 100-29204; "Liu Liangmo," file 36590/7-4, box 3429, shelf 3300E, group 85, INS, San Francisco District Office, National Archives at San Francisco; Liu Liangmo, "Xianrendao," *Funü shenghuo* 3, no. 9 (1936): 26–28. On Angel Island, see Lee, *At America's Gates*.

27. Liu Liangmo, "Shenghuo zai Meiguo," *Xiaoxi* 13, no. 5 (1940): 35–37, 43.

28. "Women de yinxiang," *Xiaoxi* 9, no. 9 (1936): 32–37.

29. "Liu Liangmo," File 36590/74, box 3429, shelf 3300E, group 85, INS, San Francisco District Office, National Archives at San Francisco.

30. Liu's Alien Registration (no. 4318630), filed with the INS office in Philadelphia on November 18, 1940, claimed that he arrived in Seattle on September 23, 1940, aboard the SS *Empress of Asia*. "Liu Liangmo," FBI files, NY 100-201676-5/7/8/10/11, PH 100-29204, WFO 100-16298; Liu Liangmo, "Shenghuo zai Meiguo," *Xiaoxi* 13, no. 5 (1940): 35–37, 43.

31. Liu Liangmo, "Shenghuo zai Meiguo," *Xiaoxi* 13, no. 5 (1940): 35–37, 43; "Liu Liangmo," FBI files, PH 100-29204, 100-201676-8/11, WFO 100-16298. Lewis, *King*, 27–37. Most of Crozer's international students came from China, including three who completed their Oriental certificates in 1949. Parr, *Seminarian*, 254n7.

32. *Time*, June 16, 1941. "Work of the U.C.R.," *China at War*, February 1942, 57–58, and November 1942, 81. For contract date of hire, see Notarized Statement of Charles Edison, Executive Vice President of UCR, September 5, 1947, UCRA. Bettis A. Garside stated to the FBI in 1943 that Liu's date of hire was September 29. "List of contacts," the East and West Association, Chinese Theater, Correspondence, Smith, Ruth, group 5, series 4, box 7, PSBH. Garside, *Within the Four Seas*; Jesperson, *American Images*, 34–35, 616–18.

33. "Liu Liangmo," FBI files, 100-201676-5/7/10, NY 100-47820. Works by Liu Liangmo: "Meiguo dui huaqiao de wuru"; "Meiguo dui Heiren de qishi."

34. "Liu Liangmo," FBI files, NY 100-47820, 100-201676-1/5, 100-3587-291, 65-16160-23, 100-3-87-A; *Daily Worker* (New York), February 10, 1941.

35. "Liu Liangmo," FBI files, PH 100-29204, 100-201676-1/2/8, 100-7045-A; *Daily Worker* (New York), June 30, 1941.

36. "Liu Liangmo," FBI files, 100-3587, 100-100201676-1/3/4/5, NY 100-47820.

37. "Liu Liangmo," FBI files, PH 100-29204, 100-201676-1/5/8/11, NY 100-47820, 100-3587-196.

38. Liu Liangmo, "Xianzai de wo shi wode pengyou zaocheng de," *Nüsheng* 3, no. 6 (1934): 25–26.

39. Zhang Gaofeng, "Daonian Liu Liangmo xiansheng," in *Liu Liangmo xiansheng jinian wenji*, 401–3; "Liu Liangmo," FBI files, NY 100-47820, or Bureau file 100-201676-10.

40. Liu Liangmo, "Chinese Have Changed and Now They Are More Militant." For teaching offer, see Robeson, *Undiscovered Paul Robeson*, 6–8, 25; Duberman, *Paul Robeson*, 174–75, 188, 201–2, 236–38, 254, 466; Liu Liangmo, "Luoboxun yu 'Yiyongjun jinxing qu.'"

41. *Camp Wo-Chi-Ca Yearbook*; Kumar Goshal, "As an Indian Sees It," *Pittsburgh Courier*, August 28, 1943.

42. Levine and Gordon, *Tales of Wo-Chi-Ca*, 36, 43–44, 86; "Liu Liangmo," FBI files, NY 100-47820, 100-201676-5; Schwartz and Schwartz, *Dance Claimed Me*, 24–28.

43. *Daily Worker* (New York), June 5, 1942; *Chicago Defender*, May 3, 23, and 26, June 19, 1941; *California Eagle*, July 9, 1942; *Lincoln University Bulletin for 1942*, 8, 14–19; *Crisis*, June 1942, 199; *Pittsburgh Courier*, October 7, 1944.

44. "Liu Liangmo," FBI files, NY 100-47820, 100-201676-1/5, 100-3587-291, 65-16160-23, 100-3587-A; *Daily Worker* (New York), February 10 and July 2, 1941; "Paul Robeson Urges Full Aid to Russia as Youth Congress Opens," *Philadelphia Inquirer*, July 4, 1941; Liu Liangmo, "Zhongguo kangzhan gequ zai Meiguo"; "American Bureau for Medical Aid to China," *China at War*, December 1942, 81. To prevent medical equipment from reaching the CCP, the American Bureau for Medical Aid to China was prohibited from sending medical supplies to institutes other than those mentioned above. For instance, Pearl S. Buck and Margaret Smythe secured $500 worth of birth control materials from the Planned Parenthood Federation of America to be distributed through Ginling College, but its president, Wu Yifang, soon learned of the prohibition. Instead, the supplies had to be steered to the National Health Institute in China. Rose to Buck, January 4, Buck Correspondence, 1944, group 1, series 2, box 20, PSBH.

45. *Chicago Defender*, May 16, 1941 (meeting with Prattis); *Lincoln University Bulletin for 1942*, 8, 14–19; Liu Liangmo, "Meiguo dui Heiren de qishi." On the *Courier*, see Buni, *Robert L. Vann*. Von Eschen, *Race against Empire*, 17–20.

46. "Liu Liangmo," FBI files, 100-201676-1, 100-135-32, 100-69266-24; "Kumar Goshal, Journalist, Dies," *NYT*, May 31, 1971; Joseph D. Bibb, "As We Read: *Courier* Makes Supreme Effort to Give Expression to Views of All Races," *Pittsburgh Courier*, December 4, 1943. Liu Liangmo, "Renshi," *Changcheng* 3, no. 2 (1935): 22–24.

47. Liu Liangmo, "China Speaks!," *Pittsburgh Courier*, January 2, 8, 9, 16, 23, February 20, 1942, February 13, August 7, 1943 (on India); January 23, February 20, May 15, September 18, 1943 (on empathy); October 31, December 12, 1942, June 12, 26, July 24, August 29, September 11, October 2, 1943, and June 3, 1944 (on Chinese Exclusion Act and poll taxes); November 21, 28, 1942 (on Black workers and unions); January 2, 8, 9, 16, 23, February 20, June 17, July 8, 1944, February 24, 1945 (on George Schuyler). "Liu Liangmo," FBI files, NY 100-47820, 100-201676-1, 100-201676-5, 100-115471-34; *Daily Worker* (New York), November 6, 1942; *Amsterdam News*, April 17, 1943.

48. Howard Taubman, "Fire Line Song Thrill Audience," *NYT*, June 27, 1942; *New York Age*, April 10, 1943; *Negro Quarterly* 1, no. 2 (Summer 1942).

49. Liu Liangmo, "China Speaks!," *Pittsburgh Courier*, May 1 and November 6, 1943,

February 12, 1944 (on Chinese seamen); "Liu Liangmo," FBI files, 100-201676-1/5, 100-135-32, NY 100-47820.

50. Liu praised Wendell Willkie's campaign for international democracy and a second war front. Liu Liangmo, "China Speaks!," *Pittsburgh Courier*, January 2, 8, 9, 16, 23, February 20, 1942. For representative examples, see "China Speaks!," *Pittsburgh Courier*, September 19, January 30, June 19, 1943, January 15 and 22, May 22, June 24, July 1, August 5, 1944, March 3, 1945 (on Japan); October 10, 1942, January 2, 1943, March 6 and 13, April 3, August 21, December 18, 1943, July 8, September 8, 1944 (on Allied effort); October 10 and 31, 1942, April 3, 1943 (on second front); January 2, June 19, August 14, 1943, January 1, June 24, July 1, August 5, November 5, 1944, January, 13, and March 10, 1945 (on Allied triumphs); January 16, October 10, 1943, January 22 and 29, August 19, December 29, 1944, February 17, 1945 (on Atlantic Charter); October 21, 1942, April 21, 1943, October 21, 1944 (on Willkie and his obituary). "Liu Liangmo," FBI files, 100-201676-1, 100-69266-24, 94-4-5785-A. *Daily Worker* (New York), September 20, 1942. Liu Liangmo, "Meiguo tongxun," *Qingnian shenghuo* (Guilin) 3, no. 1 (1942): 34–35; Liu Liangmo, "Lianheguo ge" and "Lianmengguo ge."

51. *Pittsburgh Courier*, December 18, 1943.

52. "Liu Liangmo," FBI files, 100-201676-1, 100-7045-A; *Daily Worker* (New York), June 30, 1941.

53. Buni, *Robert L. Vann*.

54. Liu Liangmo, "China Speaks!," *Pittsburgh Courier*, September 26, December 5 and 19, 1942, February 13, March 6 and 20, 1943 (on praise for Nationalists and the Chiangs); March 6 and 17, July 10, 1943, February 19, 1944 (on admiration of Sun Yat-sen and his widow).

55. Liu Liangmo, "China Speaks!," *Pittsburgh Courier*, May 22, September 2, 1943, June 10, July 29, September 2 and 30, October 7, November 11, 1944, January 6, March 5, 17, and 31, 1945 (all with sharp criticism of the Nationalists); White and Jacoby, *Thunder out of China*; So, *Transpacific Community*, 122–28.

56. For meetings at John Stilwell's home, see *Herald Statesman* (Yonkers, N.Y.), April 27, May 2, 9, and 11, 1942. For talks, see *NYT*, February 8 and July 7, 1942. For the photograph, see "Enrolls to Aid China Relief," *NYT*, May 9, 1942, or box 89, folder 13, UCRA. Liu Liangmo, "China Speaks!," *Pittsburgh Courier*, September 2 and 16, November 11, December 4, 1944, March 5, 17, and 31, 1945.

57. Works by Liu Liangmo: "China Speaks!," *Pittsburgh Courier*, January 4 and 27, February 10, 1945; "Meiguo dui Heiren de qishi." P. L. Prattis, "The Horizon," *Pittsburgh Courier*, April 21, 1945.

58. "Liu Liangmo," FBI files, 100-3587-196, 100-201676-1.

59. It seems that race played a role in the FBI's treatment of its former informants. The unredacted names in its released files on Liu Liangmo are exclusively Chinese and African Americans. "Liu Liangmo," FBI files, NY 100-47820, 100-3587-196, 100-201676-1/5; *Putnam County Courier* (Carmel, N.Y.), July 31 and August 7, 1941.

60. Liu Liangmo, "Shenghuo zai Meiguo," *Xiaoxi* 13, no. 5 (1940): 35–37, 43.

61. Liu, "China Speaks!," *Pittsburgh Courier*, February 10 and March 31, 1945.

62. The Lius to Buck, December 12; Buck to the Lius, December 27; Du Bois to Buck, December 11; Buck to Du Bois, December 27; Mrs. Hjordis Swenson to Buck, December 12; Buck to Swenson, December 27, Buck Correspondence, 1946, PSBH.

63. Dike (Liu Liangmo), "Tantan huaqiao," *Liansheng* 3, no. 2 (1940): 12.

64. Liu Liangmo, "Zhongguo kangzhan gequ zai Meiguo"; Lin Yutang, *Chinatown Family*, 218. The following sources refer to Chinatown's Patriotic Chorus, which I believe to be the same group: So, *Transpacific Community*, 146–54; Yu Renqui, *To Save China*, 122–23, Peter Kwong, *Chinatown*, 134.

65. *Zhonghua* 101 (1941): 9; "Quan Mei Zhuhua Lianhehui Di Yi Yan," *Liangyou* 166 (May 1941): 16. *Brooklyn (N.Y.) Daily Eagle*, September 17, 1943; *New York Age*, May 20, 1944.

66. Lai, "Kuomintang in Chinese American Communities," 170–212; Lai, *Chinese American Transnational Politics*, 77–100, 114–17. Tang's daughter Nancy (Wensheng) emerged as one of the few powerful radicals during the Cultural Revolution. Ji Chaozhu, *Man on Mao's Right*, 23–40, 232.

67. Liu Liangmo, "Two-Way Traffic with China," *NYT*, June 30, 1943. This may be the same Edward R. Lewis who authored *A History of American Political Thought: From the Civil War to the World War* (New York: Octagon Books, 1969).

68. Liu Liangmo, "The New Year at the Front."

69. *Baltimore Sun*, March 9, 1941.

70. *New York Post*, February 7, 1941, April 29, 1943. The fifteen-minute radio program contrasted China's new and old music, with Liu explaining and singing "Chee Lai!" and "To the Rear of the Enemy," Lee's two classic songs, and a duet of "Chinese Farmers' Song." Talks by Spaeth etc., RBML_ABMAC_record group 20, Library of Congress. For salary, see Notarized Statement of Charles Edison, UCRA.

71. "What They Say about Liu Liangmo," advertising statement, n.d. (ca. 1944), UCRA.

72. For appearances at the meetings sponsored by the American Council on Soviet Relations, see "Liu Liangmo," FBI files, 65-7045-83, 100-146964-A, 100-201676-1; and *Daily Worker* (New York), July 3, 1941, November 10, 1942. The American Council on Soviet Relations Records, Tamiment Library and Robert F. Wagner Labor Archives, Elmer Holmes Bobst Library, New York University, TAM.134. For the second Madison Square Garden rally, see *NYT*, October 3, 1941.

73. "Liu Liangmo," FBI files, 100-201676-1/5, 100-135-32, NY 100-47820; *Kingston (N.Y.) Daily Freeman*, July 23, 1942.

74. Liu Liangmo, "Yi ge Meiguo ren de Meiguo guan," *Shanghai zhoubao* 2, no. 25 (1940) and *Zhejiang chao* 126 (1940): 197; Dike (Liu Liangmo), "Zhanzheng qifen zhong de Meiguo," *Liansheng* 3, no. 3 (December 1940): 7; *Topaz (Utah) Times*, March 27, 1943, May 13 and September 6, 1944; *Manzanar (Calif.) Free Press*, May 13, 1944; *Outpost* (Rohwer, Ark.), November 14, 1942; *Official Press Daily Bulletin* (Poston, Ariz.), August 20, 1942; *Trek* (Topaz, Utah), February 1, 1943; *Minidoka Irrigator* (Hunt, Ida.), March 20, 1943, March 31, 1945; *Heart Mountain Sentinel* (Cody, Wyo.), March 20, 1943; *Tanforan Totalizer* (San Bruno, Calif.), June 13, 1942; *Pacemaker* (Santa Anita, Calif.), June 9, 1942; *Gila News-Courier* (Rivers, Ariz.), June 26, 1943; "Quotes from Ridgecrest," *Word and Way* (Kansas City, Mo.), September 2, 1943.

75. The films that Liu commented on included *Western Front, Here Is China* (UCR, 1944), *Burma Road* (directed by Chih Meng), *Glimpses of Modern China, Chung-king Rises Again, China Shall Have Our Help, Choir Night*, and *China First to Fight. Elmira (N.Y.) Star-Gazette*, April 22, 1942.

76. Example entries: "Party Saturday for China Relief," *NYT*, July 15, 1941; *New York Herald Tribune*, July 17, 1941; *Herald Statesman* (Yonkers, N.Y.), July 10, August 1, November 10 and 14, 1941, January 10 and 12, April 27, May 2, 9, and 11, 1942; *Putnam*

324

Notes to Pages 151–56

County Courier (Carmel, N.Y.), July 24 and 31, August 7 and 14, 1941, June 11, July 2 and 9, 1942; *Brooklyn (N.Y.) Daily Eagle*, August 22, 1941, April 6 and May 17, 1942; *Rochester (N.Y.) Democrat and Chronicle*, December 25, 1941; *Orangetown Telegram* (Spring Valley, N.Y.), February 20, 1942; *New York Post*, February 27, 1942; *Long Island Society*, April 13, 1942; *Daily Home News* (New Brunswick, N.J.), April 8 and 15, 1942; *California Eagle*, July 9, 1942; *Washington Post*, February 10, 1941; *Miami (Fla.) Daily News*, March 20, 1941; *Chicago Tribune*, June 19, 1941; *Morning Call* (Allentown, Penn.), October 10, 1941; *Des Moines (Iowa) Register*, October 19 and 23, 1941; *Minneapolis Star-Journal*, June 24 and December 2, 1941; *Alton (Iowa) Democrat*, December 5, 1941; *St. Louis Post-Dispatch*, December 7, 1941, April 22, 1942, October 27, 1943; *Palladium-Item and Sun Telegram* (Richmond, Ind.), March 5, 1942; *Mason City (Iowa) Globe-Gazette*, March 14, 1942; *St. Louis Star and Times*, April 21, 1942.

77. For radio appearances, see *New York Post*, May 4 and 16, 1942, April 20, 1943; *PM*, January 11, 1942; and *New York Sun*, July 3, 1943. Example entries: *Richfield Springs (N.Y.) Mercury*, August 20, 1942; *Otsego Farmer* (Cooperstown, N.Y.), August 21, 28, 1942; *Penn Yan (N.Y.) Democrat*, October 1, 1942; *California Eagle*, July 9, 1942, July 10, 1943; *NYT*, February 8, July 7, 1942, March 10, 1943; *Troy (N.Y.) Record*, May 5, 1943; *New York Post*, August 8, December 21, 1942; *Daily Worker* (New York), June 25, December 14, 1942; *Brooklyn (N.Y.) Daily Eagle*, November 16, 20, 1942, March 18, July 10, and September 17, 1943; *Herald Statesman* (Yonkers, N.Y.), November 25, 1942; *Kingston (N.Y.) Daily Freeman*, January 11, 1943; *Asbury Park (N.J.) Evening Press*, April 5, 1943; *Daily Home News* (New Brunswick, N.J.), April 30, May 4, 1943; *New York Herald Tribune*, April 19, September 23, 1943; *Ithaca (N.Y.) Journal*, September 14, 1943; *Courier-News* (Bridgewater, N.J.), October 6, 1943; "Liu Liangmo," FBI files, 100-47820, 100-201676-1/5, 61-7456-A.

78. Example entries: *Weekly Review*, September 29, 1942; *Lansing (Mich.) State Journal*, October 27, 1942; *Newark (Ohio) Advocate*, October 31, November 6, 1942; *Dispatch* (Moline, Ill.), October 10, December 8, 1942; *Daily Times* (Davenport, Iowa), December 9, 1942; *Brook (Ind.) Reporter*, December 24, 1942; *Canton (Penn.) Independent-Sentinel*, December 24, 1942; *Wilmington (Del.) Morning News*, March 17, 1941, January 15, 1943; *Evening News* (Harrisburg, Penn.), January 23, 1943; *News Journal* (Wilmington, Del.), February 17, 1943; *Gazette and Daily* (York, Penn.), March 19, 1943; *Cincinnati Enquirer*, May 2, October 25, 1943; *Suburbanite Economist* (Chicago), May 26, 30, 1943; *Hartford (Conn.) Daily Courant*, May 9, 1943; *Asheville (N.C.) Citizen*, June 18, 1943; *Times Herald* (Port Huron, Mich.), September 26, 1943; *Green Bay (Wisc.) Press-Gazette*, October 13, 1943; *Lancaster (Ohio) Eagle-Gazette*, November 6, 1943; *Philadelphia Inquirer*, October 15, 1943.

79. Edward Ballin to Liu Liangmo, January 7, April 24 and 28, 1944 (travel schedule for North Carolina, Ohio, and Indiana), UCRA; *News-Palladium* (Benton Harbor, Mich.), April 5, 8, 11, 12, 13, and 14, 1944.

80. List of meetings, Liu Liangmo, UCRA. Example entries: *Citizen Advertiser* (New York), March 14, May 31, 1944; *Herald Statesman* (Yonkers, N.Y.), April 11, 1944; *New York Sun*, May 13, 1944; *New York Age*, May 20, 1944; *Leader* (Corning, N.Y.), July 15, September 21, 1944; *Webster (N.Y.) Herald*, September 8, 1944; *Leader Republican* (New York), September 21, 1944; *Kingston (N.Y.) Daily Freeman*, September 20, December 7, 1944; *Brooklyn (N.Y.) Daily Eagle*, January 6, February 10, 1944; *Troy (N.Y.) Record*, January 11, 1944; *Pottstown (Penn.) Mercury*, February 25, 1944; *Courier-News* (Bridgewater, N.J.), March 16, 1944, February 14, 1945; *Daily Times* (Salisbury, Md.), March 31, 1944;

Morning Herald (Hagerstown, Md.), May 20, 1944; *Courier Journal* (Louisville, Ky.), May 14, June 8, 1944; *Baltimore Sun*, May 13, June 10, 1944; *Hartford (Conn.) Daily Courant*, June 17, 1944; *Des Moines (Iowa) Register*, August 21, 1944; *Rochester (N.Y.) Democrat and Chronicle*, July 4, September 9, 1944; *Ithaca (N.Y.) Journal*, September 16, 1944; *Morning Call* (Allentown, Penn.), November 17, 1944; *Detroit Free Press*, December 9, 1944; *Fort Lauderdale (Fla.) News*, January 11, 1945; *Miami (Fla.) Daily News*, January 11, September 30, 1945; *St. Petersburg (Fla.) Times*, January 13, 1945; *Clarion-Ledger* (Jackson, Miss.), April 15, 1945; *Delta Democrat-Times* (Greenville, Miss.), April 24, 1945; *Daily Press* (Newport News, Va.), May 13, 1945; *Berkshire Eagle* (Pittsfield, Mass.), July 10, 1945; *Binghamton (N.Y.) Press*, July 24, 1945; *Davenport (Iowa) Democrat and Leader*, August 13, 1945; *Minneapolis Star-Journal*, August 20, 1945; *Los Angeles Times*, September 12, 1945; *Ogden (Utah) Standard-Examiner*, September 17, 1945, September 21, 1955; *Salt Lake Tribune* (Salt Lake City, Utah), September 22, 1945; *Daily Herald* (Provo, Utah), September 23, 1945; *Morning Herald* (Uniontown, Penn.), October 2, 1945; *Wilmington (Del.) Morning News*, October 12, 1945; *Journal-Every Evening* (Wilmington, Del.), October 11, 1945.

81. "What They Say about Liu Liangmo," advertising statement, n.d. (ca. 1944), UCRA.

82. Works by Liu Liangmo: *Xiangei nü pengyou*; *Nüsheng* 1, no. 2 (1932): 5–6; 1, no. 7 (1933): 9–10; 3, no. 6 (1934): 25–26; *Nüduo* 22, no. 11 (April 1934): 3–8; 23, no. 1/2 (July 1934): 1–3; "Zenyang zuo xiandai zhongguo de zhangfu," *Nü qingnian yuekan* 14, no. 2 (1935): 9–13; *Changcheng* 2, no. 1 (1935): 16–17; 2, no. 9 (1935): 179–80; 2, no. 12 (1935): 235–37. Shilaide, "Nanzi jiao wo de," trans. by Liu Liangmo, *Nüsheng* 1, no. 6 (1932): 6–8. Liu Liangmo and Chen Weijiang, "Lian'ai yu hunyin," *Nü qingnian yuekan* 13, no. 7 (July 1934): 25–29; "Benshe jizhe Chen Weijiang nüshi nan you fu Gui," *Nüsheng* 1, no. 10 (1933): 20. Works by Chen Weijiang: *Nüsheng* 1, no. 15 (1933): 2–3; *Funü xunkan* 17, no. 15 (1933): 7–8; *Changcheng* 1, no. 1 (1934): 11–12; *Libao*, February 14, 1938; *Gudao* 1, no. 1 (1938): 19; *Nü qingnian yuekan* 13, no. 8 (1934): 35–38; 13, no. 10 (1934): 21–23; "Funü bushi ruozhe," *Nüduo* 22, no. 11 (1934): 1–3; "Ziqiang shi xuan," *Xiaoxi* 7, no. 7 (1934): 62; 8, no. 9 (1935): 1. Rudyard Kipling, "Jiaru," trans. by Chen Weijiang, *Xiaoxi* 8, no. 1 (1935): 64; *Xiaoxi* 8, no. 3 (1935): 53–54; Chen Weijing, trans., "Yonggan xie ba!," *Xiaojie* 6 (1937): 32, and *Nü qingnian yuekan* 14, no. 1 (1935): 65.

83. Roosevelt, *It's Up to the Women*; Chen Weijiang and Liu Liangmo, *Zhe shidai de nüren*; *Changcheng* 2, no. 11 (1935): 215; 2, no. 12 (1935): 241, 243. Liu met Eleanor Roosevelt at a "Youth of All Nations" meeting in New York City in early 1944. *Pittsburgh Courier*, March 25, 1944.

84. For comments on stocking movement, see *New York Post*, August 8, 1941.

85. "What They Say about Liu Liangmo," advertising statement, n.d. (ca. 1944), UCRA; "Former Chinese Army Morale Officer," the East and West Association, UCRA, group 5, series 1, box 3, PSBH.

86. *Herald Statesman* (Yonkers, N.Y.), May 11, 1942.

87. Liu to Garside, October 11, 1944, UCRA; *Daily Home News* (New Brunswick, N.J.), October 6 and 10, 1944; *Gazette and Daily* (York, Penn.), October 12, 1944; *Times-Leader* (Wilkes-Barre, Penn.), October 12, 1944; *News Journal* (Wilmington, Del.), October 11, 1944; "Liu Liangmo," FBI files, 100-47820, 100-201676-1/5, 61-7456-A.

88. Liu to Conaughy, July 19, 1944, Ballin to Liu, December 5, 1945, UCRA; *Vassar Chronicle*, October 13, 1945; "Liu Liangmo," FBI files, 100-201676-8, 100-201676-11. On Avenue Edward VII, see Hahn, *Soong Sisters*, 33. Hindus, *Red Bread*; Xinzi, *Su'e de shenghuo*; Jianbai, "Su'e de shenghuo," trans. by Chen Weijiang, *Liangcai Liutong*

Tushuguan guankan 10 (May 1937): 5; Eliat jaue way, "Moxige, Dongjing, Bolin yu meiyou zhouxin," trans. by Chen Weijiang, *Guomin gongbao* (new year supplement) (1939): 43–44; "Sulian zai Yuandong de diwei," trans. by Chen Weijiang, *Zhengzhi qingbao* 27 (1938): 7–9, and *Gongyu banyue kan* 5 (1938): 16–18; Latourette, *Toward a World Christian Fellowship*; Chen Weijiang, *Zenyang cujin shijie Jidutu tuanqi*.

89. *Vassar Chronicle*, October 13, 1945; "Liu Liangmo," FBI files, PH 100-29204, 100-201676–8/11.

90. Liu to Conaughy, July 19, 1944, Ballin to Liu, December 5, 1945, UCRA; *New York Herald Tribune*, March 23, 1945; *Daily Worker* (New York), May 26, 1945.

91. *Vassar Chronicle*, October 13, 1945; "Liu Liangmo," FBI files, PH 100-29204, 100-201676-8/11; *Morning Call* (Allentown, Penn.), October 29, 1945; *Asbury Park (N.J.) Press*, November 7 and 13, 1945, November 10, 1985; *Newburgh (N.Y.) News*, June 16, 1945.

92. "Liu Liangmo," FBI files, NY 100-47820, or Bureau file 100-201676-5/10.

93. Liu, "Suggestions to New Missionaries," Divinity Library, Yale University Library; Liu, Statement of Beliefs, October 22, 1944, UCRA.

94. Edward Ballin to Liu, November 29, December 5 and 26, 1945, January 9 and 21, February 25 (Kong), 1946, UCRA; *Nassau (N.Y.) Daily Review-Star*, February 7, 1945; *Herald Statesman* (Yonkers, N.Y.), February 2, 4, 1946; *Kingston (N.Y.) Daily Freeman*, February 8, 15, and 19, 1946; *News-Chronicle* (Shippensburg, Penn.), March 1 and 8, 1946; *Evening News* (Harrisburg, Penn.), February 23 and March 1, 1946; *Sentinel* (Carlisle, Penn.), March 2 and 7, 1946; *NYT*, April 27, 1946. Some of Liu's speeches in Syracuse were cosponsored by UCR and the Syracuse-in-China Association. *Syracuse (N.Y.) Herald American*, January 13, 1946; *Post-Standard* (Syracuse, N.Y.), January 13 and 15, 1946.

95. *Oswego (N.Y.) Palladium-Times*, August 2, 1946; "Second 'Hootenanny': Songs of Freedom of Various Origins Sung at Town Hall," *NYT*, May 17, 1946.

96. Clipping from *New York World-Telegram*, June 28, 1946, UCRA. On American politics, see Patterson, *Grand Expectations*, 105–37.

97. Helen Cornelius to Eric J. Cudd, August 20, 22, and 23, 1946, UCRA.

98. Edward M. Ballin to Liu, Office Memorandum, January 7, 1944, UCRA.

99. B. A. Garside to Helen Cornelius, August 26, 1946, UCRA.

100. The FBI spelled Liu's name variously as Liu Liang-mo, Lin Liang-mo, Liang Mo Liu, and Liang Mo Lin, and his wife's as Chen Wei-Cing or Liu Chen Wei-giang, and noted her birthdate as July 29, 1908. "Liu Liangmo," FBI files, WFO 100-16298, Bureau files 100-201676-1/5/6/7/8/9/10/11, PH 100-29204, NY 100-47820, Seattle 100-17389.

101. "Liu Liangmo, Visa, 1940, Form of Chinese Student Certificate"; Boyd to Liu, August 17, 1946; Bonham to Liu, October 3, 1946; Garside to Spengler, October 19, 1946, February 14, 1947; George Tyler to Liu, November 21, 1946, January 14, 1947; all in UCRA.

102. "China's Wartime Education Adjustments," *China at War*, August 1941, 70–73.

103. Edison to Chang, February 25, 1947; Liu to Garside, February 27, 1947; Garside to Chang, March 4, 1947; Chang to Edison, March 5, 1947; all in UCRA. For a photograph of Liu and Sah, inscribed by Liu, and their correspondence, see https://auction.artron .net/paimai-art5147765444/ (accessed February 11, 2021). Writer Bingxin's father was a colleague of Sah in the Fuzhou navy. Xie Bingxin, "Ji Sa Zhenbing xiansheng," http:// tieba.baidu.com/p/2081647777 (accessed May 23, 2017).

104. "Chinese Patriot in Plea for Aid," *Minneapolis Star-Journal*, April 19, 1947; Liu Xin, "Zhishi chuanjia, jingsheng zhuhun," in *Liu Liangmo xiansheng jinian wenji*, 432–33.

105. Garside to Liu, January 2, 1948, UCRA; *NYT*, January 20, 1947; Example entries:

New York Post, February 15, 1947; *Council Bluffs (Iowa) Nonpareil*, March 21, 1947; *Cincinnati Enquirer*, March 24 and May 17, 1947; *China Press*, March 25, 1947; *Great Falls (Mont.) Tribune*, March 25, 1947; *Hartford (Conn.) Daily Courant*, March 24, 1947; *Albuquerque (N.M.) Journal*, March 24, 1947; *Ogden (Utah) Standard-Examiner*, March 27, 1947; *Minneapolis Star-Journal*, April 19, 1947; *Pittsburgh Press*, October 25, 1947; *Pittsburgh Post-Gazette*, October 25, 1947; *Brooklyn (N.Y.) Daily Eagle*, October 28, 1947. Liu spoke on behalf of the World Student Service Fund at Carroll College in Waukesha, Wisconsin; Carnegie Hall in Lewisburg, West Virginia; Triple Cities College (SUNY-Binghamton); Hobart and William Smith Colleges in Geneva, New York; Russell Sage College in Troy, New York; Wilkes College in Wilkes-Barre, Pennsylvania; and Olivet College in Olivet, Michigan. *Waukesha (Wisc.) Daily Freeman*, February 23, 1949; *Binghamton (N.Y.) Press*, April 5, 1949; *Geneva (N.Y.) Daily Times*, April 15, 1949; *Times-Leader* (Wilkes-Barre, Penn.), April 14, 1949; *Wilkes-Barre (Penn.) Record*, March 24, 1947, April 22, 1949; *Times Record* (New York), May 2 and 3, 1949; *Olivet (Mich.) Optic*, February 24 and May 26, 1949. On UCR's dramatic drop in fundraising, see Jesperson, *American Images*, 153–55.

106. Mei Lanfang, Liu Wang Liming, C. P. Sah (Liu Liangmo's grandfather-in-law), and Weiching William Yen also attended the First NPPCC. Liu Liangmo voluntarily swapped his official membership with the alternate one of Ma Jian, the only Muslim representative at the conference. *RR*, September 22 and 28, 1949.

107. Liu Liangmo, "Yi kang Ri jiuwang geyong yundong," *Renmin yinyue* 6 (1980): 16–20, 26; Liu Liangmo, "Meiguo de jingji konghuang"; *Beckley (W.Va.) Post-Herald*, February 12, 1949.

108. "Liu Liangmo," FBI files, 100-2016676-22/23.

109. Example entries: *RR*, May 13, September 22, 23, and 26, December 30, 1949, February 22, 1956, April 15, 1958, April 18, 1959, December 14, 21, and 30, 1964, January 3, 1965, February 26, 1978, October 26, 1979, January 5, 1980, August 21, 1981, September 25, 1982, May 2 and 8, June 18, August 27, December 28, 1983, January 9, 1987.

110. Example entries: Liu Liangmo, "Zhongguo Jidujiao ge jiaohui," *RR*, April 25, 1951; Liu Liangmo, "Jiaqiang ziwo gaizao," *RR*, April 6, 1960, and *Tianfeng* 9, May 9, 1960, 13; Situleideng, "Xisheng xiaowo," *Tianfeng*, March 1, 1947; Situleideng, "Xiwang de jichu," *Tianfeng*, January 10, 1948; Song Meiling, "Nü Qingnianhui shigong yu guoji zhixu," *Tianfeng*, October 18, 1947.

111. Books by Liu Liangmo: *Mao Zedong Sixiang xuexi shouce; Renmin Zhengxie yu sanda wenjian xuexi shouce; Xin minzhu zhuyi xuexi shouce; Shenmo shi tongyi zhanxian*. Lovell, *Maoism*, 51.

112. *RR*, August 30, September 2 and 25, 1949.

113. Liu Liangmo, "Meiguo de jinbu liliang"; Hu Jiangshan, "*Xinhua shishi congkan* jinian Shimotelai," *RR*, June 21, 1950; "Shimotelai guhui yun Beijing," *RR*, February 13, 1951; "Liu Liangmo," FBI files, 100-2016676-22/23.

114. Works by Liu Liangmo: "Meiguo de jingji konghuang"; "Meiguo de fan Su fan gong kuang"; "Shou mengbi de Meiguo renmin"; "Liu Mei qiaobao shijiu tuanti kangyi Mei . . . ," *RR*, September 4, 1949.

115. Works by Liu Liangmo: "Shou mengbi de Meiguo renmin"; "Meiguo dui huaqiao de wuru."

116. Works by Liu Liangmo: "China Speaks!," *Pittsburgh Courier*, October 17, 1942 (on Lee and Douglass); November 21, 1942 (on Walker); January 23, 1943 (on Robeson and Anderson, whose concert at the Constitution Hall, sponsored by Eleanor Roosevelt, on

January 7, 1943, raised $6,500 for UCR); September 25, 1943 (on Carver); "Meiguo dui Heiren de qishi."

117. Works by Liu Liangmo: "Renmin geshou Luoboxun"; "Luoboxun yu 'Yiyongjun jinxing qu'"; "Wei zhandou de Zhongguo renmin gechang," *RR*, April 9, 1958; "Zhongguo kangzhan gequ zai Meiguo."

118. Works by Liu Liangmo: "Guanyu yuanzidan ji qita"; *RR*, April 29, 1949, June 30, 1950.

119. Works by Liu Liangmo: "Jinda qingshuan Mei di yundong"; "Tuijian *Heping wansui*," *Tianfeng*, January 24, 1953; "Tuijian *Ke'ai de Zhongguo*," *Tianfeng*, February 11, 1953; "Jianjue yonghu Chaoxian tingzhan," *Tianfeng*, August 10, 1953; "Jidujiao zai Kang Mei Yuan Chao zhong de nuli," *Tianfeng*, August 31, 1953; *RR*, October 4, 1949, January 18, and March 4, 1951, October 3 and November 9, 1952, July 1, 1965. "Liu Liangmo," FBI files, 100-2016676-22/23.

120. Liu Liangmo, *Wo suo zhidao de Meiguo*, 1–4.

121. "Zhongguo Jidujiao fabiao xuanyan," *RR*, September 23, 1950; "Zhongguo Jidujiao, Tianzhujiao renshi de aiguo yundong," *RR*, December 20, 1950; "Jianjue xiezhu zhengfu suqing Meidi," *RR*, January 7, 1951; "Shanghai Jidujiao renshi fabiao xuanyan," *RR*, January 8, 1951; "Chuli jieshou Meiguo jintie . . . ," *RR*, April 22, 1951.

122. Liu Liangmo, *Meiguo zenyang liyong zongjiao qinglue Zhongguo*, especially "Jinda qingshuan Mei di yundong."

123. *RR*, April 17, 1951; Liu Liangmo, "Zhongguo Jidujiao ge jiaohui ge tuanti daibiao lianhe xuanyan," *RR*, April 25, 1951.

124. Example Works by Liu Liangmo: *Tianfeng*, September 8, 1951, January 12, March 1, June 28, and May 17, 1952; Songs by Liu Liangmo, Liu Xingzhi, and Qian Songying: "Sanzi gexing ge," *Tianfeng*, April 28, 1951; "Qilai! Quan Zhongguo xintu" and "Zhongguo de jiaohui," *Tianfeng*, May 26, 1951.

125. "Jidujiao renshi Wu Yaozong, Deng Yuzhi, Liu Liangmo dui Gu Ren'en shijian fabiao tanhua," *RR*, April 5, 1951. Example works by Liu Liangmo: "Zenyang kaihao kongsuhui," *Tianfeng* May 19, 1951; "Sipo le zongjiao waiyi," *Tianfeng*, July 13, 1953. Lee, "Co-optation and Its Discontents."

126. Liu Liangmo, "Boxia Hu Feng de 'yangpi,'" *Tianfeng*, July 11, 1955. For a similar incident later, see "Zai Shehui zhuyi fan youpai douzheng dahui shang," *RR*, July 7, 1957.

127. Works by Liu Liangmo: "Xuexi Maozedong Sixiang, jiaqiang ziwo gaizao," *Tianfeng*, February 27, 1961, 27; *Tianfeng*, June 30 and December 1, 1958; *RR*, April 5, 1960, January 22, 1961; "Zhishi fenzi bixu jiasu ziwo gaizao," *Xueshu yuekan* 1 (1959): 35; "Chongdu shinian qian de 'Liu ping baipishu,'" *Xueshu yuekan* 10 (1959): 38-41. "Jiaqiang ziwo gaizao genshang Yuejin xingshi: Liu Liangmo weiyuan de fayan," *RR*, April 6, 1960.

128. Works by Liu Liangmo: "Dao Anhui qu canguan," *Tianfeng*, June 25, 1956; "Cong 'wan jin dao' tanqi," *Xueshu yuekan* 9 (1958): 36–37; "Xiashou shijie fang Xuxing," *Tianfeng*, June 27, 1961; "Gaijin taomi fa keyi jiesheng liangshi," *RR*, March 26, 1957; "Anhui Gaofeng She shiyantian kaifang da honghua," *RR*, August 10, 1958.

129. "Ya Fei Tuanjie Dahui daibiaotuan zucheng," *RR*, December 13, 1957.

130. Liu Liangmo, "Jianqiang de heping zhanshi Duboyisi Boshi," *Tianfeng* 4, March 2, 1959, 17–21.

131. "Daochu huanchang hongse gequ," *RR*, April 26, 1958; "Yong geming de gesheng guwu qunzhong jianshe shehui zhuyi reqing," *RR*, April 15, 1963. Liu Liangmo, "Huiyi jiuwang geyong yundong," *Renmin yinyue* 7 (1957): 24–27; 8 (1957): 18.

132. *RR*, May 22, 1966, July 9, 1973, November 6 and 13, 1977, November 13, 1982, November 13, 1983.

133. Salz, "Thunder of 10,000 Voices"; Linda Mathews, "Christian Clergy Emerge in Peking after a Decade of Forced Oblivion," *Los Angeles Times*, March 5, 1978; *Des Moines (Iowa) Register*, March 5, 1978; *Albuquerque (N.M.) Journal*, April 29, 1978; *Minneapolis Star-Journal*, March 10, 1978; *Honolulu Star-Bulletin*, March 11, 1978; *Tampa (Fla.) Times*, April 1, 1978.

134. "Shanghai shi renda daibiao . . . ," *RR*, April 21, 1981.

CHAPTER 4

1. Hughes, *I Wonder as I Wander*, 256.

2. "Sylvia Si-lan Chen," FBI files 100-30551, April 19, 1950, box 28, folder 1, JSCL (all FBI files cited in this chapter are from this source); *New York Post*, January 25, 1938.

3. Paul Robeson, "Conversation about the New China," *Freedom*, May 1951.

4. Si-lan recalled that, due to her mother's "age-wangling" to help her secure a dancing job in London, she was not "absolutely sure" of her birth year. Her death certificate and 1949 application for naturalization listed 1905 and 1909, respectively. Entry for Silan Chen Leyda, "California Death Index, 1940–1997," March 8, 1996, Department of Public Health Services, Sacramento. The 1940 U.S. Population Census registered her "estimated birth year" as 1910. Archives, "Silan Chen Leyda in the 1940 U.S. Population Census," http://www.archives.com/1940-census/silan-leyda-ny-57602177k. Since her younger brother, Jack, was born on July 3, 1908, her birth date was most likely March 20, 1905. Chen Yuan-tsung, *Minguo waijiao qiangren Chen Youren*, 14–20, 27–31, 43; Si-lan Chen Leyda, *Footnote to History*, 1–4. To distinguish members of the Chen family, I refer to them by their first names in this chapter.

5. Das, *Katherine Dunham*; Schwartz and Schwartz, *Dance Claimed Me*; Franko, *Work of Dance*, 86; Wilcox, *Revolutionary Bodies*. Shay and Sellers-Young, *Oxford Handbook of Dance and Ethnicity*, does not have an entry on China or Chinese Americans. Another noted dancer of Chinese and Black ancestry was Lily Yuen, born to Ton Yuen, an immigrant from Hong Kong who ran a laundry business, and an African American mother in Savannah, Georgia. *Afro American News*, June 20, 1925. Jennifer Wilson, "Overlooked No More: Si-lan Chen, Whose Dances Encompassed Worlds," *NYT*, May 27, 2020.

6. In the West Indies, Joseph Guixin Chen's nickname, A-Kan, was corrupted to Acham as his official family name, while the real family name, Chen, reverted to household use only. Chen Leyda, *Footnote to History*, 1. "Eugene Chen Gained His Start in Trinidad," *NYT*, April 16, 1927.

7. Chen Leyda, *Footnote to History*, 5–19. Many graduates of Stedman's Academy became first-rate ballet performers, and the famed dancer Lydia Sokolova was hired by the Imperial Russian ballet. Sokolova, *Dancing for Diaghliev*, 6–11.

8. Chen Leyda, *Footnote to History*, 29–37; "Sylvia Si-lan Chen," FBI files, 100-30551, January 27, 1951, and May 20, 1952.

9. Chen Leyda, *Footnote to History*, 10–12, 20–21, 24–25; Chen Yuan-tsung, *Minguo waijiao qiangren Chen Youren*, 41–44; "Sylvia Si-lan Chen," FBI files, 100-30551, January 27, 1951.

10. Chen Yuan-tsung, *Minguo waijiao qiangren Chen Youren*, 27–31, 40–43, 136, 211. H. H. Brayton Barff, "Eugene Chen," *NYT*, April 10, 1927.

11. Chen Leyda, *Footnote to History*, 40–49; "Sylvia Si-lan Chen," FBI files, 100-30551, January 27, 1951. Percy's account of the siblings' journey to China was somewhat different. Chen, *China Called Me*, 28–58.

12. Chen Leyda, *Footnote to History*, 55–69, 75.

13. *Illustrated London News*, January 22, 1927; *Lincoln (N.C.) Herald*, February 18, 1927; *Pittsburgh Press*, April 3, 1927; *Danville (Penn.) Morning News*, May 5, 1927; *Palm Beach (Fla.) Post*, April 4, 1927; *Clarion-Ledger* (Jackson, Miss.), May 6, 1927; *Evening News* (Wilkes Barre, Penn.), May 6, 1927; *Salem (Ohio) News*, May 4, 1927; *Indiana Gazette*, May 9, 1927; *Monroe (La.) News Star*, May 12, 1927; *Courier Journal* (Louisville, Ky.), May 14, 1927; *Minnesota Star*, May 23, 1927; *Honolulu Advertiser*, May 22, 1927; *Index Journal* (Greenwood, S.C.), May 26, 1927; *Santa Ana (Calif.) Register*, June 21, 1927; *Tampa (Fla.) Times*, June 8, 1927. Chen Leyda, *Footnote to History*, 47, 64, 67–68.

14. Chen Leyda, *Footnote to History*, 51–52, 57, 60–61, 76.

15. Chen Leyda, *Footnote to History*, 47–51, 55, 75.

16. Chen Leyda, *Footnote to History*, 68–69.

17. "Gemin zhengfu zhi waijiao," *Xinghua* 24, no. 7 (1927): 38–40; "Waijian paohun Nanjing shijian zhi zhongyao wenjian," *Dongfang zazhi* 24, no. 7 (1927): 95; "Guomin zhengfu waijiao buzhang Chen Youren zhi duiwai xuanyan," and "Han Xun Ying zujie jiaoshe xieding quanwen," *Dongfang zazhi* 24, no. 4 (1927): 104–7 (originally in *Shenbao*); Dezheng, "Chen Youren de waijiao baogao," *Xingqi pinglun* 2 (1928): 20–25; "Han an zhi sheying," *Liangyou* 12 (1927): 6; Chen Jinyu, trans., "Wairen muzhong zhi Chen Youren," *Qingnian you* 7, no. 6 (1927): 8–12; "The Independent Tattler," *Independent Weekly* 1, no. 3 (1925): 5; Qiubai, "Ji Chen Youren"; "Chen Youren yishi"; H. H. Brayton Barff, "Eugene Chen," *NYT*, April 10, 1927.

18. Chen Leyda, *Footnote to History*, 77–78, 83–85.

19. Paying a monthly rent of 120 rubles for each room, the Chen siblings made their home in suite 4 of the grand Hotel Metropole on Ploscaad Sverdlova facing Theater Square, where most African American tourists stayed. Si-lan occupied room 431, Jack, 439, and Percy, 485, before he moved to 7 Bolshoi Komsomolskii Pereulok. Chen Leyda, *Footnote to History*, 83–107, 147–55. "Sylvia Si-lan Chen," FBI files, 100-30551, January 27, 1951; "My Relatives," by Sylvia, 1944, box 29, folder 5; Jack to Sylvia, June 15, 1931, box 28, folder 12; Eugene to Sylvia, March 25, 1930, November 17, 1931, box 28, folder 10; all in JSCL; Chen, *China Called Me*, 181–242; Hughes, *I Wonder as I Wander*, 256.

20. "Sylvia Si-lan Chen," FBI files, 100-30551, January 27, 1951; "My Relatives," by Sylvia, 1944, box 29, folder 5; Jack to Sylvia, June 15, 1931, box 28, folder 12; both in JSCL.

21. Chen Leyda, *Footnote to History*, 112–18, 123–28, 147–50, 155–57, 164, 168–75.

22. Chen Leyda, *Footnote to History*, 128–47 183–86, 200; Chen to Hughes, early 1934, May 11, and June 26, 1934, Sylvia Chen 1934–46, series I, Personal Correspondence, box 43, folder 770, LHP (all correspondence from Chen to Hughes is from this source, unless otherwise noted); Mukerji, "Like Another Planet."

23. Fitzpatrick, *Cultural Front*, 136–50; Ezrahi, *Swans of the Kremlin*, 27, 60–62.

24. Chen Leyda, *Footnote to History*, 119–25, 134–43. For photographs by Grinberg, see https://unregardoblique.home.blog/tag/alexander-danilovich-grinberg/ or https://dantebea.files.wordpress.com/2013/11/alexander-grinberg-the-dancer-sylvia-chen-via-mutualart.jpeg (accessed April 26, 2018).

25. Eugene to Sylvia, March 25, 1930, November 17, 1931, box 28, folder 10, JSCL.

26. "Sylvia Si-lan Chen," FBI files, 100-30551, May 20, 1952; Jack to Sylvia, July 10, 1931,

box 28, folder 12; Eugene to Sylvia, November 17, 1931, box 28, folder 10; all in JSCL. Chen Leyda, *Footnote to History*, 163–64.

27. Chen Leyda, *Footnote to History*, 153–54, 158–60.

28. Chen Leyda, *Footnote to History*, 143–47, 151–53, 178, 183–86, 200; Chen to Hughes, May 11 and June 26, 1934.

29. Chen Leyda, *Footnote to History*, 50–51, 68–80, 153–54, 177–79, 208–14; Chen to Hughes, May 11 and June 26, 1934; Jack to Sylvia, July 10, 1931, box 28, folder 12; JSCL; "Sylvia Si-lan Chen," FBI files, 100-30551, May 20, 1952; Robeson, "I Want to Be African"; Buck, *My Several Worlds*, 321–28.

30. Chen to Hughes, June 31, 1934, LHP-HL, mssHM 64089; Chen to Hughes, December 3, 1934, June 14, 1935; Chen Leyda, *Footnote to History*, 188, 196–97.

31. Jack to Sylvia, July 10, 1931, box 28, folder 12; 1932 Moscow scrapbook, box 30, folder 9; both in JSCL; Chen to Hughes, December 3, 1934; Chen Leyda, *Footnote to History*, 123–25, 161, 196–97.

32. Chen Leyda, *Footnote to History*, 51, 119–21, 141–43, 168–71, 202–3. Leyda to Koch, [1977], box 29, folder 5; photographs of Si-lan Chen by Soichi Sunami, box 35; all in JSCL.

33. Chen Leyda, *Footnote to History*, 155–57, 164, 178, 191–92; Chen to Hughes, June 26, 1934.

34. "The Independent Tattler," *Independent Weekly* 1, no. 3 (1925): 5; "Chen Youren yingzhao dao Nanjing," *Guowen zhoubao* 8, no. 8 (1931): 1–2; Qiubai, "Ji Chen Youren"; "Chen Youren yishi."

35. "Zhongyang qidai Yue wei ru Jing," *Yishi bao*, November 28, 1931; "Sun Ke Chen Youren fu Yue," *Xinghua* 28, no. 19 (1931): 38; "Sun Ke Chen Youren deng di Yue," *Xinghua* 28, no. 44 (1931): 35–36; "Chen Youren fufu dao Ri," *Xinghua* 28, no. 28 (1931): 47–48; "Chen Youren bushu fu Ri jingguo," *Zhonghua zhoubao* 8 (1931): 128–29; Eugene to Sylvia, November 17, 1931, box 28, folder 10, JSCL.

36. "London Observer Praises Talent of Eugene Chen," *Independent Weekly* 1, no. 48 (1932): 9; "Chen Youren dui xieding zhi piping," *Zhonghua zhoubao* 28 (1932): 11; "Dui Ri juejiao wenti de douzheng," *Guomin gonglun* (Hankou), January 28, 1932, 525; *Shangbao huakan* 3, no. 27 (1932): 3; "Chen Youren cizhi," *Gongjiao zhoukan* 146 (1932): 16; *Xin shehui* 5, no. 12 (1933): 1; Zhen, "Chen Youren mishu Zhang Ke," *Shehui xinwen* 5, no. 25 (1933): 388; Gan, "Chen Youren yanjiu Tuoluosi," *Shehui xinwen* 5, no. 25 (1933): 390–91. Eugene continued to voice his opinions on China's diplomacy. He urged the government to lobby the League of Nations for a steep penalty to prevent Japan from encroaching into North China, and to cooperate with India and the United States to boycott Japanese goods. He warned the Soviet Union against selling Manchuria railroads to Japan. Yiji, "Yi zhou jian guonei yaowen," *Xunhuan* 3, no. 8 (1933): 14; "Chen Youren duiwai xuanyan," *Gongjiao zhoukan* 214 (1933): 15–16; "Qian Waizhang Chen Youren," *Zhongyang zhoubao* 254 (1933): 18–20.

37. "Jun jiang chu yang youli," *Shenbao*, March 11, 1932; "Chen Youren yishi." "Shiren jinying," *Liangyou* 63 (1931): 16; 57 (1931): cover and 11; *Shishi yuebao*, April 1931.

38. "The Independent Tattler," *Independent Weekly* 1, no. 3 (1925): 5; Xixi, "Chen Youren zhen chumai Dong Sansheng," *Riben pinglun sanri kan* 9 (1931): 5; Mo, "Buke ceduo zhi Chen Youren," *Shehui xinwen* 3, no. 19 (1933): 1; Meizi, "Zhang Liying xiajia Chen Youren zhuiji"; Juefei, "Chen Youren zhi mingming," *Qingtian huikan* 1 (1930): 8; Jin, "Chen Youren you yao xian di er ke zhadan," *Huaqiao banyue kan* 24 (1933): 28; *Zhongyang ribao*, May 23, 1933.

39. Meizi, "Zhang Liying xiajia Chen Youren zhuiji"; "Chen Youren yu qizi," *Laoshi hua* 31 (1934): 447; Lee, *Ethnic Avant-Garde*, 124.

40. Eugene to Sylvia, November 17, 1931, box 28, folder 10, JSCL; Hughes to Chen, January 1934, July 7, 1934, June 1, 1936, box 29, folder 4, JSCL, and in Rampersad, Roessel, and Fratantoro, *Selected Letters of Langston Hughes*, 157–58; Chen to Hughes, early 1934, June 26 and December 3, 1934, June 14 and August 2, 1935, February 28, 1936; Chen Leyda, *Footnote to History*, 165–66, 206.

41. Chen to Hughes, early 1934; Eugene to Sylvia, March 25, 1930, box 28, folder 10, JSCL. According to Si-lan, Percy's unspecified "senseless" behaviors led Jack to sever all relations with him, and the two returned separately to the Soviet Union through Europe. "It took many years to heal this breach." Chen Leyda, *Footnote to History*, 154–55. In his autobiography, Percy briefly mentioned the brotherly dispute over seeking funds from Madam Sun Yat-sen. Chen, *China Called Me*, 221–23.

42. Eugene to Sylvia, November 17, 1931, box 28, folder 10; Si-lan Chen passports, box 28, folder 3; all in JSCL.

43. Readers were reminded that Percy was far ahead of his father, "who could only read official documents translated into English." The magazines *Young Companion Pictorial* and *The Great Wall* featured photographs of Percy and the "daughter-in-law of Chen Youren" in high fashion, holding the Kangxi emperor's helmet stored in the Small Temple in Hohhot. Meizi, "Zhang Liying xiajia Chen Youren zhuiji"; "Overseas Events," *Dazhong huabao* 7 (1934): 5; "Wenren zai Su'e," *Liangyou* 77 (1933): 32; *Changcheng* (Suiyuan)1, no. 2 (1935): 1; "Sylvia Si-lan Chen," FBI files, 100-30551, January 27, 1951.

44. "Renwu zhi: Feisheng Ouzhou wutai de Chen Youren nü," *Liangyou* 81 (1933): 19; "Haiwai huaqiao shiling," *Liangyou* 84 (1934): 19; Gui, "Chen Youren de shanwu nü'er," *Linglong* 3 (41): 1933; "Chen Youren nü zai E tiaowu," *Linglong* 4, no. 2 (1934): 116; "Chen Youren nü gongzi jiang zi E huiguo biaoyan," *Linglong* 5, no. 181 (1935): 874–75; "Shejiao renwu," *Sheying huabao* 9, no. 27 (1933): 14; *Shenghuo huabao* 2 (1933): 53; 26 (1933), 1; "Chen Youren you nü shanwu," *Laoshi hua* 22 (1934): 197. *Shanghai Evening Post & Mercury*, January 17 and September 25, 1933.

45. Chen to Hughes, May 8 and June 14, 1935; "Sylvia Si-lan Chen," FBI files, 100-30551, April 19, 1950; "Zhu E dashiguan," *Shenbao*, October 16, 1935; Chen Yuan-tsung, *Minguo waijiao qiangren Chen Youren*, 334; Chen Leyda, *Footnote to History*, 200–229.

46. Chen to Hughes, February 28, 1936; Chen Leyda, *Footnote to History*, 196, 208–11, 215–16; *Mei Lanfang and Chinese Drama*, box 33, folder 17, JSCL.

47. Chen Leyda, *Footnote to History*, 218–19.

48. Chen Leyda, *Footnote to History*, 147–51; Eugene to Sylvia, September 16, 1930, box 28, folder 10, JSCL.

49. After divorcing Maillard, Percy married Musya (Mucia) Lukina; and Jack married Lucy Flaxman in 1931. Si-lan dismissed Lukina as the daughter of a Soviet peasant family, but Percy portrayed her as Si-lan's fellow student at the Lunacharsky Theatrical Technicum and daughter of "a Hero of Labor in Gorki on the Volgabi." Percy and Lukina later had a daughter, Eugene Marie, whom Si-lan credited for restoring "a close relationship to a brother whom I had nearly lost." Flaxman had immigrated with her parents, American Jews from Brooklyn ("the man some sort of technical advisor, the woman just a housewife," recalled Hughes), in 1917. Flaxman attended the Duncan School in Moscow. Yolanda married Alexander Shura Shelenkov (1903–96), a director, writer, and fellow cameraman for whom she worked as an assistant at the Mezhrabpofil'm in

the spring of 1932. They lived at Flat 7, House 9, Stankevich Street, in Moscow for most of their lives. Chen Leyda, *Footnote to History*, 150–55, 163; Chen, *China Called Me*, 200–202; Hughes, *I Wonder as I Wander*, 203. Chen to Hughes, June 26 and December 3, 1934; "Sylvia Si-lan Chen," FBI files, 100-30551, April 19, 1950, January 27, 1951, and May 20, 1952.

50. Eugene to Sylvia, November 17, 1931, box 28, folder 10, JSCL.

51. Chen Leyda, *Footnote to History*, 222–29.

52. "Sylvia Si-lan Chen," FBI files, 100-30551, January 27, 1951; Chen Leyda, *Footnote to History*, 154–55, 216–20. "Sylvia Chen Ill," *Shanghai Evening Post & Mercury*, December 28, 1935; "Soviet Women Lecture Topic," *North-China Daily News*, January 9, 1936; "Sylvia Chen Tells Status of Russian Women," *China Press*, January 10, 1936; "Sylvia Chen Sails, to Dance Here Later," *China Press*, January 26, 1936. It seemed that Percy was well established in Shanghai's political and cultural circles. The *Shanghai Daily* described "the oldest son of Chen Youren, as a dark-faced stout man speaking a foreign language," who rubbed shoulders with the painter Xu Beihong and the dramatist Ouyang Yuqian at a gathering presided by Shanghai mayor Wu Tiecheng. Jiping, "Jing Hu wenyi jie lianhuan suoji," *Shenbao*, April 27, 1936. On Lin's interactions with Eugene, see Lin Yutang, *Lin Yutang zizhuan*, https://www.kanunu8.com/book3/7604/167067.html, chap. 7.

53. Chen Yuan-tsung, *Minguo waijiao qiangren Chen Youren*, 334; Chen Leyda, *Footnote to History*, 220–29; Chen to Hughes, August 16, 1936; "Sylvia Si-lan Chen," FBI files, 100-30551, January 27, 1951; Si-lan Chen passports, box 28, folder 3, JSCL; *China Press*, September 6, 1936.

54. Both Si-lan's autobiography and *Essays in Honor of Jay Leyda* state that they married in 1934, but her immigration files list the date as July 10, 1936, days before Leyda returned to the United States. Since he had mentioned his break with "Carol" back in New York City when he first met Si-lan, they were probably not officially married until his divorce was finalized. Greenbaum Wolf & Ernst Office Memorandum, Reinhardt to Ernst, re: "Letter from Jay Leyda," February 2, 1937; Leyda to Si-lan Chen, n.d., box 29, folder 5, JSCL; "Sylvia Si-lan Chen," FBI files, 100-30551, May 20, 1952; "Jay Leyda: A Brief History"; Chen Leyda, *Footnote to History*, 175–99, 204–5, 222–29; Andrew L. Yarrow, "Jay Leyda, Film Historian, Writer and a Student of Sergei Eisenstein," *NYT*, February 18, 1988.

55. Chen Leyda, *Footnote to History*, 188, 222–29.

56. Here Chen is speaking of the Miora Palace in St. Petersburg, where Felix Yusupov took part in the murder of Rasputin. Chen to Hughes, August 29, 1934, LHP-HL, mssHM 64070–64101; Chen to Hughes, December 3, 1934, August 2 and 16, 1936; Chen Leyda, *Footnote to History*, 188, 196–97.

57. Chen to Hughes, February 28 and August 16, 1936.

58. Chen Leyda, *Footnote to History*, 222–29.

59. Langston Hughes, "That Powerful Drop," in *Simple Takes a Wife*, 201.

60. Chen to Hughes, August 29, 1934, and February 28, 1936; Hughes to Chen, October 18, 1934, and June 1, 1936, box 29, folder 4, JSCL; and in Rampersad, Roessel, and Fratantoro, *Selected Letters of Langston Hughes*, 163–65. P. C. Chang, Hughes's fellow Columbia University alumnus and likely acquaintance, directed Mei Lanfang's tour in the United States in 1930. Gao Yunxiang, "Soo Yong."

61. "Sylvia Si-lan Chen," FBI files, 100-30551, April 19, 1950; Leyda to Chen on MoMA letterhead, December 1936, box 29, folder 5, JSCL. While fighting for her visa to the United States in London, Si-lan heard of the Xi'an Incident, which forced the tentative united front between the Nationalist and Communist Parties against Japan. She turned her gaze

toward the ancestral home, wondering where Eugene was and whether he could serve China again. Chen Leyda, *Footnote to History*, 231, 235, 299. On December 7, 1936, the Chinese embassy in Moscow extended Si-lan's passport to January 14, 1938. Si-lan Chen passports, box 28, folder 3, JSCL.

62. Greenbaum Wolf & Ernst Office Memorandum, Reinhardt to Ernst, re: "Letter from Jay Leyda," February 2, 1937, box 29, folder 5, JSCL.

63. "Sylvia Acham-Chen-Leyda," Outward Passenger Lists, BT 27, Records of the Board of Trade and of Successor and Related Bodies, National Archives, Kew, Richmond, Surrey, England; "Passenger Lists of Vessels Arriving at New York, 1820–1897," microfilm roll 5940, Records of the U.S. Customs Service, record group 36, National Archives at Washington, D.C.; "Silan Chen Leyda in the 1940 U.S. Population Census," Archives, http://www .archives.com/1940-census/silan-leyda-ny-57602177k; "Sylvia Si-lan Chen," FBI files, 100-30551, April 19, 1950, and May 20, 1952; Lyle to Leyda, February 20, 1937; and Lyle to Uhn, February 20, 1937; both in box 29, folder 5, JSCL; Chen Leyda, *Footnote to History*, 231–75.

64. "Sylvia Si-lan Chen," FBI files, 100-30551, April 19, 1950, and May 20, 1952; "Sylvia Chen Acham Leyda," "Alphabetical Manifests of Non-Mexican Aliens Granted Temporary Admission at Laredo, Texas, December 1, 1929–April 8, 1955," microfilm roll 1; "Passenger Lists of Vessels Arriving at New York, 1820–1897," microfilm roll 6569, Records of the INS, Record Group 85, National Archives, Washington, D.C.; Chen Leyda, *Footnote to History*, 248–75; Si-lan Chen passports, box 28, folder 3, JSCL.

65. Chen Leyda, *Footnote to History*, 175–83, 189–90, 195, 204–5; "Sylvia Si-lan Chen," FBI files, 100-30551, May 20, 1952.

66. The relationship between Percy, who had become an adviser to the National Economic Council and an assistant of Sun Ke, and his siblings remained tense. Jack wrote to Si-lan, "Can't get a cent from him, but on good terms." Percy's former wife wired some money from the family estate to Moscow from Trinidad. Jack to Sylvia, March 24 and June 2, 1937, box 28, folder 12; "My Relatives," by Sylvia, 1944, box 29, folder 5; all in JSCL; Chen Leyda, *Footnote to History*, 245–46.

67. Si-lan's War Emergency and American Women's Voluntary Services IDs are preserved in box 28, folder 5, JSCL. Liu Liangmo, "Meiguo dui huaqiao de wuru."

68. *Billings (Mont.) Gazette*, July 28, 1929; *Western Weekly Magazine*, August 4, 1929; *Variety*, March 5, 1930; "Chinese Dancer Scores," *Los Angeles Times*, March 20, 1930; *Arizona Daily Star*, November 25, 1934; *Daily Worker* (New York), November 25 and 26, 1937; *Brooklyn (N.Y.) Daily Eagle*, October 4, 1935, and May 7, 1937.

69. In comparison, ticket prices for Mei Lanfang's performances in 1930, during the Great Depression, rose from $5 to $12 due to high demand. Qi Rushan, *Mei Lanfang you Mei ji*, 155; Price, *Lives of Agnes Smedley*, 245–49. "Sylvia Si-lan Chen," FBI files, 100-30551, May 20, 1952; early 1940s scrapbook, box 30, folder 9, JSCL.

70. Chen Leyda, *Footnote to History*, 239–47, 283–84, 288; John Martin, "Chinese Dancer Makes Debut Here: Si-lan Chen, Who Hails from Soviet Union, Proves a Winning Young Artist," *NYT*, January 31, 1938; *Brooklyn (N.Y.) Daily Eagle*, January 23, 1938; *New York Post*, January 29, 1938; *New York Sun*, January 31, 1938; *Daily Worker* (New York), January 28, 1938; *Kingston (N.Y.) Daily Freeman*, April 8, 1939.

71. "Anti-silk Parade Scheduled Today," *Brooklyn (N.Y.) Daily Eagle*, February 26, 1938; *Nassau (N.Y.) Daily Review-Star*, March 31, 1938.

72. "Sylvia Si-lan Chen," FBI files, 100-30551, May 20, 1952; John Martin, "Dances Given Here in Aid of Chinese," *NYT*, March 6, 1939; *Philadelphia Inquirer*, February 25, 1939;

Brooklyn (N.Y.) Daily Eagle, March 5, 1939; *Rochester (N.Y.) Democrat and Chronicle*, February 26 and March 12, 1939; *Cincinnati Enquirer*, March 23 and 26, April 3, 1939; *Indianapolis News*, March 27 and 30, 1939; *Kingston (N.Y.) Daily Freeman*, April 6, 8, 13, 15, and 18, 1939; *Baltimore Sun*, March 26, April 9 and 14, 1939; *Morning Call* (Allentown, Penn.), March 17, April 14, 15, and 17, 1939. Photographs of Si-lan by Man Ray, box 35, JSCL.

73. *New York Post*, April 23 and June 11, 1938, and April 25, 1939; *New York Sun*, April 19, 20, and 23, 1938, October 24, 1939, September 13, 1940; *Daily Worker* (New York), May 8, 1940; *Herald Statesman* (Yonkers, N.Y.), June 7 and 10, 1940; *American Dancer*, April 1942. Si-lan might have crossed paths with the Chinese American actress Soo Yong and Pauline Benton at the shadow play benefit. Hayter-Menzies, *Shadow Woman*, 49, 55–56.

74. Chen Leyda, *Footnote to History*, 83–84, 138–39, 239–47, 288; John Martin, "Dances Given Here in Aid of Chinese," *NYT*, March 6, 1939; "Chinese Girl to Fight Jap with Dance of Propaganda," *New York Post*, January 25, 1938.

75. Chen Leyda, *Footnote to History*, 83–84, 138–39, 239–47, 288; "Chinese Girl to Fight Jap with Dance of Propaganda," *New York Post*, January 25, 1938. "Sylvia Si-lan Chen," FBI files, 100-30551, May 20, 1952; "My Relatives," by Sylvia, 1944, box 29, folder 5, JSCL.

76. The book by Ayako Ishigaki (Haru Matsui) *Restless Wave* (1940) associates Japanese military aggression abroad with "feudal" restrictions on women and the poor at home. Newspaper clipping on Si-lan and Ishigaki, box 30, folder 9, JSCL; Robinson, *Great Unknown*, 17, 19. Ji Chaoding served as political adviser for *China Today*, a journal of the American Friends of the Chinese People. Price, *Lives of Agnes Smedley*, 245–49.

77. *Pittsburgh Press*, October 2 and 4, 1942; *Pittsburgh Post-Gazette*, October 3 and 5, 1942; *San Bernardino County (Calif.) Sun*, August 26 and 27, 1943, August 24, 1945; Chen Leyda, *Footnote to History*, 222–29. For more information on the aviatrixes, see Gully, *Sisters of Heaven*. MoMA blog, https://www.moma.org/explore/inside_out/2015/10/23/from-the-archives-dance-and-theater/ (accessed December 2, 2019).

78. Chen to Hughes (postcard), August 1, 1938; Chen Leyda, *Footnote to History*, 248, 253–75, 291.

79. Next to the advertisement for the Friends of the Abraham Lincoln Brigade event were news articles on Langston Hughes heading the Suitcase Theater of Harlem and Anna May Wong agreeing to be a sponsor of the San Francisco branch of the American Friends of the Chinese People. *Daily Worker* (New York), April 20, 1938, May 3, 1940, October 24, November 5, 6, and 24, 1941; *Philadelphia Inquirer*, May 25, 1940; "Canada Lee, Josh White to Aid Chinese People," *New York Amsterdam Star-News*, October 25, 1941; Taylor, *Zora and Langston*, 232; Chen to Hughes, June 26, 1942; Chen Leyda, *Footnote to History*, 204–5, 283–84; program flyers and 1940 scrapbook, box 29, folder 6, and box 30, folder 9, JSCL; Ransom, "Family Chen."

80. Leyda to Bourne, July 28 and September 7, 1943; Leyda to Thomson, April 30, 1942; "My Relatives," by Sylvia, 1944; all in box 29, folder 5, JSCL; FBI files, 105-13992-1, 100-30551, May 20, 1952; Chen Leyda, *Footnote to History*, 284–88. "Jay Leyda: A Brief History," 152–53, mistakenly notes his service dates as 1942–43.

81. *Theatre World*, March 3, 1943; *San Bernardino County (Calif.) Sun*, August 26 and 27, 1943, June 7 and August 24, 1945; *Los Angeles Times*, February 28 and March 6, 1943; *California Eagle*, March 10 and 24, 1943; Chen Leyda, *Footnote to History*, 97–98, 246. FBI files, 100-18251, 100-30551, April 19, 1950, and May 20, 1952; "My Relatives," by Sylvia, 1944, box 29, folder 5; program flyers, box 30, folder 6; all in JSCL.

82. Chen Leyda, *Footnote to History*, 284–88; Leyda to Bourne, September 7, 1943; two letters from Chen to Leyda, n.d.; memo from Leyda to Beth Mericks and Irene Margolis, February 12, 1977, box 29, folder 5; all in JSCL. For more information on H. T. Hsiang, see Hsu, *Floating Chinaman*. Local newspapers such as the *Winnipeg (Manitoba) Tribune*, May 16, 1944, and *Pittsburgh Press*, May 4, 1944, reported Si-lan's debut on the Hollywood screen.

83. Hughes to Chen, June 27, 1946, box 29, folder 4, JSCL; Chen to Hughes, July 3, 1946; Robinson, *Great Unknown*, 6, 8; *NYT*, January 16, 1950; *Shenbao*, August 23 and November 23, 1948.

84. Ransom, "Family Chen."

85. Jack to Sylvia, June 2, 1937; Jack to the Leydas, October 5 and late October 1938, box 28, folder 12; all in JSCL.

86. Sharing the page were articles reporting that Chinese in San Francisco greatly admired Anna May Wong for her contribution to China relief, Wong's response to her rumored romance with Korean American actor Philip Ahn, and a woodcut of Chinese soldiers shooting from trenches. "Chen Youren zhinü wudao mukuan," *Funü wenxian* 1 (1939): 39; "Sylvia Chen Gives Dance Recital in N.Y. for Orphan Aid," *China Press*, March 31, 1939.

87. Jack to Sylvia, March 24 and June 2, 1937; Jack to the Leydas, August 25, 1940, box 28, folder 12; all in JSCL; Chen Leyda, *Footnote to History*, 245–46; *New Masses*, February 1937.

88. Back in Hong Kong, Jack connected with *Tien Hsia Monthly* and landed a few job offers. However, convinced his "real work" was in China facing the imminent "big bust" of the world, he was determined to establish roots there with his immediate family. Chen Yuan-tsung, *Minguo waijiao qiangren Chen Youren*, 338–49; Chen Leyda, *Footnote to History*, 245–47. Works by Jack Chen: "Wei shenmo tamen wang Yan'an," trans. by Duxing, *Xu yu sheng* 1, no. 2 (1939): 62–64; "Why They Go to Yenan," *China Press*, January 12, 1939 (first appeared in *Asia*). *North-China Daily News*, December 9, 1937; *Gudao* 1, no. 1 (1938): 4; *China Press*, July 16, 1937, April 7, 1939; *Dongfang huakan* 2, no. 12 (1940): 5. "Sylvia Si-lan Chen," FBI files, 100-30551, January 27, 1951, and May 20, 1952. Jack to Sylvia, March 24 and June 2, 1937, Jack to the Leydas, October 5 and late October 1938, box 28, folder 12; Eugene to the Leydas, August 17, 1941, box 28, folder 10; all in JSCL. Bevan, *A Modern Miscellany*.

89. *Shanghai Evening Post & Mercury*, November 3, 1936; *China Press*, August 4, October 22 and 30, November 4 and 11, 1936. Jack also wrote a political pamphlet, *When Will China Win?*, published by the *Hong Kong Daily Press* and distributed by the China Defense League. Works by Jack Chen: "Crisis Gives Impetus to Cartoons," *Shanghai Evening Post & Mercury*, November 9, 1936; "Letter to Japanese Friends," *China Press*, October 27, 1936; "China's Militant Cartoons," *Asia*, May 1938, 308–12; "Guanyu muke yu manhua," trans. by Wen Zhiyi, *Daobao*, November 17, 1938. Works by Chen Yifan: "Faguo dao hechu qu?," *Dagong bao* (Hong Kong), December 20, 1938; "Yishu jia de weida liliang he weida zeren," *Guomin gonglun* (Hankou), September 21, 1938, 17; "Faguo dao hechu qu?," *Gongyu banyue kan* 8 (1939): 9–10. Jack to the Leydas, late October 1938, box 28, folder 12, JSCL.

90. Chen Yifan, "Yishu jia de weida liliang he weida zeren," *Guomin gonglun* (Hankou), September 21, 1938, 17; Jack Chen, "China's Militant Cartoons," *Asia*, May 1938, 308–12.

91. Eugene to the Leydas, August 17, 1941, box 28, folder 10; Jack to the Leydas, October 1943, box 28, folder 12; "My Relatives," by Sylvia, 1944, box 29, folder 5; all in JSCL.

92. Jack to the Leydas, August 25, 1940, box 28, folder 12; Eugene to the Leydas, August 17, 1941, box 28, folder 10; both in JSCL.

93. Eugene to the Leydas, August 17, 1941, box 28, folder 10, JSCL; "Sylvia Si-lan Chen," FBI files, 100-30551, January 27, 1951.

94. Eugene to the Leydas, August 17, 1941, box 28, folder 10; Lucy to Sylvia, March 20, 1942; Jack to the Leydas, October 1943, box 28, folder 12; "My Relatives," by Sylvia, 1944, box 29, folder 5; all in JSCL. "Sylvia Si-lan Chen," FBI files, 100-30551, January 27, 1951. Denny (Denni, Yevgeniy) Chen and his daughter Iolanda (Yolanda) Evgenievna (Yevgenievna) Chen became international long jump and triple jump athletes, respectively. Iolanda was a successful sports journalist and featured on the cover of *Playboy* (Russia, March 1996); see https://en.wikipedia.org/wiki/Yolanda_Chen (accessed April 30, 2018).

95. Eugene to the Leydas, August 17, 1941, box 28, folder 10, JSCL.

96. Chen Leyda, *Footnote to History*, 279–81; Chen Youren, "Yindu wenti yu Yazhou," *Zhengzhi yuekan* 4, no. 3 (1942): 8; Chen Youren, "Guanyu 'Wang Jingwei xiansheng zhuan,'" *Zhengzhi yuekan* 4, no. 6 (1942): 91; Chen Yaojin, "Chen Youren furen zaizhan zhi," *Dadi* 90 (1947); "Chen Youren qiangxiang dao si," *Haixing* 18 (1946): 3.

97. Li Weichen had been a close associate of China's noted reformer Kang Youwei and later rose to prominence in Singapore politics. Alumni of Nanyang University, http://www.nandazhan.com/zb/lgyjunshi.htm. He claimed Eugene's ashes were buried at the Jing'an Temple cemetery, but the magazine *Haitao* reported that they were "dispersed in the ocean." Li Weichen, "Guanyu Chen Youren xiansheng de yi ge baogao"; "Chen Youren shang yinmu," *Haitao* 24 (1946): 6.

98. Li Weichen, "Guanyu Chen Youren xiansheng de yi ge baogao."

99. Eugene to the Leydas, August 17, 1941, box 28, folder 10, JSCL.

100. When Li released his essay, Percy's long speech at a conference at the Jiaotong Bank on August 31, 1944, was made public. The conference was attended by celebrity officials including Huang Yanpei, Zhang Shengfu, Zhang Naiqi, and Shen Junru. Chen Pishi, "Weisidula he shang de Lugouqiao," *Xianshi* 2 (1939): 99; "Baozhang renshen ziyou wenti," *Xianzheng yuekan* 10 (1944): 29–52; "My Relatives," by Sylvia, 1944, box 29, folder 5, JSCL.

101. Li Weichen, "Guanyu Chen Youren xiansheng de yi ge baogao."

102. Paul Robeson, "Conversation about the New China," *Freedom*, May 1951.

103. Email from Chen Yuan-tsung to Gao Yunxiang, June 30, 2016; Chen Leyda, *Footnote to History*, 279–81. NYT, May 21, 1944.

104. Siqing, "Chen Youren furen chuguo shuhuai," *Kuaihuo lin*, July 6, 1947, 1. Georgette Chang lived in a house at no. 14 (now 18), 1136 Alley of Yuyuan Road, until its owner reclaimed it in July 1947. No. 31 (today's Children's Palace) served as Wang Jingwei's headquarters. Chang soon settled in Singapore, where she enjoyed a successful career and a comfortable life. Georgette Chen, *Georgette Chen Retrospective*. Lindsey, "Table for Three, Please"; "Estate of Georgette Chen," http://giving.nus.edu.sg/the-undying-legacy-of -georgette-chen/ (accessed November 1, 2018).

105. Jack to the Leydas, August 29 and September 27, 1949, box 28, folder 12; memo from Leyda to Mericks and Margolis, February 12, 1977, box 29, folder 5; Si-lan Chen passports, box 28, folder 3; all in JSCL; "Sylvia Si-lan Chen," FBI files, 100-30551, April 19, 1950, May 20, 1952.

106. The National Council of American-Soviet Friendship officially came "within the

Purview of Executive Order 9835" on November 24, 1947. Chen Leyda, *Footnote to History*, 246, 284–88; FBI files, 105-13992-1, 100-18251, 100-30551, April 19, 1950, May 20, 1952; "My Relatives," by Sylvia, 1944, box 29, folder 5, JSCL; *Daily People's World*, October 23, 1943.

107. The Congress of American Women and the Southern California Labor School fell "within the purview of Executive Order 9835" on May 27, 1948, and late 1949, respectively. "Sylvia Si-lan Chen," FBI files, 100-30551, April 19, 1950, May 20, 1952; *California Eagle*, December 22, 1949.

108. The Committee for a Democratic Far Eastern Policy fell "within the purview of Executive Order 9835" on April 21, 1949. "Sylvia Si-lan Chen," FBI files, 100-30551, April 19, 1950, May 20, 1952; *California Eagle*, March 16 and 23, 1950; program flyers, box 30, folder 6, JSCL.

109. "Sylvia Si-lan Chen," FBI files, 100-30551, January 27, 1951, May 20, 1952.

110. "Sylvia Si-lan Chen," FBI files, 100-30551, May 20, 1952.

111. Chen to Leyda, n.d., box 29, folder 5; Si-lan lecture notes, box 29, folder 6; all in JSCL.

112. The Senate Fact-Finding Committee on Un-American Activities in California reported that the Actors Laboratory primarily "draw ambitions young actors and actresses into an orbit of CP organizations." *Daily Peoples' World*, October 20, 1949; "Sylvia Si-lan Chen," FBI files, 105-1867, 100-30551, 105-13992, April 19, 1950, April 25, 1951, May 20, 1952; program flyers, box 30, folder 6, JSCL.

113. "Sylvia Si-lan Chen," FBI files 105-1867, 100-30551, 105-13992, April 19, 1950, April 25, 1951, May 20, 1952; Chen to Hughes, April 23, 1946.

114. The Leydas stayed in New York City in April 1947 and moved to Stockbridge, Massachusetts, where Leyda conducted research at Harvard University, until September. Then they moved to 78 Perry Street, New York City, until December 1947 and to 550 West 20th Street until January 1948. They returned to Hollywood, where Si-lan worked as a part-time instructor with the Rainbow Dance Studio at 1627 Cahuenga Boulevard. She appeared in "The Dancer Says" program at the Global Theater in July 1950. The Leydas stayed at the Prince George Hotel at 14 East 28th Street in New York City from April 20 to May 1, 1951. From May to June, they were at Cambridge, Massachusetts, staying first at the Brattle Inn at 48 Brattle Street and then in a sublet apartment at 1480 Cambridge Street. They then moved to 91 Pineapple Street, Brooklyn. "Sylvia Si-lan Chen," FBI files, 105-1867, 100-30551, 105-13992, April 19, 1950, April 25, 1951, May 20, 1952; *California Eagle*, July 7, 1950; Chen to Hughes, April 23, 1946; Leyda to Koch, [1977], box 29, folder 5; JSCL; "Jay Leyda: A Brief History," 152–53. Books by Leyda: *Melville Log, Portable Melville, Years and Hours of Emily Dickinson*.

115. Chen Leyda, *Footnote to History*, 291–99; "Yaddocast: Episode 14: Si-lan Chen," http://yaddocast.libsyn.com/episode-14-Si-lan-chen; "Chen, Si-lan," Yaddo Records "Guest," file 10813; program flyers, MoMA, Photographs, dance, ca. 1900–1950, vol. 2, nos. 58–137, Lincoln Center; all in New York Public Library.

116. Leyda to Chen, Friday night, n.d., box 29, folder 5, JSCL; "The Melville Society Archive: Finding Aid to the Jay Leyda Papers (1944–1956)," http://melvillesociety.org /ms-archive/jay-leyda-papers-finding-aid/97-overview-of-the-jay-leyda-papers-finding -aid-listings.

117. Shi Jizhe, "Chen Youren de yishu erzi,'" *Kuaihuo lin*, July 1946, 3; "Chen Youren shang yinmu," *Haitao* 24 (1946): 6; "Chen Youren nü gongzi Chen Yulan zi Su huiguo,"

Shanghai texie 16 (1946): 11; He Jun, "Chen Youren younü fanguo," *Dadi* 13 (1946); *Shanghai Evening Post & Mercury*, October 3 and November 13, 1946, January 2 and 6, 1947. "Sylvia Si-lan Chen," FBI files, 100-30551, January 27, 1951, May 20, 1952; "My Relatives," by Sylvia, 1944, box 29, folder 5; Jack to the Leydas, November 8, 1947, March 2 and August 29, 1949, box 28, folder 12; all in JSCL.

118. The INS claimed that Yolanda presented herself as a camerawoman on a mission for the Russians, and spoke "disparagingly" of Sergei Eisenstein, who was then "in disfavor with the Soviets." She declared a Leica camera. As early as 1934, Si-lan wrote to Hughes that Yolanda's "aim in life is to make enough valuta to buy herself a camera" and go to Trinidad to make a film. It seemed that at least half of her wishes were fulfilled. "Sylvia Si-lan Chen," FBI files, 105-1867, 100-30551, 05-13992, April 19, 1950, January 27 and April 25, 1951, May 20, 1952; Chen to Hughes, June 26, 1934; booking agent Clark Getts flyer on Percy Chen, box 28, folder 9, JSCL.

119. Initially the couple quarreled with director Sergei Bonderchuk, angrily left the set of the first episode of *War and Peace*, then returned to finish it and the second part. They worked on their last films in the 1970s. See IMDB entries for Shelenkov and Yolanda Chen. For quarrel, see https://en.wikipedia.org/wiki/War_and_Peace_(film_series), quoting sources in Russian.

120. Jack to the Leydas, November 8, 1947, March 2, August 29, and September 27, 1949, box 28, folder 12, JSCL.

121. Jack to the Leydas, August 25, 1940, March 2, August 29, and September 27, 1949, box 28, folder 12, JSCL.

122. Jack to the Leydas, August 25, 1940, March 2, August 29, and September 27, 1949, box 28, folder 12, JSCL; "Sylvia Si-lan Chen," FBI files, 100-30551, April 19, 1950; Chen Leyda, *Footnote to History*, 233, 299. On Dai Alian's career in China, see Wilcox, *Revolutionary Bodies*, 16–43.

123. Chen Leyda, *Footnote to History*, 298–99; "Jay Leyda: A Brief History."

124. Chen Leyda, *Footnote to History*, 299–303; Chen Leyda, "Peking Venture."

125. Chen Leyda, *Footnote to History*, 303–9.

126. Jack to Jay, n.d., box 28, folder 12, JSCL.

127. "Jay Leyda: A Brief History"; Chen Leyda, *Footnote to History*, 294–95, 310; Leyda, *Dianying*; "Films Are a Serious Business in China," *Toronto Star*, January 20, 1973.

128. "Chen, Si-lan," SJ00337, the Pioneers of Chinese Dance Digital Collection, Asia Library, University of Michigan.

129. Chen Leyda, *Footnote to History*, 303–9. On Dai's suffering, see Wilcox, *Revolutionary Bodies*, 121.

130. Jay to Koch, [1977], box 29, folder 5, JSCL; "Jay Leyda: A Brief History"; Chen Leyda, *Footnote to History*, 294–95, 310; Barbara Gail Rowes, "York Dance Program Shows Limited Success in Concert," clipping from the *Toronto Star*, ca. 1973; John Fraser, "York Students Aren't Slick, But Program Ambitious," clipping from the *Toronto Star*, ca. 1973; both in JSCL.

131. Jay to Koch, [1977]; Parker to Paige, November 9, 1976, box 29, folder 5; both in JSCL.

132. Jack to the Leydas, August 16, 1977; Chen Yuan-tsung to the Leydas, September 29, 1978, May 14, 1979, box 28, folder 12; all in JSCL. Books by Jack Chen: *Chinese Theater, New Earth, Year in Upper Felicity, Inside the Cultural Revolution, Sinking Story, Chinese of America.*

133. Entry for Silan Chen Leyda, "California Death Index, 1940–1997," March 8, 1996, Department of Public Health Services, Sacramento; email from Chen Yuan-tsung to Gao Yunxiang, July 12, 2016. After the Cultural Revolution, the Leydas heard from Jack's son, Chenny, now a father of two children and an employee of the Fushun Excavators Works in Liaoning Province. Dai Ailian survived the persecution and returned to "a good position." Chenny saw Percy during the latter's visit to Beijing from Hong Kong. Chenny to the Leydas, December 6, 1977, box 28, folder 12, JSCL. Chenny is active in the controversial anti-transgenic food movement in China as the science-consultant of former CCTV host Cui Yongyuan. See Chenny's blog at https://m.weibo.cn/u/1269923485?uid=1269923485 &luicode=10000011&lfid=1076036011503636 (accessed April 30, 2018).

CHAPTER 5

1. Hughes, "Roar China!"

2. Tang, "Echoes of *Roar, China!*"; Lee, *Ethnic Avant-Garde*, 83–119; Tyerman, "Search for an Internationalist Aesthetics," chap. 4. According to Israel Epstein, a new Chinese song, "Defend Madrid!," born out of the sentiment that China and Spain were linked antifascist fronts, became popular in Wuhan in 1938. Epstein, *My China Eye*, 77. Nancy Cunard and the Chilian poet Pablo Neruda, who had recently traveled to Spain as well, invited Hughes to contribute to a collection of poems on the embattled countries. Cunard to Hughes, March 5, 1937, Nancy Cunard, series I, Personal Correspondence, box 49, folder 918, LHP.

3. *Shanghai Times*, June 3, 1931; Sun Shiyi, "Nuhou ba Zhongguo," *Xi* 1 (1933): 44–47; Zhao Bangrong, trans., "Nuhou ba Zhongguo Ying yizhe de hua," *Xi* 1 (1933): 54; *Sheying huabao* 9, no. 33 (1933): 21; 9, no. 35 (1933): 4; *Shehui ribao*, September 17, 1933; *Jingbao*, September 19, 1933; Weidao zhe, "Riben juchang zhi *Nuhou ba, Zhongguo*," *Shanghai bao*, January 8, 1934; *Dagong bao* (Shanghai) 3 (1937): 1; "Make China Roar," *New York Times*, October 19, 1930; IBDB (Internet Broadway Database), "Roar China," https://www .ibdb.com/broadway-production/roar-china-11246; New York Public Library Digital Collections, "Scene from Roar China: NYC 1930—Theatre Guild Production," https:// digitalcollections.nypl.org/items/510d47dc-9f51-a3d9-e040-e00a18064a99.

4. Si-lan Chen Leyda, *Footnote to History*, 106. Tretiakov would be shot by the Soviet authorities five years after meeting Hughes. Hughes, *I Wonder as I Wander*, 185–86, 206, 218, 225.

5. When *The Red Poppy* was revived following the CCP victory, all instances of eroticism and opium use were removed, with the message of mutual national liberation against imperialist oppression foregrounded. Chen Leyda, *Footnote to History*, 143–47; Chen Yuan-tsung, *Return to the Middle Kingdom*, 274; Tyerman, "Resignifying *The Red Poppy*."

6. Tyerman, "Search for an Internationalist Aesthetics," 274–325. There were several versions of Chinese translations of *Roar, China!*, some from Japanese, by Ye Chen (Shen Xiling), and others. Telichakefu (Soviet Union), "Nuhou ba, Zhongguo!," trans. by Pan Zinong and Feng Ji, *Maodun yuekan* 2, no. 1 (1933): 129–71; "Make China Roar," *New York Times*, October 19, 1930; *Huangpu rikan*, July 15, 1930; *Xiju zhoukan*, July 30, 1930; *Minguo ribao*, August 27, 1930; *Shanghai tan*, September 4, 1930; *Xinsheng* 15 (1930): 115–22; Zheng Boqi, "Nuhouba, Zhongguo!," *Liangyou* 81 (1933): 14; Ying Yunwei, "Nuhou ba Zhongguo shangyan jihua," *Xi* 1 (1933): 56–59; Sun Shiyi, "Nuhou ba Zhongguo," *Xi* 1 (1933): 44–47; Ouyang Yuqian, "Nuhouba Zhongguo zai Guangdong shangyan ji," *Xi* 1 (1933): 52;

Xi 1 (1933): 49–50, 61; Bao Kehua, trans., "Guoji Diaochatuan daibiao duiyu *Nuhou ba Zhongguo* de pingping," *Xi* 2 (1933): 1; Hong Shen, "*Nuhouba! Zhongguo*," *Shehui ribao*, October 10, 1933; *Shehui ribao*, September 18 and October 8, 1933; *Xinwen bao*, September 14 and 17, October 5, 1933, August 9, 1937; *Shibao*, October 3, 1933; *Taosheng* 2, no. 41 (1933): 7; *Dazhong huabao* 1 (1933): 10; *Zhonghua yuebao* 1, no. 8 (1933): 1; *Beiyang huabao* 21, no. 1004 (1933): 2; *Mingxing* 1, no. 6 (1933): cover; *Shanhu* 3, no. 9 (1933): 4–7; *Minbao*, August 13, September 22 and 24, October 1 and 8, 1933; *Shehui yu jiaoyu* 6, no. 17 (1933): 11–13; *Dianying shibao*, September 21, 1933; *Chuban xiaoxi* 20 (1933): 16–17; *Xiao ribao*, September 16, 1933; *Wenhua jie* 1, no. 2 (1933): 1; *Folmes News*, October 10, 1933, July 23, 1937; *Lanyin ji* 1 (1934): 6–8; *Shishi xunbao* 6 (1934): 13; *Xiaoshuo* 6 (1934): 1; *Zhongyang ribao*, August 11, 1934; *Shiri tan* 45 (1934): 21; *Shanghai shangbao*, November 17, 1934; *Beichen huakan*, November 2, 1935; *Shanghai bao*, February 12, 1936.

7. *Diansheng zhoukan* 5, no. 4 (1936): 114; [Zheng] Boqi, "*Nuhou ba Zhongguo* buneng shangyan de yuanying," *Gongyu banyue kan* 2, no. 6 (July 1, 1936): 1–2; *Xiandai zhishi* 1, no. 2 (1936): 35; *Yule zhoubao* 2, no. 4 (1936): 72; 2, no. 24 (1936): 470; *Tiebao*, January 19, March 11, and June 15, 1936; *Libao*, June 1, 1936; *Shijie chenbao*, March 26, 1936; *Yule* 2, no. 19 (1936): 371; *Xunbao*, April 11, 1939; *Dazhong yingxun*, November 21, 1942; *San liu jiu huabao* 13 (1943): 21; *Haibao*, April 4, 1943; *Xin Dongxiang* 64 (1943): 16–17; *Xin juyi banyue kan* 1, no. 1 (1944): 10–11; *Dabao*, July 27, 1949; *Qingqing dianying* 17, no. 16 (1949): 1.

8. Unable to secure a foreign gunboat for the setting, Lianxing Studio aborted a film adapted from the play. Rumor had it that Sichuan warlord Yang Sen offered to sponsor a studio to resume the project, but his demand that the film concludes with him leading his army to defeat the foreign gunboat made the collaboration impossible. Leyda, *Dianying*, 85; Tian Han, "*Nuhou ba, Zhongguo!*," *Nanguo zhoukan* 9–12 (1936): 491–504; *Diansheng ribao*, September 22 and 25, October 8, and November 3, 1933; *Minbao*, August 22, 1933; *Daoguang* 1 (1933): 9; *Rensheng huabao* 2, no. 1 (1935): 30; *Shidai ribao*, February 26, 1936; Jin Ming, "*Nuhou ba Zhongguo*," *Shige* 2/3 (1936): 5; Wang Tao, "*Nuhou ba Zhongguo!*," *Shige zazhi* 1 (1936): 12–13; *Guoxun* 150 (1936): 891; *Zhongguo xueyun* 2, no. 4/5 (1936): 1; *Dafeng* (Hong Kong) 62 (February 1940): cover; *Shiyue* 3 (1943): 2; *Dazhong shenghuo* 1, no. 6 (1943): 14; *Xieli* 3, no. 1 (1944): 1; *Suichang qingnian* 1 (1945): 20–21; *Dafeng bao*, May 22, 1948. Images of *Roar, China!* stage settings: *Maodun yuekan* 2, no. 1 (1933): cover (Tsukiji Theater); *Juchang yishu* 2 (1938): cover (Meyerhold Theater); *Juchang yishu* 3, no. 1–2 (1941): cover (designed by Lee Simonson for Martin Beck Theater). Between 1935 and 1936, while working on his woodcut print *Roar, China!*," Li Hua frequently corresponded with Lu Xun, a strong advocate of the new art form. Lu Xun, *Lu Xun quanji*, 16:515, 526, 533, 542–43, 572, 601.

9. Du Bois, "I Sing to China"; "*Congo River Is Roaring*," CA00034, Pioneers of Chinese Dance Digital Collection, Asia Library, University of Michigan.

10. Lai-Henderson, "Color around the Globe"; Taketani, "Spies and Spiders"; Dickinson, *Bio-bibliography of Langston Hughes*.

11. Hughes, *Big Sea*, 83–85, 140; "To James Nathaniel Hughes," September 5, 1921, and "To Carl Van Vechten," July 15, 1927, in Rampersad, Roessel, and Fratantoro, *Selected Letters of Langston Hughes*, 6–7, 9n3, 67, 69; *Columbia Spectator*, December 7, 1908, and October 4, 1912. P. C. Chang attended Columbia University from 1913 to 1916 to earn a master's degree and from 1919 to 1924 to earn a doctoral degree. Both Liu Zhan'en's and Chang's dissertations were directed by John Dewey. Chang, "Education for Modernization in China"; Liu, "Non-Verbal Intelligence Tests for Use in China." *Columbia*

University Alumni Register 1754-1931, 146, 152, 528, and 594, https://babel.hathitrust.org/cgi/pt?id=uc1.b4525470&view=1up&seq=9.

12. Langston Hughes, "Sea Charm," *China Press*, April 12, 1925; "To Carl Van Vechten," July 15, 1927, "To Harold Jackman," August 1, 1924, and "To Claude McKay," September 13, 1928, in Rampersad, Roessel, and Fratantoro, *Selected Letters of Langston Hughes*, 37, 67–69, 77; Hughes, *Big Sea*, 83–85, 140, 292–93.

13. "To Carl Van Vechten," July 15, 1927, in Rampersad, Roessel, and Fratantoro, *Selected Letters of Langston Hughes*, 67–69; Hughes, *Big Sea*, 83–85, 140, 292–93.

14. Hughes to Chen, October 18, 1934, box 29, folder 4, JSCL (all correspondence from Hughes to Chen is from this source); Hughes, *I Wonder as I Wander*, 282.

15. Buck to Quon, January 10, Buck Correspondence, 1944, Q & R Miscellaneous, group 1, series 2, box 20, PSBH. Eugene Chen's experiences demonstrated that racial attitudes among Chinese were never as benign and simple as Buck indicated here. She had lamented, "I have been hated in China for being white; in this country people hate the Negro for being Black." Buck, "Interpretation of China to the West."

16. Hughes, *I Wonder as I Wander*, 40; "To Claude McKay," September 30, 1930, in Rampersad, Roessel, and Fratantoro, *Selected Letters of Langston Hughes*, 98; Langston Hughes, "Merry Christmas," *New Masses*, December 1930, 4.

17. Hughes to Van Vechten, November 15, 1932, in Bernard, *Remembering Me to Harlem*, 98–100.

18. Hughes, *I Wonder as I Wander*, 185–86, 206, 218, 225.

19. For Sao and other Chinese in Moscow, see McGuire, *Red at Heart*.

20. Baldwin, *Beyond the Color Line*, 90–94; "To Prentiss Taylor," March 5, 1933, and introduction, in Rampersad, Roessel, and Fratantoro, *Selected Letters of Langston Hughes*, 143, xxiv; Hughes to Van Vechtan, March 1, 1933, in Bernard, *Remembering Me to Harlem*, 101–3; Hughes, *I Wonder as I Wander*, 185–86, 206, 218, 225.

21. Chen to Hughes, March 4, 1935, and August 16, 1936, Sylvia Chen, 1934–46, series I, Personal Correspondence, box 43, folder 770, LHP (all correspondence from Chen to Hughes is from this source unless otherwise noted); Hughes to Chen, June 1, 1936; Chen Leyda, *Footnote to History*, 151–52, 208–9; Hughes, *I Wonder as I Wander*, 256.

22. Box 29, folder 4, JSCL; Chen Leyda, *Footnote to History*, 151–53.

23. Hughes, *I Wonder as I Wander*, 256; "To James A. Emanuel," September 19, 1961, in Rampersad, Roessel, and Fratantoro, *Selected Letters of Langston Hughes*, 375; Emanuel, *Langston Hughes*.

24. Chen to Hughes, [1933].

25. It seemed Hughes cared to hear from Chen. During his brief stay in Reno, Nevada, he instructed that only mail from his publisher (Knopf) and Chen be forwarded to him. "To Noel Sullivan," October 29, 1934, in Rampersad, Roessel, and Fratantoro, *Selected Letters of Langston Hughes*, 168; Chen to Hughes, early 1934, June 26, August 29 and October 18, 1934, March 4, June 14, and August 2, 1935, February 28, 1936; Hughes to Chen, June 1, 1936.

26. Hughes to Chen, October 18, 1934; Chen to Hughes, August 29, 1934, LHP-HL, mssHM 64070–64101; Chen to Hughes, [ca 1933], May 11, June 26, and December 3, 1934.

27. Hughes to Chen, n.d.; Chen to Hughes, early 1934 and May 11, 1934; "To Sylvia Chen (Leyda)," July 7, 1934, in Rampersad, Roessel, and Fratantoro, *Selected Letters of Langston Hughes*, 157–58.

28. Chen to Hughes, December 3, 1934, March 4, 1935, August 16, 1936; Hughes to Chen, June 1, 1936; Chen Leyda, *Footnote to History*, 208–9; Hughes, *I Wonder as I Wander*, 256.

29. Koestler, *Invisible Writing*, 137–41. Koestler was best known for his 1941 anti-Stalinist novel *Darkness at Noon*. Lee, *Ethnic Avant-Garde*, 119–20.

30. Als, "The Sojourner"; Rampersad, *Life of Langston Hughes*.

31. Meanwhile, West explored a homosexual relationship with another member of the cast, Mildred Jones, who fell in love with Russian men. Sherrard-Johnson, *Dorothy West's Paradise*, 93–96; Dorothy to Rachel West, March 5–7, 1933, Dorothy West Papers, MC676 series II, folders 1.16 and 2.13, Schlesinger Library, Radcliffe Institute, Harvard University; Hughes and West photographs, series XII, Photographs, Langston Hughes Chronology, 1930s, box 460, folder 11127, and box 459, folder 11105, LHP.

32. Chen to Hughes, June 26, 1934, March 4, May 8, June 14, and August 2, 1935.

33. Hughes to Chen, [between December 1934 and January 1935], June 1, 1936; Chen to Hughes, August 2, 1935, August 16, 1936; Williams and Tidwell, *My Dear Boy*.

34. Chen to Hughes, [1933], August 29, 1934; Hughes to Chen, March 29, 1933, October 18, 1934; Hughes, "Goodbye Christ."

35. Chen to Hughes, early 1934, June 26 and December 3, 1934, March 4, May 8 and 11, August 2, 1935, August 2 and 16, 1936. Hughes said that "The Vigilantes Knock at My Door" would appear in *New Masses*, but it never did. Hughes to Chen, July 7 and October 18, 1934, June 1, 1936.

36. Hughes referred to Lloyd Patterson and his marriage to Vera Aralovna. Hughes to Chen, July 7 and October 18, 1934; Chen to Hughes, June 26, August 29, and December 3, 1934, March 4, May 8 and 11, August 2, 1935.

37. "To Prentiss Taylor," March 5, 1933, in Rampersad, Roessel, and Fratantoro, *Selected Letters of Langston Hughes*, 143; Hughes to Chen, June 1, 1936; Chen to Hughes, February 28 and August 16, 1936. W. E. B. Du Bois decided that *Mulatto*, which he had not yet seen, could not be bad, because Joseph Wood Krutch of Tennessee, a writer for the *Nation* who "has never yet seen anything decent in 'niggers,'" did not like it. W. E. B. Du Bois, "A Forum of Fact and Opinion," *Pittsburgh Courier*, May 30, 1936.

38. Rampersad mistook the Carmons for Jack's in-laws. "To Sylvia Chen (Leyda)," July 7, 1934, and "To Prentiss Taylor," March 5, 1933, in Rampersad, Roessel, and Fratantoro, *Selected Letters of Langston Hughes*, 143; Hughes, *I Wonder as I Wander*, 256.

39. Hughes, *I Wonder as I Wander*, 185–86, 206, 218, 225; Chen to Hughes, [1933]; Price, *Lives of Agnes Smedley*, 50, 55–56, 161, 168, 189–200.

40. Holt performed in Shanghai nightclubs off and on from 1932 to 1937. Hughes to Van Vechten, November 15, 1932; Van Vechten to Hughes (postcard), December 31, 1932, in Bernard, *Remembering Me to Harlem*, 99–100, and Rampersad, Roessel, and Fratantoro, *Selected Letters of Langston Hughes*, 136; Dorothy to Rachel West, March 5–7, 1933, Dorothy West Papers, MC676 series II, folders 1.16 and 2.13, Schlesinger Library, Radcliffe Institute, Harvard University; *Kansas City (Kans.) Plaindealer*, September 2, 1932, April 20, 1934.

41. At Vladivostok, the end of the Trans-Siberian Railway, Hughes noted scenes that symbolically foreshadowed the grim situation he would find in China: "Much of the area was marked off limits," and pedestrians on the main street walked around the dead body of what was seemingly a Chinese person. Hughes, *I Wonder as I Wander*, 206, 218, 225, 239, 245. "James Langston Hughes left here in the N.Y.K. S S Taiyo Maru," *North-China Daily News*, July 21, 1933.

42. Hughes, *I Wonder as I Wander*, 206, 218, 225, 239, 245.

43. Hughes, *I Wonder as I Wander*, 275–76; Bernard, *Remembering Me to Harlem*, 107.

44. Hughes, *I Wonder as I Wander*, 247, 250. P. Dai to W. E. B. Du Bois, November 27, 1936, WDBP.

45. Bernard, *Remembering Me to Harlem*, 58; Taylor, *Zora and Langston*, 125.

46. Langston Hughes, "Big Round World," in *Return of Simple*, 156; Langston Hughes, "Fancy Free," in *Best of Simple*, 122; Hughes, *I Wonder as I Wander*, 246. Contemporary postcards and other caricature drawings frequently featured African Americans consuming watermelons.

47. Hughes, *I Wonder as I Wander*, 247–52; Liu Liangmo, "Chinese Have Changed."

48. Although Hughes was well paid in rubles for his work published in the Soviet Union, the funds could not be used abroad. To fund his China trip, he requested that Golden Stair Press forward his royalties to Shanghai rather than his bank in New York City, lest the debt he accumulated publishing *Scottsboro Limited* overdraw his account. "To Prentiss Taylor," March 5, 1933, in Rampersad, Roessel, and Fratantoro, *Selected Letters of Langston Hughes*, 143.

49. Hughes's encounter with the African American diaspora in Shanghai went beyond the casual greetings during the serendipitous rickshaw moment. As in Europe, he quickly connected to the established community of African American jazz musicians and dancers who provided entertainment in metropolises across the globe "from Paris to the Orient." Hughes, *I Wonder as I Wander*, 246–47, 251–57.

50. Hughes, *I Wonder as I Wander*, 249–52.

51. Harold Isaacs had moved in with Smedley as her bodyguard following the arrest of Hilaire Noulens (or Paul Ruegg, Yakov Rudnik) and his wife, Gertrude (Tatyana Moiseenko), of the Comintern's Far Eastern Bureau by the Shanghai Municipal Police in 1931. Madam Sun Yat-sen helped to launch an international campaign that involved Albert Einstein and Jawaharlal Nehru to win their release. Apparently, Smedley introduced Hughes to Isaacs. Price, *Lives of Agnes Smedley*, 217–22, 224–45. Hughes, *I Wonder as I Wander*, 248–51. "Famous American Negro Poet Says Shanghai Not Nice Place," *Shanghai Evening Post & Mercury*, July 19, 1933.

52. Hughes, *I Wonder as I Wander*, 256–57; Hughes, *Not without Laughter*.

53. *Wenxue* 1, no. 2 (1933): 1; *Xiandai* 3, no. 4 (August 1933): 1. See advertisements of the two issues with table of contents in *Shenbao*, July 31, August 1 and 6, 1933. "Xiushi guo Hu," *Sheying huabao* 9, no. 28 (1933): 19; "Zuojia yu chuban jie," *Xiandai chuban jie* 15 (1933): 8–9; Xing, "Heiren zuojia Xiusi you Hu fu Ri," *Shidai ribao*, August 9, 1933.

54. Wu Shi (Fu Donghua), "Xiushi zai Zhongguo"; Lee, *Ethnic Avant-Garde*, 122. For Walter White's investigation of lynching in the Deep South in 1919, see Lewis, *W. E. B. Du Bois*, 8–9. Kiang Kang-hu, "A Chinese Scholar's View of Mrs. Buck's Novels," and Pearl S. Buck, "Mrs. Buck Replies to Her Chinese Critic," *NYT*, January 15, 1933.

55. Zhang Chenglu (Lu Xun), "Weilai de guangrong," in Lu Xun, *Lu Xun quanji*, 5:443–45; "Ziyou tan," *Shenbao*, January 11, 1934; "Beiping texun," *Shenbao*, December 11, 1933; Price, *Lives of Agnes Smedley*, 156.

56. Wu Shi (Fu Donghua), "Xiushi zai Zhongguo"; Rampersad, *Life of Langston Hughes*, 1:78.

57. Hughes, *I Wonder as I Wander*, 243; "Xiushi zai Riben fabiao shigao," *Wenxue* 1, no. 4 (1933): 586; Wu Shi (Fu Donghua), "Xiushi zai Zhongguo"; Lu Xun, *Lu Xun quanji*, 5:493.

58. Lu Xun, *Lu Xun quanji*, 16:361, 363. *Chenbao*, March 18, 1933. In addition to his intense debates with Lu Xun regarding the class nature of literature, the noted cultural

figure Liang Shiqiu argued that the physics of Shaw and Lu were imbalanced, as was the quality of their works. Liang Shiqiu, "Guanyu Lu Xun," http://www.millionbook.com /mj/l/liangshiqiu/lsq/10.htm (accessed April 15, 2018).

59. "Bidding" was later included in *Wei ziyou shu*, and "Gawking," in *Nanqiang beidiao ji*. Lu Xun, *Lu Xun quanji*, 5:227–30, 249, 269–70, 278–80, 297–99; 8:377–81, 510. Lu Xun, Qu Xiubai, and Yue Wen, *Xiaobona zai Shanghai*.

60. Wu Shi (Fu Donghua), "Xiushi zai Zhongguo"; Lu Xun, *Lu Xun quanji*, 5:493. Lu Xun made negative comments about Mei in several essays.

61. Hughes, *I Wonder as I Wander*, 206, 218, 225, 256–57; Smedley to Hughes, October 31, 1934, LHP-HL, mssHM 64098.

62. Chen to Hughes, [1933], June 26 and December 3, 1934, May 8, June 14, and August 2, 1935, February 28, 1936; Hughes to Chen, early 1934, July 7, 1934, June 1, 1936; Chen Leyda, *Footnote to History*, 206.

63. Hughes, *I Wonder as I Wander*, 206, 218, 225, 256–57; Shen Pengnian, "Lu Xun huijian Xiushi jiqi beiwu shijian." Lu Xun was associated with both domestic and international leftist circles. He received materials from *New Masses* in 1931. Edgar Snow was translating and editing *Living China*, a collection of Lu Xun's short stories, around the time of Hughes's visit. Smedley, a close friend who had started to correspond with him in 1929, brought a Western doctor to his residence on May 31, 1936, a few months before his death. Lu Xun, *Lu Xun quanji*, 4:420–21; 16:164, 187, 190, 251, 378, 380, 609–10. "Tongxing," *Wenxue* 1, no. 3 (1933): 498-500; Qiutao, "Jian Xiao yu jian Xiushi," *Zhongyang ribao*, September 5, 1933.

64. "Mei jizhe Aisake fu Ri, yin qi Riren zhuyi," *Shenbao*, August 9, 1933; Hughes, "From Moscow to Shanghai"; Price, *Lives of Agnes Smedley*, 217–28; Hughes, *I Wonder as I Wander*, 247–52.

65. Hughes, *I Wonder as I Wander*, 268, 276; "Dongjing Mei qiao bei zhu," *Shenbao*, July 26, 1933; "Mei jizhe Aisake fu Ri, yinqi Riren zhuyi," *Shenbao*, August 9, 1933"; "Wentan xiaoxi," *Chuban xiaoxi* 17 (1933): 15; "Xiushi zai Sulian," *Wenxue* 1, no. 3 (1933): 476; "Mei ren Xiushi zai Ri," *Minbao*, July 26, 1933; "Langston Hughes Is Told to Leave Japan," *China Press*, July 26, 1933; *China Press*, October 1, 1933.

66. Smedley to Hughes, October 31, 1934, LHP-HL, mssHM 64098.

67. Shao Xunmei, "Xiandai Meiguo shitan gaiguan," *Xiandai* 5, no. 6 (October 1934): 874–90; Hahn, *Soong Sisters*.

68. "Houji," in Lu Xun, *Lu Xun quanji*, 5:411, 432n8.

69. Shao was married to his cousin Sheng Peiyu, a granddaughter of Sheng Xuanhuai. You Guang (Lu Xun), "Wen chuang qiu meng," in Lu Xun, *Lu Xun quanji*, 5:307; "Ziyou tan," *Shenbao*, September 11, 1933; Wei Suo (Lu Xun), "'Huaji' lijie," in Lu Xun, *Lu Xun quanji*, 5:361; "Ziyou tan," *Shenbao*, October 26, 1033; Bao Dao (Lu Xun), "Zhongqiu er yuan," in Lu Xun, *Lu Xun quanji*, 5:594; "Dongxiang," *Zhonghua ribao*, September 28, 1934; Weisuo (Lu Xun), "Denglong shu shiyi," in Lu Xun, *Lu Xun quanji*, 5:291–93; "Ziyou tan," *Shenbao*, September 1, 1933; "Xuyan," in Lu Xun, *Lu Xun quanji*, 5:438. Lu Xun named the 1935 series that he edited for the young leftist authors (including Xiao Hong, Xiao Jun, and Ye Zi) "Slaves." Lu Xun, *Lu Xun quanji*, 16:520, 524.

70. Zhang Chenglu (Lu Xun), "Weilai de guangrong," and Runiu (Lu Xun), "Dianying de jiaoxun," both in Lu Xun, *Lu Xun quanji*, 5:443–45 and 309–11; "Ziyou tan," *Shenbao*, September 11, 1933. Finding domestic cinema "extremely shallow and ridiculous," Lu Xun frequented theaters from 1928 to 1936 to see foreign (mainly Hollywood) films with

families and friends, including Kanzo Uchiyama. His diary indicates that, in addition to Charlie Chan movies, films about adventures in the Amazon and the South Pole, and a Mickey Mouse series for kids, he was particularly interested in African themes. Lu Xun watched *Son of Tarzan* (1920), *Monster Hunting in Africa* (1929), *Byrd at the South Pole* (1929), *Trade Horn* (1930), *Morocco* (1930), *Ingagi* (1931), *The Cohens and Kellys in Africa* (1931), *East of Borneo* (1931), *Rango* (1931), *Tarzan: The Ape Man* (one of a series of six by MGM), *Wild Women of Borneo* (1931), *Ubangi* (1931), *Jungle Adventure* (1933), *Tarzan the Fearless* (1933), *White Cargo* (1935), *Song of King Kong* (1935), *Warfare in Africa* (1935), and the first and second parts of *Queen of the Jungle* (1935). Lu Xun, *Lu Xun quanji*, 16:4, 6, 102–3, 251, 256–57, 264–67, 272–78, 280, 355, 358, 402–5, 428, 431, 440–41, 458–60, 472, 475, 478, 482, 532, 535, 557–61, 565, 569, 586–89, 591, 594.

71. Runiu (Lu Xun), "Dianying de jiaoxun," in Lu Xun, *Lu Xun quanji*, 5:309–11; Langston Hughes, "The Moon," in *Return of Simple*, 40; Hughes, *I Wonder as I Wander*, 246.

72. Taozui (Lu Xun), "Dating yingxiang," in Lu Xun, *Lu Xun quanji*, 5:325–27; "Ziyou tan," *Shenbao*, September 24, 1933. Another noted writer, Shen Congwen, shared Lu Xun's view that asking foreigners about their impression of China was ridiculous. In his novel *Alice in China*, Shen wrote, "Even visiting dogs would harbor their impression of China." Shen Congwen, *Alisi Zhongguo youji*, http://www.dushu369.com/zhongguomingzhu /HTML/70777.html (accessed October 18, 2018), chap. 1.

73. Hughes, *Big Sea*, 267–68.

74. Mu Mutian, "Nuobei'er wenyi jiang yu wangguo," *Shenbao*, November 19, 1933.

75. Lu Xun, *Lu Xun quanji*, 8:491; Xu Maoyong, "Ji Lili Kebei," *Shenbao*, September 3, 1934.

76. Hughes, *Big Sea*, 81–85.

77. Hughes to Van Vechtan, March 1, 1933, in Bernard, *Remembering Me to Harlem*, 101–3; Hughes, *Zdrastvui Revoliutsiia*; Hughes, *A Negro Looks at Soviet Central Asia*.

78. Knopf to Hughes, March 12, 1933, in Bernard, *Remembering Me to Harlem*, 122–23.

79. Van Vechten to Hughes, April 3, 1933, and Hughes to Van Vechten, May 23, 1933, in Bernard, *Remembering Me to Harlem*, 103–5, 122–23. Langston Hughes, "Advertisement for the Opening of the Waldorf-Astoria," *New Masses*, December 1931, 11–12. As one of the world's largest and most expensive hotels, the Waldorf-Astoria attracted as guests U.S. presidents, royalty, Hollywood stars, and other rich and powerful people, such as H. H. Kung. It was purchased by the Chinese Anbang Insurance Group, headed by Deng Xiaoping's grandson-in-law, for nearly $2 billion in 2015 and closed for renovations in 2017. The Chinese government seized the Anbang Insurance Group and took over ownership of the hotel one year later. *Toronto Star*, March 2, 2017; *NYT*, February 22, 2018.

80. Hughes to Van Vechten, March 5 and October 3, 1934, and Van Vechten to Hughes, March 20, 1934, in Bernard, *Remembering Me to Harlem*, 120–25.

81. Hughes to Van Vechten, September 22, 1933, in Bernard, *Remembering Me to Harlem*, 107; "To Blanche Knopf," June 5, 1934, and "To Noel Sullivan," January 29, 1936, in Rampersad, Roessel, and Fratantoro, *Selected Letters of Langston Hughes*, 157, 191; Carrie Hughes to Langston, February 28, 1936, in Williams and Tidwell, *My Dear Boy*, 141.

82. Langston Hughes, "Good Morning, Revolution," *New Masses*, September 1932, 5; Hughes, *Scottsboro Limited*; Wu Shi (Fu Donghua), "Xiushi zai Zhongguo"; Zheng Linkuan, "Lansidun Xiushi"; Du Bois, *Souls of Black Folk*, 7–8.

83. Wu Shi (Fu Donghua), "Xiushi zai Zhongguo"; Zheng Linkuan, "Lansidun Xiushi";

Bernard, *Remembering Me to Harlem*, 45; Hughes, "Negro Artist and the Racial Mountain" (published in the *Nation* on June 23, 1926, although Zheng mistook the date for July 23). Shanghai's English-language press reported on Du Bois attending the 1923 Pan-African Congress in London and featured his review of novels *Precipice* (1948) by Hugh MacLennan and *The Fires of Spring* (1949) by James A. Michener for the *New York Times*. "A Negro Leader: Dr. E. B. Burghardt Du Bois," *North-China Daily News*, December 15, 1923; William Du Bois, "Book Review," *China Press*, December 16, 1948 and March 28, 1949.

84. Wu Shi (Fu Donghua), "Xiushi zai Zhongguo"; Zheng Linkuan, "Lansidun Xiushi." Hughes, *Weary Blues*.

85. Wu Shi (Fu Donghua), "Xiushi zai Zhongguo"; Zheng Linkuan, "Lansidun Xiushi." Langston Hughes, "Ruby Brown," *Crisis*, August 1926, 181, in Hughes, *Fine Clothes*, 30; Langston Hughes, "Song for a Dark Girl," *Crisis*, May 1927, 94, in Hughes, *Fine Clothes*, 75; Hughes, "New Cabaret Girl," in *Fine Clothes*, 31.

86. Wu Shi (Fu Donghua), "Xiushi zai Zhongguo"; Zheng Linkuan, "Lansidun Xiushi."

87. Langston Hughes, "Call to Creation," *New Masses*, February 1931, 4; Wu Shi (Fu Donghua), "Xiushi zai Zhongguo"; Zheng Linkuan, "Lansidun Xiushi."

88. Langston Hughes, "Our Spring," *International Literature* 2 (1933): 4; Wu Shi (Fu Donghua), "Xiushi zai Zhongguo"; Xiushi, "Women de chuntian." Yang Cunren joined the CCP in 1925 but publicly announced he would "leave the trench of party life." In 1933 he called for "raising the banner of petty bourgeois revolutionary literature." Yang Cunren, "Likai zhengdang shenghuo de zhanhao," *Dushu zazhi* 3, no. 1 (February 1933): 1–10; Yang Cunren, "Jieqi xiao zichan jieji geming wenxue zhi qi," *Xiandai* 2, no. 4 (February 1933): 623–25; Liushi (Yang Cunren), "Xin Rulin waishi," *Da wanbao*, June 17, 1933; Lu Xun, *Lu Xun quanji*, 5:195, 16:383–85.

89. Zheng Linkuan, "Lansidun Xiushi"; Lydia Filatova, "Langston Hughes: American Writer," *International Literature* 2 (1933): 106–7. For Hughes's encounters with Mayakovsky, see Lee, *Ethnic Avant-Garde*, 55, 68–72. Dickinson, *Bio-bibliography of Langston Hughes*, 53–56, 148.

90. Langston Hughes, "People without Shoes," *New Masses*, October 1931, 12; Hughes, *Dream Keeper*; Bontemps and Hughes, *Popo and Fifina*; Zheng Linkuan, "Lansidun Xiushi"; Dickinson, *Bio-bibliography of Langston Hughes*, 53–56, 148; Xiushi, "Meiyou xiezi de renmen," trans. by Wu Shi (Fu Donghua), *Wenxue* 1, no. 2 (1933): 159–261.

91. Zhang Jiabi, "Xiushi," *Zhongyang ribao*, August 28, 1934; Jin Ge, "Heiren wenxue jia Xiushi," *Zhongyang ribao*, August 23, 1935; Ruoruo, "Xiushi," *Zhongguo xuesheng* 2, no. 9 (1935): 23; Ye Junjian, "Meizhou de Heiren shiren," *Wenyi dianying* 1, no. 4 (1935): 10–11.

92. "Wentan xiaoxi," *Chuban xiaoxi* 17 (1933): 14; "Xiushi guo Hu," *Sheying huabao* 9, no. 28 (1933): 19; "Xiushi zai Sulian," *Wenxue* 1, no. 3 (1933): 476.

93. In his interview with *Shanghai Evening Post & Mercury*, Hughes argued that the Soviet Union, which swiftly uplifted its darker citizens from conditions closely resembling those in the American South, showed the way to solve the "Negro problem." To prove his point, Hughes cited the examples of twelve African Americans who rose to the positions of "chemists in the cotton-seed laboratories, road engineers, and experts in the machine and tractor stations" in Soviet Asia. "Famous American Negro Poet Says Shanghai Not Nice Place," *Shanghai Evening Post & Mercury*, July 19, 1933; Langston Hughes, "Moscow and Me," *International Literature* 3 (July 1933): 61–67; 4 (1934): 78–81; Xiushi Lansidun, "Wo he Mosike," trans. by Mengze, *Wenshi* (Beiping) 1, no. 4 (1934): 83–92; trans. by Zuoyun, *Qinghua shuqi zhoukan* 3/4 (1934): 148–52; and trans. by Di, *Xunhuan* 4, no. 5

(1934): 68–70; 4, no. 6 (1934): 84–87. For controversies over aborting *Black and White*, see Lee, *Ethnic Avant-Garde*, 119–48. Dickinson, *Bio-bibliography of Langston Hughes*, 53–56, 148; Carew, *Blacks, Reds, and Russians*, 134.

94. Lu Xun, *Lu Xun quanji*, 16:373, 5:109–14; "Ziyou tan," *Shenbao*, April 19, 1933.

95. L. Xiushi, "Bushi meiyou xiaode," trans. by Xiuxia and Zhengnong, *Wenyi* 1, no. 1 (1933): 74–89; 1, no. 2 (1933): 282–99; 1, no. 3 (1933): 435–59. Zhu Xiuxia also published a review of Pearl Buck's *Good Earth* in the second issue, calling it "a masterpiece for white ladies and gentlemen." Xiuxia, "Ping Buke Furen de *Dadi*," *Wenyi* 1, no. 2 (1933): 300–305. See *Shenbao*, October 15, November 1 and 15, 1933, for advertisements of the above issues of *Wenyi*. Ruoruo, "Xiushi," *Zhongguo xuesheng* 2, no. 9 (1935): 23.

96. Xiushi, *Bushi meiyou xiaode*; *Shenbao*, January 5, 1937; "Heiren zuojia Xiushi di yi bu changpian xiaoshuo Zhong yi ben," *Tiebao*, November 6, 1936; Carrie Hughes to Langston, January 20, 1936, January 10, 1938, in Williams and Tidwell, *My Dear Boy*, 132, 157.

97. Dong, "Xiushi de xinzuo," *Qinghua zhoukan* 42, no. 9/10 (1934): 145. Works by Xiushi: "Yuehanxun jiejie de wangshi," trans. by Miss Xiyu, *Wenyi* 1, no. 1 (1933): 135–40; "Di wu nianji," trans. by Zhengnong, *Dushu shenghuo* 1, no. 1 (1934): 74–76; "Yi wei kelian de xiao Heiren," trans. by Yuliu, *Xin shidai* 6, no. 2 (1934): 83–86; "Zumu de jimo," trans. by Zhengnong, *Xin wenxue* 2 (1935): 244–49; "Tingyuan qinqu," trans. by Yun, *Zuotan* 1 (1934): 11; "Gei Adademy de xing," trans. by Yang Zhe, *Dangdai wenxue* 1, no. 3 (1934): 37 (see advertisement of the issue with the table of contents in *Shenbao* [September 16, 1934]). Works by Xiushi Lansidun: "Xiao youmo: SH-SSS-SS-S!," trans. by Zhuang Qidong, *Chuban xiaoxi* 21 (1933): 3–4; "Wo, ye," *Wenxue* 1, no. 4 (1933): 603; "Gongyuan de changdeng," trans. by Zhuang Qidong, *Shige yuebao* 1, no. 1 (1934): 8; "Liti," trans. by Zhuang Qidong, *Shige yuebao* 1, no. 2 (1934): 16–17; "Xiushi shichao" ("Hei zhongzi," "Gei yi ge Heiren zhidao zhe," "Heiren didai"), trans. by Yang Ren, *Shige* 1, no. 4 (1935): 33. Yang Changxi, *Heiren wenxue*; Liaoliao, "Xiushi de duanpian xiaoshuo ji," *Libao*, April 22, 1936.

98. Works by Langston Hughes, "Luosifu xiaodiao," *Yanda zhoukan* 7, no. 9 (1936): 8–10; "Laughter in Madrid," *China Press*, April 29, 1938. Lanshidun Xiushi, "Heiren," trans. by Aiyi, *Qianxian ribao*, January 7, 1937. Works by L. Xiushi: "Shangdi gei ji'e de haizi," *Wenxue congbao* 1, no. 5 (1936): 344; "Shengdan de qianxi," trans. by Yao Ke, *Yiwen* 1, no. 3 (1936): 658–66; "Madeli," trans. by Liu Jin, *Wenyi tuji* 1, no. 4 (1939): 99–102; "Madeli zai xiaozhe," *Qiyue* 3, no. 4 (1938): 121–22. Works by Xiushi: "Xiushi shi er shou" ("Ojibwa de zhange" and "Wo ye lai"), trans. by Li Ronghua, *Meiyue shige* 2, no. 3 (1936): 29–31; "Wu lianchi de Kela," trans. by Chonggang, *Xin Zhonghua* 5, no. 3 (1937): 49–54; "Bairen," trans. by Lu Xi, *Renjian shiri* 3 (1937): 13; "Hei nü Jialan," trans. by Zhou Huaguo, *Fudan xuebao* 3 (1936): 1–11; "Anni," trans. by Li Jin, *Xin shidai* 7, no. 1 (1937): 48–57; "Basaluona de kongxi," *Gongyu banyue kan* 6 (1938): 37; "Basailongna de kongxi," trans. by Ma Er, *Daobao*, November 29, 1938; "Madeli de renmen," trans. by Shi, *Daobao*, January 26, 1939.

99. This volume also introduced Rabindranath Tagore and Shudha Mazumdar of India; Melek Hanum of Turkey; Andri Holovko of Ukraine; Olive Schreiner of South Africa; Milan Ogrizovic of Croatia; Russian Jewish writers I. L. Peree and David Binksi; Zhang Hezhou, a Korean writing in Japanese; Mongolian writer Makhmud Galyan; a Persian fable; and "Aladdin." Some were translated by Ye Lingfeng and Zhou Zuoren. The editor noted that the pro-British Mazumdar, "a daughter of a land owner and wife of the viceroy of Bangladesh, fully illustrates the true color of Indian intellectuals educated by whites." Xiushi, "Xin di de liwu," trans. by Zhu Xiuxia, in Shi Leying, *Ruoguo xiaoshuo mingzhu*, 99–108.

100. Lee, *Ethnic Avant-Garde*, 68–72; Mayakefusiji (Soviet Union), "Zai Hawala deng'an" and "Gunchu Zhongguo," *Yizuo* 1 (1937): 95–104.

101. "To Maxim Lieber," December 30, 1940, and "To Arthur Spingarn," January 30, 1941, in Rampersad, Roessel, and Fratantoro, *Selected Letters of Langston Hughes*, 223, 225, 237; Langston Hughes, "Goodbye Christ," *Saturday Evening Post*, December 21, 1940, 34.

102. "To Carl Van Vechten," June 21 [22] and October 8, 1941, in Rampersad, Roessel, and Fratantoro, *Selected Letters of Langston Hughes*, 230–31, and Bernard, *Remembering Me to Harlem*, 190.

103. "To Miss Jessie Parkhurst Guzman, Negro Year Book, Department of Records and Research, Tuskegee Institute," December 2, 1947, and "To Horace Bond," April 30, 1948, in Rampersad, Roessel, and Fratantoro, *Selected Letters of Langston Hughes*, 276–77, 280–81.

104. Eslanda Robeson to Hughes, February 28, 1944, March 10 and April 16, 1948, Eslanda Goode Robeson, series I, Personal Correspondence, box 138, folder 2562, LHP.

105. Robeson was alleged to be associated with fifty-one to sixty communist front organizations; Du Bois, eleven to twenty; and Shirley Graham, Marlon Brando, and Aubrey Pankey, one to ten. House Un-American Activities Committee, "Review of the Scientific and Cultural Conference for World Peace," Washington, D.C., April 19, 1949, 17–20. "To Richard Morford, Executive Director, National Council of American-Soviet Friendship, Inc.," May 27, 1952, in Rampersad, Roessel, and Fratantoro, *Selected Letters of Langston Hughes*, 309–10.

106. Hughes, *I Wonder as I Wander*, 256.

107. Chen Leyda, *Footnote to History*, 238; Chen to Hughes (postcard), March 3, 1937.

108. "To Salvia Chen," March 4, 1937, in Rampersad, Roessel, and Fratantoro, *Selected Letters of Langston Hughes*, 198; Chen to Hughes, March 3 (postcard), March 11, and 19, 1937, February 2 and August 1, 1938; Chen Leyda, *Footnote to History*, 238.

109. Hughes to Chen, January 30, June, July 1 and 16, 1938; Chen to Hughes, February 2 and July 5, 1938 (postcards); *Daily Worker* (New York), November 5, 1938.

110. Hughes to Chen, n.d., October 26, 1942; Chen to Hughes, September 10, 1942, April 23, May 28, and July 3, 1946, n.d.

111. *Amsterdam News*, October 17, 1942; Van Vechten to Hughes, October 13, 1942, and Hughes to Van Vechten, November 25, 1949, in Bernard, *Remembering Me to Harlem*, 213, 264.

112. For Van Vechten photographs, see Beinecke Rare Book and Manuscript Library, "Carl Van Vechten's Portraits," https://beinecke.library.yale.edu/collections/highlights /carl-van-vechtens-portraits, and "Loh Tsei," http://brbl-dl.library.yale.edu/vufind /Record/3558098?image_id=1245024; Van Vechten to Gertrude Stein and Alice Toklas (postcard), December 17, 1937, in Burns, *Letters of Gertrude Stein and Carl Van Vechten*, 582. Hilda Yen rejoined the Chen children in Moscow while working at the Chinese embassy, where her uncle Weiching Williams Yen was the ambassador. Chen Yuan-tsung, *Return to the Middle Kingdom*, 214. In his letters to Si-lan, Jack noted that Yen sold her jewelry for her passage to the United States in late 1937 to learn aviation. He inquired of Yen's plane crash in 1938 and affectionately requested, "By the way look out for my aviatrix." Jack to the Leydas, October 1938, box 28, folder 12, JSCL. Percy recorded his interactions with Ya-ching Lee in his autobiography, and Jack also wrote about her. Chen, *China Called Me*, 274–75, 282, 300, 305; Jack Chen, "Miss Lee Ya-ching Tells Experience on Air Tour," *China Press*, February 19, 1937.

113. Hughes to Van Vechtan, March 1, 1933, February 21, 1934, in Bernard, *Remembering Me to Harlem*, 118–20; Van Vechten to Hughes, April 3, 1933, [after February 21, 1934]; Chen to Hughes, early 1934, June 26, and December 3, 1934, March 4, May 8 and 11, August 2, 1935; Hughes to Chen, July 7 and October 18, 1934; Bernard, *Remembering Me to Harlem*, 103–4.

114. Chen to Hughes, June 26 and September 10, 1942; Hughes to Chen, October 26, 1942; Jack to the Leydas, October 1943, Buck to Chen, September 10 and November 20, 1945, box 28, folders 8 and 12, JSCL. Buck's East West Association had sponsored Lin Peifen, acclaimed as "the first creative modern dancer to emerge from war-torn China," who toured the United States from 1948 to 1950. The perceived competition between the two dancers might have affected Buck's attitude toward Si-lan. *Pittsburgh Post-Gazette*, May 22, 1949; *Detroit Free Press*, March 12, 1949; *Cincinnati Enquirer*, December 26, 1948.

115. Chen to Hughes, April 23, May 28, and July 3, 1946; Hughes to Chen, May 20 and June 27, 1946.

116. Chen to Hughes, May 10, 1948.

117. Hughes, *Fields of Wonder*, 82; *Opportunity*, July 1948, 99.

118. Chen Leyda, *Footnote to History*, 151–52.

119. "To Maxim Lieber," April 23, 1941, "To Marie Short," November 15, 1942, "To Arna Bontemps," August 5, 1943, and "To Countee Cullen," July 23, 1943, in Rampersad, Roessel, and Fratantoro, *Selected Letters of Langston Hughes*, 228, 247, 253, 255; Bernard, *Remembering Me to Harlem*, 206.

120. De Santis, *Langston Hughes and the "Chicago Defender,"* 60.

121. Langston Hughes, "The Underground: Antifascists of the Occupied Countries of Europe and Asia," *New Masses*, September 28, 1943, 14; Rampersad, *Collected Poems*, 656, 683, 279–80, 299, 303; Dickinson, *Bio-bibliography of Langston Hughes*, 82, 207, 243; De Santis, *Langston Hughes and the "Chicago Defender,"* 123; *Chicago Defender*, May 23, 1943.

122. De Santis, *Langston Hughes and the "Chicago Defender,"* 60; "To Mr. Melvin B. Tolson," June 18, 1949, in Rampersad, Roessel, and Fratantoro, *Selected Letters of Langston Hughes*, 285; Melvin B. Tolson, "African China," *Voices*, Fall 1949.

123. Lanjun, "Meiguo Hei shiren Xiushi," *Zazhi* 5, no. 6 (1939): 48–49. Works by Xiushi: "Jingjichang de nuli," trans. by Guan Lu, *Shanghai funü* 3, no. 10 (1939): 18–21; "Luoyi xiansheng yu Baolin," trans. by Guan Lu, *Shanghai funü* 3, no. 11 (1939): 20–22; "Wuchi de Kela," trans. by Zhang Youlan, *Xingjian* 3, no. 1 (1940): 130–35. Works by L. Xiushi: "Jia," trans. by Guan Lu, *Wenyi xinchao* 1, no. 12 (1939): 412–15; "Jin fanwan dasui le," trans. by Bai Ying, *Zazhi* 10, no. 2 (1942): 103–8; "Bulang jiaoshou," trans. by Guo Min, *Shidai Zhongguo* 7, no. 1 (1943): 45–48. Works by Lasidong Xiushi and trans. by Zhang Youlan: "Kelian de xiao Heiren," *Xianzheng yuekan* 1, no. 1 (1940): 125–33; "Fu yu zi," *Xianzheng yuekan* 1, no. 2 (1940): 103–10; 1, no. 3 (1940): 103–11; "Yi ge Shengdanjie de wanshang," *Xianzheng yuekan* 1, no. 4 (1940): 105–7; "Bailei," *Zhengzhi yuekan* 1, no. 1 (1941): 139–42; "Muqin he haizi," *Shanghai minzhong* 1, no. 1 (1940): 47–49. Lansidong Xiushi, "Mingri de mengya," trans. by Zhao Qian, *Wenyi yuekan* (Nanjing) 5, no. 1 (1940): 5. Cai Dengshan, *Chong kan Minguo renwu*, 16–17.

124. Other authors formally included in the volume were "world-level poets" J. W. Goethe, Heinrich Heine, Friedrich Rückert, Friedrich Nietzsche, Percy Bysshe Shelley, Lord Byron, John Keats, William Wordsworth, Alphonse de Lamartine, Charles Baudelaire, Victor Hugo, Jorge Luis Morales, Mikhail Lermontov, Anton Chekhov, Ivan

Turgenev, Gabriele D'Annunzio, Sándor Petőfi, Walt Whitman, and Carl Sandburg; Chinese poets Yu Pingbo, Xu Zhimo, Li Jinfa, Dai Wangshu, and Zang Kejia; and five Japanese ones. Shanding, *Manwen jindai shijie shi xuan*, 1–2, 206–7, 251–61; L. Xiushi, "Jiaoshou," trans. by Li Zelan, *Wenyi yuebao* (Jilin) 1 (1948): 36–38.

125. *Shi chuangzuo* (Guilin) 15 (1942): 2; "Langsideng Xiushi jinzuo er shou," trans. by Yuan Shuipai, *Wenxue yuebao* (Chongqing) 3, no. 1 (1941): 27–28; Xiushi, "Diao le yi jian hao chaishi," trans. by Chen Souzhu, *Shichao yu wenyi* (Chongqing) 2, no. 2 (1943): 65–69; Xiushi, *Hei Lide*.

126. L. Xiushi, "Xiegei Chaqisi de shi," *Wenyi shenghuo* (Guilin) 10 (1946): 2–3; Lansidun Xiushi, "Heiren shige" ("Tong tanyu" and "Xiangjia lange"), *Shijie wenyi jikan* 1, no. 3 (1946): 70–73; Langsitun Xiushi, "Ziyou lieche," trans. by He Mo, *Beida banyue kan* 5 (1948): 13; L. Xiushi, "Ziyou lieche," trans. by Yuan Shuipai, *Zhongguo xinshi* 1 (1948): 38–40; Yuan Shuipai, "Heiren shiren Xiusi shi xuan: zhu tade sishiwu sui shengri," *Shuizhun* 1 (1947): 18–20.

127. "To L. B. Smith," March 9, 1952, in Rampersad, Roessel, and Fratantoro, *Selected Letters of Langston Hughes*, 307.

128. "To Frank D. Reeves," April 8, 1953, and "To Arna Bontemps," January 28, 1961, in Rampersad, Roessel, and Fratantoro, *Selected Letters of Langston Hughes*, 292, 313–14, 369.

129. Robeson to Hughes, September 18, 1950, Paul Robeson, Shirley Graham Du Bois, and John Howard Lawson et al. to Hughes, September 25, 1951, Paul Robeson, series I, Personal Correspondence, box 138, folder 2563; Du Bois to Hughes, January 8, 1945, August 17, 1951, February 15, 1952; Hughes to Du Bois, January 27, 1945, W. E. B. Du Bois, series I, Personal Correspondence, box 57, folder 1073; all in LHP. "Dr. W. A. Hunton, Expert on Africa," *NYT*, January 16, 1970.

130. Hughes, *Famous American Negroes*; Hughes, *Famous Negro Music Makers*; "To W. E. B. Du Bois," May 22, 1956, in Rampersad, Roessel, and Fratantoro, *Selected Letters of Langston Hughes*, 335; Lewis, *W. E. B. Du Bois*, 556; Du Bois, *Autobiography*, 396–97.

131. Hughes to Van Vechten, September 20, 1953, in Bernard, *Remembering Me to Harlem*, 274–75; Langston Hughes, "Mysterious Madam Shanghai," in *Laughing to Keep from Crying*, 1952.

132. Hughes, *Best of Simple*, 56, 59.

133. De Santis, *Langston Hughes and the "Chicago Defender,"* 60.

134. Rampersad, *Collected Poems*, 385–86, 449.

135. "China," box 224, folder 3711, LHP.

136. Rampersad, *Collected Poems*, 557, 670, 682.

137. Xiushi et al., *Heiren shixuan*, trans. by Zou Jiang (1952) and Zhang Qi (1957). Zhang translated from the English version of the bilingual "Auch ich bin Amerika," published by Volk und Welt Verlag in Berlin. Xiushi et al., *Heiren duanpian xiaoshuo ji*; Xiushi et al., *Heiren duanpian xiaoshuo xuan*.

138. Xiushi et al., *Heiren duanpian xiaoshuo ji*, iii–viii; Xiushi et al., *Heiren duanpian xiaoshuo xuan*, 1–3.

139. Xiushi et al., *Heiren shixuan* (1957), 21–35; Xiushi et al., *Heiren duanpian xiaoshuo xuan*, 1–3. Books by Langston Hughes: *Negro Mother, Dream Keeper, Dear Lovely Death*.

140. Xiushi et al., *Heiren duanpian xiaoshuo ji*, iii–viii; Xiushi et al., *Heiren duanpian xiaoshuo xuan*, 1–3.

141. Hughes, *An African Treasury*; Bingxin, "Jiana shixuan," *Shijie wenxue*, December

1962; Sun Wentao, "Wo yu Meiguo Heiren shiren Xiusi shi 'Ziyou' de yuanfen," *Shige bao*, January 6, 2007, http://www.shigebao.com/html/articles/34/2157.html (accessed March 15, 2021); Langston Hughes, "Merry-Go-Around," *Common Ground*, Spring 1942, 27; Langston Hughes, "Brass Spittoons," *New Masses*, December 1926; 10; Xiushi et al., *Heiren shixuan* (1974), 190–98.

142. Xiusi, *Dahai*; Luo Xingqun, *Lansidun Xiushi duanpian xiaoshuo ji*, 1–6, 453–55; Hughes, *Something in Common*.

143. Luo Xingqun, *Lansidun Xiushi duanpian xiaoshuo ji*, 1–19.

EPILOGUE

1. Shinn and Eisenman, *China and Africa*; French, *China's Second Continent*; Gadzala, *Africa and China*; Lee, *Specter of Global China*.

2. Shu Zhang, "Jinian Duboyisi danchen 125 zhounian ji," *Xiya Feizhou* 1 (1994): 65, 73–74; "Jinian Duboyisi danchen 125 zhounian," *Xiya Feizhou* 1 (1994): 1–9, 21–23; Aipositan, "Dui Duboyisi Boshi de yidian zhuiyi," *Xiya Feizhou* 1 (1994): 4–5; Gao Jinyuan, "Mo bu diao de guanghui," *Xiya Feizhou* 4 (1994): 63–64; Du Bois to students of Tianjin Normal University, December 2, 1959, WDBP; interview with David Du Bois, National Visionary Leadership Project, http://www.visionaryproject.org/duboisdavid.

3. "Baoluo Luoboxun danchen 110 zhounian jinianhui zai Jing juxing," China Net, http://www.china.com.cn/photo/txt/2008-04/09/content_14704104.htm (accessed March 13, 2021); Xiang Yansheng, "Meiguo Heiren Gewang Luoboxun yu 'Yiyongjun jinxing qu'"; China Central TV on Paul Robeson and "Chee Lai!," http://tv.cntv.cn/video/C10634/487f661cb56140480f0996a2f859cfdd (accessed February 17, 2015); Chen Yiming, "Cong jinian Luoboxun xiangdao Liu Liangmo," *Shiji* 4 (2009): 64–65; Li Guowen, "Baoluo Luoboxun de Zhongguo qingyuan," *Jinri Zhongguo* 5 (2008): 48–49; He Dazhang, "Ta changchu le renlei de xinsheng," *Guangming ribao*, April 17, 2008.

4. Yang, *China, Christianity, and the Question of Culture*.

5. Wilcox, *Revolutionary Bodies*, 32–44.

6. Xiushi, *Fu yu zi*. The other foreign poem included in this textbook is "Motherland" by the Russian poet Mikhail Lermontov; see http://old.pep.com.cn/czyw/jszx/ztts/fenxj/jx/dydy/4/201008/t20100825_738162.htm (accessed April 25, 2017).

7. Example entries: Xiusi, *Lansidun Xiusi shixuan* (two versions by Shanghai Yiwen Chubanshe and Shanghai Wenyi Chubanshe); Tang Gengjin and Wan Hua, *Ying Mei shige daodu*, Shanghai: Shanghai Daxue Chubanshe, 2014; Tao Shan, "'Zaoqiu' de wenti tedian fenxi," *Kaoshi zhoukan* 22 (2010): 30–31; Tian Zaigeng, "Lansidun Xiusi jiqi Heiren shi," *Chengdu daxue xuebao* 2 (1993): 40–42; Ou Rong and Li Tingting, "Chaoyue *Pijuan De Bulusi*," *Meiyu xuekan* 1 (2018): 61–66; Wang Chao and Zhang Wenqing, "Bulusi yinyue yu Lansidun Xiusi de guanxi," *Jiannan wenxue* 7 (2011): 83–85; Liu Wei, "*Lansidun Xiusi shixuan*: Jueshi shiren de shenchen yongtan," *Zhonghua dushu bao*, September 30, 2018.

Bibliography

ARCHIVAL SOURCES

Archives of the Pearl S. Buck House, 520 Dublin Road, Perkasie, Pa.
Arthur and Elizabeth Schlesinger Library, Radcliffe Institute for
    Advanced Study, Harvard University, Cambridge, Mass.
    Shirley Graham Du Bois Papers, MC476
    Dorothy West Papers, MC676
Asia Library, University of Michigan
    The Pioneers of Chinese Dance Digital Collection
Beinecke Rare Book and Manuscript Library, Yale University Library, New Haven, Conn.
    Langston Hughes Papers, JWJ MSS 26
        Series I, Personal Correspondence
            Sylvia Chen, 1934–46, Box 43, Folder 770
            "China," Box 224, Folder 3711
            Nancy Cunard, Box 49, Folder 918
            W. E. B. Du Bois, Box 57, Folder 1073
            I Wonder as I Wander, draft, Box 304, Folder 4999
            Eslanda Goode Robeson, Box 138, Folder 2562
            Paul Robeson, Box 138, Folder 2563
        Series XII, Photographs
            Langston Hughes Chronology, 1930s, Box 460,
                Folder 11127, and Box 459, Folder 11105
    Photographs of Prominent African Americans, JWJ MSS 76
        Paul Robeson, Box 16, Folder 169
"California Death Index, 1940–1997." Department of Public Health Services, Sacramento, Calif.
    Entry for Silan Chen Leyda, March 8, 1996
Divinity Library, Yale University Library
    Liu Liangmo, "Suggestions to New Missionaries from a Chinese Brother," 1943, A169.19
Elmer Holmes Bobst Library, New York University
    Tamiment Library and Robert F. Wagner Labor Archives

The American Council on Soviet Relations Records, TAM.134
Jay and Si-lan Chen Leyda Papers and Photographs, TAM.083
FBI files
"Sylvia Si-lan Chen"
"W. E. B. and Shirley Graham Du Bois"
"Langston Hughes"
"Liu Liangmo"
"Paul and Eslanda Goode Robeson"
Huntington Library, Manuscript Department, San Marino, Calif.
Langston Hughes Papers (1932–34), mssHM 64089 and mssHM 64070–64101
Library of Congress, Washington, D.C.
Talks by Spaeth etc., RBML_ABMAC_Record Group 20
Lincoln Center, New York Public Library
Program fliers, MoMA, Photographs, Dance, ca. 1900–1950, vol. 2, nos. 58–137
Moorland-Spingarn Research Center, Manuscript Division,
Howard University, Washington, D.C.
Paul and Eslanda Goode Robeson Archives
National Archives, Kew, Richmond, Surrey, England
Records of the Board of Trade and of Successor and Related Bodies
"Sylvia Acham-Chen-Leyda," Outward Passenger Lists, BT27
National Archives, San Francisco, Calif.
Records of the Immigration and Naturalization Service (INS), Record Group 85
"Liu Liangmo." File 36590/7-4, Box 3429, Shelf 3300E
National Archives, Washington, D.C.
Records of the INS, Record Group 85
"Alphabetical Manifests of Non-Mexican Aliens Granted Temporary
Admission at Lerado, Texas, Dec. 1, 1929–April 8, 1955." Microfilm Roll 1
"Passenger Lists of Vessels Arriving at New York, 1820–1897," Microfilm Roll 6569
New York Public Library
"Chen, Si-lan," Yaddo Records "Guest," File 10813
Seeley G. Mudd Manuscript Library, Princeton University, Princeton, N.J.
United China Relief Archives
University of Massachusetts Amherst Libraries, Amherst, Mass.
Special Collections and University Archives
W. E. B. Du Bois Papers, MS 312

RECORD ALBUMS

Robeson, Paul, and Keynote Orchestra and Chorus. *Anthem of the U.S.S.R.* New York: Keynote Recordings, 1944.
Robeson, Paul, Liu Liangmo, and the Chinese People's Chorus. *Chee Lai!: Songs of New China.* New York: Keynote Recordings, 1941.

FILMS, VIDEOS, AND AUDIO RECORDINGS

China Central TV. Lunar New Year Gala 2018. https://www.youtube.com/watch?v=FeRi86DcfyA.

China Central TV. Lunar New Year Gala 2021. https://www.youtube.com/watch?v
=MZ8MpS6tLcY.

China Central TV. Paul Robeson and "Chee Lai." http://tv.cntv.cn/video/C10634
/487f661cb56140480f0996a2f859cfdd.

China Central TV. "Salute to Classics: Wang Luobing." https://www.youtube.com
/watch?v=6Rky-2kP240.

Documentary *Welcome, Dr. William E. B. Du Bois!* on W. E. B. and Shirley Graham Du
Bois's 1959 visit to China, made by the Central News and Documentary Film Studio
on behalf of the Chinese People's Association for Cultural Relations with Foreign
Countries, May 1959. https://credo.library.umass.edu/view/full/mums312-b246-
i002.

Madam Chiang Kai-shek address to the U.S. Congress, February 18, 1943. https://archive
.org/details/MadameChiangToCongress.

"Paul Robeson Speaks! International Peace Arch, Blaine, Washington State, May 18, 1952."
https://www.youtube.com/watch?v=VLCndkx1e10.

Paul Robeson testimony before the House Un-American Activities Committee, July 13,
1956. https://www.youtube.com/watch?v=VhnCrHZkgNk.

Why We Fight: The Battle of China, 1944. http://www.imdb.com/title/tt0184254/?ref_
=nv_sr_6.

WEBSITES

Archives. "Silan Chen Leyda in the 1940 U.S. Population Census." http://www.archives
.com/1940-census/silan-leyda-ny-57602177k.

"Baoluo Luoboxun danchen 110 zhounian jinianhui zai Jing juxing." China Net. http://
www.china.com.cn/photo/txt/2008-04/09/content_14704104.htm.

Beinecke Rare Book and Manuscript Library. "Carl Van Vechten's Portraits." https://
beinecke.library.yale.edu/collections/highlights/carl-van-vechtens-portraits.

————. "Loh Tsei." Photographs by Carl Van Vechten. http://brbl-dl.library.yale.edu
/vufind/Record/3558098?image_id=1245024.

China Ministry of Education prescribes a translation of Langston Hughes's "The Negro
Speaks of Rivers" in the approved textbook of Chinese language and literature
mandated for ninth graders. http://old.pep.com.cn/czyw/jszx/ztts/fenxj/jx
/dydy/4/201008/t20100825_738162.htm.

Columbia University Alumni Register, 1754–1931. https://babel.hathitrust.org/cgi/pt?id
=uc1.b4525470&view=1up&seq=9.

Du Bois, David. Interview. National Visionary Leadership Project. http://www.visionary
project.org/duboisdavid.

"Estate of Georgette Chen." http://giving.nus.edu.sg/the-undying-legacy-of-georgette
-chen/.

Fairbank Center for Chinese Studies at Harvard University. "Teaching China through
Black History: A Reading and Teaching Guide to the History of Black and African
American Connections with China." https://medium.com/fairbank-center/teaching
-china-through-Black-history-30e3cdc32f03.

Grinbert, Alexander. Photographs. https://unregardoblique.home.blog/tag/alexander
-danilovich-grinberg/ or https://dantebea.files.wordpress.com/2013/11/alexander
-grinberg-the-dancer-sylvia-chen-via-mutualart.jpeg.

IBDB (Internet Broadway Database). "Roar China." https://www.ibdb.com/broadway
-production/roar-china-11246.

Liang Shiqiu. "Guanyu Lu Xun." http://www.millionbook.com/mj/l/liangshiqiu/lsq
/10.htm.

Lin Yutang. *Lin Yutang zizhuan.* https://www.kanunu8.com/book3/7604/167067.html.

Lü Qiqing and Zhao Le. "Gesheng zhong de kangzhan chuanqi." China National Radio.
http://gscq.cnr.cn/gbgx/20150921/t20150921_519921389_4.shtml.

"The Melville Society Archive: Finding Aid to the Jay Leyda Papers (1944–1956)." http://
melvillesociety.org/ms-archive/jay-leyda-papers-finding-aid/97-overview-of-the-jay
-leyda-papers-finding-aid-listings.

MoMA blog. https://www.moma.org/explore/inside_out/2015/10/23/from-the
-archives-dance-and-theater/.

New York Public Library Digital Collections. "Scene from Roar China: NYC 1930—
Theatre Guild Production." https://digitalcollections.nypl.org/items/510d47dc
-9f51-a3d9-e040-e00a18064a99.

Shen Congwen. *Alisi Zhongguo youji.* http://www.dushu369.com/zhongguomingzhu
/HTML/70777.html.

Wang Xueqi. "Dianying xiju mingxing Wang Ying he Heiren Gewang Luoboxun de you
yi jiaowang." China Society for People's Friendship Studies. http://www.cspfs.com.cn
/speechbyWangXuexin.html.

Xie Bingxin. "Ji Sa Zhenbing xiansheng." http://tieba.baidu.com/p/2081647777.

"Yaddocast: Episode 14: Si-lan Chen." http://yaddocast.libsyn.com/episode-14-Si
-lan-chen.

CHINESE-LANGUAGE NEWSPAPERS AND PERIODICALS

Beida banyue kan

Beilei

Beiyang huabao

Changcheng (Suiyuan)

Changcheng (Shanghai)

Chenbao

Chuban xiaoxi

Dadi

Dafeng (Hong Kong)

Dafeng (Jinhua)

Dagong bao (Guilin)

Dagong bao (Hong Kong)

Dagong bao (Shanghai)

Dagong bao (Tianjin)

Dangdai wenxue

Daobao

Da wan bao

Dazhong dianying

Dazhong huabao

Diantong huabao

Dianying huabao

Dianying shibao

Dikang sanri kan

Dongfang huabao

Dongfang zazhi

Dushu

Dushu shenghuo

Ertong zhishi

Fudan xuebao

Fujian daobao

Funü shenghuo

Funü wenxian

Gongjiao zhoukan

Gongyu banyue kan

Guangming ribao

Guangzhou qingnian

Guansheng

Gudao

Guomin gongbao

Guomin gonglun (Hankou)

Guowen zhoubao

Haitao

Haixing

Honglu

Huanian

Huaqiao banyue kan

Huchao

Huda zhoukan

Jiefang ribao

Jinhua dongnan zhanxian

Jinri Zhongguo

Kangjian fukan

Kangzhan

Kangzhan huabao

Kangzhan huakan

Kangzhan sanri kan

Kangzhan yuebao

Kuaihuo lin

Laosao yuekan (Tianjin)

Laoshi hua

Liangyou

Liansheng

Libao

Linglong

Maodun yuekan

Meiyue shige

Meizhou huaqiao ribao

Minbao

Minguo ribao

Mingxing

Nüduo

Nü qingnian yuekan

Nüsheng

Qianxian ribao

Qinghua zhoukan

Qingnian dazhong

Qingnian shenghuo (Guilin)

Qingnian you

Qiyue

Quanmin kangzhan sanri kan

Quanmin kangzhan zhoukan

Renjian shiri

Renmin ribao

Renmin yinyue

Renwu

Riben pinglun sanri kan

Shangbao huakan

Shanghai funü

Shanghai zhoubao

Shehui xinwen

Shenbao

Shenghuo huabao

Shenghuo jiaoyu

Shenghuo zhoukan

Sheying huabao

Shi chuangzuo

Shibao

Shichao yu wenyi (Chongqing)

Shidai manhua

Shidai ribao

Shidai Zhongguo

Shige

Shige bao

Shige yuebao

Shiji

Shijie wenyi jikan

Shishi yuebao

Shuizhun

Tianfeng

Tianjin qingnian

Tiebao

Tonggong

Tuanxun (Changsha)

Wenshi (Beiping)

Wenxue

Wenxue congbao

Wenxue yuebao

Wenyi

Wenyi shenghuo (Guilin)

Wenyi tuji

Wenyi xinchao

Wenyi yuebao

Wenyi yuekan (Nanjing)

Xiandai

Xiandai chuban jie

Xianggang qingnian

Xianzheng yuekan

Xiao pengyou

Xiaojie

Xiaoxi

Xin ertong banyue kan

Xin Hunan xunkan

Xin shehui

Xin shidai

Xin wenxue

Xin Zhonghua

Xinghua
Xingjian
Xingqi pinglun
Xinhua yuebao
Xinhuashe dianxun gao
Xinya
Xiya Feizhou
Xuesheng zazhi
Xunhuan
Yibao zhoukan
Yinyue shijie
Yishi bao
Yiwen
Yizuo
Zazhi

Zhange (Shaoxing)
Zhanshi huakan
Zhanshi jiaoyu
Zhejiang chao
Zhengyi bao
Zhengzhi qingbao
Zhengzhi yuekan
Zhongguo xinshi
Zhonghua zhoubao
Zhongyang ribao
Zhongyang zhoubao
Zhoubao
Zixiu daxue
Zuotan

ENGLISH-LANGUAGE NEWSPAPERS AND PERIODICALS

Abilene (Tex.) Reporter-News
Afro American News
Albuquerque (N.M.) Journal
Alton (Iowa) Democrat
American Dancer
Amsterdam News
Argus-Leader (Sioux Falls, S.D.)
Arizona Daily Star
Asbury Park (N.J.) Evening Press
Asbury Park (N.J.) Press
Asheville (N.C.) Citizen
Asia
Atlantic Monthly
Baltimore Afro-American
Baltimore Sun
Beckley (W.Va.) Post-Herald
Berkshire Eagle (Pittsfield, Mass.)
Billings (Mont.) Gazette
Binghamton (N.Y.) Press
Black Scholar
Brook (Ind.) Reporter
Brooklyn (N.Y.) Daily Eagle
California Eagle
Canton (Penn.) Independent-Sentinel
Chicago Defender
Chicago Globe
Chicago Tribune
China at War
China Pictorial

China Press (Shanghai)
Cincinnati Enquirer
Citizen Advertiser (New York)
Clarion-Ledger (Jackson, Miss.)
Common Ground
Council Bluffs (Iowa) Nonpareil
Courier Journal (Louisville, Ky.)
Courier-News (Bridgewater, N.J.)
Crisis
Daily Herald (London)
Daily Herald (Provo, Utah)
Daily Home News (New Brunswick, N.J.)
Daily Missoulian (Mont.)
Daily People's World
Daily Press (Newport News, Va.)
Daily Times (Davenport, Iowa)
Daily Times (Salisbury, Md.)
Daily Worker (London)
Daily Worker (New York)
Daily World (Aberdeen, Wash.)
Danville (Penn.) Morning News
Davenport (Iowa) Democrat and Leader
Delta Democrat-Times (Greenville, Miss.)
Des Moines (Iowa) Register
Detroit Free Press
Dispatch (Moline, Ill.)
Elmira (N.Y.) Star-Gazette
Evening News (Harrisburg, Penn.)
Evening News (Wilkes Barre, Penn.)

Fisk News
Fort Lauderdale (Fla.) News
Freedom
Gazette and Daily (York, Penn.)
Geneva (N.Y.) Daily Times
Gila News-Courier (Rivers, Ariz.)
Great Falls (Mont.) Tribune
Green Bay (Wisc.) Press-Gazette
Hartford (Conn.) Daily Courant
Heart Mountain Sentinel (Cody, Wyo.)
Herald Statesman (Yonkers, N.Y.)
Honolulu Advertiser
Honolulu Star-Bulletin
Illustrated London News
Independent Weekly (Yinghua duli
    zhoubao)
Index Journal (Greenwood, S.C.)
Indiana Gazette
Indianapolis News
International Literature
Ithaca (N.Y.) Journal
Journal-Every Evening
    (Wilmington, Del.)
Kansas City (Kans.) Plaindealer
Kingston (N.Y.) Daily Freeman
Labour/Le Travail
Lancaster (Ohio) Eagle-Gazette
Lansing (Mich.) State Journal
Leader (Corning, N.Y.)
Leader (Manchester, N.H.)
Leader Republican (New York)
Lincoln (N.C.) Herald
London Morning Post
Long Island Society
Los Angeles Times
Manzanar (Calif.) Free Press
March of Labor
Mason City (Iowa) Globe-Gazette
Messenger
Miami (Fla.) Daily News
Minidoka Irrigator (Hunt, Ida.)
Minneapolis Star-Journal
Minnesota Star
Monroe (La.) News Star
Monthly Review
Morning Call (Allentown, Penn.)
Morning Herald (Hagerstown, Md.)

Morning Herald (Uniontown, Penn.)
Nassau (N.Y.) Daily Review-Star
National Guardian
National News
Negro Digest
New Africa
Newark (Ohio) Advocate
Newburgh (N.Y.) News
New Masses
New Republic
News-Chronicle (Shippensburg, Penn.)
News Journal (Wilmington, Del.)
News-Palladium (Benton Harbor, Mich.)
New Statesman and Nation
New World Review
New York Age
New York Amsterdam Star-News
New York Herald Tribune
New York Post
New York Sun
New York Times
New York World-Telegram
North-China Daily News (Shanghai)
Official Press Daily Bulletin
    (Poston, Ariz.)
Ogden (Utah) Standard-Examiner
Olivet (Mich.) Optic
Opportunity: A Journal of Negro Life
Orangetown Telegram
    (Spring Valley, N.Y.)
Oswego (N.Y.) Palladium-Times
Otsego Farmer (Cooperstown, N.Y.)
Outpost (Rohwer, Ark.)
Pacemaker (Santa Anita, Calif.)
Palladium-Item and Sun Telegram
    (Richmond, Ind.)
Palm Beach (Fla.) Post
Peace Reporter (New York)
Peking Review
Penn Yan (N.Y.) Democrat
Philadelphia Inquirer
Phylon: The Atlanta University Review
    of Race and Culture
Pittsburgh Courier
Pittsburgh Post-Gazette
Pittsburgh Press
PM

Post-Standard (Syracuse, N.Y.)
Pottstown (Penn.) Mercury
Putnam County Courier (Carmel, N.Y.)
Reader's Digest
Reynolds News (London)
Richfield Springs (N.Y.) Mercury
Rochester (N.Y.) Democrat and Chronicle
Salem (Ohio) News
Salt Lake Tribune (Salt Lake City, Utah)
San Bernardino County (Calif.) Sun
Santa Ana (Calif.) Register
Santa Fe New Mexican
Saturday Evening Post
Sentinel (Carlisle, Penn.)
Shanghai Evening Post & Mercury
Shanghai Times
Spectator (London)
St. Louis Post-Dispatch
St. Louis Star and Times
St. Petersburg (Fla.) Times
Staats-Zeitung und Herold (New York)
Suburbanite Economist (Chicago)
Syracuse (N.Y.) Herald American
Tampa (Fla.) Times
Tanforan Totalizer (San Bruno, Calif.)

Theatre World
Time
Times Herald (Port Huron, Mich.)
Times-Leader (Wilkes-Barre, Penn.)
Times Record (New York)
Topaz (Utah) Times
Toronto Star
Trek (Topaz, Utah)
Troy (N.Y.) Record
United Asia
Variety
Vassar Chronicle
Voices
Washington Post
Waukesha (Wisc.) Daily Freeman
Webster (N.Y.) Herald
Weekly Review
West African Review
Western Weekly Magazine
Wilkes-Barre (Penn.) Record
Wilmington (Del.) Morning News
Winnipeg (Manitoba) Tribune
Word and Way (Kansas City, Mo.)
Worker (New York)

DISSERTATIONS AND THESES

Chang, Pengchun. "Education for Modernization in China." PhD diss., Columbia University, 1923.

Liu, Herman Zhan'en. "Non-Verbal Intelligence Tests for Use in China." PhD diss., Columbia University, 1922.

Tyerman, Edward. "The Search for an Internationalist Aesthetics: Soviet Images of China, 1920–1935." PhD diss., Columbia University, 2014.

Zhang Wei. "Yi 'Zaina yaoyuan di defang.'" MA thesis, Zhongyang Yingyue Xueyuan, 2010.

ARTICLES AND BOOKS IN CHINESE AND RUSSIAN

Baoluo Luoboxun. Beijing: Yinyue Chubanshe, 1958.

Bingxin. "Dao Duboyisi Boshi." Shejie wenxue 9 (1963).

Cai Dengshan. Chong kan Minguo renwu. Taiwan: Duli Zuojia, 2014.

Chen Weijiang, trans. Zenyang cujin shijie Jidutu tuanqi. Shanghai: Qingnian Xiehui Shuju, 1939.

Chen Weijiang and Liu Liangmo, trans. Zhe shidai de nüren. Shanghai: Changcheng Shuju, 1935.

Chen Yiming. "Gesheng jili aiguo qing." *Lianhe shibao*, November 6, 2009.

"Chen Youren yishi." *Zhenguan zazhi* 30, no. 4 (1931): 84–85.

Chen Yuan-tsung. *Minguo waijiao qiangren Chen Youren—yi ge jiazu de chuanqi*. Hong Kong: Sanlian Shudian Youxian Gongsi, 2009.

Duboyisi, Wei Ai Bo. *Feizhou: Feizhou dalu jiqi jumin de lishi gaishu*. Translated by Cai Hui et al. Beijing: Shijie Zhishi Chubanshe, 1964.

———. *Mengsa de kaoyan, Mengsa ban xuexiao, Youse renzhong de shijie*. Translated by Cai Hui et al. Shanghai: Zuojia Chubanshe, 1966.

Duboyisi, Wei Ai Bojiate. *Heiren de linghun*. Translated by Weiqun. Beijing: Renmin Wenxue Chubanshe, 1959.

———. *Wei heping er zhan*. Translated by Weiqun. Beijing: Shijie Zhishi Chubanshe, 1953.

———. *Yuehan Bulang*. Translated by Weiqun. Beijing: Sanlian Shudian, 1959; Renmin Chubanshe, 1976.

———. *Yuehan de guilai*. Translated by Weiqun. Beijing: Shangwu Yinshuguan, 1960.

Gelanmu, Xiulai. *Heiren geshou Luoboxun*. Translated by Fang Yingyang. Shanghai: Zhengfeng Chubanshe, 1950; Changsha: Hunan Renmin Chubanshe, 1981.

Geleihanmu, Xiulai. *Congqian you ge nuli*. Translated by Bei Jin. Beijing: Renmin Wenxue Chubanshe, 1959.

Geleimu. *Heiren kexue jia Kafo*. Hong Kong: Jinri Shijie She, 1960.

Geleimu and Lisike. *Heiren kexue jia Qiaozhi Huashengdun Kafo'er zhuan*. Translated by Nie Miao. Shanghai: Shanghai Guang Xuehui, 1949.

Hanmi'erdun, Fojiniya. *Heiren Gewang Luoboxun*. Translated by Cheng Cheng. Tianjin: Tianjin Renmin Chubanshe, 1981.

He Dazhang. *Yi ge zhenshi de Song Qingling*. Hong Kong: Xianggang Zhonghe Chuban Youxian Gongsi, 2013.

Hughes, Langston. *Zdrastvui Revoliutsiia*. Translated by U. Anisimov. Moscow: Gosudarstvennoe Izdatel'stvo Khudozhestvennoi Literatury, 1933.

Lin Shu and Wei Yi, trans. *Heinu yutian lu*. 4 vols. Wulin: Weishi, 1901.

Li Runxin. *Jiebai de mingxing Wang Ying*. Beijing: Zhongguo Qingnian Chubanshe, 1987.

Li Shizhao. *Baoluo Luoboxun yanchang de Heiren minge*. Beijing: Renmin Yinyue Chubanshe, 1991.

Liu Liangmo. "Guanyu yuanzidan ji qita." *Guangming ribao*, September 28, 1949; *Meizho huaqiao ribao*, July 19, 21, and 22, 1950; and in Liu Lianmo, *Wo suo zhidao de Meiguo*, 32–36. Shanghai: Qingnian Xiehui Shuju, 1951.

———. *Huangjia Zhuang*. Shenghuo Shudian, 1938.

———. "Jinda qingshuan Mei di yundong." *Guangming ribao*, February 1, 1951; and in Liu Liangmo, *Meiguo zenyang liyong zongjiao qinglue Zhongguo*, 17–27. Shanghai: Qingnian Xiehui Shuju, 1951.

———. "Luoboxun yu 'Yiyongjun jinxing qu.'" Appendix to Xiulai Gelanmu, *Heiren geshou Luoboxun*, translated by Fang Yingyang, 384–88. Shanghai: Zhengfeng Chubanshe, 1950.

———. *Mao Zedong sixiang xuexi shouce*. 1950. Shanghai: Qingnian Xiehui Shuju, 1971.

———. "Meiguo de fan Su fan gong kuang." *Guangming ribao*, September 7, 1949; *Meizhou huaqiao ribao*, July 8 and 9, 1950; and in Liu Liangmo, *Wo suo zhidao de Meiguo*, 6–11. Shanghai: Qingnian Xiehui Shuju, 1950.

———. "Meiguo de jinbu liliang." *Guangming ribao*, September 15, 1949; *Meizhou huaqiao ribao*, July 22, 24, 25, 1950; and in Liu Liangmo, *Wo suo zhidao de Meiguo*, 37–41. Shanghai: Qingnian Xiehui Shuju, 1950.

———. "Meiguo de jingji konghuang." *Guangming ribao*, September 5, 1949; *Meizhou huaqiao ribao*, July 6 and 7, 1950; and in Liu Liangmo, *Wo suo zhidao de Meiguo*, 1–5. Shanghai: Qingnian Xiehui Shuju, 1950.

———. "Meiguo dui Heiren de qishi." *Guangming ribao*, September 10, 1949; *Meizhou huaqiao ribao*, July 13, 1950; and in Liu Liangmo, *Wo suo zhidao de Meiguo*, 16–19. Shanghai: Qingnian Xiehui Shuju, 1950.

———. "Meiguo dui huaqiao de wuru." *Guangming ribao*, September 9, 1949; *Meizhou huaqiao ribao*, July 10 and 11, 1950; and in Liu Liangmo, *Wo suo zhidao de Meiguo*, 12–15. Shanghai: Qingnian Xiehui Shuju, 1950.

———. *Meiguo zenyang liyong zongjiao qinglue Zhongguo*. Shanghai: Qingnian Xiehui Shuju, 1951.

———. *Minzhong geyong abc*. Kunming: Yunnan Shengli Minzhong Jiaoyu Guan Minzhong Geyong tuan, 1937.

———. *Qingnian ge ji*. Shanghai: Qingnian Xiehui Xiaohui Zu, 1937.

———. "Renmin geshou Luoboxun." *Shijie zhishi* 20, no. 15 (September 23, 1949); and *Meizhou huaqiao ribao*, July 13 14, 15, and 17, 1950; and in Liu Liangmo, *Wo suo zhidao de Meiguo*, 20–26. Shanghai: Qingnian Xiehui Shuju, 1950.

———. *Renmin Zhengxie yu sanda wenjian xuexi shouce*. Shanghai: Qingnian Xiehui Shuju, 1950.

———. "Riben feiji he Zhongguo xiaohai." *Dikang sanri kan* 14 (1937): 9–10; and in *Huzhan xiezhen*, edited by Hu Tian, 175–78. Chengdu: 1938.

———. "Shanghai kang Ri jiuwang de geyong yundong." *Wenshi ziliao xuanji* 1 (1978).

———. *Shenmo shi tongyi zhanxian*. Shanghai: Qingnian Xiehui Chubanshe, 1950.

———. *Shiba ge yue zai qianfang*. Hong Kong: Qingnian Xiehui Shuju, 1939.

———. "Shou mengbi de Meiguo renmin." *Guangming ribao*, October 4, 1949; *Meizhou huaqiao ribao*, July 17, 18, and 19, 1950; and in Liu Liangmo, *Wo suo zhidao de Meiguo*, 27–31. Shanghai: Qingnian Xiehui Shuju, 1950.

———. "Suiyuan de minzhong liliang." *Guomin zhoukan*, May 12, 1937; and *Wenzhai* 1, no. 6 (1937): 203–4.

———. *Wo suo zhidao de Meiguo*. Shanghai: Qingnian Xiehui Shuju, 1950.

———. *Xin minzhu zhuyi xuexi shouce*. Shanghai: Qingnian Xiehui Shuju, 1950.

———. *Zhanshi de junren fuwu*. Hankou: Xinzhi Shudian, 1938.

———. "Zhongguo kangzhan gequ zai Meiguo." *Renmin yinyue* 9 (1982): 41.

———, ed. *Minzu husheng*. Changsha: Changsha Qingnianhui, 1938.

———, ed. *Xiangei nü pengyou: fu lian'ai xue abc*. Shanghai: Changcheng Shuju, n.d.

———, trans. "Lianheguo ge." *Gemin qingnian* 1, no. 23 (1943): 25; *Lianhe zhoubao* 14 (1944): 5.

———, trans. "Lianmengguo ge." *Yinyue zhishi* 1, no. 4 (1943): 59.

Liu Liangmo and Lu Shaofei. "Kangzhan changshi manhua." *Guojia zong dongyuan huabao* 33 (April 1938): 2.

Liu Liangmo xiansheng jinian wenji. Shanghai: Zhongguo Jidujiao Quanguo Xiehui, 2010.

Li Weichen. "Guanyu Chen Youren xiansheng de yi ge baogao." *Zhengzhi yuekan* 8, no. 2 (1944): 70–78.

Luoboxun, Baoluo. *Wo jiu zhanzai zhe'er.* Translated by Zhao Zelong. Beijing: Shijie Zhishi Chubanshe, 1958.

Luoboxun, Baoluo, and Li Shishao. *Baoluo Luoboxun yanchang de Heiren minge.* Beijing: Zhongyang Yuetan Ziliao Zu, 1956.

Luo Xingqun, trans. *Lansidun Xiushi duanpian xiaoshuo ji.* Chongqing: Chongqing Chubanshe, 1988.

Lu Xun. *Lu Xun quanji.* Vols. 4, 5, 8, and 16. Beijing: Renmin Wenxue Chubanshe, 2005.

Lu Xun, Qu Qiubai, and Yue Wen, eds. *Xiaobona zai Shanghai.* Shanghai: Yecao Shuju, 1933.

Meiguo Heiren yao ziyou. Beijing: Yinyue Chubanshe, 1964.

Meiguo mingge xuan. Beijing: 199 Zhongxue, 1980.

Mei Shaowu. *Wode fuqin Mei Lanfang.* Tianjin: Baihua Wenyi Chubanshe, 1984.

Meizi. "Zhang Liying xiajia Chen Youren zhuiji." *Shanghai zhoubao* 1, no. 12 (1932): 234–35.

Qi Rushan. *Mei Lanfang you Mei ji.* Shenyang: Liaoning Jiaoyu Chubanshe, 2005.

Qiubai. "Ji Chen Youren." *Daya huabao,* February 25, 1931, 2.

Shanding. *Manwen jindai shijie shi xuan.* Shenyang: Manzhou Tushu Zhushi Huishe, 1942.

Shao Yanxiang and Fang Cheng. "Huida he bu huida." *Lingdao wencui* 10 (2000); *Minzhu yu kexue* 2 (2000).

Shen Pengnian. "Lu Xun huijian Xiushi jiqi beiwu shijian." *Shaoxing Lu Xun yanjiu* 27 (2005): 119–27.

Shi Leying, ed. *Ruoguo xiaoshuo mingzhu.* Shanghai: Qiming Shuju, 1937.

Sun Ruizhen and Zou Jin. *Malaiya qingren: Wang Ying zhuan.* Chengdu: Sichuan Wenyi Chubanshe, 1987.

Suolu duofu ni kefu (Soviet Union). "Luoboxun." *Xinhua yuebao* 1, no. 1 (1949): 301–2; originally published in *Pravda,* June 11, 1949.

Weilian, Luobote. *Daiqiang de Heiren.* Translated by Lu Ren. Beijing: Shijie Shudian Chubanshe, 1963.

Wu Shi (Fu Donghua). "Xiushi zai Zhongguo." *Wenxue* 1, no. 2 (1933): 254–58; 1, no. 4 (1933): 586.

Xiang Yansheng. "Meiguo Heiren Gewang Luoboxun yu 'Yiyongjun jinxing qu.'" *Minzu yinyue* 6 (2009).

Xia Yan. *Lan xun jiumeng lu.* Beijing: Sanlian Shudian, 1985.

Xinzi. *Su'e de shenghuo.* Translated by Chen Weijiang. Shanghai: Changcheng Shuju, 1933.

Xiushi. *Fu yu zi.* Shanghai: Shanghai Guji Chubanshe, 2008.

———. *Hei Lide.* Translated by Zhu Xiuxia. Chongqing: Duli Chubanshe, 1945.

——— et al. *Heiren shixuan.* Translated by Zou Jiang. Shanghai: Wenhua Gongzuoshi, 1952.

Xiushi, Langsidun, et al. *Heiren shixuan.* Translated by Zhang Qi. Beijing: Zuojia Chubanshe, 1957.

Xiushi, Lansidong. *Bushi meiyou xiaode.* Translated by Zhu Xiuxia and Xia Zhengnong. Shanghai: Liangyou Tushu Yinshua Gongsi, 1936.

Xiushi, Lansidun. "Women de chuntian." Translated by Yang Cunren, *Shengcun yuekan* 4, no. 8 (1933): 153–54; translated by Peng Lie, *Wenyi yuebao* (Beiping) 1, no. 3 (1933): 347–48; translated by Meng Zong, *Shige yuebao* 2, no. 1 (1934): 17–18.

Xiushi, Lansidun, et al. *Heiren duanpian xiaoshuo ji.* Translated by Huang Zhong. Beijing: Zhongguo Qingnian Chubanshe, 1955.

———. *Heiren duanpian xiaoshuo xuan.* Translated by Shi Xianrong. Shanghai: Xin Wenyi Chubanshe, 1957.

———. *Heiren shixuan.* Translated by Li Kuixian. Taizhong: Guangqi Chubanshe, 1974.

Xiusi, Lansidun. *Dahai: Lansidun Xiusi zizhuan.* Translated by Wu Keming and Shi Qin. Shanghai: Shanghai Yiwen Chubanshe, 1986.

———. *Lansidun Xiusi shixuan.* Translated by Ling Yue and Liang Jiaying, Shanghai: Shanghai Wenyi Chubanshe, 2018.

———. *Lansidun Xiusi shixuan.* Translated by Zhou Zhongzi. Shanghai: Shanghai Yiwen Chubanshe, 2018.

Yang Changxi. *Heiren wenxue.* Shanghai: Liangyou Tushu Gongsi, 1933.

Yingang (Lu Xun). "Jiebao yi ban." In Lu Xun, *Lu Xun quanji,* 8:278–84. Beijing: Renmin Wenxue Chubanshe, 2005.

Yinyue hui. Shanghai: Zhongguo Renmin Duiwai Wenhua Xiehui, 1955.

Yu Minsheng. "Guanghui de shiye, heping de zhanshi—Duboyisi fufu fangwen ji." *Renmin ribao,* February 23, 1959.

Zheng Da. "Bailaohui Zhongguo xiju daoyan di yi ren—ji Xiong Shiyi zai Meiguo daoyan *Wang Baochuan.*" *Meiguo yanjiu* 4 (2013).

Zheng Linkuan. "Lansidun Xiushi." *Qinghua zhoukan* 42, no. 9/10 (1934): 131–39.

Zhirun. "Liu Liangmo zai Meiguo jiao Heiren Gewang chang 'Yiyongjun jinxing qu.'" *Shijie chenbao* (Shanghai), February 12, 1946.

Zhu Mo, ed. *Luoboxun zhuan.* Shanghai: Taipingyang Chubanshe, 1951.

Zhu Shengjun and Lin Caibing, eds. *Baoluo Luoboxun yanchang gequ ji.* Shanghai: Shanghai Yinyue Chubanshe, 1958; Shanghai Wenyi Chubanshe, 1958.

ARTICLES AND BOOKS IN ENGLISH

"AHR Conversations: Black Internationalism." *American Historical Review* 125, no. 5 (December 2020): 1699–1739.

Als, Hilton. "The Sojourner: The Elusive Langston Hughes." *New Yorker,* February 23 and March 2, 2015.

Appiah, Kwame Anthony. *Cosmopolitanism: Ethics in a World of Strangers.* New York: W. W. Norton, 2006.

Aptheker, Herbert, ed. *The Correspondence of W. E. B. Du Bois.* Vol. 3: *Selections, 1944–1963.* 1978. Amherst: University of Massachusetts Press, 1997.

———. *Pamphlets and Leaflets by W. E. B. Du Bois.* 1960. White Plains, N.Y.: Kraus-Thomson, 1986.

Balaji, Murali. *Professor and Pupil: The Politics and Friendship of W. E. B. Du Bois and Paul Robeson.* New York: Nation, 2007.

Baldwin, Kate A. *Beyond the Color Line and the Iron Curtain: Reading Encounters between Black and Red, 1922–1963.* Durham, N.C.: Duke University Press, 2002.

Bandele, Ramla M. *Black Star: African American Activism in the International Political Economy.* Urbana: University of Illinois Press, 2008.

Bay, Mia. *Traveling Black: A Story of Race and Resistance.* Cambridge, Mass.: Belknap Press of Harvard University Press, 2021.

Bernard, Emily, ed. *Remembering Me to Harlem: The Letters of Langston Hughes and Carl Van Vechten, 1925–1964*. New York: Knopf, 2001.

Bevan, Paul. *A Modern Miscellany: Shanghai Cartoon Artists, Shao Xunmei's Cricle and the Travels of Jack Chen, 1926–1938*. Leiden: Brill, 2016.

Blain, Keisha N. *Set the World on Fire: Black Nationalist Women and the Global Struggle for Freedom*. Philadelphia: University of Pennsylvania Press, 2018.

Bontemps, Arna, and Langston Hughes. *Popo and Fifina*. New York: Macmillan, 1932.

Bosworth, Patricia. *Marlon Brando*. New York: Viking, 2001.

Boyle, Sheila Tully, and Andrew Bunie. *Paul Robeson: The Years of Promise and Achievement*. Amherst: University of Massachusetts Press, 2001.

Brady, Anne-Marie. *Making the Foreign Serve China: Managing Foreigners in the People's Republic*. Lanham, Md.: Rowman & Littlefield, 2003.

Brazinsky, Gregg A. *Winning the Third World: Sino-American Rivalry during the Cold War*. Chapel Hill: University of North Carolina Press, 2017.

Buck, Pearl S. *The Good Earth*. New York: John Day, 1931.

———. "Interpretation of China to the West." In *China as I See It*, edited by Theodore F. Harris, 10–15. London: Methuen, 1970.

———. *My Several Worlds: A Personal Record*. New York: John Day, 1954.

Buck, Pearl S., and Eslanda G. Robeson. *American Argument*. New York: John Day, 1949.

Buni, Andrew. *Robert L. Vann of the "Pittsburgh Courier": Politics and Black Journalism*. Pittsburgh: University of Pittsburgh Press, 1974.

Burke, Roland. *Decolonization and the Evolution of International Human Rights*. Philadelphia: University of Pennsylvania Press, 2010.

Burns, Edward, ed. *The Letters of Gertrude Stein and Carl Van Vechten*, vol. 2, *1935–1946*. New York: Columbia University Press, 1986.

Camp Wo-Chi-Ca Yearbook. Hackettstown, N.J., 1948.

Carby, Hazel V. *Race Men*. Cambridge, Mass.: Harvard University Press, 1998.

Carew, Joy Gleason. *Blacks, Reds, and Russians: Sojourners in Search of the Soviet Promise*. New Brunswick, N.J.: Rutgers University Press, 2008.

Chang, Gordon. *Fateful Ties: A History of America's Preoccupation with China*. Cambridge, Mass.: Harvard University Press, 2015.

Chen, Georgette. *Georgette Chen Retrospective*. Singapore: National Museum Art Gallery, 1985.

Chen, Jack. *The Chinese of America*. San Francisco: Harper and Row, 1980.

———. *The Chinese Theater*. London: Dobson, 1960.

———. *Inside the Cultural Revolution*. London: Sheldon, 1976.

———. *New Earth*. 1957. Carbondale: Southern Illinois University Press, 1972.

———. *The Sinking Story*. New York: Macmillan, 1977.

———. *A Year in Upper Felicity: Life in a Chinese Village during the Cultural Revolution*. New York: Macmillan, 1973.

Chen, Percy. *China Called Me: My Life Inside the Chinese Revolution*. Boston: Little, Brown, 1979.

Chen, Yuan-tsung. *Return to the Middle Kingdom*. New York: Union Square, 2008.

Cheng, Cindy I-Fen. *Citizens of Asian America: Democracy and Race during the Cold War*. New York: New York University Press, 2013.

Chen Leyda, Si-lan. *Footnote to History*. New York: Dance Horizons, 1984.

———. "Peking Venture: Out of the Goose Pond and Into the Common Pot, or Better a Little Lake Than a Big Swan." *Dance Magazine*, May 1972, 34–39.

Clemons, Michael L., ed. *African Americans in Global Affairs*. Boston: Northeastern University Press, 2010.

Das, Joanna Dee. *Katherine Dunham, Dance, and the African Diaspora*. New York: Oxford University Press, 2017.

Dent, Robert Yancy, and Marilyn Robeson, eds. *Paul Robeson, Tributes, Selected Writings*. New York: Paul Robeson Archives, 1976.

De Santis, Christopher C., ed., *Langston Hughes and the "Chicago Defender": Essays on Race, Politics, and Culture, 1942–62*. Urbana: University of Illinois Press, 1995.

Dickinson, Donald C. *A Bio-bibliography of Langston Hughes*. New Haven, Conn.: Archon, 1967.

Dikotter, Frank. *Mao's Great Famine: The History of China's Most Devastating Catastrophe, 1958–1962*. New York: Walker, 2010.

Duberman, Martin B. *Paul Robeson: A Biography*. New York: Knopf, 1988.

Du Bois, W. E. B. "The African Roots of War." *Atlantic Monthly* 115 (May 1915): 707–14; and in Foner, *W. E. B. Du Bois Speaks: Speeches and Addresses, 1890–1919*, 244–57.

———. *The Autobiography of W. E. B. Du Bois*. 1968. New York: Oxford University Press, 2007.

———. *Color and Democracy: Colonies and Peace*. New York: Harcourt, Brace, 1945.

———. *Darkwater: Voices from within the Veil*. New York: Harcourt, Brace, 1921.

———. *Dusk of Dawn: Concept of Race: An Essay toward an Autobiography of a Race Concept*. 1940. New York: Oxford University Press, 2007.

———. "The Evolution of the Race Problem." *Proceedings of the National Negro Conference*, New York, 1909, 142–58; and in Foner, *W. E. B. Du Bois Speaks: Speeches and Addresses, 1890–1919*, 196–210.

———. *In Battle for Peace: The Story of My Eighty-Third Birthday*. 1952. New York: Milwood, 1976.

———. "I Sing to China: Dedicated to Kuo Mo-jo." *China Reconstructs* 8 (June 1959): 24–26.

———. "Normal US-China Relations." *New World Review* 22 (August 1954): 13–15.

———. "The Pan-African Movement" (speech at the sixth Pan-African Congress in Manchester in 1945). In Foner, *W. E. B. Du Bois Speaks: Speeches and Addresses, 1920–1963*, 161–78.

———. "Prospect of a World without Race Conflict." *American Journal of Sociology* 49 (March 1944): 450–56; and in Foner, *W. E. B. Du Bois Speaks: Speeches and Addresses, 1920–1963*, 124–36; and condensed in *Negro Digest* 2 (August 1944): 45–47.

———. *The Souls of Black Folk*. 1903. New York: Signet Classics, 1995.

———. "The Vast Miracle of China Today." *National Guardian*, June 8, 1959.

Edwards, Brent Hayes. *The Practice of Diaspora: Literature, Translation, and the Rise of Black Internationalism*. Cambridge, Mass.: Harvard University Press, 2003.

Emanuel, James A. *Langston Hughes*. New York: Twayne, 1967.

Epstein, Israel. *My China Eye: Memoirs of a Jew and a Journalist*. San Francisco: Long River, 2005.

———. *Woman in World History: Life and Times of Soong Ching Ling (Madame Sun Yatsen)*. Beijing: New World, 1993.

Essays in Honor of Jay Leyda. Cambridge, Mass.: MIT Press, 1979.

Bibliography

Ezrahi, Christina. *Swans of the Kremlin: Ballet and Power in Soviet Russia.* Pittsburgh: University of Pittsburgh Press, 2012.

Fitzpatrick, Sheila. *The Cultural Front: Power and Culture in Revolutionary Russia.* Ithaca, N.Y.: Cornell University Press, 1992.

Foner, Philip S., ed. *Paul Robeson Speaks: Writings, Speeches, Interviews, 1918–1974.* New York: Citadel, 1978.

———. *W. E. B. Du Bois Speaks: Speeches and Addresses, 1890–1919.* New York: Pathfinder, 1970.

———. *W. E. B. Du Bois Speaks: Speeches and Addresses, 1920–1963.* New York: Pathfinder, 1970.

Franko, Mark. *The Work of Dance: Labor, Movement, and Identity in the 1930s.* Middletown, Conn.: Wesleyan University Press, 2002.

Frazier, Robeson Taj. "The Assault of the Monkey King on the Hosts of Heaven." In *African Americans in Global Affairs,* edited by Michael L. Clemons, 313–45. Boston: Northeastern University Press, 2010.

———. *The East Is Black: Cold War China in the Black Radical Imagination.* Durham, N.C.: Duke University Press, 2015.

French, Howard W. *China's Second Continent: How a Million Migrants Are Building a New Empire in Africa.* New York: Knopf, 2014.

Friedman, Jeremy. *Shadow Cold War: The Sino-Soviet Competition for the Third World.* Chapel Hill: University of North Carolina Press, 2015.

Fukuzawa, Yukichi. "Disassociating Asia" (1885). In *Japan: A Documentary History,* edited by David J. Lu, 2:353. New York: Routledge, 2005.

Gadzala, Aleksandra W., ed. *Africa and China: How Africans and Their Governments Are Shaping Relations with China.* Lanham, Md.: Rowman & Littlefield, 2015.

Gallicchio, Marc. *The African American Encounter with Japan and China: Black Internationalism in Asia, 1895–1945.* Chapel Hill: University of North Carolina Press, 2000.

Gao Yunxiang. "Soo Yong (1903–1984): Hollywood Celebrity and Cultural Interpreter." *Journal of American-East Asian Relations* 17, no. 4 (2010): 372–99.

———. *Sporting Gender: Women Athletes and Celebrity Making during China's National Crisis, 1931–45.* Vancouver: UBC Press, 2013.

———. "W. E. B. and Shirley Graham Du Bois in Maoist China." *Du Bois Review: Social Science Research on Race* 10, no. 1 (2013): 59–85.

Garside, B. A. *Within the Four Seas: The Memoirs of B. A. Garside.* New York: Frederic C. Bell, 1985.

Gilroy, Paul. *Darker than Blue: On the Moral Economies of Black Atlantic Culture.* Cambridge, Mass.: Harvard University Press, 2010.

Gordon, Eugene. "A Great Negro Artist Puts His Genius to Work for His People." *Sunday Worker,* June 4, 1939.

Graham, Shirley. *Paul Robeson: Citizen of the World.* New York: Julian Messner, 1946.

———. *There Was Once a Slave: The Heroic Story of Frederick Douglass.* New York: J. Messner, 1947.

Graham, Shirley, and George Dewey Lipscomb. *Dr. George Washington Carver, Scientist.* New York: J. Messner, 1944.

Graham Du Bois, Shirley. *His Day Is Marching On: A Memoir of W. E. B. Du Bois.* Philadelphia: J. P. Lippincott, 1971.

Gully, Patti. *Sisters of Heaven: China's Barnstorming Aviatrixes*. Berkeley, Calif.: Long River, 2007.

Hahn, Emily. *The Soong Sisters*. New York: Doubleday, Doran, 1941.

Hamilton, Virginia. *Paul Robeson: The Life and Times of a Free Black Man*. New York: Harper & Row, 1974.

Hayter-Menzies, Grant. *Shadow Woman: The Extraordinary Career of Pauline Benton*. Montreal: McGill-Queen's University Press, 2013.

Higbee, Mark D. "A Letter from W. E. B. Du Bois to His Daughter Yolanda, Dated 'Moscow, Dec. 10, 1958.'" *Journal of Negro History* 78, no. 3 (1993): 190–91.

Hindus, Maurice. *Red Bread: Collectivization in a Russian Village*. New York: J. Cape & H. Smith, 1931.

Ho, Fred. "The Inspiration of Mao and the Chinese Revolution on the Black Liberation Movement and the Asian Movement on the East Coast." In Ho and Mullen, *Afro Asia*, 155–65.

Ho, Fred, and Bill V. Mullen, eds. *Afro Asia: Revolutionary Political and Cultural Connections between African Americans and Asian Americans*. Durham, N.C.: Duke University Press, 2008.

Hodges, Graham R. G. *Anna May Wong: From Laundryman's Daughter to Hollywood Legend*. 2nd ed. Hong Kong: Hong Kong University Press, 2012.

Hollander, Paul. *Political Pilgrims: Travels of Western Intellectuals to the Soviet Union, China, and Cuba, 1928–1978*. New York: Oxford University Press, 1981.

Horne, Gerald. *Black and Red: W. E. B. Du Bois and the Afro-American Response to the Cold War, 1944–1963*. Albany: State University of New York Press, 1986.

———. *Race Woman: The Lives of Shirley Graham Du Bois*. New York: New York University Press, 2002.

Hsu, Hua. *A Floating Chinaman: Fantasy and Failure across the Pacific*. Cambridge, Mass.: Harvard University Press, 2016.

Hsu, Madeline. *Dreaming of Gold, Dreaming of Home: Transnationalism and Migration between the United States and South China, 1882–1943*. Palo Alto, Calif.: Stanford University Press, 2000.

Huang Yunte. *Charlie Chan: The Untold Story of the Honorable Detective and His Rendezvous with American History*. New York: W. W. Norton, 2010.

———. *Inseparable: The Original Siamese Twins and Their Rendezvous with American History*. New York: Liveright, 2018.

Hughes, Langston, ed. *An African Treasury*. New York: Pyramid Books, 1961.

———. *Autobiography: I Wonder as I Wander*. 1956. Vol. 14 of *The Collected Works of Langston Hughes*. Columbia: University of Missouri Press, 2003.

———. *The Best of Simple*. New York: Hill and Wang, 1961.

———. *The Big Sea*. 1940. New York: Hill and Wang, 1993.

———. *Dear Lovely Death*. New York: Troutbeck, 1931.

———. *The Dream Keeper and Other Poems*. New York: Knopf, 1932.

———. *Famous American Negroes*. New York: Dodd Mead, 1954.

———. *Famous Negro Music Makers*. New York: Dodd Mead, 1955.

———. *Fields of Wonder*. New York: Knopf, 1947.

———. *Fine Clothes to the Jew*. New York: A. A. Knopf, 1927.

———. "From Moscow to Shanghai." *China Forum*, July 14, 1933, 5.

———. "Goodbye Christ." *Negro Worker*, November/December 1932, 32.

————. *Laughing to Keep from Crying*. New York: Henry Holt, 1952.

————. "The Negro Artist and the Racial Mountain." *Nation*, June 23, 1926.

————. *A Negro Looks at Soviet Central Asia*. Moscow: Co-Operative Publishers Society of Foreign Workers in the U.S.S.R., 1934.

————. *The Negro Mother*. New York: Golden Stair, 1931.

————. *Not without Laughter*. New York: Random House, 1930.

————. *The Return of Simple*. New York: Hill and Wang, 1994.

————. "Roar China!" *Volunteer for Liberty*, September 6, 1937, 3.

————. "Roar China!" *New Masses*, February 22, 1938, 20.

————. "Roar China!" In *Anthology of Magazine Verse, 1938–1942*, edited by Alan Pate, 223–25. New York: Paebar, 1942.

————. *Scottsboro Limited*. New York: Golden Stair, 1932.

————. *Simple Takes a Wife* (1952). In *The Langston Hughes Reader*, 244–313. New York: George Braziller, 1958.

————. *Something in Common and Other Stories*. New York: Hill and Wang, 1963.

————. "That Powerful Drop." In *The Langston Hughes Reader*. New York: George Braziller, 1958.

————. *The Weary Blues*. New York: Knopf, 1926.

"Jay Leyda: A Brief History." In *Essays in Honor of Jay Leyda*, edited by Rosalind Krauss. Cambridge, Mass.: MIT Press, 1979.

Jesperson, T. Christopher. *American Images of China, 1931–1945*. Palo Alto, Calif.: Stanford University Press, 1999.

Ji Chaozhu. *The Man on Mao's Right*. New York: Random House, 2008.

Jones, Andrew F. *Yellow Music: Media Culture and Colonial Modernity in the Chinese Jazz Age*. Durham, N.C.: Duke University Press, 2001.

Kaplan, Carla. *Miss Anne in Harlem: The White Women of the Black Renaissance*. New York: Harper, 2013.

Kawakami, Kiyoshi Karl. *Japan Speaks on the Sino-Japanese Crisis*. New York: Macmillan, 1932.

Kelley, Robin D. G. "But a Local Phase of a World Problem: Black History's Global Vision, 1883–1950." *Journal of American History* 86, no. 3 (December 1999): 1045–77.

Kelley, Robin D. G., and Betsy Esch. "Black Like Mao: Red China and Black Revolution." In Ho and Mullen, *Afro Asia*, 97–155.

Koestler, Arthur. *The Invisible Writing*. 1954. New York: Vintage, 2005.

Kwong, Peter. *Chinatown, N.Y.: Labor & Politics, 1930–1950*. New York: Monthly Review Press, 1979.

Lai, Him Mark. *Chinese American Transnational Politics*. Urbana: University of Illinois Press, 2010.

————. "The Koumintang in Chinese American Communities before World War II." In *Entry Denied: Exclusion and the Chinese Community in America, 1882–1943*, edited by Sucheng Chan, 170–212. Philadelphia: Temple University Press, 1991.

Lai-Henderson, Salina. "Color around the Globe: Langston Hughes and Black Internationalism in China." *MELUS* 45, no. 2 (Summer 2020): 88–107.

Larkin, Bruce D. *China and Africa, 1949–1970: The Foreign Policy of the People's Republic of China*. Berkeley: University of California Press, 1973.

Latourette, Kenneth Scott. *Toward a World Christian Fellowship*. New York: Associate, 1938.

Lee, Ching Kwan. *The Specter of Global China: Politics, Labor, and Foreign Investment in Africa*. Chicago: University of Chicago Press, 2017.

Lee, Erica. *At America's Gates: Chinese Immigration during the Exclusion Era, 1882–1943*. Chapel Hill: University of North Carolina Press, 2003.

Lee, Joseph Tse-Hei. "Co-optation and Its Discontents: Seventh-Day Adventism in Maoist China." *Frontiers of History in China* 7, no. 4 (2012): 582–606.

Lee, Steven S. *The Ethnic Avant-Garde: Writers, Artists, and the Magic Pilgrimage to the Soviet Union*. New York: Columbia University Press, 2015.

Levine, June, and Gene Gordon. *Tales of Wo-Chi-Ca: Blacks, Whites and Reds at Camp*. San Rafael, Calif.: Avon Springs, 2002.

Lewis, David Levering. *King: A Critical Biography*. New York: Praeger, 1970.

———. *W. E. B. Du Bois: The Fight for Equality and the American Century, 1919–1963*. New York: Henry Holt, 2000.

Leyda, Jay. *Dianying: Electric Shadows—An Account of Films and the Film Audience in China*. Cambridge, Mass.: MIT Press, 1972.

———. *The Melville Log: A Documentary Life of Herman Melville, 1819–1891*. New York: Harcourt, Brace, 1951.

———. *The Portable Melville*. New York: Viking, 1952.

———. *The Years and Hours of Emily Dickinson*. New Haven, Conn.: Yale University Press, 1960.

Lincoln University Bulletin for 1942. Lincoln, Penn.: Lincoln University Bulletin, 1943.

Lindsey, Ellen Anne. "Table for Three, Please." In *Young Wives' Tales: New Adventures in Love and Partnership*, edited by Jill Corral and Lisa Miya-Jervis. Seattle: Seal, 2001.

Lin Yutang. *Chinatown Family*. 1948. New Brunswick, N.J.: Rutgers University Press, 2007.

———. *My Country and My People*. New York: John Day, 1935.

———. "Singing Patriots of China." *Asia* 41 (February 1941): 70–73; *Time*, June 16, 1941, 3; and condensed in *Reader's Digest*, March 1941. All in Box 23, Folder 9, United China Relief Archives.

Liu Liangmo. "Chinese Have Changed and Now They Are More Militant." *Detroit Tribune*, June 21, 1943.

———. "The New Year at the Front." *Asia* 41 (February 1941): 72–73.

Liu Liangmo and Evelyn Modoi. *China Sings: Folk-Songs and Fighting Songs of China*. New York: Carl Fischer, 1945.

Liu Liangmo and Helen Simon. *Young China*. New York: American Youth Congress, 1941.

Lovell, Julia. *Maoism: A Global History*. New York: Knopf, 2019.

Makalani, Minkah. *In the Cause of Freedom: Radical Black Internationalism from Harlem to London, 1917–1939*. Chapel Hill: University of North Carolina Press, 2011.

Marable, Manning. *Malcolm X: A Life of Reinvention*. New York: Viking, 2011.

McGuire, Elizabeth. *Red at Heart: How Chinese Communists Fell in Love with the Russian Revolution*. Oxford: Oxford University Press, 2017.

Mei Lanfang and Chinese Drama. New York: China Institute, 1930.

Meng, Chih. *China Speaks: On the Conflict between China and Japan*. New York: Macmillan, 1932.

———. *Chinese American Understanding: A Sixty-Year Search*. New York: China Institute in America, 1981.

Meriwether, James H. *Proudly We Can Be Africans: Black Americans and Africa, 1935–1961.* Chapel Hill: University of North Carolina Press, 2002.

Moon, Henry Lee. *The Emerging Thought of W. E .B. Du Bois: Essays and Editorials from "The Crisis."* New York: Simon and Schuster, 1972.

Morath, Inge, and Arthur Miller. *Chinese Encounters.* New York: Farrar, Straus and Giroux, 1979.

Mukerji, S. Ani. "'Like Another Planet to the Darker Americas': Black Cultural Work in 1930s Moscow." In *Africa in Europe,* edited by Eve Rosenhaft and Robbine John Macvicar Aitken, 120–41. Liverpool: Liverpool University Press, 2013.

Mullen, Bill V. *Afro-Orientalism.* Minneapolis: University of Minnesota Press, 2004.

———. *Un-American: W. E. B. Du Bois and the Century of World Revolution.* Philadelphia: Temple University Press, 2015.

Mullen, Bill V., and Cathryn Watson, eds. *W. E. B. Du Bois on Asia: Crossing the World Color Line.* Jackson: University Press of Mississippi, 2005.

Ottley, Roi. *New World A-Coming: Inside Black America.* Boston: Houghton Mifflin, 1943.

Parr, Patrick. The Seminarian: Martin Luther King Jr. Comes of Age. Chicago: Lawrence Hill Books, 2018.

Patterson, James T. *Grand Expectations: The United States, 1945–1971.* New York: Oxford University Press, 2003.

Perry, Imani. *May We Forever Stand: A History of the Black National Anthem.* Chapel Hill: University of North Carolina Press, 2018.

Plummer, Brenda. *Rising Wind: Black Americans and U.S. Foreign Affairs, 1935–1960.* Chapel Hill: University of North Carolina Press, 1996.

Pomfret, John. *The Beautiful Country and the Middle Kingdom: America and China, 1776 to the Present.* New York: Henry Holt, 2016.

Price, Ruth. *The Lives of Agnes Smedley.* New York: Oxford University Press, 2005.

Rampersad, Arnold, ed. *The Collected Poems of Langston Hughes.* New York: Vintage Classics, 1994.

———. *The Life of Langston Hughes: I, Too, Sing America. 2 vols.* Oxford: Oxford University Press, 2002.

Rampersad, Arnold, David Roessel, and Christina Fratantoro, eds. *Selected Letters of Langston Hughes.* New York: Knopf, 2015.

Ransby, Barbara. *Eslanda: The Large and Unconventional Life of Mrs. Paul Robeson.* New Haven, Conn.: Yale University Press, 2013.

Ransom, Llewellyn. "The Family Chen: East Met West, Mixed with Brilliant Results." *People's Voice,* July 18, 1942.

Rasberry, Vaughn. *Race and the Totalitarian Century: Geopolitics in the Black Literary Imagination.* Cambridge, Mass.: Harvard University Press, 2016.

Reilly, Thomas. "Wu Yaozong and the YMCA: From Social Reform to Social Revolution, 1927–1937." *Journal of American–East Asian Relations* 19 (2012): 263–87.

Robeson, Eslanda G. *African Journey.* New York: John Day, 1945.

Robeson, Paul. "China: Promise of a New World" (speech at the Sun Yat-sen tribute dinner, New York, March 12, 1944). In Foner, *Paul Robeson Speaks,* 155–56.

———. "Happy Birthday, New China!" *Freedom,* October 1952; and in Foner, *Paul Robeson Speaks,* 327–28.

———. *Here I Stand.* New York: Othello, 1958.

———. "I Want to Be African." In *What I Want from Life*, edited by E. G. Cousins, 71–77. London: George Allen & Unwin, 1934.

Robeson, Paul, Jr. *The Undiscovered Paul Robeson: Quest for Freedom, 1939–1976*. Hoboken, N.J.: John Wiley, 1976.

Robinson, Greg. *The Great Unknown: Japanese American Sketches*. Boulder: University Press of Colorado, 2016.

Roosevelt, Eleanor. *It's Up to the Women*. New York: Frederick W. Stokes, 1933.

Roth, Hans Ingvar. *P. C. Chang and the Universal Declaration of Human Rights*. Philadelphia: University of Pennsylvania Press, 2018.

Salz, Morris. "The Thunder of 10,000 Voices." *New China* (Spring 1977): 17–20.

Schwartz, Peggy, and Murray Schwartz. *The Dance Claimed Me: A Biography of Pearl Primus*. New Haven, Conn.: Yale University Press, 2011.

Scott, A. C. *Mei Lan-Fang: Leader of the Pear Garden*. Hong Kong: Hong Kong University Press, 1959.

Shay, Anthony, and Barbara Sellers-Young, eds. *Oxford Handbook of Dance and Ethnicity*. New York: Oxford University Press, 2016.

Sherrard-Johnson, Cherene M. *Dorothy West's Paradise: A Biography of Class and Color*. New Brunswick, N.J.: Rutgers University Press, 2012.

Shinn, David H., and Joshua Eisenman. *China and Africa: A Century of Engagement*. Philadelphia: University of Pennsylvania Press, 2012.

Singh, Nikhil Pal. *Black Is a Country: Race and the Unfinished Struggle for Democracy*. Cambridge, Mass.: Harvard University Press, 2004.

Smedley, Agnes. *Battle Hymn of China*. New York: Knopf, 1943.

Snow, Philip. *The Star Raft: China's Encounter with Africa*. Ithaca, N.Y.: Cornell University Press, 1989.

So, Richard Jean. *Transpacific Community: America, China, and the Rise and Fall of a Cultural Network*. New York: Columbia University Press, 2016.

Sokolova, Lydia. *Dancing for Diaghliev: The Memoirs of Lydia Soklova*. New York: Macmillan, 1961.

Soong Chingling. *The Struggle for New China*. Peking: Foreign Languages Press, 1953.

Soothill, William Edward. *The Student's Four Thousand Tzu and General Pocket Dictionary*. Shanghai: Kwang Hsueh, 1932.

Spence, Jonathan. *To Change China: Western Advisers in China*. New York: Little, Brown, 1969.

Stowe, Leland. *They Shall Not Sleep*. New York: Knopf, 1944.

Strong, Tracy B., and Helene Keyssar. "Anna Louise Strong: Three Interviews with Chairman Mao Zedong." *China Quarterly* 103 (September 1985): 489–509.

Taketani, Etsuko. *The Black Pacific Narrative: Geographic Imaginings of Race and Empire between the World Wars*. Hanover, N.H.: Dartmouth College Press, 2014.

———. "'Spies and Spiders': Langston Hughes and Transpacific Intelligence Dragnets." *Japanese Journal of American Studies* 25 (2014): 25–48.

Tang Xiaobing. "Echoes of *Roar, China!* On Vision and Voice in Modern Chinese Art." *Positions* 14, no. 2 (2006): 467–94.

Taylor, Jay. *The Generalissimo: Chiang Kai-shek and the Struggle for Modern China*. Cambridge, Mass.: Belknap Press of Harvard University Press, 2009.

Taylor, Yuval. *Zora and Langston: A Story of Friendship and Betrayal*. New York: W. W. Norton, 2019.

Tyerman, Edward. "Resignifying *The Red Poppy*." *Slavic and East European Journal* 61, no. 3 (Fall 2017): 445–66.

Tyson, Timothy B. *Radio Free Dixie: Robert F. Williams and the Roots of Black Power*. Chapel Hill: University of North Carolina Press, 1999.

Von Eschen, Penny M. *Race against Empire: Black Americans and Anticolonialism, 1937–1957*. Ithaca, N.Y.: Cornell University Press, 1997.

———. *Satchmo Blows Up the World: Jazz Ambassadors Play the Cold War*. Cambridge, Mass.: Harvard University Press, 2004.

West, Michael O., William G. Martin, and Fanon Che Wilkins, eds. *From Toussaint to Tupac: The Black International since the Age of Revolution*. Chapel Hill: University of North Carolina Press, 2009.

White, Theodore, and Annalee Jacoby. *Thunder out of China*. New York: William Sloane, 1946.

Wilcox, Emily. *Revolutionary Bodies: Chinese Dance and the Socialist Legacy*. Berkeley: University of California Press, 2018.

Williams, Carmaletta M., and John Edgar Tidwell, eds. *My Dear Boy: Carrie Hughes's Letters to Langston Hughes, 1926–1938*. Athens: University of Georgia Press, 2013.

Wright, Richard. *The Color Curtain: A Report on the Bandung Conference*. Cleveland: World, 1956.

Xu Guoqi. *Chinese and Americans: A Shared History*. Cambridge, Mass.: Harvard University Press, 2014.

Yang Huilin. *China, Christianity, and the Question of Culture*. Waco, Tex.: Baylor University Press, 2014.

Yan Xu. *The Soldier Image and State-Building in Modern China, 1924–1945*. Lexington: University Press of Kentucky, 2019.

Yeh, Diana. *The Happy Hsiungs: Performing China and the Struggle for Modernity*. Hong Kong: Hong Kong University Press, 2014.

Yung, Judy. *The Chinese Exclusion Act and Angel Island: A Brief History with Documents*. Boston: Bedford/St. Martin's, 2019.

Yu Renqui. *To Save China, To Save Ourselves: The Chinese Hand Laundry Alliance of New York*. Philadelphia: Temple University Press, 1995.

Index

Page references in italics refer to illustrative matter.

passports and citizenship (*continued*)
56, 62, 294; of Eugene Chen, 222; of Jack
Chen, 198, 219; of Yolanda Chen, 229; of
Liu, 165–66; of Madam Sun Yat-sen, 84;
of Robeson, 84, 91, 93, 97–98, 100, 108,
116–17, 120, 313n57, 317n114
Paul Robeson (booklet), 109, 111
Paul Robeson: Citizen of the World (Graham),
30, 36–37, 54, 81, 93, 100, 105, 113–14
Peace Information Center, 35
peace prizes: for Bunche, 118; for Du Bois,
40, 55, 303n79; for Robeson, 94, 98,
313n61
Peach-Blossom Lady (dance by Chen
Leyda), 206
Peekskill Riots (1949), 84, 91, 94–96, 105,
112, 113, 115, 171
Peking Review, 12, 231
People's Choral Societies. *See* mass singing
movement
"People's Singer Robeson" (Liu), 104, 171
"People without Shoes" (Hughes), 273
Picasso, Pablo, 34, 92
Pittsburgh Courier: Du Bois's column
and other essays in, 21, 24, 25, 34; Liu's
column in, 34, 142–48, 150, 152, 161, 170–
71. *See also* Goshal, Kumar
poll tax, 34, 79, 143–44
Popo and Fifna (Bontemps and Hughes),
273
Powell, Adam Clayton, 141, 144, 155, 216
Prattis, P. L., 142, 148
Primus, Pearl, 141, 152, 179
Progressive Party (U.S.), 32, 105, 169
Progressive Women's Council, 207
Proud Valley (film), 107
Pushkin, Alexander, 72, 94, 113–14, 282–83,
316n89

Qian Junrui, 99, 100, 109, 131
Qu Qiubai, 260

race mixing (miscegenation), 291; Chen
family, 9, 178–79, 181–83, 192–93, 201–4,
214, 215–16, 221–22, 231, 248–50; Creole,
4, 179, 182, 250, 294; Redroso, 243. *See
also* "Father and Son"; *Mulatto*

racism, 261; "Blackfaces," 102, 241, 316n91;
Buck on, 243, 343n15; in cartoons, 218;
by whites in China, 22–23, 252–54; in
Hollywood films, 214–15; in India, 143;
in Japan, 251; in U.S., 5–6, 28, 34, 137–38,
143–44, 256. *See also* African Americans;
Black "primitivism"; coolies and
rickshaw pullers; immigration process
and policies, U.S.; Jim Crow; lynching;
poll taxes; race mixing; Scottsboro case;
white colonialism
Ray, Man, 207
Reagan, Ronald, 225
The Red Detachment of Women, 233
red music, 176
The Red Poppy (play), 238, 341n5
Redroso, Rigino, 243, 276
Red Spear (dance by Chen Leyda), 189
Ren Guang, 128
"Roar, China!" (poem by Hughes), 236–37,
241, 256, 276, 291
"Roar, China!" theme, global circulation of,
236–41, 341n6
Roaring Voices of the Nation (Liu), 130
Roar of Women (film), 255
Robeson, Eslanda Goode, 82, 100, 123, 277,
309n19; 1949 trip to PRC, 86–87, 97,
171, 224–25; Buck and, 76–79, 100–101;
Chen Leyda and, 189–90, 225; death of,
294; Hughes and, 277; Mei and, 80–81,
82; political work of, 2, 37, 78–79, 117–18;
publications by, 79, 81, 86
Robeson, Paul, 293; 1958–62 travels by,
4, 116–18, 120; alliances with CCP and
PRC, 84–100; biographies of, 30, 36–37,
54, 81, 103–7, 109, 111–13, 122; birthday
celebrations of, 77, 89, 97, 99–100, 103,
105–11, 115, 119, 121, 122, 171, 285, 293;
Buck and, 76–79, 87, 189; Chen family
and, 189, 217, 222; on Chiang Kai-shek
and Nationalists, 84–85, 91, 119–20;
concerts by, 71–72, 76, 86, 94–96, 99,
116–17; cultural and political exile of,
97–99; death of, 122, 294; Du Bois and,
40, 91–93, 285–86; FBI surveillance of,
6–7, 70, 74, 97, 98, 140–41; films of, 101–3,
107, 115, 122, 196; friendship with Liu,